1 MONTH OF
FREE
READING

at

www.ForgottenBooks.com

By purchasing this book you are eligible for one month membership to ForgottenBooks.com, giving you unlimited access to our entire collection of over 1,000,000 titles via our web site and mobile apps.

To claim your free month visit:

www.forgottenbooks.com/free975758

ISBN 978-0-260-84541-2
PIBN 10975758

Forgotten Books is a registered trademark of FB &c Ltd.
Copyright © 2018 FB &c Ltd.
FB &c Ltd, Dalton House, 60 Windsor Avenue, London, SW19 2RR.
Company number 08720141. Registered in England and Wales.

For support please visit www.forgottenbooks.com

United States
Circuit Court of Appeals
For the Ninth Circuit.

WILLIAM E. STRAW,

Appellant,

vs.

UNITED STATES OF AMERICA,

Appellee.

Transcript of Record.

Upon Appeal from the United States District Court for the **Southern** District of California, Central Division.

Parker, Stone & Baird Co., Law Printers, Los Angeles.

INDEX.

[Clerk's Note: When deemed likely to be of an important nature, errors or doubtful matters appearing in the original record are printed literally in italic; and, likewise, cancelled matter appearing in the original record is printed and cancelled herein accordingly. When possible, an omission from the text is indicated by printing in italics the two words between which the omission seems to occur.]

PAGE

Amended Complaint 8

Answer 5

Bond on Appeal.. 47

Citation 2

Clerk's Certificate 51

Complaint 3

Conclusions of Law... 19

Demurrer to Amended Complaint....................................... 11

Engrossed Bill of Exceptions.. 32

   Plaintiff's Exhibit No. 10 (Letter Jan. 15, 1929,
     Straw to General Hines)... 34

   Plaintiff's Exhibit No. 11 (Letter April 10, 1929,
     Smith to Straw).. 35

   Plaintiff's Request for Special Findings....................... 36

Findings of Fact and Conclusions of Law........................ 26

Judgment 29

Names and Addresses of Attorneys.................................. 3

Notice of Appeal.. 43

Order Allowing Appeal... 45

Order Extending Time to Lodge Proposed Bill of Exceptions and Extending Term of Court........................ 30

Order Extending Time Within Which to Serve and
   File Bill of Exceptions and Extending Term............. 31

Order Settling Bill of Exceptions...................................... 41

Petition for Appeal.. 44

Praecipe 49

Request for Special Findings... 22

Second Amended Complaint... 15

Stipulation 17

Stipulation Waiving Jury... 18

Names and Addresses of Attorneys.

For Plaintiff and Appellant:

DAVID SPAULDING, Esq.,

Waters Building,

West Los Angeles, California.

For Defendant and Appellee:

SAMUEL W. McNABB, Esq.,

United States Attorney,

CLYDE THOMAS, Esq.,

Assistant United States Attorney,

Federal Building,

Los Angeles, California.

United States of America, ss:

To UNITED STATES OF AMERICA, SAMUEL W.
McNABB, CLYDE THOMAS and H. C. VEIT,
Attorneys for defendant—GREETING:

You are hereby cited and admonished to be and appear
at a United States Circuit Court of Appeals for the Ninth
Circuit, to be held at the City of San Francisco, in the
State of California, on the 20th day of January, A. D.
1932, pursuant to an Appeal filed in the Clerk's Office
of the District Court of the United States, in and for the
Southern District of California, in that certain cause entitled WILLIAM E. STRAW, plaintiff vs. UNITED
STATES OF AMERICA, defendant, No. 3583-M.
Wherein William E. Straw is the Appellant and you are
the Appellee and you are required to show cause, if any
there be, why the judgment in the said action mentioned,
should not be corrected, and speedy justice should not be
done to the parties in that behalf.

WITNESS, the Honorable PAUL J. McCORMICK
United States District Judge for the Southern District of
California, this 21st day of December, A. D. 1931, and
of the Independence of the United States, the one hundred
and fifty-*five*

Paul J. McCormick
U. S. District Judge for the Southern District of
California.

Received copy.
Clyde Thomas.

[Endorsed]: Filed Dec. 21, 1931. R. S. Zimmerman,
Clerk, by Edmund L. Smith, Deputy Clerk

UNITED STATES DISTRICT COURT
SOUTHERN DISTRICT OF CALIFORNIA.
CENTRAL DIVISION.

WILLIAM E. STRAW,
 	
               Plaintiff
 	
 vs.
 	
 UNITED STATES OF AMERICA,
 	
             Defendant.
	No. 3583-M
	
	 COMPLAINT.

Comes now the plaintiff and for cause of action against the defendant, alleges as follows, to-wit:—

I.

That the plaintiff is a resident of Los Angeles, County of Los Angeles, State of California. That he enlisted for military service in the United States, Army on the 5th day of June, 1915, and was honorably discharged on the 19th day of May, 1919.

II.

That while in the military service of the United States, during the war time period, desiring to be insured against the risks of war, said William E. Straw applied for a policy of War Risk Insurance in the sum of Ten Thousand Dollars thereafter there were deducted from his monthly pay certain sums of money as premium for said insurance. That a Certificate of War Risk Insurance was duly issued to him by the terms whereof the defendant agreed to pay said plaintiff, or his estate, the sum of $57.50 per month in the event he suffered permanent and total disability, but said policy was never delivered to the plaintiff.

III.

That while the said insurance policy was in force, the said plaintiff contracted the following disabilities, to-wit:

bronchiactasis, pulmonary tuberculosis, hemorroids and tubercular peritonitis.

IV.

That by reason of the foregoing the plaintiff was discharged, as aforesaid, totally and permanently disabled from bronchiactasis, pulmonary tuberculosis, hemorroids and tubercular peritonitis, and plaintiff has been informed and believes, and therefore alleges as true, that he will always be so disabled and never again be able to follow any substantially gainful occupation, by reason whereof he became entitled to receive from the defendant, $57.50 per month commencing on the 19th day of May, 1919.

V.

That the plaintiff has made due proof of said total and permanent disabilities to the said defendant and demanded payments of the aforesaid amounts, but the defendant disagreed with plaintiff as to his claim of disability and has failed to pay to the plaintiff the sum of $57.50 per month, defendant has paid the plaintiff the sum of $11.21 per month commencing January 28th, 1925. That at this time the plaintiff is totally and permanently disabled and has been since the date of said discharge.

WHEREFORE, The plaintiff demands judgment against the defendant in the sum of   per months from the date of said disabilities together with interest thereon at the rate of six per cent. per annum, from the several dates same became due and payable, and for his costs and disbursements herein incurred.

David Spaulding
David Spaulding
Attorney for Plaintiff.

Verified.

[Endorsed]: Filed Jun 20, 1929 R. S. Zimmerman, Clerk By Edmund L. Smith Deputy Clerk

[TITLE OF COURT AND CAUSE.]

ANSWER

COMES NOW the United States of America, defendant in the above entitled cause, by its Attorneys, Samuel W. McNabb, United States Attorney for the Southern District of California, and Sharpless Walker, Assistant United States Attorney for said District, and R. M. Chenoweth, of Counsel, and answering plaintiff's Complaint, admits, denies and alleges:

I.

Answering Paragraph I of plaintiff's Complaint, defendant denies that plaintiff enlisted in the United States Army on June 5, 1915, and alleges that plaintiff enlisted in the United States Army on June 8, 1915, but admits that the plaintiff was honorably discharged therefrom on May 19, 1919. Defendant alleges that it has no information or belief on the remaining allegation of said Paragraph sufficient to enable it to answer, and on that ground it denies each and every allegation of said Paragraph not herein specifically admitted to be true.

II.

Answering Paragraph II of plaintiff's Complaint, defendant admits that on February 3, 1918, plaintiff applied for and was granted a policy of War Risk Term Insurance in the amount of Ten Thousand Dollars ($10,-000.00), and that the premiums on the aforesaid insurance were deducted from plaintiff's monthly pay while in the Military Service. Defendant alleges that the aforesaid insurance was payable in monthly payments of Fifty-seven Dollars and Fifty Cents ($57.50) each, only in the event plaintiff suffered permanent and total disability while said insurance was in force and effect, and that plaintiff permitted said *said* insurance policy to lapse on July 1, 1919, for nonpayment of premium due thereon on June 1, 1919. Defendant denies each and every allegation in said Paragraph not herein specifically admitted to be true.

III.

Answering Paragraph III of plaintiff's Complaint, defendant denies each and every allegation contained therein.

IV.

Answering Paragraph IV of plaintiff's Complaint, defendant denies each and every allegation contained therein.

V.

Answering Paragraph V of plaintiff's Complaint, defendant admits that the defendant disagreed with plaintiff as to plaintiff's claim of disability, and has failed to pay to plaintiff the sum of Fifty-seven Dollars and Fifty Cents ($57.50) per month, or any part thereof, except the sum of Eleven Dollars and Twenty-one Cents ($11.21) per month commencing January 8, 1925. Defendant denies each and every allegation in said Paragraph not herein specifically admitted to be true.

FOR A FURTHER AND SEPARATE ANSWER AND DEFENSE TO PLAINTIFF'S COMPLÅINT, AND FOR COUNTER CLAIM THERETO, THE DEFENDANT, UNITED STATES OF AMERICA, ALLEGES:

I.

That on or about February 3, 1918, plaintiff applied for and was granted a War Risk Term Insurance policy in the amount of Ten Thousand Dollars ($10,000.00), and that said policy lapsed on July 1, 1919, for nonpayment of premium due thereon on June 1, 1919; that under the provisions of Section 305 of the World War Veterans' Act of 1924, as amended, said insurance, in the amount of Two Thousand and Fifty-six Dollars

($2056.00) was revived by reason of uncollected compensation found to be due plaintiff; that said insurance is subject to a lien of One Hundred and Five Dollars and Ninety-five Cents ($105.95), on account of premiums due from plaintiff to defendant for the period from June, 1919 to January, 1925. That there is now due and owing to defendant from plaintiff, by reason of said premiums, the sum of One Hundred and Five Dollars and Ninety-five Cents ($105.95), no part of which has been paid.

WHEREFORE, defendant, United States of America, prays:

That plaintiff take nothing by this action, and that plaintiff's Complaint be dismissed;

That the Court allow the counter claim of defendant, in the amount of One Hundred and Five Dollars and Ninety-five Cents ($105.95);

That judgment be rendered in favor of the defendant for costs herein;

And for such other and further relief as may be meet and just in the premises.

Samuel W. McNabb

SAMUEL W. McNABB

United States Attorney

Sharpless Walker

SHARPLESS WALKER

Assistant U. S. Attorney

R. M. Chenoweth

R. M. CHENOWETH

Of Counsel

Attorneys for Defendant

Verified.

[Endorsed]: Filed Dec 13 1929 R. S. Zimmerman, Clerk By Edmund L. Smith Deputy Clerk

AMENDED COMPLAINT

COMES NOW the plaintiff and for its first cause of
action against the defendant alleges as follows, to-wit:

I.

That the plaintiff is a resident of Los Angeles, County
of Los Angeles, State of California. That he enlisted
for military service in the United States Army on the
8th day of June, 1915, and was honorably discharged on
the 19th day of May, 1919.

II.

That while in the military service of the United States,
during the war time period, desiring to be insured against
the risks of war, said William E. Straw applied for a
policy of war risk insurance in the sum of ten thousand
dollars ($10,000.00) thereafter there were deducted from
his monthly pay certain sums of money as premium for
said insurance. That a certificate of war risk insurance
was duly issued to him by the terms whereof the defendant agreed to pay said plaintiff, or his estate, the sum of
$57.50 per month in the event he suffered permanent and
total disaibility, but said policy was never delivered to the
plaintiff.

III.

That while the said insurance policy was in force the
said plaintiff contracted the following disabilities, to-wit:
bronchiectasis, pulmonary tuberculosis and tubercular peritonitis.

IV.

That by reason of the foregoing the plaintiff was discharged, as aforesaid, totally and permanently disabled

from bronchiectasis, pulmonary tuberculosis and tubercular peritonitis, and plaintiff has been informed and believes, and therefore alleges as true, that he will always be so disabled and never again be able to follow any substantially gainful occupation, by reason whereof he became entitled to receive from the defendant the sum of $57.50 per month commencing on the 19th day of May, 1919.

V.

That the plaintiff has made due proof of said total and permanent disabilities to the said defendant and demanded payments of the aforesaid amounts, but the defendant disagreed with plaintiff as to his claim of disability and has failed to pay to the plaintiff the sum of $57.50 per month; that defendant has paid the plaintiff the sum of $11.21 per month commencing January 28th, 1925. That at this time the plaintiff is totally and permanently disabled and has been since the date of said discharge.

WHEREFORE, plaintiff demands judgment against the defendant in the sum of $57.50 per month from the date of said disabilities, together with interest thereon at the rate of six per cent per annum from the several dates same became due and payable, and for his costs and disbursements herein incurred.

COMES NOW the plaintiff and for its second cause of action against the defendant alleges as follows, to-wit:

I.

Plaintiff includes Paragraph One of its first cause of action as if it were here specifically set out.

II.

Plaintiff includes Paragraph Two of its first cause of action as if it were here specifically set out.

III.

Plaintiff includes Paragraph Three of its first cause of action as if it were here specifically set out.

IV.

That at the time of plaintiff's discharge from service he ceased paying premiums on said policy of insurance. That at the time of plaintiff's discharge from said service plaintiff was suffering from a compensable disability. That a rating for compensation from the date of plaintiff's discharge was given plaintiff by representatives of the defendant on the 2nd day of November, 1922. That if plaintiff was not permanently and totally disabled on the date of his said discharge from service then the plaintiff was totally and permanently disabled from September 12, 1922. That on the 12th day of September, 1922, plaintiff was entitled to due and uncollected compensation, and that by reason of said due and uncollected compensation plaintiff's insurance was in full force and effect on the 12th day of September, 1922. That the plaintiff became entitled to receive from the defendant the sum of $57.50 per month commencing on the 12th day of September, 1922, less the unpaid premiums and interest thereon at five per cent per annum, compounded annually, from the date of plaintiff's discharge to the 12th day of September, 1922.

V.

That plaintiff has made due proof of said total and permanent disability to the said defendant and demanded payment of the aforesaid amounts, but the defendant disagreed with plaintiff as to his claim of disability and has failed to pay the plaintiff the sum of $57.50 per month from the 12th day of September, 1922. That at this time the plaintiff is totally and permanently disabled, and has been since the 12th day of September, 1922.

WHEREFORE, the plaintiff demands judgment against the defendant in the sum of $57.50 per month from the 12th day of September, 1922, less the amount of unpaid premiums and interest thereon at the rate of five per cent per annum, compounded annually, from the date of plaintiff's discharge to the 12th day of September, 1922.

> David Spaulding
> DAVID SPAULDING
> Attorney for Plaintiff.

Verified.

[Endorsed: Filed Aug 21 1931   R. S. Zimmerman, Clerk   By Thomas Madden, Deputy Clerk.

———

[TITLE OF COURT AND CAUSE.]

DEMURRER TO AMENDED COMPLAINT.

COMES NOW the defendant, by Samuel W. McNabb, United States Attorney for the Southern District of California, and Clyde Thomas, Assistant United States Attorney for said district, and for cause of demurrer to plaintiff's amended complaint, alleges:

I.

That said complaint does not state facts sufficient to constitute a cause of action against this defendant.

II.

That said complaint does not state facts in its second cause of action sufficient to constitute a cause of action against this defendant.

III.

That said second cause of action does not state facts sufficient to show a right in this plaintiff to sue this defendant.

IV.

That said second cause of action is ambiguous, uncertain and unintelligible for the reason that it cannot be determined, in paragraph IV thereof, by what authority or claim of right the plaintiff is entitled to collect on his insurance policy because of total and permanent disability on the 12th day of September, 1922, after his policy had lapsed.

V.

That said second cause of action is barred by the statute of limitations.

WHEREFORE defendant demands that it be hence dismissed with its costs.

SAMUEL W. McNABB,
United States Attorney.

Clyde Thomas
CLYDE THOMAS,
Assistant United States Attorney.

POINTS and AUTHORITIES.

POINT I.

The matter of rating for compensation purposes is entirely within the discretion of the Veterans' Administration and cannot be reviewed by the court unless arbitrary, capricious or contrary to law. Armstrong v. United States, 16 Fed. (2nd) 387-389, C. C. A. 8.

"This is the precise language of the Supreme Court in Silberschein v. United States, 266 U. S. 221, 45 S. Ct.

69, 69 L. Ed. 256. No claim is made that the decision
of the Director upon the compensation awarded was unsupported by evidence, arbitrary, or capricious, nor that
he has refused or denied any application for readjust-
ment."

- - - - - - - - - - - -

"The application of the schedules and the determination
of the compensation due cannot well be made except
through the elaborate organization provided by law within
the Bureau itself. It is on this account that exclusive
control over matters of compensation are lodged in the
Bureau. The courts have no authority to determine and
adjust compensation, as such, even to the extent of reviewing the findings of the Bureau, except as hereinabove
stated. They may not do indirectly what they cannot do
directly."

It follows that the policy can only be revived, as the
plaintiff is apparently attempting to allege, by the action
of the Bureau.

POINT II.

Paragraph IV of the second cause of action is ambiguous and uncertain, as it cannot be determined therefrom
whether the Veterans' Administration did, by its action,
revive the veteran's policy or not, and that during the
time that such policy was in effect by such revival, the
plaintiff became totally and permanently disabled. It will
be noted from the statute itself that the permanent and

total disability of the plaintiff is necessary to create such revival. (38 USCA 516.)

POINT III.

Plaintiff's allegation of disagreement in paragraph V is a conclusion of law, and as such, will not sustain the plea. In addition to that, it should show that the claim was made to the Bureau as a claim for a revival of the policy under Section 516 of Title 38 USCA, before a disagreement exists as to a claim based on such circumstances, as distinguished from a claim made on the original policy, as relied on in the first cause of action. Berntsen v. United States, 41 Fed. (2nd) 663, C. C. A. 9, quoting on page 665:

"Such a disagreement so manifested, however, cannot justify the inauguration or maintenance of this suit, because the purpose of Congress in enacting the legislation herein relied upon by the appellant was to give the government, through its Veterans' Bureau, an opportunity to fully consider and pass upon the claim before a submission of the claim to a court was permitted. The disagreement contemplated by the statute must be a rejection by the government through the Bureau of the very claim which the applicant later presents by his suit."

In this case judgment of non-suit was affirmed by our own circuit.

POINT IV.

The second cause of action is barred by the statute of limitations by virtue of Section 445 of Title 38 USCA, as amended May 29th, 1928.

[Endorsed]: Filed Aug 28 1931 R. S. Zimmerman Clerk By Theodore Hocke Deputy Clerk

[TITLE OF COURT AND CAUSE.]

SECOND AMENDED COMPLAINT

COMES NOW the plaintiff and for cause of action against the defendant alleges as follows, to-wit:

I.

That the plaintiff is a resident of Los Angeles, County of Los Angeles, State of California. That he enlisted for military service in the United States Army on the 8th day of June, 1915, and was honorably discharged on the 19th day of May, 1919.

II.

That while in the military service of the United States, during the war time period, desiring to be insured against the risks of war, said William E. Straw applied for a policy of War Risk Insurance in the sum of Ten Thousand Dollars ($10,000.00). That a Certificate of War Risk Insurance was duly issued to him by the terms whereof the defendant agreed to pay the said plaintiff, or his estate, the sum of $57.50 per month in the event he suffered permanent and total disability to such an extent that he would be unable to follow continuously any substantially gainful occupation.

III.

That while the said insurance policy was in force and effect the plaintiff contracted the following disabilities, to-wit: bronchiectasis and pulmonary tuberculosis.

IV.

That by reason of the foregoing the plaintiff was discharged, as aforesaid, totally and permanently disabled from bronchiectasis and pulmonary tuberculosis; and plaintiff has been informed and believes, and therefore alleges as true, that he will always be so disabled and never again be able to follow any substantially gainful occupation, by reason whereof he became entitled to receive from the defendant the sum of $57.50 per month commencing on the 19th day of May, 1919.

V.

That if the plaintiff was not totally and permanently disabled on the 19th day of May, 1919, then plaintiff's said policy of War Risk Insurance remained in full force and effect up to and including the month of October, 1922. That if said plaintiff was not totally and permanently disabled on the 19th day of May, 1919, plaintiff was so disabled on the 1st day of September, 1922, and entitled to benefits of said policy as provided by law from September 1, 1922.

VI.

That the plaintiff has made due proof of said total and permanent disabilities to the said defendant and demanded payments of the aforesaid amounts, but the defendant disagreed with plaintiff as to his claim of disability and has failed to pay to the plaintiff the sum of $57.50 per month. That at this time the plaintiff is totally and permanently disabled and has been since the date of said discharge.

WHEREFORE, The plaintiff demands judgment against the defendant in the sum of $57.50 per month from the date of said disabilities.

David Spaulding

‛DAVID SPAULDING

Attorney for Plaintiff.

Verified.

[Endorsed]: Filed Sept 10, 1931. R. S. Zimmerman, Clerk By B. B. Hansen   Deputy Clerk

[TITLE OF COURT AND CAUSE.]

STIPULATION

Whereas the minutes of the trial in the above entitled action did not show fully proceedings that took place at that time,

IT IS HEREBY STIPULATED and agreed by the plaintiff and defendant in the above entitled action that an order may be entered de novo by the trial judge making a minute order showing as follows:

That the plaintiff dismissed his first Amended Complaint;

That following the objection and exception of the defendant to the plaintiff being allowed to file a Second Amended Complaint, it was stipulated and ordered by the court that the trial would proceed with the understanding that the defendant had demurred to the Second Amended Complaint and had made a motion to strike paragraph V in the Second Amended Complaint and that the demurrer had been overruled and the motion to strike had been denied and exception noted to each; that the said demurrer to the Second Amended Complaint was particularly based on the ground that the Second Amended Complaint did not show any disagreement as to the cause of action set out in the paragraph added to the Second Amended Complaint and not appearing in the first Amended Complaint;

That it was further stipulated and agreed that the defendant would be considered to have answered the Second Amended Complaint as set out in the Answer to the original Complaint with the addition of a denial of a disagreement as to the claim set out in the new paragraph and a plea of the statute of limitations as to the cause of action attempted to be set out in the new paragraph.

DATED: January   , 1932.

> David Spaulding
> > Attorney for Plaintiff.
>
> SAMUEL W. McNABB,
> > United States Attorney,
>
> Clyde Thomas
> CLYDE THOMAS
> Assistant United States Attorney,
> > Attorneys for Defendant.

[Endorsed]: Filed Feb. 15, 1932   R. S. Zimmerman, R. S. Zimmerman, Clerk.

[Title of Court and Cause.]

STIPULATION WAIVING JURY

IT IS HEREBY STIPULATED AND AGREED, by and between the respective parties to this action, that the above entitled cause be tried before the Court without a jury, trial by jury being hereby expressly waived.

DATED THIS 3rd day of September, 1931.

> David Spaulding
> > Attorney for Plaintiff,
>
> SAMUEL W. McNABB
> > United States Attorney,
>
> Clyde Thomas
> CLYDE THOMAS,
> Assistant United States Attorney
> > Attorneys for Defendant.

[Endorsed]: Filed Sep 3 1931   R. S. Zimmerman, Clerk   By Thomas Madden, Deputy Clerk

[TITLE OF COURT AND CAUSE.]

DAVID SPAULDING, Esq. of Los Angeles, Calif. for Plaintiff.

CLYDE THOMAS, Asst. U. S. Attorney for the United States.

CONCLUSIONS OF THE COURT

Under the allegations of the Second Amended complaint plaintiff veteran claims that he became totally and permanently disabled on May 19, 1919. He failed to establish such contention. The evidence proves that he worked sufficiently immediately subsequently to his discharge from the army until January 1921, with such regularity and vigor that he could not be classified as totally and permanently disabled during that period.

The amended complaint further alleges that if it be found as a fact that plaintiff was not totally and permanently disabled on the 19th of May, 1919, then and in that case, it is claimed that he became totally and permanently disabled within the meaning of his war risk insurance on September 1, 1922, when under his policy of war risk insurance and under applicable acts of Congress relative thereto, his insurance was in full force and effect. I am satisfied from the evidence that such contention has been sustained.

The Veterans' Bureau has admitted that for compensation purposes, under appropriate legislation, the veteran has suffered a total and permanent disability since January 8th, 1925, and he has been so rated by the Bureau for such compensation purposes, and has been receiving compensation under such rating since said date. The record proves a much earlier disability of total and permanent character within the meaning of the war risk insurance provisions of applicable acts of Congress and it is well within the established facts to conclude that on September 22, 1922, plaintiff was wholly disabled to the extent that since that date he is properly classified as totally and permanently disabled under his war risk insurance contract.

There is however, a serious legal obstacle that prevents recovery by the plaintiff in this action. It is elementary and has been uniformly established by the decisions of the Federal Courts that jurisdiction to judicially hear this cause arises only after disagreeement between the veteran and the Veterans' Bureau as the agency of the United States, and such disagreement must be upon the precise claim that is the basis of this suit. See Berntsen vs. United States, C. C. A. 9, 41 Fed. 2nd), 663. The only evidence of disagreement in the case at bar consists of a letter of the plaintiff to the director of the Veterans' Bureau dated January 15th, 1929, and a reply thereto from the General Counsel of the Veterans' Bureau to the plaintiff dated April 10th, 1929, these letters being plaintiff's exhibits 10 and 11 respectively. It appears from them, that the claim that is now the basis of this suit, that is to say, the claim of total and permanent disability from September 1, 1922, was never urged or presented by plaintiff to the Bureau and has never been considered or passed on by the Veterans' Bureau, and that there has therefore never been any disagreement between the parties over such claim. It is perfectly clear from the two letters that the claim asserted by the veteran was with reference solely to a discharge from the service, to-wit: in 1919, and such claim has not been substantiated, this, in my opinion, does not justify a finding that there has been any disagreement between the parties over a claim under the contract and/or insurance for total and permanent disability arising September 1, 1922, and for this reason, this Court is without jurisdiction to grant the plaintiff the relief prayed for in the Second Amended Complaint.

In view of the conclusions herein announced, it becomes unnecessary to consider or determine the merits of the counterclaim of the defendant asserted in its answer or other defenses claimed because if this Court has no jurisdiction to determine the subject matter of the suit as laid in the Second amended complaint, it likewise has no power to pass upon the counterclaim of the United States, and it becomes unnecessary to consider other defenses. The Veterans' Bureau should be given an opportunity to consider and pass upon the plaintiff's claim before he has the right to the Court's consideration.

For the foregoing reasons findings and judgment are ordered for the defendant in accordance with the views herein expressed, and the United States Attorney will accordingly prepare, serve and present the same under the rules of this Court.

Dated at Los Angeles, California, October 3, 1931.

Paul J. McCormick
Paul J. McCormick
United States District Judge

[Endorsed]: Filed Oct 3 1931 R. S. Zimmerman, Clerk By B. B. Hansen Deputy Clerk

[TITLE OF COURT AND CAUSE.]

PLAINTFF'S REQUEST FOR SPECIAL FINDINGS.

COMES NOW the plaintiff, William E. Straw, by his attorney, David Spaulding, and hereby respectfully requests the Court that in rendering and making its judgment in the above entitled cause, which has been submitted to the Court, that said Court make special findings of fact and law upon the following facts and issues included in said cause, as follows:

SPECIAL FINDINGS OF FACT.

Plaintiff requests the Court to find:

I.

That the plaintiff, William E. Straw, enlisted for military service in the United States Army on the 8th day of June, 1915, and was honorably discharged on the 19th day of May, 1919.

II.

That while in the military service of the United States, during the war time period, on February 3, 1918, plaintiff applied for and was granted a policy of war risk insurance in the amount of Ten Thousand Dollars ($10,-000.00). That if said plaintiff was not permanently and totally disabled on May 19, 1919, he was so disabled on or before October 1, 1922, when, under his policy of war risk insurance and under applicable acts of Congress relative thereto, his insurance was in full force and effect.

III.

That prior to October 1, 1922, plaintiff contracted bronchiectasis and pulmonary tuberculosis, which at all times since September 22, 1922, have resulted in plaintiff's permanent and total disability.

IV.

That a disagreement existed between plaintiff and defendant as to plaintiff's physical condition at any time between May· 19, 1919, and January 8, 1925. That the particular evidence upon which said disagreement is founded is plaintiff's exhibit No. 10, which is in words and figures as follows, to-wit:

"January 15, 1929

General Frank T. Hines
Director
United States Veterans Bureau
Washington, D. C.
Dear Sir:—

I hereby make formal application for the payment of my insurance in the amount of $57.50 per month to me by the Veterans Bureau of the United States Government, for the reason that I have been permanently and totally disabled ever since my discharge from the service due to my disabilities incurred in the service.

The facts will show that I have been unable to continuously follow any substantially gainful occupation ever since my discharge by reason of these disabilities.

Please notify me as soon as possible your decision on this request. I believe that I am entitled to the benefits of my insurance, and in the event of an unfavorable reply from the Director it is my intention to enter suit in civil courts for this insurance benefit.

Address all communications to me care P. O. Box 1031, Sawtelle, California.

I desire to cooperate with the Veterans Bureau in every respect.

Respectfully yours,

William E. Straw

C-1035790"

and plaintiff's exhibit No. 11, which is in words and figures as follows, to-wit:

"United States Veterans Bureau
Washington, D. C.

April 10, 1929

In reply refer to LL-35 C-1035790

Mr. William E. Straw
c/o Mr. Ashmun Brown, Adjutant-Treasurer
Disabled American Veterans of the World War
Chandler Porter Wright Chapter No. 10
Room 3, Waters Building
11340 Santa Monica Boulevard
Sawtelle, California

Dear Sir:—

Further reference is made to the claim submitted by you for a permanent and total disability rating from date of discharge.

You are advised that the Director, after a careful review, has decided the evidence is insufficient to warrant a permanent and total disability rating prior to January 8, 1925. Under this decision, the benefits claimed must be denied. However, this decision does not affect in any way the insurance benefits now payable.

This letter is evidence of a disagreement under Section 19 of the World War Veterans Act, 1924, as amended.

By direction,

William Wolff Smith

General Counsel"

CONCLUSIONS OF LAW.

I.

From the foregoing findings of fact the Court concludes as a matter of law that a disagreement existed between the plaintiff and defendant as to total permanent disability on September 22, 1922, and that jurisdiction was placed in the Courts to hear and determine all controversies under said contract of insurance and plaintiff's physical condition on September 22, 1922.

II.

. That plaintiff is entitled to judgment, as provided by law, under his contract of war risk insurance from and after September 22, 1922.

Dated this 2nd day of November, 1931.

David Spaulding

DAVID SPAULDING

Attorney for Plaintiff

These special findings, upon consideration, are hereby refused as being unjustified by the record.

Dated: Nov. 2nd, 1931.

Paul J. McCormick

UNITED STATES DISTRICT JUDGE

We hereby except to the above refusal of the Court.
Dated: Nov. 2nd, 1931.

David Spaulding

David Spaulding

Attorney for Plaintiff

[Endorsed]: Filed Nov. 2 1931 R. S. Zimmerman Clerk By Thomas Madden Deputy Clerk.

[TITLE OF COURT AND CAUSE.]

FINDINGS OF FACT AND CONCLUSIONS OF LAW.

This matter coming on regularly to be heard before the undersigned, one of the judges of the above entitled court, plaintiff appearing in person and by his counsel, David Spaulding, and the defendant appearing by Samuel W. McNabb, United States Attorney for the Southern District of California, and Clyde Thomas, Assistant United States Attorney for said District and from the evidence submitted, the following Findings of Fact were made:

FINDINGS OF FACT.

I.

At the time this action was commenced, plaintiff was and still is citizen of the United States and a resident of the County of Los Angeles, State of California.

II.

That plaintiff enlisted for military service in the United States Army on the 8th day of June, 1915, and was honorably discharged on the 19th day of May, 1919.

III.

That while in the military service of the United States during the war time period, plaintiff, William E. Straw, applied for a policy of War Risk Insurance in the sum of Ten Thousand Dollars ($10,000.00) and thereafter there was deducted from his monthly pay certain sums of money as premiums for said insurance; that a certificate of War Risk Insurance was duly issued to him by the terms whereof the defendant agreed to pay the said plaintiff, or his estate, the sum of $57.50 per month in the event he suffered permanent and total disability while said policy was in force; that by reason of the payment of premiums by plaintiff to the defendant, the said policy of insurance remained in full force and effect up to and including July 1, 1919.

IV.

That plaintiff became permanently and totally disabled within the meaning of his War Risk Insurance contract on September 1, 1922, when under his contract of War Risk Insurance and under applicable acts of Congress relative thereto, his insurance was in force and effect.

V.

That the plaintiff was not permanently and totally disabled on the 19th day of May, 1919, or at any time previous to January 1, 1921.

VI.

That plaintiff was totally and permanently disabled on the 22nd day of September, 1922, but that the only evidence of a disagreement between the plaintiff and defendant was the plaintiff's letter to the Director of the Veterans' Bureau dated January 15, 1929, and a reply thereto from the General Counsel of the Veterans' Bureau dated April 10, 1929, which letters were a claim for and denial thereof of total and permanent disability from discharge, to-wit, 1919; that said claim was not substantiated at the trial and that said claim and denial did not justify the finding that the same was or could be considered a disagreement between the parties over a claim under the contract of insurance for total disability arising September 1, 1922, and that the court was, therefore, without jurisdiction to grant a claim never theretofore considered or denied by the Veterans' Bureau. That likewise the court had no power to pass upon the counterclaim of the defendant herein for the same reason.

CONCLUSIONS OF LAW.

From the above Findings of Fact the court makes the following Conclusions of Law:

The plaintiff was not totally and permanently disabled at any time prior to January 1, 1921, and that there exists no disagreement as to any claim the plaintiff had against the Veterans' Bureau at any time subsequent to the 1st day of July, 1919, and the defendant is entitled to judgment against the plaintiff, that said plaintiff take nothing by this action and that the United States of America be allowed its costs.

> Paul J. McCormick
> United States District Judge.

Dated November 2nd, 1931.

APPROVED as to form as provided in Rule 44:

> David Spaulding,
> David Spaulding,
> Attorney for Plaintiff.

To all of which plaintiff excepts.

> David Spaulding,
> Att. for Plaintiff.

[Endorsed]: Filed Nov 12 1931   R. S. Zimmerman Clerk   By B. B. Hasen Deputy Clerk.

[TITLE OF COURT AND CAUSE.]

JUDGMENT.

The above entitled cause having come duly on for trial on the 10th day of September, 1931, before the Honorable Paul J. McCormick, one of the judges of the above entitled court, plaintiff appearing in person and by his atttorney, David Spaulding, the defendant, United States of America, appearing by Samuel W. McNabb, United States Attorney for the Southern District of California, and Clyde Thomas, Assistant United States Attorney for said District, a jury having been duly waived by written stipulations filed herein, and the court having duly considered the evidence introduced by both parties, and having on the 2nd day of October, 1931, rendered an opinion in favor of the defendant to the effect that the plaintiff was not entitled to recover by this said action and that the defendant was entitled to its costs.

NOW, THEREFORE, IT IS ORDERED, ADJUDGED AND DECREED that the plaintiff take nothing by his said Second Amended Complaint and that the defendant be given judgment for its costs in the sum of $128.90.

DATED: November 2nd, 1931.

Paul J. McCormick
United States District Judge.

APPROVED as to form as provided in Rule 44:

David Spaulding
Attorney for Plaintiff.

Judgment entered November 12th, 1931. R. S. Zimmerman, Clerk. By B. B. Hansen, Deputy Clerk.

To which plaintiff excepts.

David Spaulding,

Att. for Pl.

[Endorsed]: Filed Nov. 12, 1931 R. S. Zimmerman, Clerk By B. B. Hansen Deputy Clerk

———

[TITLE OF COURT AND CAUSE.]

ORDER FIXING TIME TO LODGE PROPOSED BILL OF EXCEPTIONS AND EXTENDING TERM OF COURT.

Upon application of the plaintiff herein, good cause appearing therefor, IT IS HEREBY ORDERED that plaintiff herein may have up to and including the 11th day of January, 1932, in which to lodge its proposed bill of exceptions herein; and

IT IS FURTHER ORDERED that the present term of court may be extended for that purpose.

DONE IN OPEN COURT this 2nd day of Nov. 1931.

Paul J. McCormick,

UNITED STATES DISTRICT JUDGE

[Endorsed]: Filed Nov. 2, 1931. R. S. Zimmerman, Clerk. By Thomas Madden, Deputy Clerk.

[TITLE OF COURT AND CAUSE.]

ORDER EXTENDING TIME WITHIN WHICH TO SERVE AND FILE BILL OF EXCEPTIONS AND EXTENDING TERM.

On Motion of Samuel W. McNabb, United States Attorney for the Southern District of California, and Clyde Thomas, Assistant United States Attorney for said District, and good cause appearing therefor;

IT IS ORDERED that the time within which the defendant herein may serve and file its proposed Bill of Exceptions herein as well as for the presentation settlement and allowance thereof is hereby extended to and including the 15th day of February, 1932.

IT IS FURTHER ORDERED that for the purpose of making and filing Bill of Exceptions herein, and the making of any and all motions necessary to be made within the term in which the Judgment herein was entered, the term of this Court is hereby extended to and including the 15th day of February, 1932.

Dated: December 31, 1931.

> Paul J. McCormick
> United States District Judge

[Endorsed]: Filed Dec 31 1931 R. S. Zimmerman, Clerk By Edmund L. Smith, Deputy Clerk

32   *William E. Straw vs.*

[TITLE OF COURT AND CAUSE.]

ENGROSSED BILL OF EXCEPTIONS.

BE IT REMEMBERED that the above entitled cause came on regularly for trial on the 10th day of September, 1931, before the Honorable Paul J. McCormick, one of the Judges of the above entitled Court; a jury having been waived by a stipulation in writing filed herein; the plaintiff appearing in person and by his attorney, David Spaulding; the defendant appearing by its attorneys, Samuel W. McNabb, United States Attorney for the Southern District of California, Clyde Thomas, Assistant United States Attorney, and H. C. Veit, Regional Attorney for the United States Veterans Bureau; it appearing that on August 21, 1931, plaintiff had filed his first amended complaint herein; it appearing that thereafter the defendant had filed a demurrer to the first amended complaint, and that on September 7, 1931, said demurrer came on regularly to be heard; it appearing that at the time of the hearing of the demurrer to the first amended complaint, plaintiff, by his attorney, David Spaulding, moved to strike said first amended complaint and asked leave to file his second amended complaint, whereupon the defendant demurred to the second amended complaint and made a motion to strike paragraph five of said second amended complaint, whereupon the Court reserved its ruling on said demurrer and motion until the date of trial.

WHEREUPON the following proceedings took place:

The COURT—The demurrer to the second amended complaint is overruled and motion to strike is denied, and an exception is noted to each ruling.

WHEREUPON it was stipulated by the parties and ordered by the Court that the trial would proceed and that the record would show that the said demurrer to the second amended complaint was particularly based on the ground that the second amended complaint did not show any disagreement as to the cause of action set out in the paragraph added to the second amended complaint and not appearing in the first complaint; that it was further stipulated and agreed that the defendant would be considered to have answered the second amended complaint, as set out in the answer to the original complaint, with the addition of a denial of a disagreement as to the claim set out in paragraph five of plaintiff's second amended complaint and a plea of the statute of limitations as to the cause of action set out in said paragraph five.

WHEREUPON the following proceedings took place:

William C. Rawlings, a witness on behalf of the plaintiff herein, after being first duly sworn on oath, testified as follows:

My name is William C. Rawlings. I am employed by the United States Veterans Bureau in the capacity of field examiner. In that capacity I have control and custody of the official records of the beneficiaries of the United States Veterans Bureau. I have the records of William E. Straw, a beneficiary of the United States Veterans Bureau. I have, as a part of the records, a letter dated January 15, 1929, wherein claim is made for the benefits of William E. Straw's war risk insurance.

WHEREUPON plaintiff's exhibit No. 10 was admitted in evidence. Plaintiff's exhibit No. 10 is, in words and figures, as follows:

"January 15, 1929.

General Frank T. Hines
Director
United States Veterans Bureau
Washington, D. C.

Dear Sir:—

I hereby make formal application for the payment of my insurance in the amount of $57.50 per month to me by the Veterans Bureau of the United States Government, for the reason that I have been permanently and totally disabled ever since my discharge from the service due to my disabilities incurred in the service.

The facts will show that I have been unable to continuously follow any substantially gainful occupation ever since my discharge by reason of these disabilities.

Please notify me as soon as possible your decision on this request. I believe that I am entitled to the benefits of my insurance, and in the event of an unfavorable reply from the Director it is my intention to enter suit in civil courts for this insurance benefit.

Address all communications to me care Post Office Box 1031, Sawtelle, California.

I desire to cooperate with the Veterans Bureau in every respect.

Respectfully yours,
William E. Straw
C-1035790"

I have with me, as a part of the records and files of the United States Veterans Bureau, a copy of a letter of disagreement, dated April 10, 1929.

WHEREUPON plaintiff's exhibit No. 11 was admitted in evidence. Plaintiff's exhibit No. 11 is, in words and figures, as follows:

"United States Veterans Bureau
Washington, D. C.

April 10, 1929

In reply refer to LL-35 C-1035790

Mr. William E. Straw
c/o Mr. Ashmun Brown, Adjutant-Treasurer
Disabled American Veterans of the World War
Chandler Porter Wright Chapter No. 10
Room 3, Waters Building
11340 Santa Monica Boulevard
Sawtelle, California

Dear Sir:—

.Further reference is made to the claim submitted by you for a permanent and total disability rating from date of discharge.

You are advised that the Director, after a careful review, has decided the evidence is insufficient to warrant a permanent and total disability rating prior to January 8, 1925. Under this decision, the benefits claimed must be denied. However, this decision does not affect in any way the insurance benefits now payable.

This letter is evidence of a disagreement under Section 19 of the World War Veterans Act, 1924, as amended.

By direction,
William Wolff Smith
General Counsel"

THEREAFTER plaintiff and defendant rested and the case was submitted to the Court.

THEREAFTER plaintiff submitted to the Court plaintiff's request for special findings and conclusions of law. Plaintiff's request for special findings and conclusions of law is, in words and figures, as followings, to-wit:

"UNITED STATES DISTRICT COURT
SOUTHERN DISTRICT OF CALIFORNIA
CENTRAL DIVISION

WILLIAM E. STRAW,   )
              Plaintiff,   )
)
        VS   )   No. 3583-M
)
UNITED STATES OF AMERICA,)
              Defendant.)
)

PLAINTIFF'S REQUEST FOR SPECIAL
FINDINGS.

COMES NOW the plaintiff, William E. Straw, by his attorney, David Spaulding, and hereby respectfully requests the Court that in rendering and making its judgment in the above entitled cause, which has been submitted to the Court, that said Court make special findings of fact and law upon the following facts and issues included in said cause, as follows:

SPECIAL FINDINGS OF FACT.

Plaintiff requests the Court to find:

I.

That the plaintiff, William E. Straw, enlisted for military service in the United States Army on the 8th day of June, 1915, and was honorably discharged on the 19th day of May, 1919.

II.

That while in the military service of the United States, during the war time period, on February 3, 1918, plaintiff applied for and was granted a policy of war risk insurance in the amount of Ten Thousand Dollars ($10,000.00). That if said plaintiff was not permanently and totally disabled on May 19, 1919, he was so disabled on or before October 1, 1922, when, under his policy of war risk insurance and under applicable acts of Congress relative thereto, his insurance was in full force and effect.

III.

That prior to October 1, 1922, plaintiff contracted bronchiectasis and pulmonary tuberculosis, which, at all times since September 22, 1922, have resulted in plaintiff's permanent and total disability.

IV.

That a disagreement existed between plaintiff and defendant as to plaintiff's physical condition at any time between May 19, 1919, and January 8, 1925. That the particular evidence upon which said disagreement is founded is plaintiff's exhibit No. 10, which is, in words and figures, as follows, to-wit:

"January 15, 1929

General Frank T. Hines
Director
United States Veterans Bureau
Washington, D. C.
Dear Sir:—

I hereby make formal application for the payment of my insurance in the amount of $57.50 per month to me by the Veterans Bureau of the United States Government, for the reason that I have been permanently and totally disabled ever since my discharge from the service due to my disabilities incurred in the service.

The facts will show that I have been unable to continuously follow any substantially gainful occupation ever since my discharge by reason of these disabilities.

Please notify me as soon as possible your decision on this request. I believe that I am entitled to the benefits of my insurance, and in the event of an unfavorable reply from the Director it is my intention to enter suit in civil courts for this insurance benefit.

Address all communications to me care Post Office Box 1031, Sawtelle, California.

I desire to cooperate with the Veterans Bureau in every respect.

Respectfully yours,
William E. Straw
C-1035790"

and plaintiff's exhibit No. 11, which is, in words and figures, as follows, to-wit:

"UNITED STATES VETERANS BUREAU

Washington, D. C., April 10, 1929

In reply refer to LL-35   C-1035790

Mr. William E. Straw
c/o Mr. Ashmun Brown, Adjutant-Treasurer
Disabled American Veterans of the World War
Chandler Porter Wright Chapter No. 10
Room 3, Waters Building
11340 Santa Monica Boulevard
Sawtelle, California

Dear Sir:
Further reference is made to the claim submitted by you for a permanent and total disability rating from date of discharge.

You are advised that the Director, after a careful review, has decided the evidence is insufficient to warrant a permanent and total disability rating prior to January 8, 1925. Under this decision, the benefits claimed must be denied. However, this decision does not affect in any way the insurance benefits now payable.

This letter is evidence of a disagreement under Section 19 of the World War Veterans Act, 1924, as amended.

By direction,
William Wolff Smith
General Counsel"

CONCLUSIONS OF LAW.

I.

From the foregoing findings of fact the Court concludes as a matter of law that a disagreement existed between the plaintiff and defendant as to total permanent disability on September 22, 1922, and that jurisdiction was placed in the Courts to hear and determine all controversies under said contract of insurance and plaintiff's physical condition on September 22, 1922.

II.

That plaintiff is entitled to judgment, as provided by law, under his contract of war risk insurance from and after September 22, 1922.

Dated this 12th day of November, 1931.

DAVID SPAULDING
Attorney for Plaintiff

These special findings, upon consideration, are hereby refused as not warranted by the record.

Dated November 12, 1931.

PAUL J. McCORMICK
United States District Judge

We hereby except to the above refusal of the Court. Dated November 12, 1931.

> DAVID SPAULDING
> Attorney for Plaintiff"

THEREAFTER the Court made and entered its findings of fact. Finding of fact No. 4 is as follows:

"That plaintiff became permanently and totally disabled within the meaning of his War Risk Insurance contract on September 1, 1922, when under his contract of War Risk Insurance and under applicable acts of Congress relative thereto, his insurance was in force and effect."

Finding of fact No. 5 is as follows:

"That plaintiff was totally and permanently disabled on the 22nd day of September, 1922, but that the only evidence of a disagreement between the plaintiff and defendant was the plaintiff's letter to the Director of the Veterans' Bureau dated January 15, 1929, and a reply thereto from the General Counsel of the Veterans' Bureau dated April 10, 1929, which letters were a claim for and denial thereof of total and permanent disability from discharge, to-wit: 1919; that said claim was not substantiated at the trial and that said claim and denial did not justify the finding that the same was or could be considered a disagreement between the parties over a claim under the contract of insurance for total disability arising September 1, 1922, and that the Court was, therefore, without jurisdiction to grant a claim never theretofore considered or denied by the Veterans' Bureau. That likewise the Court had no power to pass upon the counterclaim of the defendant herein for the same reason.

To which finding the plaintiff excepted.

The plaintiff herein prays that this, his proposed bill of exceptions, be allowed, settled and signed.

David Spaulding

DAVID SPAULDING

Attorney for Plaintiff

Received copy of within proposed bill of exceptions this 11 day of February, 1932.

Clyde Thomas

Attorney for Defendant.

UNITED STATES DISTRICT COURT
SOUTHERN DISTRICT OF CALIFORNIA
CENTRAL DIVISION

WILLIAM E. STRAW,

Plaintiff

vs.   No. 3583-M

United States of America,

Defendant

ORDER SETTLING BILL OF EXCEPTIONS.

The above cause coming on for hearing on this day, on the application of the plaintiff to settle his bill of exceptions heretofore duly lodged in this cause, and it appearing to the Court that the time within which to serve and file his bill of exceptions in the foregoing cause has been duly extended, and that said bill of exceptions as heretofore lodged with the Clerk is duly and seasonably presented for settlement and allowance; and it fur-

ther appearing that said bill of exceptions contains all
the material facts occurring upon the trial of the case,
together with the exceptions thereto, and all of the material matters and things occurring upon the trial, except
the exhibits introduced in evidence, which are hereby
made a part of said bill of exceptions by reference and
incorporation; and the Court being fully advised, it is by
the Court

ORDERED, that the said bill of exceptions be and
the same hereby is settled as a true bill of exceptions
in said cause, which contains all of the material facts,
matters, things and exceptions thereto occurring upon
the trial of said cause, and the same is hereby certified
accordingly by the undersigned Judge of this court, who
presided at the trial of the said cause, as a true, full and
correct bill of exceptions, and the Clerk of the court is
hereby ordered to file the same as a record in said cause,
and transmit it to the Honorable Circuit Court of Appeals
for the Ninth Circuit.

Signed in open court this 15th day of February, 1932.

                    Paul J. McCormick
          UNITED STATES DISTRICT JUDGE
Presented by:

                    David Spaulding
                    DAVID SPAULDING
                         Attorney for Plaintiff.

O. K. and complete and correct.

                    Clyde Thomas
                    Attorney for the United States

Filed: February 15, 1932.

[Endorsed]: Filed Feb. 15, 1932. R. S. Zimmerman.
R. S. Zimmerman, Clerk.

[TITLE OF COURT AND CAUSE.]

NOTICE OF APPEAL.

UNITED STATES OF AMERICA, SOUTHERN DISTRICT OF CALIFORNIA, CENTRAL DIVISION.

TO: THE UNITED STATES OF AMERICA, Defendant, and SAMUEL W. McNABB, CLYDE THOMAS and H. C. VEIT, Attorneys for said Defendant.

You, and each of you, will please take notice that William E. Straw, plaintiff in the above entitled cause, hereby appeals to the United States Circuit Court of Appeals for the Ninth Circuit from the judgment, decree and order entered in the above entitled cause on the 12th day of November, 1931, and that the certified transcript of record will be filed in said Appellate Court within thirty days from the filing of this notice.

David Spaulding
DAVID SPAULDING
Attorney for Plaintiff.

Received copy of the within notice of appeal this 17 day of December, 1931.

Clyde Thomas
Attorney for Defendant

[Endorsed]: Filed Dec. 21, 1931. R. S. Zimmerman, Clerk. By Edmund L. Smith, Deputy Clerk.

[TITLE OF COURT AND CAUSE.]

PETITION FOR APPEAL.

TO: THE HONORABLE, THE JUDGES OF THE UNITED STATES DISTRICT COURT, SOUTHERN DISTRICT OF CALIFORNIA

COMES NOW the plaintiff, William E. Straw, by his attorney, David Spaulding, and feeling himself aggrieved by the judgment entered in this case on the 12th day of November, 1931, hereby prays that an appeal may be allowed from the United States District Court for the Southern District of California to the United States Circuit Court of Appeals for the Ninth Circuit, and in connection with this petition petitioner hereby presents his assignments of error; and said plaintiff prays that his appeal be allowed and citation be issued as provided by law, and that a transcript of the record, proceedings and papers, upon which said judgment was based, duly authenticated, be sent to the United States Circuit Court of Appeals for the Ninth Circuit as by the rules of said Court in such cases made and provided.

David Spaulding
DAVID SPAULDING
Attorney for Plaintiff.

Received copy of within petition for appeal this 17 day of December, 1931.

Clyde Thomas
Attorney for Defendant.

[Endorsed]: Filed Dec. 21, 1931. R. S. Zimmerman, Clerk. By Edmund L. Smith, Deputy Clerk.

[TITLE OF COURT AND CAUSE.]

ORDER ALLOWING APPEAL

On the application of the plaintiff herein, IT IS HERE-BY ORDERED that an appeal to the United States Circuit Court of Appeals for the Ninth Circuit from the judgment heretofore entered and filed herein on the 12th day of November, 1931, be, and the same is, hereby allowed with bond in the sum of Two hundred and fifty Dollars ($250.00).

IT IS FURTHER ORDERED that a certified transcript of the record, exhibits, and stipulations and all proceedings be forthwith transmitted to the United States Circuit Court of Appeals for the Ninth Circuit.

DONE in open Court this 21 day of December, 1931.

Paul J. McCormick
UNITED STATES DISTRICT JUDGE.

[Endorsed]: Filed Dec. 21, 1931. R. S. Zimmerman, Clerk, by Edmund L. Smith, Deputy Clerk.

————

[TITLE OF COURT AND CAUSE.]

ASSIGNMENTS OF ERROR

COMES NOW William E. Straw, plaintiff in the above entitled action, by David Spaulding, the attorney of record, and in connection with his notice of appeal herein and petition for appeal herein, assigns the following errors, which he avers occurred at the trial of said case, upon which plaintiff will rely upon his prosecution of his appeal in this case from the judgment entered herein on the 12th day of November, 1931.

I.

That the District Court erred in making and entering its finding herein that plaintiff's letter to the Director, dated January 15, 1929, (plaintiff's exhibit No. 10) and a reply thereto from the General Counsel of the Veterans Bureau, dated April 10, 1929, (plaintiff's exhibit No. 11) did not justify the finding that the same was, or could be, considered a disagreement between the parties over a claim under the contract of insurance for total disability arising September 1, 1922.

II.

That the District Court erred in making and entering its finding herein that from the evidence no disagreement existed over a claim for insurance at any time other than from plaintiff's discharge, to-wit: 1919.

III.

That the District Court erred in making and entering its finding herein that there was no disagreement between the parties over a claim under a contract of insurance for a total disability arising in September, 1922.

IV.

That the District Court erred in making and entering its finding herein that there was no jurisdiction in the Court to hear and determine a claim for total disability arising in September, 1922.

V.

That the District Court erred in making and entering herein as its conclusion of law: "That there exists no disagreement as to any claim the plaintiff had against the Veterans Bureau at any time subsequent to the 1st day of July, 1919."

VI.

That the District Court erred in making and entering as its conclusion of law herein: "That the defendant is entitled to judgment against the plaintiff. That the plaintiff take nothing by this action."

VII.

That the District Court erred in making and entering its judgment herein for the defendant.

David Spaulding

DAVID SPAULDING

Attorney for Plaintiff

Received copy of within assignments of error this 17 day of December, 1931.

Clyde Thomas

Attorney for Defendant

[Endorsed]: Filed Dec. 21, 1931. R. S. Zimmerman, Clerk By Edmund L. Smith Deputy Clerk.

[TITLE OF COURT AND CAUSE.]

BOND

KNOW ALL MEN BY THESE PRESENTS that WILLIAM E. STRAW, as principal, and Two Hundred Fifty Dollars ($250.00) cash as surety, are held and firmly bound unto the UNITED STATES OF AMERICA, in the full and just sum of Two Hundred Fifty Dollars ($250.00) to be paid to said UNITED STATES OF AMERICA to which payment well and truly to be made we bind ourselves, our heirs, executors and adminis-

trators, jointly and severally, by these presents. Sealed
with our seals and dated this 25th day of February, 1932.

WHEREAS, lately at a District Court of the United
States for the Southern District of California in a suit,
pending in said court between WILLIAM E. STRAW,
Plaintiff, and UNITED STATES OF AMERICA, Defendant, a decree was rendered against the said WIL-
LIAM E. STRAW, and the said WILLIAM E. STRAW
having obtained an appeal and filed a copy thereof in the
Clerk's office of said court to reverse the decree in the
aforesaid suit, and ordering that a citation issue directed
to the said UNITED STATES OF AMERICA, as provided by law, citing and admonishing it to be and appear
at a session of the United States Circuit Court of' Appeals
for the Ninth Circuit, to be held at the City of San Francisco   ;

NOW, the condition of the above obligation is such,
that if the said WILLIAM E. STRAW shall prosecute
his appeal to effect and answer all costs on said appeal, if
he fail to make his plea good, then the above obligation to
be void; else to remain in full force, virtue and effect.

SEALED and delivered in the presence of:

William E. Straw.

APPROVED:

Geo. Cosgrave

U. S. District Judge

Examined and recommended for approval

David Spaulding

Solicitor for Appellant.

[Endorsed]:   Filed Feb 25 1931.   R. S. Zimmerman
Clerk.

[TITLE OF COURT AND CAUSE.]

PLAINTIFF'S PRAECIPE FOR TRANSCRIPT OF RECORD.

TO THE CLERK OF THE ABOVE ENTITLED COURT:

You will please issue certified copy of the following papers in the above entitled cause to comprise the transcript of record on appeal and transmit the same, duly authenticated, to the Clerk of the United States Circuit Court of Appeals for the Ninth Circuit at San Francisco, California:

1—Complaint

2—Answer

3—Amended Complaint

4—Demurrer to Amended Complaint

5—Second Amended Complaint

6—Minute Order of September 10, 1931, relative to filing Second Amended Complaint, demurrer thereto, motion to strike, answer thereto

7—Stipulation Waiving Jury

8—Conclusions of the Court

9—Plaintiff's request for special findings of fact and conclusions of law

10—Findings of fact and Conclusions of Law

11—Judgment

12—Order of 12th day of November, 1931, fixing time to lodge proposed bill of exceptions and extending term of court to the 11th day of January, 1932

13—Notice of appeal

14—Petition for appeal

15—Plaintiff's assignments of error

16—Order allowing appeal,

17—Plaintiff's bill of exceptions

18—Citation on appeal

19—This praecipe

20—Order and stipulation for transmission of original exhibits

21—Order extending time within which to serve and file bill of exceptions and extending term,

omitting titles, verifications, and acceptance of service on all said documents, except Citation on Appeal and Complaint.

David Spaulding

David Spaulding

Attorney for Plaintiff.

Received copy of within praecipe this   day of December, 1931.

Clyde Thomas

Attorney for Defendant.

[Endorsed]: Filed Feb. 15, 1932   R. S. Zimmerman, R. S. Zimmerman   Clerk.

[TITLE OF COURT AND CAUSE.]

CLERK'S CERTIFICATE.

I. R. S. Zimmerman, clerk of the United States District Court for the Southern District of California, do hereby certify the foregoing volume containing 50 pages, numbered from 1 to 50 inclusive, to be the Transcript of Record on Appeal in the above entitled cause, as printed by the appellant, and presented to me for comparison and certification, and that the same has been compared and corrected by me and contains a full, true and correct copy of the citation; complaint; answer; amended complaint; demurrer to amended complaint; second amended complaint; stipulation; stipulation waiving jury; conclusions of the court; plaintiff's request for special findings; findings of fact and conclusions of law; judgment; order fixing time to lodge proposed bill of exceptions and extending term of court; order extending time within which to serve and file bill of exceptions and extending term; bill of exceptions and order settling bill; notice of appeal; petition for appeal; order allowing appeal; assignment of errors; bond on appeal, and praecipe.

I DO FURTHER CERTIFY that the amount paid for printing the foregoing record on appeal is $ and that said amount has been paid the printer by the appellant herein and a receipted bill is herewith enclosed, also that the fees of the Clerk for comparing, correcting and certifying the foregoing Record on Appeal amount to................ and that said amount has been paid me by the appellant herein.

William E. Straw vs.

IN TESTIMONY WHEREOF, I have hereunto set my
hand and affixed the Seal of the District Court of the
United States of America, in and for the Southern
District of California, Central Division, this..............
day of March in the year of Our Lord One Thousand Nine Hundred and Thirty-two, and of our
Independence the One Hundred and Fifty-sixth.

R. S. ZIMMERMAN,

Clerk of the District Court of the
United States of America, in and
for the Southern District of
California.

By

Deputy.

IN THE

United States
Circuit Court of Appeals,

FOR THE NINTH CIRCUIT. 2

William E. Straw,

Appellant,

vs.

United States of America,

Appellee.

BRIEF OF APPELLANT.

DAVID SPAULDING,
P. O. Box 581, West Los Angeles
Attorney for Appellant

FILED

APR 8 - 1932

PAUL P. O'BRIEN,
CLERK

Parker, Stone & Baird Co., Law Printers, Los Angeles.

TOPICAL INDEX.

PAGE

Argument 7

Assignment of Errors.. 5

Conclusions 15

Insurance Remaining in Force by Reason of Section
   305 13

Pertinent Statutes and Regulations................................... 6

Statement of the Case... 3

The Amendment of July 3, 1930...................................... 10

The Effect of Plaintiff's Exhibit No. 10......................... 12

The Effect of Plaintiff's Exhibit No. 11......................... 11

The Purpose of a Disagreement...................................... 15

TABLE OF CASES.

PAGE

Bernsten v. United States (C. C. A. 9) 41 F. (2d) 663 15

LaMarche v. United States (C. C. A. 9) 28 F. (2d)
828 10

United States v. DeArmond (C. C. A. 8) 48 F. (2d)
465 at page 467...11, 15

United States v. Gianakourous (C. C. A. 6) 41 F.
(2d) 521 9

United States v. Hendrickson (C. C. A. 10), 53 F.
(2d) 797 ....14, 15

United States v. Scott (C. C. A. 6), 50 F. (2d) 773...... 10

United States v. Vance (C. C. A. 8), 48 F. (2d) 472
at page 474.. 9

STATUTES.

PAGE

Section 19 of the World War Veterans Act of October
6, 1917, as amended, Section 445, Title 38, United
States Code (38 U. S. C. A. 445)................................ 6

Section 19 of the Act of October 6, 1917, as amended
by the Act of July 3, 1930, Section 445, Title 38,
U. S. C. A.. 7

IN THE

United States
Circuit Court of Appeals,
FOR THE NINTH CIRCUIT.

William E. Straw,

Appellant,

vs.

United States of America,

Appellee.

BRIEF OF APPELLANT.

Statement of the Case.

William E. Straw, appellant, hereinafter called plaintiff, brought suit on a policy of war risk insurance. He filed an amended complaint and a second amended complaint. The issue was heard before the trial court under the allegations of the second amended complaint. By the second amended complaint plaintiff alleged military service, the issuance of the policy, the maturity of the policy by reason of total and permanent disability on the date of plaintiff's discharge from service, to-wit, May 19, 1919; and, in the alternative, that if plaintiff was not totally and permanently disabled on the 19th day of May, 1919, then his said policy of insurance remained in full force and effect up to and including the month of October, 1922; that if plaintiff was not totally and permanently disabled on the 19th day of May, 1919, he was so disabled on the 1st day of September, 1922, and entitled to the benefits of his policy as provided by law from September 1, 1922. Plaintiff alleged a disagreement existed between plaintiff and defendant.

The appellee, hereinafter called the defendant, filed an answer to the original complaint. Said answer admitted military service, admitted the existence of the policy, admitted a disagreement as to the claim laid in the original complaint, alleged the policy lapsed on June 1, 1919, by reason of non-payment of premium due on that date; affirmatively alleged a claim due the defendant by reason of certain insurance kept in force under the provisions of section 305 of the World War Veterans Act of 1924, as amended. By stipulation it was agreed that defendant's answer to the original complaint should be considered an answer; to the second amended complaint with the addition of a denial of a disagreement to the claim set out in paragraph five of said second amended complaint and a plea to the statute of limitations to the claim set out in paragraph five of said second amended complaint.

A jury was regularly waived in writing and from the evidence the court determined the plaintiff was not permanently and totally disabled on the date of his discharge, to-wit, May 19, 1919; that the plaintiff was so disabled on September 1, 1922; that plaintiff's insurance was in full force and effect on September 1, 1922 [Tr. p. 27]. The trial court determined that there was no disagreement under a claim of total and permanent disability in 1922, and ordered judgment for the defendant.

Prior to judgment the court was requested to make special findings of fact and conclusions of law on the question of a disagreement at any ¦time between plaintiff's discharge, to-wit, May 19, 1919, and January 8; 1925 [Tr. pp. 23-24]. An exception was saved to the trial court's adverse ruling.

From the findings of the court and the exceptions thereto the question before this court is whether or not there was justification in the trial court to hear and determine any rights plaintiff may have had under a policy of war risk insurance during the month of September, 1922.

Assignment of Errors.

The plaintiff will rely upon and argue the assignment of errors, or parts thereof, as are here set out.

I.

That the District Court erred in making and entering its finding herein that the plaintiff's letter to the director, dated January 15, 1929 (Plaintiff's Exhibit No. 10), and a reply thereto from the General Counsel of the Veterans Bureau, dated April 10, 1929 (Plaintiff's Exhibit No. 11), did not justify the finding that the same was or could be considered a disagreement between the parties over a claim under the contract of insurance for total disability arising September 1, 1922.

II.

That the District Court erred in making and entering its finding herein that from the evidence no disagreement existed over a claim for insurance at any time other than the plaintiff's discharge, to-wit, 1919.

III.

That the District Court erred in making and entering its finding herein that there was no disagreement between the parties over a claim under the contract of insurance for a total disability arising in September, 1922.

IV.

That the District Court erred in making and entering its finding herein that there was no jurisdiction to hear and determine a claim for total disability arising in September, 1922.

V.

That the District Court erred in making and entering its conclusion of law that there exists no disagreement as to any claim the plaintiff had against the Veterans Bureau at any time subsequent to the 1st. day of July, 1919.

VII.

That the District Court erred in making and entering its judgment herein for the defendant.

Pertinent Statutes and Regulations.

Section 19 of the Act of October 6, 1917, as amended, section 445, title 38, U. S. Code (38 USCA 445):

> "In the event of a disagreement as to claim under a contract of insurance between the bureau and any person or persons claiming thereunder, an action on the claim may be brought against the United States either in the Supreme Court of the District of Columbia or the District Court of the United States in and for the district in which said persons or any one of them reside, and jurisdiction is hereby conferred upon such courts to hear and determine all such controversies."

The act as amended by the act of July 3, 1930, section 445, title 38, USCA:

> "The term 'claim' as used in this section means any writing which alleges permanent and total disability at a time when the contract of insurance was in force, or which uses words showing an intention to claim insurance benefits; and the term 'disagreement' means a denial of the claim by the director or someone acting in his name on an appeal to the director."

Argument.

There can be no question that the proof of a statutory "disagreement" was a necessary part of plaintiff's case. To prove said necessary allegation plaintiff offered in evidence a letter to the director of the United States Veterans Bureau, dated January 15, 1929 [Tr. p. 34], Plaintiff's Exhibit No. 10. It is as follows:

"January 15, 1929.

General Frank T. Hines
Director
United States Veterans Bureau
Washington, D. C.

Dear Sir:—

> I hereby make formal application for the payment of my insurance in the amount of $57.50 per month to me by the Veterans Bureau of the United States Government, for the reason that I have been permanently and totally disabled ever since my discharge from the service due to my disabilities incurred in the service.

> The facts will show that I have been unable to continuously follow any substantially gainful occupation ever since my discharge by reason of these disabilities.

Please notify me as soon as possible your decision on this request. I believe that I am entitled to the benefits of my insurance, and in the event of an unfavorably reply from the Director it is my intention to enter suit in civil courts for this insurance benefit.

Address all communications to me care Post Office Box 1031, Sawtelle, California.

I desire to cooperate with the Veterans Bureau in every respect.

Respectfully yours,

William E. Straw
C-1 035 790"

The reply thereto, Plaintiff's Exhibit No. 11 [Tr. p. 35], is as follows:

"United States Veterans Bureau

Washington, D. C.

April 10, 1929

In reply refer to LL-35 C-1 035 790

Mr. William E. Straw
c/o Mr. Ashmun Brown, Adjutant-Treasurer
Disabled American Veterans of the World War
Chandler Porter Wright Chapter No. 10
Room 3, Waters Building
11340 Santa Monica Boulevard
Sawtelle, California

Dear Sir:—

Further reference is made to the claim submitted by you for a permanent and total disability rating from date of discharge.

You are advised that the Director, after a careful review, has decided the evidence is insufficient to warrant a permanent and total disability rating prior to January 8, 1925. Under this decision, the benefits claimed must be denied. However, this decision does not affect in any way the insurance benefits now payable.

This letter is evidence of a disagreement under section 19 of the World War Veterans Act, 1924, as amended.

By direction,

William Wolff Smith

General Counsel"

From Plaintiff's Exhibit No. 10 it is apparent there was a claim made to the bureau for insurance benefits prior to the instituting of this suit; and from Plaintiff's Exhibit No. 11 it is equally apparent that said claim was formally denied by the bureau prior to filing suit for, on the face of Plaintiff's Exhibit No. 11, there is a statement of what said letter purports to be. Said letter states: "This letter is evidence of a disagreement under section 19."

In *United States v. Vance* (C. C. A. 8), 48 F, (2d) 472, at page 474, the court stated:

"By section 19 of the act, as amended (section 445, title 38, United States Code (38 USCA, section 445)), jurisdiction is conferred upon the District Court to hear and determine all controversies between the policyholder and the government 'in the event of disagreement as to claim under a contract of insurance.'"

In *United States v. Gianakourous* (C. C. A. 6), 41 F. (2d) 521, the court stated:

"There arose under the policy a disagreement because of which suit was brought. The court therefore had jurisdiction as to any controversy under the policy."

In *United States v. Scott* (C. C. A. 6), 50 F. (2d) 773, the court stated:

> "And while the burden is on the plaintiff to prove total and permanent disability and that such disability existed during the life of the policy, mere inability to prove the exact time when the disability arose, if it began during the life of the policy, is not fatal. (LaMarche v. United States (C. C. A. 9), 28 F. (2d) 828.)"

It would then seem apparent that one of the questions open to evidence after disagreement is the date·the policy lapsed or the length of time the policy remained in force. Such question is open to contention and is susceptible to evidence. It would also seem apparent that plaintiff is not required in the bureau more definitely to prove his claim than he is in court.

The Amendment of July 3, 1930.

If ever there existed doubt concerning the meaning of the phrase "in the event of disagreement as to claim under a contract of insurance," that doubt must be dispelled by the action of Congress in the amendment of July 3, 1930. By said amendment it is apparent that Congress intended that a claimant should advise the bureau in writing that he claimed permanent and total disability at a time when the contract of insurance was in force and, in order that a veteran claimant would not become entangled in technicalities, any writing using words showing an intention to claim insurance benefits was sufficient to put the defendant on notice. It is equally apparent that the burden was then placed on the bureau and no limit was made as to time for their review or preparation. Plaintiff's Exhibits Nos. 10 and 11 squarely meet the requirements as stated by Congress in its latest amendment on the subject.

The Effect of Plaintiff's Exhibit No. 11.

In *United States v. DeArmond* (C. C. A. 8), 48 F. (2d) 465, the Eighth Circuit Court of Appeals had occasion to consider a very similar claim by a veteran, or his representative, and the answer from defendant thereto On page 467 there appears the claim:

"He was discharged with S. C. D. and from and after the date of discharge he has been totally incapacitated. Because of his physical condition he is unquestionably permanently and totally unfit to carry on any substantially gainful occupation."

It will be observed that plaintiff there, as plaintiff here, claimed total and permanent disability and fixed as the starting date the date of his discharge. In reply thereto there appears in said case:

"Reference is made to previous correspondence in which you stated the above-named veteran had been permanently and totally disabled since his discharge from the service and requested payment of insurance benefits.

"You are informed that after considering the case the Director has decided that the evidence was not sufficient to warrant a permanent and total rating prior to September 12, 1922. In view of the fact that the veteran's insurance lapsed for non-payment of premiums due long prior to the effective date of the total and permanent rating, the insurance claimed cannot be paid."

It will be observed that the representatives of the bureau there, as in the instant case, fixed the earliest date under which they would consider the claimant totally and permanently disabled. It will be observed that what difference there is in the bureau's reply in the DeArmond case, *supra,* and the bureau's reply in the instant case, is the difference in dates as to their contention under which total and permanent disability arose. In that case, in view of the claimant's request and the bureau's reply thereto, the court stated:

> "The foregoing was tantamount to a denial of total and permanent disability at any time prior to September 12, 1922. This would amount to a disagreement as to the total and permanent disability of the assured on June 1, 1920.

> "The amendment was not a departure and neither did the amended petition attempt to state a cause of action where there had been no disagreement with the Director of the Veterans Bureau so as to deny jurisdiction of the court."

The Effect of Plaintiff's Exhibit No. 10.

It will be observed that in Plaintiff's Exhibit No. 10 plaintiff stated:

> "I have been permanently and totally disabled *ever* since my discharge from the service."

> "I have been unable to continuously follow any substantially gainful occupation *ever* since my discharge."

Webster says the word "ever" means at all times, at any time, always.

Plaintiff then said at all times subsequent to his discharge he had been totally and permanently disabled. One of the times subsequent to his discharge and prior to January 15, 1929, was the month of September, 1922. The very claim made by claimant then was that he was, during the month of September, 1922, totally and permanently disabled. It is submitted that his claim would be no more inclusive and certainly no more intelligent had he chronologically set out the days covered by the word "ever". That the defendant understood and observed the word "ever" would appear from their answer, otherwise they should have answered simply that the claimant was not totally and permanently disabled on the date of his discharge and left the road open to the claimant to suggest subsequent dates. In view of Plaintiff's Exhibit No. 11, it would have been a useless gesture again to call to the attention of the defendant the plaintiff's condition on any date prior to January 8, 1925, for such inquiry had already been specifically answered.

Insurance Remaining in Force by Reason of Section 305.

It will be observed in the conclusions of the court [Tr. p. 19] that:

> "under applicable Acts of Congress relative thereto, his insurance was in full force and effect,"

and from the findings of fact and from finding of fact No. 3 [Tr. p. 27]:

> "that by reason of payment of premiums by plaintiff to defendant the said policy of insurance remained in full force and effect up to and including July 1, 1919."

The evidence relied on by the plaintiff to meet the defense of lapsation was the provisions of section 305 of the World War Veterans Act, or section 516, title 38, United States Code (38 USCA, section 516).

In *United States v. Hendrickson* (C. C. A. 10), 53 F. (2d) 797, the court was considering a claim with many similar aspects. In that case:

> "A jury found that the appellee has been permanently and totally disabled within the meaning of his policy of war risk insurance since February 2, 1920. * * * The appellee paid his premiums in cash until his discharge from the army in February, 1919, * * * but he was paid nothing on account of his compensation until June, 1920, when his back pay was remitted in a lump sum without deducting for insurance premiums. It appears then without dispute that his uncollected compensation in February, 1920, was more than enough to have kept his insurance in force."

The court stated:

> "A war risk insurance policy does not lapse for non-payment of premiums as long as the government fails to pay the soldier installments of compensation to which he is entitled under the ratings of the bureau. * * * Under the precise words of the statute, his policy had not lapsed when it matured. * * * The appellee had, therefore, a policy of insurance in good standing on February 2, 1920; he became totally and permanently disabled on that day."

The court then sets out what is necessary to obtain jurisdiction in such a case. It is precisely the same as in any other case and requires no extraordinary allegations on the part of the claimant to the bureau.

The Purpose of a Disagreement.

It has heretofore been stated to this court that the purpose of a disagreement is obvious. It is not a technical trap for the unwary but, rather, an orderly procedural step which redounds to the benefit of both the veteran and the government. The requirement that the government be put upon notice by a claim for insurance benefits affords the Veterans Bureau the opportunity to avoid litigation and, if litigation be deemed necessary, to take steps necessary to the maintenance of an adequate defense. If, however, the government has been put upon notice, as is required by the statute, if the government has made a review and has announced its contention, such statutory provision has served its function. It is the claim for benefits, the review, the denial, and the statement that this claim was considered such a claim as required a denial, as contemplated by section 19 of the act, which distinguishes this case from the case of *Berntsen v. United States* (C. C. A. 9), 41 F. (2d) 663, upon which case the defendant relied in the lower court.

Conclusion.

In conclusion it is respectfully submitted:

1. In view of the findings of the trial court and in view of *United States v. Hendrickson, supra,* this plaintiff had on September 1, 1922, a policy of war risk insurance in full force and effect, upon which date he became totally and permanently disabled.

2. In view of Plaintiff's Exhibit No. 11 and *United States v. DeArmond, supra,* a disagreement existed be-

tween the plaintiff and defendant as to his total and permanent disability on that day and jurisdiction was thereby placed in the court.

3. In view of finding of fact No. 4 made by the trial court, judgment should have been ordered for the plaintiff.

4. That the judgment entered by the trial court should be reversed and judgment ordered for the plaintiff.

Respectfully submitted,

DAVID SPAULDING,
Attorney for Appellant.

IN THE

United States
Circuit Court of Appeals,
FOR THE NINTH CIRCUIT.

William E. Straw,

                Appellant,

      vs.

United States of America,

                Appellee.

BRIEF OF APPELLEE.

FILED

MAY 1 2 1932

PAUL P. O'BRIEN,
           CLERK

Samuel W. McNabb,
      United States Attorney;
Clyde Thomas,
      Assistant United States Attorney.

Parker, Stone & Baird Co., Law Printers, Los Angeles.

Statement of Case... 3

Argument 5

    Amendment of July 3, 1930.. 6

    Effect of Plaintiff's Exhibits 10 and 11....................... 6

    Insurance Remaining in Effect by Reason of Sec.
       305 9

    Plaintiff's Action Barred by Statute of Limitations.... 10

Conclusion 10

———

AUTHORITIES RELIED ON.

PAGE

Berntsen v. U. S., 41 Fed. (2nd) 663 (9th C.
    C. A.) 9

World War Veterans' Act, Sec. 19 (38 U. S. C. A.
    445) as amended... 10

World War Veterans' Act, Sec. 305 (38 U. S. C. A.
    516) 4

No. 6772.

IN THE

United States
Circuit Court of Appeals,
FOR THE NINTH CIRCUIT.

William E. Straw,

Appellant,

vs.

United States of America,

Appellee.

BRIEF OF APPELLEE.

STATEMENT OF CASE.

It seems pertinent, before discussing the issues in this case, to make a more complete statement of the conditions under which it was tried than is set out in Appellant's Brief.

After issue joined on the original Complaint plaintiff, appellant herein, filed an Amended Complaint [Tr. p. 8]. The first cause of action in the Amended Complaint was identical with the original Complaint and alleged that the plaintiff was totally and permanently disabled at the date of his discharge from the United States Army on May 19, 1919, at which time his war risk insurance policy was still

in force. The second cause of action set out in effect that
by virtue of Section 305 of the World War Veterans' Act
(38 U. S. C. A. 516), the plaintiff was entitled to the
benefits of such act in keeping his war risk insurance
policy in force until September 12, 1922, at which time he
was alleged to be totally and permanently disabled and
entitled to the benefits of said policy.

To this Amended Complaint, defendant filed a demurrer
[Tr. p. 11]. Thereafter, plaintiff asked leave to withdraw
the Amended Complaint and on the date of trial filed a
Second Amended Complaint [Tr. p. 15] in which it was
sought to avoid the objections set out by defendant's
demurrer to the Amended Complaint by combining the two
causes of action. This was done by the simple process of
adding paragraph V of the Second Amended Complaint
to the cause of action as originally set out, stating in the
alternative that

"if the plaintiff was not totally and permanently disabled on the 19th day of May, 1919, then plaintiff's
said policy of War Risk Insurance remained in full
force and effect up to and including the month of
October, 1922. That if said plaintiff was not totally
and permanently disabled on the 19th day of May,
1919, plaintiff was so disabled on the 1st day of September, 1922, and entitled to benefits of said policy
as provided by law from September 1, 1922."

The defendant stated its desires to file a demurrer to the
Second Amended Complaint and a motion to strike paragraph V thereof on all grounds set out in the demurrer to
the Amended Complaint, and to urge particularly that the
Second Amended Complaint did not show any disagreement as to the cause of action set out in the said para-

graph V, and that on such demurrer being overruled the defendant be considered to have answered the Complaint denying all material matters therein alleged, and particularly denying a disagreement as to any claim set out in paragraph V of the said Second Amended Complaint and a plea of the Statute of Limitations as to the cause of action set out in said paragraph V [Tr. p. 33]. The demurrer and motion to strike was overruled by the Court and exception noted to each ruling [Tr. p. 32]. Thereupon the Court proceeded to the trial of the matter as set out in appellant's statement.

ARGUMENT.

Plaintiff has based its entire argument on the issue of whether or not the claim filed by plaintiff with the Veterans' Bureau and the Veterans' Bureau's reply thereto constitutes a disagreement as to the plaintiff's claim by virtue of Section 305 as of September, 1922. There is admittedly a disagreement as to any claim the veteran might have as of the date of his discharge. Appellee argued and the Court found that the disagreement as of the date of discharge did not contemplate and did not constitute a disagreement as to any claim arising subsequently to discharge by reason of Section 305. Appellant first cites the cases of *United States v. Vance* and *United States v. Gianakourous*. In both of these cases the question raised was as to the jurisdiction of the Court over the cause, a disagreement not being denied in either case. Appellant then cites the case of *United States v. Scott* in which the defendant sought to require the plaintiff to prove the exact date on which the disability arose and the Court held that if the plaintiff proved the disability to have arisen during the life of the policy, the dates of which were not in dispute, that the defendant was not entitled to a directed verdict merely because the plaintiff had not fixed the exact date on which the disability began. The case of *La Marche v. United States,* a Ninth Circuit case, was to like effect. Disagreement was not an issue in either of these cases.

Amendment of July 3, 1930.

Appellant attempts to broaden his disagreement and in effect relax the requirement for a disagreement by arguing that Congress so intended when it provided that any writing, using words showing an intention to claim insurance benefits, was sufficient. Obviously, Congress' only intention by such provision was to prevent the bureau becoming supertechnical in its defenses. On the other hand, it is just as apparent on reading the said Act and the Amendments thereto that Congress fully intended that no insurance claim should be litigated in the courts until the bureau had had an opportunity to pass fully thereon.

Effect of Plaintiff's Exhibits 10 and 11.

Appellant argues that Plaintiff's Exhibit 11 [Tr. p. 35] denying plaintiff's claim is broader and more inclusive than the claim itself [Plaintiff's Ex. 10, Tr. p. 34]. Plaintiff claimed disability from date of discharge due to disabilities incurred in the service. In denying this claim, the Veterans' Bureau stated:

"Further reference is made to the claim submitted by you for a permanent and total disability rating *from date of discharge.*

"You are advised that the Director after careful review, has decided the evidence is insufficient to warrant a permanent and total rating prior to January 8, 1925. Under this decision *the benefits claimed* must be denied. *However, this decision does not effect in any way the insurance benefits now payable.*"

It will be noted that this denial referred to the claim as "from date of discharge" and that it denied "the benefits claimed." It then recites that such decision does not effect in any way the insurance benefits now payable. It will thus be seen that the disagreement itself refers to insurance benefits arising subsequent to the claim denied but does not in any way attempt to pass on such claim. It thus negatives any idea that the bureau was denying any claim arising under and by virtue of Section 305.

Appellant attempts to broaden this denial under the authority of *United States v. De Armond,* 48 Fed. (2d) 465. However, on examination of that case it will be found that the claim relied on by the defendant was based on a war risk insurance contract kept in force by the payment of premiums. "It was undisputed that all premiums were paid up to and including September, 1921" (page 466). "The original petition fixed the date of his incapacity as June 20, 1919. Appellant objected to the amendment which changed the date from June 1, 1920" (page 466). It will be noted that both dates were within the life of the policy. No reliance was made on Section 305 to maintain the policy in effect after the insured had ceased paying premiums thereon. The Court held that under such claim and disagreement based on the same policy, that the date of disability was immaterial and, as held in the previous cases, the only question was as to disability during the life of the policy. In the instant case, we have the additional question as to whether or not the policy was kept in force and effect by operation of Section 305. Such would be an entirely new question to be passed on by the Veterans' Bureau and, if not claimed by the veteran, would not and need not, in the natural course of events, be passed upon by the Veterans' Bureau. Not only is this true but ajudication of such claim was excepted from the disagreement as heretofore pointed out.

No claim was ever made by the plaintiff to the bureau that he considered his policy in force and effect by virtue of Section 305, subsequent to the 19th day of May, 1919. He now rests his appeal on the proposition that the bureau only has to pass on the date of his total and permanent disability. Appellee contends and believes that the bureau has as much right to pass on the question of whether or not a contract of insurance is in force as it has to pass on the question of the disability of the claimant. Obviously, the question does not often arise for the policy is in effect as long as the premiums are paid thereon. But when it is claimed by act of law or otherwise, the policy is in force and effect for a longer period, or if it should be claimed that the policy was in effect by payment of premiums for a longer period than is shown by the Veterans' Bureau records, it is submitted that it would be necessary to have a disagreement with the Veterans' Bureau as to the existence of such policy. In the present case, there is no claim shown to have been made to the Veterans' Bureau that the policy was in force and effect subsequent to the 19th day of May, 1919, and consequently no disagreement as to the policy being in force and effect subsequent to that time. This question has been very definitely passed upon by this Court in the case of *Berntsen v. United States,* 41 Fed. (2d) 663, in which this Court says:

> "Such a disagreement so manifested, however, cannot justify the inauguration or maintenance of this suit, because the purpose of Congress in enacting the legislation herein relied upon by the appellant was to give the government, through its Veterans' Bureau, an opportunity to fully consider and pass upon the claim before a submission of the claim to a court was permitted. The disagreement contemplated by the statute must be a rejection by the government through the Bureau of the very claim which the applicant later presents by his suit."

Insurance Remaining in Force by Reason of Section 305.

Appellant relies on the case of *United States v. Hendrickson,* 53 Fed. (2d) 797, to establish the fact that his insurance policy was still in force and effect after he ceased paying premiums thereon. The statement made by the Court in that case is true when all the provisions of Section 305 have been complied with. The law provides that under certain conditions, the insurance policy shall be construed to have been continued in force and effect. This is not in conflict with the government's position in this case, that the Veterans' Bureau should pass on the claim based on such conditions before the insured is entitled to sue on his policy. It will be noted that the Hendrickson case was one in which a disagreement was admitted and the defense was based on the claim that no action could be maintained thereon. In other words, in that case, the plaintiff had secured the very disagreement on which the action was based and the lack of which the government is setting up as a defense in this case.

Plaintiff's Action Barred by Statute of Limitations.

Appellee also relies on the Statute of Limitations as a defense to the cause of action set out as of September, 1992. A demurrer was filed to the Amended Complaint on the grounds that the second cause of action was barred by the Statute of Limitations [Tr. p. 11]. When the Second Amended Complaint was filed, it was stipulated that the same demurrer would be deemed to have been filed thereto. This demurrer was overruled and exception noted [Tr. p. 32]. The Second Amended Complaint was filed September 10, 1931 [Tr. p. 16], and the Amended Complaint, on August 21, 1931 [Tr. p. 11], which was the first pleading claiming disability as of September, 1922. This was more than six years after the alleged disability and more than one year after the 3rd day of July, 1930, which is the period of limitation established by law. (38 U. S. C. A. 445.) It follows that defendant's demurrer should have been sustained and is sufficient reason for affirming the judgment from which this appeal is taken.

CONCLUSION.

1. No claim was filed by the appellant with the Veterans' Bureau claiming a policy of insurance to be in force by virtue of Section 305 and that appellant was disabled during such time.

2. The claim filed by appellant was definitely based on the policy in force by virtue of his having paid premiums thereon and not a continuation thereof by operation of law.

3. The denial was of the exact claim filed with the bureau.

4. Such denial did not in any manner pass on the question as to whether or not there was a continuation of the appellant's policy by force of Section 305 but to the contrary stated that such was not the case.

5. No disagreement existing between the appellant and the Veterans' Bureau as to such claim, the present action cannot be maintained against the United States.

6. Appellant's cause of action is barred by the Statute of Limitations.

Wherefore, appellee asks that the judgment of the lower court be affirmed and that it be awarded its costs.

Respectfully submitted,

SAMUEL W. McNABB,
United States Attorney;
CLYDE THOMAS,
Assistant United States Attorney.

No. 6779

United States

Circuit Court of Appeals

For the Ninth Circuit. ⁴⁄

EDWARD L. HAFF, AS ACTING
~~JOHN D. NAGLE~~, as Commissioner of Immigration for the Port of San Francisco,

Appellant,

vs.

TOM TANG SHEE,

Appellee.

Transcript of Record.

Upon Appeal from the United States District Court for
the Northern District of California,
Southern Division.

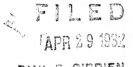

No. 6779

United States

Circuit Court of Appeals

For the Ninth Circuit.

JOHN D. NAGLE, as Commissioner of Immigration for the Port of San Francisco,

Appellant,

vs.

TOM TANG SHEE,

Appellee.

Transcript of Record.

Upon Appeal from the United States District Court for the Northern District of California, Southern Division.

INDEX

[Clerk's Note: When deemed likely to be of an important nature, errors or doubtful matters appearing in the original certified record are printed literally in italic; and, likewise, cancelled matter appearing in the original certified record is printed and cancelled herein accordingly. When possible, an omission from the text is indicated by printing in italic the two words between which the omission seems to occur.]

Page

Assignments of Errors.. 25

Certificate of Clerk to Transcript of Record........ 30

Citation on Appeal.. 30

Exhibit "A" 9

Exhibit "B" 12

Notice of Appeal....................... 23

Order to Show Cause.... 20

Order Granting Petition for Writ................................. 22

Order of Discharge.. 22

Order Allowing Appeal.. 27

Order Transmitting Original Exhibits......................... 28

Petition for Writ of Habeas Corpus............................ 2

Petition for Appeal.. 24

Praecipe for Transcript of Record on Appeal...... 29

Stipulation for Introduction of Original Immigration Records 21

In the Southern Division of the United States
District Court,

Northern District of California.

No. 20588-S.

In the Matter of

TOM TANG SHEE

On Habeas Corpus.

NAMES OF ATTORNEYS:

For Respondent and Appellant:

UNITED STATES ATTORNEY, San Francisco, Calif.

For Petitioner and Appellee:

STEPHEN M. WHITE, ESQ., 576 Sacramento St., San Francisco, Calif.

In the Southern Division of the United States
District Court, in and for the Northern
District of California.

Second Division.

No. 20588-S.

In the Matter of

TOM TANG SHEE

On Habeas Corpus.

No. 29996/2-9; ex SS Taiyo Maru,
January 14, 1931.

PETITION FOR WRIT OF HABEAS CORPUS.

To the Honorable, the Southern Division of the United States District Court, for the Northern District of California:

The petition of Tom Wong respectfully shows:

I.

That he is a native born citizen of the United States, having been born at San Francisco, California, on February 20, 1894.

II.

That he has resided and remained continuously in the United States ever since his birth, save for the following trips to China: departed on May 9, 1902, and returned on September 29, 1911; departed on December 30, 1927, and returned on January 14, 1931; that on each occasion of his departure from and return to the United States, his status as a native born citizen of the United States was investigated by the United States Immigration authorities and, as a result, it was found and conceded that he was born in the United States and subject to the jurisdiction thereof.

III.

That on March 3, 1910, at Mow Peng Village, Hoy Ping District, China, he married a Chinese person by the name of Tom Tang Shee, who is now and has ever since been his wife.

IV.

That on January 14, 1931, his said wife arrived in the United States from China and thereupon applied to the United [1*] Immigration authorities for the Port of San Francisco for admission to the United States under the status of a wife of an American citizen who was married prior to May 26, 1924, as provided for in Section 13, paragraph (c), subdivision (4), of the Immigration Act of 1924, approved May 26, 1924 and as amended by an Act of Congress of June 13, 1930; that her application for admission was heard by a Board of Special Inquiry, which was convened by the Commissioner of Immigration for the Port of San Francisco and, as a result of the testimony and evidence introduced before the said Board of Special Inquiry, it was found and decided, as follows:

1. That your petitioner is a native born citizen of the United States.

2. That the said Tom Tang Shee is the wife of your petitioner and that she was married to your petitioner prior to May 26, 1924.

3. That the said Tom Tang Shee is not in possession of a non-quota immigration visa,

that, having found that the said Tom Tang Shee was not in possession of a non-quota immigration visa, the said Board of Special Inquiry thereupon excluded her from admission to the United States

---

*Page-number appearing at the foot of page of original certified Transcript of Record.

and ordered her deportation to China; that an appeal was taken to the Secretary of Labor and that, as a result, the excluding decision of the said Board of Special Inquiry was affirmed.

V.

That the said Tom Tang Shee is now in custody of John D. Nagle, Commissioner of Immigration for the Port of San Francisco, at the United States Immigration Station at Angel Island, State and Northern District of California, and the said John D. Nagle, acting under the orders of the Secretary of Labor, has given notice of his intention to deport the said Tom Tang Shee on the first available steamer.

VI.

That your petitioner alleges, as he is advised and be- [2] lieves, that the Board of Special Inquiry and the Secretary of Labor and each of them, in denying the application for admission to the United States of the said Tom Tang Shee and the said John D. Nagle, in holding her in custody so that her deportation may be effected, are unlawfully confining, imprisoning and restraining her of her liberty, in the following particulars, to wit:—

1.   That Section 13 of the Immigration Act approved May 26, 1924, Subdivision (c) thereof, provides as follows:

"No alien ineligible to citizenship shall be admitted to the United States unless such alien

* * * (4) is the Chinese wife of an American citizen who was married prior to the approval of the Immigration Act of 1924, approved May 26, 1924.''

That your petitioner alleges that the said statute does not require that the Chinese wife of an American citizen who was married prior to the approval of the Immigration Act of May 26, 1924, possess a non-quota Immigration Visa or any Visa, in order to be admissible to the United States; that the said immigration authorities, namely, the Board of Special Inquiry and the Secretary of Labor, in denying the said Tom Tang Shee admission to the United States on the ground that she was not in possession of a non-quota Immigration Visa, have added and imposed a condition or requirement not prescribed by the statute in such cases made and provided for and that they have thereby acted arbitrarily and in excess of the power and authority committed to them.

2. That your petitioner alleges that on or about December 3, 1930, the said Tom Tang Shee applied to the United States Consulate at Hongkong, China for an immigration visa, which would permit her to proceed to the United States under the status of a Chinese wife of an American citizen who was married prior to May 26, 1924; that, upon the occasion of her said application, she presented to the said American Consulate evidence of the fact that she was a Chinese person, that her husband, who is

your petitioner, was a native born citizen of [3] the United States and that she was married to your petitioner prior to May 26, 1924; that the said American Consulate thereupon executed a document designated as a petition for the issuance of an immigration visa, in which document there was incorporated all the evidence aforesaid, and thereupon informed the said Tom Tang Shee that she had permission to proceed to the United States; that your petitioner alleges that under Section 2, Paragraph (a), and Section 13, Paragraph (a) of the Immigration Act approved May 26, 1924, the said American Consulate is authorized to issue an immigration visa to an immigrant, who is about to proceed to the United States and, in this connection, your petitioner further alleges that it was the duty of the said American Consulate, who had the evidence before him that the said Tom Tang Shee was the Chinese wife of an American citizen who was married prior to the approval of the Immigration Act approved May 26, 1924, to issue an immigration visa to the said Tom Tang Shee and that his failure to issue a proper immigration visa or any visa was through no fault of the said Tom Tang Shee, but that the failure and omission to issue a proper immigration visa or any visa are wholly due to the said American Consulate; that your petitioner alleges that in view of the circumstances and evidence aforesaid equity will consider that as done, which should have been done and will, therefore, consider that the said American Con-

sulate issued to the said Tom Tang Shee a proper
immigration visa; that the said immigration authorities, namely, the Board of Special Inquiry and the
Secretary of Labor, in denying the said Tom Tang
Shee admission into the United States on the ground
that she was not in possession of a proper immigration visa, have failed and omitted to consider the
equity in the case and have thereby acted arbitrarily
and in excess of the power and authority committed
to them in such cases made and provided for.

VII.

That your petitioner, has filed herewith, as Exhibit "A", [4] a copy of the decision of the Board
of Special Inquiry and hereby refers to the same
with the same force and effect as if set forth in full
herein; that your petitioner has, also, filed herewith, as Exhibit "B", a copy of the brief of Washington Counsel, which was filed before the Secretary of Labor, and which is hereby referred to as
a memorandum of points and authorities in behalf
of the said Tom Tang Shee in this proceeding.

VIII.

That the said Tom Tang Shee is, as hereinbefore
alleged, confined at the United States Immigration
Station at Angel Island, California; that she is
between five and six months advanced in pregnancy
and for said reason cannot withstand a further and
continued detention at the said station without suffering severe hardship and impairment of health.

IX.

That your petitioner, as the husband of the said Tom Tang Shee, verifies this petition upon behalf of the said Tom Tang Shee and as and for the act of the said Tom Tang Shee.

WHEREFORE, your petitioner prays that a writ of habeas corpus be issued and directed to John D. Nagle, Commissioner of Immigration for the Port of San Francisco, California, commanding and directing him to hold the body of the said Tom Tang Shee, within the jurisdiction of this Court, at a time and place to be specified in this order, together with the time and cause of her detention, so that the same may be inquired into the end that the said Tom Tang Shee may be restored to her liberty and go hence without day.

Dated at San Francisco, California, April 15, 1931.

STEPHEN M. WHITE,
Attorney for Petitioner. [5]

United States of America,
State of California,
City and County of San Francisco.—ss.

Tom Wong, being first duly sworn, deposes and states as follows:

That he is the petitioner named in the foregoing petition; that he has read the petition and knows the contents thereof; that the same is true of his own knowledge, except as to those matters stated therein on information and belief and, as to those matters, he believes it to be true.

TOM WONG.

Subscribed and sworn to before me this 14th day of April, 1931.

(Seal)   STEPHEN M. WHITE,
        Notary Public in and for the City and County
        of San Francisco, State of California.

(Endorsed): Filed Apr. 15, 1931. [6]
29996/2-9   2-5-31

SUMMARY

By CHAIRMAN:

(Exhibit "A")
(Finding and Decision of Special
Board of Inquiry)

Applicant is seeking admission as the wife of Tom Wong, whose status as a native of the U. S. is established by the records at hand. Tom Wong, who gave his age as 38 testified that he was born in S. F. and that he has made two trips to China, first departing for that country when he was nine years old, File 29996/2-8 shows that he apparently departed from this port on May 9, 1902 on the S. S. Nippon Maru for China, and that subsequent to his arrival here on the S. S. China on Sept. 29, 1911, he was admitted as a native. He last departed for China in Dec. 1927, in possession of duly approved Form 430, and returned to the U. S., accompanied by the present applicant.

Tom Wong was the only witness presented in behalf of the present applicant. Applicant has also given her age as 38 years, and according to the testimony given, the couple were married at the Mow Peng Village in St 2-1-22 (Mar. 3, 1910). It is noted that when Tom Wong returned to this port from China in Oct. 1911 he stated that he was married to Ong (Tang) Shee on the date just mentioned and that his wife was then at the Mow Village, Hpd. China. He further claimed that he had one son Jim Jar born in St 2-10 (Nov. or Dec. 1910), and said son apparently was admitted as of the relationship claimed at Seattle, in Oct. 1927 (their file 7555/13-16).

Applicant proved to be a rather unsatisfactory witness; she at times stated that she had forgotten about matters which she could reasonably be expected to know. She seemed too reluctant in giving many answers and also wept at intervals. She has the appearance of a respectable hardworking country woman, and I am satisfied she is at least the age claimed. She stated that she has never attended school and that she is able to count only up to ten. [7]

The testimony of applicant and her alleged husband is in substantial accord, except concerning two or three matters which are not deemed of vital importance. After carefully considering all of the evidence in hand, and the fact that applicant appears to be quite ignorant, the members of the Board are of the opinion that it should be conceded that Tom Tang Shee is the wife of Tom Wong, a native of the United States.

Applicant is without the required non-quota immigration visa, but there was presented in her behalf petition in duplicate, for such a visa, executed by the alleged husband at the United States Consulate at Hong Kong on December 3, 1930. The petition bears the seal of the American Consulate General; American Foreign Service Fee Stamp in the sum of $2.; and notation "H.K. 2403 $6.80". Applicant asserted that she did not know whether she had applied for an immigration visa "because her husband attended to everything." Tom Wong's testimony is to the effect that applicant is not in possession of an immigration visa; that he just filled out the petition for issuance of immigration visa; that he was informed at the Consulate that it was "all right"—that he should go to the ship with applicant and present the Forms (633) when he purchased tickets; that he was not informed at the Consulate that any other document was necessary; that he knew that it was necessary for applicant to have immigration visa and that he thought that the documents mentioned (Forms 633) were visa.

It is noted that on Jan. 15, 1931, applicant was certified by the Medical Examiner of Aliens at this Station as being afflicted with "uncinariasis (hookworm Disease) Class 'B'—which, in my opinion, may affect her ability to earn a living."

It is therefore moved that the applicant be denied on the grounds that she is an alien not in possession of an unexpired immigration visa or return permit, is not exempted from the said requirements in said respect under any of the provisions of the immigration laws; that she has been certified by Public [8] Health Surgeons as afflicted with a physical defect, Class B, which said defect may affect her ability to earn a living; and that the burden of proof has not been sustained as required by Section 23 of the Act of 1924.

(Endorsed): Filed Apr. 15, 1931. [9]

George W. Hott,
Attorney & Counsellor at Law,
Evans Building,
Washington, D. C.
Exhibit "B"
(Brief of Washington Counsel filed with the Secretary of Labor in behalf of Tom Tang Shee)

IN THE DEPARTMENT OF
LABOR
CHINESE DIVISION
No. 55742/689
In re: Tom Tang Shee, Wife of Native.
BRIEF FOR APPLICANT
Statement

The above mentioned applicant arrived at San Francisco, January 14, 1931, and applied for admission as the wife of Tom Wong, (Tom Moon

Suey), a native-born citizen of the United States.

The citizenship of the husband and the applicant's relationship to him are conceded. The applicant was excluded on the ground that she was "not in possession of an unexpired immigration visa or return permit, and not exempted from the requirements in said respect under any of the provisions of the immigration laws."

The husband was born in San Francisco February 20, 1894. He made two trips to China, departing from this country on or about May 9, 1902, and returning to this country September 29, 1911. He departed on his last trip December 30, 1927, in possession of a duly approved Form 430 certificate and he returned to this country January 14, 1931, accompanied by the present applicant. His only child Hom (Tom) Gam Gow, was admitted to this country through the port of Seattle (No. 7555/13-16) on October 29, 1927.

VISA NOT REQUIRED

I.

It is not believed that the provisions of the immigration Act of 1924, relating to visas, have any application to Chinese aliens. This act embraces two separate and dis- [10] tinct systems of exclusion which have individual fields of operation.

(1) The quota provisions and the visa provisions are part and parcel of the quota-visa system of exclusion, where they find their exclusive field of operation. Under the plan of this law, the neces-

sity for the use of the immigration visa grows out of the establishment of quotas, the office of the visa being to assure that every immigrant who should be, is counted against his proper quota and counted currently. The visa has no other field of operation under this law. The possession of an immigration visa is a wholly useless document for any purpose except to keep check on the quota and furnish credentials to the holder of his right to proceed to this country for the purpose of having his eligibility to admission inquired into by the proper officers of the United States Government, (Section 2, Subdivision g). This system is merely a modification and extension of the quota system which had been in operation for several years prior to the passage of the Immigration Act of 1924 and had no application to Chinese persons.

(2) The second system of exclusion relates to aliens who are ineligible to citizenship (section 13, subdivision c) and is in part supplemental to the Chinese Exclusion Laws which have been in force for many years, with some modification of the prior laws which is not material in this case. This class of aliens has no quota, and where no quota exists, there is no office for the visa to perform. Under the authority conferred by subdivision (e) of section 12, the Secretaries of State, Commerce and Labor, and the President, through the proclamation issued by the President, on the recommendation of said secretaries, have authoritatively construed the law as requiring that the quota-visa provisions shall

not be applied to aliens covered by the separate in-eligible-to-citizenship excluding system. See procla-mation of the President (No. 1872) establish- [11] ing immigration quotas, incorporated in the im-migration Rules of January 1, 1930, page 106, wherein it is stated, (at page 108); "all quotas hereby established are available only for persons who are eligible to citizenship in the United States and admissible under the immigration Laws of the United States."

II.

In an event it is submitted that the Chinese wife of an American citizen is specifically excepted from the quota-visa excluding provisions of the Immigra-tion Act of 1924, but if required to have a visa, it should have been given to her by the American Consul at Hong Kong when she appeared before him prior to her embarkation for the United States. By virtue of the amendment of June 13, 1930, sec-tion 13 (c) of the Act of 1924 now reads:

"No alien ineligible to citizenship shall be ad-mitted to the United States unless such alien (1) is admissible as a non-quota immigration under the provisions of subdivisions (b), (d), or (e) of Sec-tion 4, or (2) is the wife, or the unmarried child under eighteen years of age, of an immigrant admis-sible under subdivision (d), and is accompanying or following to join him, (3) is not an immigrant as defined in section 3, or (4) is the Chinese wife of an American citizen who was married prior to May 26, 1924." (8 U. S. C. A., section 213c).

It will be noted that the statute itself does not classify the Chinese wife of an American citizen as a non-quota immigrant, and the amendment does not increase the classes of non-quota immigrants as provided for in section 4; as to aliens ineligible to citizenship, the statute specifies only three classes, namely, (b) returning residents; (d) teachers or ministers and their wives and children, and (e) students, who are admissible as non-quota immigrants. Of course, section 4 (a), as it stood prior to the amendment, does not comprehend within its meaning the Chinese wife of an American citizen, [12] (Chang Chan et al. v. Nagle, 268 U. S. 346, 45 S. Ct. 540), and it is not believed that the amendment itself, either expressly or impliedly, brings the Chinese wife of an American citizen within section 4 (a), as a non-quota immigrant.

It is therefore respectfully submitted that the Chinese wife of an American citizen is an alien who by virtue of Section 13 (c) (4), belongs to an excepted class, absolutely independent of other excepted classes, and it follows that this applicant was entitled to obtain an immigration visa directly from the American Consul, the same as other immigrants (section 2 (a) of the Immigration Act of 1924), rather than making application to the Commissioner General of Immigration for the issuance of the visa, the procedure required of non-quota immigrants under section 9. It will be noted that section 9 (a) relates to non-quota immigrants by reason of relationship under the provision of subdivision (a) of section 4 which, as above mentioned, does not apply to the Chinese wives of American citizens, (Chang Chan et al. v. Nagle, supra), and under section 6 which relates to preferences within the quotas and has no application in the pending case because no person ineligible to citizenship comes within the quota provisions. It therefore appears certain that the American Consul has the authority to issue a visa to the Chinese wife of an American citizen and that it was his duty to issue the same. This case appears to come squarely within the decisions of the courts in re Spinella, 3 Fed. (2d) 195, and Ex parte Seid Soo Hong, 23 Fed. (2) 847, in each of which it was held that the omission or neglect of the American Consul to issue the proper visa should not be chargeable to the applicants and that equity would consider that as done which should have been done.

It will be noted that this applicant and her husband both appeared before the American Consul for the purpose of securing the necessary documents to permit the applicant [13] to accompany her husband to this country, but the applicant being unable to read English and the husband having no knowledge as to the procedure in such cases relied upon the American Consul and they believed that he had issued to the wife all of the documents that were necessary to insure her admission to the United States, but instead it appears that the American Consul merely had the applicant's husband execute before him a petition, Form 633, for the issuance of an immigration visa. However, this document and the testimony taken before the board of special inquiry, contains all of the necessary facts showing conclusively that the applicant is entitled to admission to this country as the wife of a native-born citizen. In the case of Ex parte Seid Soo Hong, supra, the son of a merchant who came to the United States without a visa and had not made the affidavit upon the special form prepared by the State Department, as required by the Immigration Rules, the court said: "all of the necessary information has come before the immigration authorities and they have found the facts essential to his admission."

It was conceded by the board of special inquiry that this applicant has satisfactorily established the fact that she is the wife of a native of the United States and she was excluded solely on the ground that she did not have an immigration visa which they believed the law required. In view of this fact, it would seem to be a useless thing to require this applicant to return to China for the purpose of securing such visa, and for no other reason, when it is conceded that she has established all the necessary facts to secure her admission to the United States. In principle the case of Tsoi Sim v. U. S., 116 Fed. 920, directly applies as showing that the doing of a vain thing is to be avoided. The Circuit Court of Appeals of the Ninth Circuit said:

"If appellant was to be deported she would have the unquestioned right to immediately return, and would be entitled to land and remain in this country, upon the sole [14] ground that she is the lawful wife of an American citizen." The court further stated:

"By this act her status was changed from that of a Chinese laborer to that of a wife of a native-born citizen (American). Her husband is not before this court, but his rights, as well as hers, are involved. * * * On the contrary, the native-born, by virtue of his birth, becomes a citizen of the United States, and is entitled to greater rights and privileges than the alien merchant. The wife has the right to live with her husband, enjoy his society; receive his support and maintenance and all the comforts and privileges of the marriage relations. These are hers, as well as his, natural rights. By virtue of her marriage, her husband's domicile became her domicile, and thereafter she was entitled to live with her husband, and remain in this country." It is respectfully submitted that the appeal should be sustained.

Respectfully submitted,

GEORGE W. HOTT,

Attorney for Applicant.

Feb. 26, 1931.

Note—

The triplicate copy of the testimony is submitted herewith.

G. W. H.

(Endorsed): Filed Apr. 15, 1931. [15]

(Title of Court and Cause.)

ORDER TO SHOW CAUSE.

Good cause appearing therefor, and upon reading the verified petition on file herein:—

IT IS HEREBY ORDERED that John D. Nagle, Commissioner of Immigration for the Port of San Francisco, appear before this Court on the 27th day of April, 1931, at the hour of 10 o'clock AM of said day, to show cause, if any he has, why a writ of habeas corpus should not be issued herein, as prayed for, and that a copy of this order be served upon the said Commissioner, and a copy of the petition and said order be served upon the United States Attorney for this District, his representative herein.

AND IT IS FURTHER ORDERED that the said John D. Nagle, Commissioner of Immigration, as aforesaid, or whoever, acting under the orders of the said Commissioner, or the Secretary of Labor, shall have the custody of the said Tom Tang Shee, or the Master of any steamer upon which she may have been placed for deportation by the said Commissioner, are hereby ordered and directed to retain the said Tom Tang Shee, within the custody of the said Commissioner of Immigration, and within the jurisdiction of this Court until its further order herein.

Dated at San Francisco, California, April 15, 1931.

A. F. ST. SURE,
United States District Judge.

(Endorsed): Filed Apr. 15, 1931. [16]

(Title of Court and Cause.)

STIPULATION

for Introduction of Original Immigration Records.

IT IS HEREBY STIPULATED by and between the attorneys for the respective parties hereto that the original immigration records pertaining to the application for admission to the United States of the above named, Tom Tang Shee, may be introduced in evidence and filed herein as exhibits in the above entitled proceedings.

Dated this 19th day of October, 1931.

STEPHEN M. WHITE,
Attorney for Petitioner.

GEORGE J. HATFIELD,
U. S. Attorney,

by H. A. VAN DER ZEE,
Assistant U. S. Attorney.

So Ordered:

A. F. ST. SURE,
U. S. District Judge.

(Endorsed): Filed Oct. 20, 1931. [17]

District Court of the United States,
Northern District of California.
Southern Division.

AT A STATED TERM of the Southern Division of the United States District Court for the Northern District of California, held at the Court Room thereof, in the City and County of San Francisco, on Monday the 19th day of October, in the year of our Lord one thousand nine hundred and thirty-one.

PRESENT: the Honorable, A. F. ST. SURE, Judge.

No. 20588.

In the Matter of

TOM TANG SHEE

On Habeas Corpus.

The application for Writ of Habeas Corpus (by order to show cause) came on this day to be heard. S. M. White, Esq., appearing as Attorney for petitioner and H. A. van der Zee, Esq., Asst. U. S. Atty., appearing for Respondent. After argument by the Attorneys, it is ordered that said application for writ of habeas corpus be and the same is hereby granted, and that the detained be and she is hereby discharged. Further ordered that Respondent have a stay of execution for period of 10 days. On motion of Mr. White, it is ordered that the detained person be admitted to bail in the sum of $500.00. [18]

———

(Title of Court and Cause.)

This matter having been regularly brought on for hearing upon the issues joined herein, and the same having been duly heard and submitted, and due consideration having been thereon had, it is by the Court now here ORDERED that the said named person in whose behalf the Writ of Habeas Corpus was sued out is illegally restrained of his liberty, as alleged in the petition herein, and that he be, and he is hereby discharged from the custody from which he has been produced, and that he go hence without delay.

Entered this 19th day of October, 1931.

WALTER B. MALING, Clerk,

By C. W. CALBRAITH,

Deputy Clerk.

(Endorsed): Filed Oct. 19, 1931. [19]

———

(Title of Court and Cause.)

NOTICE OF APPEAL.

To the Clerk of the above-entitled court, to Tom Wong, the petitioner in the above-entitled matter, to Tom Tang Shee, the detained person, and to Stephen M. White, Esq., their attorney:

YOU AND EACH OF YOU will please take notice that John D. Nagle, Commissioner of Immigration at the Port of San Francisco, respondent in the above-entitled matter and appellant herein, hereby appeals to the United States Circuit Court of Appeals for the Ninth Circuit, from an order and judgment made and entered in the above-entitled cause on the 19th day of October, 1931, discharging the said Tom Tang Shee from the custody of the said John D. Nagle, Commissioner of Immigration at the Port of San Francisco, the respondent and appellant herein.

Dated: December 8, 1931.

> GEO. J. HATFIELD,
> United States Attorney.

(Endorsed): Service of the within by copy admitted this 10th day of Dec., 1931. Stephen M. White, Attorney for Petitioner.

Filed Dec. 10, 1931. [20]

(Title of Court and Cause.)

PETITION FOR APPEAL.

To the Honorable Judge of the District Court of the United States for the Northern District of California:

JOHN D. NAGLE, as Commissioner of Immigration at the Port of San Francisco, respondent in the above-entitled matter and appellant herein, feeling aggrieved by the order and judgment made and entered in the above-entitled cause on the 19th day of October, 1931, discharging Tom Tang Shee from the custody of said respondent, does hereby appeal from said order and judgment to the United States Circuit Court of Appeals for the Ninth Circuit, for the reasons set forth in the Assignment of Errors filed herewith.

WHEREFORE, petitioner prays that his appeal be allowed and that citation be issued, as provided by law, and that a transcript of the record, proceedings and documents, and all papers upon which said order and judgment were based, duly authenticated, be sent to the United States Circuit Court of Appeals for the Ninth Circuit, under the rules of such court, and in accordance with the law in such case made and provided.

Dated: December 8, 1931.

GEO. J. HATFIELD,

United States Attorney. [21]

(Endorsed): Service of the within by copy admitted this 10 day of Dec., 1931.

STEPHEN M. WHITE,

Attorney for Petitioner.

Filed Dec. 10, 1931. [22]

(Title of Court and Cause.)

ASSIGNMENT OF ERRORS.

Comes now John D. Nagle, Commissioner of Immigration at the Port of San Francisco, respondent in the above entitled cause, by Geo. J. Hatfield, United States Attorney, and in connection with his petition for an appeal in the above entitled cause, assigns the following errors which he avers occurred upon the hearing of the above-entitled cause and upon which he will rely upon appeal to the United States Circuit Court of Appeals for the Ninth

Circuit from the order and judgment made by this Honorable Court on October 19, 1931:

(1) The court erred in granting the petition for a writ of habeas corpus;

(2) The court erred in ordering discharged the detained person referred to in said petition for writ of habeas corpus;

(3) The court erred in holding that the allegations contained in said petition for writ of habeas corpus were sufficient in law to justify the granting and issuing of a writ of habeas corpus.

(4) The court erred in holding that the detained person Tom Tang Shee was entitled to enter the United States without an immigration visa;

(5) The court erred in judicially determining the right of said Tom Tang Shee to enter the United States. [23]

WHEREFORE, said respondent and appellant prays that the order and judgment of the United States District Court for the Southern Division of the Northern District of California made and entered herein in the office of the clerk of said Court on the 19th day of October, 1931, discharging the said Tom Tang Shee from the custody of John D. Nagle, Commissioner of Immigration, be reversed, and that the said Tom Tang Shee be remanded to the custody of said Commissioner of Immigration.

Dated: December 10, 1931.

GEO. J. HATFIELD,
United States Attorney.

(Endorsed): Service of the within by copy admitted this 10th day of Dec., 1931.

STEPHEN M. WHITE,
Attorney for Petitioner.

Filed Dec. 10, 1931. [24]

———

(Title of Court and Cause.)

ORDER ALLOWING APPEAL.

On motion of Geo. J. Hatfield, United States Attorney for the Northern District of California, attorney for respondent, and appellant in the above entitled cause,

IT IS HEREBY ORDERED that an appeal to the United States Circuit Court of Appeals for the Ninth Circuit from an order and judgment theretofore made and entered in the above-entitled cause, be, and the same is hereby allowed, and that a certified transcript of the records, testimony, exhibits, stipulations and all proceedings be forthwith transmitted to the said United States Circuit Court of Appeals for the Ninth Circuit, in the manner and time prescribed by law.

IT IS FURTHER ORDERED that the appeal operate as a supersedeas.

Dated: January 13th, 1932.

HAROLD LOUDERBACK,
United States District Judge.

(Endorsed): Service of the within order allowing appeal by copy admitted this 14 day of Jan., 1932.

S. M. WHITE,

Attorney for Appellee.

Filed Jan. 14, 1932. [25]

———

(Title of Court and Cause.)

ORDER TRANSMITTING ORIGINAL EXHIBITS.

GOOD CAUSE APPEARING THEREFORE, it is hereby ordered that the Immigration Records filed as Respondent's Exhibits herein, may be transmitted by the Clerk of the above-entitled Court to and filed with the Clerk of the United States Circuit Court of Appeals for the Ninth Circuit to be taken as a part of the record on appeal in the above-entitled cause with the same force and effect as if embodied in the transcript of record and so certified by the clerk of this court.

Dated: March 2, 1932.

A. F. ST. SURE,

United States District Judge.

(Endorsed): Filed Mar. 3, 1932. [26]

(Title of Court and Cause.)

PRAECIPE.

To the Clerk of Said Court:

Sir:

Please issue copies of the following papers to be used in preparing transcript on appeal:

1. Petition for writ of habeas corpus.

2. Petitioner's exhibits "A" and "B" annexed to said petition.

3. Order to show cause.

4. Stipulation and order for introduction of original immigration records.

5. Minutes of court of October 19, 1931, including order that petition be granted, that detained be discharged, that execution be stayed, that detained be admitted to bail pending appeal, etc.

6. Order of discharge.

7. Notice of appeal.

8. Petition for appeal.

9. Assignment of errors.

10. Order allowing appeal.

11. Order transmitting original exhibits.

12. Citation.

13. Praecipe for record on appeal.

GEO. J. HATFIELD,
United States Attorney,
Attorney for Appellant.

(Endorsed): Filed Mar. 1, 1932. [27]

District Court of the United States
Northern District of California.

I, Walter B. Maling, Clerk of the United States District Court, for the Northern District of California, do hereby certify that the foregoing 27 pages, numbered from 1 to 27, inclusive, contain a full, true, and correct transcript of the records and proceedings in the Matter of Tom Tang Shee, On Habeas Corpus, No. 20588-S, as the same now remain on file and of record in my office.

I further certify that the cost of preparing and certifying the foregoing transcript of record on appeal is the sum of Ten Dollars and Seventy Five Cents ($10.75) and that the said amount has not been paid to me by the Attorney for the appellant herein.

In WITNESS WHEREOF, I have hereunto set my hand and affixed the seal of said District Court, this 11th day of March, A.D. 1932.

(Seal)   WALTER B. MALING, Clerk,
              By C. M. TAYLOR,
                           Deputy Clerk. [28]

———

United States of America.—ss.

The President of the United States of America

To Tom Tang Shee, to Tom Wong and to Stephen
    M. White, Esq., their attorney herein:
GREETING:

YOU ARE HEREBY CITED AND ADMONISHED to be and appear at a United States Circuit Court of Appeals for the Ninth Circuit, to be holden at the City of San Francisco, in the State of California, within thirty days from the date hereof, pursuant to an order allowing an appeal, of record in the Clerk's Office of the United States District Court for the Southern Division of the Northern District of California, Second Division wherein John D. Nagle, as Commissioner of Immigration for the Port of San Francisco is appellant, and you are appellees, to show cause, if any there be, why the decree or judgment rendered against the said appellant, as in the said order allowing appeal mentioned, should not be corrected, and why speedy justice should not be done to the parties in that behalf.

WITNESS, the Honorable A. F. St. Sure, United States District Judge for the Southern Division of the Northern District of California, this 13th day of January, A. D. 1932.

HAROLD LOUDERBACK,
United States District Judge.

(Endorsed): Service of the within Citation by copy admitted this 14th day of Jan., 1932.

S. M. WHITE,
Attorney for Appellee.

Filed Jan. 14, 1932. [29]

[Endorsed]: No. 6779. United States Circuit Court of Appeals for the Ninth Circuit. John D. Nagle, as Commissioner of Immigration for the Port of San Francisco, Appellant, vs. Tom Tang

Shee, Appellee. Transcript of Record. Upon Appeal from the United States District Court for the Northern District of California, Southern Division. Filed March 11, 1932.

PAUL P. O'BRIEN,

Clerk of the United States Circuit Court of Appeals for the Ninth Circuit.

United States Circuit Court of Appeals

For the Ninth Circuit

JOHN D. NAGLE, as Commissioner of
Immigration for the Port of San
Francisco,

Appellant,

VS.

TOM TANG SHEE,

Appellee.

BRIEF FOR APPELLANT.

GEO. J. HATFIELD,
United States Attorney,

I. M. PECKHAM,
Assistant United States Attorney,
Attorneys for Appellant.

ARTHUR J. PHELAN,
*United States Immigration Service,
on the Brief.*

Parker Printing Company, 545 Sansome Street, San Francisco.

FIL

DEC

Subject Index

	Page
Statement of the Case	1
Facts of the Case	1
Specification of Errors	2
The Issue	3
Argument	3
Appellee is prohibited from entering the United States without an Immigration Visa	3
Conclusion	16

Table of Authorities Cited.

Pages

Chang Chan, et al. v. Nagle, 268 U. S. 346.............. 4

Chinese Rule 2, as amended by Chinese General
Order No. 17.. 8

Chun Shee v. White (C. C. A. 9), 9 Fed. (2d) 342 8

Ex parte Seid Soo Hong, 33 Fed. (2d) 847.......... 14

Fok Yung Yo v. United States, 185 U. S. 296...... 8

In re Spinnella, 3 Fed. (2d) 196............................. 14

Kaichiro Sugimoto v. Nagle (C. C. A. 9), 38
Fed. (2d) 207.. 15

Karnuth v. United States, 279 U. S. 231............... 4

Marty v. Nagle (C. C. A. 9), 44 Fed. (2d) 695..... 15

Sec. 3, Immigration Act of 1924 (8 U. S. C. A.,
Sec. 203) 3

Sec. 13 (a) Immigration Act of 1924 (8 U. S.
C. A., Sec. 213 (a)).. 5

Sec. 2, Immigration Act of 1924 (8 U. S. C. A.,
Sec. 202 (a)) 5

Sec. 8, Immigration Act of 1924 (8 U. S. C. A.,
Sec. 208) 6

Sec. 9, Immigration Act of 1924 (8 U. S. C. A.,
Sec. 209) 6

Sec. 24, Immigration Act of 1924 (8 U. S. C. A.,
Sec. 222) 7

Sec. 372 of the Consular Regulations, as amend-
ed July 1, 1930.. 8

Takeyo Koyama v. Burnett (C. C. A. 9), 8 Fed.
(2nd) 940 13

Tsoi Sim v. United States, 116 Fed. 920.. 15

Pages

U. S. ex rel. Graber v. Karnuth, 29 Fed. (2d)
314 .... 6.

U. S. ex rel. Johansen v. Phelps, 14 Fed. (2d)
679 6

U. S. ex rel. London v. Phelps (C. C. A. 2), 22
Fed. (2d) 288. 5

U. S. ex rel. Polymeris v. Trudell, 284 U. S. 279;
52 S. Ct. 143 11

No. 6779

United States Circuit Court of Appeals

For the Ninth Circuit

JOHN D. NAGLE, as Commissioner of
Immigration for the Port of San
Francisco,

Appellant,

vs.

TOM TANG SHEE,

Appellee.

BRIEF FOR APPELLANT.

STATEMENT OF THE CASE.

This appeal is from an order of the United States District Court for the Southern Division of the Northern District of California granting a writ of habeas corpus and discharging appellee from the custody of appellant (Tr. pp. 22 and 23).

FACTS OF THE CASE.

Appellee, a native and citizen of China, is the wife of Tom Wong, a citizen of the United States, having married him in China on March 3, 1910 (Tr. p. 2). She was denied admission to the United States by a Board of Special Inquiry (Tr. pp. 9 to 12 inclusive). That decision was affirmed by the Secretary of Labor (Exhibit "A", p. 51). Its basis is shown by the following excerpt from the memorandum of the Secretary of Labor:

"It appears from the record that the applicant in company with her alleged husband appeared at the American Consulate General in Hongkong on December 3, 1930, and that the alleged husband there executed a Form 633 petition for the issuance of a non quota immigration visa to the applicant. The applicant testifies that she supposed that the required arrangements were made by her husband because he 'attended to everything'. The alleged husband says he knew of the requirement of an immigration visa and supposed that the Form 633 petition was the required visa. So far as the record shows both the applicant and her husband have acted in good faith. However, in the opinion of the Board of Review there is no provision in the law for the exemption of this applicant from the requirement to be in possession of an unexpired immigration visa * * *". (Exhibit "A", p. 51.)

SPECIFICATION OF ERRORS.

The errors assigned and relied upon on this appeal are that:

(1) The court erred in granting the petition for a writ of habeas corpus;

(2) The court erred in ordering discharged the detained person referred to in said petition for writ of habeas corpus;

(3) The court erred in holding that the allegations contained in said petition for writ of habeas corpus were sufficient in law to justify the granting and issuing of a writ of habeas corpus;

(4) The court erred in holding that the detained person Tom Tang Shee was entitled to enter the United States without an immigration visa;

(5) The court erred in judicially determining the right of said Tom Tang Shee to enter the United States. (Tr. p. 26.)

THE ISSUE.

The issue presented is whether appellee is entitled to enter the United States without an immigration visa under the Immigration Act of 1924.

ARGUMENT.

1. APPELLEE IS PROHIBITED FROM ENTERING THE UNITED STATES WITHOUT AN IMMIGRATION VISA.

Appellee is an "immigrant" by definition.

Section 3 of the Immigration Act of 1924 (8 U. S. C. A., Section 203) provides:

"When used in this Act the term "immigrant" means any alien departing from any place outside the United States destined for the United States, except * * *".

Then follow six excepted classes, to none of which appellee claims to belong.

"The term thus includes every alien coming to this country either to reside permanently or for a temporary purpose, unless he can bring himself within one of the exceptions."

Karnuth v. United States, 279 U. S. 231, at 242, 243.

Appellee therefore is an "immigrant".

By the Amendment of 1930, she is a "non quota immigrant".

Subdivision (a) of Section 4 of the Act (8 U. S. C. A., Section 204(a)) classifies "the wife of a citizen of the United States" as a "non quota immigrant".

Originally Chinese wives of citizens could not enter under that Section because Section 13(c) (8 U. S. C. A., Section 213(c)) prohibited the admission of aliens ineligible to citizenship.

Chang Chan, et al., v. Nagle, 268 U. S. 346 at 353.

On June 13, 1930, an amendment to Section 13(c), supra, was enacted excepting Chinese wives of American citizens married before May 26, 1924, from the prohibition against the entry of aliens ineligible to citizenship. This placed them in the same position as other wives of American citizens.

Appellee therefore is directly within the definition of "immigrant" in Section 3 and within the definition of "non quota immigrant" in Section 4(a).

As an immigrant, whether quota or non quota, she could not enter without the required immigration visa.

Section 13(a) of the Act (8 U. S. C. A., Section 213(a)) provides:

"No immigrant shall be admitted into the United States unless he (1) has an unexpired immigration visa * * *".

We have already shown that appellee is an "immigrant" as expressly defined in the Act.

While the consul is the proper officer to issue a visa, he can only do so subject to the conditions in the Act and regulations.

Section 2 of the Act (8 U. S. C. A., Section 202(a)), provides:

"A consular officer upon the application of any immigrant (as defined in the following section) *may* (under the conditions hereinafter prescribed * * *) issue to such immigrant an immigration visa * * *".

Now, the issuance of an immigration visa is discretionary with the Consul and is beyond the control of the courts.

United States ex rel London v. Phelps, (C. C. A. 2) 22 Fed. (2d) 288;

United States ex rel Johansen v. Phelps, 14
   Fed. (2d) 679;

United States ex rel Graber v. Karnuth, 29
   Fed. (2d) 314.

But this discretion is a controlled discretion. It is controlled by the Act and regulations. Section 9 of the Act controls non quota visas.

Section 8 of the Act (8 U. S. C. A., Section 208), provides:

> "A consular officer *may,* subject to the limitations provided in Sections 2 and 9, issue an immigration visa to a non quota immigrant as such upon satisfactory proof, *under regulations prescribed* under this Act, that the applicant is entitled to be regarded as a non quota immigrant."

Section 9, supra, (8 U. S. C. A., Section 209), provides:

> "(a) In case of any immigrant claiming in his application for an immigration visa to be a non quota immigrant by reason of relationship under the provisions of subdivision A of Section 4 * * * the *consular officer shall not issue such immigration visa * * * until he has been authorized to do so as hereinafter in this section provided.*

> "(b) Any citizen of the United States claiming that any immigrant is a relative, and that such immigrant is properly admissible to the United States as a non quota immigrant under the provisions of subdivision A of Section 4 * * * *may file with the Commissioner Gene-*

ral a petition in such form as may be by regulations prescribed *   *   *".

That section provides further that said petition shall be under oath, that if executed outside the United States the oath shall be administered by a consular officer, that the petition shall be accompanied by the statements of two or more responsible American citizens setting forth certain facts, and that

> "(e) If the *Commissioner General finds* the facts stated in the petition to be true, and that the immigrant in respect of whom the petition is made is entitled to be admitted to the United States as a non quota immigrant under subdivision A of Section 4 * * * *he shall*, with the approval of the Secretary of Labor, *inform the Secretary of State* of his decision, *and the Secretary of State shall then authorize* the consular officer with whom the application for the immigration visa has been filed to issue the immigration visa.   *   *   *".

Both statute and regulations prohibit issuance of immigration visas in these cases unless non quota status for the alien wife has been authorized as provided in Section 9 of the Act.

Section 24 of the Act (8 U. S. C. A., Sec. 222), provides:

> "The *Commissioner General*, with the approval of the Secretary of Labor, *shall prescribe rules and regulations* for the enforcement of the provisions of this act; but all such rules and

regulations, insofar as they relate to the administration of this act by *consular officers,* shall be prescribed by the *Secretary of State* on the recommendation of the Secretary of Labor."

Pursuant to this statutory mandate, the Secretary of State has prescribed Section 372 of the Consular Regulations, as amended July 1, 1930, which reads in part as follows:

> "The *Chinese wives* of American citizens by marriages occurring prior to May 26, 1924, (Sections 4a and 13c, Act of 1924) * * * *must present non quota immigration visas* issued under Section 4a of the Act of 1924. *Such visas* should not be issued *unless non quota status* for the alien wife *has been authorized as provided in* Section 9 of the Act of 1924."

The Commissioner General of Immigration, with the approval of the Secretary of Labor, prescribed a similar regulation on June 27, 1930 (Chinese Rule 2, as amended by Chinese General Order No. 17).

Such regulations, prescribed pursuant to law, have the force and effect of law.

> *Fok Yung Yo v. United States,* 185 U. S. 296;
> *Chun Shee v. White* (C. C. A. 9), 9 Fed. (2d) 342.

Appellee says that the statute does not require the *Chinese* wife of an American citizen who was married prior to May 26, 1924, to obtain a non quota immigration visa, or any visa. The contention is without merit. We have already shown that she is an "immigrant" by definition, and a "non quota immigrant" by classification. The amendment of 1930 exempting Chinese wives of American citizens from the bar against aliens ineligible to citizenship, did not purport to exempt them from any other requirement of the Act. It simply abolished an exception. It simply raised a bar. It is absurd to say that Chinese wives of American citizens may come in without an immigration visa, but that other wives of American citizens may not. It is equally absurd to say that Chinese wives of American citizens might obtain an immigration visa without securing authorization from the Commissioner General and the Secretary of State, although other wives of American citizens might not. Yet that is the interpretation contended for by appellee. Such an interpretation would involve holding that by the amendment of 1930 excepting such aliens from the prohibition against the entry of aliens ineligible to citizenship, Congress impliedly exempted them from all the other provisions of the Immigration Act of 1924; that in letting down one bar it let down all. Further discussion of such a theory is entirely unnecessary. Obviously by the 1930 amendment Congress merely removed the prohibition which had prevented Chinese wives of American citizens from enjoying the same rights of entry as other wives of American citizens.

Even if it were to be assumed that Chinese wives of American citizens are not within the terms of Section 4(a), supra, nevertheless the Act provides for regulations relating to its administration. There can be no doubt of the entire reasonableness and validity of a regulation which prescribes for Chinese wives of citizens the same procedure which the statute itself prescribes for wives of citizens generally.

In view of the statutory provisions there can be no escape from the conclusion that appellee is an "immigrant," that she is required to have an immigration visa, and that she could only obtain one by authorization of the Commissioner General and the Secretary of State upon the prescribed petition, the same as any other foreign born wife of an American citizen.

Let us now revert to the facts in the case at bar.

On December 3, 1930, the husband of appellee executed before the American Consul at Hongkong the required petition (Exhibit "A", p. 1) but never filed said petition with the Commissioner General of Immigration and took no further steps to obtain the necessary authorization for the issuance of the immigration visa. The petition itself expressly states on its face:

> "1· Under the provisions of Section 9 of the Immigration Act of 1924 consular officers are not permitted to issue immigration visas to relatives claiming a non quota or quota preference status unless authorized by the Secretary of State.

> "2· Any citizen of the United States claiming that any immigrant is his relative and properly admissible to the United States as a non quota

immigrant * * * may file a petition (Form 633) with the Commissioner General of Immigration for the issuance of an immigration visa to such relative. If the Commissioner General finds that such relative is entitled to be admitted to the United States, either as a non quota or quota preference, he shall, with the approval of the Secretary of Labor, so inform the Secretary of State, who, thereupon, will authorize the proper consular officer to issue the visa.''

(Exhibit ''A'', p. 1.)

The position taken by appellee before the Department and in the Court below was that when she appeared before the American Consul it was his duty to issue her an immigration visa, that the failure to issue such a visa was wholly due to the fault of the Consul and hence that she should be allowed to enter without an immigration visa.

This contention is disposed of by the recent decision of the United States Supreme Court in

U. S. ex rel Polymeris v. Trudell, 284 U. S. 279; 52 S. Ct. 143.

In that case the relators were non quota aliens, domiciled in the United States, who went abroad in 1923 for a temporary visit. In 1924 and thereafter, they made several unsuccessful applications to the American Consul for immigration visas. Finally they presented themselves at an American border port without immigration visas. Mr. Justice Holmes said:

''The relators have no right to enter the United States unless it has been given to them by the

United States. The burden of proof is upon them to show that they have the right. Immigration Act of 1924, Sec. 23, 43 Stat. 165 (U. S. Code, tit. 8, Sec. 221, 8 U. S. C. A., Sec. 221). By section 13 of the Act (8 U. S. C. A., Sec. 213) and the regulations under it, as remarked by the court below, a returning alien cannot enter unless he has either an immigration visa or a return permit. The relators must show not only that they ought to be admitted, but that the United States *by the only voice authorized to express its will* has said so. Obviously it has not done so, and therefore the judgment must be affirmed.''

The assertion that the consular officer informed appellee that she had permission to proceed to the United States flies directly in the face of the consular regulations above quoted, (fair warning of which was expressly printed on the face of appellee's petition for a visa), and of the statutory provisions relative to the necessity and function of immigration visas and petitions for authority to issue such visas.

Consuls are public officers whose acts are attended with the presumption of official regularity. The petition for issuance of an immigration visa (Exhibit ''A'', page 1) itself shows that the Consul intended to and did merely take the petitioner's oath as required by the statute and charged a fee of the equivalent of $2.00 in American funds for this notarial act (8 U. S. C. A., Section 209 (c); 22 U. S. C. A., Sections 98, 128). The petition is neither in form nor in content an immigration visa (8 U. S. C. A., Sections 202 and 207). That the Consul was merely performing the notarial act required in connection with the verification of such petitions (8 U. S. C. A., Section 209(c)) and did not purport to be granting a visa, is also clear from the fact that the statutory fees for issuance of an immigration visa are $9.00 for issuance and $1.00 for verification of the application therefor (8 U. S. C. A., Sections 202 and 207).

In any event, even if made, any mistaken representation that the appellee might enter without an immigration visa would be immaterial.

The case of

> *Takeyo Koyama v. Burnett* (C. C. A. 9), 8 Fed. (2d) 940,

is directly in point. In that case the appellant was denied admission under a statute prohibiting her entry without a passport. She presented affidavits executed before a consular officer, showing that she was the wife of an American citizen. It was contended that the Consul had represented to her that such affidavits would be sufficient to entitle her to enter the United States. This Court said:

> "Nor is there any merit in the claim that the affidavits made before departing from Honolulu and before returning thereto constituted a passport, or an official document in the nature of a passport. Equally without merit is the claim that the government is estopped by representations made by its consular officers in Japan, if any such were in fact made."

The cases which were relied upon by appellee are not in point.

In the case of

In re Spinnella, 3 Fed. (2d) 196,

the American Vice Consul issued a visa but noted thereon that it was issued "in lieu of a non quota visa". The Court said:

> "In other words, the American Vice Consul in Italy did not give the alien a non quota visa, because, apparently he had no such forms."

In

Ex parte Seid Soo Hong, 33 Fed. (2d) 847,

the applicant being a minor son of a merchant *was not required to present a visa.* The regulations merely required that he present an affidavit on the application form of the State Department. He presented an affidavit on the form prescribed for sons of citizens, his papers at the time of appearance at the consulate having been made out on the theory that he was admissible as of the latter status. The Court said:

> "The granting or denying of a visa involves the exercise of discretion by consular officers with which the courts will not interfere, but the same rule does not apply to the form upon which an application is prepared."

Neither case is in point because in the case at bar the Consul has not issued an immigration visa in any form, and *could not issue such a visa until the petition therefor had been approved by the Commissioner General of Immigration and the Secretary of State.*

The case of

Tsoi Sim v. United States, 116 Fed. 920,

merely involved the question whether a Chinese woman who had entered the United States lawfully and subsequently married an American citizen could be deported on the ground that she was an unregistered laborer. That case is clearly not in point.

Regarding the suggestion that if appellee returned to China and obtained the proper immigration visa there would be nothing to prevent her admission, it is sufficient to point out that what her rights would be on attempting to reenter with the necessary document which the Act requires is not now before the Court.

> *Marty v. Nagle* (C. C. A. 9), 44 Fed. (2d) 695;
> *Kaichiro Sugimoto v. Nagle* (C. C. A. 9), 38 Fed. (2d) 207.

In the *Marty* case this Court said:

> "It would, no doubt, be to the interest of the appellants to have their right to reenter the United States determined at this time, but the right to make such advance determination is vested in neither the Secretary of Labor nor in the courts."

The court may ask, why put the applicant to the trouble of returning to China, when the same document introduced here as a "visa" can be withdrawn from the record here, filed with the Commissioner General, and upon his approval a proper visa be issued to applicant by the Consul at Hong Kong? In other words, if we can be held to concede that applicant would be entitled to the visa, if she applied for it in the right manner, why compel the applicant to return to Hong Kong to get the visa?

Perhaps it would be sufficient to say *"lex ita scripta est"*. The statute has so said. The statute has so ridden its arbitrary way.

Perhaps it would be better if an administrative discretion were reposed in some officer, board or tribunal to relieve from hardship in individual cases. But Congress in its wisdom has not seen fit to so provide. Perhaps it has occurred to Congress, as will readily occur to the court, that if such a scheme were provided thousands of intending immigrants would sail for our shores, presuming on the favorable exercise of such discretion in their particular cases, and our immigration facilities would be taxed to feed and care for them pending the outcome of their applications. Such a situation would only multiply the hardships of the instant case. At any rate this is a prospect that Congress has very wisely refused to invite. Far better that the right of entry be ironed out on the other side before departure, than to allow the cases to accumulate on this side pending quasi judicial or judicial solution. Here the applicant is returned to China at the expense of the steamship company who presumed to sell her a ticket without seeing her visa, and they must refund her passage money. There is no excuse for them. She is only out one month's time. Let her comply with the law.

Appellee's admission is specifically prohibited by express terms of the statute unless she has an unexpired immigration visa, and she has no such visa.

CONCLUSION.

Appellee is an "immigrant" as expressly defined in the Act. She has no immigration visa. The Act prohibits her entry without one. To obtain such a visa the petition which she presented should have been filed by her husband with the Commissioner General of Immigration for his decision as to whether an immigration visa should issue and for authorization of the Secretary of State for the issuance of such a visa. We submit that the courts have no power to exempt an alien from the mandatory requirement of presenting an immigration visa, nor to say that she must be admitted without an immigration visa because she could be admitted if she had one. There is, furthermore, no merit whatever in the contention that it was the duty of the American Consul to issue her an immigration visa at the time the husband's petition was sworn to before him, because under the law and regulations the consular officer

could not issue an immigration visa until the petition
had been approved by the Commissioner General of
Immigration and until authorization for issuance of
the visa had been received from the Secretary of
State.

It is submitted that the order of the Court below
was erroneous and should be reversed.

Respectfully submitted,

GEO. J. HATFIELD,
United States Attorney,

I. M. PECKHAM,
Asst. United States Attorney,
Attorneys for Appellant.

ARTHUR J. PHELAN,
United States Immigration Service,
on the Brief.

No. 6779

IN THE

United States Circuit Court of Appeals

For the Ninth Circuit

JOHN D. NAGLE, as Commissioner of
Immigration for the Port of San
Francisco, California,

Appellant,

vs.

TOM TANG SHEE,

Appellee.

BRIEF FOR APPELLEE.

STEPHEN M. WHITE,
576 Sacramento Street,
San Francisco, Cal.,

Attorney for Appellee.

Parker Printing Company, 545 Sansome Street, San Francisco.

No. 6779

IN THE

United States Circuit Court of Appeals

For the Ninth Circuit

JOHN D. NAGLE, as Commissioner of
Immigration for the Port of San
Francisco, California,

Appellant,

vs.

TOM TANG SHEE,

Appellee.

BRIEF FOR APPELLEE.

Facts of the Case.

Tom Wong, a native born American citizen of
Chinese descent, married the appellee, an alien of
Chinese descent, in China on March 3, 1910. In 1927,
contemplating a trip to China, Tom Wong applied to
the immigration authorities for a citizen's return cer-
tificate, which was issued to him and upon which he
departed for China in December of the same year.
On December 3, 1930, when about to return to the
United States, he appeared with the appellee at the
American Consulate at Hongkong for the purpose of

obtaining the documents necessary to enable her to proceed to this country with him. To the American Consul, he presented his return certificate, which evidenced his American citizenship, and before this official executed, in behalf of the appellee, a document designated as "Form 633" and entitled "Petition for Issuance of Immigration Visa" (Exhibit "A", p. 1). No immigration visa was, however, issued to the appellee.

Upon arriving at San Francisco, on January 14, 1931, the appellee applied for admission under the status of a wife of an American citizen who was married prior to May 26, 1924. A Board of Special Inquiry at the port and the Secretary of Labor conceded that the appellee was the wife of her alleged husband, Tom Wong, through a marriage occurring prior to May 26, 1924, and that Tom Wong was an American citizen. The denial of admission was based upon the ground that the appellee was not in possession of an immigration visa (Exhibit "A", p. 51). A petition for a writ of habeas corpus was presented to the Court below (Tr. of R., pp. 2-9) and from an order granting the petition and discharging the appellee this appeal comes (Tr. of R., p. 22).

Issues in the Case.

In behalf of the appellee, we contend:

1. That the American Consul at Hongkong was empowered to issue the appellee an immigra-

tion visa without first obtaining the authorization of the Secretary of State.

2. That the appellee should not be penalized and deported for failure to present an immigration visa, where the facts established that she made application for the visa, but that the American Consul, in neglect of official duty, failed to issue the same; "equity will consider that as done which ought to have been done.".

Argument.

THE APPELLEE WAS NOT A NON-QUOTA IMMIGRANT AND THE AMERICAN CONSUL WAS, THEREFORE, EMPOWERED TO ISSUE HER AN IMMIGRATION VISA WITHOUT FIRST OBTAINING AUTHORIZATION FROM THE SECRETARY OF STATE.

Section 13 (a) of the Immigration Act of May 26, 1924 (8 U. S. C. A., Sec. 213 (a)) provides:

"No immigrant shall be admitted to the United States unless he (1) has an unexpired immigration visa or was born subsequent to the issuance of the immigration visa of the accompanying parent, (2) is of the nationality specified in the visa in the immigration visa, (3) is a non-quota immigrant if specified in the visa in the immigration visa as such, and (4) is otherwise admissible under the immigration laws."

Section 13 (c) of the Act (8 U. S. C. A., Sec. 213 (c)), as originally enacted, provided as follows:

"No alien ineligible to citizenship shall be admitted to the United States unless such alien (1) is admissible as a non-quota immigrant under the provisions or subdivision (b), (d), or (e) of Sec. 4, or (2) is the wife, or the unmarried child under eighteen years of age, of an immigrant admissible under such subdivision (d), and is accompanying or following to join him, or (3) is not an immigrant as defined in Section."

Subdivisions (b), (d), and (e) of Section 4 of the Act (8 U. S. C. A., Sec. 204) apply to (1) immigrants previously lawfully admitted who are returning from a temporary visit abroad, (2) immigrants who are teachers or ministers and their families, and (3) immigrants who are students. An immigrant is defined in Section 3 of the Immigration Act of May 26, 1924 (8 U. S. C. A., Sec. 203), as "any alien departing from any place outside the United States destined for the United States", except (1) a government official and his household, (2) a tourist or a visitor for business or pleasure, (3) an alien in continuous transit through the United States, (4) an alien lawfully admitted to the United States who later goes in transit from one part of the United States to another through foreign contiguous territory, (5) a seaman, (6) a merchant.

It is clear that an alien Chinese wife of an American citizen was, as the Act originally stood, inadmissible to the United States under Section 13 (c), supra, in that she was an alien ineligible to citizenship and did not fall within any of the excepted classes mentioned in that section.

Chang Chan et al. v. Nagle, 268 U. S. 346, at
page 353.

By amendment approved June 13, 1930, as follows:

"Be it enacted by the Senate and House of Representatives of the United States of America in
Congress assembled, That subdivision (c) of section 13 of the Immigration Act of 1924, approved
May 26, 1924, as amended, is amended by striking
out 'or' before '(3)', and by inserting after 'section 3' the following: 'or (4) is the Chinese wife
of an American citizen who was married prior to
the approval of the Immigration Act of 1924, approved May 26, 1924.''

Section 13 (c) of the Act now reads:

"No alien ineligible to citizenship shall be admitted to the United States unless such alien (1) is
admissible as a non-quota immigrant under the
provisions of subdivision (b), (d), or (e) of Section 4, or (2) is the wife, or the unmarried child
under 18 years of age, of an immigrant admissible
under such subdivision (d) and is acompanying
or following to join him, (3) is not an immigrant
as defined in Section 3, *or (4) is the Chinese wife
of an American citizen who was married prior to
the approval of the Immigration Act of 1924,
approved May 26, 1924.*"

Hence, an alien Chinese wife of an American citizen who was married prior to May 26, 1924, is now
admissible to the United States.

Appellant advances the contention that the appellee
falls within the definition of a "non-quota immigrant"

under Section 4 (a) of the Act (8 U. S. C. A., Sec. 204) providing as follows:

> "Sec. 4, (as amended by sections 1 and 2 of joint resolution approved May 29, 1928, 45 Stat. 1009). When used in this act the term 'non-quota immigrant' means—
>
> (a) An immigrant who is the unmarried child under twenty-one years of age, or the wife, of a citizen of the United States, or the husband of a citizen of the United States by a marriage occurring prior to June 1, 1928."

Upon this premise, he concludes that the appellee is required to have a non-quota immigration visa issued in accordance with Section 9 of the Act (8 U. S. C. A., Sec. 209), which provides that, if an American citizen claims an immigrant as his relative and that such immigrant is admissible to the United States as a "non-quota immigrant" under Section 4 (a), supra, application for the immigration visa must be filed with the Commissioner General of Immigration, who, with the approval of the Secretary of Labor, shall inform the Secretary of State of his decision, and the Secretary of State shall then authorize the Consular officer to issue the visa.

Unless an alien is particularly specified as a "non-quota immigrant", he is not admissible as a "non-quota immigrant" by reason of relationship to any individual, who is so specified *or by reason of being excepted from the operation of any other law regulating or forbidding immigration.*

Section 5 of the Immigration Act of May 26th, 1924 (8 U. S. C. A., Section 205), provides:

> "When used in this act the term 'quota immigrant' means any immigrant who is not a nonquota immigrant. An alien who is not particularly specified in this act as a non-quota immigrant or a nonimmigrant shall not be admitted as a nonquota immigrant or a nonimmigrant by reason of relationship to any individual who is so specified or by reason of being excepted from the operation of any other law regulating or forbidding immigration."

Section 4(a), supra, is descriptive of a wife of an American citizen, who is admissible as a "non-quota immigrant", regardless of the time of her marriage and against whom there is no inhibition on account of her race (Sec. 13 (a), supra). The section does not *particularly specify* an alien Chinese wife of an American citizen, who was married prior to May 26, 1924, as a "non-quota immigrant" and, consequently, under the clear language of Section 5, supra, she is not admissible as a "non-quota immigrant". Manifestly, an alien Chinese wife, who is ineligible to citizenship and whose admissibility depends upon a marriage to an American citizen occurring prior to May 26, 1924, is not in the same class as a wife, who is eligible to citizenship and who is admissible, without any requirement as to time of marriage.

Moreover, Section 13 (c), supra, positively precludes the appellee's entry as a "non-quota immigrant". It will be noted that this section specifies, among aliens ineligible to citizenship, only three classes, who are admissible as "non-quota immigrants", these classes being (1) aliens who are returning to the United States from a temporary visit abroad, (2) teachers or ministers and their families, and (3) students. The amendment of June 13, 1930, to Section 13 (c), supra, did not in any manner increase the classes of non-quota immigrants, but merely added a new class, entirely independent of other excepted classes, of admissible immigrants, who were ineligible to citizenship, this class being alien Chinese wives of American citizens, who were married prior to May 26, 1924.

It must be conceded that the appellee is admissible, if at all, solely by virtue of Section 13 (c), supra, as amended. If the section, under its specific terms, does not render her admissible under the status of a "non-quota immigrant," it would be by implication only that it could be held that she was admissible under that status. Against such implication, the Supreme Court, in *Chang Chan, et al., v. Nagle,* supra, spoke, as follows:

> "Nor can we approve the suggestion that the provisions contained in subdivision (a) of Section 4 were omitted from the exceptions in Sec. 13 (c) because of some obvious oversight, and should now be treated as if incorporated therein. Although descriptive of certain 'non-quota immigrants,' the subdivision is subject to the positive inhibition against all aliens ineligible to citizenship who do not fall within definitely specified and narrowly restricted classes."

Appellant states (p. 9 of brief), that it is absurd to say that Chinese wives are not required to possess "non-quota" immigration visas issued by the American Consul upon authorization from the Commissioner General of Immigration and the Secretary of State, when other wives of American citizens are required. Of course, the statute may not be substituted for a rule based upon notions of policy or justice.

In *Commissioner of Immigration v. Gottlieb,* 265 U. S. 310, 68 L. Ed. 1031, 44 Sup. Ct. 528, the contention was made that it was absurd to hold that the families of ministers from the Asiatic barred zone were admissible, irrespective of quota limitations, and, at the same time, to hold that families of ministers who did not come from the Asiatic barred zone were subject to the quota limitations. The Supreme Court said:

"* * * . The contention that it is absurd and unreasonable to say that the wives and children of ministers from the barred Asiatic zone are to be admitted and those outside of it denied admission does not require consideration, since the result we have stated necessarily follows from the plain words of the law, for which we are not at liberty to substitute a rule based upon other notions of policy or justice. That aliens from one part of the world shall be admitted according to their status, and those from another part according to fixed numerical proportions, is a matter wholly within the discretion of the law-making body, with which the courts have no authority to interfere."

It is, therefore, submitted that the Chinese wife of an American citizen, who was married prior to May 26, 1924, is not, either by the specific terms of the statute or by implication, admissible as a "non-quota immigrant," but that she is admissible purely as an immigrant belonging to an excepted class, absolutely independent of the classes of admissible "non-quota immigrants," which, in respect to aliens ineligible to citizenship, are limited to three classes, namely, returning residents, teachers or ministers and their families and students. (Section 13 (c), supra, as amended.)

Admittedly, if the appellee be not a "non-quota immigrant," she was not required to file an application for an immigration visa with the Commissioner General of Immigration and the American Consul was not required to have authorization from the Secretary of State before issuing the visa, the procedure required of "non-quota immigrants" under Section 9, supra, of the Act. She was entitled to receive an immigration visa directly from the American Consul, the same as other immigrants (Sec. 2 (a) of Immigration Act of 1924, 8 U. S. C. A., Sec. 202 (a)).

———

APPLICATION FOR THE ISSUANCE OF AN IMMIGRATION VISA WAS MADE TO THE AMERICAN CONSUL, WHO, IN NEGLECT OF OFFICIAL DUTY, FAILED TO ISSUE THE SAME.

It is conceded that the appellee and her husband appeared at the American Consulate at Hongkong on December 3, 1930, and that the husband, in behalf of the appellee, filed a document designated as "Form 633" and entitled "Petition for Issuance of Immigration Visa" (Exhibit A, p. 1). This document.was completed and executed before the American Consul, who attached the photographs of the appellee and her husband thereto and who appended thereto the following notation:

> "Petitioner is holder of Form 430 No. 12017/33436 issued by the Acting Commissioner of Immigration at San Francisco, California, on December 8, 1927. *   *   *".

This Form 430, to which the consul made reference, was a certificate issued by the immigration authorities confirming the appellee's husband's status as an American citizen.

At the hearing before the Board of Special Inquiry, the appellee testified that she, with her husband, before leaving China, called at the American Consulate at Hongkong, that her husband attended to everything there, that three papers were there executed, two of which were given to the husband and one of which was retained by the consul, that the documents (referring to Form 633 and duplicate thereof) were given to the husband at the American Consulate (Exhibit A, p. 13).

Tom Wong, the appellee's husband, testified before the Board of Special Inquiry that he appeared, with the appellee, at the American Consulate at Hongkong, that he filled out the papers (referring to Form 633 and duplicate thereof), that these were stamped by the consul, who kept one and gave two to him, that he was informed by the consul "that it was all right and I should go on the ship with the applicant and present these forms (633) at the steamship office when I bought the tickets," that he was not informed at the consulate that any other document was necessary in order to show appellee's admissibility to the United States, that the consul gave him these papers (referring to Form 633) and asked him for $6.80, which he paid and told him it was all right, that he took the papers to the steamship company and purchased the tickets, that no other document was issued at the American Consulate, that he knew that it was necessary for the appellee to have an immigration visa, that he thought these documents (Form 633) were visas, that he was under the impression that he had complied with all the requirements in regard to obtaining a visa (Exhibit A, pp. 14-15).

It is conceded by the Secretary of Labor that the appellee and her husband acted in good faith in endeavoring to obtain an immigration visa from the American Consul. The Secretary of Labor states:

"It appears from the record that the applicant in company with her alleged husband appeared at the American Consulate General in Hongkong on December 3, 1930, and that the alleged husband there executed a Form 633 petition for the issuance of a non quota immigration visa to the applicant. The applicant testifies that she supposed that the required arrangements were made by her husband because he 'attended to everything'. The alleged husband says he knew of the requirement of an immigration visa and supposed that the Form 633 petition was the required visa. So far as the record shows both the applicant and her husband have acted in good faith. * * *''. (Exhibit "A," p. 51.)

Have made application to the American Consul for the visa, having exhibited the evidence to the American Consul necessary to enable the latter to issue the visa, the American Consul having, in effect, assured the appellee's husband that he had issued the proper documents to enable the appellee to proceed to the United States, we submit that it was unfair and unreasonable for the immigration authorities to hold the appellee to a high degree of formalism and to deny her admission merely because she was without an immigration visa. The appellee and her husband did all in their power to obtain the visa and it is conceded that they acted in good faith throughout. While the issuance of an immigration visa is discretionary with the American Consul, nevertheless, it is apparent, if we accept the testimony of the appellee's husband, that he (American Consul) was willing and, in effect, considered that he had exercised his discretion in favor of the appellee, although, in fact, he omitted to issue the formal document.

The Courts have consistently held that where an immigrant in good faith has endeavored to obtain a

Consular document, but that the American Consul, through neglect of official duty, has failed to issue the document, "equity will consider that as done which ought to have been done."

> *In re Spinnella,* 3 Fed. (2d) 196;
> *Ex parte Seid Soo Hong,* 23 Fed. (2d) 847;
> *Ex parte Yee Gee,* (D. C.) 17 Fed. (2d) 653;
> *Ex parte Woo Show How,* (D. C.) 17 Fed. (2d) 652.

The cases of *Ex parte Yee Gee,* supra, and *Ex parte Woo Show How,* supra, were expressly approved in *Li Bing Sun v. Nagle,* 56 Fed. (2d) 1000, C. C. A. 9th, at pages 1003 and 1004.

In *Lytle et al. v. The State of Arkansas,* 13 L. Ed. 153, at page 160, the Supreme Court said:

"It is a well-established principle, that where an individual in the prosecution of a right does everything which the law requires him to do, and he fails to attain his right by the misconduct or neglect of a public officer, the law will protect him. In this case the pre-emption right of Cloyes having been proved, and an offer to pay the money for the land claimed by him, under the Act of 1830, nothing more could be done by him, and nothing more could be required of him under that act. And subsequently, when he paid the money to the receiver, under subsequent acts, the surveys being returned, he could do nothing more than offer to enter the fractions, which the register would not permit him to do. This claim of pre-emption stands before us in a light not less favorable than it would have stood if Cloyes or his representatives had been permitted by the land officers to do what, in this respect, was offered to be done.''

In *Camp v. Boyd,* 229 U. S. 530, 57 L. Ed. 1317, at page 1330, the Supreme Court said:

"The equitable principles upon which our decision must turn are simple and fundamental. Equity regards that as done which ought to be done. It looks to the true intent and meaning, rather than to the form. It relieves against the consequences of accident and mistake, as well as of fraud."

In *Storti v. Massachusetts,* 183 U. S. 138, 46 L. Ed. 120, at page 124, the Supreme Court said:

'' * * *. The command of the section is 'to dispose of the party as law and justice require.' All the freedom of equity procedure is thus prescribed; and substantial justice, promptly administered, is ever the rule in habeas corpus.''

In *Tsoi Sim v. U. S.,* 116 Fed. 920, C. C. A. 9th, at page 926, the Court said:

"It is true that the views of the Department do not reach the standard of judicial decisions, but are entitled to great respect, and are here given for the persuasive and sound reasoning therein contained. In arriving at the conclusions stated, we are not opening the door for the commission of fraud, or departing from the true construction of the statute. Conceding that, by applying the literal language of the statute, it might be held she should be deported, yet is it not evident that such a construction would necessarily lead to absurd results without any benefit to the United States? The object and intent of the law was to deport Chinese not entitled to remain. If appellant was to be deported, she would have the unquestioned right to immediately return, and would be entitled to land, and remain in this country upon the sole ground that she is the lawful wife of an American citizen.

Is it not manifest that Congress never intended by the passage of the law to have it apply to a case like the present? One of the cardinal rules as to the interpretation of statutes is that they should receive a sensible construction. In U. S. v. Kirby, 7 Wall. 482, 486, 19 L. Ed. 278, Mr. Justice Field, in speaking for the Court, said:

'All laws should receive a sensible construction. General terms should be so limited in their application as not to lead to injustice, oppression, or an absurd consequence. It will always, therefore, be presumed that the Legislature intended exceptions to its language, which would avoid results of this character. The reason of the law, in such cases, should prevail over its letter.' "

Appellant refers to the case of *U. S. ex rel. Polymeris v. Trudell,* 284 U. S. 279; 52 Sup. Ct. 143. There, the immigrants had been refused visas by the American Consul, but, notwithstanding, proceeded to the United States and endeavored to gain admission.

Inasmuch as the American Consul acted upon the applications for visas, there was no omission or neglect of duty on his part. In the case at bar, the American Consul did not refuse to issue a visa to the appellee, but he omitted and neglected to take action either one way or the other, although it is manifest that if he had taken action it would have been favorable to the appellee.

Appellant, also, refers to the case of *Koyama v. Burnett,* 8 Fed. (2) 940, C. C. A. 9th, wherein a Japanese alien attempted to gain admission without a passport. Being a Japanese subject, she could obtain a passport only from the government of Japan. Hence, the American Consul was not empowered to issue her a passport and no question of omission or neglect of duty on his part was involved.

CONCLUSION.

It is submitted that the order of the Court below in granting the petition for a writ of habeas corpus and discharging the appellee was right and should be affirmed.

Respectfully submitted,

STEPHEN M. WHITE,
576 Sacramento Street,
San Francisco, Cal.,
Attorney for Appellee.

United States
Circuit Court of Appeals
For the Ninth Circuit.

E. M. ALLISON, as Administrator of the Estate of
Thomas J. Kelly, deceased,

Appellant,

vs.

STANDARD AIR LINES, INC., a corporation,

Appellee.

Transcript of Record.

Upon Appeal from the United States District Court for the Southern
District of California, Central Division.

FILED

MAR 25 1932

PAUL P. O'BRIEN,
CLERK.

Parker, Stone & Baird Co., Law Printers, Los Angeles.

United States
Circuit Court of Appeals
For the Ninth Circuit.

E. M. ALLISON, as Administrator of the Estate of
Thomas J. Kelly, deceased,

Appellant,

vs.

STANDARD AIR LINES, INC., a corporation,

Appellee.

Transcript of Record.

Upon Appeal from the United States District Court for the Southern
District of California, Central Division.

Parker, Stone & Baird Co., Law Printers, Los Angeles.

TOPICAL INDEX.

[Clerk's Note: When deemed likely to be of an important nature, errors or doubtful matters appearing in the original record are printed literally in italic; and, likewise, cancelled matter appearing in the original record is printed and cancelled herein accordingly. When possible, an omission from the text is indicated by printing in italics the two words between which the omission seems to occur.]

PAGE

Answer 6

Assignments of Error.. 68

Bill of Exceptions... 15

Defendant's Exhibit No. E—Ticket............................ 38

Instructions to the Jury... 42

Insufficiency of the Evidence..................................... 61

Notice of Motion for a New Trial............................... 57

Order Denying Motion for New Trial........................ 66

Plaintiff's Points and Authorities in Support of Motion for New Trial... 58

Specifications of Error.. 61

Specifications of Error in Law Occurring at the Trial and Excepted to by the Plaintiff 62

Testimony on Behalf of Plaintiff:

Allison, E. M.. 25

Covington, C. L... 18

Kelly, Blanche Vance.. 25

Kujeneck, George 16

Lindenberger, Mr. 17

Phillips, Bert C.. 23

Rawlings, C. E... 21

Sawyer, Brooks.. 24

Smith, Luther T.. 22

Virchow, Arthur 19

Wallace, John L.. 24

Williams, W. H.. 18

PAGE

Testimony on Behalf of Defendant:

    Hamilton, Ray 36

    Leary, George 35

    Martin, John Leslie 36

    Navey, Mr. 35

    Rexter, Paul E., Jr. 25

    Russell, Harold B. 35

    Thompson, Mrs. 36

    Tomlinson, Lieut. 30

Citation 2

Complaint 3

Cost Bond on Appeal 83

Judgment 14

Names and Addresses of Attorneys 1

Order Allowing Appeal 81

Order Approving Bond on Appeal 82

Petition for Appeal 67

Praecipe 86

Verdict 13

Names and Addresses of Attorneys.

For Plaintiff and Appellant:

OLIVER O. CLARK, Esq.,
Garfield Building,

SAMUEL A. ROSENTHAL, Esq.,
Wright & Callender Building,
Los Angeles, California.

For Defendant and Appellee:

O'MELVENY, TULLER & MYERS, Esqs.,
HARRY D. PARKER, Esq.,
HOMER I. MITCHELL, Esq.,
Title Insurance Building,
Los Angeles, California.

UNITED STATES OF AMERICA, SS:

To STANDARD AIR LINES, INC., a corporation, defendant and respondent:—GREETING:

You are hereby cited and admonished to be and appear at a United States Circuit Court of Appeals for the Ninth Circuit, to be held at the City of San Francisco, in the State of California, on the 25th day of May, A. D. 1931, pursuant to an order allowing appeal of record in the Clerk's Office of the District Court of the United States, in and for the Southern District of California, in that certain cause No. 3516-H, in the records of said Court, wherein E. M. Allison, as Administrator of the Estate of Thomas J. Kelly, is plaintiff and appellant and Standard Air Lines, Inc., a corporation, is defendant and respondent, and you are required to show cause, if any there be, why the final judgment in said cause made and entered on the 20th day of September, 1930, in the said above entitled cause mentioned, should not be corrected, and speedy justice should not be done to the parties in that behalf.

WITNESS, the Honorable GEO. COSGRAVE, United States District Judge for the Southern District of California, this 25 day of April, A. D. 1931, and of the Independence of the United States, the one hundred and fifty-fifth.

Geo. Cosgrave

U. S. District Judge for the Southern District of California.

Received copy of the within Citation this 27th day of April, 1931.   John F Dahl and Kirke T Moore Attorneys for Defendant

[Endorsed]: In the United States Circuit Court of Appeals for the Ninth Circuit E. M. Allison, as Administrator of the Estate of Thomas J. Kelly, plaintiff and appellant vs. Standard Air Lines, Inc., a corporation, defendant and respondent. Citation Filed Apr 27 1931 R. S. Zimmerman, Clerk By Edmund L. Smith Deputy Clerk

---

IN THE DISTRICT COURT OF THE UNITED STATES, IN AND FOR THE SOUTHERN DISTRICT OF CALIFORNIA, CENTRAL DIVISION.

E. M. Allison, as Admininstrtor
of the estatte of Thomas J.
Kelly, deceased,

Plaintiff	No. 3516-H
vs	Ation for money
STANDARD AIR LINES, INC.	damages.
a corporation,	COMPLAINT.
Defendant.	

Now comes the plaintiff above named and for his cause of action against defendant above named complains:

I.

That plaintiff, E. M. Allison, is the duly appointed, acting and qualified administrator through appointment made by the Superior Court of Los Angeles County, California, of the estate of Thomas J. Kelly, deceased, who at the time of his death was forty-one years of age and was a citizen of the state of California and resided in the City of Los Angeles in said state.

II.

That defendant, Standard Air Lines, Inc. is a corporation organized and existing under and by virtue of the laws of the state of Nevada and has and maintans its offices and principal place of business in Reno in said state and is engaged generally in the business of a common carrier of passengers for hire by means of air planes and especially in carrying passengers by air planes from Los Angeles California to points within and without said state.

III

That the amount in controversy in this action exceeds the sum of Ten Thousand Dollars.

IV.

That the death of Thomas J. Kelly was caused by the wrongful act and neglect of defendant, and said Thomas J. Kelly left as his sole and only heir, Blanche Vance Kelly, his widow, on whose behalf this action is brought.

V.

That on or about March 30th, 1929 Thomas J. Kelly, having paid the fare demananded therefor by defendant, became a passneger on a certain air plane operated by defendant company and on said date at a point at or near Banning in the state of California by reason of the negligence of defendant in operating said air plane the same was wrecked and destroyed and Thomas J. Kelly was killed.

VI.

That Jhomas J. Kelly was capable of earing about Ten Thousand Dollars per year.

VII.

That the death of said Thomas J. Kelly was caused by the negligence of defendant and his widow, Blanche Vance

Kelly, has been damaged through and by the negligence of defendant in the death of her husband, Thomas J. Kelly, in the sum of Fifty Thousand Dollars.

VIII.

WHEREFORE plaintiff prays judgment against defendant in and for the sum of Fifty Thousand Dollars and costs.

Edwin S Earhart
Plaintiff's Attorney.

STATE OF CALIFORNIA
COUNTY OF LOS ANGELES, ss.

E. M. Allison being first duly sworn on oath says: That he is the plaintiff in the foregoing and above entitled action, that he has read the within complaint and knows the contents thereof; and that the same is true of his own knowledge except as to those matters therein stated on his information and belief and that as to those matters and things he believes it to be true.

E. M. Allison

Subscribed and sowrn to before me this 21st. day of May 1929.

[Seal] Lillian A. Skillen
Notary Public in and for said County and State.
My Commission Expires July 10, 1929.

[Endorsed]: No. 3516-H United States District Court Southern District of California Central Division E. M. Allison, Admr. estate Thomas J. Kelly, deceased. Plaintiff vs. Standard Air Lines, Inc a corporation, Defendant Complaint. Money Damages. Filed May 21 1929 R. S. Zimmerman, Clerk By Edmund L. Smith Deputy Clerk Edwin S. Earhart 1330 Wildwood Trail Albany 2237. Plaintiff's Attorney.

IN THE DISTRICT COURT OF THE UNITED
STATES IN AND FOR THE SOUTHERN
DISTRICT OF CALIFORNIA
CENTRAL DIVISION

E. M. ALLISON, as Administrator of the Estate of Thomas J. Kelly, deceased,	)))	No. 3516-H
Plaintiff,	))	ANSWER TO PLAINTIFF'S
-v-		COMPLAINT.
	)	
STANDARD AIR LINES, INC., a corporation,	)	
Defendant.	))	

Comes now the defendant and for its answer to the
complaint herein admits, denies and alleges as follows:

I.

Alleges that as to the allegations contained in paragraphs I and VI of the complaint defendant has no
knowledge, information or belief sufficient to answer
thereto and placing its denial on that ground denies each
and every allegation in said paragraphs contained;

II.

Admits the allegations of Paragraphs II and III of said
complaint; except it denies that it was a common carrier
of passengers as to the said Thomas J. Kelly;

III.

Answering the allegations of paragraph IV denies
specifically that the death of said Thomas J. Kelly was
caused by any wrongful act or neglect of the defendant;
and alleges that as to whether Blanche Vance Kelly was

the widow of said Thomas J. Kelly, and as to whether she was his sole and only heir, defendant has no knowledge, information or belief sufficient to answer and placing its denial on that ground denies said allegation;

IV.

Answering the allegations of paragraphs V and VII of said complaint, defendant admits that on or about March 30, 1929, said Thomas J. Kelly was a passenger on an airplane operated by defendant and on said date at a point near Banning, in the State of California, said airplane was wrecked and destroyed and said Thomas J. Kelly was killed, but specifically denies that said wreck or the death of said Kelly was caused by any negligence whatsoever on the part of this defendant; and defendant denies that said Blanche Vance Kelly has been damaged by any negligence of this defendant or by the death of Thomas J. Kelly in the sum of $50,000, or in any sum whatsoever.

AND FOR A FURTHER, SEPARATE AND SECOND COMPLETE DEFENSE TO PLAINTIFF'S CAUSE OF ACTION, DEFENDANT ALLEGES AS FOLLOWS:

I.

That since the 28th day of November, 1927, the Standard Air Lines, Inc. has been operating an air line to Tucson, Arizona, using the San Gorgonio Pass as a portion of its route to Arizona; that the cities of Beaumont and Banning are located in this Pass;

That all during the operations of the Standard Air Lines through this Pass, it has made close observation of weather conditions in said Pass in the vicinity of Beaumont, Banning and March Field, Riverside, California; that the majority of the time said Pass is free and clear of clouds and fogs, but that a portion of the season the pass is filled with high fogs and clouds, which, however, have rarely obscured visibility for a distance of less than 100 feet above the floor of the Pass;

That on the morning of March 30, 1929, the aeroplane mentioned in plaintiff's complaint left the airport of the Standard Air Lines, Inc. at 94th and Southwestern Avenue in Los Angeles in good mechanical condition and order, bound for El Paso, Texas, through the San Gorgonio Pass over the usual route of the Standard Air Lines;

That at the time said ship left Los Angeles with Thomas J. Kelly as a passenger, weather conditions in Los Angeles were favorable to flight, being slightly hazy with the sun shining through high clouds;

That in normal flying time the aeroplane of the Standard Air Lines would reach the entrance to the San Gorgonio Pass at approximately 9:05 o'clock a. m.;

That defendant has been informed and believes and basing this allegation upon said information and belief alleges the fact to be that at the time said aeroplane of the Standard Air Lines entered the San Gorgonio Pass, in which the accident occurred, the pilot had a clear and unobstructed vision for the whole distance of the Pass below overhanging clouds;

That said Pass, at the time the accident occurred, was filled with misty haze and low hanging clouds, which, however, did not obscure visibility through the Pass nor view of the terrain below the aeroplane; that all of said terrain on the floor of said San Gorgonio Pass is well suited to the emergency landing of an aeroplane, being flat and level;

That after said aeroplane entered the Pass a disturbance took place in the arrangement of the low hanging clouds which suddenly obscured the vision of the pilot of the aeroplane and completely shut off visibility through the Pass and covered the ground below the aeroplane in such a manner that a person in an aeroplane would be unable to see the ground, so that said aeroplane became enveloped in a cloud of fog, completely obscuring visibility in any direction;

That said aeroplane, at the time it entered the Pass, was traveling at a minimum speed of approximately 80 miles an hour when it became suddenly enveloped in a low lying cloud displaced from its normal position by an unforeseen force;

That said pilot became enveloped in the clouds and lost his course and in endeavoring to extricate the aeroplane from the position in which it was suddenly placed by the sudden unforeseen action of the elements, lost his way and said aeroplane was wrecked and destroyed at a point near Banning; that said accident was due to unforeseen events and Act of God.

AND FOR A FURTHER AND SEPARATE AND THIRD COMPLETE DEFENSE TO PLAINTIFF'S CAUSE OF ACTION, DEFENDANT ALLEGES AS FOLLOWS:

I.

That at the time said Thomas J. Kelly engaged passage on the aeroplane of the Standard Air Lines, he entered into a contract with the Standard Air Lines, Inc., which embodied the conditions of flying and the terms upon which the said Thomas J. Kelly was carried as a passenger in the aeroplane operated by the Standard Air Lines, Inc.; that one of the conditions embodied in said written agreement entered into between Thomas J. Kelly and the Standard Air Lines, Inc. provided as follows:

"Should the Company accept the holder hereof for a flight in one of its airplanes, such acceptance shall not be deemed to make the Company a common carrier, but it is specifically agreed and understood between the holder and the Company that the Company is a private carrier and is liable to the holder not as an insurer, but only for proven negligence of its employees and agents, and the mere occurrence of an accident resulting in injury or loss of life to the holder shall not be any evidence of negligence."

and that under the terms and conditions of said contract the defendant is not liable for any injury to passengers carried in its planes except for the proven negligence of its employees and agents and that the mere occurrence of an accident resulting in the death of the plaintiff does not in any way constitute evidence of negligence.

WHEREFORE, defendant prays that it be dismissed hence with its costs herein expended.

John F. Dahl

John F. Dahl

NEWBY & NEWBY

By Nathan Newby Jr.

Nathan Newby, Jr.

Attorneys for Defendant.

STATE OF CALIFORNIA)
) SS:
COUNTY OF LOS ANGELES)

JACK FRYE, being first duly sworn deposes and says: That he is the president of the STANDARD AIR LINES, INC., a corporation, the defendant in the above entitled action; that he has read the foregoing answer and knows the contents thereof; and that the same is true of his own knowledge, except as to the matters which are therein stated upon his information and belief, and as to those matters that he believes it to be true.

Jack Frye

Subscribed and sworn to before me this 21 day of June, 1929.

[Notarial seal] Howard Rockefeller
Notary Public, in and for the State and County aforesaid.

[Endorsed]: Original No. 3516-H In the District Court of the United States In and for the Southern District of California Central Division E. M. Allison, as Adm. of the Estate of Kelly, dec. Plaintiff vs. Standard Air Lines, Inc., a corp. Defendant Answer of Defendant Corporation Received copy of the within Answer this 21 day of June 1929 Edwin S. Earhart Attorney for Plaintiff Filed Jun 21 1929 R. S. Zimmerman, Clerk By Francis E. Cross Deputy Clerk John F. Dahl Newby and Newby Los Angeles, Cal. 1102 W. M. Garland Bldg., 117 W. 9th St.—Va 5547. Attorneys for Defendant

At a stated term, to wit: The September Term, A. D. 1930 of the District Court of the United States of America, within and for the Central Division of the Southern District of California, held at the Court Room thereof, in the City of Los Angeles on Friday the 19th day of September in the year of our Lord one thousand nine hundred and twenty-

Present:

The Honorable GEORGE COSGRAVE, District Judge.

E. M. Allison as Administrator of)
Estate of Thomas J. Kelly,   )
                     Plaintiff,) No. 3516-H-Law
)
         vs.   )
)
Standard Air Lines, Inc., a corpora-)
tion,   Defendant.)

This cause coming on for further trial; * * * * *

The counsel for the defendant stipulates that in case judgment is in favor of the plaintiff, that the defendant may have stay of execution on the judgment for a period of ten days after motion for a new trial shall have been disposed of. * * * * * *

Now, at the hour of 11:05 o'clock a. m., court reconvenes, the jury being present, and all others appearing as before, the jury present their verdict in favor of the defendant. The verdict, as presented to the Court, is read in open court and ordered filed and entered herein; the verdict, as filed, being as follows, to-wit: * * * *

IN THE DISTRICT COURT OF THE UNITED
STATES IN AND FOR THE SOUTHERN
DISTRICT OF CALIFORNIA
CENTRAL DIVISION.

----oOo----

E. M. Allison, as Administrator of) No. 3516-H-Civil.
)

the Estate of Thomas J. Kelly, De-)
)

ceased,   Plaintiff,)
)   VERDICT.
            Vs.

Standard Air Lines, Inc., a Corpora-)
)

tion,   Defendant.)

----oOo----

We, the Jury in the above-entitled action, find the issues
in favor of the defendant.

Los Angeles, California, September 19, 1930.

William A. Monten
FOREMAN OF THE JURY.

[Endorsed]: Filed Sep 19 1930 R. S. Zimmerman,
Clerk By Francis E. Cross Deputy Clerk

IN THE DISTRICT COURT OF THE UNITED
STATES, SOUTHERN DISTRICT OF CALI-
FORNIA, CENTRAL DIVISION.

***

E. M. ALLISON, as Administrator of the Estate of Thomas J. Kelly, Deceased, Plaintiff,	No. 3516-H
vs.	JUDGMENT
STANDARD AIR LINES, INC., a corporation, Defendant.	

***

The issues in the above entitled action having been duly
brought on for trial and tried before the Honorable
George Cosgrave, District Judge, and a jury, at a stated
term of this court held in and for the Southern District
of California, Central Division, at the Post Office Building, in the City of Los Angeles, State of California, in
said district, on the 17th, 18th and 19th days of September, 1930, and a verdict for the defendant having been
duly rendered on the 19th day of September, 1930, against
the plaintiff:

Now, on motion of John F. Dahl, attorney for said
defendant, it is adjudged that the plaintiff take nothing by
his suit and that the defendant recover against the plaintiff
his costs and charges incurred herein to be taxed, and that
said defendant have execution against the plaintiff therefor. Costs taxed at $157.14.

Judgment signed this 20th day of September, A. D.
1930.

Geo. Cosgrave
Judge

JUDGMENT ENTERED SEPTEMBER 20th, 1930.
R. S. ZIMMERMAN, Clerk,
By Francis E. Cross
Deputy Clerk.

Dock & Index
9/20/30

[Endorsed]: No. 3516-H In the District Court of the United States, Southern District of California, Central Division. E. M. Allison, as Administrator of the Estate of Thomas J. Kelly, Deceased, Plaintiff, vs. Standard Air Lines, Inc., a corporation, Defendant. Judgment Filed Sep 20 1930 R. S. Zimmerman, Clerk By Francis E. Cross Deputy Clerk John F. Dahl, 1102 W. M. Garland Building, 117 West Ninth Street, Los Angeles, California. Attorney for Defendant.

IN THE DISTRICT COURT OF THE UNITED STATES SOUTHERN DISTRICT OF CALIFORNIA CENTRAL DIVISION.

E. M. ALLISON, as Administrator of the Estate of Thomas J. Kelly, deceased,

Plaintiff and Appellant,

vs.

STANDARD AIR LINES, INC., a corporation,

Defendant and Respondent.

No. 3516-H

BILL OF EXCEPTIONS

PROPOSED BILL OF EXCEPTIONS OF THE PLAINTIFF, E. M. Allison, as Administrator of the Estate of Thomas J. Kelly, deceased, in the above numbered and entitled action, to be used on said Plaintiff's

(Testimony of George Kujeneck)

Appeal from the Judgment in said action, and for any and all purposes for which such Bill of Exceptions may properly be used:

BE IT REMEMBERED that the above entitled action came on regularly for trial, in the above entitled Court, and was tried on the 17th, 18th and 19th day of September, 1930, before the Honorable Geo. Cosgrave, U. S. District Judge presiding, sitting with a jury; the plaintiff, E. M. Allison, appearing in person and by his attorneys, Oliver O. Clark and Samuel A. Rosenthal, and the defendant appearing by its attorneys John F. Dahl and Kirke T. Moore; and thereupon the following proceedings were had and the following evidence, both oral and documentary, was introduced, to-wit:

GEORGE KUJENECK

called as a witness on behalf of the plaintiff, testified as follows:

On March 30th, 1929, at about 9:20 a.m., I was working on the property of Paul Hainey, about a quarter of a mile from the point where the Standard Airlines airplane, involved in this proceeding, crashed against the side of a hog-back hill. I had been attracted by this airplane, which was flying low right around where I was working. It came down as low as 50 feet from the ground. I was wondering why it was flying so low. He then attempted to fly over the hill north of me and then he circled around northeast and low, and then he swung northerly right into the hill, and crashed. I left my mule standing when he flew over me, because he flew so low and was heading in my direction. I saw the plane at all times from the

(Testimony of Mr. Lindenberger)

time I first saw it until it crashed. He could have landed in the field in which I was working. There was all of four or five acres right there in which he could have landed at the time of the crash and before it. I could see the crest of the hill into which the airplane crashed and the fog level was above the top of that hill. The crest of the mountain was about the same height on the north side as it was on the west side, where he crashed. I didn't see the aeroplane exactly when it crashed because it went into kind of a canon before it crashed. So far as I know the motor sounded all right. When he tried to make the hill it sounded like a buzz saw; the motor was running the entire time.

MR. LINDENBERGER

called as a witness on behalf of the plaintiff, testified as follows:

On the morning of March 30th, 1929, between 8 and 9 o'clock in the morning, I was at the Tri-City Airport in Redlands, which is between Redlands and Colton. It was quite foggy. While I was there, a plane of the Standard Airlines, which was the plane that crashed in the accident involved in this proceeding, circled overhead the airport two or three times, flying low, and then proceeded southeast towards San Timoteo Canyon, which runs into San Gorgonio Pass. At that time, there was a ceiling of about 200 feet at the airport. The Tri-City Airport is about twenty miles from the scene of the accident.

(Testimony of C. L. Covington—W. H. Williams)

C. L. COVINGTON

called as a witness on behalf of the plaintiff, testified as
follows:

On the morning of March 30, 1929, I was on my ranch
about a mile southwest of the ranch where Kujeneck was
working. I did not see the plane prior to the crash. I
heard the plane circling over me ten or fifteen minutes
before it crashed. Just before the plane came through
the fog the motor sounded like he opened it wide open
and that caused me to look around just as he came through
the fog, as he came down and crashed. I had heard it
for ten or fifteen minutes. It seemed to be circling overhead, more than one circle. From where I was when the
plane crashed I could see the ridge of the mountain immediately above the place where it crashed, and the fog
there I would say was five hundred feet high. I heard
the crash and the instant it crashed I saw the smoke and
flame. While it was circling there would be a minute
or two when I couldn't hear it and then I would hear
it again and that intermittency occurred several times.

W. H. WILLIAMS

called as a witness on behalf of the plaintiff, testified as
follows:

I run the Lighthouse Cafe and Gas Station on the Redlands Highway No. 99, about one mile in a direct line
from where the airplane crash involved in this proceeding
occurred. At about nine o'clock in the morning of March
30th, 1929, I witnessed the crash of this airplane. I was
first attracted by the missing of the motor on the plane.

(Testimony of Arthur Virchow)

The plane was then going easterly and then it began to circle around the field in which Mr. Belford was working. He circled around two or three times and started up. The ceiling of the fog right above my gas station at that time was about 200 feet. There are many large fields here in the vicinity of the crash, where a landing of an airplane could have been made. One of such fields contains about 50 to 60 acres and was then being plowed. While the plane was circling, it circled within a quarter of a mile of my station and was at times as close as 20 to 50 feet from the ground.

ARTHUR VIRCHOW

called as a witness on behalf of the plaintiff, testified as follows:

I am a rancher and live at Beaumont. At the time of the accident in question I lived next door to the place of Mr. Kujeneck. On the morning of March 30, 1929, I saw the aeroplane crash about four hundred feet north of the north end of my ranch.

I was about half way between my house and the highway on the south end of my ranch, probably six hundred feet from the house. When I first saw the aeroplane it was traveling in a westerly direction and he came out of the fog just over my head and then he came down low enough so I could see the lettering on the wing very plain and he flew for a quarter of a mile below the fog and then he disappeared again and the next time I saw him he came up right over the top of my house and missed it probably seventy-five or one hundred feet and he flew over the house or barn traveling almost east and

(Testimony of Arthur Virchow)
just after he got over the barn he turned to the left and
then he disappeared again and I could still hear the motor
running.   Then after he got over the barn I couldn't tell
which direction he was going but the next time he appeared he came out of the fog and I didn't see him only
for a split part of a second from the time he left the fog
and he hit the hill.

I should judge the fog was about three or four hundred
feet high that morning.

He made two complete circles just west of the house
and then he flew going east, flew over the house and then
he made that turn and went north and from the time he
made the turn over the house I couldn't see what he did
because he was in the fog from where I was standing.
While he was circling about he was below the fog and in
my view.   The land on my property consisted of about
thirty-seven and one-half acres set out solid in trees and
Volunteer field on the south end which was bare, the
grapes having just been taken off, which is fairly level
but one small wash through it.   That particular area was
probably between one and two thousand feet from which
I saw the plane circle beneath the fog.   There were other
comparatively level areas which were not covered with
trees or other obstructions in that vicinity.   When I saw
the plane he was over a solid orchard all the time practically until he started going up the canon.   The bare field
I described was right near and there were grain fields
close by.

The Cranes are up the road about a quarter of a mile
from where I was standing and there were other unob-
scured fields near the Crane place, a grain field across the

(Testimony of C. E. Rawlings)
road of one hundred sixty acres but which has a couple
of big washes in it.

I have had experience with internal combustion engines,
gasoline motors and other motors, and I heard the motor
of the aeroplane clearly that morning and it seemed to be
running smoothly and in an orderly way; as far as I could
tell it was running, perfectly.

I went to the scene of the crash after the accident and
when I got there the plane was still burning; the cover
on it was afire and the tire was afire.

C. E. RAWLINGS

called as a witness on behalf of the plaintiff, testified as
follows:

I witnessed the airplane crash involved in this proceeding. I was working in my orchard in the morning, a
little after 9 o'clock and was first attracted by the noise
of the motor on this plane. I could not see it on account
of its being above the fog. I watched for it and soon
saw it come out of the fog. It then took a northwesterly
direction toward the canyon. It seemed to me that the
motor stopped while he was in the fog. Then as he came
out of the fog, he started up again and he sailed a little
way and the motor stopped again, and after that started
again, and he was sailing in approximately a northwesterly
direction, and then took a drop down and into the foothills. I saw the plane drop approximately 150 to 250
feet during the time it was visible to me. I saw the flash
of the flame and heard the crash. It was perfectly clear
in the canyon where the plane crashed and I could see the
tops of the foothills through the canyon. I could see the

(Testimony of Luther T. Smith)
tail of the plane when it hit. There were no leaves on
the trees in the orchard where I was at that time. The
place where I was standing was as high, or perhaps a
little higher, than the point of the accident. The plane
was about a half mile from the scene of the accident when
I first saw it and was about 150 or 200 feet over the
hilltop.

LUTHER T. SMITH

called as a witness for the plaintiff, testified as follows:

On the morning of the airplane crash involved here,
while I was working in my field where I reside I was attracted to the sound of an airplane in that vicinity. I
could see the airplane over my property at a height of
about 300 feet and it was headed in an easterly direction.
I kept watching him and he traveled a short way easterly
and then swung back in a westerly direction about over
the State Highway, which fronts my property. Then he
went almost due north into and around the foothills to
where the crash occurred. When the plane was headed
easterly, it was traveling in what appeared to me to be
the right direction of its course, because my property lies ·
in the San Gorgonia Pass. The ceiling of the fog where
I was standing was about 300 and 500 feet above the
ground and watching the plane, I could see it clearly to
about the point where the crash occurred. My property
is about a mile from the point of the crash, that is, about
a mile south and about 400 acres of my property is level
land upon any of which an airplane could have landed

(Testimony of Bert C. Phillips)
safely. The fog did not appear to me to be a spotted fog.
I could plainly see the point of the crash from where I
was standing. As I saw the plane the motor was hitting
regularly. I don't recall that I heard it slow off at all.
I heard the motor going at all times. In my acreage there
are not very many ditches.

BERT C. PHILLIPS

called as a witness on behalf of the plaintiff, testified as
follows:

On the morning of the airplane crash involved here, I
was howing weeds on my property about a mile and a
half east of the point of the crash. I heard the plane
about 9 o'clock. It was a little south of west at first, then
to the west; I would estimate it was a mile and a half
away; I could hear the plane definitely although it didn't
run regularly,—that was what called my attention to it.
It sounded so bad that I naturally observed closer. The
plane circled around and the ceiling of the fog was about
150 feet high above the ground where I was. There were
places where the plane could land in my vicinity. I heard
the crash and saw the smoke and flame. From what I
heard the plane seemed to be flying low and it seemed
to be circling and the engine,—I didn't hear it distinctly,—
and from there I crossed over the field so that I could see
better. There were a good many trees about and I couldn't
see over them. The first I heard the plane was to the
west and yet it seemed as I listened to be going around
and seemed to be low down. I didn't see it. I don't deny
that I testified at the Coroner's inquest that it seemed like
he was trying to make a landing.

BROOKS SAWYER

called as a witness on behalf of the plaintiff, testified as follows:

I live at Redlands, California, and am in the insurance business. On the morning of the airplane crash involved here, I drove to the scene of this accident and saw the wreck of the ship. The plane when it struck was heading in a westerly direction. The nose of the plane was between 15 and 20 feet below the crest of the hog-back and I would say that it struck while in a climbing altitude. I have been connected with the sale of aeroplanes, have managed an aeroplane concern and have done quite a bit of flying around Southern California. My opinion was that the plane was attempting to rise over the Hog Back; the machine was headed in a westerly direction, the nose being towards the top of the hill, and from the position of the motor and the position of the fuselage I would judge that the pilot had been attempting to pull the ship over and make the nose rise over the top of this ridge. He lacked a very few feet of safety. The ceiling of the fog at Redlands was about one thousand five hundred feet.

JOHN· L. WALLACE

called as a witness on behalf of the plaintiff, testified as follows:

I saw the plane on the morning of its crash circling about my farm near Beaumont. I knew it was circling by the sound of the motor, although the plane was not visible. I first saw the plane when it came out of the fog and crashed.

(Testimony of E. M. Allison—Blanche Vance Kelly—Paul
E. Rexter, Jr.)

E. M. ALLISON

called as a witness on behalf of the plaintiff, testified as
follows:

That he was the regularly appointed, qualified and acting Administrator of the Estate of Thomas J. Kelly,
deceased.

BLANCHE VANCE KELLY

called as a witness on behalf of the plaintiff, testified as
follows:

That she was the widow of Thomas J. Kelly, deceased,
and that at the time of his death and for a long time
prior thereto, the deceased was making substantial con-
tributions to her care and support.

PAUL E. REXTER, JR.

called as a witness on behalf of the defendant, testified as
follows:

That at the time of the airplane crash involved here,
he was an officer of the defendant and was a transport
pilot. That the defendant maintained a systematic method
for the checking of all planes prior to a flight for the
purpose of determining their condition. That before this
flight was undertaken, this plane was thoroughly checked
and was found to be in good mechanical condition. That
this plane had been in use since about the 4th day of
February, 1929. That the pilot on this ship at the time
of the crash had been employed by the defendant about
two months, was known to the witness about six or seven
months, was familiar with this route, had made three

(Testimony of Paul E. Rexter, Jr.)

round trips per week during the period of his employment and was a good pilot. That this plane left the airport at 84th and Western Streets, in Los Angeles, California, at eight o'clock on the morning of the accident
and was en route to El Paso, Texas, over a route which
would take it up through and over the San Gorgonio Pass.
That he visited the scene of the accident on the day of
the accident and that it appeared that at the time of the
crash, the plane was heading west; that the hill into which
the plane crash sloped about sixty degrees and that the
plane was evidently climbing at the time of the crash.
That no pilot would fly blind and that evidently the pilot
of this ship was seeking a landing place at the time of
the crash. That the ceiling of the fog that morning was
about 200 feet high at Redlands and about 1500 feet high
at Beaumont. That an exhaust from an airplane might
give an uneven sound when heard from the ground, even
though the engine should be working perfectly. That it
was evident from the scene at the crash that the power
was on when the crash occurred. That the crash occurred
on the west side of the San Gorgonio Pass. That in the
opinion of the witness the pilot was seeking a suitable
place for a landing which he had theretofore seen, when
the crash occurred and that the plane struck while climbing. That the circling by this plane at the Tri-City Airport at Redlands indicated to his mind that the pilot
thought it was safe to proceed on his journey. That in
his opinion the low flying done by the pilot of this ship
after leaving the Tri-City Airport was due to fog conditions in front of the pilot; otherwise, he would not have
come down so low. That sometimes a pilot may be able

(Testimony of Paul E. Rexter, Jr.)

to see the ground beneath him and yet ground observers would not be able to see the pilot.

The plane left on time, at 8 o'clock in the morning; at the time of the start visibility was five miles, the ceiling was unlimited and there was a very light haze.

Immediately adjoining the hill on which the plane crashed, at its eastern foot, was a little valley and right there at the foot of the hill there was an area, and the only one within a considerable distance, upon which a pilot could have landed safely.

The structure of the fuselage of the plane was not seriously damaged, the forward portion of the fuselage was not injured back of the engine mount; the plane was in a stalling position at the moment of impact, meaning that it was in a position in which it was climbing at as high an angle of climb as it could make; the brush on the hillside showed that it had climbed upwardly in this position for at least seventy-five feet before it struck the ground. The propeller was of steel alloy and was driven by the motor in such a way as to carve a curved section out of the rocky soil showing that the motor was running at the time of the impact.

The plane and the motor were both of type approved by the Department of Commerce of the United States; the plane was licensed by that Department, and flown by a pilot also licensed by that Department.

Immediately before the flight the plane and motor and every part thereof had been duly inspected and passed by an aeroplane mechanic also duly licensed by the United States Department of Commerce. The plane was powered with a five hundred twenty-five horse power Pratt-Whit-

(Testimony of Paul E. Rexter, Jr.)

ney Hornet Radial Engine having two exaust stacks, one of which exausted five cylinders and the other four cylinders, one exausting on one side of the fuselage, the other on the other side, thus making an uneven exaust beat which might create an impression that the motor was missing as compared with the even exaust beat of any engine having an even number of cylinders.

A plane could not have arrived at the climbing position in which this plane was when it struck without having the power of the engine to pull it into that position.

The only conclusion I can arrive at is in his circling around the point of the accident it became his judgment that he could not proceed further and tried to make a landing at the only spot available in the region which he was in which he had theretofore observed.

There are many factors and conditions to be taken into consideration and dealt with by a pilot in making a landing. He must first determine from what direction to approach the available landing spot; he must know his altitude in order to estimate distance required and the angle of glide which he must assume; he must also adjust all of these factors in such a way that he may at the proper point and then only reduce his speed to a point where it is safe to contact the ground. He must further study the contour of the ground in order not to be overturned by striking bumps or wrecked by hidden ditches, stumps, fences or other obstructions.

This plane had a cruising speed of about one hundred miles per hour and had a landing speed of about sixty miles.

(Testimony of Paul E. Rexter, Jr.)

The pilot was on schedule time when he reached the point where the fog conditions became such as to make a landing desirable and necessary and going into and out of the fog as he was doing he didn't have much time to make decisions and those that he made had to be made quickly. The accident was such as might have befallen the most capable and experienced pilot under the same conditions. These fogs come in from the ocean and quite often terminate near Redlands and very rarely extend as far as Banning. I have flown this line as a pilot and have on more than one occasion seen a two hundred feet ceiling at the Tri-City Airport and passed on through the Gorgonio Pass without encountering any trouble at all in the pass.

A pilot in the air can frequently see weather conditions ahead which cannot be seen by an observer on the ground.

In my opinion he did not return to the Tri-City Airport because of the fact that the fog in the meantime had closed in behind him and cut off his visibility and course in that direction.

The pilot had received all the weather reports that were available at the time he left the ground and they showed flying conditions to be favorable throughout his division.

The plane was fully equipped with compass, altimeter, revolution indicator, bank and turn indicator and all other instruments required by law, all of which had been tested as required by law before the flight. In circling, the card of the compass, of course, remained stationary and the other part is rotating; it is therefore under such conditions inaccurate until it has had an opportunity to adjust itself and establish direction in normal flight.

(Testimony of Lieut. Tomlinson)

Under the conditions shown by the testimony I would not have sought to climb up through an indeterminate depth of cloud and fogs with the mountains surrounding me as they were. I would seek a landing and in my opinion that is what the pilot of this plane was doing at the time of the accident.

LIEUT. TOMLINSON

called as a witness on behalf of the defendant, testified as follows:

I am manager of operations for the western division T. A. T.-Maddux. I have been flying since 1918 and have had two thousand nine hundred sixty-eight hours of flying. I was in the U. A. Naval Air Service until January, 1929; led the Sea Hawks, and was in command of the navy squadron at Mines Field. I have flown through the San Gorgonio Pass probably twenty times carrying passengers and am familiar with fog conditions prevailing there. I have been through the pass in practically every type and condition of fog, stratus fog, rain, high cumulus clouds and wind conditions and sand storms. Exhibit B shows the north side of the approach to the San Gorgonio Pass with the San Bernardino Mountains in the immediate foreground. There is a very noticeable wash which leads off to the north and slightly east at the center of the picture, where the accident took place. Exhibit F is a photograph in which I can identify the spot in which the accident took place.

There is nothing in the fact that Everett circled the Tri-City Airport for a time with a ceiling of about two hundred feet to negative the advisability of continuing on

(Testimony of Lieut. Tomlinson)

his trip. In circling over the airport it is entirely probable that he saw toward the pass an area of slightly higher visibility.

The conditions under which he was flying are known as stratus fog. The fog drifts in from the ocean and comes in waves. The bottom of the fog is not a continuous plane as some people think of it, the bottom of the fog is like waves in the ground swell at sea, if you could make that comparison; the bottom of the fog dips and is in rolls. There may have been a part of one of these rolls over the Tri-City Airport and a trough to the east which he may have seen so the visibility immediately east of the Tri-City Airport and in the direction of his course may have appeared better to him.

Q Assuming after he left the Tri-City Airport he was heard by a man living about three-quarters of a mile or a mile southwest of the place where the airplane crashed; he was heard either in the fog or above a layer of fog, traveling east; shortly thereafter he was seen to come out of the fog, come very close to the ground, proceed up that little draw that is so plainly shown in the picture and turn to the right, northeast; and go up into the clouds; he was seen next zooming some poles near a house; seen to turn to the left and go into a cloud and when next seen was coming out of the cloud just before he hit the hillside. What in your opinion would account for that kind of maneuvering on the part of the pilot?

A I can best describe that with reference to this picture.

Q Hold it so the jury can see it.

(Testimony of Lieut. Tomlinson)

A   The main pass lies in this direction here (indicating). The rolls of fog I spoke of usually come in parallel to the coast line and your wind in that direction, so your rolls of fog would be coming at a slight angle to the pass. It is very reasonable to assume that one of these rolls of fog coming up in here (indicating) would be down very low on this flat ground, but where it hit a range of hills such as we see here (indicating) it would have a tendency to carry it up and leave a draw such as this with a greater ceiling than you, would have down here (indicating). I have encountered that condition—a flat plain with a fifty foot ceiling, and a man down here (indicating) could not see me any distance at all, but it will hit against the hills and rise, due to the fact that instead of flowing directly up the draw, it was at an angle. Probably that man decided he had to land, and down in here (indicating) he saw this open channel over those fields and started circling to reach a point from which he could drop his ship into it. Due to the speed he was traveling and the low ceiling—probably from one hundred to one hundred and fifty feet, possibly more—it is probable he could not recognize any of these fields quick enough to cut his motors and make a safe landing, particularly as the wind would carry him up in this direction (indicating). Remember, the fog was rolling in from the ocean towards the mountains so any wind would tend to strike that draw. When he got here (indicating) he saw it closing in, and perhaps realized that if he could but turn around he could cut his motors and make a safe landing, so he pulled up and turned to the right and started to drop

(Testimony of Lieut. Tomlinson)

down, keeping ground contact while making the turn, hoping to land down wind in some of these fields. He might damage the ship, but he would get out all right. In making the turn he was possibly blind. He probably could get glimpses of the ground from time to time, but the fog was boiling over there and during a time when he was flying blind he missed the angle of the valley and saw this ridge in front of him, knew he could not turn in time and the only thing to do was to open his motors and try to go over.

In making a landing under the conditions that prevailed at this time a man has got to spot a field and then he has got to maneuver to get back into it, preferably into the wind. It is very difficult to do this under fog conditions. You spot your field and while you are maneuvering your ship one of these rolls of fog may come along and for a time you are flying blind; then when you spot your field again, such a ship as he was flying you can't throw up on its ear and turn on a dime. It takes perhaps half a mile to make a good, safe turn, and before you can get back, your field, like as not, is fogged out.

He has got to consider obstructions; the type of country he is flying over; rows of trees, rows of wires and ditches.

You have got to make a very flat turn there passing over the field, to see that it is a fit field to land in. You have got to turn to the left. You have got to swing to the left and then make a right turn to run down the field, because if you make a left turn, you are going to be a mile or so from the field. You see what I mean? You have got to be headed down the field to make a landing.

(Testimony of Lieut. Tomlinson)

It is a rather complicated maneuver, and requires considerable skill and judgment.

He probably found the floor of the pass itself was resting in the bottom of one of these rolls of fog. If you can picture your ground from the Tri-City Airport going up on a gradual slope and then sort of leveling off near Banning and then as it goes through the pass, and then picture rolls of fog rolling in, you have got a greatly decreased ceiling. A man could fly along and come into the upper reaches of this pass while one of those troughs is at that point. The fog is rolling along at the rate of fifteen or twenty miles an hour, and then he finds the bottom of the wave is on the ground. He turns to go back. By the time he gets back to where he got in, the next wave has blanketed that over. Particularly in that area where you have those hills the action I have described in that draw is not peculiar to that one point. You will find a point where the fog will hit one hill and give a space of visibility and then it is on the ground again. With such a condition the proper thing would be to land.

I think the man tried to get back in that draw and land as I have described, I believe there was a channel of visibility up that draw.

Under the conditions existing there at the time, according to the testimony, he suffered an accident which could have happened to any skillful pilot.

I think at the time of the accident he was either effecting a landing or determining the suitability of landing in that field which he may not have been able to observe at the instant of passing over it. I believe he circled as many as three or four times over that particular area to determine more accurately the feasibility of landing in that field and at the time of the accident I think he was making a turn with the intention of landing there.

(Testimony 'of Harold B. Russell—George Leary—Mr. Navey)

HAROLD B. RUSSELL

called as a witness on behalf of the defendant, testified as follows:

That he was an experienced and capable pilot of an airship; that there was a landing field at Beaumont, northeast of the point of this crash. That in his opinion, the pilot of this ship was undertaking to make a landing at a point he had selected for that purpose at the time when the crash occurred. That in his opinion, the pilot of this ship was circling at the Tri-City Airport in order to obtain a better visibility and must have seen a better spot ahead of him, or else he never would have left. That an emergency landing in the vicinity of this crash was feasible; that he is familiar with the fog conditions which ordinarily obtain in this Pass and that the fog did not have an even ceiling in this Pass.

GEORGE LEARY

called as a witness on behalf of the defendant, testified as follows:

That he is an airplane mechanic; that he examined this plane before it started on this trip and that the engine and plane were in good condition.

MR. NAVEY

called as a witness on behalf of the defendant, testified as follows:

That he is an airplane mechanic; that he examined this plane before it started on this trip and that the engine and plane were in good condition.

(Testimony of Ray Hamilton—Mrs. Thompson—John Leslie Martin)

RAY HAMILTON

called as a witness on behalf of the defendant, testified as follows:

That in his opinion this plane was reasonably on its course when it crashed.

MRS. THOMPSON

called as a witness on behalf of the defendant, testified as follows:

On the morning of this airplane crash, Mrs. Thompson was at her home in the vicinity of the crash, was attracted by the zooming of the plane as it roared over her place, and that the fog was heavy and low. That she saw the plane come northwest and just miss a heavy wire lower than her house. That she could see the home of Mr. Wallace from where she was. That Mr. Wallace's home was 100 or more feet lower than her home. That about two minutes elapsed between the time she first heard the plane zooming and the time when she again heard it zooming.

JOHN LESLIE MARTIN

called as a witness on behalf of the defendant, testified as follows:

I am an aeroplane pilot employed by the Western Air Express, licensed by the Department of Commerce, and have been flying since 1923, teaching students to fly until two years ago, since when I have been flying a regular line. For nearly a year I flew for the Standard Airlines through the San Gorgonio Pass, making two round trips

(Testimony of John Leslie Martin)

weekly. I had made several trips with the pilot Everett in the same ship with him; he was an experienced pilot.

I am acquainted with the fog conditions obtaining in the terrain approaching the pass. In my opinion when Everett circled the Tri-City Airport it was only to give him a chance to look over conditions and that had he not seen a light spot or some spot where the ceiling was high enough and visibility good enough he would not have proceeded. There is no doubt he had very good visibility or he would not have proceeded. When he got near the scene of the accident I believe the fog was getting too low for him and he was maneuvering around for the purpose of finding out whether the visibility warranted his going on and that he turned around and saw conditions behind as bad as in front and figured on making a landing and was maneuvering for a landing at some particular spot around there. In my opinion he had observed this valley and the ground there with reference to the feasibility of landing there and that he made a circle to the left to get into this field and throttled his motor back coming down out of the fog and that he saw this Hog Back in front of him and then put on all the gun he had and hauled the yoke back in and endeavored to clear it and settle down in this field that he had picked out. It was an accident that might have happened to any experienced pilot.

The defendant stipulated that at the time in question, the deceased, Thomas J. Kelly, was a passenger for hire on the airplane here involved and that said airplane was owned and operated by the defendant in the carriage of passengers for hire; and that said airship was on its regular run from Los Angeles to El Paso, Texas, and that there had been issued to the deceased, Thomas J. Kelly, a ticket containing the provisions set forth in the answer of the defendant on file herein, and which said ticket is in words and figures as follows, to-wit:

STANDARD AIRLINES, INC.

NON-TRANSFERABLE
Good for
One Continuous Passage
To Destination Shown Below

SUBJECT TO THE FOLLOWING TERMS AND CONDITIONS:

Reservations must be made and space assigned before ticket is good for passage.

Going Trip must begin, and Return Trip must be completed on dates shown hereon.

It is agreed between the holder of this ticket, and the STANDARD AIRLINES, Inc., that the same is a personal license, revocable at the will of the Company, with or without cause, and the holders' recourse in such event is limited to the amount paid therefor and marked hereon.

Should the Company accept the holder hereof for a flight in one of its airplanes, such acceptance shall not be deemed to make the Company a common carrier, but it is specifically agreed and understood between the holder and the Company that the Company is a private carrier and is liable to the holder not as an insurer, but only for proven negligence of its employees and agents, and the mere occurrence of an accident resulting in injury or loss of life to the holder shall not be any evidence of negligence.

It is further agreed and understood between the Company and the holder of this ticket that the Company is not liable for any loss or claimed loss caused by the delay or failure of aircraft to depart from any point or arrive at any point according to schedule, agreement or otherwise, nor for any loss or damage or injury to person or property caused by weather conditions, acts of God, or any other causes beyond the control of the Company.

BAGGAGE: 25 pounds of baggage will be transported free for each passenger. Limited additional baggage charged for at the company's excess baggage rate. It is further agreed that the company's liability for baggage is limited, in any event, to one-hundred dollars ($100.00) per passenger.

If in the judgment of the Company's agents, it is not deemed safe to proceed with the passenger, the company may cancel the entire trip or any portion thereof and refund the part of the fare equal to the unused portion of this ticket.

This ticket is non-transferable, and if presented for passage by any other than the original purchaser, may be taken up and cancelled.

STANDARD AIRLINES, INC.
Jack Frye
PRESIDENT, LOS ANGELES

I have read the terms and conditions printed hereon, and agree thereto.

Signature of Purchaser.

Agent.

(Sample)

STANDARD AIRLINES, INC.

Good for One Passage
When attached to contract Bearing
Purchaser's Signature

From..

To..

Date ....,

Fare $...............................

Baggage

No.   00702   Checked................................

— — — — — — — — — — — — — — — — — — —

(Sample)

STANDARD AIRLINES, INC.

PASSENGER'S COUPON
(Not Good For Passage)

From..

To..

Date................................... Seat No..................... .....

Fare $...............................

Baggage

No.   00702   Checked................................

(Sample)

STANDARD AIRLINES, INC.

AUDITOR'S COUPON
(Not Good For Passage)

From..

To..

Date.. Seat No......................

Fare $............................

Baggage

No. 00702   Checked................................

— — — — — — — — — — — — — — — — —

(Sample)

STANDARD AIRLINES, INC.

AGENT'S COUPON
(Not Good For Passage)

From..

To..

Date.. Seat No......................

Fare $............................

Baggage

No. 00702   Checked................................

[Endorsed]: No. 3516-H. Allison vs. Std Air Lines Deft Exhibit No. E for ident Filed 9/17 1930 R. S. Zimmerman, Clerk By Francis E. Cross Deputy Clerk Admitted and that this ship was a commercial ship and regularly licensed as such, and that at the time and place alleged in the complaint herein said airplane crashed upon a mountain side and said Thomas J. Kelly was thereby killed.

That thereupon the cause was argued to the jury by counsel for the plaintiff and defendant.

That thereupon, the Court read the instructions to the jury, as follows:

TITLE OF COURT AND CAUSE.

INSTRUCTIONS TO THE JURY.

THE COURT: Gentlemen of the jury:

It becomes the duty of the Court to give you certain instructions regarding the law in the case presented to you for your consideration, and it is also the privilege of the Court to comment upon the evidence if he sees fit. Such comments, in the event they are made, are merely the Court's ideas of what conclusions you may properly draw from the evidence. They are in no sense binding upon you. You are at all times the sole judges of the effect of evidence and of where the truth lies and within certain limitations, of the inferences that may be drawn from a proven set of facts.

In this action E. M. Allison, as administrator of the estate of Thomas J. Kelly, deceased, seeks to recover for the benefit of the surviving wife of the decedent damages against the Standard Air Lines, Inc., arising by reason of the death of Thomas J. Kelly.

The complaint states that Mr. Kelly, on March 30th, 1930, became a passenger on the defendant's airplane and in the vicinity of Banning in this state, by reason of the negligence of the defendant in operating the airplane was killed; that Blanche Vance Kelly, the surviving wife of the decedent, has been damaged in the sum of *$5000.00* thereby.

The defendant admits that Thomas J. Kelly was a passenger upon its airplane, and does not deny that he was killed in an accident. It does deny that his death was caused by or was due to any negligence on the part of the defendant, or that the decedent's surviving wife has been damaged in any sum at all.

As a further defense the defendant. claims that it operates an airline to Tucson, Arizona, through the San Gorgonio Pass; that this pass is generally but not always free from clouds and fogs; that the airplane left the airport at Los Angeles in good condition and order, flying the usual route under favorable weather conditions; that after entering the pass the plane became enveloped in a fog completely obscuring the vision; that by reason thereof the pilot lost his way, and the airplane was wrecked due to unforeseen events, and the Act of God.

As a further defense, the defendant claims that by reason of the conditions printed upon the ticket issued to the deceased, the defendant is not liable except for the proven negligence of its employees and the mere occurrence of the accident, resulting in the death of the decedent, is not of itself evidence of negligence.

Generally, with respect to the testimony in all cases, you are instructed that it is the exclusive province of the Judge of this court to instruct you as to the law that is applicable to these cases, that you may render a verdict as determined by you on the law as given to you by the judge. It would be a violation of your duty for you to attempt to determine the law or to base a verdict upon any other view of the law than that given you by the Court.

On the other hand, it is your exclusive province to determine the facts of the case, and to consider the evidence for that purpose. The Court cannot determine the facts, nor aid you in arriving at them, except by giving you the rules of law to be used by you in arriving at the truth. You are the sole judges of the effect and value of the evidence. Your power, however, of judging of the effect and value of the evidence is not arbitrary, but is to be exercised with legal discretion.

You are not bound to decide in conformity with the declarations of any number of witnesses which do not produce conviction in your minds, against a lesser number or against a presumption of law or evidence which satisfies your minds. In other words, it is not the greater number of witnesses which should control you, where their evidence is not satisfactory to your minds, as against a lesser number whose testimony does satisfy your minds.

In civil cases a preponderance of evidence is all that is required. That is, such evidence as, when weighed with that opposed to it, has more convincing force, and from which it results that the greater probability is in favor of the party upon whom the burden rests.

In weighing the evidence you are to consider the credibility of all witnesses who have testified in the case. You are the sole and exclusive judges of their credibility. The conduct of the witnesses, their character, as shown by the evidence, their manner on the stand, their relation to the parties, if any; their degree of intelligence, the reasonableness or unreasonableness of their statements, and the strength or weakness of their recollection may be taken into consideration for the purpose of determining their credibility. A witness is presumed to speak the truth. This presumption, however, may be repelled by the manner in which the witness testifies, by the character of the witness for truth, honesty or integrity, or his motive or by contradictory evidence.

A witness false in one part of his testimony is to be distrusted in others; that is to say, you may reject the whole of the testimony of a witness who has wilfully sworn falsely as to a material point, and being convinced that a witness has stated what was untrue, not as the result of mistake or inadvertence, but wilfully and with a design to deceive, you must treat all of his testimony with distrust and suspicion.

The testimony of one witness entitled to full credit is sufficient for the proof of any fact.

You should not consider as evidence any statement of counsel made during the trial, unless such statement is made as an admission or stipulation conceding the existence of a fact or facts. Neither should you consider any statement or comment of the Court made during the trial of the case. You are not to consider for any purpose, any evidence offered or rejected or stricken out by the Court, and such evidence is to be treated as though it never had been given. You are to decide this case solely upon the evidence that has been introduced before you, and the inferences which you may deduce therefrom, and such presumptions as the law may deduce therefrom as stated in these instructions and upon the law as given you in these instructions.

You must weigh and consider this case without regard to sympathy, prejudice or passion for or against either party to the action.

In the event your verdict should be for the plaintiff, you will give such damages as under all the circumstances of the case as shown by the evidence, you may deem proper. An action of this kind may be brought by the administrator of the estate. It is brought for the benefit of the heirs of the decedent which in this case is the surviving wife alone. It is admitted that according to the mortality tables the expectancy of life of the decedent was twenty-six years. This, however, is not conclusive or binding upon you, but is evidence to be considered by you along with other evidence in the case in arriving at the amount of damages, if any. You may properly take into consideration the relations between the decedent and his surviving wife as shown by the evidence.

Negligence is the failure to observe, for the protection of the interests of another person, that degree of care, protection and vigilance which the circumstances justly demand, whereby such other person suffers injury. It may be active or passive in character and may consist in heedlessly doing an improper thing or in heedlessly refraining from doing a proper thing. On who does not do what he should do is chargeable with negligence equally with him who does that which he should not do.

Negligence is never presumed, but the burden is upon the plaintiff to prove such negligence by a preponderance of the evidence and to further prove that such negligence on the part of the defendant was the proximate cause of Mr. Kelly's death. On both of these issues, the burden is upon the plaintiff, and unless the plaintiff proves such negligence and that it was the proximate cause of the decease of said Kelly, there can be no recovery herein and the verdict must be for the defendant and against the plaintiff.

Proximate cause is that cause which in natural and continuous sequence, unbroken by any efficient intervening cause, produces the injury and without which the result would not have occurred. It is the efficient cause, which acts and sets the other cause in operation.

No one is responsible for the results of an unavoidable accident, nor for casualties which not have been known to occur before, and which might not reasonably have been anticipated, and a defendant is not liable for an injury which is not caused by his negligence but which results from some overwhelming natural agency over which he has no control.

One who, without negligence on his part, is suddenly confronted with imminent danger or seeming imminent danger is not required to exercise that degree of care and skill which is required in the commission of an act after careful deliberation; he is required to act only as a reasonably prudent man would act under similar circumstances. Accordingly, where a situation requires an immediate choice between alternative courses of conduct, negligence may not be inferred from an unwise choice, if a reasonable man under similar circumstances, would choose similiarly.

One of the defenses in this case interposed by the defendant is by reason of a ticket issued to the decedent, the defendant could be liable only for negligence. In other words, it seeks to differentiate between the position of the defendant in this case and what is known as a common carrier of passengers. You are instructed that the law does not permit such a difference arising by reason of the issuance of a ticket. The issuance of a ticket with provisions printed thereon such as have been placed in evidence here does not change the relations of the parties to this action.

If you should find from the evidence that the pilot Everett acted in such a manner as a person of ordinary prudence and caution and skill would use under the same circumstances, he was not negligent.

He was only required to exercise such care and skill as is ordinarily possessed by those engaged in the same business, or art, and if you find from the evidence that he exercised such care and skill, he was not negligent, although the danger might have been avoided if he had acted in a different manner.

Hence his acting in the particular manner which he did would not necessarily be negligence merely because there may have been a safer manner of doing it.

All of the circumstances attending the transaction must be taken into consideration. However, these circumstances must be those which the evidence shows may reasonably be supposed to have been known to him and to have influenced his mind at the time, for after an event has transpired it is often easy to demonstrate means whereby it might have been prevented from occurring.

If you should find from the evidence that the pilot Everitt was an experienced and skillful pilot, and without any negligence on his part encountered fog conditions, and that bringing to bear all his previous experience and skill he weighed the facts and circumstances surrounding him and of which he had knowledge and decided upon a course of action which he tried to carry out, that is, to make an emergency landing, then his want of success would be due to error of judgment and not to negligence. That is, if he exercised his best judgment and if his acts would have been approved by competent experts.

You are instructed that the carrier of persons for reward must use the utmost of care and diligence for their safe carriage, must provide everything necessary for that purpose and must exercise toward that end a reasonable degree of skill.

The carrier of persons for reward is bound to provide vehicles fit for that purpose and is not excused for failure in this respect by any degree of care.

While the law demands the utmost care for the safety of passengers, it does not require airplane companies to exercise all the care, skill and diligence of which the human mind can conceive nor such as will free the transportation of passengers from all possible perils.

The deceased in this case necessarily took upon himself all the usual and ordinary perils incident to airplane travel and if you find from the evidence that the defendant exercised all the care, skill and diligence required by law as defined in these instructions and that nevertheless the accident occurred, the defendant would not be responsible therefor, and your verdict should be for the defendant.

A carrier is not an insurer of the safety of its passengers and is not bound absolutely and at all events to carry them safely and without injury. All passengers take the risk of those dangers which cannot be averted by the carrier by the exercise of the degree of care which the law requires.

The defendant in this case, in addition to its defense that it was not guilty of negligence has presented the defense that the accident in question was due to unforeseen events, inevitable accident or Act of God. You are advised that if either of these defenses are established by the evidence, the plaintiff cannot recover, and your verdict must be for the defendant.

No matter how great and imminent might have been the danger or serious consequences of an accident, the plaintiff would not be entitled to recover if the death of Thomas J. Kelly was the result of an inevitable or unavoidable accident; that is, if the accident could not have been prevented by the exercise of that degree of care and caution required of the defendant under the instructions heretofore given. A pure accident without negligence on the part of the defendant is not actionable, and if you are convinced that the accident was of such a character, it would come under the head of an inevitable accident, then in such event, the plaintiff could not recover.

There is in the law of accidents the further principle that I will briefly state to you.

When any person is confronted with a sudden emergency, he is not required to exercise the same degree of caution, that natural and deliberate judgment exercised when there is plenty of time to determine what would be the wise thing to do. The law makes note of those things.

Now, gentlemen, with reference to the application of these instructions to these particular facts, I feel like observing to you that of course it is admitted Mr. Kelly was a passenger for hire upon this airplane. It is un-contradicted that the airplane was sufficient for its pur-pose. In fact, its capacity was more than its load. It was inspected as required by the government regulations; that the air was clear and suitable for flying when it left Los Angeles. We have no direct evidence as to when or where it encountered the fog. It is without dispute that it circled the Tri-City Airport several times and was later seen by several of the witnesses, you will remember their names, who describe it as flying around in the vicinity of the place where the accident occurred. Several of the witnesses described it as at times invisible because of the fog. Other witnesses that it appeared and later dis-appeared in the fog. It emerged from the fog and later disappeared into the fog.

There is considerable contradiction as to how high the fog was or what the visibility was. That you must de-termine for yourselves from a consideration of all the evidence. The testimony of all the witnesses is such that you must reasonably draw the inference that the plane was off its course and had lost its bearings. Whether or not the terrain was visible to the aviator may be reason-ably doubted from the evidence. Undoubtedly it was not always visible. As I remember, several witnesses heard the plane, when they could not see it. One witness, I believe, stated the plane appeared to be directly overhead, yet was obscured from his view by the fog. All the expert testimony seems to agree that in the opinion of the witnesses testifying, the pilot was seeking a landing place. Those, however, were all witnesses presented by the defendant. The plaintiff contends that by rejecting the landing place which the plaintiff claims must have been visible, and seeking to find his way out of the fog, he suffered this accident. The plaintiff, as I understand its position, maintains that it was negligent to attempt to fly through fog in any event; that not to have landed at the Tri-City Airport, and not to have landed in the field or in the places where a landing might have been made in the vicinity of the accident, constituted negligence.

There is one feature in this case, however, to which I desire to call your particular attention. That is, that there is no witness, no living witness, who is able to tell us what the aviator actually saw. One of the experts stated with reference to his circling over the airport— the Tri-City Airport—that it might have been he saw what he thought was clear weather, or clearing atmospheric conditions beyond him.

Applying the principle regarding the error of judgment, which you will bear in mind, if in the judgment of this aviator he saw what appeared to be favorable conditions ahead of him, then the defendant is not to be held for negligence because he chose that course rather than to land upon the field in safety.

Now, that is more or less of a new science, as we all recognize, and admittedly it is a branch of the law where we have very few precedents, that is, adjudicated cases. In order to hold the defendant for negligence, you must, as I explained to you, find that the pilot in this case— because the pilot represents the defendant—the corporation is able to act only through its employee in this case, and therefore the pilot in this case is for all purposes of the case, so far as your verdict goes, the defendant itself. The pilot must have done something which good judgment did not approve, or would not approve, and on account of the fact that we cannot know what the aviator saw, what appeared to him it is a rather difficult thing in my judgment to know that the conditions that appeared to him did not justify his doing what he did.

You, gentlemen are the exclusive judges of the evidence in this case, and you are to make up your minds from the evidence before you what the situation was.

One other thing may be suggested to you. An airplane is a thing that must be kept going, and going at a very rapid rate, to insure anything like safety. If a man sees danger ahead of him when he is driving an automobile, he may stop. It is not so with an airplane. Stopping means danger, often death, unless of course a landing is made.

Gentlemen, your verdict must be according to the preponderance of the evidence. That has been explained to you. This case requires a unanimous verdict. When you retire, you will choose one of your number as foreman. There are submitted to you two forms of verdict. Are there any exceptions to the charge, gentlemen?

MR. CLARK: Are exceptions to the charge reserved to each side, your Honor?

THE COURT: You must, according to procedure, state your exceptions now. You may state them in as informal a manner as you wish.

MR. DAHL: The only exception we would like to take, would be to your honor's instruction with respect to the ticket for transportation.

MR. CLARK: The only exception I desire to take is on the question of whether or not your Honor covered thoroughly the distinction between the exercise of ordinary care and the highest degree of care. In other words, pointing out to the jury if any negligence, however slight, of the defendant contributed to the accident, that would render the defendant iiable. Second, if the jury should find it was the concurrence of an Act of God and a slight negligence, even, of the defendant, that would make the defendant liable. Those are the only two exceptions we note, your Honor.

That at the proper time, the plaintiff requested the Court to instruct the jury as follows, which instructions, so requested by the plaintiff, were refused by the Court, to-wit:

You are instructed that in determing what would amount to reasonable and ordinary care in the operation of an airship you may and should consider all the conditions as they existed at the time so far as they were apparent to the defendant and insofar as those conditions should have been apparent to the defendant had it been in the exercise of reasonable and ordinary care.

The defendant in this cause has set up the defense that the injury complained of was due to an inevitable accident.

As to this defense, you are instructed that if you find from the evidence that the accident could have been avoided by the defendant by the exercise of the highest degree of care, then you must also find that the accident was not inevitable and that the defense of inevitable accident has not been sustained.

You are instructed that the defendant as a carrier of said T. J. Kelly, as a passenger, for pay, is liable for the death of said T. J. Kelly, if such death was occasioned or proximately contributed to by the negligence, however slight, of any of the servants of said defendant, including the pilot of said airplane, while such servants were engaged in the general scope of their employment, and regardless of whether the negligent act or omission, if any, was or was not authorized by the defendant.

You are instructed that if you find from the evidence that the accident complained of was the result of a combination of extraordinary weather conditions and any negligence, however slight, of the defendant, which contributed thereto, then you must find for the plaintiff and against the defendant.

You are instructed that if you should find from the evidence that the accident complained of was the result of the concurrence of an Act of God and of any negligence, however slight, of the defendant, then your verdict must be for the plaintiff and against the defendant.

The Court erred as a matter of law in receiving the verdict of the jury and causing the Clerk of the Court to enter Judgment thereon, for the reason that the same verdict and judgment are not sustained and justified by the evidence, and that the evidence introduced in the trial of said action is insufficient to sustain or justify the verdict of the jury and the judgment entered thereon.

The Court erred as matter of law in overruling and refusing to grant the motion for new trial of the plaintiff, E. M. Allison, as Administrator of the estate of Thomas J. Kelly, deceased, for the reasons and upon the grounds set forth in said Motion, and in this Bill of Exceptions.

The Court erred in accepting the verdict of the jury and in causing the Clerk of said Court to enter Judgment thereon.

The Court erred in accepting the verdict of the jury and entering Judgment thereon, because the said verdict was rendered and given under the influence of passion and prejudice or passion or prejudice.

The Court erred in accepting the verdict of the jury and entering judgment thereon, because the said verdict was not sustained or justified by the evidence introduced at the trial of said action.

The Court erred in accepting the verdict of the jury and entering judgment thereon because the evidence introduced at the trial of said action is insufficient to sustain or justify said verdict.

The Court erred in accepting the verdict of the jury and entering judgment thereon because said verdict is contrary to and against the evidence introduced in the trial of said action.

The Court erred in accepting the verdict of the jury and entering judgment thereon because evidence introduced in the trial of said action showed and proved by a preponderance thereof, that the accident in question, and the injury to, and the death of, the deceased, were caused by and proximately contributed to by the negligence of the defendant.

That thereafter, on the 19th day of September, 1930, the jury returned into open court a verdict in said action in favor of the defendant and against the plaintiff.

That thereupon the court ordered said verdict in said action recorded and judgment entered thereon, which was accordingly done by the Clerk of said Court.

That thereafter, on to-wit: the 30th day of September, 1930, and within the time required by law, the plaintiff, E. M. Allison, as Administrator of the Estate of Thomas

J. Kelly, deceased, served on the attorney for the defendant in said action, and filed in said action, said plaintiff's Motion for a New Trial, which said Motion and Notice are in words and figures as follows, to-wit:

TITLE OF COURT AND CAUSE.

NOTICE OF MOTION FOR A NEW TRIAL.

TO THE DEFENDANT HEREIN AND TO JOHN F. DAHL, ESQ., AND KIRKE T. MOORE, ESQ., ITS ATTORNEYS:

YOU, AND EACH OF YOU, WILL PLEASE TAKE NOTICE that on Monday, the 6th day of October, 1930, at the hour of ten o'clock A. M., the plaintiff will move the above entitled Court and the Honorable Judge George Cosgrave, Judge presiding, in Room 422 of said Court, at the Federal Building, in Los Angeles, California, for an order vacating and setting aside the judgment heretofore made and entered herein and the verdict of the jury herein, and the implied findings of fact herein, and granting plaintiff a new trial herein.

Said motion will be made upon each of the following grounds, to-wit:

1. Irregularity in the proceedings of the Court, jury and adverse party and orders of the Court and abuse of discretion by which plaintiff was prevented from having a fair trial.

2. Accident or surprise, which ordinary prudence could not have guarded against.

3. Newly discovered evidence material for the plaintiff, which plaintiff could not with reasonable diligence have discovered and produced at the trial.

4.   Insufficiency of the evidence to justify the verdict or decision and that the verdict and the decision is against law.

5.   Error in law occurring at the trial, and excepted to by the plaintiff.

6.   Errors of the Court in the instructions given to the jury and in the instructions requested by the plaintiff and refused, and in instructions given by the Court upon its own motion and in instructions requested but modified by the Court.

Said motion will be made and based upon the papers, records and pleadings herein and upon the notes of the reporter who took down the testimony and instructions upon the trial of said cause and upon affidavits to be hereafter prepared, served and filed.

Dated: Los Angeles, California, September 30, 1930.

Oliver O. Clark
S. A. Rosenthal
Attorneys for Plaintiff.

CERTIFICATE OF COUNSEL.

I hereby certify that the above motion is made in good faith and is not interposed for purposes of delay.

Oliver O. Clark

TITLE OF COURT AND CAUSE.

PLAINTIFF'S POINTS AND AUTHORITIES IN SUPPORT OF MOTION FOR NEW TRIAL.

Plaintiff urges that a new trial should be granted herein upon the grounds specified in the Notice of Motion to which this Memorandum is attached, for the following reasons, among others:

1. That the evidence is insufficient to justify or to support the implied findings or the verdict or the judgment for the reason that it appears from the evidence that the cause of the injury was under the exclusive control and management of the defendant and that, therefore, the doctrine of res ipso loquitur applies and that under said doctrine the negligence of the defendant is presumed and the burden rests upon the defendant to show its freedom from negligence; and that, in the absence of such showing, the verdict and the judgment must be in favor of such negligence and against the defendant; and that in the case at bar, there is no evidence to show the defendant's freedom from negligence and therefore under said presumption of negligence and the doctrine of res ipso loquitur, the verdict and the judgment should have been in favor of plaintiff and against the defendant.

Judson v. Giant Powder Company; 107 Cal. 549-562;

Redfield v. Oakland C. S. Ry. Co.; 112 Cal. 220;

Pecheco v. Judson Mfg. Co., 113 Cal., 541;

Arnold v. Calif. etc. Cement Co., 161 Cal. 522;

Barboza v. Pacific Portland Cement Co., 162 Cal. 36;

Paiva v. California Door Company, 48 Cal. App. Dec. 636-640;

Willard v. Valley Gas & Fuel Company, 171 Cal., 9;

Rathbun v. White, 157 Cal. 348;

Hallawell v. Union Oil Company, 36 Cal. App. Rep., 672-681;

Diller v. Northern California Powder Co., 162 Cal., 537.

2. That the Court erred in the instructions which it gave respecting the degree of care which the defendant was bound to exercise under the circumstances shown by the evidence in this case and also erred in the instructions requested by plaintiff, which it refused to give or gave as modified respecting said degree of care in this: that under the law it was the duty of the defendant here to have exercised the utmost care and the defendant was liable for any negligence, however slight, and yet the instructions of the Court as given stated in effect to the jury that the defendant was held only for the exercise of ordinary care.

3. That under the law the deceased did not assume any hazards of his transportation arising from any negligence, however slight, of the defendant, but under the instructions as given to the jury by the Court, the jury were told in substance that because of the hazardous character of the means of transportation here employed, the deceased would be held to have assumed the extraordinary hazards.

4. That there is not any evidence in the record sufficient to show the defendant's freedom from negligence and that, therefore, as a matter of law and in accordance with the presumption of negligence, the verdict and decision is contrary to the evidence and is not supported by the evidence and is against law.

Oliver O. Clark
S. A. Rosenthal
Attorneys for Plaintiff.

That thereafter said Motion was set down for hearing in said Court and was heard by said Court on the 24th day of November, 1930, and submitted upon briefs. That thereafter briefs were filed by the parties hereto and thereafter, to-wit: on the 24th day of January, 1931, said Motion for New Trial was denied by said Court, to which ruling an exception was made and allowed by the Court.

SPECIFICATIONS OF ERROR:

The plaintiff, E. M. Allison, as Administrator of the Estate of Thomas J. Kelly, deceased, now specifies the errors urged by him on his Motion for a New Trial in said action and being the errors upon which he now relies on this his appeal from the verdict and judgment in said action, and each and every part thereof.

I.

INSUFFICIENCY OF THE EVIDENCE.

Said plaintiff now specifies the following particulars wherein the evidence is insufficient to sustain or justify the verdict of the jury and the judgment entered thereon.

1. The evidence is insufficient to sustain or justify the finding and verdict of the jury and the judgment entered thereon.

2. The evidence is insufficient to sustain or justify the finding and decision that the defendant was free from negligence proximately contributing to the injuries and death complained of in plaintiff's complaint.

3. The evidence is insufficient to sustain or justify the finding and decision that the injuries and death complained of in plaintiff's complaint was due to risks and dangers assumed by the plaintiff.

4. The evidence is insufficient to sustain or justify the finding and decision that the injuries and death complained of in plaintiff's complaint was proximately contributed to by any negligence of the deceased.

II.

SPECIFICATIONS OF ERROR IN LAW

OCCURING AT THE TRIAL AND EXCEPTED TO BY THE PLAINTIFF.

The plaintiff, E. M. Allison, as Administrator of the Estate of Thomas J. Kelly, deceased, now specifies the following errors in law occurring at the trial of said action, being the errors of law urged by plaintiff on his Motion for a New Trial herein and here now urged and complained of, and specified on this his appeal from the Verdict and Judgment in said action, and each and every part thereof:

1. The Court erred in refusing to instruct the jury as requested by the plaintiff, which instructions so requested by said plaintiff are hereinbefore set forth in full commencing at line 4 on page 35 hereof, to and including line 13 on page 36 hereof.

2. The Court erred in instructing the jury, which instructions so given by the Court to the jury and the plaintiff's exceptions thereto, are hereinbefore set forth in full commencing at line 10 on page 25 hereof, to and including line 26 on page 33 hereof.

3. The Court erred as matter of law in denying the Motion for a New Trial of the plaintiff, which Motion for a New Trial and the Court's Order in denying and refusing to grant the same are hereinbefore set forth in full commencing at line 6 on *on* page 41 hereof, to and including line 12 on the same page.

4. The Court erred as matter of law in accepting the Verdict of the jury herein and causing the Clerk of the Court to enter a Judgment in accordance with said Verdict and in thereby holding that the evidence introduced in the trial of this action was sufficient to sustain and justify said Verdict and the Judgment entered thereon.

III.

THE VERDICT AND JUDGMENT ARE AGAINST THE LAW.

The plaintiff, E. M. Allison, as Administrator of the Estate of Thomas J. Kelly, deceased, now specifies the particulars wherein the Verdict and Judgment are against the law, being the points relied upon by said plaintiff on his Motion for a New Trial herein and here now urged and assigned by him on this, his appeal, from the Verdict and Judgment in said action and each and every part thereof, to-wit:

1. Irregularity in the proceedings of the Court, jury and adverse party and orders of the Court and abuse of discretion by which plaintiff was prevented from having a fair trial.

2. Accident or surprise, which ordinary prudence could not have guarded against.

3. Newly discovered evidence material for the plaintiff, which plaintiff could not with reasonable diligence have discovered and produced at the trial.

4. Insufficiency of the evidence to justify the verdict or decision and that the verdict and the decision is against law.

5. Error in law occurring at the trial, and excepted to by the plaintiff.

6. Errors of the Court in the instructions given to the jury and in the instructions requested by the plaintiff and refused, and in instructions given by the Court upon its own Motion and in instructions requested but modified by the Court.

That each and all of said errors and exceptions hereinbefore complained of and specified were urged by said plaintiff on his Motion for a New Trial herein and are here now reassigned and urged on this, his appeal from the Verdict and Judgment in said action, and each and every part thereof, which Specifications of Error are more fully set forth in the Assignments of Error heretofore served and filed herein.

WHEREFORE, to the end that the proceedings and exceptions aforesaid may be and remain of record, the plaintiff, E. M. Allison, as Administrator of the Estate of Thomas J. Kelly, deceased, within the time allowed by law, and stipulation of counsel, and order of this Court, here now presents the within and foregoing Bill of Exceptions, and prays that the same be settled and allowed as said Plaintiff's Engrossed Bill of Exceptions on his appeal from the Verdict and Judgment in said action, and for any and all purposes for which said Bill of Exceptions may properly be used.

DATED: Los Angeles, California, December 16th, 1931.

Oliver O. Clark

Samuel A. Rosenthal

Attorneys for Plaintiff, E. M. Allison, as Administrator of the Estate of Thomas J. Kelly, deceased.

STIPULATION.

IT IS HEREBY STIPULATED by and between the parties hereto, that the foregoing Bill of Exceptions may be settled and adopted and certified to and used as the Bill of Exceptions on appeal herein.

DATED this 16th day of December, 1931.

> Oliver O. Clark,
>
> Samuel A Rosenthal

Attorneys for Plaintiff, E. M. Allison, as Administrator of the Estate of Thomas J. Kelly, deceased.

> Harry D. Parker
>
> O'Melveny, Tuller & Myers
>
> and Homer I. Mitchell
>
> Attorneys for Defendant.

The foregoing is hereby allowed, settled and approved as the Bill of Exceptions for the record on appeal herein.

DATED this 11th day of January, 1932.

> Geo. Cosgrave
>
> JUDGE.

[Endorsed]: No. 3516-H   In the District Court of the United States Southern District of California Central Division.   E. M. Allison, as Administrator of the Estate of Thomas J. Kelly, deceased, plaintiff and Appellant, vs. Standard Air Lines, Inc., a corporation, Defendant and Respondent.   Plaintiff's Proposed Bill of Exceptions.   Filed Jan 11 1932   R. S. Zimmerman, Clerk By Thomas Madden, Deputy Clerk   Law Offices Oliver O. Clark Los Angeles, California 1203 Garfield Building

IN THE DISTRICT COURT OF THE UNITED
STATES FOR THE SOUTHERN DISTRICT OF
CALIFORNIA CENTRAL DIVISION

E. M. ALLISON, as administrator
of the Estate of Thomas J. Kelly)
deceased,   No. 3516-H.

                    Plaintiff,   DECISION

        -vs-   On Motion For
)   New Trial.
STANDARD AIR LINES, INC., a)
corporation,

                    Defendant.

_____

Motion for new trial is denied.

                        Geo. Cosgrave
                        Geo. Cosgrave,
                            U. S. District Judge.

[Endorsed]: Filed Jan 27 1931 R. S. Zimmerman,
Clerk By Francis E. Cross Deputy Clerk

IN THE DISTRICT COURT OF THE UNITED
STATES FOR THE SOUTHERN DISTRICT OF
CALIFORNIA CENTRAL DIVISION

* * *

E. M. ALLISON, as Administrator)
of the Estate of Thomas J. Kelly,)
Deceased,)   No. 3516-H
)
     Plaintiff and Appellant,) PETITION FOR
) APPEAL
vs.)
)
STANDARD AIR LINES, INC.,)
a corporation,)
)
    Defendant and Respondent)

E. M. Allison, as Administrator of the Estate of Thomas J. Kelly, deceased, plaintiff in the above numbered and entitled action, feeling himself aggrieved by the Verdict of the Jury and the Judgment entered thereon in the above entitled action on September 20th, 1930, comes now by his attorneys Oliver O. Clark and Samuel A. Rosenthal, and files herewith Assignments of Errors and petitions this Honorable Court for an Order allowing plaintiff to prosecute an appeal in the Honorable, the Circuit Court of Appeals for the Ninth Circuit of the United States of America, under and according to the laws of the United States in that behalf made and provided, to the end that said Judgment may be reviewed and reversed by the said Circuit Court of Appeals.

Dated: · April 24th, 1931.

Oliver O. Clark
Samuel A. Rosenthal
Attorneys for Plaintiff and Appellant.

[Endorsed]: No. 3516-H   In the District Court of the United States for the Southern District of California Central Division E. M. Allison, as Administrator of the Estate of Thomas J. Kelly, deceased, Plaintiff and Appellant vs. Standard Air Lines, Inc, a corporation, Defendant and Respondent Petition for Appeal. Received copy of the within Petition this ·25th day of April, 1931 John F Dahl Attorney for defendant Filed Apr 25 1931 R. S. Zimmerman, Clerk By Edmund L Smith Deputy Clerk Oliver O. Clark Samuel A. Rosenthal 1203 Garfield Building Los Angeles, California Attorneys for plaintiff

---

IN THE DISTRICT COURT OF THE UNITED
STATES SOUTHERN DISTRICT OF
CALIFORNIA CENTRAL
DIVISION

* * *

E. M. ALLISON, as Administrator)
of the Estate of Thomas J. Kelly,)
Deceased,)
)
     Plaintiff and Appellant)   No. 3516-H
)
        vs.)   ASSIGNMENTS
)   OF ERROR.
STANDARD AIR LINES, INC.,)
a corporation,)
)
   Defendant and Respondent)

Comes now E. M. Allison, as Administrator of the Estate of Thomas J. Kelly, Deceased, plaintiff in the above numbered and entitled action, by Oliver O. Clark and Samuel A. Rosenthal, his attorneys of record, and files the following Assignments of Error upon which he will rely on the prosecution of his appeal in the above entitled cause, petition for which appeal is filed at the same time as this Assignments of Error.

I.

The Court erred in instructing the jury as follows, which instruction given to the jury by the Court was then and there excepted to by the plaintiff and an exception allowed, to-wit:

"The carrier of persons for reward must use the utmost care and diligence for their safe carriage, must provide everything necessary for that purpose and must exercise toward that end a reasonable degree of skill."

"The carrier of persons for reward is bound to provide vehicles fit for that purpose and is not excused for failure in this respect by any degree of care."

II.

The Court erred in instructing the jury as follows, which instruction given to the jury by the Court was then and there excepted to by the plaintiff and an exception allowed, to-wit:

"While the law demands the utmost care for the safety of passengers, it does not require airplane companies to exercise all the care, skill and diligence of which the human mind can conceive nor which will free the transportation of passengers from all possible perils."

III.

The Court erred in instructing the jury as follows, which instruction given to the jury by the Court was then and there excepted to by the plaintiff and an exception allowed, to-wit:

"If you should find from the evidence that the pilot
Everett acted in such a manner as a person of ordinary
prudence and caution and skill would use under the same
circumstances, he was not negligent."

IV.

The Court erred in instructing the jury as follows,
which instruction given to the jury by the Court was
then and there excepted to by the plaintiff and an exception allowed, to-wit:

"He was only required to exercise such care and skill
as is ordinarily possessed by those engaged in the same
business or art, and if you find that he exercised such
care and skill, he was not negligent although the danger
might have been avoided if he had acted in a different
manner."

V.

The Court erred in instructing the jury as follows,
which instruction given to the jury by the Court was then
and there excepted to by the plaintiff and an exception
allowed, to-wit:

"hence his acting in the particular manner which he did
would not necessarily be negligence merely because there
may have been a safer manner of doing it."

VI.

The Court erred in instructing the jury as follows,
which instruction given to the jury by the Court was
then and there excepted to by the plaintiff and an exception allowed, to-wit:

"All of the circumstances attending the transaction
must be taken into consideration. However, these circumstances must be those which the evidence shows may
reasonably be supposed to have been known to him and

to have influenced his mind at the time, for after an event has transpired it is often easy to demonstrate means whereby it might have been prevented from occurring."

VII.

The Court erred in instructing the jury as follows, which instruction given to the jury by the Court was then and there excepted to by the plaintiff and an exception allowed, to-wit:

"If you should find from the evidence that the pilot Everett was an experienced and skillful pilot, and without any negligence on his part encountered fog conditions, and that bringing to bear all his previous experience and skill he weighed the facts and circumstances surrounding him and of which he had knowledge and decided upon a course of action which he tried to carry out, that is, to make an emergency landing, then his want of success would be due to error of judgment and not to negligence. That is if he exercised his best judgment and if his acts would have been approved by competent experts."

VIII.

The Court erred in instructing the jury as follows, which instruction given to the jury by the Court was then and there excepted to by the plaintiff and an exception allowed, to-wit:

"The deceased in this case necessarily took upon himself all the usual and ordinary perils incidental to airplane travel, and if you find from the evidence that the defendant exercised all the care, skill and diligence required by law as defined in these instructions and that nevertheless the accident occurred, the defendant would not be responisble therefor, and your verdict should be for the defendant."

IX.

The Court erred in instructing the jury as follows, which instruction given to the jury by the Court was then and there excepted to by the plaintiff and an exception allowed, to-wit:

"The defendant in this case, in addition to its defense that it was not guilty of negligence has presented the defense that the accident in question was due to unforseen events, inevitable accident or Act of 'God. You are advised that if either of these defenses are established by the evidence, the plaintiff cannot recover, and your verdict must be for the defendant.

X.

The Court erred in instructing the jury as follows, which instruction given to the jury by the Court was then and there excepted to by the plaintiff and an exception allowed, to-wit:

"When any person is confronted with a sudden emergency, he is not required to exercise the same degree of caution that natural and deliberate judgment exercised when there is plenty of time to determine what would be the wise thing to do. The law takes note of these things."

XI.

The Court erred in instructing the jury as follows, which instruction given to the jury by the Court was then and there excepted to by plaintiff and an exception allowed, to-wit:

"Applying the principle regarding the error of judgment, which you will bear in mind, if in the judgment of this aviator he saw what appeared to be favorable conditions ahead of him, then the defendant is not to be held for negligence because he chose that course rather than to land upon the field in safety."

XII.

The Court erred in instructing the jury as follows, which instruction given to the jury by the Court was then and there excepted to by the plaintiff and an exception allowed, to-wit:

"In order to hold the defendant for negligence, you must, as I explained to you, find that the pilot in this case * * * * * * must have done something which good judgment did not approve, or would not approve."

XIII.

The Court erred in instructing the jury as follows, which instruction given to the jury by the Court was then and there excepted to by the plaintiff and an exception allowed, to-wit:

"On account of the fact that we cannot know what the aviator saw, what appeared to him, it is a rather difficult thing in my judgment to know that the conditions that appeared to him did not justify his doing what he did."

XIV.

The Court erred in instructing the jury as follows, which instruction given to the jury by the Court was then and there excepted to by the plaintiff and an exception allowed, to-wit:

"Negligence is never presumed, but the burden is upon the plaintiff to prove such negligence by a preponderance of the evidence* * * and unless the plaintiff proves such negligence * * * there can be no recovery herein and the verdict must be for the defendant and against the plaintiff."

XV.

The Court erred in instructing the jury as follows, which instruction given to the jury by the Court was then and there excepted to by the plaintiff and an exception allowed, to-wit:

"As a further defense, the defendant claims that by reason of the conditions printed upon the ticket issued to the deceased, the defendant is not liable except for the proven negligence of its employees and the mere occurrence of the accident, resulting in the death of the defendant, is not of itself evidence of negligence."

XVI.

The Court erred in instructing the jury as follows, which instruction given to the jury by the Court was then and there excepted to by the plaintiff and an exception allowed, to-wit:

"One who, without negligence on his part is suddenly confronted with imminent danger or seeming imminent danger is not required to exercise that degree of care and skill which is required in the commission of an act after careful deliberation; he is required to act only as a reasonably prudent man would act under similar circumstances. Accordingly, where a situation requires an immediate choice between alternative courses of conduct, negligence may not be inferred from an unwise choice, if a reasonable man under similar circumstances, would choose similarly."

XVII.

The Court erred in instructing the jury as follows, which instruction given to the jury by the Court was then and there excepted to by the plaintiff and an exception allowed, to-wit:

"If you should find from the evidence that the pilot Everett acted in such a manner as a person of ordinary prudence and caution and skill would use under the same circumstances, he was not negligent. He was only required to exercise such care and skill as is ordinarily possessed by those engaged in the same business or art, and if you find from the evidence that he exercised such care and skill, he was not negligent although the danger might have been avoided if he had acted in a different manner; hence his acting in the particular manner which he did would not necessarily be negligence merely because there may have been a safer manner of doing it. All of the circumstances attending the transaction must be taken into consideration. However, these circumstances must be those which the evidence shows may reasonably be supposed to have been taken into consideration. However, these circumstances must be those which the evidence shows may reasonably be supposed to have been known to him and to have influenced his mind at the time, for after an event has transpired it is often easy to demonstrate means whereby it might have been prevented from occurring."

XVIII.

The Court erred in instructing the jury as follows, which instruction given to the jury by the Court was then and there excepted to by the plaintiff and an exception allowed, to-wit:

"The defendant in this case, in addition to its defense that it was not guilty of negligence has presented the defense that the accident in question was due to unforeseen events, inevitable accident or Act of God. You are advised that if either of these defenses are established by the evidence, the plaintiff cannot recover, and your verdict must be for the defendant."

XVIX.

The Court erred in instructing the jury as follows, which instruction given to the jury by the Court was then and there excepted to by the plaintiff and an exception allowed, to-wit:

"There is one feature in this case, however, to which I desire to call your particular attention. That is, that there is no witness, no living witness, who is able to tell us what the aviator actually saw. One of the experts stated with reference to his circling over the airport—the Tri-City airport, that it might have been he saw what he thought was clear weather, or clearing atmospheric conditions beyond him. Applying the principle regarding the error of judgment, which you will bear in mind, if in the "judgment of this aviator" he saw what appeared to be favorable conditions ahead of him, then the defendant is not to be held for negligence because he chose that course rather than to land upon the field in safety.

"Now, this is more or less of a new science, as we all recognize, and admittedly it is a branch of the law where we have very few precedents, that is, adjudicated cases. In order to hold the defendant for negligence, you must, as I explained to you, find that the pilot in this case—because the pilot represents the defendant—the corporation is able to act only through its employee in this case, and therefore the pilot in this case is for all purposes of the case, so far as your verdict goes, the defendant itself. The pilot must have done something which good judgment did not approve, or would not approve, and on account of the fact that we cannot know what the aviator saw, what appeared to him, it is a rather difficult thing in my judgment to know that the conditions that appeared to him did not justify his doing what he did."

XX.

The Court erred in refusing to instruct the jury as requested by the plaintiff, which instruction so requested by the plaintiff and not given by the Court is as follows:

"You are instructed that in determining what would amount to reasonable and ordinary care in the operation of a passenger train on approaching this crossing, you may and should consider all the conditions as they existed at the crossing so far as they were apparent to the defendants and insofar as those conditions should have been apparent to the defendants had they been in the exercise of reasonable and ordinary care."

XXI.

The Court erred in refusing to instruct the jury as requested by the plaintiff, which instruction so requested by the plaintiff, and not given by the Court, is as follows:

"The defendant in this cause has set up the defense that the injury complained of was due to an inevitable accident.

As to this defense, you are instructed that if you find from the evidence that the accident could have been avoided by the defendant by the exercise of the highest degree of care, then you must also find that the accident was not inevitable and that the defense of inevitable accident has not been sustained."

XXII.

The Court erred in refusing to instruct the jury as requested by the plaintiff which instruction so requested by the plaintiff and not given by the Court, as as follows:

"You are instructed that the defendant as a carrier of said T. J. Kelly, as a passenger, for pay, is liable for the death of said T. J. Kelly, if such death was occasioned or proximately contributed to by the negligence, however slight, of any of the servants of said defendant, including the pilot of said airplane, while such servants were engaged in the general scope of their employment, and regardless of whether the negligent act or omission, if any, was or was not authorized by the defendant."

XXIII.

The Court erred in refusing to instruct the jury as requested by the plaintiff which instruction so requested by the plaintiff and not given by the Court, is as follows:

"You are instructed that if you find from the evidence that the accident complained of was the result of a combination of extraordinary weather conditions and any negligence, however slight, of the defendant, which contributed thereto, then you must find for the plaintiff and against the defendant."

XXIV.

The Court erred in refusing to instruct the jury which was requested by the plaintiff, which instruction so requested by the plaintiff and not given by the Court is as follows:

"You are instructed that if you should find from the evidence that the accident complained of was the result of the concurrence of an Act of God and of any negligence, however slight, of the defendant, then your verdict must be for the plaintiff and against the defendant."

XXV.

The Court erred as matter of law in receiving the verdict of the jury and causing the Clerk of the court to enter judgment thereon, for the reason that the same verdict and judgment are not sustained and justified by the evidence, and that the evidence introduced in the trial of said action is insufficient to sustain or justify the verdict of the jury and the judgment entered thereon.

XXVI.

The Court erred as matter of law in overruling and refusing to grant the motion for new trial of the plaintiff, E. N. Allison, as administrator of the estate of Thomas J. Kelly, deceased, for the reasons and upon the grounds set forth in said Motion, and in this Bill of Exceptions.

XXVII.

The Court erred in accepting the verdict of the jury and in causing the clerk of said court to enter judgment thereon.

XXVIII.

The Court erred in accepting the verdict of the jury and entering judgment thereon, because the said verdict was rendered and given under the influence of passion and prejudice or passion or prejudice.

XXIX.

The Court erred in accepting the verdict of the jury and entering judgment thereon, because the said verdict was not sustained or justified by the evidence introduced at the trial of said action.

XXX.

The Court erred in accepting the verdict of the jury and entering judgment thereon because the evidence introduced at the trial of said action is insufficient to sustain or justify said verdict.

XXXI.

The Court erred in accepting the verdict of the jury and entering judgment thereon because said verdict is contrary to and against the evidence introduced in the trial of said action.

XXXII.

The Court erred in accepting the verdict of the jury and entering judgment thereon because evidence introduced in the trial of said action showed and proved by a preponderance thereof, that the accident in question and the injury to, and the death of, the deceased, were caused by and proximately contibuted to by the negligence of the defendant.

XXXIII.

Upon the foregoing Assignment of Error and upon the record in said cause, plaintiff prays that judgment entered in said action on September 20th, 1930, be reversed.

                    Oliver O. Clark
                    Samuel A. Rosenthal
                    Attorneys for Plaintiff.

[Endorsed]: No. 3516-H In the District Court of the United States for the Southern District of California Central Division E. M. Allison, as Administrator of the Estate of Thomas J. Kelly, Deceased, Plaintiff and Appellant vs. Standard Air Lines, Inc., a corporation, Defendant and Respondent Assignments of Error. Received copy of the within Assignments of Error this 25th day of April, 1931 John F. Dahl Attorney for defendant Filed Apr 25 1931 R. S. Zimmerman, Clerk By Edmund L. Smith Deputy Clerk Oliver O. Clark Samuel A. Rosenthal 1203 Garfield Building Los Angeles, California Attorneys for plaintiff

IN THE DISTRICT COURT OF THE UNITED
STATES FOR THE SOUTHERN DISTRICT
OF CALIFORNIA CENTRAL DIVISION

* * *

E. M. ALLISON, as Administrator)
of the Estate of Thomas J. Kelly,)
Deceased,)
)
         Plaintiff and Appellant)   No. 3516-H
)
)
            vs.)   ORDER
)   ALLOWING
STANDARD AIR LINES, INC.,)   APPEAL.
a corporation,)
     Defendant and Respondent)

Upon motion of Oliver O. Clark and Samuel A. Rosenthal, attorneys for plaintiff in the above numbered and
entitled action, and upon reading and filing its Petition
for Appeal and Assignments of Error;

IT IS ORDERED that an appeal be and it is hereby
allowed to have reviewed in the United States Circuit
Court of Appeals, for the Ninth Circuit, the verdict and
judgment heretofore rendered and entered on the 20th
day of September, 1930.

DONE this 25th day of April, 1931.

                       Geo. Cosgrave
UNITED STATES DISTRICT JUDGE, LOS
ANGELES, CALIFORNIA.

[Endorsed]: No. 3516-H In the District Court of the
United States For the Southern District of California
Central Division E. M. Allison, as Administrator of the
Estate of Thomas J. Kelly, deceased Plaintiff and Appel-

lant vs. Standard Air Lines, Inc., a corporation, Defend-
ant and Respondent Order Allowing Appeal. Filed
Apr 25 1931 R. S. Zimmerman, Clerk By Edmund
L. Smith Deputy Clerk Oliver O. Clark Samuel A.
Rosenthal 1203 Garfield Building Los Angeles, Cali-
fornia Attorneys for plaintiff

IN THE DISTRICT COURT OF THE UNITED
STATES FOR THE SOUTHERN DISTRICT
OF CALIFORNIA CENTRAL DIVISION

---oOo---

E. M. ALLISON, as Administrator of the Estate of Thomas J. Kelly, deceased,	No. 3516-H
Plaintiff and Appellant	ORDER APPROVING BOND ON APPEAL
vs.	
STANDARD AIR LINES, INC., a corporation, Defendant and Respondent	

---oOo---

Whereas the plaintiff, E. M. Allison, as the Administrator of the Estate of Thomas J. Kelly, Deceased, in
the above numbered and entitled action, has filed his Bond
on Appeal herein, in the sum of Two Hundred and Fifty
($250.00) Dollars, to answer for all costs on said appeal;
and whereas the said Bond appears to be a good and
sufficient bond in every particular as required by law.

IT IS HEREBY ORDERED that the said Bond is
hereby approved both in sufficiency and form.

DONE this 27th day of April, 1931.

Geo. Cosgrave
United States District Judge, Los Angeles, California.

[Endorsed] : No. 3516-H In the District Court of the United States For the Southern District of California Central Division E. M. Allison, as Admx., of the Estate of Thomas J. Kelly, Deceased, Plaintiff and Appellant, vs. Standard Air Lines, Inc., a corporation, Defendant and Respondent, Filed Apr 28 1931 R. S. Zimmerman, Clerk By Edmund L. Smith Deputy Clerk Law Offices Samuel A. Rosenthal Oliver O. Clark Attorneys for Plaintiff and Appellant

---

GENERAL
CASUALTY COMPANY
OF AMERICA.
Seattle, Washington.

IN THE DISTRICT COURT OF THE UNITED
STATES SOUTHERN DISTRICT OF
CALIFORNIA CENTRAL
DIVISION

E. M. ALLISON, Administrator of the Estate of Thomas J. Kelley, Deceased Plaintiff vs. STANDARD AIR LINES, INC., a corporation Defendant.	No. 3516-H COST BOND ON APPEAL

KNOW ALL MEN BY THESE PRESENTS:

THAT, We, E. M. ALLISON, Administrator of the Estate of Thomas J. Kelley, Deceased, as Principal and GENERAL CASUALTY COMPANY OF AMERICA, a Corporation duly licensed and qualified to become Surety on bonds or undertakings under the laws of the state of

California, as Surety, are held and firmly bound unto
STANDARD AIR LINES, INC., a Corporation, in the
full and just sum of TWO HUNDRED FIFTY
($250.00) Dollars, to be paid to said STANDARD AIR
LINES, INC., a Corporation, their successors or assigns,
to which payment, well and truly to be made we bind ourselves, our heirs, executors and administrators, jointly
and severally, by these presents.

SIGNED, SEALED AND DATED this 27th day of
April, 1931.

WHEREAS, the Plaintiff in the above entitled action
is about to appeal to the United States Circuit Court of
Appeals for the Ninth Circuit from the verdict of the jury
and the judgment thereon in the above entitled action
entered against him on September 20, 1930 in the District
Court of the United States, Southern District of California, Central Division, and is required to furnish an
appeal bond in connection with said appeal.

NOW, THEREFORE, in consideration of the premises, and of such appeal, the undersigned GENERAL
CASUALTY COMPANY OF AMERICA, does under-
take and promise on the part of the appellant that the said
appellant will pay all damages and costs which may be
awarded against him on the appeal, or on a dismissal
thereof, not exceeding TWO HUNDRED FIFTY
($250.00) Dollars, to which amount it acknowledges itself
bound.

E. M. ALLISON
GENERAL CASUALTY COMPANY
OF AMERICA
By: A. W. SCHRODER
Its Attorney-in-Fact.

Examined and recommended for approval as provided in Rule 28.

    SAMUEL A. ROSENTHAL

    OLIVER O. CLARK

      By Hyman Bradley Attorneys   [Seal]

State of California   )
County of Los Angeles) ss.

On this 27th day of April, A. D. 1931, before me, Esther McLaughlin, a Notary Public in and for the County and State aforesaid, duly commissioned and sworn, personally appeared W. H. SCHRODER, Attorney-in-Fact of the GENERAL CASUALTY COMPANY OF AMERICA, to me personally known to be the individual and officer described in and who executed the within instrument, and he acknowledged the same, and being by me duly sworn, deposes and says that he is the said officer of the Company aforesaid, and the seal affixed to the within instrument is the corporate seal of said Company, and that the said corporate seal and his signature as such officer were duly affixed and subscribed to the said instrument by the authority and direction of the said corporation.

IN WITNESS WHEREOF, I have hereunto set my hand and affixed my official seal at my office in the City of Los Angeles, County of Los Angeles, the day and year first above written.

  [Seal]   ESTHER McLAUGHLIN,

  Notary Public in and for the County of Los Angeles,

    State of California.

[Endorsed]: 3516–H General Casualty Company of America Seattle, Washington on behalf of E. M. Allison, administrator of the estate of Thomas J. Kelley, deceased to Standard Airlines, Inc., a corporation.

Filed Apr 28 1931. R. S. Zimmerman, clerk By Edmund L. Smith, deputy clerk.

IN THE DISTRICT COURT OF THE UNITED STATES FOR THE SOUTHERN DISTRICT OF CALIFORNIA CENTRAL DIVISION

E. M. ALLISON, as Administrator of the Estate of Thomas J. Kelly, deceased,

                    Plaintiff and Appellant

          vs.

STANDARD AIR LINES, INC., a corporation,

                    Defendant and Respondent

No. 3516-H

PRAECIPE FOR TRANSCRIPT OF RECORD.

To the Clerk of Said Court:

SIR:

Please issue and certify a transcript for appellant upon appeal to the Circuit Court of Appeals for the Ninth Judicial Circuit of the United States of America, of the record in the above entitled cause, and include therein:

1. Complaint,
2. Answer,
3. Verdict,
4. Judgment,
5. Bill of Exceptions,
6. Petition for Appeal and Supersedeas,
7. Assignments of Error,
8. Order Allowing Appeal,
9. Order Approving Bond on Appeal,
10. Bond on Appeal,
11. Citation,
12. Minute Order Denying Motion for New Trial,
13. This Praecipe
14. Certificate of Clerk Authenticating Record.

Done at Los Angeles, California, May ...... 1931.

Samuel A. Rosenthal

Oliver O. Clark

Attorneys for Plaintiff E. M. Allison, as Administrator of the Estate of Thomas J. Kelly, deceased.

[Endorsed]: No. 3516-H In the District Court of the United States For the Southern District of California Central Division E. M. Allison, as Administrator of the Estate of Thomas J. Kelly, deceased, Plaintiff and Appellant vs. Standard Air Lines, Inc., a corporation, Defendant and Respondent Praecipe for Transcript of Record. Received copy of the within praecipe this 14th day of May, 1931 John F. Dahl Attorney for Defendant Filed May 14 1931 R. S. Zimmerman, Clerk By Edmund L. Smith Deputy Clerk Oliver O. Clark Samuel A. Rosenthal 1203 Garfield Building Los Angeles, California Attorneys for plaintiff and appellant

IN THE DISTRICT COURT OF THE UNITED
STATES FOR THE SOUTHERN DISTRICT OF
CALIFORNIA CENTRAL DIVISION

*   *   *

E. M. ALLISON, as Administrator)
of the Estate of Thomas J. Kelly,)
Deceased,   )   No. 3516-H
)
        Plaintiff and Appellant,)
)
            vs.   )
)
STANDARD. AIR LINES, INC.,   )
a corporation,   )
)
        Defendant and Respondent)

CLERK'S CERTIFICATE.

I. R. S. Zimmerman, clerk of the United States District
Court for the Southern District of California, do hereby
certify the foregoing volume containing 87 pages, numbered from 1 to 87 inclusive, to be the Transcript of
Record on Appeal in the above entitled cause, as printed
by the appellant, and presented to me for comparison and
certification, and that the same has been compared and
corrected by me and contains a full, true and correct copy
of the citation; complaint; answer; verdict, judgment; bill
of exceptions; order overruling demurrer; petition for
appeal; assignment of errors; order allowing appeal; bond,
and praecipe.

I DO FURTHER CERTIFY that the fees of the Clerk
for comparing, correcting and certifying the foregoing
Record on Appeal amount to..............and that said amount
has been paid me by the appellant herein.

IN TESTIMONY WHEREOF, I have hereunto set my hand and affixed the Seal of the District Court of the United States of America, in and for the Southern District of California, Central Division, this................ day of March in the year of Our Lord One Thousand Nine Hundred and Thirty-two, and of our Independence the One Hundred and Fifty-sixth.

R. S. ZIMMERMAN,

Clerk of the District Court of the United States of America, in and for the Southern District of California.

By

Deputy.

No. 6802.

IN THE

United States

Circuit Court of Appeals,

FOR THE NINTH CIRCUIT.

E. M. Allison, as Administrator for the
Estate of Thos. J. Kelly, deceased,
Appellant,

vs.

Standard Air Lines, Inc., a corporation,
Respondent.

APPELLANT'S OPENING BRIEF.

OLIVER O. CLARK,
Garfield Bldg., 403 W. 8th St., Los Angeles,
SAMUEL A. ROSENTHAL,
Wright & Callender Bldg., 4th and Hill, L. A.,
Attorneys for Appellant.

FILED

JAN 23 1933

Parker, Stone & Baird Co., Law Printers, Los Angeles. O'BRIEN,

TOPICAL INDEX.

PAGE

The Questions Stated.. 3

Statement of the Case... 4

Specifications of Error... 6

Argument 7

    As to Specification of Error Number I...................... 7

I.

In California, Is One Who, for a Reward, Carries a
    Passenger by Airship, Required to Exercise the
    Utmost Care for the Safety of the Passenger, or
    Is Ordinary Care All That Is Required?................. 7

II.

If Utmost Care Is Required of Such a Carrier, Does
    the Court's Charge to the Jury, in This Case,
    State That Duty With Sufficient Clearness and
    Certainty 9

    As to Specification of Error. Number II..................... 22

III.

Does the Doctrine of Res Ipsa Loquitur Apply to
    Accidents Arising in the Carrying of Passengers,
    for Reward, by Airplane?... 23

IV.

If the Doctrine of Res Ipsa Loquitur Applies to Air-
    plane Passenger Carrying, May Such Presump-
    tion of Negligence Be Considered by the Court,
    When the Jury Was Not Instructed Upon the
    Subject, in Determining the Sufficiency of the
    Evidence to Sustain a Verdict for the Defendant? 24

V.

Assuming the Doctrine of Res Ipsa Loquitur to Be
Applicable Here, Is the Evidence Sufficient to
Sustain the Verdict for the Defendant?.............. 26

VI. `

If the Application of the Doctrine of Res Ipsa
Loquitur Applies to Airplane Passenger Carrying,
Is the Application Thereof in Any Way Limited,
in California, by Provisions in the Contract of
Carriage, Which Say That the Carrier Shall Be
Deemed to Be a Private, Not a Common, Carrier;
That the Carrier Shall Be Liable Only for Proven
Negligence, and That the Mere Occurrence of an
Accident Shall Not Be Any Evidence of Any
Negligence of the Carrier?.. 29

Conclusion 30

TABLE OF CASES AND AUTHORITIES CITED.

PAGE

Bank of the Metropolis v. New England Bank, 6 Howard, 212 20

Barrett v. Southern Pacific Co., 207 Cal. 165 20

Estate of Dolbeer, 149 Cal. 227 25

Hill v. Finigan, 77 Cal. 267 25

Housel v. Pacific Electric Ry. Co., 167 Cal., p. 245 24

Housel v. Pacific Elec. Ry. Co., 167 Cal. 247 26

Matteson v. Bank of Italy, 97 Cal. App. 643 27

Olsen v. Standard Oil Company, 188 Cal. p. 24 24

Pierce v. United Gas & Electric Co., 161 Cal., pp. 176 185 21

Pulsifer v. Berry, 87 Me. 405, 32 Atl. 986 12

Rudd v. Byrnes, 156 Cal. 636 12

Sinan v. A. T. & S. F. Ry. Co., decided by the California District Court on Appeal, on February 4th, 1930, and in which a rehearing was denied by the Supreme Court in March, 1930 22

Thompson v. Davis, 172 Cal. 491 24

————

California Jurisprudence, Vol. 4, p. 920 29

California Jurisprudence, Vol. 4, p. 980 23

4 California Jurisprudence, Vol. 4; at p. 932 ....8, 10

Civil Code of California, Sec. 2175 29

No. 6802.

IN THE

United States
Circuit Court of Appeals,

FOR THE NINTH CIRCUIT.

E. M. Allison, as Administrator for the
Estate of Thos. J. Kelly, deceased,
Appellant,

vs.

Standard Air Lines, Inc., a corporation,
Respondent.

APPELLANT'S OPENING BRIEF.

The Questions Stated.

I.

In California is one who, for a reward, carries a
passenger *by airship,* required to exercise the *utmost* care
for the safety of the passenger, or is *ordinary* care all
that is required?

II.

If *utmost* care is required of such a carrier, does the
court's charge to the jury, in this case, state that duty
with sufficient clearness and certainty?

III.

Does the doctrine of *res ipsa loquitur* apply to accidents arising in the carrying of passengers, for reward, by airplane?

IV.

If the doctrine of *res ipsa loquitur* applies to airplane passenger carrying, may such presumption of negligence be considered by the court, when the jury was not instructed upon the subject, in determining the sufficiency of the evidence to sustain a verdict for the defendant?

V.

Assuming the doctrine of *res ipsa loquitur* to be applicable here, is the evidence sufficient to sustain the verdict for the defendant?

VI.

If the application of the doctrine of *res ipsa loquitur* applies to airplane passenger carrying, is the application thereof in any way limited, in California, by provisions in the contract of carriage, which say that the carrier shall be deemed to be a *private,* and not a *common* carrier; that the carrier shall be liable *only* for *proven* negligence, and that the mere occurrence of an accident shall not be any evidence of any negligence of the carrier?

Statement of the Case.

This is an action for damages, prosecuted by the administrator of the estate of one Thomas J. Kelly, against Standard Airlines, Inc., for the death of said Kelly in an airship crash near Banning, California, on March 30th, 1929.

At the time in question the defendant was the owner and operator of airships used in the transportation of passengers, for reward, from Los Angeles, California, to El Paso, Texas.

The deceased, Kelly, was a passenger upon one of these ships, and held a ticket issued to him, that day, by the defendant, for reward, for the carriage of himself by airline from Los Angeles, California, to El Paso, Texas. [Tr. p. 37.]

While the airship was flying in the fog, several miles off its regular course, it crashed into a mountain near Banning, California, and the pilot, and Kelly and the other passengers were instantly killed.

The ticket held by Kelly contained the following printed provision [Tr. pp. 38, 39]:

> "Should the Company accept the holder hereof for a flight in one of its airplanes, such acceptance shall not be deemed to make the Company a common carrier, but it is specifically agreed and understood between the holder and the Company that the Company is a private carrier and is liable to the holder not as an insurer, but only for proven negligence of its employees and agents and the mere occurrence of an accident resulting in injury or loss of life to the holder shall not be any evidence of negligence."

The complaint pleads that the defendant was a *common* carrier for reward; that Kelly was a passenger, for reward, upon one of defendant's airships en route from Los Angeles, California, to El Paso, Texas; the crash of the airship, and Kelly's resulting death, and further pleads, *in general terms,* that the crash of the airship was due to the defendant's negligence.

The answer denies any negligence, and pleads the provisions of Kelly's ticket which undertake to limit the defendant's liability.

Upon the trial, with a jury, the verdict was for the defendant, and upon that verdict judgment, for the defendant, was entered.

In due time plaintiff moved for a new trial. The motion was denied and plaintiff prosecutes this appeal.

Specifications of Error.

Appellant specifies as errors of the learned trial court to be considered and urged upon this appeal, the following, to-wit:

I.

That the learned trial court erred in its instructions to the jury as to the care required to be exercised by the defendant.

These instructions are separately designated in appellant's *"Assignments of Error"* set forth in the *"Transcript of Record"* upon this appeal, as follows: Numbers II and III at page 69; Numbers IV, V and VI, at page 70; Numbers VII and VIII, at page 71; Numbers IX, X and XI, at page 72; Numbers XII, XIII and XIV, at page 73; Numbers XVI and XVII, at page 74; Number XVIII at page 75, and Number XVIX at page 76, of the transcript.

II.

That the evidence is insufficient to support the verdict, or the judgment, in favor of the defendant, and that the learned trial court erred in denying appellant's motion for a new trial.

This specification of error is set forth, in detail, under assignments of error Number XXV, at page 78; Numbers XXVI, XXVII, XXVIII, XXIX, XXX and XXXI at page 79, and Number XXXII at page 80, of the *Transcript of Record* upon this appeal.

In the interest of brevity and clarity said *Specification of Error No. I,* will be considered under questions numbers I and II, heretofore stated in this brief.

For the same reasons *Specification of Error Number II* will be considered under questions numbers III, IV, V and VI, heretofore stated in this brief.

ARGUMENT.

As to Specification of Error Number I.

This specification of error presents two questions as separately stated—numbers I and II—on page 6 of this brief. We shall consider these in the order there stated.

I.

In California Is One Who, for a Reward, Carries a Passenger By Airship, Required to Exercise the Utmost Care for the Safety of the Passenger, or Is Ordinary Care All That Is Required?

In California the care required of a common carrier of passengers for reward, is stated in section 2100 of the Civil Code.

That section provides that:

> "A carrier of persons for reward must use the *utmost care and diligence* for their safe carriage * * *."

In Volume 4, California Juris., at page 932, the rule is stated to be that:

> "The carrier must exercise *the highest degree of care* in their transportation, and is responsible for injuries received by them while in the course of transportation which might have been avoided by the exercise of *such care.* As the rule is otherwise expressed, passenger carriers bind themselves to carry safely those whom they admit into their coaches, *as far as human care and foresight will go,* and *they are responsible for any, even the slightest,* negligence."

In these statements of the rule no distinction, as to the care required, is made between carriers because of any method of transportation employed.

We do not find, otherwise, in the law of this state, any such distinction between carriers because of the method of transportation.

The rule, *as stated,* is broad enough to include all carriers of passengers for reward, regardless of the means by which such carriage is undertaken, whether by land, by sea, by air, or by any combination of two, or more, of these.

Obviously *the reason for the rule* is a desire to provide for passengers, carried for hire, the utmost safety of which such a carrier is capable of providing.

In that *reason for the rule* the means of conveyance is of no importance excepting as one of the considerations in determining what the conduct of the carrier should be while in the exercise of the *utmost care.*

There is, therefore, no basis either in the *rule as stated* or in the reason *for the rule,* upon which to deny the application of this rule to *airplane* passenger carrying, for reward.

Therefore, the defendant here was held to the exercise of the *utmost* care and diligence in the airplane transportation of Kelly, and is liable in damages for any, *even the slightest,* neglect contributing to Kelly's death.

II.

If Utmost Care Is Required of Such a Carrier, Does the Court's Charge to the Jury, in This Case, State That Duty With Sufficient Clearness and Certainty.

In the charge to the jury the learned judge of the trial court, feeling, no doubt, that in actions like this, the plaintiff is usually well cared for by the hands of Providence and the jurors, has exhibited a very commendable desire to be perfectly fair to this defendant as one of the pioneers in a comparatively new field of passenger transportation.

But this spirit of fairness, we believe, has resulted in a charge which contains so many conflicting and confusing instructions as to the care required of the defendant that it cannot be said, at all, that the verdict here was based upon a proper notion of the defendant's duty to Kelly.

The court instructed the jury [Tr. p. 49] that:

"the carrier of persons for reward must use the utmost care and diligence for their safe carriage,

must provide everything necessary for that purpose
and must exercise toward that end a reasonable
degree of skill."

"the carrier of persons for reward is bound to provide
vehicles fit for that purpose and is not excused for
failure in this respect by any degree of care."

Unquestionably these two instructions, standing alone,
correctly state the law, and if they had not been nullified
by contrary statements, we would not complain upon this
point.

The fault is that both before and after the giving of
these instructions, the court gave many other instructions
which clearly told the jury that *in this case a different and
lesser* degree of care, only, was required.

Immediately following this instruction the court instructed the jury [Tr. p. 49] that:

"While the law demands the utmost care for the
safety of passengers, it does not require *airplane*
companies to exercise all the care, skill and diligence
of which the human mind can conceive nor which will
free the transportation of passengers from all possible perils."

This instruction is *directly contrary* to the rule stated
in 4 Cal. Jur., page 932, above quoted, which requires the
carrier:

"to carry safely * * * *as far as human care and
foresight will go*".

This instruction expressly told the jury that a carrier
of passengers could be said to have exercised the *utmost
care and diligence* and yet not have provided, *as far as*

human care and foresight could go, for the safe carriage of the passenger.

This we submit *is a manifest contradiction, is entirely confusing to the jury,* and is *not a correct statement of the law.*

Another criticism of this instruction is that it singles out and emphasizes *airplane transportation* in a way which when considered with other instructions indicates that a *"carrier by airplane"* is held to a *lesser* degree of care than a *"carrier by other means".* Yet *the law makes no such distinction.*

The court also instructed the jury [Tr. p. 48] that:

> "If you should find from the evidence that the pilot Everett acted in such a manner as a person of *ordinary prudence and caution and skill* would use under the same circumstances, *he was not negligent."*

Clearly this instruction defines and applies *ordinary care* only, and expressly exonerates the defendant if the jury finds that the pilot exercised *ordinary* care.

Again, on page 48 of the transcript, the court instructed that:

> "He was only required to exercise such care and skill as is *ordinarily* possessed by those engaged in the same business or art, and if you find that he exercised *such* care and skill, he was not negligent although the danger might have been avoided if he had acted in a different manner."

Here again *ordinary* care, only, is defined and applied, and the jury is expressly told that *in this case* the defendant is exonerated if the pilot exercised such—*ordinary*—care.

Another just criticism of this instruction is that here the jury is told that if this pilot exercised the care *ordinarily* exercised *by those engaged in the same business or art,* then he was not negligent.

This is not the law.

In *Rudd v. Byrnes,* 156 Cal. 636, 642, the court said:

> "The standard of care required of persons under given circumstances is not to be established by proof that others have been in the habit of acting in a certain manner."

In *Pulsifer v. Berry,* 87 Me. 405, 32 Atl. 986, which is cited approvingly by the California Supreme Court in *Rudd v. Byrnes, supra,* it is said:

> "Not even a general custom can be deemed a relevant fact in an action for negligence. * * * It may be stated as a general rule that, where a party is charged with negligence, he *will not be allowed to show that the act complained of was customary among those engaged in a similar occupation, or those placed under like circumstances,* and owing the same duties."

This error of the instruction is of much importance here because of the testimony [Tr. pp. 25 to 37 inc.] of the several pilots called by the defendant, and of the license which this instruction gives to the jury to set up the testimony of these pilots as the standard of care required of defendant.

For *each* of these two reasons the instruction of which we here complain, was erroneous and highly prejudicial to the plaintiff.

Again [Tr. p. 48], the court instructed that:

> "hence his acting in the particular manner which he did would not necessarily be negligence merely because there may have been a *safer* manner of doing it."

Certainly it needs no argument, in face of the law, above quoted, to sustain the point that where two or more courses of action are open, one of which is safer than the others, that a person who is held to the exercise of *the utmost care,* and who is required to *"carry safely * * * as far as human care and foresight will go",* must adopt the *safer* course or be guilty of negligence.

The instruction correctly states the rule of *ordinary* care, but grievously errs when applied to *utmost* care.

Again the court instructed [Tr. p. 48] that:

> "All of the circumstances attending the transaction must be taken into consideration. However, these circumstances must be those *which the evidence shows may reasonably be supposed to have been known to him and to have influenced his mind at the time,* for after an event has transpired it is often easy to demonstrate means whereby it might have been prevented from occurring."

This instruction does not correctly describe *ordinary* care, and much less *utmost* care.

The circumstances which control are *not only* those *"which the evidence shows may reasonably be supposed to have been known to him* (the pilot) *and to have influenced his mind at the time",* but are those which *"in the exercise of the utmost care and diligence"* for the safe carriage of the passenger, *should have been known to the pilot,* and *should have influenced his mind at the time.*

This instruction, directed as it was to the particular facts in this case, was highly prejudicial.

Again the court instructed the jury [Tr. pp. 48, 49], that:

> "If you should find from the evidence that the pilot Everett was an experienced and skillful pilot, and without any negligence on his part encountered fog conditions, and that bringing to bear all his previous experience and skill he weighed the facts and circum-- stances surrounding him and of which he had knowledge and decided upon a course of action which he tried to carry out, that is, to make an emergency landing, then his want of success would be due to *error of judgment* and not to negligence. That is if he exercised his best judgment and if his acts would have been approved by competent experts."

This instruction is erroneous in several vital and highly prejudicial respects. It is not a correct statement of either ordinary or utmost care.

The instruction requires that it be shown, as the predicate for its conclusion, that the pilot without any negligence contributing thereto, encountered fog.

Admittedy [Tr. p. 17] this pilot *encountered fog* as early as while he was at the Tri-City Airport, and there is no evidence that he was negligent before or up to the time when he encountered this fog.

The instruction requires that it be shown that he was an *experienced and skillful* pilot, and undoubtedly the evidence so shows.

The instruction also requires that it be shown that:

> "bringing to bear all his previous *experience and skill* he weighed the facts and circumstances surrounding him and of which he had knowledge and decided upon a course of action which he tried to carry out, that is, to make an emergency landing. * * * that in so doing he exercised his best judgment, and that his acts would have been approved by competent experts."

The instruction then tells the jury that if these things are all shown:

> "then his want of success would be due to error of judgment *and not to negligence*".

The vices of the instruction are these:

> 1. *It substitutes "experience and skill" for "care and diligence"* as the yard stick of negligence.

The law expressly requires the exercise of *the utmost "Care and Diligence" and nowhere recognizes or condones "Experience and Skill" as a substitute.*

A pilot may be every so *"Experienced and Skillful"* and yet under many circumstances be *neither "Careful nor Diligent".*

> 2. *This instruction limits "the facts and circumstances surrounding him" and which he weighed,* to those *"of which he had knowledge"* and *utterly excludes* those of which, in the exercise of the utmost *"Care and Diligence"* he should have had knowledge.

This is patently erroneous, because it is well settled that in the law of negligence one is charged not only with what he knows, but also with that which in the exercise of that degree of care with which he is charged, *he ought to have known.*

3. *This instruction* expressly approves any course of action which represented *his best judgment* provided it would have been approved by experts.

As heretofore pointed out, *the "Opinion of Experts"* has nothing to do with his course of action and it cannot be justified by their opinion.

His *"best judgment"*, regardless of how experienced or skillful he was, is not the test of the care required.

The *true test* of his care is whether his course of action *from the time he encountered the fog at the Tri-City Airport,* was the *safest* course of action open to him, because in the exercise of *utmost* care he was required to adopt the *safest* course—*he could not experiment.*

4. *This instruction* expressly tells the jury that *error of judgment* is *not negligence* under the conditions stated.

We know of no principle of law which sustains this conclusion.

If under the law one could escape the charge of negligence by showing that he was *"experienced and skillful"* and under the circumstances exercised *his best judgment,* then damages for negligence would seldom be recovered.

The test is not *what this pilot* did, or what other pilots would have done, but rather what this pilot, or any other pilot, *should have done,* in the exercise of the *utmost* care, to carry this passenger safely. *Anything less than everything* which *could* have been done *"as far as human care and foresight will go", is negligence,* and any negligence, *however slight,* makes the carrier liable.

Again the court instructed the jury [Tr. p. 49], that:

> "the deceased in this case necessarily took upon himself all the *usual and ordinary* perils incidental to airplane travel, and if you find from the evidence that the defendant exercised all the care, skill and diligence required by law *as defined in these instructions* and that nevertheless the accident occurred, the defendant would not be responsible therefor, and your verdict should be for the defendant."

The principal vice in this instruction is that the *care and diligence* required of the defendant *were not correctly or clearly defined* in the instructions to which this instruction refers.

Another just and substantial criticism of this instruction is that it plainly tells the jury that the passenger assumed all the perils not due to the failure of an *experienced* and *skillful* pilot to exercise his best judgment which would be approved by *competent experts.*

Such is not the law. Such *best judgment* might fall far short of even ordinary care, when measured by the proper yard stick.

Again the court instructed the jury [Tr. p. 50], that:

> "The defendant in this case, in addition to its defense that it was not guilty of negligence has presented the defense that the accident in question was due to *unforeseen events,* inevitable accident or Act of God. You are advised that if either of these defenses are established by the evidence, the plaintiff cannot recover, and your verdict must be for the defendant."

This instruction is prejudicially faulty in that it does not define *"unforeseen events"* but plainly permits the jury to believe that if the accident was due to an *"unforeseen event"* the defendant is not liable, notwithstanding that the event *might have been foreseen* had the defendant exercised the *utmost care, and this the defendant was bound to do.*

Again the court instructed the jury [Tr. p. 50], that:

> "When any person is confronted with a *sudden emergency,* he is not required to exercise the same degree of caution that natural and deliberate judgment exercised when there is plenty of time to determine what would be the wise thing to do. The law takes note of these things."

This does not correctly state the law. The law is that if one, *because of his negligence,* is confronted with sudden danger, *he is nevertheless liable because of his negligence which made possible the sudden danger,* notwithstanding that when thus suddenly confronted with danger he did the best he could.

Applied to this case the error in this instruction was very damaging because under it the jury could well believe that the defendant was exonerated if the pilot did all that he could do *immediately before the crash* (that being the sudden danger), notwithstanding their belief that if he had exercised the *utmost* care and landed at the Tri-City Airport *he never would have been confronted with this sudden danger.*

Again the court instructed the jury [Tr. p. 52], that:

> "Applying the principle regarding the *error of judgment,* which you will bear in mind, if *in the judg-*

ment of this aviator he saw what *appeared to be* favorable conditions ahead of him, then *the defendant is not to be held for negligence* because he chose that course *rather than to land upon the field in safety."*

This instruction completely ignores the rule not only of *utmost care,* but even of *ordinary* care.

It incorporates the several vices of the former instruction as to *"Error of Judgment"* (this brief, p. 14) and adds the additional one that if he saw *"what appeared to be favorable conditions ahead of him"* then he could not be held negligent because he chose to go ahead *rather than to land upon the field in safety.*

Certainly no one will say that one who is *required to do the utmost that human care and foresight will do* for the safety of a passenger, is permitted, *when confronted with danger,* to forsake a known safe course—(to land)—and instead to venture forth into the danger of mountains and fog, solely upon *"Appearances"* of favorable conditions.

We repeat that this instruction *directs a verdict for the defendant* in absolute disregard of every element of the law of care.

Again the court instructed the jury [Tr. p. 52], that:

"*In order to hold the defendant for negligence,* you must, as I explained to you, find that the pilot in this case * * * must have done something which *good* judgment did not approve, or would not approve."

This instruction, in common with many others, as above pointed out, erroneously substitutes *"good judgment"* for *"utmost care"* as the test of defendant's liability.

Such a substitution is contrary to the law.

We respectfully submit that further argument or citation is *not* necessary to show conclusively that the instructions as to negligence were *conflicting, confusing* and *erroneous*.

It is, of course, elementary that where instructions are conflicting and misleading, a new trial should be granted, and this is the rule in the federal, as well as in the state courts.

In *Haight v. Vallet,* 89 Cal. 246, 249, the Supreme Court of California states the rule to be that:

"Where the instructions on a material point are contradictory, it is impossible for the jury to decide which should prevail, and *it is equally impossible, after the verdict, to know that the jury was not influenced by that instruction which was erroneous,* as the one or the other must necessarily be, where the two are repugnant."

To the same effect is:

Barrett v. Southern Pacific Co., 207 Cal. 165.

In *Rea v. Missouri,* 17 Wall. 532, 21 Lawyers Edition. 707, the Supreme Court of the United States held that where the manifest tendency of additional instructions upon a material issue in a case is to give the jury an impression different from that they first held, the instructions are calculated to mislead the jury, and *constitute reversible error.*

Again, in *Bank of the Metropolis v. New England Bank,* 6 Howard, 212 and 12 Lawyers Edition, 409, the Supreme Court of the United States stated that if the Circuit Court to which a case has been remanded for a new trial gives to the jury instructions which are inconsistent in themselves, from which it would be impossible for the jury to comprehend distinctly the issue of fact from which they were to find their verdict, *the judgment must be reversed.*

Under the rule, therefore, both in the state and federal courts, *the giving of the several instructions here complained of necessitates a new trial.*

The mere fact that in the first instruction which the court gave concerning the duty of the carrier the correct rule was stated in the language of the Code, *does not cure the error* in the giving of the later instructions in which different degrees, and tests, of care were emphasized.

The true rule is stated in *Pierce v. United Gas & Electric Co.,* 161 Cal., pp. 176-185, as follows:

"It is true that other instructions were given at the request of defendant that stated the law in these respects as favorably to defendant as was warranted, if not more favorably. *But the giving of these instructions simply produced a clear conflict in the instructions given the jury by the court and it is impossible for us to say which instruction the jury followed in arriving at a verdict in favor of plaintiff.* Learned counsel for plaintiff make no reply to the claim of defendant in this behalf."

Concerning the several instructions here complained of in which the jury was told that under certain conditions therein named, the defendant was not liable or their verdict should be for the defendant, and in which instructions the true test of the care required was not contained, we direct the court's attention to the case of *Sinan v. A. T. & S. F. Ry. Co.*, decided by the California District Court of Appeal, on February 4th, 1930, and in which a rehearing was denied by the Supreme Court in March, 1930, and in which decision the court said:

> "Counsel for respondent cites a number of authorities to the general rule that instructions must be considered as a whole and that if the instructions thus considered fairly state the law, the insufficiency of some single instruction will not be considered reversible error. We do not think that this general rule corrects the present situation. The instruction complained of distinctly states a certain condition under which the defendant is entitled to a verdict and in addition directs if that state of facts is found by the jury that their verdict shall be for the defendant. Under this instruction, the jury may well have understood that if the misplaced switch caused the accident and that its displacement was occasioned by trespassers over which the defendant had no control, these facts alone require the verdict as directed."

This rule is clearly applicable to the instructions here complained of.

From any reading, or analysis, of these instructions, it clearly appears that they are so hopelessly confusing and contradictory as to require a reversal of the judgment.

As to Specification of Error Number II.

This specification of error presents four questions as separately stated—numbers III, IV, V and VI—on page 4 of this brief. We shall consider these in the order there stated.

III.

Does the Doctrine of Res Ipsa Loquitur Apply to Accidents Arising in the Carrying of Passengers, For Reward, by Airplane?

The law has ever jealously guarded the safety of passengers carried for hire.

In accord with this policy the law has set up a *"Presumption of Negligence"* from the sole fact of an injury to a passenger.

The rule is well stated, and supported by the citation of a long line of cases, in Volume 4, California Jurisprudence, at page 980, as follows:

> "PRESUMPTION OF NEGLIGENCE AND BURDEN OF PROOF. It has been long and continuously settled that, in an action by a passenger against a carrier for injuries received *a prima facie case is established* when the plaintiff shows that he was injured while being carried as a passenger by the defendant, and that the injury was caused by the manner in which the defendant used or directed some agency or instrumentality under its control."

Nowhere in the statement of that rule, or in the many cases in which the rule has been applied, have we found any indication—much less any holding—that this doctrine is inapplicable to a carrier of passengers by airplane.

From the plain statement of the rule, and from the multitudinous cases in which it has been applied, it indisputably appears that this rule applies to every carrier of passengers for hire, regardless of the means of transportation employed.

IV.

If the Doctrine of Res Ipsa Loquitur Applies to Airplane Passenger Carrying, May Such Presumption of Negligence Be Considered by the Court, When the Jury Was Not Instructed Upon the Subject, in Determining the Sufficiency of the Evidence to Sustain a Verdict for the Defendant?

The presumption of negligence, under this rule, *is evidence*.

This *evidence* may not be disregarded by the jury, in the absence of substantial evidence to the contrary.

This evidence, in the absence of any other substantial evidence in reference to negligence, *necessitates a verdict in favor of the plaintiff*.

The rule is well stated in *Housel v. Pacific Electric Ry. Co.,* 167 Cal., page 245, 247, as follows:

> "The presumption that the injury was caused by the negligence of the carrier, which is raised upon the proof by the plaintiff that he was injured while being carried as a passenger, is itself a fact which the jury must consider in determining its verdict, and which, in the absence of any other evidence in reference to the negligence, *necessitates a verdict in favor of the plaintiff.*"

In *Thompson v. Davis,* 172 Cal. 491, the Supreme Court stated the rule to be:

> "That a presumption is evidence and may in certain cases outweigh positive evidence adduced against it has long been the settled law of this state."

In *Olsen v. Standard Oil Company,* 188 Cal. page 24, the court said:

"The presumption is that every man obeys the law and the presumption in this case is that the plaintiff was traveling at a lawful rate of speed and on the proper side of the highway at all times. *This presumption is in itself a species of evidence and it shall prevail and control your deliberations until and unless it is overcome by satisfactory evidence.*"

In *Estate of Dolbeer,* 149 Cal. 227, it is held that:

"From the nature of presumptions it is apparent that the burden is not ordinarily upon the one in whose favor the presumption exists, to sustain it, but rather upon the one attacking it, to rebut it."

In *Hill v. Finigan,* 77 Cal. 267, it is held that:

"An unrebutted presumption has the same effect as an admission."

From the very nature of this presumption, and its character and force as evidence, as shown in the foregoing decisions, there is no room to doubt but that this presumption *remains as evidence in the case* even though the court does not instruct the jury as to the presumption of negligence.

Of course, if neither party requests an instruction as to this presumption then neither party may complain because such an instruction was not given.

But, it seems clear, the presumption remains—whether instructed upon, or not—as evidence in the case, and, therefore, as any other evidence, must be considered by the court in determining the sufficiency of the evidence to support a verdict for the defendant.

V.

Assuming the Doctrine of Res Ipsa Loquitur To Be Applicable Here, Is the Evidence Sufficient to Sustain the Verdict for the Defendant?

Plaintiff proved that at the time of his death, the deceased, Kelly, was a passenger for hire, in one of the defendant's airships, en route from Los Angeles, California, to El Paso, Texas; that this airship while under the control of the defendant and its servants, and upon its regular run, crashed into a mountain, in the daytime, near Banning, in California, and that thereby Kelly was killed.

Upon these facts the law *presumes* defendant's negligence and this presumption is *evidence* which the *defendant* is required to overcome by evidence.

There is no evidence in the record to destroy this presumption, and, therefore, the presumption "necessitates a verdict in favor of the plaintiff", (Housel v. Pacific Elec. Ry. Co., 167 Cal. 247, supra, p. 14) and a verdict contrary thereto is unsupported by the evidence and must be set aside.

The only attempt which was made to meet this *prima facie* case was by means of the pilots called by the defendant.

None of these pilots was in the vicinity of this crash until many hours after the fatal accident occurred.

None of them could testify as to what the conditions actually were as encountered by this ill-fated pilot that morning.

All that any of them could, or did, say was that, *in his opinion,* this pilot *must* have seen a favorable opening through the fog *else he would not have left the safety of the Tri-City Airport.*

This mere speculation is not evidence; and in no way meets the *presumption of negligence* in favor of a *passenger.* (See *Matteson v. Bank of Italy,* 97 Cal. App. 643, 648.)

Not one of the witnesses made any attempt to justify the action of this pilot in leaving the safety of the Tri-City Airport, in the prevailing fog, except to say, as Lieut. Tomlinson said, that "he (the pilot) *probably* saw an opening along his route through the fog that *gave evidence* of a clearing through which he could continue his trip."

The learned trial judge clearly recognized the entire absence of any evidence on this matter when he stated to the jury [Tr. p. 52], that:

> "there is no witness, no living witness, who is able to tell us what the aviator actually saw."

Notwithstanding this state of the evidence, the jury was mislead into thinking that the plaintiff could not recover unless *he proved* that the *pilot was not justified* in what he did, whereas, under the law the burden rested *on the defendant to prove that the pilot was justified* in doing as he did—*an impossible thing to prove here.*

The court told the jury [Tr. pp. 52, 53], that:

> "On account of the fact that we cannot know what the aviator saw, what appeared to him, *it is a rather difficult thing* in my judgment *to know that the conditions that appeared to him did not justify his doing what he did.*"

The court also told the jury [Tr. p. 46], that:

"*negligence is never presumed,* but the burden is upon the *plaintiff* to prove such negligence by a preponderance of the evidence * * * and *unless the plaintiff proves such negligence* * * * *there can be no recovery herein* and the verdict must be for the defendant and against the plaintiff."

The instruction last mentioned is especially erroneous and prejudicial in that it is a formula instruction which directs a verdict in favor of the defendant in certain events, and the events stated are incorrect and improper.

It was incorrect to say that *"negligence is never presumed,"* because, *under the state of the record here, "negligence is presumed in favor of a passenger".*

It was incorrect to say that *"the burden is on plaintiff to show negligence"* because, *under the state of the record here, the burden is on the defendant to show, as against the presumption, freedom from negligence.*

Certainly nothing more need be said to show conclusively that *the verdict is not supported by the evidence,* for the reasons that:

1. The law *presumes negligence from the fact of injury to a passenger;*

2. This presumption throws upon *the carrier* the burden of meeting this presumption with evidence of the *exercise* of *utmost care;* and that

3. In this case *there is no evidence whatsoever to meet this presumption,* and *therefore the presumption stands unimpaired and "necessitates a verdict in favor of the plaintiff."*

We respectfully submit that the judgment is not supported by the evidence, and should be reversed.

VI.

If the Application of the Doctrine of Res Ipsa Loquitur Applies to Airplane Passenger Carrying, Is the Application Thereof in Any Way Limited, in California, by Provisions in the Contract of Carriage, Which Say That the Carrier Shall Be Deemed To Be a Private, Not a Common, Carrier; That the Carrier Shall Be Liable Only for Proven Negligence, and That the Mere Occurrence of An Accident Shall Not Be Any Evidence of Any Negligence of the Carrier?

It is not an answer to the defendant's liability here for the defendant to say that the ticket excused liability except for proven negligence and that negligence is not to be presumed from the fact of injury.

All such contracts are expressly forbidden by section 2175 of the Civil Code of California, which provides that:

"CERTAIN AGREEMENTS VOID. A common carrier cannot be exonerated, by any agreement made in anticipation thereof, from liability for the gross negligence, fraud, or wilful wrong of himself or his servants."

In Volume 4, California Jurisprudence, at page 920, the rule is also stated as follows:

"Independent of statutory provisions, it is almost universally held that any contract purporting to exempt a common carrier of persons from liability for negligence of itself or its servants to a passenger carried for compensation is void as being against public policy, and it is immaterial in such cases that the attempted limitation on such liability is agreed to by the passenger in consideration of special concessions in the matter of rate of fare or other departure from the rules applicable to passengers paying full fare, provided there is any consideration whatever for the carriage."

Under the law, the court very properly instructed the jury [Tr. p. 48], that:

"The issuance of a ticket with provisions printed thereon such as have been placed in evidence here does not change the relations of the parties to this action."

CONCLUSION.

We feel that the verdict of the jury is also largely a reflection of the attitude of the learned trial judge which indicated a belief that:

1. *Passenger carrying upon scheduled airways is unusually hazardous,* and that:

2. *Because of the newness of the science of aviation, there exists a branch of the law wherein there are few precedents to guide in an action such as this.* [Tr. p. 52.]

We submit that the records do not support either of these conclusions.

Statistics, of which this court may take judicial notice, show that *passenger travel upon scheduled airways (and this was one)* is one of the safest means of travel. In support of this we refer to a statistical report compiled by the U. S. Department of Commerce in late November, 1930.

This fact is clearly and definitely recognized by the management of *scheduled* airways who advertise the fact extensively to promote airway travel by passengers.

We also submit that there is nothing new in the *Law of Negligence* as applied to passenger carrying on scheduled airways.

The principals of substantive law; of the burden of proof, and of evidence are well and long settled and understood, and are applicable alike to the carrier of passengers whether by land or sea, or beneath or above either.

It is the novelty of any injury to a passenger while being carried over scheduled airways which adds interest in a suit for damages, but this, in no way, adds anything to the problem of determining the law applicable thereto, or in applying the law.

We, therefore, respectfully submit that because of the inaccurate, confusing and misleading instructions to the jury, upon the defendant's duty to the deceased, and also because of the insufficiency of the evidence to support the verdict, or the judgment, in defendant's favor, the judgment should be reversed and a new trial ordered.

OLIVER O. CLARK,
SAMUEL A. ROSENTHAL,
Attorneys for Appellant.

No. 6802.

IN THE
United States
Circuit Court of Appeals,
FOR THE NINTH CIRCUIT. ⁴/

E. M. Allison, as Administrator for the
Estate of Thos. J. Kelly, deceased,
Appellant,

vs.

Standard Air Lines, Inc., a corporation,
Respondent.

RESPONDENT'S BRIEF.

Harry D. Parker,
White McGee, Jr.,
601-602 Pacific National Bldg., Los Angeles, Cal.,
O'Melveny, Tuller & Myers,
Walter K. Tuller,
Homer I. Mitchell,
900 Title Insurance Bldg., Los Angeles, Cal.,
W. Jefferson Davis,
1140 Rowan Bldg., Los Angeles, Cal.,
Attorneys for Respondent.

Parker, Stone & Baird Co., Law Printers, Los Angeles.

TOPICAL INDEX.

PAGE

Statement of Respondent's Contentions............................ 3

Argument 4

I.

The Jury Was Clearly and Correctly Instructed on
the Care Required of Respondent as a Common
Carrier 4

II.

Appellants Cannot Complain of Instructions on the
Care Required and on Inevitable Accident Because
no Proper Exception Was Taken to Said Instruc-
tions 21

III.

The Doctrine of Res Ipsa Loquitur Is Not Applicable.... 23

A. The Applicability of Res Ipsa Loquitur Is Not
    Affected by the Fact That Defendant Was a
    Common Carrier. Where Facts Exist Bringing
    a Case Within the Definition of Res Ipsa
    Loquitur, the Doctrine Is Applicable Whatever
    May Be the Relationship Between the Plaintiff
    and Defendant.. 23

B. The Doctrine of Res Ipsa Loquitur Should Not
    Be Invoked in This Case, Because Two of the
    Essential Elements Which Warrant the In-
    voking of the Doctrine Are Missing...................... 26

    1. It cannot be said that accidents in air trans-
        portation do not ordinarily occur except
        where the carrier is negligent.......................... 26

    2. It cannot be said that plaintiff has shown
        that the thing that caused the accident was
        under the exclusive control of defendant...... 36

PAGE

C. One California·Case Applies Res Ipsa Loquitur
to an Airplane Accident, but the Decision Is
Not Supported by Reason or Logic and Is Not
Binding upon This Court.............................. 41

D. The Sound Rule Should Be That Res Ipsa Loquitur Should Not Be Invoked in Accidents Occurring in Air Transport, but That the Jury
Should Be Permitted to Draw Such Inferences
of Negligence From All of the Facts and Circumstances as Such Facts and Circumstances
Fairly Justify 51

IV.

Appellants Cannot Complain of Instructions Which
Disregarded Res Ipsa Loquitur Because no Exception Was Taken to Said Instructions...................... 53

V.

Even if the Doctrine of Res Ipsa Loquitur Had Been
Applicable to This Case, There Is Substantial Evidence That the Defendant Was Not Negligent.......... 54

1. Evidence that the plane and engine were in good
condition 54

2. The pilot was capable.............................. 56

3. Defendant was not negligent in permitting the
plane to leave Los Angeles on its scheduled flight
to Phoenix 56

4. The pilot was not negligent in proceeding beyond
the Tri-City Airport towards San Gorgonio
Pass 57

5. The pilot was not negligent in seeking a landing.. 58

Conclusion 62

TABLE OF CASES AND AUTHORITIES CITED.

CASES.   PAGE

Alewel v. East St. Louis & S. Ry. Co. (Mo.), 26 S. W.
(2nd) 869 9

Atlas Powder Co. v. Benson (C. C. A. 3rd), 287 Fed.
797, p. 798..37, 49

Bartlett v. Town Taxi Inc. (Mass.), 160 N. E. 797.... 46
Bush v. L. A. Railway Co., 178 Cal. 538.......................... 44

Carlsen v. Diehl, 57 Cal. App. 731.................................. 38
Carney v. Boston Elevated Ry. (Mass.), 98 N. E. 605.. 46
Cesco & N. E. Rly. Co. v. Proctor (Tex.), 272 S. W.
308 10
Chicago & E. I. R. Co. v. Grimm (Ind.), 57 N. E. 640.. 7
Chicago, etc. Ry. Co. v. Kendall (C. C. A. 8th), 167
Fed. 62, 71... 49

Delaware & H. Co. v. Dix (C. C. A. 3rd), 188 Fed.
901 25
Diamond v. Weyerhaeuser, 178 Cal. 540.......................... 44
Di Leo v. Eastern Mass. St. Ry. Co. (Mass.), 150 N.
E. 891 45
Dwyer v. Connecticut Co. (Conn.), 131 Atl. 838........... 9

Erie Railroad Co. v. Murphy (C. C. A. 2d), 9 Fed. 2d
525, at p. 526... 26

Grace v. St. Louis R. Co. (Mo.), 36 S. W. 1121............ 9
Griffin v. Manice (N. Y.), 59 N. E. 925.......................... 25

Harrison v. Sutter St. Ry. Co., 134 Cal. 549................ 44
Herman Chemical Co. v. Burlington, etc. Co. (C. C. A.
3rd), 9 Fed. (2nd) 289... 53
Hocking Valley R. R. Co. v. New York Coal Co. (C. C.
A. 6th), 217 Fed. 727... 50

PAGE

Housel v. Pacific Electric, 167 Cal. 245............................ 44

Judson v. Giant Powder Co., 107 Cal. 549...................... 43

Keller v. Cushman, 104 Cal. App. 186................. 38

Lindsay v. Burgess, 156 U. S. 208................................. 53
Louisiana & Northwest Rly. Co. v. Crumpler, 122 Fed.
425 (C. C. A. 8th)... 7
Lucid v. E. I. Du Pont de Nemours Powder Co. (C. C.
A. 9th), 199 Fed. 377, at p. 378...................................... 37

Massachusetts Bonding & Insurance Co. v. Norwich
Pharmacal Co. (C. C. A. 2nd), 18 Fed. (2nd) 934.... 50

New York N. H. & H. R. Co. v. Lincoln, 223 Fed.
896, 899 (C. C. A. 2nd)... 7
Niland v. Boston Elevated Ry. Co. (Mass.), 100 N.
E. 554 46

Olson v. Whitthorne & Swan, 203 Cal. 206.................. 38
Osgood v. L. A. Railway, 137 Cal. 280............................ 44

Parker v. Elgin (C. C. A. 6th), 5 Fed. (2nd) 562...... 53
Parramore v. Denver & R. G. W. R. Co. (C. C. A.
2nd) 912 48
Pontecoro v. Clark, 95 Cal. App. 162, p. 181.................. 10

Robinson v. Consolidated Gas Co. (N. Y.), 86 N. E.
805 39
Rocker v. Deering South Western Ry. Co. (Mo.),
226 S. W. 69.. 10

San Joaquin Light & Transit Co. v. Requena, 224 U.
S. 89, at pp. 98-99.. 24
Scott v. Kansas City Rys. Co. (Mo.), 229 S. W. 178.... 9
Simmons Hdw. Co. v. Rhodes (C. C. A. 8th), 7 Fed.
(2nd) 352... 53

Singer Sewing Machine Co. v. Springfield St. Ry. Co. (Mass.), 103 N. E. 283 46

Smith v. O'Donnell, 84 C. D. 6 ....41, 47, 50, 51

Southern Pac. Co. v. Schuler, 135 Fed. 1015 (C. C. A. 9th) 8

Southern Ry. Co. v. Smith (C. C. A. 6th), 214 Fed. 942 48

St. Clair v. McAlister, 84 C. D. 97, 99 44

St. Louis, etc. R. R. Co. v. Cason (Tex.), 129 S. W. 394 49

St. Mary's Gas Co. v. Brodbeck (Ohio), 151 N. E. 323 49

Sweeney v. Erving, 228 U. S. 233 39

Teale v. Southern Pacific Co., 120 Cal. App. at p. 580..6, 8

Thompson v. Green, 174 Fed. 404 (C. C. A. 3rd) 9

Tower v. Humboldt Transit Co., 176 Cal. 602 44

Trafnell v. Hines, 268 Fed. 504, 505 (C. C. A 3rd) 8

Union Pacific Ry. Co. v. Yates (C. C. A. 8th), 79 Fed. 584 50

Valente v. Sierra Rly. Co., 158 Cal. at p. 417 ....6, 10

Veuve de Courson de la Villeuve v. Societe Aeronautique Latecocere, February 7, 1927, 11 Revue Internationale de la Locomotion Aerienne 239 41

Wadsworth v. Boston Elevated (Mass.), 66 N. E. 421 39

Western & Atlantic R. R. Co. v. Henderson, 279 U. S. 639 46

W. Tenn. Grain Co. v. J. C. Shaffer & Co. (C. C. A. 6th), 299 Fed. 197 50

Wilson v. Colonial Air Transport, 180 N. E. 212 31

Yazoo & M. V. R. Co. v. Wright (C. C. A. 6th), 207 Fed. 281 53

vi.

AUTHORITIES.

PAGE

2 Air Law Review, 9, 24 28

2 Air Law Review 26 41

Air Commerce Bulletin, published by the Department
    of Commerce May 1, 1931 .... 3?

American Bar Association Journal (July 1930),
    "Transportation by Air and the Doctrine of Res
    Ipsa Loquitur 34

California Jurisprudence, Vol. 4, at p. 934 5

Civil Code, Sec. 2100 .... 4, 6, 8, 10

25 Corpus Juris, 846 47

No. 6802.

United States
Circuit Court of Appeals,

FOR THE NINTH CIRCUIT.

E. M. Allison, as Administrator for the
Estate of Thos. J. Kelly, deceased,

Appellant,

vs.

Standard Air Lines, Inc., a corporation,

Respondent.

RESPONDENT'S BRIEF.

STATEMENT OF RESPONDENT'S CONTENTIONS.

I.

The jury was clearly and correctly instructed on the care required of respondent as a common carrier.

II.

Appellant cannot complaint of instructions on the care required and on inevitable accident because no proper exception was taken to said instructions.

III.

The doctrine of *res ipsa loquitur* is not applicable.

IV.

Appellant cannot complain of instructions which disregard *res ipsa loquitur,* because no exception was taken to said instructions.

V.

Even if the doctrine of *res ipsa loquitur* had been applicable to this case there is substantial evidence that the defendant was not negligent.

ARGUMENT.

I.

The Jury Was Clearly and Correctly Instructed on the Care Required of Respondent as a Common Carrier.

The first question raised by appellant is one concerning which there need be no dispute. California has adopted the same rule as to the *quantum* of care exacted of a common carrier that is almost universally followed in the United States. But in quoting the California statute declaring that rule, appellant has omitted the portion which defines, not the *quantum* of care, which is one thing, but the extent to which a carrier must go to exercise that *quantum* of care, which is a different thing. It is through appellant's failure to recognize this distinction, which will be elaborated elsewhere in this brief, that we believe have arisen appellant's principal objections to the charge of the lower court. Section 2100, Civil Code, provides:

> "General duties of carrier. A carrier of persons for reward must use the utmost care and diligence for their safe carriage, must provide everything

necessary for that purpose, *and must exercise to that end a reasonable degree of skill."* (The portion omitted by appellant is italicized by us.)

Thus, although passengers must be carried as safely as human care and foresight will go, that care and foresight need be only such as issues from *reasonable* skill. The quotation from California Jurisprudence, therefore, presents only one phase of the rule; indeed, in the same article of that work (Vol. 4, at page 934), it is stated:

"The above rule does not, however, require the utmost degree of care which the human mind is capable of imagining, nor the use of every possible prevention of accident which the highest scientific skill might suggest. The degree of care and diligence which is to be exercised is such only as can reasonably be exercised consistently with the character and mode of conveyance adopted and the practical operation of the business of the carrier."

With these observations in mind, we will pass to the instructions attacked by appellant and will consider them in the order followed in appellant's brief.

It is conceded by appellant that the court correctly instructed the jury in the language of the statute above quoted, and also correctly instructed the jury that "the carrier of persons for reward is bound to provide vehicles fit for that purpose *and is not excused for failure in this respect by any degree of care."* (Italics ours.) But the complaint is made that in other instructions a different and lesser degree of care was laid down. The first one criticised [App. Brief p. 10; Tr. p. 49] is that which declares that although the law demands the utmost care for the safety of passengers, it does not require all the care, skill and diligence of which the human mind can conceive, nor which will free the transportation of passengers from all possible perils. It is urged that this contradicts the rule of utmost care. We believe, however, that this is an entirely correct statement of law. To hold otherwise will be to make a common carrier virtually an insurer of the safety of the passenger, whereas the proper test, as we have pointed out, is *reasonable skill*.

If it is necessary to go any further than section 2100, Civil Code—"and must exercise to that end reasonable skill"—to justify the instruction there is abundant authority in support of it.

In *Valente v. Sierra Rly. Co.*, 158 Cal. at p. 417, the California Supreme Court recognized the rule that the degree of care and diligence required "is such only as can reasonably be exercised consistent with the character and mode of conveyance adopted and the practical operation of the road and transaction of the business of the carrier."

In *Teale v. Southern Pacific Co.*, 120 Cal. App. at p. 580 (a hearing was denied by the Supreme Court, and the case accordingly expresses the law of California), it is said:

> "In brief, the rule may be stated to be that where, in the conduct of a certain business, it must be known that unusual or uncommon danger must necessarily coexist with certain conditions, which are capable of being controlled to a large extent by the use of *reasonable and available means,* the law will hold casual-

ties resulting from an omission to so control such conditions as among those which could *'reasonably be anticipated'* and against the happening of which, therefore, it was the duty of the person conducting such business to adopt and enforce precautionary measures." (Italics ours.)

In *Louisiana & Northwest Rly. Co. v. Crumpler,* 122 Fed. 425 (C. C. A. 8th), an instruction was held to be substantially correct which used language almost identical with that of ours:

"The duty resting upon the defendant as a carrier of passengers did not compel it to exercise all the care and diligence the human mind can conceive of, nor such care as would render the transportation of passengers free from any possible danger to them"

Other decisions in point are:

Chicago & E. I. R. Co. v. Grimm (Ind.), 57 N. E. 640;

New York N. H. & H. R. Co. v. Lincoln, 223 Fed. 896, 899 (C. C. A. 2nd).

The next instructions to which appellant directs our attention are those cited on page 11 of appellant's brief. [Tr. p. 48.]

In criticising these instructions, appellant has failed again to distinguish between the *quantum* of care required—the utmost care—and the measuring stick provided by the law to determine whether that degree of care has been exercised. *Th utmost care is imperative, but it necessarily can be only the utmost care that a person of ordinary prudence would use under the same circumstances.* In other words the test is the "reasonable degree of skill" test of section 2100, Civil Code. "Utmost care," yes, but the carrier "must exercise to that end a reasonable degree of skill" only; and the jury having been instructed that the carrier must use the utmost care and diligence and must exercise to that end a reasonable degree of skill, and that the pilot was required to exercise such care and skill as is ordinarily possessed by those engaged in the same business or art, it is a mere quibbling over words to argue that the expression "ordinary prudence and caution and skill" indicated a different and lesser degree of care, especially as the expression was qualified by the words "under the same circumstances."

Instructions of like import have been approved in many decisions involving common carriers, as in the following:

> *Trafnell v. Hines,* 268 Fed. 504, 505 (C. C. A. 3rd):
>
> "If the plaintiff was a passenger on a train of the defendant carrier the defendant owed him the duty to exercise for his safety every degree of care, diligence and skill which a reasonable man would use under the circumstances."

> *Southern Pac. Co. v. Schuler,* 135 Fed. 1015 (C. C. A. 9th):
>
> "But, if on the other hand, the defendant could not discover the condition of this embankment by the exercise of such diligence, and prudence as skillful men engaged in that kind of business might fairly be expected to use under like circumstances, it would not be chargeable with negligence, and would not be liable in this case."

Dwyer v. Connecticut Co. (Conn.), 131 Atl. 838:

" 'The railway is not an insurer by its contract of passage of the safety· of passengers, but it must use the utmost care to avoid injury to such passengers that a *reasonably prudent person* would use *under similar circumstances.* It must use the utmost care consistent with the nature of the business to guard passengers against a danger arising from whatever source it may reasonably and naturally be expected to occur; and *the duty of the motorman and conductor of the car is to operate the car as a reasonably prudent motorman and conductor, skilled in the business, would operate a car under like circumstances.'* " (Italics ours.)

Thompson v. Green, 174 Fed. 404 (C. C. A. 3rd). In this case an instruction was approved which declared that the carrier must exercise "the highest degree of care which reasonable, prudent·and careful men would under like cir-· cumstances exercise."

Grace v. St. Louis R. Co. (Mo.), 36 S. W. 1121. A high degree of care "such as practical and skillful railroad men would have used."

Scott v. Kansas City Rys. Co. (Mo.), 229 S. W. 178. The highest practicable care and skill "which might reasonably be expected of ordinary careful and prudent persons engaged in like business in running and operating its cars."

Alewel v. East St. Louis & S. Ry. Co. (Mo.), 26 S. W. (2nd) 869. "Such care as an ordinarily prudent motorman would exercise under the same or similar circumstances, . . . and the highest degree of care, skill, and foresight."

Cesco & N. E. Rly. Co. v. Proctor (Tex.), 272 S. W. 308. "Such a high degree of care as would be used by a cautious, or prudent, and competent person under the same or similar circumstances."

Rocker v. Deering South Western Ry. Co. (Mo.), 226 S. W. 69. "That high degree of care which a person of ordinary prudence would use under like circumstances."

We have already cited the California cases of *Valente v. Sierra Ry. Co.* and *Teale v. Southern Pac. Co.* in which is recognized the rule that the degree of care is only such as can *reasonably be exercised* consistent with the mode and character of conveyance. The same rule was stated in the California case of *Pontecoro v. Clark,* 95 Cal. App. 162, at pages 181, 182:

> "Reading the two instructions in this case together, they fairly and with sufficient clarity state the principles of law to which they are addressed in the following form, which is substantially in the form in which they are separately given in this case: 'While common carriers are not insurers of the safety of their passengers, they are bound to exercise the highest degree of care and caution for the safety of their passengers, and to do all that human foresight and viligance *can reasonably do, consistent with the mode of conveyance and the practical operation of its rule,* to prevent accident to their passengers while riding on their cars.' " (Italics ours.)

Indeed, in view of the concluding clause of section 2100, Civil Code—"and must exercise to that end a reasonable degree of skill"—it is difficult to see how the rule could be otherwise in California.

It appears, therefore, that the instructions complained of were in no way inconsistent with the instructions as to utmost care, but on the other hand correctly state the other phase of that rule. It would be an anomaly to single out any one pilot of a common carrier and say that he must exercise a greater degree of care and skill than that ordinarily possessed by other pilots of common carriers; yet that would seem to be the requirement implicit in appellant's criticism. All that any passenger can require is, first, that the utmost care be exercised in his behalf, and next, that the one charged with the exercise of that degree of care must do so in the manner of those possessing ordinary care and skill as operators of common carriers under similar circumstances. And that in substance is precisely what the court told the jury: "The carrier of persons for reward must use the utmost care and diligence for their safe carriage. . . . He was only required to exercise such care and skill as is ordinarily possessed by those engaged in the same business or art. . . ."

A further contention of appellant as to the instruction last quoted is that it was equivalent to an instruction that the standard of care required could be established by proof of customary acts of others under like circumstances, which appellant states is not the law. It is obvious to us, however, that the instruction could not have been so understood by the jury. It was not an instruction as to any specific act or acts of the pilot, but was a definition of the degree of care and skill which the pilot was required to possess and use in the exercise of the utmost care. That degree was such as was ordinarily possessed and exercised by pilots of common carriers. Appellant could not require that he be a better pilot than the ordinary pilot of an airplane operating as a common carrier, or that he exercise greater diligence than such as the ordinarily prudent common carrier would use in the exercise of utmost care.

The next instruction attacked by appellant (App Brief p. 13) immediately follows the one last considered above [Tr. p. 48]:

> "Hence his acting in the particular manner which he did would not necessarily be negligence merely because there may have been a safer manner of doing it."

The instruction states a universally recognized principle of the law of negligence. The objection to it is based upon the false assumption that a common carrier of passengers is bound at his peril to carry them safely, and to guard against and prevent every conceivable danger. We have already cited authority for the correct rule, and will not further deal with this contention of appellant which so plainly has no foundation in the law.

Appellant next complains (App. Brief p. 13) of the following instructions [Tr. p. 48]:

> "All of the circumstances attending the transaction must be taken into consideration. However, these circumstances must be those which the evidence shows may reasonably be supposed to have been known to him, and to have influenced his mind at the time, for after an event has transpired it is often easy to demonstrate means whereby it might have been prevented from occurring."

These instructions must be construed with reference to certain other instructions [Tr. pp. 47, 48]:

"One who, without negligence on his part, is suddenly confronted with imminent danger or seeming imminent danger is not required to exercise that degree of care and skill which is required in the commission of an act after careful deliberation; he is required to act only as a reasonably prudent man would act under similar circumstances. Accordingly, where a situation requires an immediate choice between alternative courses of conduct, negligence may not be inferred from an unwise choice, if a reasonable man under similar circumstances, would choose similarly."

    *   *   *   *   *   *   *   *

"If you should find from the evidence that the pilot Everett was an experienced and skillful pilot, and without any negligence on his part encountered fog conditions, and that bringing to bear all his previous experience and skill he weighed the facts and circumstances surrounding him and of which he had knowledge and decided upon a course of action which he tried to carry out, that is, to make an emergency landing, then the want of success would be due to error of judgment, and not to negligence. That is if he exercised his best judgment and if his acts would have been approved by competent experts."

The criticism made by appellant of the first instruction of this group is that it fails to include circumstances which "in the exercise of the utmost care and diligence for the safe carriage of the passenger should have been known to the pilot, and should have influenced his mind at the time."

The second instruction of this group is not criticised by appellant, but the last one is attacked upon the following grounds:

1. That it substitutes "negligence and skill" for "care and diligence."

2. That it limits the facts and circumstances surrounding the pilot and which he weighed to those of which he had knowledge.

3. That it expressly approves of any course of action which represented his best judgment provided it would have been approved by experts.

4. That it tells the jury that error of judgment is not negligence under the conditions stated.

We must first bear in mind that the proviso "without negligence on his part" was twice stated to the jury. It must be assumed, therefore, that the jury understood that the condition precedent to the rule stated by the court was that the pilot must be free from negligence. Next, the instruction that "these circumstances must be those which the evidence shows may reasonably be supposed to have been known to him, and to have influenced his mind at the time," was immediately followed by the statement that "if you should find from the evidence that the pilot Everett was an experienced and skillful pilot, *and without negligence on his part* encountered fog conditions, and that bringing to bear all his previous experience and skill he weighed the facts and conditions surrounding him and of which he had knowledge and decided upon a course of conduct which he tried to carry out . . . then his want of success would be due to error of judgment. . . ." (Italics ours.)

In the first place, the jury having been previously instructed that the utmost care was required and that in the exercise of the utmost care the duty upon the pilot was to use such care and skill as is ordinarily possessed and exercised by those engaged in the same business or art, could not have placed any construction upon the criticized language other than that those circumstances which reasonably may be supposed to have been known to him would be such circumstances as a pilot exercising the utmost care according to the standards of ordinarily prudent pilots of common carriers, would have known to exist. In the second place, it is hard to conceive how a higher standard of care could reasonably be required than the standard set up in the language which requires, first, that the pilot be an experienced and skillful pilot, and secondly, that he bring to bear upon the situation all his previous experience and skill in weighing the facts and circumstances surrounding him. If he was an experienced and skillful pilot, and if he brought to bear upon the situation all his previous experience and skill, then he would have knowledge of all the surrounding circumstances which should have been known to him. Furthermore, the court lays down as a final condition that his course must be such as would have been approved by competent experts. Can a common carrier be compelled to exercise any higher care than such as would have been approved of by competent experts in the same business or art? With the instructions as a whole in mind, it would appear that appellant is quarreling with a mere matter of phraseology, and such phraseology as a jury could not have misunderstood. If a pilot was experienced and skillful, and brought to bear upon a situation

all his previous experience and skill, he necessarily would
have used due care and diligence; by the same token, he
necessarily would have known of all the surrounding facts
and circumstances which he could reasonably have been
required to know. If the court erred in these instructions it erred favorably to appellants, because one of the
conditions laid down was that the pilot's course must be
such as would have been approved by competent experts.
It is our contention that this statement of the court stated
the law more favorably to appellant than he had a right
to demand. The course of conduct followed by the most
skillful pilot might very well be disapproved of by experts who have had the advantage of mature deliberation;
yet if in the exercise of the utmost care he acted as any
ordinarily prudent pilot of a common carrier possessing
reasonable skill would have acted under the circumstances
he would not be negligent. But certainly no greater safe-
guard could be required to protect passengers on common
carriers than that the conduct of a carrier be such as
would be approved of by competent experts who can view
his conduct through the eyes of mature deliberation.

Appellant further contends that the instruction tells
the jury that error of judgment is not negligence, but in
so contending appellant misconstrues the plain import of
the instruction and again falls into the error of assuming
that a common carrier is bound at his peril safely to
transport passengers. The instruction does not say
merely that an error of judgment is not negligence, but
the instruction does say that if an experienced and skillful
pilot using all his previous experience and skill in weighing the surrounding circumstances pursues a certain
course of conduct, which course of conduct would be ap-

proved by competent experts, then his want of success would be due to error of judgment and not to negligence. We submit that this is a correct statement of the law.

Appellant complains (App. Brief p. 17) of the instruction [Tr. p. 49] that the deceased necessarily assumed the usual and ordinary perils incidental to airplane travel, and that if the defendant exercised all the care, skill and diligence required by law as defined in the instructions, and that, nevertheless an accident occurred, defendant would not be negligent. As the only objection to this instruction is that the law as to care and diligence was not correctly defined elsewhere in the instructions, further comment on this instruction in view of our previous discussion is unnecessary.

The court instructed the jury [Tr. p. 50]:

"The defendant in this case in addition to its defense that it was not guilty of negligence has presented the defense that the accident in question was due to unforeseen events, inevitable accident, or Act of God. You are advised that if either of these defenses are established by the evidence the plaintiff cannot recover, and your verdict must be for the defendant;"

and again [Tr. p. 50]:

"When any person is confronted with a sudden emergency, he is not required to exercise the same degree of caution, that natural and deliberate judgment exercised when there is plenty of time to determine what would be the wise thing to do."

Appellant's criticism of the first of these instructions is that it does not state that the unforeseen events mentioned are only those which might not have been foreseen by the utmost care; and of the second, that the sudden emergency rule applies only when the person in whose favor it is invoked is free from negligence.

The first instruction, however, obviously does not purport to be a definitive statement of the unforeseen events—inevitable accident doctrine. It was merely a general statement of the defenses pleaded by defendant, and a general statement that if those defenses were established by the evidence the plaintiff could not recover. It is analogous to the often heard instruction that a defendant has pleaded contributory negligence, and that if such defense is established it bars a recovery.

In attacking this and the second instruction, appellant has ignored other portions of the charge in which the rule was stated so clearly that we believe no intelligent jury could have misunderstood the principle. One of the first instructions given was [Tr. p. 47]:

> "No one is responsible for the results of an unavoidable accident, nor for casualties which could not have been known to occur before, *and which might not have reasonably been anticipated,* and a defendant is not liable for an injury which is not caused by his negligence, but which results from some overwhelming natural agency over which he has no control." (Italics ours.)

This is a correct statement of the law, and is stated as clearly as language could express it.

We have already called attention to the instruction immediately following the one just quoted [Tr. p. 47], and which contains the qualification "one who without negligence on his part is suddenly confronted with imminent

danger . . ."; also the instruction [Tr. p. 48] in which
the qualification is again stated: "If you find from the
evidence that the pilot Everett was an experienced and
skillful pilot and without any negligence on his part . . ."
Still another instruction [Tr. p. 50] asserted the principle
with the utmost clarity:

> "No matter how great and imminent might have
> been the danger or serious consequences of an acci-
> dent the plaintiff would not be entitled to recover if
> the death of Thomas J. Kelly was the result of an
> inevitable, or unavoidable accident, that is, *if the ac-
> cident could not have been prevented by the exercise
> of that degree of care and caution required of the de-
> fendant under the instructions heretofore given. A
> pure accident without negligence on the part of the
> defendant is not actionable,* and if you are convinced
> that the accident was of such a character, it would
> come under the head of an inevitable accident, then in
> such event the plaintiff could not recover." (Italics
> ours.)

The rule that instructions must be construed as a whole
is so universally recognized that we will not burden this
brief with citation of authority respecting it. A trial
court is not required to state all the law applicable to a
case in a single instruction. The instructions must be
considered in connection with each other, and if they
harmonize as a whole and fairly and accurately state the
law, prejudicial error cannot be based upon isolated sen-
tences and phrases which may be open to criticism, or because a single instruction does not contain all of the conditions and limitations which are to be gathered from the
entire charge.

Appellant's criticism of the statements made by the court in applying the law to the facts [Tr. p. 52] must also be considered in the light of the rule just stated. The court's statement that "when applying the principle regarding the error of judgment, which you will bear in mind, if in the judgment of this aviator he saw what appeared to be favorable conditions ahead of him then the defendant is not to be held for negligence because he chose that course rather than to land upon the field in safety"; and the further statement that "in order to hold the defendant for negligence, you must, as I explained to you, find that the pilot in this case . . . must have done something which good judgment did not approve, or would not approve . . ." could not reasonably have been understood to be the declaration of all the law of the case or a declaration of all the law on this particular phase of the case. In so far as the statements purported to go, they were entirely correct and were in no way inconsistent with any of the other instructions. In stating that if in the judgment of the pilot he saw what appeared to be favorable conditions ahead of him he would not be negligent for proceeding on his course rather than landing upon the field in safety, the court was referring to the evidence as to the weather conditions which prevailed when the plane circled the field at the Tri-City Airport. Certainly it was not necessary for the court while making this statement applying the law to the facts to restate all the principles concerning the use of care and diligence which had previously been expounded. And in stating, also while applying the law to the facts, that in order to hold the defendant it was necessary for the jury to find that the pilot did something of which good judgment did not or would not approve, the court was not compelled to give a resume of the principles previously declared as to the exercise of skill and caution. To meet the requirements contended for by appellant it would be necessary that a charge be so overburdened with reiterations that the mind of the jury would be confused rather than clarified.

Appellant has argued that where instructions are conflicting and misleading a new trial should be granted. We submit, however, from the foregoing discussion of the instructions, that none of them are in conflict and none of them misleading. The argument of appellant is based upon the erroneous theory that a single instruction must state all the law on that point, which contention is completely out of accord with the rule that the charge is to be considered as a whole. We submit that the charge in this case considered in its entirety fairly and accurately states the principles of law applicable thereto.

II.

Appellants Cannot Complain of Instructions on the Care Required and on Inevitable Accident Because No Proper Exception Was Taken to Said Instructions.

The exceptions taken by appellant were the following [Tr. p. 53]:

"Mr. Clark: The only exception I desire to take is on the question of whether or not Your Honor covered thoroughly the distinction between the exercise of ordinary care and the highest degree of care. In other words, pointing out to the jury if any negligence, however slight, of the defendant contributed to the accident, that would render the defendant liable. Second, if the jury should find it was the concurrence of an Act of God and a slight negligence, even, of the defendant, that would make the defendant liable. Those are the only two exceptions we note, Your Honor."

Thus, appellant did not except to any specific portion of the charge. None of the instructions defining degree of care and none of the instructions on inevitable accident, including the instruction on "unforeseen events" now complained of, were assigned as error. The court could not have gathered from the exceptions taken whether the appellant excepted to any specific instruction or instructions. The most that can be inferred from the exceptions, if even such an inference is justified, is that the appellant desired additional instructions on the distinction between ordinary care and the highest degree of care, and on the concurrence of slight negligence with an Act of God. But the jury having been fully and fairly instructed, we believe that additional instructions were unnecessary; and appellant on this appeal does not complain of the court's failure to give additional instructions. Appellant directs his attack solely to the given instructions, but in his exceptions none of them were properly assigned as error. That in order for objections to be made to instructions on appeal, proper exceptions at the time of trial must taken, is, of course, the rule. (Authorities therefor are cited under Point III of this brief.)

III.

THE DOCTRINE OF RES IPSA LOQUITUR IS NOT APPLICABLE.

A. The Applicability of Res Ipsa Loquitur Is Not Affected by the Fact That Defendant Was a Common Carrier. Where Facts Exist Bringing a Case Within the Definition of Res Ipsa Loquitur, the Doctrine Is Applicable Whatever May Be the Relationship Between the Plaintiff and Defendant.

The question of whether or not the doctrine of *res ipsa loquitur* is applicable to accidents occurring in travel by airplane is one of vital importance in the development of air transport and deserves the most careful and mature consideration of the court.

The encouragement of air transport is unquestionably a public service of real importance. It has been so recognized by Congress through the expenditure of public funds and by many of the states.

No statute requires the application of the *res ipsa loquitur* rule to air transport nor are there any decisions controlling upon this court. This court must make the law for this Circuit and is free to adopt the rule that is right and proper. If logic and reason clearly require that the rule be applied to air transport, then we concede it should be done, notwithstanding the fact that so to do may hamper the development of an industry that has a most remarkable degree of public importance, both in time of peace and in time of war. This court is free to determine whether logic and reason do clearly require that the rule be applied. If it finds that logic and reason do not clearly require the application of the rule to air transport, then we respectfully submit that this court should not apply it but leave the matter to be determined by the legislative bodies.

At page 23 of his brief appellant asserts that the rule "applies to every carrier of passengers for hire regardless of the means of transportation employed." The question of whether or not the rule is applicable to a given set of circumstances depends not on whether the defendant is a carrier of passengers for hire but depends upon whether the circumstances are such that the case may be said to fall within the definition of the rule of *res ipsa loquitur*. The rule is not confined to accidents occurring to passengers of carriers for hire, nor is it applicable to every accident which may occur to a passengers upon a carrier for hire. Indeed, the fact that defendant was a common carrier has nothing to do with the question of whether the doctrine is applicable.

The first requisite is an understanding of the scope of the doctrine. In *San Joaquin Light & Transit Co. v. Requena*, 224 U. S. 89, at pages 98-99, the doctrine is defined as follows:

> ". . . when a thing which causes injury, without fault of the injured person, is shown to be under the exclusive control of the defendant, and the injury is such as in the ordinary course of things does not occur if the one having such control uses proper care, it affords reasonable evidence, in the absence of an explanation, that the injury arose from the defendant's want of care."

From this statement of the rule it is apparent that the applicability of the rule is in no way affected by the question of whether or not the defendant is a common carrier but is entirely dependent upon whether the thing causing the injury was under the exclusive control of the defendant and whether the injury was such as in the ordinary course of things would not have occurred if the one having such control had used proper care. This has been recognized by all courts which have made any careful analysis of the doctrine.

Griffin v. Manice (N. Y.), 59 N. E. 925, 926:

> "Primarily, it is argued that the principle which usually passes under the name of *"res ipsa loquitur"* applies only to cases where the relation between the parties is the contractual one of carrier or bailee, or in which the party injured has been injured while on a public highway. While there are some expressions to be found in text-books and decisions which seem to support this claim, in my judgment it is unfounded, and *the application of the principle depends on the circumstances and character of the occurrence, and not on the relation between the parties,* except indirectly, so far as that relation defines the measure of duty imposed on the defendant." (Italics ours.)

Delaware & H. Co. v. Dix (C. C. A. 3rd), 188 Fed. 901, 905:

> "The presumption originates from the nature of the act, not from the nature of the relations between the parties."

The question of whether the doctrine is applicable is therefore not controlled or even affected by the fact that the defendant is a carrier for hire.

B. The Doctrine of Res Ipsa Loquitur Should Not Be Invoked in This Case, Because Two of the Essential Elements Which Warrant the Invoking of the Doctrine Are Missing.

1. IT CANNOT BE SAID THAT ACCIDENTS IN AIR TRANSPORTATION DO NOT ORDINARILY OCCUR EXCEPT WHERE THE CARRIER IS NEGLIGENT.

One of the elements of *res ipsa loquitur* is that the accident must be such "as in the ordinary course of things does not occur" in the absence of negligence on the part of the defendant. At this stage in the development of air transportation it cannot be fairly said that accidents occurring in air transportation do not occur unless there has been some negligence on the part of the carrier. *We do not yet have sufficient information as to the cause of airplane accidents* to say that in any specified percentage of cases the accident would not have happened but for the negligence of the operator. The doctrine of *res ipsa loquitur* has for its basis the fact that under certain circumstances *experience* has shown us that an accident would not have occurred had the defendant used proper care. It should not be applied where we have not had sufficient experience to enable us to say with some degree of certainty that an accident would not probably have occurred had not there been some negligence on the part of the operator. This thought has been lucidly expressed in *Erie Railroad Co. v. Murphy* (C. C. A. 2d), 9 Fed. 2d 525, at page 526, where the court stated, with regard to a set of facts where *res ipsa loquitur* was applicable:

"It is regrettable that this situation has been so often spoken of as governed by the rule of *res ipsa loquitur,* for that can hardly be called a *rule* which depends for existence on a court's view of possible facts; nor is the matter made clearer by concealing the difficulty of definition in a tag of Latin.

Nothing, not even a man, speaks until experience and observation have given it or him power to speak and say something; and the phrase really means that what metaphorically *speaks* is experience, and experience that leads observing judges to hold that reasonable laymen may infer negligence from facts which experience teaches do not follow due exercise of care and skill. The standard illustration of the so-called *rule* is a boiler explosion, and since experience teaches observers that steam boilers, well made and properly cared for, do not explode without warning, the inference is justified that an exploding boiler failed either in construction, upkeep or management. Rose v. Stephens etc, Co. (C. C.), 11 F. 438; The Rambler (C. C. A.), 290 F. 791.

But observation must rely on experience confidently to hold this, no court would have announced such doctrine if the engine that 100 years ago pulled the first train on the Stockton & Darlington road had exploded; nor was there place for it, had one of the first gasoline explosion engines that took to the open road in competition with each other in 1894 similarly behaved.

But now there are 30 years of experience with gasoline engines of many kinds and under all conditions of use and misuse, and it has become common knowledge that such apparatus, made with ordinary care and managed with ordinary skill, does not either explode or burst into flame."

It must be evident that we have not yet had sufficient experience to say that airplane accidents would not occur but for the negligence of the operator. The doctrine of *res ipsa loquitur* applies only in those cases where *experience* has shown that the accident ordinarily would not happen except for negligence of the defendant. Can it be fairly said that from the mere fact that an accident occurs in air travel, logic and reason clearly require the court to hold that it probably would not have happened except for the negligence of the operator? We submit that reason and logic do not require such a holding. The fact that the law of gravitation is always working is in itself a strong reason why the rule should not be applied. Whenever any object heavier than air is lifted into the air there is an ever-present pull drawing it back to earth. Nothing that mortal man can do can change the force of this ever-present law. Everyone knows of its existence. Everyone who goes into the air goes with the knowledge of the constant application of this force of gravity. Furthermore, everyone knows that there are unseen and, to a large extent, unforeseeable currents in the air and that it is filled with spaces of relative vacuum or "pockets." These natural conditions created by the Almighty and beyond the regulation and control of any human power create a difference that is fundamental and inevitable as between travel on land and travel through the air.

As was stated by Howard Osterhout in his learned discussion, "The Doctrine of *Res Ipsa Loquitur* as Applied to Aviation," (2 Air Law Review 9, 24):

"The known experience of aviation accidents indicates that fogs, poor visibility, unchartered uprushing currents of air, snow storms, rapidly gathering

thunderstorms and quick changes in weather, all tran-
spiring after the plane has ascended into the heavens,
play a very great part in causing disaster to aircraft otherwise sound and well-piloted. If these
forces of nature might have caused the accident, or
if the crash might as well have been attributed to
such a force of nature—the act of God—or to unknown causes, as to negligence; or, if there is reasonable doubt as to the exact cause of the accident,
then and under these circumstances, it would be contrary to legal precedent, as well as to the dictates
of common sense, to apply the rule of presumptive
negligence."

Moreover, travel through the air requires close decision
of judgment on the part of the pilot. No one can contend that liability can be predicated upon a mere error of
judgment. No matter how carefully trained and how
skillful a pilot may be, conditions frequently arise where
a decision must be made quickly and where between two
or more courses which may be taken, the decision is an
exceedingly close matter of judgment. Suppose he chooses
the wrong course and an accident results, clearly this
alone does not show negligence and should not be sufficient to create liability. Should the court in such a case
say there is a *presumption* of negligence. Suppose, for
example, that a sudden storm arises or that the pilot, who
had been proceeding under a reasonably high ceiling of
fog, suddenly finds not only a heavy bank of fog
lying upon the ground ahead of him but also that fog
has closed in behind him. Suppose there is no good landing field close by but that there is a rough field or a small
one. The plane is proceeding at close to 100 miles per
hour, for it must maintain that speed in order to stay in

the air. The pilot must determine immediately whether to try to go through the storm or fog or to take his chances on a forced landing. Either course may result in an accident or, on the other hand, either course may bring his passengers to safety. If he tries to make the forced landing and passengers are injured, shall the law lay down a presumption that he was negligent, *non constat* that if he had attempted to go through this storm there might have been a more serious accident; or suppose he tries to go through the storm and an accident results, does this fairly raise a presumption that he was negligent in failing to attempt the forced landing?

Suppose a passenger is moving about in a plane and it suddenly strikes an air pocket, throwing the passenger against the side or to the floor to his injury? If such a sudden jerk occurred in a railroad train a presumption of negligence might well arise and the doctrine of *res ipsa loquitur* might be applied. But to make such a presumption in air transport is simply to lay down a presumption of law that is not in accord with the facts but is directly contrary to the facts. Such sudden jerks are not inevitable in air travel; the pilot cannot control pockets in the air, neither can he see them nor anticipate them.

Illustrations might be multiplied but would probably serve no useful purpose. The point we wish to emphasize is that reason and logic do not require a holding that because an accident happens in air travel there has probably been negligence.

In the handling of ordinary methods of transportation and in the handling of machinery and in like cases where the rule of *res ipsa loquitur* ordinarily applies, man has had long experience and methods have been developed under which, with the exercise of ordinary care, accidents probably would not occur, but air travel is still in its infancy. For thousands of years men have been traveling by land and sea. Air travel of any considerable extent is less than a quarter of a century old. We know it to be a fact that ordinarily accidents do not happen in land or sea transport without negligence but we equally know it to be a fact that in the newly developing air industry, at least in the transportation end, most accidents that happen are in spite of great care exercised by the operator. This is particularly true because we still have much to learn about control of the air. It is particularly true because of the natural forces and conditions, gravity, air currents, air pockets, fogs, sudden storms and the like, which are beyond any human control.

If the court should adopt the *res ipsa loquitur* rule based upon the assumption that such accidents in air transport ordinarily do not happen except where there has been negilgence, it would be adopting a rule based upon an assumption that is simply false in fact. It needs no argument to show that this would be unfair, unjust, illogical and wrong.

> "When the reason for the rule ceases, the rule itself ceases."

The logic of this argument has been recognized by the highest court of the state of Massachusetts in *Wilson v. Colonial Air Transport,* 180 N. E. 212, considering a case where the right wing motor of a tri-motored plane went dead a few seconds after leaving the ground. The right side of the plane tipped, and in spite of the frantic efforts of the pilot to right the plane it made a nose dive into the water resulting in damage to plaintiff's property, for which he sued. The court said, speaking of *res ipsa loquitur:*

> ". . . the doctrine will not be applied if there is any other reasonable or probable cause from which it might be inferred there was no negligence at all; . . ."

> ". . . we are not as yet, in respect to the operation, care and characteristics of aircraft in a position where the doctrine can be applied."

We do not ask the court to rely on our statement that experience in air transport has not yet been sufficient to warrant a presumption that accidents do not ordinarily occur except when the operator is negligent. Available statistics disclose that such a presumption was not warranted on the date of trial, and indeed is not today warranted.

Reliable statistics in the causes of accidents of *regularly operated air transport companies* are not yet available. The Department of Commerce of the United States has compiled statistics of *all air accidents* and their causes, but has not segregated accidents occurring in air transport from accidents occurring during student instruction, experimental and pleasure flying, and commercial flying other than by scheduled transport operators. This action was tried in September, 1930, and there were at that time available statistics for the years 1927, 1928 and 1929. Statistics for those years show that less than 7% of all air accidents reported to the Department of Commerce took place on regularly operated air transport systems. Of all the air accidents, 93% occurred during student instruction, experimental and pleasure flying, and commercial flying other than by scheduled transport operators. The statistics which we are about to give will obviously show a greater percentage of accidents due to negligence or incompetence than would be shown had the statistics been confined to air transport. In air transport the equipment and pilots are ordinarily of the highest order and their operations are systemized and carried out along lines which experience has taught them to be the least likely to result in danger to the passengers and the pilot. On the other hand, the independent flyer is often without proper training; his equipment is apt to be faulty and probably is not inspected regularly. Accidents in experimental flying and student instruction are much more apt to be due to the human element than in the case of regular transport operation. It is therefore apparent that statistics compiled from the whole field of airplane operation tend to show a greater percentage of accidents due to preventable causes than would statistics confined to air transport.

The Department of Commerce in compiling statistics on the causes of air accidents during the years 1927, 1928, and 1929 (Air Commerce Bulletin, published by the Department of Commerce May 1, 1931), divides the causes of accidents into four classifications, so that during these years the causes were as follows:

1. Accidents due to personnel, including errors of judgment, poor technique, disobedience of orders and negligence on the part of pilots   54%

2. Accidents due to material, including defective materials and structural defects   24%

3. Miscellaneous, including accidents due to weather, darkness, landing fields and other causes   15%

4. Accidents arising from doubtful and undetermined causes   6%

From these classifications it may be readily seen that of all accidents reported to the Department of Commerce, fully 21% were due to causes for which the operator was without blame. As we have heretofore pointed out, had these statistics been confined to accidents occurring in air transport, where greater care is used in the selection of pilots and the purchase and inspection of equipment, the percentage due to causes for which the operator was without blame would probably be much greater. Even using these figures, can it be said that the operator is guilty of negligence in the remaining 79% of the accidents? Of this 79%, 24% are due to power, plant, and structural defects. Defects sometimes develop in first class equipment during a flight which were not discoverable by inspection prior to the flight. If the operator uses high grade equipment which is maintained in good condition and is subjected to rigid inspection, should he nevertheless be held guilty of negligence when an accident occurs by reason of a defect in the plane or motor undiscoverable prior to flight? At the present time, and certainly in September, 1930, when this case was tried, the answer to that question was and is "No."

An article in the American Bar Association Journal (July 1930), "Transportation by Air and the Doctrine of *Res Ipsa Loquitur*," by William M. Allen, quotes the executive of one of our largest air mail and passenger companies as follows:

"It has been our experience that the majority
our accidents are due to causes beyond our contr
For example, bad weather is one of our greatest er
mies. Despite close attention to weather repo:
our pilots are sometimes caught in blizzards, fog
smoke. We make a practice of giving a plane
thorough inspection before commencing a flight, t
even the most minute inspection will not reveal
defective conditions in need of correction.

"I would think that the experience of other lar
air transport operators must be similar to ours.
the present stage of development it is my opinion th
*many of the accidents occurring on the lines of fir.
class companies are due to causes beyond the conti
of those companies."* (Italics ours.)

From this expression of opinion and such statistics as a
available at the present time in regard to a new and i
fant industry, the writer of this article draws the f(
lowing conclusion:

"It would seem that the inherent nature of tran
portation by air, together with the fact that aviati(
is as yet an infant, must lead to the conclusion th
an aircraft operator should not be held guilty
negligence for accidents arising from defects develo
ing in the plane or motor when he has used eve
effort to guard against such defects."

The compilation of reliable statistics as to causes
air accidents has just been begun. Perhaps after travel
air has become more or less universal, it will be possit
to determine accurately when, and under what circu
stances, airplane accidents may be said to ordinarily res
from the negligence of the operator.

Before invoking the doctrine of *res ipsa loquitur,* however, it must be clearly determined from the evidence that the facts, based on common knowledge and experience, warrant the inference of negligence, which is a condition precedent to the application of the doctrine of *res ipsa loquitur.* At the present writing, and certainly at the time of the trial of this action, experience and common knowledge furnish no basis for a statement that accidents do not ordinarily occur in air transportation unless there has been negligence on the part of the operator. Since the application of the doctrine of *res ipsa loquitur* depends upon the presence of such experience and common knowledge, it would be an arbitrary act to apply the doctrine where such experience and knowledge are lacking. Since neither experience nor logic nor reason support the application of the doctrine to the facts of this case, we respectfully contend that there was no presumption that the defendant was negligent.

2. IT CANNOT BE SAID THAT PLAINTIFF HAS SHOWN THAT THE THING THAT CAUSED THE ACCIDENT WAS UNDER THE EXCLUSIVE CONTROL OF DEFENDANT.

We are not only faced with the fact that our experience in air transport is insufficient to enable us to honestly say that ordinarily an accident will not occur except where the carrier is negligent, but also with the fact that the circumstances of this accident were such as to fairly indicate that it was caused by forces beyond the control of defendant.

In order that the thing may be said to be "under the *exclusive* control of the defendant," it must appear by a fair preponderance that causes beyond defendant's *exclusive* control did not produce the accident. This court has so interpreted the doctrine in *Lucid v. E. I. Du Pont de Nemours Powder Co.* (C. C. A. 9th), 199 Fed. 377, at page 378:

> ". . . The doctrine of *res ipsa loquitur* involves an exception to the general rule that negligence must be affirmatively shown, and is not to be inferred, and the doctrine is to be applied only when the nature of the accident itself, not only supports the inference of the defendant's negligence, *but excludes all others.*" (Italics ours.)

In discussing the definition adopted by the Supreme Court and quoted above, the Circuit Court of Appeals of the Third Circuit stated in *Atlas Powder Co. v. Benson* (C. C. A. 3rd), 287 Fed. 797, at pages 798 and 799:

> "This definition has been termed a legal classic (1 Thomp. Negl. §15; 20 R. C. L. 187), and was adopted by the Supreme Court in San Juan Light & Transit Co. v. Requena, 224 U. S. 89, 99, 32 Sup. Ct. 399, 56 L. Ed. 680. In order effectively to invoke this principle of law it is essential that it shall appear from the circumstances that the transaction in which the accident occurred was in the exclusive management of the defendant, and *all the elements of the occurrence within its control,* and that the result was so far out of the usual course that there is no fair inference that it could have been produced by any other cause than negligence. *If there was any other cause apparent to which, in the minds of the jurors, it may with equal fairness be attributed, the doctrine cannot be invoked.*" (Italics ours.)

The decisions of other courts are to the same effect.

Olson v. Whitthorne & Swan, 203 Cal. 206, 208 :

"It does not apply 'where an unexplained accident might have been caused by plaintiff's negligence, or been due to one of several causes, for some of which the defendant is not responsible.' (19 Cal. Jur., pp. 710, 711.)"

Carlsen v. Diehl, 57 Cal. App. 731, 737:

"It does not apply where there is direct evidence of the cause, or where the facts are such that an inference that the mishap was due to a cause other than the defendant's negligence could be as reasonably drawn as that it was due to his negligence (29 Cyc. 624)."

Keller v. Cushman, 104 Cal. App. 186, 189:

"In 45 C. J. 1212, section 780, the text, supported by an abundance of authorities, reads: 'The doctrine of *res ipsa loquitur* does not dispense with the general rule requiring plaintiff to prove that defendant's negligence was the proximate cause of the injury complained of, but in order to render the doctrine applicable and a presumption of negligence to attach to defendant, the nature and circumstances of the accident must be of such a character that there could be no reasonable inference but that the injury complained of was due to the negligence of the defendant or of others for whose acts he is legally responsible. Accordingly, where there are two or more persons or causes which might have produced the injury, some, but not all of which were under the control of the defendant, or for which he was legally responsible, *plaintiff, in order to invoke the doctrine,*

*must exclude the portion of those causes for which
the defendant is under no legal obligation.'* " (Italics
ours.)

Robinson v. Consolidated Gas Co. (N. Y.), 86 N. E.
805, 807:

> "If, however, proof of the occurrence shows that
> the accident might have happened from some cause
> other than the negligence of the defendant, the pre-
> sumption does not arise and the doctrine cannot prop-
> erly be applied."

Wadsworth v. Boston Elevated (Mass.), 66 N. E. 421,
422:

> "But where, as in the present case, it is as
> inferable that the accident occurred without negli-
> gence on the part of the defendant or its servants or
> agents as that it did, the ground for such an infer-
> ence is wanting. *If causes other than the negligence
> of the defendant or its servants or agents might
> have produced the accident, the plaintiff was bound to
> exclude the operation of such causes by a fair pre-
> ponderance of the evidence.*" (Italics ours.)

The Supreme Court recognizes that *res ipsa loquitur* is
not applicable unless the circumstances of the occurrence
point to negligence on the part of defendant and not to
either such negligence or some other cause which might
equally well have caused the accident.

Sweeney v. Erving, 228 U. S. 233, 238.

In the case at bar, the circumstances disclose that it
is just as likely, if not more likely, that the accident was
caused by the forces of nature as by any negligence on
the part of defendant. The airplane passed over Redlands

with a fog ceiling of between 200 and 1500 feet. The witness who testified that the ceiling was 1500 feet had had flying experience and his testimony was no doubt entitled to greater weight than the inexperienced witness who estimated the ceiling at 200 feet. Fog conditions were such at Redlands that the presence of even a 200 foot ceiling there did not indicate the presence of fog in San Gorgonio Pass [Tr. p. 29.] The plane proceeded into the pass. We do not know what the pilot saw, because he and all passengers were killed, but the testimony shows that there was fog in the pass and that in places it was very close to the ground, whereas in others it was as high as 500 feet. The presence of this fog was not due to any act of defendant. It necessitated an immediate landing. The pilot proceeded to attempt to put his plane down at the only available field [Tr. p. 27.] In maneuvering for a landing, the fog over which defendant had no control obscured a hill adjoining the proposed emergency landing field [Tr. p. 20] and prevented the pilot from seeing it until it was too late. The plane crashed and burst into flames.

What caused the accident? Was it defendant's negligence or was it this overpowering force of nature,—fog, one of the unconquered enemies of aviation? With the fog relentlessly rolling in the pass in great waves or swells, who can say but that the most cautious operator might be caught in its clutches. The fair inference from the evidence is that but for the fog the accident would have never occurred. The plaintiff has not proved by a fair preponderance of the evidence that "all of the elements of the occurrence" were within defendant's control. Rather, the circumstances show that "the accident might

ned from some cause other than the negligence
nt." In the presence of these circumstances,
e of *res ipsa loquitur* does not apply. The ele-
ifying its application are not present.

s the view of the Court of Appeals of Paris
*!e Courson de la Villeuve v. Societe Aeronau-
·ocere,* decided February 7, 1927, and reported
ue Internationale de la Locomotion Aerienne
fused to apply the doctrine of *res ipsa loquitur*
d to grant plaintiff relief, stating, as translated
aw Review 26:

the absence of all evidence, many other causes
accident could, with equal probability, be as-
, certain of which exclude all responsibility on
rt of the defendant company."

aifornia Case Applies Res Ipsa Loquitur to
rplane Accident, but the Decision Is Not
rted by Reason or Logic and Is Not Bind-
ɔon This Court.

30, 1932, the Supreme Court of California in
ntitled *Smith v. O'Donnell,* 84 C. D. 6, in-
collision between two airplanes, in one of
tiff was a passenger, held that under the facts
hat case the doctrine of *res ipsa loquitur* was
The court recognized that the doctrine should
only "when it is shown that the occurrence
loes not ordinarily happen without negligence
of those in charge of the instrumentality;" but
:ussing the fact that information is not avail-
whether collisions in midair ordinarily occur

by reason of negligence of one or both of the operators, and if by the negligence of only one, which one, held:

> "If the proper degree of care is used, a collision in midair does not ordinarily occur, and for that reason the doctrine was properly submitted to the jury."

We respectfully submit that the statement of the Supreme Court has no foundation in fact. No figures are available, and experience in air transportation has not been sufficiently broad to justify the statement that collisions in midair are ordinarily caused by negligence of both of the operators, to say nothing of being able to state that collisions in midair are ordinarily caused by negligence of the operator of the particular plane in which plaintiff was a passenger. As we have heretofore pointed out, to state that in air transportation a particular accident does not ordinarily occur except where the operator is negligent is simply to assume as a fact that which we do not know. It seems to us that to apply the doctrine of *res ipsa loquitur* in a case like this is to fly in the face of reason and logic and to simply arbitrarily decide that the doctrine will apply without regard to whether the facts and circumstances bring the accident within the definition of the doctrine.

Indeed, to hold that the doctrine of *res ipsa loquitur* applies where there has been a collision is itself an arbitrary application of the doctrine, since how can it be fairly said that the accident would not have happened but for the negligence of the defendant in whose vehicle the plaintiff was riding? Is it not just as likely that if the accident was due to any negligence, it was due to the negligence of the operator of the vehicle with which the defendant collided? In holding the doctrine applicable to collision cases, we respectfully submit the California Supreme Court fails to carefully analyze the scope of and reason for the doctrine. There seems to be great confusion in California as to the applicability of this doctrine. Academically, the California Supreme Court concedes that the basis of the rule is past experience and that it should only be applied where it can be inferred from said experience that the accident would not have happened but for negligence on the part of the defendant. In *Judson v. Giant Powder Co.,* 107 Cal. 549, 556, the court states:

> "Presumptions arise from the doctrine of possibilities. The future is measured and weighed by the past, and presumptions are created from the experience of the past. What has happened in the past, under the same conditions, will probably happen in the future, and ordinary and probable results will be presumed to take place until the contrary is shown."

We state that the concession is made academically, for in practice the court has applied the doctrine to cases where it cannot be fairly inferred that experience has shown that the accident would not have happened but for negligence on the part of defendant. For instance, the doctrine has been applied in cases where a passenger has been injured by reason of the collision of the vehicle in which he was riding with some other vehicle. We cannot understand how it can be fairly said that experience has shown that the accident would not have happened but for negligence on the part of the operator of the particular vehicle in which plaintiff happened to be riding. Rather, experience has shown us that sometimes the accident is due to the negligence of the operator of the vehicle in which the plaintiff happens to be riding, and sometimes is due to the negligence of the operator of the other vehicle involved in the collision. The cases to which we refer are:

> *St. Clair v. McAlister,* 84 C. D. 97, 99;
>
> *Housel v. Pacific Electric,* 167 Cal. 245;
>
> *Osgood v. L. A. Railway,* 137 Cal. 280.

These are not the only cases in California involving collisions; there are others which hold that *res ipsa loquitur* is not applicable to collision cases because there is no more reason to presume that the accident was caused by the negligence of the operator of one vehicle than that it was caused by the negligence of the operator of the other vehicle. The law in California with respect to collisions seems to be in hopeless confusion. The cases holding that *res ipsa loquitur* is not applicable to collision cases are:

> *Harrison v. Sutter St. Ry. Co.,* 134 Cal. 549, 552;
>
> *Tower v. Humboldt Transit Co.,* 176 Cal. 602, 607;
>
> *Bush v. L. A. Railway Co.,* 178 Cal. 538, 539;
>
> *Diamond v. Weyerhaeuser,* 178 Cal. 540, 542.

Massachusetts has adopted the logical rule that where an injury occurs as a result of a collision, such injury may as well be due to the acts of the other party to the collision, over whom the defendant has no control, as to the acts of the defendant himself, and the doctrine of *res ipsa loquitur* is not applicable. There are many cases to that effect:

v. Eastern Mass. St. Ry. Co. (Mass.), 150
, 842:

. . Concerning this doctrine it was said in
v. London General Omnibus Co. (1909), 2 K.
2, 664, quoted with approval in Reardon v.
n Elevated Railway, 141 N. E. 853, 247 Mass.
26:

'he mere occurrence of such an accident is not
 ʒlf evidence of negligence. Without attempt-
ι lay down any exhaustive classification of the
in which the principle of *res ipsa loquitur* ap-
it may generally be said that the principle
ιpplies when the direct cause of the accident,
o much of the surrounding circumstances as
ssential to its occurrence, were within the sole
 ιl and management of the defendants, or their
 ιts, so that it is not unfair to attribute to them
 ιa *facie* responsibility for what happened. An
nt in the case cf traffic on a highway is in
d contrast to such a condition of things.
 vehicle has to adapt its own behaviour to the
our of other persons using the road, and over
ιctions those in charge of the vehicle have no
l. Hence the fact that an accident has hap-
either to or through a particular vehicle is
ʒlf no evidence that the fault, if any, which
it was committed by those in charge of that
,
.

e primary difficulty with the plaintiffs' conten-
that the assumed inference is not a necessary
ut is one that rests upon surmise, conjecture,
gination; the second difficulty is that the facts
ually consistent with an assumption that the
for some undisclosed reason was driven be-

tween the tarvia and the track and that the driver in the act of returning the truck to the tarvia surface turned it in a direction that brought the right rear end of the truck within the line of the overhang of the electric car. In such a situation, the collision may have resulted merely as an unavoidable accident in spite of the observance of all proper precautions. In either case the presumption of fact upon which the doctrine of *res ipsa loquitur* is based does not arise and the burden remains on the plaintiffs to prove by affirmative evidence the negligence of the defendant."

> *Bartlett v. Town Taxi Inc.* (Mass.), 160 N. E. 797, 798;
>
> *Singer Sewing Machine Co. v. Springfield St. Ry. Co.* (Mass.), 103 N. E. 283;
>
> *Niland v. Boston Elevated Ry. Co.* (Mass.), 100 N. E. 554;
>
> *Carney v. Boston Elevated Ry.* (Mass.), 98 N. E. 605.

The United States Supreme Court recognizes that there is no place for a *presumption* of negligence on the part of the operator of one of two colliding vehicles. In *Western & Atlantic R. R. Co. v. Henderson,* 279 U. S. 639, the court had under consideration a statute which raised a presumption of negligence on the part of a railroad whenever an accident occurred. This statutory presumption was similar to the presumption which the courts have created by the doctrine of *res ipsa loquitur.* The court said, holding the statute arbitrary and therefore unconstitutional:

"The mere fact of collision between a railway train and a vehicle at a highway grade crossing furnishes no basis for any inference as to whether the accident was caused by negligence of the railway company or of the traveler on the highway or of both or without fault of anyone. Reasoning does not lead from the occurrence back to its cause." (P. 642.)

We have felt it our duty to call attention to the decision in *Smith v. O'Donnell* although said decision is in no way controlling upon this court in reaching a determination in the case at bar as to whether or not the doctrine of *res ipsa loquitur* applies.

In the first place the question of whether the doctrine applies is a question to be determined in each individual case. We have already demonstrated that the facts do not justify its application in the case at bar. Inasmuch as the facts here are entirely different from those in the California case, the fact that the doctrine was applied in the California case does not furnish any guide for its application here.

In the second place, the doctrine of *res ipsa loquitur* rests upon principles of general law. It does not arise out of statute, but out of the common law. Therefore, the mere fact that the California courts have interpreted it as applicable to aviation accidents does not make it necessary for this court to follow said interpretation. It is well settled that if a question depends upon principles of general jurisprudence or rests upon general or commercial law, the federal courts will decide for themselves and are not bound by state decisions.

25 *Corpus Juris* 846, citing many cases.

This well settled rule has been applied to interpretations of questions of negligence.

>*Parramore v. Denver & R. G. W. R. Co.* (C. C. A 2nd) 912, 914.

"It was a decision on a question of general law, the question of contributory negligence, and in the consideration of that and other questions of general or commercial law the national courts are not bound by or required to follow the decisions of the state courts. On the other hand, the power is granted to them and the duty is imposed upon them, in cases in which, as in this case, their jurisdiction is properly invoked, to consider and decide questions of general and commercial law, with proper respect and esteem for the opinions of the state courts, but nevertheless as their own knowledge, wisdom, and judgment dictate. The court below was not required to follow the decisions of the Supreme Court of Utah upon the question of contributory negligence, or upon the question of the submission of the question of contributory negligence to the jury, but it was required to determine these questions by its own knowledge and judgment." (Citing cases.)

>*Southern Ry. Co. v. Smith* (C. C. A. 6th), 214 Fed. 942, 947.

In the third place the doctrine of *res ipsa loquitur* is generally regarded as a rule of evidence. It is not a rule of evidence prescribed by any statute but is merely a rule. enforced by the courts where the facts warrant such enforcement. The sound rule seems to be that state decisions on questions of evidence are not binding upon the federal courts.

That the doctrine of *res ipsa loquitur* is a rule of evidence creating an inference or presumption of negligence, is well settled.

> *Atlas Powder Co. v. Benson* (C. C. A. 3rd), 287 U. S. 797, 798.
>
> "* * * The doctrine is strictly evidentiary and supplies in given circumstances not a presumption of negligence but evidence of negligence on which recovery can be based."

> *St. Mary's Gas Co. v. Brodbeck (Ohio)*, 151 N. E. 323, 326.
>
> "It is not a substantive rule of law, * * * It is a rule of evidence which permits or requires the inference of negligence where an accident occurs under circumstances where, in the ordinary course of events, such accidents do not occur. It is at best an evidential inference not binding upon a jury, but to be considered by it under proper instructions."

> *St. Louis, etc. R. R. Co. v. Cason* (Tex.), 129 S. W. 394, 397.
>
> "The rule * * * is not one of substantive law but is a rule of evidence only."

There has been some conflict as to whether federal courts are bound by the decisions of state courts with reference to rules of evidence and cases can be found supporting each side of the question. The better rule seems to be that federal courts are not so bound.

In *Chicago, etc. Ry. Co. v. Kendall* (C. C. A. 8th), 167 Fed. 62, 71, the court painstakingly reviews the conflicting decisions and analyzes the question with great learning, arriving at the conclusion:

> "We are satisfied that the practice which has heretofore obtained in federal courts is sound practice, and that local decisions on questions of evidence ought not to constitute authoritative rules binding upon those courts."

In a more recent case, *Massachusetts Bonding & Insurance Co. v. Norwich Pharmacal Co.* (C. C. A. 2nd), 18 Fed. (2nd) 934, 939, the court states, after briefly reviewing the question:

> "We should therefore feel free, if the occasion demanded, to adopt the common law as we understood it, even though we were at variance with that recognized by the courts of the state in which the cause was tried."

Other cases to the same effect are:

> *Union Pacific Ry. Co. v. Yates* (C. C. A. 8th), 79 Fed. 584, 588;
>
> *Hocking Valley R. R. Co. v. New York Coal Co.* (C. C. A. 6th), 217 Fed. 727, 731;
>
> *W. Tenn. Grain Co. v. J. C. Shaffer & Co.* (C. C. A. 6th), 299 Fed. 197, 200.

To hold that the doctrine of *res ipsa loquitur* is not applicable here will not conflict with the decision in *Smith v. O'Donnell,* inasmuch as the facts are quite different. To hold that the doctrine of *res ipsa loquitur* does not apply to aviation accidents would give rise to a conflict with the decision in *Smith v. O'Donnell*. This court should feel free to render such a conflicting decision because the decision of the California Supreme Court is not controlling upon this court. Its persuasive effect, we respectfully urge, is nullified by the fact that it is contrary to reason and logic. This court is free to adopt the sound logical rule applicable to the particular facts of this case. We respectfully submit that *res ipsa loquitur* is not applicable here.

D. The Sound Rule Should Be That Res Ipsa Loquitur Should Not Be Invoked in Accidents Occurring in Air Transport, but That the Jury Should Be Permitted to Draw Such Inferences of Negligence From All of the Facts and Circumstances as Such Facts and Circumstances Fairly Justify.

We are not attempting to contend for any rule which will free operators of airplanes from liability for negligence. We simply ask that the court not adopt an arbitrary rule, which has no foundation in fact, that the occurrence of an accident gives rise to a presumption that the operator of the plane was negligent. We certainly do not ask the court to adopt an arbitrary rule prescribing that in such case there is *not* negligence. When an accident occurs in air transport, let the question of liability be determined by the fair inferences to be drawn from the evidence in that particular case, without any arbitrary presumption one way or the other. This is fair and just to all concerned, will keep the law entirely logical, and will neither unduly promote or unduly hamper the development of an industry that means much to the welfare of this country in times of peace, and perhaps even more in times of war.

We freely concede that accidents may occur in air transport of such a nature that an inference of negligence can be fairly drawn. In such cases let the trier of fact draw the inference. This is an entirely different proposition from adopting the doctrine of *res ipsa loquitur*. For example, if a wing should drop off a plane in ordinary flight when it was not subjected to any unusual stress, the jury might well infer that there had been negligence either in construction or in inspection. If all the engines of a multiple motor plane should cease to function, the jury might well infer that there was fault in inspection of the engines or in the use of a poor quality gasoline. Other illustrations of particular cases might be given where it is fair to *infer* negligence. Even these, however, are not cases for the application of the doctrine of *res ipsa loquitur,* but straight cases of logical deduction or inference from the facts. The point we urge is that there should not be laid down a general principle of the doctrine of *res ipsa loquitur* applied to aviation accidents. The reasons on which the rule is founded do not require it; no statute requiries it; public policy does not require it, but, rather, requires the opposite holding. Hence, no such rule should be adopted by the courts, but each case should be left to be determined on its own facts.

IV.

PPELLANTS CANNOT COMPLAIN OF IN-
STRUCTIONS WHICH DISREGARDED RES
IPSA LOQUITUR BECAUSE NO EXCEP-
TION WAS TAKEN TO SAID INSTRUC-
TIONS.

At page 28 of appellant's brief complaint is made that
ᵉ jury was instructed:

> "Negligence is never presumed, but the burden is
> upon plaintiff to prove such negligence by a pre-
> ponderance of the evidence * * *"

ιis instruction is a correct statement of the law. Even
it were not, appellant is not in a position to complain
:ause no exception was taken to this instruction, nor
ιs any objection raised that the court did not apply the
:trine of *res ipsa loquitur*. It is well settled that errors
instructions will not be reviewed unless excepted to.

> *Lindsay v. Burgess,* 156 U. S. 208;
> *Simmons Hdw. Co. v. Rhodes* (C. C. A. 8th),
>   7 Fed. (2nd) 352, 354;
> *Herman Chemical Co. v. Burlington, etc. Co.* (C.
>   C. A. 3rd), 9 Fed. (2nd) 289;
> *Parker v. Elgin* (C. C. A. 6th), 5 Fed (2nd) 562.
> *Yazoo & M. V. R. Co. v. Wright* (C. C. A. 6th)
>   207 Fed. 281, 287.

Ϋot being entitled to raise the question of *res ipsa*
uitur by complaining of instructions, appellant presents
question by contending that even though the jury was
so instructed, the law raises a presumption of negli-
ιce and that there is no substantial evidence to rebut
ᵢ presumption. Hence appellant contends there was
ontradicted evidence of negligence.

V.

EVEN IF THE DOCTRINE OF RES IPSA LO-QUITUR HAD BEEN APPLICABLE TO THIS CASE, THERE IS SUBSTANTIAL EVIDENCE THAT THE DEFENDANT WAS NOT NEGLIGENT.

We respectfully submit that there is substantial evidence that defendant was not negligent so that even assuming the doctrine of *res ipsa loquitur* applies (which we do not concede except for the purpose of argument) the verdict must, nevertheless, be upheld because there is substantial evidence which is in conflict with the presumption or inference of negligence raised by the doctrine of *res ipsa loquitur*.

1. EVIDENCE THAT THE PLANE AND ENGINE WERE IN GOOD CONDITION.

"The plane was powered with a 525 horse-power Pratt-Whitney Hornet radial engine." [Tr. pp. 27-28.]

"The plane and the motor were both of the type approved by the Department of Commerce of the United States; the plane was licensed by that Department . . . ." [Tr. p. 27.]

"This plane had been in use since about the 4th day of February, 1929." [Tr. p. 25.]

(Since the accident happened on March 30, 1929, it had been in use less than two months.)

"The plane was fully equipped with compass, altimeter, revolution indicator, bank and turn indicator and all other instruments required by law, all of which had been tested as required by law before the flight." [Tr. p. 29.]

"The defendant maintained a systematic method for checking these planes prior to a flight for the purpose of determining their condition. Before this flight was undertaken this plane was thoroughly checked and was found to be in good mechanical condition." [Tr. p. 25.]

Mr. Leary and Mr. Navey each testified that

"he is an airplane mechanic; that he examined this plane before it started on this trip and that the engine and plane were in good condition." [Tr. p. 35.]

The following evidence rather conclusively establishes that the accident was not due to a failure of the motor:

"It was evident from the scene at the crash that the power was on when the crash occurred." [Tr. p. 26.]

"A plane could not have arrived at the climbing position in which this plane was when it struck without having the power of the engine to pull it into that position." [Tr. p. 28.]

"The structure of the fuselage of the plane was not seriously damaged, for the forward portion of the fuselage was not injured back of the engine mount; the plane was in a stalling position at the moment of impact, meaning that it was in a position in which it was climbing at as high an angle of climb as it could make; the brush on the hillside showed that it had climbed upwardly in this position for at least seventy-five feet before it struck the ground. The propellor was of steel alloy and was driven by the motor in such a way as to carve a curved section out of the rocky soil showing that the motor was running at the time of the impact." [Tr. p. 27.]

2. THE PILOT WAS CAPABLE.

An officer of defendant who was also a transport pilot, testified:

"That the pilot on this ship at the time of the crash had been employed by the defendant about two months, was known to the witness about six or seven months, was familiar with this route, had made three round trips per week during the period of his employment and was a good pilot." [Tr. pp. 25-26.]

"The plane was . . . flown by a pilot . . . licensed by that department (Department of Commerce of the United States.)" [Tr. p. 27.]

A licensed pilot who had made several trips with Everett, the pilot of the ill-fated ship, testified:

"He was an experienced pilot." [Tr. p. 37.]

3. DEFENDANT WAS NOT NEGLIGENT IN PERMITTING THE PLANE TO LEAVE LOS ANGELES ON ITS SCHEDULED FLIGHT TO PHOENIX.

"The plane left on time at eight o'clock in the morning; at the time of the start visibility was five miles; the ceiling was unlimited and there was a very light haze." [Tr. p. 27.]

"The pilot had received all the weather reports that were available at the time he left the ground and they showed flying conditions to be favorable throughout his division." [Tr. p. 29.]

It must be kept in mind that this accident happened on March 30, 1929. Since that date great strides have been made in the air transport business enabling the operator to communicate with the pilot by radio, thus making it possible to keep him constantly advised of weather conditions immediately ahead. In 1929, however, communication with planes by radio had not been perfected so that it was not possible to arrange to have weather reports given to the pilot by various weather stations along his route.

4. The Pilot Was Not Negligent in Proceeding Beyond the Tri-City, Airport Towards San Gorgonio Pass.

The Tri-City Airport is located between Colton and Redlands. In a flight from Los Angeles a plane would pass over Colton; thence over the Tri-City Airport; thence over Redlands and thence into the San Gorgonio Pass. There was testimony as to the height of the fog at the Tri-City Airport:

"Between eight and nine o'clock in the morning at the Tri-City Airport, located between Redlands and Colton and about twenty miles from the scene of the accident, there was a ceiling of about 200 feet." [Tr. p. 17.]

There was testimony as to the height of the fog at Redlands:

"The ceiling of the fog at Redlands was about one thousand five hundred feet." [Tr. p. 24.]

This evidence justifies the inference that as the pilot proceeded beyond the Tri-City Airport the ceiling of fog became higher and offers ample justification for attempting to complete his scheduled flight to Phoenix.

An experienced pilot who had flown ships on the Los Angeles to Phoenix line through San Gorgonio Pass testified:

> "These fogs come in from the ocean and quite often terminate near Redlands and very rarely extend as far as Banning. I have flown this line as a pilot and have on more than one occasion seen a two hundred-foot ceiling at the Tri-City Airport and passed on through the Gorgonio Pass without encountering any trouble at all in the pass." [Tr. p. 29.]

An experienced flyer who had been flying since 1918, had had 2,968 hours of flying, was in the United States Naval Air Service until January, 1929, led the famous squadron known as the "Sea Hawks," had flown San Gorgonio Pass about twenty times carrying passengers and who was familiar with fog conditions prevailing there, who had been through the pass in practically every type and condition of fog, rain, high cumulus clouds, wind conditions and sandstorms, testified:

> "There is nothing in the fact that Everett (the pilot) circled the Tri-City Airport for a time with a ceiling of about two hundred feet to negative the advisability of continuing on his trip." [Tr. p. 30.]

5. THE PILOT WAS NOT NEGLIGENT IN SEEKING A LANDING.

An experienced air transport pilot testified:

> "Under the conditions shown by the testimony, I would not have sought to climb up through an

indeterminate depth of cloud and fogs wi
mountains surrounding me as they were. I
seek a landing and in my opinion that is wh
pilot of this plane was doing at the time
accident." [Tr. p. 30.]

Another experienced pilot testified:

"That an emergency landing in the vicinity
crash was feasible * * * ." [Tr. p. 35.

An experienced air transport flyer testified:

"Immediately adjoining the hill on which the
crashed, at its eastern foot, was a little valle
right there at the foot of the hill there was ar
and the only one within a considerable distanc
which a pilot could have landed safely." [Tr.

The same witness also testified:

"The accident was such as might have b
the most capable and experienced pilot und
same conditions." [Tr. p. 29.]

The leader of the Sea Hawks heretofore mer
testified:

"Under the conditions existing there at th
according to the testimony he suffered an a
which could have happened to any skillful
[Tr. p. 34.]

An experienced pilot who had been flying since
who had flown the line through San Gorgonio Pa
nearly a year, making two trips weekly, and wh

made several trips with the pilot Everett in the same ship with him, testified:

"It was an accident that might have happened to any experienced pilot." [Tr. p. 37.]

In view of the fact that the pilot and all of the passengers were killed in the accident it was impossible for defendant to have offered any further evidence of its lack of negligence. Indeed, further evidence could hardly be more convincing of the care exercised by defendant than the rather overwhelming evidence to which we have called attention above. The evidence shows that the plane and motor were in good condition; that they were properly inspected before leaving Los Angeles; that the pilot was capable and experienced; that weather conditions were favorable when he took off; that the presence of a two hundred-foot fog at the Tri-City Airport was not indicative of trouble in San Gorgonio Pass; that as a matter of fact, the ceiling of fog became higher as he flew over Redlands approaching the pass; that when beyond Redlands, the pilot found it impossible to proceed by reason of a fog which was settling or had settled close to the ground and which had perhaps closed in behind him, he did that which a cautious and prudent pilot would do under the same circumstances, *i. e.,* endeavored to effect a landing and in doing so, he crashed into a hillside which the fog obscured from him until it was too late to successfully rise over it.

ately, an airplane can not be handled with the
ı as can a bicycle. The cruising speed of this
one hundred twenty miles per hour and it
nd at less than sixty miles an hour. As one
ienced witnesses said:

making a landing under the conditions that
d at this time a man has got to spot a field
n he has got to maneuver back into it, pre-
into the wind. It is very difficult to do this
og conditions. You spot your field and while
maneuvering your ship, one of these rolls of
y come along and for a time you' are flying
hen you spot your field again, such a ship as
flying you can't throw up on its ear and
a dime." [Tr. p. 33.]

nce shows that the pilot was endeavoring to
ous and prudent thing; that he was capable
iced and that in spite of it all, an accident
f the doctrine of *res ipsa loquitur* is applica-
·s a presumption of negligence, that presump-
n entirely dissipated by substantial and con-
ence that the operator of the plane exercised
degree of care. The most that can be said
doctrine creates a conflict of evidence and in
jury's verdict that conflict must be resolved
he defendant.

CONCLUSION.

The jury was fully and fairly instructed in accordance with well established principles of law. There is no presumption of negligence on the part of respondent, because the evidence does not embrace the elements upon which the doctrine of *res ipsa loquitur* is based. The fact that there is substantial evidence that respondent was not negligent should result in resolving all conflicts of evidence in favor of respondents, whether such conflicts result from presumptions or from the testimony of witnesses.

We respectfully submit that the judgment should be affirmed.

Harry D. Parker,
White McGee, Jr.,
O'Melveny, Tuller & Myers,
Walter K. Tuller,
Homer I. Mitchell,
W. Jefferson Davis,

Attorneys for Respondent.

In the United States Circuit Court of Appeals

FOR THE NINTH CIRCUIT /

UNITED STATES OF AMERICA,
                              Appellant,

   vs.

ELMER J. HILL,

                              Appellee.

Transcript of Record

Upon Appeal from the United States District Court
for the District of Oregon

Names and Addresses of Attorneys of Record:

   GEORGE NEUNER,
   United States Attorney for the District of Oregon.

REX KIMMELL,
   Assistant United States Attorney
   Federal Building, Portland, Ore.
         For Appellant.

   ALLAN A. BYNON,
      Portland, Oregon
      For Appellee.

In the United States Circuit Court of Appeals

FOR THE NINTH CIRCUIT

UNITED STATES OF AMERICA,

 Appellant,

vs.

ELMER J. HILL,

 Appellee.

Transcript of Record

Upon Appeal from the United States District Court
for the District of Oregon

Names and Addresses of Attorneys of Record:

 GEORGE NEUNER,
 United States Attorney for the District of Oregon.

REX KIMMELL,
 Assistant United States Attorney
 Federal Building, Portland, Ore.
 For Appellant.

 ALLAN A. BYNON,
 Portland, Oregon
 For Appellee.

INDEX

Page

Answer 11

Assignments of Error... 27

Bill of Exceptions 29

Citation on Appeal... 5

Complaint 7

Judgment 14

Motion for New Trial.. 16

Notice of Appeal... 26

Order Allowing Appeal.. 25

Order Allowing Appellant to and including March 10 to tender and lodge Bill of Exceptions 23

Order Denying Motion for New Trial.................... 21

Petition for Order of Appeal................................. 24

Praecipe for Transcript of Record........................ 74

Stipulation that Appellant have extension of time to March 10 to tender and lodge Bill of Exceptions 22

Stipulation as to what Transcript of Record shall contain 72

Verdict 13

DISTRICT COURT OF THE UNITED STATES OF AMERICA, DISTRICT OF OREGON

To ELMER J. HILL and ALLAN A. BYNON, his Attorney, Greeting:

WHEREAS, the United States of America has lately appealed to the United States Circuit Court of Appeals for the Ninth Circuit from a judgment rendered in the District Court of the United States for the District of Oregon, in your favor, and has given the security required by law;

YOU ARE THEREFORE HEREBY CITED AND ADMONISHED to be and appear before said United States Circuit Court of Appeals for the Ninth Circuit, at San Francisco, California, within thirty days from the date hereof, to show cause, if any there be, why the said judgment should not be corrected, and speedy justice should not be done to the parties in that behalf.

Given under my hand, at Portland, in said District, this 27 day of February, in the year of our Lord, one thousand nine hundred and thirty-two.

JAMES ALGER FEE,

Judge.

UNITED STATES OF AMERICA, ⎱
⎰ ss.
District of Oregon

Due and legal service of the within CITATION ON APPEAL is hereby admitted and accepted in the State and District of Oregon, this 26th day of February, 1932, by receiving a copy thereof, duly certified to be a true and correct copy of the original, by Rex Kimmell, Assistant United States Attorney for the District of Oregon.

ALLAN A. BYNON,
Attorney for Plaintiff.

Endorsed:

U. S. DISTRICT COURT
District of Oregon
Filed February 29, 1932
G. H. Marsh, Clerk
By F. L. Buck, Chief Deputy

IN THE DISTRICT COURT OF THE UNITED STATES FOR THE DISTRICT OF OREGON
July Term, 1930

Be It Remembered, That on the 14th day of October, 1930, there was duly filed in the District Court of the United States for the District of Oregon, a

COMPLAINT

in words and figures as follows, to-wit:

IN THE DISTRICT COURT OF THE UNITED STATES FOR THE DISTRICT OF OREGON

ELMER J. HILL,
                              Plaintiff,
        vs.
UNITED STATES OF AMERICA,
                              Defendant.

COMPLAINT

Comes now the plaintiff and for cause of action against the defendant complains and alleges:

I.

Plaintiff is now a bona fide resident and inhabitant of the County of Marion, State of Oregon, and is a citizen of the United States of America.

II.

Heretofore, and upon the 21st day of September, 1917, plaintiff joined the military forces of the United States of America and thereafter served with said military forces during the late World War and was honorably discharged from said service on or about the 4th day of April, 1919.

III.

During said service with said military forces plaintiff applied for and received a policy of War Risk Insurance from the United States of America in the sum of Five Thousand Dollars ($5,000.00), by the terms and conditions of which the defendant agreed to pay the plaintiff, in case of permanent and total disability, the sum of Twenty-eight and 75/100 Dollars ($28.75) per month during the continuation of said condition of permanent total disability, all on the condition that the plaintiff pay to the defendant premiums on said policy of insurance as as provided by law, and said premiums were duly paid by said plaintiff on said policy of insurance to and including the date of his said honorable discharge, as is hereinbefore set forth, and upon the date of his said honorable discharge said policy was in full force and effect and so continued for a period of thirty-one days thereafter.

IV.

Commencing on or about July 1, 1918, and continuing until about October 20, 1918, plaintiff suffered from exposure, deprivation and malnutrition incident to front line warfare, during which time plaintiff developed and suffered from dysentery and stomach disorders brought on by drinking gas poisoned water; thereafter, and on or about January 1, 1919, plaintiff developed and suffered from pulmonary tuberculosis; thereafter, plaintiff suffered continuously from stomach trouble and duodenal ulcers, nervousiness, weakness and sleeplessness. Said disabilities persisted and grew worse and by reason thereof plaintiff was, at the time of his said honorable discharge, permanently and totally disabled in that he was at that time, and has been at all times subsequent thereto, is now, and will ever be, unable to follow continuously any substantially gainful occupation. Said disabilities and said conditions so existing at the date of plaintiff's said honorable discharge were founded on conditions reasonably certain to prevail throughout his lifetime.

V.

Several years prior to the filing of this action, plaintiff made due proof to the defendant of his said condition of permanent and total disability as of April 4, 1919, and on February 6, 1930, demanded payment of the moneys due plaintiff under said policy of insurance, but defendant has never responded to said demand, although more than seven months have elapsed since the same was made, and by failure to acknowledge its obligations under said contract, and by failure to discharge the same, and by failure to disavow said obligations and the right of plaintiff to the payments herein demanded, and by failure and refusal to act with respect to said demand or to allow or to deny said claim, has disagreed with the plaintiff as to his claim and now disagrees with the plaintiff as to his rights under said policy of insurance which are herein set forth, and a disagreement exists between said plaintiff and said defendant by reason thereof.

WHEREFORE, plaintiff prays for judgment against the defendant that he be adjudged to have been permanently and totally disabled upon the date of his discharge and for judgment at the rate of

Twenty-eight and 75/100 Dollars ($28.75) per month from the said date of discharge, to-wit, April 4, 1919, to the date of judgment, and for plaintiff's costs and disbursements incurred herein.

(Sgd.) EMMONS, LUSK & BYNON,

Attorneys for Plaintiff.

STATE OF OREGON,
County of Multnomah, } ss.

I, ELMER J. HILL, being first duly sworn, depose and say that I am the plaintiff in the above entitled action; and that the foregoing Complaint is true, as I verily believe.

(Sgd.)   ELMER J. HILL.

Subscribed and sworn to before me this 6th day of September, 1930.

(Sgd.)   ALLAN A. BYNON,

Notary Public for the State of Oregon.

My commission expires July 8, 1931.

(Notarial Seal)

STATE OF OREGON,
County of Multnomah, } ss.

Due, timely and legal service by copy admitted at Portland, Oregon this 14th day of October, 1930.

GEORGE NEUNER, K.H.

United States District Attorney.

Endorsed:

U. S. DISTRICT COURT
District of Oregon
Filed Oct. 14, 1930
G. H. Marsh, Clerk
By F. L. Buck, Chf. Deputy

And Afterwards, to-wit, on the 4th day of February, 1931, there was duly Filed in said Court, an

ANSWER

in words and figures as follows, to-wit:

COMES NOW the United States of America, by George Neuner, United States Attorney for the District of Oregon, and Rex Kimmell, Assistant United States Attorney, and for its answer to the Bill of Complaint of plaintiff herein admits, denies and alleges as follows:

I.

Alleges that the defendant herein has no information or knowledge sufficient to enable it to form a belief as to the truth or falsity of any of the allegations contained in Paragraph I of Plaintiff's complaint and, therefore, denies the same and puts the plaintiff on proof thereof.

II.

Admits the allegations of Paragraph II of plaintiff's complaint.

III.

Answer Pargraph III of plaintiff's complaint, it

is admitted that plaintiff applied for and was granted $5,000 War Risk Insurance and that premiums were paid thereon to and including the month of April, 1919. All the other allegations of said Paragraph III are denied.

IV.

Denies the allegations of Paragraph IV of plaintiff's complaint.

WHEREFORE, defendant having fully answered plaintiff's complaint, demands that plaintiff take nothing thereby and that the defendant go hence without day and recover of and from the plaintiff its costs and disbursements herein.

GEORGE NEUNER,
United States Attorney
REX KIMMELL,
Assistant United States Attorney.

STATE OF OREGON,   } ss.
County of Multnomah,

I, Rex Kimmell, being first duly sworn, depose and say:

That I am a duly appointed, qualified and acting Assistant United States Attorney for the District of Oregon; that I am possessed of information concerning the above-named plaintiff, from which I have prepared the foregoing ANSWER; that I have prepared and read the foregoing Answer and that the allegations therein contained are true, as I verily believe.

REX KIMMELL,
Assistant United States Attorney.

Subscribed and sworn to before me this 3rd day of February, 1931.

FRANK L. BUCK,
Notary Public for Oregon.

My Commission Expires: October 16, 1932.

(Seal)

Endorsed:

U. S. DISTRICT COURT

District of Oregon

Filed Feb. 4, 1931

G. H. Marsh, Clerk

By F. L. Buck, Chf. Deputy

And Afterwards, to-wit, on the 3rd day of October, 1931, there was duly Filed in said Court, a

VERDICT

in words and figures as follows to-it:

We, the jury, duly impaneled and sworn to try the above entitled cause, do find in favor of the plaintiff and against the defendant, and find that the above named plaintiff was, on the 4th day of April, 1919, and ever since has been, totally and permanently disabled.

14

Dated at Portland, Oregon, this 2 day of October, 1931.

MILLARD A. LIBBY,

Foreman.

Endorsed:

U. S. DISTRICT COURT
District of Oregon
Filed Oct. 3, 1931
G. H. Marsh, Clerk

And Afterwards, to-wit, on Tuesday, the 6th day of October, 1931, the same being the 69th Judicial day of the Regular July Term of said Court; present the Honorable John H. McNary, United States District Judge, presiding, the following proceedings were had in said cause, to-wit:

JUDGMENT

The above entitled cause came on regularly to be heard on the 2nd day of October, 1931, before the Honorable John H. McNary, Judge of the above entitled Court, plaintiff appearing in person and by his counsel, Allan A. Bynon, the defendant, United States of America, appearing by its counsel, Rex Kimmel, Metta G. Walker and Francis Wade, a jury having been duly impaneled and sworn to try said cause, the opening statements of counsel having been made, witnesses having been sworn and heard, the closing arguments of respective counsel having been made, the jury, having been instructed by the Court, did, upon the 2nd day of October, 1931, return its verdict that the plaintiff, above named, was, upon the 4th day of April, 1919, and ever since has been and is now totally and permanently disabled;

NOW, THEREFORE, the Court, being advised in the premises, and according to said verdict, does enter its judgment; and

IT IS ORDERED AND ADJUDGED that Elmer J. Hill became totally and permanently disabled upon the 4th day of April, 1919, and ever since said date has been and now is permanently and totally disabled, and judgment is entered herein in favor of the plaintiff, and against the defendant, United States of America, and that there is now due said Elmer J. Hill upon said policy of War Risk Insurance carried by him which is referred to in the Complaint herein, the accrued payments of Twenty-eight and 75/100 Dollars ($28.75) per month from the 4th day of April, 1919, until this date; and

IT IS FURTHER ORDERED AND ADJUDGED that there be and hereby is allowed to said plaintiff's attorney, Allan A. Bynon, as a reasonable attorney's fee herein, ten per centum of the amount recovered by the plaintiff herein, that is to say, ten per centum of each payment the plaintiff shall hereunder and hereafter collect from such insurance, to be paid to

16

said Allan A. Bynon by the Veterans' Bureau of the United States out of the payments to be made under this judgment at the rate of one-tenth of each such payments;

AND IT IS SO ORDERED.

Dated this 6th day of October, 1931.

(Sgd.)   JOHN H. McNARY,

Judge.

Endorsed:

U. S. DISTRICT COURT
District of Oregon
Filed Oct. 6, 1931
G. H. Marsh, Clerk
By H. S. Kenyon, Deputy

And Afterwards, to-wit, on the 30th day of October, 1931, there was duly Filed in said Court, a

MOTION FOR NEW TRIAL

in words and figures as follows, to-wit:

COMES NOW the defendant, United States of America, by George Neuner, United States Attorney for the District of Oregon, and Rex Kimmell, Assistant United States Attorney, and moves the court for an order setting aside the verdict heretofore rendered by the jury in the above-entitled cause on the 22d day of October, 1931, and the judgment rendered on said verdict on said 22d day of October, and granting said defendant a new trial on the following grounds:

(1) On the ground that the court erred in overruling and disallowing defendant's motion for an order directing the jury to return a verdict for the defendant, which motion was made at the conclusion of all the evidence and after both, the plaintiff and defendant, had rested their case, and which motion was based upon the ground that the evidence failed to show that plaintiff was totally and permanently disabled at any time during the life of his policy of war risk insurance;

(2) On the further ground that said verdict and judgment are against the law and evidence in the case, for the reason that the evidence on behalf of plaintiff showed affirmatively and conclusively that plaintiff was not totally and permanently disabled or totally or permanently disabled at the time his policy of war risk insurance lapsed;

(3) On the ground that since the trial of said cause defendant has discovered evidence which was not available and was not known to exist at the time of or prior to said trial, and that such newly discovered evidence is material and when introduced will probably have the effect of changing the result of the trial.

This motion, insofar as the ground of newly discovered evidence is concerned, is supported by the affidavit attached hereto and made a part hereof.

GEORGE NEUNER,
United States Attorney for the
District of Oregon.

REX KIMMELL,
Assistant United States Attorney.

STATE OF OREGON, $\left.\right\}$ ss.

County of Multnomah.

I, Francis T. Wade, being first duly sworn, on oath depose and say:

That on or about the 15th day of June, 1931, I directed a letter to the Regional Manager of the Veterans' Bureau at Buffalo, New York, directing that the activities of Elmer J. Hill in that vicinity during the years, 1921, 1922, and 1923, be investigated and a report made as soon as possible;

That on or about the 1st day of September, 1931, I addressed a special delivery, air mail letter to the Regional Attorney at Philadelphia, Pennsylvania, instructing an investigation of the activities and work of Elmer J. Hill in and about art schools in Philadelphia and in particular to contact one Frank Godwin, artist;

That on September 28, 1931, I received a communication from the Regional Attorney at Newington, Connecticut, stating that an effort had been made to contact Mr. Godwin by calling at his address in Riverside, Connecticut, which place is located in the extreme eastern end of the State of Connecticut, but it was found that Mr. Godwin was away and could not be contacted;

That on October 2, 1931, a day after the trial of the case of Elmer J. Hill vs. United States, I received a communication from the Regional Attorney at Buffalo, New York, enclosing a report of the Field Examiner from that office, which stated that the witness, Mr. Frank Godwin, had been contacted, after considerable difficulty, at his summer cottage on Lake Skaneateles, in the State of New York;

That the report of the Field Examiner above referred to, who interviewed Mr. Godwin, states that Mr. Godwin furnished substantially the following information:

In the year 1922, Mr. Godwin was instructing a class of fifty or sixty World War Veterans, who were then receiving vocational training as artists and illustrators at La Porte, Pennsylvania; that at that time he was well acquainted with one Jack Hill, who was not in the class but who was working about the studios; that in March or April of 1923 Hill called at the studio of Mr. Godwin in Philadelphia and asked for a job as an artist model at Mr. Godwin's summer home in the mountains, where Mr. Godwin was doing considerable painting at that time; that Hill stated to Mr. Godwin that he had been an acrobat in a circus and he wanted to keep in shape and do some training; that Mr. Godwin employed Hill and took him to his summer home, where Hill procured an old barn, which he turned into a gymnasium and while there used it for the purpose of training and physical culture.

Mr. Godwin further stated that Hill had an excellent physique, large and well-developed shoulders, slender waist and legs, and that during that time Hill worked for him as a model, posing for numerous pictures, among others being that of a pirate in illustrations for "Treasure Island," and that during that time Hill appeared to be in very good health and made no complaint of any ailment; that Hill was with Mr. Godwin during the entire summer of 1923, during which time he also posed for other artists; for his work as artist model Hill was paid $1 per hour.

As the plaintiff, at the time of the trial of this case, testified that he was working in and around the studios of Philadelphia at that time, there is no question but that he is the Jack Hill referred to by Mr. Godwin;

In the event a new trial is granted in this case,

I believe that Mr. Godwin will testify substantially as hereinabove set out, and such testimony would materially affect the result of the trial.

FRANCIS T. WADE,

Subscribed and sworn to before me this 30 day of Oct., 1931.

J. W. McCULLOCH,
Notary Public for Oregon.

My commission expires June 23, 1935.

(Seal)

Endorsed:

U. S. DISTRICT COURT

District of Oregon

Filed Oct. 30, 1931

G. H. Marsh, Clerk

By F. L. Buck, Chief Deputy

And Afterwards, to-wit, on Monday, the 30th day of November, 1931, the same being the 20th Judicial day of the Regular November Term of said Court; present the Honorable John H. McNary, United States District Judge, presiding, the following proceedings were had in said cause, to-wit:

Now at this day comes the plaintiff by Mr. Allan A. Bynon, of counsel, and the defendant by Mr. Rex Kimmell, Assistant United States Attorney, whereupon this cause comes on to be heard upon the motion of the defendant for a new trial herein. And the Court having heard the argument of counsel and being now fully advised in the premises,

IT IS ORDERED that the said motion be and the same is hereby denied, to which ruling of the court defendant excepts and its exception is allowed.

And Afterwards, to-wit, on the 4th day of March, 1932, there was duly Filed in said Court, a

STIPULATION

in words and figures as follows, to-wit:

IT IS HEREBY STIPULATED by and between the plaintiff, through Allan A. Bynon, his attorney, and the defendant, through Rex Kimmell, Assistant United States Attorney, that the defendant may have a further extension of time within which to tender and file the bill of exceptions herein to and including the 10th day of March, 1932.

ALLAN A. BYNON,
Attorney for Plaintiff.
REX KIMMELL,
Assistant United States Attorney,
Attorney for Defendant.

Endorsed:
U. S. DISTRICT COURT
District of Oregon
Filed March 4, 1932
G. H. Marsh, Clerk
By F. L. Buck, Chief Deputy

And Afterwards, to-wit, on Friday, the 4th day of March, 1932, the same being the 97th Judicial day of the Regular November Term of said Court; present the Honorable John H. McNary, United States District Judge, presiding, the following proceedings were had in said cause, to-wit:

ORDER EXTENDING TIME WITHIN WHICH TO TENDER AND LODGE BILL OF EXCEPTIONS

PURSUANT to Stipulation heretofore entered into by the parties,

IT IS HEREBY ORDERED, ADJUDGED AND DECREED that the time within which defendant may tender a Bill of Exceptions herein be and the same hereby is extended to and including the 10th day of March, 1932, and the Court does hereby waive the rule requiring the Bill of Exceptions to be tendered and lodged within ten days after judgment and retains jurisdiction to settle said Bill of Exceptions to and including March 10, 1932.

JOHN H. McNARY,
District Judge.

Endorsed:
U. S. DISTRICT COURT
District of Oregon
Filed March 4, 1932
G. H. Marsh, Clerk
By F. L. Buck, Chief Deputy

And Afterwards, to-wit, on the 27th day of February, 1932, there was duly Filed in said Court, a

PETITION FOR ORDER OF APPEAL

in words and figures as follows, to-wit:

The above-named defendant, United States of America, conceiving itself aggrieved by the judgment filed and entered on the 6th day of October, 1931, in the above-entitled action, does hereby appeal from said judgment, and the whole thereof, to the United States Circuit Court of Appeals for the Ninth Judicial Circuit, for the reason and upon the ground specified in the assignment of error filed herewith, and prays that this, its appeal, be allowed; that a citation issue as provided by law, and that a transcript of the record and proceedings of said cause, duly authenticated, may be sent to the United States Circuit Court of Appeals for the Ninth Judicial Circuit, sitting at San Francisco, California.

Dated at Portland, Oregon, this 26 day of February, 1932.

GEORGE NEUNER,
United States Attorney for the
District of Oregon.
REX KIMMELL,
Assistant United States Attorney.

Endorsed:

U. S. DISTRICT COURT
District of Oregon

Filed Feb. 27, 1932

G. H. Marsh, Clerk

By F. L. Buck, Chief Deputy

And Afterwards, to-wit, on Saturday, the 27th day of February, 1932, the same being the 92nd Judicial day of the Regular November Term of said Court; present the Honorable James Alger Fee, United States District Judge, presiding, the following proceedings were had in said cause, to-wit:

ORDER ALLOWING APPEAL

Upon petition of the United States of America, defendant in the above-entitled cause,

IT IS ORDERED that the appeal of said defendant from the judgment herein to the United States Circuit Court of Appeals for the Ninth Circuit be, and the same is hereby, allowed.

Dated at Portland, Oregon, this 27 day of February, 1932.

JAMES ALGER FEE,

Judge.

Endorsed:

U. S. DISTRICT COURT

District of Oregon

Filed Feb. 27, 1932

G. H. Marsh, Clerk

By F. L. Buck, Chief Deputy

And Afterwards, to-wit, on the 27th day of February, 1932, there was duly Filed in said Court, a

NOTICE OF APPEAL

in words and figures as follows, to-wit:

To the above-named Plaintiff, ELMER J. HILL, and
    his Attorney, ALLAN A. BYNON:

You and each of you, will take notice that the
defendant, United States of America, appeals to the
United States Circuit Court of Appeals for the Ninth
Circuit from that certain judgment and decree made
and entered in the above-entitled cause and court and
signed by the Honorable John H. McNary, one of the
judges of said District Court, on the 6th day of
October, 1931, which judgment and decree was and
is to the effect that the plaintiff, Elmer J. Hill, became totally and permanently disabled upon the 4th
day of April, 1919, and ever since said date has been
and now is permanently and totally disabled, and
that judgment be entered in favor of the plaintiff,
and against the defendant, The United States of
America, and that there are now due the said Elmer
J. Hill upon the policy of War Risk Insurance carried by him the accrued payments of Twenty-eight
and 75/100 ($28.75) Dollars per month from the
4th day of April, 1919, and the defendant appeals
from the whole of said judgment and decree.

Dated this 26 day of February, 1932.

GEORGE NEUNER,

United States Attorney for the

District of Oregon.

REX KIMMELL,

Assistant United States Attorney.

Endorsed:

U. S. DISTRICT COURT

District of Oregon

Filed Feb. 27, 1932

G. H. Marsh, Clerk

By F. L. Buck, Chief Deputy

And Afterwards, to-wit, on the 27th day of February, 1932, there was duly Filed in said Court

ASSIGNMENTS OF ERROR

in words and figures as follows, to-wit:

The United States of America being the defendant in the above-entitled cause and appearing by George Neuner, United States Attorney for the District of Oregon, and Rex Kimmell, Assistant United States Attorney, and having filed its notice of appeal as required by law, that the defendant appeals to the United States Circuit Court of Appeals for the Ninth Circuit from the final order and judgment made and entered in said cause against said defendant herein, now makes and files, in support of said appeal, the following Assignments of Error upon which it will rely for a reversal of said final order and judgment upon the said appeal and which said error is to the great detriment, injury and prejudice of this defendant, and said defendant says that in the records and proceedings upon the hearing and determination thereof in the District Court of the United States for the District of Oregon, there is manifest error in this, to-wit:

I.

That the Court erred in overruling the motion of the defendant for a directed verdict, for the reason that the evidence adduced at the trial of the above-entitled cause was insufficient to justify a verdict for the plaintiff.

II.

That the Court erred in overruling the motion for a directed verdict for the reason that the evidence adduced at the trial of the above entitled cause establishes the fact that plaintiff was not permanently and totally, nor permanently or totally, disabled on or before the 4th day of April, 1919, or at any time during the life of his contract of War Risk Insurance upon which this action is predicated.

WHEREFORE, on account of the errors above assigned, defendant prays that the judgment of this Court be reversed and that this case be remanded to said District Court and that such directions be given that the above errors may be corrected and law and justice be done in the matter.

Dated at Portland, Oregon, this 26th day of

February, 1932.

> GEORGE NEUNER,
>> United States Attorney for the
>> District of Oregon.
>
> REX KIMMELL,
>> Assistant United States Attorney.

Endorsed:

U. S. DISTRICT COURT

District of Oregon

Filed Feb. 27, 1932

G. H. Marsh, Clerk

By F. L. Buck, Chief Deputy

And Afterwards, to-wit, on the 15th day of March, 1932, there was duly Filed in said Court, a

BILL OF EXCEPTIONS

in words and figures as follows, to-wit:

BE IT REMEMBERED: That on the 21st day of October, 1931, at 10 o'clock A.M., the above-entitled cause came on for trial before John H. McNary, District Judge, Allan A. Bynon, appearing as attorney for plaintiff, and Rex Kimmell, Assistant United States Attorney for the District of Oregon, and Francis T. Wade, of the United States Veterans Bureau, appearing as attorneys for defendant;

WHEREUPON the following proceedings were had:

ELMER J. HILL, called and sworn as a witness in

his own behalf, testified as follows:

(Direct Examination by Mr. Bynon.)

I am Elmer J. Hill, the plaintiff, and live at Williams, in Josephine County, Oregon. I have been residing in Oregon a year, and am now residing here, and expect to reside here.

When I entered the service for the World War I lived at Herkimer, New York. Before that time I worked on farms, and construction companies. I had an eighth grade education.

I went overseas with the 303rd Infantry, 76th Division. I was transferred to the First Division, 18th Infantry.

(Plaintiff's Exhibit "A" admitted without objection — Copy of Discharge Certificate.)

Following is a substantial copy of Plaintiff's Exhibit "A":

HONORABLE DISCHARGE FROM
THE UNITED STATES ARMY
TO ALL WHOM IT MAY CONCERN:

This is to certify, That Elmer J. Hill 1659940, Pvt. Co. D, 18th Infantry — Thru 12th Co. 152nd D.B., THE UNITED STATES ARMY, as a Testimonial of Honest and Faithful Service is hereby HONORABLY DISCHARGED from the military service of the United States by reason of Cir. No. 73

Nov. 18, 1919.

Said Elmer J. Hill was born in Johnstown, in the State of N.Y.; when enlisted he was 22 years of age, and by occupation a Am. Worker; he had Blue eyes; Brown hair, Medium complexion, and was 5 feet 7 inches in height.

Given under my hand at Camp Upton, N.Y., this 4th day of April, one thousand nine hundred and nineteen.

JAMES F. COOPER,

Major Infanrty, Commanding.

(Reverse Side)

Name: Elmer J. Hill.   Grade: Private.

Enlisted or Inducted: Sept. 21, 1917, at Herkimer, N. Y.

Serving in First enlistment period at date of discharge.

Battles, engagements, skirmishes, expeditions:
St. Mihiel, Verdun, Argonne.

Knowledge of any vocation: Am. Worker.

Wounds received in service: None.

Physical condition when discharged: Good.

Character: Excellent.

Remarks: No AWOL under GO 31-12 and GO 4514
Co. A 303 Inf 9-22-17 to 8-6-18; Co. B 162 Inf. 8-6-18 to 8-14-18; Co. D 18th Inf. and Casual Co. S 8-14-18 to date of discharge.

Signature of soldier: Elmer J. Hill.

E. P. CJRISTOPHERSON,
Captain Infantry
Commanding 12th Co. 152nd D. Bn.

(Continuing testimony of Elmer J. Hill) When we arrived overseas my organization was first sent to the Toule Sector, and was moved from there to Saint Mihiel.

I participated in that offensive and was in the infantry and was in the front line. While there I was exposed all the time; in mud and water; several days without any rest, and part of the time we had no food. There was active fighting at that time; we was through the whole thing there. Altogether, I was in active front line service about three weeks.

My organization was moved from Saint Mihiel to the Verdun sector. I became sick at Verdun, and was sent to the receiving station.

I was taken out of the front line service and sent away just before I got to Verdun. Just before I was taken away from the front line I had dysentery, high fever and a kind of nervous breakdown. I was under lots of shell fire during my front line service.

I got dysentery from drinking poisoned water in the Saint Mihiel sector — in the Saint Mihiel Battle. This water was in a hole that was supposed to be a well, but it was night and we were all thirsty and hadn't had a drink for quite a while, so we took a drink to satisfy our thirst. I became violently sick to my stomach a couple of hours after, and after that I contracted a bad case of dysentery which lasted about six weeks altogether. In connection with that I was sent to Base 23.

(Plaintiff's Exhibit "B" was admitted in evidence without objection.)

Plaintiff's Exhibit "B" consists of photostatic copies of A.G.O. records concerning Elmer J. Hill during the time he was in the United States Army. The record shows the following pertinent facts:

Physical Examination under the Selective Service Act of May 18, 1917

Statement of Person Examined

Have you found that your health and habits in any way interfere with your success in civil life? If so, give details: No.

Do you consider that you are now sound and well? If not, state details: No, do not know.

Have you ever been under treatment in a hospital or asylum? If so, for what ailment? No.

I certify that the foregoing questions and my answers thereto have been read over to me; that I fully understand the questions and that my answers thereto are correctly recorded and true in all respects.

ELMER HILL.

R. P. HUYEK, M.D.
Examining Physician.

Place: Herkimer.
Date: Aug. 7, 1917.

Physical Examination by Examining Physician of Local Board

Weight, 141 lbs; height 5-ft, 7-in.

Girth of chest: at Expiration 32 inches.

at Inspiration 35 inches.

Head, chest, abdomen, extremities, nose and throat, heart, genito-urinary organs: Normal.
No hernia or hemorrhoids: No flat feet or other deformities of feet.

I certify that I have carefully examined the person named on the first page hereof and have carefully recorded the results of the examination, and that it is my judgment and belief that he is physically qualified for military service.

R. P. HUYEK, M.D.
Examining Physician.

Place: Herkimer.
Date: Aug. 7, 1917.

Physical Examination at Place of Mobilization

Weight, 141 lbs.; height, 67 inches.

Girth of chest: At expiration, 32 inches.

At inspiration, 35 inches.

Head, chest, abdomen, extremities, nose and

throat, heart: Normal.

Genito-urinary organs: DK left varicocele.

No hernia, hemorrhoids, flat foot or other deformities of feet.

I certify that I have carefully examined the person named on the first page hereof and have carefully recorded the results of the examination, and that it is my judgment and belief that he is physically qualified for military service. All defects noted existed prior to enlistment.

LEE F. HUNT,
Capt. M. R. C.

Place: Camp Devens, Mass.

Date: Sept. 24, 1917.

REGISTER INDEX CARD

Hill, Elmer J.

Pvt. D, 18 Infantry.

Age, 23 yrs; Race, W.; Nativity, N.Y.; Service 1-1/12 yrs.

Register No. 1659940.

Date of Admission, Oct. 1, 1918.

Source of Admission, Souilly.

Transferred from Fr San Tr No. 24.

Cause of admission: Dysentery, acute.

In Line of Duty? Yes.

Oct. 3, 1918. Change Influenza, acute.

Disposition: Duty APO 712 Nov. 22, 1918.

U.S.A. BASE HOSPITAL No. 23, A.E.F.

E.J.F.

1st Lieut. San C.

Days of Treatment in Current Case

Current Year

	In Hospital
October	31
November	21
Total	52

FIELD MEDICAL CARD

Name, Rank, etc.

Sick

Line of Duty

Base Hospital No. 23

Diagnosis: Dysentery

Change to Influenza, ac. Oct. 3, 1918

Date of Entry: Oct. 1, 1918

Patient complains of a severe diarrhea; passed some blood

Diag. Dysentery

Nov. 7: (Reference to treatment)

11-16-18 Has had no diarrhea in 7 days. Is in good condition. Has been working in kitchen. To duty 11-22-18.

H. F. May, Capt. M.C.

Report of Physical Examination of Enlisted Man Prior to Separation from Service in the United States Army

Hill, Elmer J. 1659940 Pvt. Co. D, 18 Inf.
Occupation Prior to entry into service:
Am. Worker.

Declaration of Soldier

Have you any reason to believe that at the present time you are suffering from the effects of any wound, injury, or disease, or that you have any disability or impairment of health, whether or not incurred in the military service?
No.
(Stamped on). Soldier did not desire to execute Form 526 B.W.R.

I declare that the foregoing questions and my answers thereto have been read over to me, and that I fully understand the questions, and that my replies to them are true in every respect and are correctly recorded.

ELMER J. HILL.
Witness:
Henry A. Potter, 2nd Lt. Inf.
Place: Camp Upton, N.Y. Apr. 2, 1919.

Certificate of Immediate Commanding Officer

I CERTIFY THAT: Aside from his own statement I do not know, nor have I any reason to believe, that the soldier who made and signed the foregoing declaration has a wound, injury or disease at the present time, whether or not incurred in the military service of the United States.

HENRY A. POTTER,

Commanding.

Apr. 2, 1919.

Certificate of Examining Surgeon

I CERTIFY THAT: The soldier named above has this date been given a careful physical examination, and it is found that he is physically and mentally sound.

R. G. PORTER,

1st Lt.

Camp Upton, N.Y. Apr. 2, 1919.

REPORT OF BOARD OF REVIEW

Not executed, except it has stamp "Soldier did not desire to execute Form 526 B.W.R."

(Continuing testimony of Elmer J. Hill) I had influenza, and was laid up with that about two weeks.

"Q. When did you first discover you were suffering from nervousness?

A. At the hospital at

Q. How did you happen to know you were suffering from nervousness?

A. I couldn't stay still.

Q. What brought that on you?

A. High explosives; high explosive shells."

I believe I returned to the United States the 25th of March. I was discharged April 4, 1919, and after I was discharged I went home to Herkimer, New York.

At the time I was discharged I was suffering from nervousness, stomach trouble, and I had a bad chest condition. I didn't have any more dysentery for quite a while after I was discharged. I had a hemorrhage a few years later. Doctors at the hospital where I was at told me it came from the effects of the dysentery I had had previously.

"Q. Your condition at the time you got out of service, you allege pulmonary tuberculosis. Did you know at that time you had it?

A. I didn't know it until the doctor told me.

Q. What were your symptoms on April 4th, 1919? Tell us how you felt.

A. I had a fever all the time. I used to have awful sweats at night. I coughed a whole lot, and expectorated; lots of times my sputum was tinged with blood."

The first thing I did after I got back into civil life was to go to Detroit to see my sister. It was six weeks before I attempted a job, and during that six weeks I rested.

I first took a job with the Studebaker and stayed there about two months. During those two months I lost a few days, because I didn't feel like working. I ceased work for the Studebaker people because I couldn't stand the work; too much smoke.

I rested up a while at my sister's, and then I took a job with the Dodge people. To the best of my belief I don't believe I worked for them over two weeks. I had to leave there for the same reason.

I next worked at the Ford plant, Highland Park. I worked there ten weeks, during which I lost a little time on account of sickness.

There was quite a long interval between the time I ceased work for the Dodge people and went to work for Ford.

I quit working for Ford because the work was too hard. It was on a punch press, drill press.

After that I went to work for the Cadillac Company, and worked, I think, about six weeks. I did not work steadily six weeks; I lost time. I ceased work for the Cadillac people because the work was too hard; so much smoke and gas.

The gas and smoke nauseated me, and made my chest condition worse.

"Q. What did you do about that chest condition?

A. I thought I better go where I could get more

fresh air.

Q. Where did you go; what did you do?

A. I went back east; I went to the lumber woods in Northern New York State."

I was there about a month. I felt better, but I couldn't stand the work; it was too hard.

Then I came back to Detroit, and stayed around there for a while. I didn't do any work there.

I saw Dr. Hyatt after I got out of the service. He was located in Herkimer, New York. I did not get any treatment under Dr. Hyatt.
"Q. When did you start any treatment?

A. Well, I never had any treatment."

After I consulted with Dr. Hyatt I went to Arizona. I stayed there two years. I didn't do anything down there; I went down there for my health, to cure this t.b.

I went to work for a washing machine outfit; I didn't make good. I met another fellow who was a pioneer representative. He was going to Prescott, and he told me he would give me a job if I would go to Prescott. That was known to be the best place in Arizona for a t.b. condition, so I went with him and tried it for a while; but riding over the rough roads, going from house to house, was too much for me. I couldn't stand it, and finally gave that up too. I came back and contracted a case of eczema on both feet. I went to the hospital, and they examined me and sent me to the Presidio, San Francisco, and I stayed there all winter. It was while I was there I started to receive compensation.

To the best of my knowledge, I was in the Letterman General Hospital in 1926. After that I went back to Pennsylvania, and lived with my wife's people about a year.

I worked on a couple of farms, and then I took a job in the Pennsylvania Highway Department. During that year, working for the Pennsylvania Highway and working on a farm, I made about $300.

"Q. How long did you work any one time continuously, without interruption? A. About a week.

Q. Did you have any other employment of any kind that brought you any substantial returns from then until you came to Oregon?

A. Yes, I had a job in South Bend, where I worked for the Banks Brake Company about two weeks.

Q. South Bend, Indiana? A. Yes.

Q. Was there any other job?

A. I went to Indianapolis and went to work for the Marmon people.

Q. How long did you work there for the Marmon company?

A. About four weeks.

Q. Why did you quit that work?

A. I couldn't stand it."

On my way out here I stopped in Jerome, Idaho, and worked about two weeks. At that time I was suffering continually from stomach trouble.

"Q. How does that stomach trouble affect you? Tell us what it does to you.

A. I have gnawing pains all the time; I can't sleep nights, and after I eat I have all kinds of distress and agony.

Q. Have you had that pain since you were in France?

A. No. (?)

Q. When did it start?

A. I had it at intervals off and on the last eight years."

I had this stomach trouble in France; it started at the receiving station in Souile when I was in there for treatment. I did not have it before I went into the service. I did not have any pulmonary trouble before I entered the service.

Idaho was my last employment before I came to Oregon. The next job I had was for six weeks for a contractor named Miles Stuper at Grants Pass,

Oregon. They were building new water works down there. I worked every day for six weeks.

At the end of that time I was ready to collapse. My stomach condition became so bad that I couldn't stand it to work any longer. There was work for me if I could have continued, but it just happened the day I was going to quit the job, they built a pile driver and had two men to drive the piling, and only two men could do it, so they laid me off. Since then I haven't had any jobs in Oregon.

I went to Williams, Josephine County, to live because I couldn't afford to live in town. I didn't have to pay anything for wood out there, and I got my water free. Another reason I went out there to live is it is high out there where I am living. I feel a little bit better when I am there.

"MR. BYNON: It is stipulated that there is a disagreement existing between us, Your Honor."

(Cross Examination by Mr. Kimmell.)

I was discharged regularly with the other soldiers in my oufit and at the same time.

At the time of my discharge my condition was not good. We were lined up and were all examined at that time. I made no complaint to anyone about my physical condition at that time.

The first time I made any complaint about my

physical condition was to Dr. Ralph P. Hyatt. He was not connected with the government at that time.

The first time I notified the government of any disability of any kind was in 1921, to the best of my belief. That was in Detroit, Michigan. They sent me to the Great Lakes Naval Training Station 30 days for observation. I was in Great Lakes 30 days for observation and was released at the end of that 30 days without treatment. They didn't give me any treatment.

The first place I went after I got out of the service was Detroit. I was discharged at Camp Upton, Long Island.

"Q. I assume you were in Detroit within a week or two, were you?

A. No; I didn't go to Detroit right away. I stayed around home and rested up for quite a while."

My home was in New York State. I left home and went to visit my sister in Detroit. I did not go to Detroit for the purpose of obtaining work with the automobile companies there. I had not worked there before I went into the service. I went to Detroit to see my sister. I hadn't seen her for a long time.

To the best of my knowledge I went to work for the Studebaker Company in about six weeks; not six weeks after I was discharged, it was over two months after I was discharged before I went to work.

I had to wait about a week after I made application before I went to work.

I was with the Studebaker Company for the purpose of learning the business—motor business—and I used to help make tests on motors. There was no strenuous labor connected with making these tests. During the two months I was there I didn't do anything else but help make these tests.

Then I went to work a while for the Dodge people. I had to rest up a while after my work with the Studebaker Company before I went to work with Dodge.

There was too much gas and smoke at the Studebaker Company; I couldn't stand that.

Then I applied for work with the Dodge Company. It was a different kind of work. I was on light repair; that is where they take the cars for final test, before they send them to the proving ground; just had to get in and drive them around. All I did was drive them around. Besides driving the cars around we had to check up on the transmission, and if they were noisy we had to take the top off and use a little hammer on the gears. It wasn't much of a job; that is about all there was to it. There was not a great deal of work connected with that.

I worked there about two weeks. I couldn't stand that work either; I couldn't stand the smoke. There is gas and smoke in connection with that work at times, because they may have two or three cars running at the same time. The reason I couldn't stand the work was because of the gas and smoke.

Then I applied to the Ford people after I left there. At the Ford plant I ran a drill press and punch press. One reason I had to leave there was because the work was too hard for me. They kept changing us from days to nights. I got run down so bad I had to leave.

I was there ten weeks. That was mostly foot work. I had to stand up all the time. There was some gas and smoke around there, but not to any great extent. It didn't bother me so much around the Ford plant. It was the standing up and using my feet that bothered me there. I used to get so tired I couldn't carry on.

To the best of my belief, I think it was 1922 — '21 or 22 — that I left the Ford plant. It was before I was in the Great Lakes Hospital under observation.

I ran a wet grinder when I was with the Cadillac people. I had a job cutting — that is a Gleason cutter, sort of a gear cutter. I had to stand up on that job.

After I left the Ford plant I didn't go to the Cadillac people for some time. I was sick, and thought I better rest up. That was before I was at the Great Lakes Hospital. All of these places were before I went to the Great Lakes Hospital for observation.

"Q. What were you receiving in wages about this time? Was it about the same at all these places?

A. Approximately, yes.

Q. What were you being paid there?

A. Well, the Studebaker, I used to get — I got $25 a week while I was there. And at the Ford it ran a little more than that at the Ford. And the Cadillac was about the same; and Dodge Brothers was a little less than that."

When I left there, first went to Chicago, Great Lakes Veterans' Hospital, for observation. When I left the hospital I came back to Detroit. I did not work for any of these companies in Detroit after I got out of the hospital.

From Detroit I went back East for a while — Little Falls, New York. I went back to see my brother. I did not work for my brother there. He was not farming.

I did not do any work while I was in New York,

before I went to Arizona. I didn't work on a farm there.

I was married at that time. I was married after I got out of the service, while I was in Detroit; about a year after I got out of the service.

I stayed in New York — around Little Falls — about two months. I was not treating with any physician while I was at Little Falls for the disability I am claiming here.

From Little Falls I believe I went to Philadelphia, where I worked for a couple of art schools. I was just working in the school, helping to straighten the class rooms, doing janitor work. I worked in these art schools off and on about three months.

The only treatments I took for my condition during that time was what I took myself. I used to buy medicine. I had two or three examinations in Philadelphia, but they never gave me any treatment; that was for the chest condition. I had two or three examinations by physicians connected with the Veterans' Bureau; they sent for me every little while because I had applied for compensation. But I didn't receive any treatment while I was there.

"Q. Is that when you went to the Northern New York woods, when you left Philadelphia?

A. No, that wasn't when I went up there.

Q. Where did you go?

A. When I left New York I came west.

Q. Had you been up on this job in the woods of Northern New York prior to the time you first came west, that you testified about?   A.   Yes.

Q. That was before you went to Philadelphia?

A. Yes sir.

Q. Before you went to Little Falls?

A. Yes sir.

Q. You went from Detroit up to that job there?

A. Yes sir.

Q. About how long were you up there?

A. In the woods?

Q. Yes.   A.   I was up there about a month.

Q. What were you doing there?   Falling trees?

A. No, I worked in a lumber camp; I was helping a lumber scaler."

Before I went into service I worked in the camp of a construction company at Bangor, Maine. I have no trade; I was just a laborer. I had worked for the construction company about four weeks before I went into the service.

I came to Arizona after I left Philadelphia.   The

only thing I did there was trying to sell washing machines. I had never tried salesman work before. I did not have any success at that.

"Q. Did you make any money at it?

A. When I got to Prescott this representative gave me some prospects to go and see. He knew they were good ones. I made a little on the work for him; I made about $75.

Q. How long were you working to make that $75?

A. That was about four or five months.

Q. During all that time were you calling on customers? It was just because you didn't have the ability to sell them; is that the idea?

A. I don't get you.

Q. Were you trying to sell machines, calling on customers all that four months?

A. No; part of the time I would have to lay in and rest up.

Q. How were you traveling at that time?

A. The representative had a car. He used to take me to a town, and go on to the next one. I would stay there and try to work that town."

I stayed in Arizona about two years altogether. Then I went east to see a brother at Flint, Michigan. I went back to see a brother there that was ill, and after I got back there I was taken ill myself.

I had a car when I went back there. I went back there and stayed about a year. It was in '26 when I left there. That was after I had been in Letterman's Hospital.

I went to Letterman's Hospital for eczema. I did not contract that in service. I got that down in Arizona or California, just a short time before I went to the hospital. I was in Letterman's Hospital, I believe, about six or seven weeks altogether.

While I was there they gave me treatment for eczema and not for anything else. I was not under observation and had no general physical examinations while I was there.

They wanted to take my tonsils out. I had a bad throat condition, and I caught a cold about two or three days before they could take them out, and I wouldn't let them take them out.

The only thing I complained of and asked treatment for while I was in the hospital was tonsils and eczema.

After I left my brother in Flint I came to Jerome, Idaho, where I took a job on a farm. That was in the summer time. I didn't work there very long; about two weeks.

Then I came on to Oregon. At this time I was

driving. I had my family with me. My wife has been with me on all these trips west I made.

I first came into Oregon two years ago, into The Dalles. I lived there a week or so, working in a garage.

Then I left and came to Portland, arriving in the fall of 1929. I first applied for work at Swenson's Employment Agency. They couldn't do anything for me. I used to get a job a day or two around in a garage. Jobs were kind of hard to find at that time. I did some work at different times in different garages.

"Q. About how long did that continue in Portland before you left?

A. Then about four months before I left. I had nothing to do for about four months before I left.

Q. How long were you in Portland altogether?

A. I came here in the fall, and left next spring.

Q. Came here in the fall of 1929, and left in the spring of 1930?   A. Yes.

Q. That four months you couldn't get a job?

A. I wasn't able to work.

Q. Did you apply for work any place?

A. Yes; once in a while I would go out and try to

find a job."

When I left here in the spring of 1930 I did not go right down to Williams; I went to Oakland. I took the stage down to Oakland. I had my family with me.

I got to Oakland in the spring and stayed until fall — the fall of 1930. Then I came to Grants Pass, where I worked about six weeks for Miles Stuber. I was receiving 50c an hour on that job.

I had two short jobs while I was in Oakland the winter of '29 and '30· I did not go down there to look for work. I went down to see if the climate would do me any good. It was so damp and cold here I began to feel bad again. I went down there to try that climate down there.

It must have been about April I left to go down there — April, 1930. I had never been in Oakland before, but had been in San Francisco.

Then I came back to Grants Pass and did that work for Mr. Stuber. I did not do any other work in Grants Pass. Then I went from there to Williams.

I live about five miles from Williams. It is not a farm. It used to be a homestead; it is a dry farm, no stock or anything on it. I do not cultivate any of it. It was a homestead relinquishment. I got it this spring.

When I went into the service I weighed 175, to the best of my knowledge. When I got out of the service I believe I weighed 140. I weigh about 165 now.

"Q. You said the first time your stomach bothered you was over at that well. Did all of you drink out of that well?

A. No, there was only about four of us drank out of that.

Q. How long was it before you began to have those pains. I understood it was after you got out of service.

A. No, I got those pains after I drank the water. They lasted about six weeks, then I didn't have any more until some time after that.

Q. Until some time after that?

A. No; I didn't have any more dysentery until some time after."

I would say it came back in '26· That was the first time I had dysentery after that.

"Q. Where was the first place you started taking treatments after you got out of the service?

A. I never have taken any treatments. I just went to Arizona. They told me that was the only place I could be cured.

Q. That wouldn't be treatment for your stomach?

A. Never had any."

I have applied to the Veterans' Bureau for treatment for my stomach. They gave me examinations, and no treatments.

"A JUROR: I would like to know if the gentleman ever was gassed in service, on the front?

THE WITNESS: I never got very much gas, but I got a little. At the time I got it, it didn't do any more than just choke me, and it kind of passed off. I had sort of a cold after that, but it didn't last long.

Q. The gas you got you didn't think disabled you?

A. I couldn't say.

Q. You got over it, and felt all right, as far as you know?

A. Well, yes.

Q. Let me see your hands. (Witness exhibits hands to counsel.) You don't do anything on this homestead?

A. No sir."

I just live down there. I am living down there at this time.

(Redirect Examination by Mr. Bynon.)

"Q. Just briefly name the different veterans' bureau hospitals, or offices, you have been in since you got out of the service?

A. The first one was Detroit; the next one Great Lakes, Illinois; examined in Indianapolis, Indiana; and the one in Philadelphia, Pennsylvania. I was in the University Hospital, Oklahoma, for stomach examination.

Q. How about Arizona?

A. I had several examinations in Arizona — Phoenix."

I have been examined at Letterman's. Dr. Read examined me the last time I was examined. There were four doctors altogether examined me, looked at me through the fluoroscope.

A diagnosis of pulmonary tuberculosis was made. That was after I went to Phoenix, Arizona.

(Recross Examination by Mr. Kimmell.)

I believe I was examined by Dr. Seid at San Francisco in about 1926.

I don't know the doctors' names who examined me in Arizona, but there were two of them in the bureau at Phoenix.

MRS. A. J. ANDERSON, called and sworn as a witness in behalf of plaintiff, testified as follows:

(Direct Examination by Mr. Bynon.)

I live at 1523½ East Glisan, Portland.

Mr. Anderson and I know Mr. Hill. We knew him and his family when they lived here. We met them about two years ago, the latter part of December. We were neighbors; they lived next door. I was in their home practically every day.

I know Mr. Hill complained of his stomach all the time he lived there. Every time he ate a meal he had trouble afterwards. I know he wasn't working while he was there.

I don't know what kind of trouble he seemed to have after eating; seemed like it burned his stomach. He always took some kind of medicine afterwards.

During the period of time I saw him he was nervous; didn't look at all well; hasn't since I have met him.

I have personal knowledge of his condition at home; I saw him there. He had some kind of spells after he ate. I know he had to go to bed several times. I saw him in bed in the daytime a short time, possibly three or four times.

(Cross Examination by Mr. Kimmell.)

We only lived near each other a few months. I have known them since they moved away; I just corresponded with them since they moved away.

(Redirect Examination by Mr. Bynon.)

I saw something of the family when they were at Lents. The same conditions existed there. They were there about three months.

"Q. That is about four or five months you knew them altogether in Portland?

A. No; I have known them ever since they have been here. We kept in touch with them; we visited back and forth.

Q. Your testimony covers just while you were living there, and all the time they were living there?

A. All the time they were living there."

A. J. ANDERSON, called and sworn as a witness in behalf of plaintiff, testified as follows:

(Direct Examination by Mr. Bynon.)

I am the husband of the lady just on the stand.

My business is hardwood floor contractor, part of the time.

I know Mr. Hill, the plaintiff here, and met him the same time as my wife, in December, 1929. They were next door neighbors.

I was in and out of their home, sometimes every day, or every day or two. We were constantly in touch with them. If I wasn't there every day or so, the women visited back and forth.

At this time I thought Mr. Hill was a sick man. He was complaining all the time I knew him; still is, that he was sick; and he looked sick. And different times I have seen him taking medicine. The last couple of weeks he has been continually taking medicine, and I surmised it was his stomach.

Mr. Hill is very high strung; he is nervous. If he gets his mind set on any one thing, or tells you about something, one particular thing — pretty soon he gets so loud you can hear him a block away.

"Q. Do you know what kind of nights he spends?

A. I have come home twelve, one or two o'clock, and see a light. I would drop in, and Mr. Hill was complaining he couldn't sleep. I tried to sympathize with him different ways; I felt sorry for him."

He has not worked during this time that I know of. After they moved to Lents, my wife kept in touch with them, but I didn't.

He has been at my place since this came on for trial. He also came to my place in August — or October — a year ago, for a visit. His condition has always been the same.

(Cross Examination by Mr. Kimmell.)

They lived neighbors to us about two months;

December to February, '29 and '30· All the time I had close contact with him was those two months, except when he came to visit for a day about a year ago. He was at my place about a year ago. I believe he traveled by automobile; he drove, himself. Regarding his appearance at the time I saw him there during the two months and his appearance now, his appearance is very much the same as when I first met him.

ELMER J. HILL, recalled, testified as follows:

(Direct Examination by Mr. Bynon.)
The car I had was a 1920 Hudson. It cost me $20.

(Cross Examination by Mr. Kimmell.)
I had this car a year now. Besides that I had a 1918 Buick. That cost $20.

(Plaintiff's Exhibit "C", consisting of photograph of plaintiff taken before he went overseas, was admitted in evidence without objection.)

Whereupon plaintiff rested and defendant offered the following:

DEPOSITION OF DR. R. C. FOSTER, taken on behalf of defendant, on oral interrogatories submitted by J. S. Wheeler appearing for defendant; no appearance for plaintiff:

My name is Doctor Robert C. Foster. I reside at Phoenix, Arizona. I am a physician, a graduate of the University of Arkansas, Medical Department. I graduated in 1923. My business since graduation in 1903 has been the practice of medicine. I followed that continuously since that time.

Since my graduation I have had occasion to specialize in pulmonary tuberculosis.

"Q. How long have you specialized in that branch of the work, Doctor?

A. Practically since graduation.

Q. That would be about twenty-eight years, Doctor?

A. I might amplify that to this extent, general practice with special attention to tuberculosis prior to eleven years ago, and tuberculosis since then — 1920.

Q. Continuously?   A. Yes."

The document you have handed me is a report of a complete physical examination of Elmer J. Hill, November 29, 1926, made by Dr. J. T. McDonald, the Goss Laboratory, and myself. My signature is attached to that document.

I made a chest examination of the plaintiff, Elmer J. Hill, on or about the 29th day of November, 1926. My examination consisted of an examination of his chest by inspection, palpation, percussion and auscultation.

Inspection is looking at the chest to determine the shape and whether or not it appears to be a normal chest in shape and size, or to discover any other visible abnormalities of the chest. Palpation is placing the back edge of the hand on the chest while the claimant speaks to determine the sensation transmitted by the spoken voice to the hand. Percussion is lightly striking the chest with the first finger of the right hand over the second finger of the left hand to determine the sound produced by such action and to evidence whether or not the normal air contained in that portion of the lung exists. Auscultation is the listening to the chest through the instrument called stethoscope during quiet breathing and upon coughing in order to find out whether or not the lung is normal or diseased.

These are the usual and customary tests used by the medical profession for the purpose of making this examination.

As a result of the examination I made, I found only a mild bronchitis. Bronchitis is no evidence of tuberculosis.

As a result of my examination, I did not find any evidence of tuberculosis on Elmer J. Hill when I examined him on the 29th of November, 1926.

My prognosis, as a result of my examination of Elmer J. Hill, was good.

"Q. Doctor, have you had occasion either as a private physician or examiner for the Government to observe the relative degree of disability, if any, or impairment of mind or body from disease or injury from following a substantial and gainful occupation continuously by men?

A. I have."

As a result of my examination and experience, will state that the plaintiff, Elmer J. Hill, in my opinion, was not permanently and totally disabled at the time I examined his chest November 29, 1926. There was nothing in that examination that would indicate that he might have been or could have been totally and permanently disabled prior to that time.

"Q. By the way, Doctor, I call your attention to an X-ray report made by the Goss Laboratory here in the City of Phoenix, and I will ask you if you have made an examination of that X-ray report. This X-ray report is dated the same date as your physical examination. Now, Doctor, what does that X-ray report show in connection with your physical examination?

A. The X-ray report substantiates my physical examination."

That X-ray report does not show past or present evidence of pulmonary tuberculosis. Had Elmer J. Hill been a sufferer from pulmonary tuberculosis prior to the date of my examination and prior to the date of the X-ray examination, that fact would have been capable of ascertainment by my examination, except for a very minute and very old infection that would be of no physical handicap. It would not constitute any impairment of his body or mind at this time.

If there had been any tuberculosis in the plaintiff prior to the time of taking the X-ray, any pulmonary tuberculosis of appreciable degree or even of slight disability would have been noted by the X-ray.

I have made considerable examination of X-ray plates, have read a considerable number of them, and am thoroughly familiar with them.

"Q. And are able to testify from your expert knowledge of the condition of this plate?

A. By the report of it.

Q. From the result of your examination of this X-ray report, would you say that Elmer J. Hill was suffering from pulmonary tuberculosis on the 29th day of November, 1926?

A. I will say that he was not suffering from any degree of tuberculosis at that time."

(Questionnaire and photostatic copy of report of physical examination of Elmer J. Hill on November 29, 1926, by Dr. R. C. Foster, including X-ray report of Dr. H. L. Goss, offered in evidence, marked Defendant's Exhibit "A".)

Deposition of DR. JOHN T. McDONALD, taken on behalf of defendant, on oral interrogatories submitted by J. S. Wheeler appearing for defendant; no appearance for plaintiff:

My name is John T. McDonald. I live at Phoenix, Arizona, My profession is the medical profession. I am a graduate of the University of Louisville, Kentucky. I graduated in 1900, and have followed my profession ever since that time. I have not specialized in any particular branch of my profession, to exclude other work.

I am now connected with the United States Veterans' Bureau in Phoenix in a medical capacity; this bureau is now called the Bureau of Veterans' Affairs and I am employed there full time.

As such employee, I had occasion, on or about the 29th day of November, 1926, to make an examination of Elmer J. Hill.

The document which you show me is an examination made by me for the files of the Veterans' Bureau office. The general examination was made by myself and signed by me with other examiners to complete the Board.

This examination covered all the complaints except lungs. I am referring to my examination.

There is nothing given here in any active nature except hypertrophied tonsils bi-lateral with enlarged lymph glands in the neck that were non-separating, and a slight chronic eczema on the toes of both feet. Otherwise the examination is entirely negative.

The term "negative", as applied to the examination of Elmer J. Hill, means no diseased condition found in the parts referred to.

His muscular development was normal; the eye, ear, nose and throat, tonsils only noted as wrong; the thyroid gland located in the neck was negative or normal; the heart tone, action and position normal; the abdomen was negative, the genito-urinary organs were normal; the groins are normal. That completes the examination.

My prognosis was favorable — good.

I would not say, as a result of my examination of Elmer J. Hill on the 29th day of November, 1926, that he was suffering from any mental or physical impairment or disability that would render him unfit to successfully carry on any gainful occupation.

"Q. Did you find anything that would impair his ability in that direction to carry on an ordinary gainful occupation?

A. Let me ask for a little information: to impair—,

this disability, it just depends on the degree you have in mind.

Q. I mean any ordinary case for ordinary gainful occupation?

A. No, but just a moment if I can explain; you know a man could have a large tonsil and if he would get an abscess he probably would be disabled for the time being. You are referring to chronic?

Q. That is exactly what I am referring to, did you find any total impairment of his physical condition?

A. No sir."

This man was not totally or permanently disabled at the time of my examination.

I did not make an examination of the X-ray report of Dr. Goss at the time I made my physical examination of this man. I did not examine the lungs, and this X-ray report is all entirely on the lung condition.

I did not make any examination of the lungs with reference to an inquiry as to whether he was suffering with tuberculosis. I do sometimes on the Board, but in this instance I did not listen to his lungs at all.

"Q. Was there anything to indicate to you, Doctor,

from your examination of this man at that time, that there was anything wrong with him in any way; that is, any serious physical impairment that would include lungs and anything else?

A. I could not say that there was nothing wrong with him but there was nothing of a disabling nature.

Q. Disabling nature?

A. Nothing to disable him from earning a living by his working."

(Record of Examination of Elmer J. Hill made made by Dr. J. T. McDonald on November 29, 1926, offered in evidence, marked Defendant's Exhibit "B".)

ELMER J. HILL, called in rebuttal, testified as follows:

(Direct Examination by Mr. Bynon.)

Dr. R. B. Hyatt who examined me before I entered the service was the same doctor that treated me after I got back. He lives at Herkimer.

I gained weight after I went to camp. The most I weighed any time before I became sick overseas was 175. That was Camp Devens before we sailed.

"Q. I am handing you Plaintiff's Exhibit "B", and call your attention to the report of the Adjutant

General prior to your entering service, and ask if that bears your signature, at the bottom of the page?

A. Yes sir.

Q. Now, in answer to this question: 'Declaration of Soldier. Have you any reason to believe that at the present time you are suffering from any disability or impairment of health, whether or not incurred in the military service?'; the answer is 'no'. Did you write that answer in?

A. No sir, I never did.

Q. Was that there before you signed it, or not? When was it written in there? If you don't know, say so.

A. I really couldn't say for sure."

I have no explanation to make to the jury about the signature that appears in answer to that question. I was then suffering from a physical disability. I was sick; I was discouraged; I though if I could get out of the service and get home I would get better.

Referring to Plaintiff's Exhibit "C", the soldier sitting down is me. That picture was taken of me just before I went overseas.

At the conclusion of all of the testimony, the defendant filed the following MOTION FOR DIRECTED VERDICT:

COMES NOW the defendant, United States of America, by its attorneys, at the close of the introduction of all the testimony, and moves the Court for an order directing the jury to return a verdict in favor of the defendant and against the plaintiff for the reason that the testimony fails to show that the plaintiff was totally and permanently disabled at any time during the time when his policy of insurance was in force and effect.

This motion was denied by the court and an exception allowed.

Thereupon counsel for plaintiff and defendant argued the case to the jury, and at the conclusion of such arguments, the court instructed the jury as to the law. No exceptions to the court's instructions were noted.

IT IS HEREBY CERTIFIED that the foregoing proceedings were had upon the trial of this cause, and that the Bill of Exceptions contains all the evidence produced at said trial.

IT IS FURTHER CERTIFIED that the foregoing exceptions asked and taken by the defendant were allowed by the Court, and this Bill of Exceptions was duly presented within the time fixed by law and the order of this court, and is by me duly allowed and signed this 15 day of March, 1932.

JOHN H. McNARY,

One of the Judges of the District Court of the United
States for the District of Oregon.

Endorsed:

U. S. DISTRICT COURT

District of Oregon

Filed March 15, 1932

G. H. Marsh, Clerk

By F. L. Buck, Chief Deputy

And Afterwards, to-wit, on the 16th day of March,
1932, there was duly Filed in said Court, a

STIPULATION

in words and figures as follows, to-wit:

IT IS HEREBY STIPULATED by and between
the respective parties to the above-entitled action that
the record and transcript to be prepared by the Clerk
of the Court and transmitted to the United States
Circuit Court of Appeals for the Ninth Circuit shall
consist of the following:

Citation on Appeal

Complaint

Answer

Verdict

Judgment

Motion for New Trial

Order Denying Motion for New Trial

Stipulation that Appellant Have an Extension
of Time to and Including March 10 within

which to tender and lodge Bill of Exceptions

Order Allowing Appellant to and Including March 10 within which to tender and lodge Bill of Exceptions

Petition for Order of Appeal

Order Allowing Appeal

Notice of Appeal

Assignments of Error

Bill of Exceptions

Stipulation as to what Transcript of Record shall contain

Praecipe for Transcript of Record,

omitting titles, verifications, and acceptance of service on all said documents, except Citation on Appeal and Complaint.

> (Sgd.)   ALLAN A. BYNON,
>   Attorney for Plaintiff.
> (Sgd.)   REX KIMMELL,
>   Assistant United States Attorney.

Endorsed:

U. S. DISTRICT COURT

District of Oregon

Filed March 16, 1932

G. H. Marsh, Clerk

By F. L. Buck, Chief Deputy

And Afterwards, to-wit, on the 16th day of March, 1932 there was duly Filed in said Court a

PRAECIPE

in words and figures as follows to-wit:

To the Clerk of the above-entitled Court:

You are hereby directed to please prepare and certify the record in the above cause for transmission to the United States Circuit Court of Appeals for the Ninth Circuit, including therein a certified copy of all papers filed and proceedings had in the above-entitled cause, which are necessary to a determination thereof in said Appellate Court, and especially including therein the following documents:

Citation on Appeal

Complaint

Answer

Verdict

Judgment

Motion for New Trial

Order Denying Motion for New Trial

Stipulation that Appellant Have an Extension of Time to and Including March 10 within which to tender and lodge Bill of Exceptions

Order Allowing Appellant to and Including March 10 within which to tender and lodge Bill of Exceptions

Petition for Order of Appeal

Order Allowing Appeal

Notice of Appeal

Assignments of Error

Bill of Exceptions

Stipulation as to what Transcript of Record
shall contain

Praecipe for Transcript of Record,

omitting titles, verifications, and acceptance of service on all said documents, except Citation on Appeal and Complaint.

Dated this 16th day of March, 1932.

(Sgd.) REX KIMMELL,

Assistant United States Attorney.

Endorsed:

U. S. DISTRICT COURT

District of Oregon

Filed March 16, 1932

G. H. Marsh, Clerk

By F. L. Buck, Chief Deputy

No. 6805

In the United States Circuit Court of Appeals

FOR THE NINTH CIRCUIT

UNITED STATES OF AMERICA,

Appellant,

vs.

ELMER J. HILL,

Appellee.

Appellant's Brief

Upon appeal from the United States District Court for the District of Oregon.

Names and Addresses of Attorneys of Record:

GEORGE NEUNER,
 United States Attorney for the District of Oregon

REX KIMMELL,
 Assistant United States Attorney,
  Federal Building, Portland, Oregon
   For Appellant.

ALLAN A. BYNON,
 Portland, Oregon.
  For Appellee.

FILED

AUG 11 1932

PAUL P. O'BRIEN,
CLERK

The Adam Printing Co., Portland, Ore.   40—8-9-32

No. 6805

In the United States Circuit Court of Appeals

FOR THE NINTH CIRCUIT

UNITED STATES OF AMERICA,

Appellant,

vs.

ELMER J. HILL,

Appellee.

Appellant's Brief

Upon appeal from the United States District Court for the District of Oregon.

Names and Addresses of Attorneys of Record:

GEORGE NEUNER,
United States Attorney for the District of Oregon
REX KIMMELL,
Assistant United States Attorney,
Federal Building, Portland, Oregon
For Appellant.

ALLAN A. BYNON,
Portland, Oregon.
For Appellee.

INDEX

Page

Argument

    Assignment of Error No. 1 8

    Assignment of Error No. 2 21

Assignments of Error 6

Conclusion 21

Points and Authorities 7

Statement of Facts 5

Authorities Cited:

    Ewing vs. Goode, 78 Fed. 442, 444 7

    Gunning vs. Cooley, 281 U. S. 90, 94 7

    Louisville & N. R. Co. v. E. Tenn. V. & G.
        R.R. Co., 60 Fed. 993-999 7

    United States vs. Golden, 34 F. (2d) 367, 370   7

    United States vs. Thomas, 53 F. (2d) 192 7

    United States vs. McLaughlin, 53 Fed. (2)
        450 7

STATEMENT OF FACTS

Elmer J. Hill, hereinafter called plaintiff, enlisted in the military forces of the United States on the 21st day of September, 1917, and on the 4th day of April, 1919, was honorably discharged therefrom. While serving in said military forces, plaintiff applied for and was granted a policy of war risk insurance in the sum of $5,000, and premiums were duly paid thereon to and including the month of April, 1919, and said policy of insurance lapsed midnight, May 31, 1919.

On the 6th day of September, 1930, plaintiff sued on his original war risk insurance policy and alleged that from July 1, 1918, to October 20, 1918, he suffered from exposure, deprivation and malnutrition incident to front line warfare, during which time he developed and suffered from dysentery and stomach disorders brought on by drinking gas-poisoned water, and that thereafter and about January 1, 1919, plaintiff developed and suffered from pulmonary tuberculosis, and thereafter he suffered continuously from stomach trouble, duodenal ulcers, nervousness, weakness, and sleeplessness, and that by reason of such disabilities he was, at the time of his discharge from service, permanently and totally disabled.

The Government, hereinafter called the defendant, in its answer denied the above allegations of the complaint and denied that plaintiff was permanently and totally disabled at any time during the life of the policy of insurance. The only issue of fact raised by the pleadings was the one presented by the above allegations and denials.

After all the evidence had been introduced in the case, the defendant moved for a directed verdict in its behalf on the ground that there was no substantial evidence to support the allegation of permanent and total disability at any time during the life of plaintiff's policy of war risk insurance. The motion was overruled and an exception to the ruling allowed.

The case was thereupon submitted to the jury and a verdict was returned in favor of plaintiff, finding that plaintiff was on the 4th day of April, 1919, totally and permanently disabled. Based on such verdict, judgment was entered by the court in favor of plaintiff on the 6th day of October, 1931, and from that judgment defendant appeals.

ASSIGNMENTS OF ERROR

I.

The court erred in overruling the motion of defendant for a directed verdict, for the reason that the evidence adduced at the trial of the case was insufficient to justify a verdict for the plaintiff.

II.

The court erred in overruling the motion for a directed verdict, for the reason that the evidence adduced at the trial of the above-entitled cause establishes the fact that plaintiff was not permanently and totally disabled, nor permanently or totally disabled on or before the 4th day of April, 1919, or at any time during the life of his contract of war risk insurance upon which this action is predicated.

POINTS AND AUTHORITIES

I.

When a plaintiff, with the burden on him, introduces evidence consistent with two different states of fact, he proves neither.

> Louisville & N. R. Co. vs. E. Tennessee, V. & G. R.R. Co., 60 Fed. 993-999;
>
> Ewing vs. Goode, 78 Fed. 442, at 444;
>
> Gunning vs. Cooley, 281 U. S. at p. 94.

II.

There are no degrees of disability recognized by a war risk insurance contract; there must be total disability to entitle the insured to recover.

> United States vs. Golden, 34 F. (2d) 367, 370;
>
> United States vs. Thomas, 53 F. (2d) 192;
>
> United States vs. McLaughlin, 53 F. (2) 450.

III.

Unless there is substantial evidence supporting

the allegations of plaintiff, a timely motion for a directed verdict should be allowed.

Gunning vs. Cooley, 281 U. S. 90.

ARGUMENT
Assignment of Error No. 1

The attention of the court is called to the fact that this case is unusual in the following particulars:

(a) The only testimony produced by plaintiff as to his condition during the life of the contract sued upon or as to his condition at any time prior to 1929 (10 years after the contract terminated) was the testimony of plaintiff himself; (Tr. 30-57)

(b) No doctors testified on behalf of plaintiff;

(c) Plaintiff himself introduced the Adjutant General's Office report, which showed, among other things,

(1) At time of discharge plaintiff declared that he had no reason to believe that he was suffering from the effect of any wound, injury or disease, or impairment of health;

(2) The certificate of plaintiff's immediate commanding officer that he had no reason to believe that plaintiff had any wound, injury or disease at the time of plaintiff's discharge;

(3) Certificate of examining surgeon, dated April 2, 1919, that plaintiff was given a careful physical examination and found to be physically and mentally sound; (Exhibit "B", Tr. 33-38)

(d) Plaintiff himself introduced his honorable discharge from the United States Army, which showed plaintiff received no wounds while in service, and that at that time his physical condition was good. (Exhibit "A", Tr. 30-31)

We believe that it is a sound proposition of law that when a plaintiff introduces evidence to show that a fact **existed,** and also introduces evidence to show that that fact **did not exist,** his proof tends to establish neither. If such is the law, an examination of the record herein will clearly show that plaintiff has produced no substantial evidence to establish the fact of permanent and total disability during the life of his policy of insurance.

Plaintiff testified, insofar as his allegation of stomach trouble and dysentery, and duodenal ulcer is concerned — and, in fact, that is all the evidence in the record in support of that allegation — as follows:

"I got dysentery from drinking poisoned water in the St. Mihiel Sector in the St. Mihiel battle. This water was in a hole that was supposed to be a well, but it was night and we were all thirsty and hadn't had a drink for quite a while, so we took a drink to satisfy our thirst. I became violently sick to my stomach a couple of hours after and after that **I contracted a bad case of dysentery, which lasted about six weeks altogether.**" (Tr. 32, 33)

* * *

"Q. How does that **stomach trouble** affect you? Tell us what it does to you?

A. I have gnawing pains all the time; I can't sleep nights and after I eat I have all kinds of distress and agony.

Q. **Have you had that pain since you were in France?**

A. No.

Q. When did it start?

A. I had it at intervals off and on **the last eight years.**"

* * *

"I had this stomach trouble in France; it started at the receiving station in Souile, when I was in there for treatment." (Tr. 43)

* * *

"Q. You state the first time your stomach

bothered you was over at that well. Did all
of you drink out of that well?

A. No. There was only about four of us drank
out of that.

Q. How long was it before you began to have
those pains? I understood it was after you
got out of service.

A. No. I got those pains after I drank the water.
They lasted about six weeks. Then I didn't
have any more until some time after that.

Q. Until some time after that?

A. **No. I didn't have any more dysentery until
some time after that. I would say it came
back in '26. That was the first time I had
dysentery after that.**

Q. Where was the first place you started taking
treatments after you got out of the service?

A. I never have taken any treatments. I just
went to Arizona. They told me that was the
only place I could be cured."
(Tr. 55)

★ ★ ★

The evidence is that plaintiff went to Arizona in
1925.

"At the time I was discharged I was suffering from nervousness, stomach trouble, and I

had a bad chest condition. I didn't have any more dysentery for quite a while after I was discharged. I had a hemorrhage a few years later. The doctors at the hospital where I was at told me it came from the effects of the dysentery I had had previously."

Plaintiff testified in support of his allegation of tuberculosis as follows:

"Q. Your condition at the time you got out of service, you allege pulmonary tuberculosis. Did you know at that time you had it?

A. I didn't know it until the doctor told me.

Q. What were your symptoms on April 4, 1919? Tell us how you felt?

A. I had a fever all the time. I used to have awful sweats at night. I coughed a whole lot and expectorated. Lots of times my sputum was tinged with blood." (Tr. 39)

* * *

"I saw Dr. Hyatt after I got out of service. He was located in Herkemer, New York. I did not get any treatment under Dr. Hyatt."

* * *

"Q. When did you start in treatment?

A. Well, I never had any treatment."

* * *

"After I consulted with Dr. Hyatt I went to

Arizona. I stayed there two years. I didn't do anything down there. I went down there for my health, to cure this t.b." (1925)

*   *   *

"I had two or three examinations in Philadelphia, but they never gave me any treatment; that was for the chest condition. I had two or three examinations by physicians connected with the Veterans Bureau. **They sent for me every little while because I had applied for compensation,** but I didn't receive any treatment while I was there."

We have quoted substantially all the testimony in the record tending to show that plaintiff, on or before date of discharge, was suffering from the disabilities which he alleges permanently and totally disabled him at that time. We seriously doubt, even though plaintfif had not gone further and produced evidence that contradicts his testimony, whether or not there would be more than a scintilla of evidence to be submitted to the jury. However, **plaintiff having produced evidence,** by way of his own testimony, **of the existence of his alleged condition,** and also evidence, by way of the records; namely, plaintiff's Exhibits "A" and "B", **of the non-existence of that condition,** certainly it can not be said that there is substantial evidence furnished by plaintiff that the condition existed at all.

This principle of law is established by the following authorities:

> "When a party with the burden on him introduces evidence consistent with two different states of fact, he proves neither."
>> Louisville & N. R. Co. vs. E. Tennessee V. & G. Ry. Co., 60 Fed. 993, at p. 999.

> "When a plaintiff produces evidence that is consistent with a hypothesis that the defendant is not negligent and also with one that he is, his proof tends to establish neither."
>> Ewing, et al, vs. Goode, 78 Fed. 442, at p. 444.

These decisions are quoted from and this principle is cited with approval in the United States Supreme Court case of Gunning vs. Cooley, 281 U. S. 90, at p. 94.

If there is no substantial evidence in the record of plaintiff's disability on or before the date of his discharge, plaintiff's testimony concerning his activities subsequent to the date his policy of insurance terminated in itself can not sustain the judgment that has been entered in this case.

Plaintiff has produced evidence not only that he was suffering from disability during the life of his contract of insurance, but also that he was not suffering from disability during the life of his contract of insurance. Therefore, there is no evidence of either fact. The burden is upon plaintiff to establish the allegation of his complaint. That being true, we contend that it is wholly immaterial, insofar as this case is concerned, what he did or what his condition was after the 31st day of May, 1919.

Although we contend the matters hereinbefore set forth are sufficient to establish error in overruling defendant's motion for a directed verdict, we, nevertheless, desire to direct the court's attention to the insufficiency of plaintiff's testimony concerning his activities and efforts after his discharge to sustain the finding that he was permanently and totally disabled during the life of his contract of insurance.

It will be conceded by counsel that the test of total disability is: **Could** insured follow continuously **any** substantially gainful occupation, and it is not: **Did** the insured carry on some **particular** occupation continuously.

The evidence in this case is that plaintiff attempted to work for the Studebaker Automobile Company for about two months and stopped because there was too much smoke; that he next attempted to work for the Dodge Automobile Company for two weeks, where he stopped because there was too much smoke; that he next attempted to work for the Ford Automobile Company for about ten weeks, where he stopped because the work was too hard; that he next attempted to work for the Cadillac Automobile Company for about six weeks, where he stopped because of too much smoke and gas; that he next attempted to work in the woods in Northern New York for about a month, where he stopped because the work was too hard; that he next went to Detroit, where he stayed around a while without working, and that he then went to Arizona .(Tr. 40, 41)

The evidence shows that plaintiff went to Arizona in the year 1925.

It is a significant fact that the evidence goes only so far as to show that plaintiff worked or attempted to work for one automobile company after the other —in all for a period of twenty-six weeks—each of which jobs he quit because of the same unfavorable conditions under which he was compelled to work; namely, gas and smoke; that he worked in the woods in Northern New York State for a period of four weeks, during which time he felt better, but which work he quit because it was too hard. And that was the extent of his efforts "to carry on any substantially gainful occupation" during the six years immediately following the termination of his policy of insurance.

Other than that thirty weeks of attempted work, it can not be ascertained from the evidence what plaintiff was doing or what his condition was during the remainder of that six-year period.

Courts have held, and it seems a good principle of law, that the bare evidence that insured tried unsuccessfully to follow one line of work is no evidence that he was in such condition that it was impossible for him to follow continuously some other line of work, had he tried to do so.

In the case of United States vs. Thomas, 53 Fed. (2) 192, at p. 195 the court so holds. The evidence in that case was that the insured lost the use of his left arm while in service and lost the third finger of his right hand, and he alleged that those disabilities totally and permanently disabled him during the life of his policy of insurance. The evidence showed that he was first employed in the cotton mills of South Carolina, which was the only type of work he had ever done before service; that he was unable to work even as long as a week at a time because of his disabilities, and that he attempted to do mechanical work intermittently, but, because of his disabilities, could not carry on continuously. At the conclusion of the testimony a motion for a directed verdict was made, which was overruled, and the case was submitted to the jury. An appeal was taken from the order overruling the motion for a directed verdict and the lower court was reversed. In commenting upon the evidence in that case, the court, among other things, said:

"The claim of the insured does not fail because of intermittent efforts on his part to engage in two-handed occupations, but rather because he offered no substantial evidence to show that he is unable to do the kind of work which a one-armed man can successfully perform. We do not overlook the fact that, in addition to the injuries to the left arm, the right middle finger, and the jaw, plaintiff has suffered from nervousness, loss of sleep, and inability to eat hard food, and doubtless these afflictions have affected his ability to work. Nevertheless, there was no showing at the trial that all of the injuries combined made it impossible for him to follow with reasonable regularity **any** substantially gainful occupation. It may be that such evidence is in the possession of the insured; but from the evidence offered to the court it would appear that the insured has made no attempt to take up any calling except two-handed ones, and this failure on his part must be contrasted with the testimony of all the physicians in the case, including that of his own doctor, which shows, in accordance with the common knowledge open to all, that there are a number of occupations open to a partially crippled man."

The attention of the court is directed to the fact that there is no medical evidence in the record to show that plaintiff was suffering from tuberculosis. The plaintiff testified that he consulted a Dr. Hyatt after he got out of the service and that in 1925 he went to Arizona to cure his t.b. condition. (Tr. 41)

While in Arizona plaintiff was carefully examined by two doctors, one a general practitioner and the other a specialist in diseases of the chest. The defendant introduced in evidence the testimony of those two doctors as to plaintiff's condition while in Arizona.

Dr. R. C. Foster, chest specialist, testified that he found plaintiff suffering from a mild bronchitis; that there was no evidence of tuberculosis, and that the prognosis, as a result of the examination, was good. (Tr. 63.) He testified further as follows:

"Q. Doctor, have you had occasion, either as a private physician or examiner for the government, to observe the relative degree of disability, if any, or impairment of mind or body from disease or injury from following a substantially gainful occupation continuously by men.

A. I have."

"As a result of my examination and experience will state that the plaintiff, Elmer J. Hill, in my opinion, was not permanently and totally disabled at the time I examined his chest, November 29, 1926. **There was nothing in that examination that would indicate that he might have been or could have been totally and permanently disabled prior to that time.**"

Dr. John T. McDonald, general practitioner, testified:

"This examination covered all the complaints except lungs. I am referring to my examination. There is nothing given here in any active nature except hypertrophied tonsils bi-lateral with enlarged lymph glands in the neck that were non-separating, and a slight chronic eczema on the toes of both feet. Otherwise the examination is entirely negative. * * *

"My prognosis was favorable, good. * * *

"This man was not totally or permanently disabled at the time of my examination."
(Tr. 67, 68)

The testimony of Dr. Foster and Dr. McDonald, introduced by the defendant, and the certificate of the examining surgeon made at the time of plaintiff's discharge, introduced by plaintiff, constitute the entire medical evidence in this case. It should be noted that there is no conflict in the medical evidence. It is positively to the effect that plaintiff was not suffering from the alleged diseases and disabilities prior to 1926.

Two witnesses, Mr. and Mrs. A. J. Anderson, testified in this case on behalf of plaintiff. They each testified that they met plaintiff for the first time about two years prior to the date of trial, and that since that time they observed that plaintiff had been suffering stomach disorders; that plaintiff did no work during the time that they were neighbors, about five months during the winter of 1929.

Assignment of Error No. 2

The argument under Assignment of Error No. 1 is urged in support of Assignment of Error No. 2.

CONCLUSION

The verdict and judgment in this case are supported only by the testimony of plaintiff himself. The government does not seriously contend that plaintiff was not suffering from some disability in 1929. Plaintiff has alleged that he had stomach trouble, duodenal ulcers, dysentery, tuberculosis, sleeplessness, nervousness, and weakness, and that those conditions rendered him permanently and totally disabled on or prior to May 31, 1919.

The allegation of stomach disorders, duodenal ulcers, and dysentery is supported only by plaintiff's testimony that he had pains in his stomach for about six weeks after drinking poisoned water in the St. Mihiel Sector, and that he had such pains at intervals off and on during the last eight years, or since 1923, and that the dysentery returned in 1926.

There is no testimony in support of the allegation of sleeplessness, nervousness, and weakness.

The allegation of tuberculosis is supported only by plaintiff's testimony that on the day he was discharged,

> "I had fever all the time. I used to have awful sweats at night. I coughed a whole lot and expectorated. Lots of times my sputum was tinged with blood."

He went to see a Dr. Hyatt in Herkemer, New York, right after he got out of the service in 1919, and in 1925 he went to Arizona to cure t.b.

As opposed to that testimony, plaintiff introduced evidence that when he was discharged he was not suffering from disability of any kind, and the defendant introduced evidence showing positively that he was not suffering from any serious disability when he was in Arizona. Medical evidence on behalf of both plaintiff and defendant, shows positively that plaintiff did not suffer either total or permanent disability prior to 1926.

If the decision in this case sustains the lower court's ruling in submitting this evidence to the jury, that decision will constitute an authority of this Circuit, by which any veteran who has worked but little since discharge can come into court and, without other witnesses — either lay or medical — take the stand and testify and be entitled to have his case submitted to the caprices of a sympathetic jury, regardless of any defense that can possibly be interposed.

Plaintiff has failed to sustain the burden of proof imposed upon him, and there is no substantial evidence to support the finding of the jury or the judgment. Therefore, defendant respectfully submits that the judgment should be set aside and a new trial granted.

Respectfully submitted,

GEORGE NEUNER,

United States Attorney for the District of Oregon.

REX KIMMELL,

Assistant United States Attorney

Attorneys for Appellant.

In the United States Circuit Court of Appeals

For the Ninth Circuit

UNITED STATES OF AMERICA,
　　　　　　　　　　Appellant,

　　vs.

ELMER J. HILL,
　　　　　　　　　　Appellee.

APPELLEE'S BRIEF

Upon Appeal from the United States District Court
for the District of Oregon

Names and Addresses of Attorneys of Record:

GEORGE NEUNER,
　　United States Attorney for the District of Oregon,

REX KIMMELL,
　　Assistant United States Attorney,
　　　　Federal Building, Portland, Oregon,
　　　　　　For Appellant.

ALLAN A. BYNON,
　　Portland, Oregon,
　　　　For Appellee.

THE IVY PRESS

TABLE OF CASES CITED

Page

Alabama Great Southern Ry. Co. v. Taylor, 71 So.
676 22

B. & A. Electric Ry. Co. v. Cross, 142 Md. 500, 121
Atl. 374 22

Bangor & Arrostook R. R. v. Jones, 36 F. (2d) 886 4

Burns v. Polar Wave Ice & Fuel Co., 187 S. W. 145 22

Chapman v. Kansas City Ry. Co., 217 S. W. 623.. 22

Clark v. United States, 48 Fed. (2d) 291, 293..... 23

23 C. J. 9, Sec. 1733........................... 19

Ford v. United States, 44 Fed. (2d) 754.......3-5-24

Gray, Administratrix, v. Davis, Director General of
R. R., 294 F. 57........................... 4

Hayden v. United States (C. C. A., 9th), 41 Fed.
(2d) 614, 617 24

Heisson v. Dickinson, 35 F. (2d) 270........... 4

Humble v. United States, 49 Fed. (2d) 600....... 21

Marathon Lumber Co. v. Dennis, 296 F. 471..... 3

McGovern v. United States, 294 Fed. 108, (C. C.
A.) 299 Fed. 302......................... 21

McNalley v. United States, 52 Fed. (2d) 440, 443. 4

Mt. Adams & E. P. Inclined Ry. Co. v. Lowery, 74
F. 463, 20 C. C. A. 596................... 3

Nichols v. United States, 48 Fed. (2d) 293, 296... 23

Rochford v. Pennsylvania Co., 174 F. 81, 98 C. C.
A. 105 3

Smith-Booth-Usher Co. v. Detroit Copper Mining
Co., 220 F. 600, 136 C. C. A. 58............. 3

Sprencel v. United States, 47 Fed. (2d) 501, 505.. 23

TABLE OF CASES CITED

PAGE

Travelers' Ins. Co. v. Randolph, 78 F. 754, 24 C. C. A. 305 3

United States Fidelity & Guaranty Co. v. Blum, 270 F. 946 3

United States v. Burke, 50 Fed. (2d) 653, 655, 656   2

United States v. Cox, 24 F. (2d) 944............ 19

United States v. Eliasson, 20 F. (2d) 821......... 19

United States v. Lesher, 59 Fed. (2d) 53......... 5

United States v. Phillips, 44 F. (2d) 689......... 19

United States v. Scarborough, 57 Fed. (2d) 137... 4

United States v. Schweppe, 38 F. (2d) 595....... 19

United States v. Sligh, 31 F. (2d) 735............ 19

United States v. Tyrakowski, 50 Fed. (2d) 766, 768, 771 18

United States v. Woltman, 57 Fed. (2d) 418...... 4

White v. United States, 270 U. S. 175, 180, 46 S. Ct. 274, 275, 70 L. Ed. 530..................4-24

In the United States Circuit Court of Appeals

For the Ninth Circuit

UNITED STATES OF AMERICA,

                  Appellant,

    vs.

ELMER J. HILL,

                  Appellee.

APPELLEE'S BRIEF

Upon Appeal from the United States District Court
for the District of Oregon

Names and Addresses of Attorneys of Record:

GEORGE NEUNER,
    United States Attorney for the District of Oregon,

REX KIMMELL,
    Assistant United States Attorney,
        Federal Building, Portland, Oregon,
            For Appellant.

ALLAN A. BYNON,
    Portland, Oregon,
        For Appellee.

ARGUMENT

The sole question involved in this appeal is whether the lower Court erred in overruling defendant's Motion for a Directed Verdict. It is the contention of the defendant that its motion should have been allowed by reason of the fact that plaintiff had failed to prove that he was permanently and totally disabled and unable to follow continuously any substantially gainful occupation on and after the 4th day of April, 1919, within the meaning of his War Risk Insurance policy.

Before examining the sufficiency of the evidence to support the verdict in this case, we wish to call to the Court's attention certain established principles that control the Federal Appellate Courts in passing upon the question as to whether the trial Court erred in refusing to direct a verdict, especially in cases involving War Risk Insurance policies.

In this Circuit, the rules governing the question as to when a given case should be left to the decision of a jury, are laid down in United States v. Burke (C. C. A., 9th Circuit) 50 Fed. (2d) 653, 655, 656, where Judge Sawtelle says:

> "The question is whether the evidence tending to establish total and permanent disability while the policy was in effect was sufficient to take the case to the jury. We do not weigh the evidence, but inquire merely whether there was sufficient evidence to sustain the verdict and judgment. * * *
> "Courts often experience great difficulty in determining whether a given case should be left to the decision of the jury or whether a verdict should be directed by the Court. Fortunately, however, the rule in this Circuit has been definitely settled and almost universally observed. Judge Gilbert, for many years and until recently the distinguished senior Judge of this Court, whose gift for expres-

sion was unsurpassed, has stated the rule as follows:

" 'Under the settled doctrine as applied by all the Federal Appellate Courts, when the refusal to direct a verdict is brought under review on writ of error, the question thus presented is whether or not there was any evidence to sustain the verdict, and whether or not the evidence to support a directed verdict as requested, was so conclusive that the trial Court in the exercise of a sound judicial discretion should not sustain a verdict for the opposing party.

" 'And on a motion for a directed verdict the Court may not weigh the evidence, and if there is substantial evidence both for the plaintiff and the defendant, it is for the jury to determine what facts are established even if their verdict be against the decided preponderance of the evidence. Travelers' Ins. Co. v. Randolph, 78 F. 754, 24 C. C. A. 305; Mt. Adams & E. P. Inclined Ry. Co. v. Lowery, 74 F. 463, 20 C. C. A. 596; Rochford v. Pennsylvania Co., 174 F. 81, 98 C. C. A. 105; United States Fidelity & Guaranty Co. v. Blum (C. C. A.) 270 F. 946; Smith-Booth-Usher Co. v. Detroit Copper Mining Co., 220 F. 600, 136 C. C. A. 58. In the case last cited this Court said:

" ' "The right to a jury trial is guaranteed by the Constitution, and it is not to be denied, except in a clear case." ' * * *

"Again, 'such an instruction would be proper only where, admitting the truth of the evidence for the plaintiff below, as a matter of law, said plaintiff could not have a verdict.' Marathon Lumber Co. v. Dennis, 296 F. 471 (C. C. A. 5.)"

In Ford v. United States (C. C. A.), 44 Fed. (2d) 754, the Court said:

"It is well settled that, on such a question as is here presented, the plaintiff is entitled to the most favorable construction that a jury might be warranted in putting on the evidence. Heisson v. Dickinson (C. C. A.), 35 F. (2d) 270, and cases cited; Bangor & Arrostook R. R. v. Jones (C. C. A.), 36 F. (2d) 886; Gray, Administratrix v. Davis, Director General of R. R. (C. C. A.), 294 F. 57.

"And the act itself is to be liberally construed in favor of such claimants. In White v. United States, 270 U. S. 175, 180, 46 S. Ct. 274, 275, 70 L. Ed. 530, Mr. Justice Holmes said of such contracts: 'The insurance was a contract, to be sure, for which a premium was paid, but it was not one entered into by the United States for gain. All soldiers were given a right to it and the relation of the Government to them if not paternal was at least avuncular. It was a relation of benevolence established by the Government at considerable cost to itself for the soldier's good'."

See to the same effect, McNalley v. United States (C. C. A.), 52 Fed. (2d) 440, 443; also, United States v. Woltman, 57 Fed. (2d) 418.

In the recent case of United States v. Scarborough, (C. C. A., 9th Circuit) 57 Fed. (2d) 137, Judge Sawtelle states the law as follows:

"The sole question to be determined is the sufficiency of the evidence to support the judgment; in other words, whether there is substantial evidence to establish plaintiff's claim that the deceased veteran was totally and permanently disabled prior to the date upon which the policy lapsed.

"The applicable rules of law in cases of this character are so familiar and have been so often announced by this and other Courts in recent cases that it would seem futile to refer to or repeat them here. It is fundamental that this Court, in determining the question here presented, must view the evidence in the light most favorable to the appellee, and must affirm the findings and conclusions of the trial Court if they are supported by any substantial evidence."

The last expression on this subject by the Circuit Court of Appeals for this Circuit appears in the case of United States v. Lesher, 59 Fed. (2d) 53, wherein Judge Neterer states the law as follows:

"Under the Seventh Amendment to the Constitution, a jury trial is guaranteed in a civil action; and that it is error to direct a verdict for defendant if there is any substantial evidence is stare decisis. * * *

"The Court does not weigh the evidence, but considers whether there is any or sufficient evidence to sustain a verdict. See Ford v. United States (C. C. A.), 44 F. (2d) 754. And in war risk cases the most favorable construction should be given the evidence that is produced. Ford v. United States, supra. The trial Judge must, in the exercise of sound discretion, determine whether upon the evidence produced a verdict can be sustained, not weigh the evidence. If there is evidence, it must be submitted; if not, it is pronouncedly his duty to direct a verdict."

Keeping in mind the rules as laid down in the foregoing decisions, let us examine the evidence in this case in order to ascertain whether there is substantial evidence that on or before the 4th day of April, 1919, plaintiff had an impairment of mind or body which rendered it impossible for him to follow continuously any substantially gainful occupation and that such impairment was then founded on conditions which rendered it reasonably certain that it would continue throughout his life.

Plaintiff, Elmer J. Hill, gave the following substantial evidence:

Plaintiff, on direct examination, testified (Tr. pp. 30, 32, 33, 38, 39):

"When I entered the service for the World War I lived at Herkimer, New York. Before that time I worked on farms, and construction companies. I had an eighth grade education. * * *

"When we arrived overseas my organization was first sent to the Toule Sector, and was moved from there to St. Mihiel.

"I participated in that offensive and was in the infantry and was in the front line. While there I was exposed all the time; in mud and water; several days without any rest, and part of the time we had no food. There was active fighting at that time; we was through the whole thing there. Altogether, I was in active front line service about three weeks.

"My organization was moved from Saint Mihiel to the Verdun sector. I became sick at Verdun and was sent to the receiving station.

"I was taken out of the front line service and sent away just before I got to Verdun. Just before I was taken away from the front line I had dysentery, high fever and a kind of nervous breakdown. I was under lots of shell fire during my front line service.

"I got dysentery from drinking poisoned water in the Saint Mihiel sector—in the Saint Mihiel Battle. This water was in a hole that was supposed to be a well, but it was night and we were all thirsty and hadn't had a drink for quite a while, so we took a drink to satisfy our thirst. I became violently sick to my stomach a couple of hours after, and after that I contracted a bad case of dysentery which lasted about six weeks altogether. In connection with that I was sent to Base 23. * * *

"I had influenza, and was laid up with that about two weeks."

Q. When did you first discover you were suffering from nervousness?

A. At the hospital at—

Q. How did you happen to know you were suffering from nervousness?

A. I couldn't stay still.

Q. What brought that on you?

A. High explosives; high explosive shells. * * *

The Register Index Card of U. S. A. Base Hospital No. 23 (Tr. p. 35), shows the following:

"Cause of admission: Dysentery, acute.
In Line of Duty? Yes.
Oct. 3, 1918. Change Influenza, acute."

Plaintiff further testified (Tr. pp. 39, 40, 41, 42, 43, 44):

"At the time I was discharged I was suffering from nervousness, stomach trouble, and I had a bad chest condition. I didn't have any more dysentery for quite a while after I was discharged. I had a hemorrhage a few years later. Doctors at the hospital where I was at told me it came from the effects of the dysentery I had had previously."

Q. Your condition at the time you got out of service, you allege pulmonary tuberculosis. Did you know at that time you had it?

A. I didn't know it until the doctor told me.

Q. What were your symptoms on April 4th, 1919? Tell us how you felt.

A. I had a fever all the time. I used to have awful sweats at night. I coughed a whole lot, and expectorated; lots of times my sputum was tinged with blood.

"The first thing I did after I got back into civil life was to go to Detroit to see my sister. It was six weeks before I attempted a job, and during that six weeks I rested.

"I first took a job with the Studebaker and stayed there about two months. During those two months I lost a few days, because I didn't feel like working. I ceased working for the Studebaker people because I conuld't stand the work; too much smoke.

"I rested up a while at my sister's, and then I took a job with the Dodge people. To the best of my belief I don't believe I worked for them over two weeks. I had to leave there for the same reason.

"I next worked at the Ford plant, Highland Park. I worked there ten weeks, during which I lost a little time on account of sickness.

"There was quite a long interval between the time I ceased work for the Dodge people and went to work for Ford.

"I quit working for Ford because the work was too hard. It was on a punch press, drill press.

"After that I went to work for the Cadillac Company, and worked, I think about six weeks. I did not work steadily six weeks; I lost time. I ceased work for the Cadillac people because the work was too hard; so much smoke and gas.

"The gas and smoke nauseated me, and made my chest condition worse."

Q. What did you do about that chest condition?

A. I thought I better go where I could get more fresh air.

Q. Where did you go; what did you do?

A. I went back East; I went to the lumber woods in Northern New York State.

"I was there about a month. I felt better, but I couldn't stand the work; it was too hard. * * *

"I saw Dr. Hyatt after I got out of the service. He was located in Herkimer, New York. I did not get any treatment under Dr. Hyatt." * * *

"After I consulted with Dr. Hyatt I went to Arizona. I stayed there two years. I didn't do anything down there; I went down there for my health, to cure this T. B.

"I went to work for a washing machine outfit; I didn't make good. I met another fellow who was a pioneer representative. He was going to Prescott, and he told me he would give me a job if I would go to Prescott. That was known to be the best place in Arizona for a T. B. condition, so I went with him and tried it for a while; but riding over the rough roads, going from house to house, was too much for me. I couldn't stand it, and finally gave that up, too. * * *

"To the best of my knowledge, I was in the Letterman General Hospital in 1926. After that I went back to Pennsylvania, and lived with my wife's people about a year.

"I worked on a couple of farms, and then I took a job in the Pennsylvania Highway Department. During that year, working for the Pennsylvania Highway and working on a farm, I made about $300.00."

Q. How long did you work any one time continuously, without interrupation?

A. About a week. * * *

"On my way out here I stopped in Jerome, Idaho, and worked about two weeks. At that time I was suffering continually from stomach trouble."

Q. How does that stomach trouble affect you? Tell us what it does to you.

A. I have gnawing pains all the time; I can't sleep nights, and after I eat I have all kinds of distress and agony.

Q. Have you had that pain since you were in France?

A. No. (?)

Q. When did it start?

A. I had it at intervals off and on the last eight years.

"I had this stomach trouble in France; it started at the receiving station in Souile when I was in there for treatment. I did not have it before I went into the service. I did not have any pulmonary trouble before I entered the service.

"Idaho was my last employment before I came to Oregon. The next job I had was for six weeks for a contractor named Miles Stuper at Grants Pass, Oregon. They were building new water works down there. I worked every day for six weeks.

"At the end of that time I was ready to collapse. My stomach condition became so bad that I couldn't stand it to work any longer. There was work for me if I could have continued, but it just happened the day I was going to quit the job, they built a pile driver and had two men to drive the piling, and only two men could do it, so they laid me off. Since then I haven't had any jobs in Oregon.

"I went to Williams, Josephine County, to live because I couldn't afford to live in town. I didn't have to pay anything for wood out there, and I got my water free. Another reason I went out there to live is it is high out there where I am living. I feel a little bit better when I am there."

On cross-examination, plaintiff testified as follows (Tr. pp. 44-57):

"At the time of my discharge my condition was not good. We were lined up and were all examined at that time. I made no complaint to anyone about my physical condition at that time.

"The first time I made any complaint about my physical condition was to **Dr. Ralph P. Hyatt.** He was not connected with the government at that time. * * *

"I was with the Studebaker Company for the purpose of learning the business—motor business—and I used to help make tests on motors. There was no strenuous labor connected with making these tests. During the two months I was there I didn't do anything else but help make these tests.

"Then I went to work a while for the Dodge people. I had to rest up a while after my work with the Studebaker Company before I went to work with Dodge.

"There was too much gas and smoke at the Studebaker Company; I couldn't stand that.

"Then I applied for work with the Dodge Company. It was a different kind of work. I was on light repair; that is, where they take the cars for final test, before they send them to the proving ground; just had to get in and drive them around. All I did was drive them around. Besides driving the cars around we had to check up on the transmission, and if they were noisy we had to take the top off and use a little hammer on the gears. It wasn't much of a job; that is about all there was to it. There was not a great deal of work connected with that.

"I worked there about two weeks. I couldn't stand that work either; I couldn't stand the smoke. There is gas and smoke in connection with that work at times, because they may have two or three cars running at the same time. The reason I couldn't stand the work was because of the gas and smoke.

"Then I applied to the Ford people after I left there. At the Ford plant I ran a drill press and punch press. One reason I had to leave there was because the work was too hard for me. They kept changing us from days to nights. I got run down so bad I had to leave.

"I was there ten weeks. That was mostly foot work. I had to stand up all the time. There was some gas and smoke around there, but not to any great extent. It didn't bother me so much around the Ford plant. It was the standing up and using my feet that bothered me there. I used to get so tired I couldn't carry on.

"To the best of my belief, I think it was 1922—'21 or '22—that I left the Ford plant. It was before I was in the Great Lakes Hospital under observation.

"I ran a wet grinder when I was with the Cadillac people. I had a job cutting—that is a Gleason cutter, sort of a gear cutter. I had to stand up on that job.

"After I left the Ford plant I didn't go to the Cadillac people for some time. I was sick, and thought I better rest up. That was before I was at the Great Lakes Hospital. All of these places were before I went to the Great Lakes Hospital for observation. * * *

"When I left there, first went to Chicago, Great Lakes Veterans' Hospital, for observation. When I left the hospital I came back to Detroit. I did not work for any of these companies in Detroit after I got out of the hospital. * * *

"The only treatments I took for my condition during that time was what I took myself. I used to buy medicine. I had two or three examinations in Philadelphia, but they never gave me any treatment; that was for the chest condition. I had two or three examinations by physicians connected with the Veterans' Bureau; they sent for me every little while because I had applied for compensation. But I didn't receive any treatment while I was there. * * *

"I came to Arizona after I left Philadelphia. The only thing I did there was trying to sell washing machines. I had never tried salesman work before. I did not have any success at that. * * *"

Q. Were you trying to sell machines, calling on customers all that four months?

A. No; part of the time I would have to lay in and rest up. * * *

"I stayed in Arizona about two years altogether. Then I went East to see a brother at Flint, Michigan. I went back to see a brother there that was ill, and after I got back there I was taken ill myself. * * *

"After I left my brother in Flint I came to Jerome, Idaho, where I took a job on a farm. That was in the summer time. I didn't work there very long; about two weeks.

"Then I came on to Oregon. At this time I was driving. * * *

"I first came to Oregon two years ago, into The Dalles. I lived there a week or so, working in a garage.

"Then I left and came to Portland, arriving in the Fall of 1929. I first applied for work at Swenson's Employment Agency. They couldn't do anything for me. I used to get a job a day or two around in a garage. Jobs were kind of hard to find at that time. I did some work at different times in different garages."

Q. About how long did that continue in Portland before you left?

A. Then about four months before I left. I had nothing to do for about four mouths before I left.

Q. How long were you in Portland altogether?

A. I came here in the Fall, and left next Spring.

Q. Came here in the Fall of 1929, and left in the Spring of 1930? A. Yes.

Q. That four months you couldn't get a job?

A. *I wasn't able to work.*

"I had two short jobs while I was in Oakland the winter of '29 and '30. I did not go down there to look for work. I went down to see if the climate would do me any good. It was so damp and cold here I began to feel bad again. I went down there to try that climate down there. * * *

"Then I came back to Grants Pass and did that work for Mr. Stuber. I did not do any other work in Grants Pass. Then I went from there to Williams.

"I live about five miles from Williams. It is not a farm. It used to be a homestead; it is a dry farm, no stock or anything on it. I do not cultivate any of it. It was a homestead relinquishment. I got it this Spring. * * *"

Q. You said the first time your stomach bothered you was over at that well. Did all of you drink out of that well?

A. No, there was only about four of us drank out of that.

Q. How long was it before you began to have those pains? I understood it was after you got out of service.

A. No, I got those pains after I drank the water. They lasted about six weeks, then I didn't have any more until some time after that. * * *

Q. Where was the first place you started taking treatments after you got out of the service?

A. I never have taken any treatments. I just went to Arizona. They told me that was the only place I could be cured. * * *

Q. Let me see your hands. (Witness exhibits hands to counsel.) You don't do anything on this homestead?

A. No, sir.

"I just live down there. I am living down there at this time."

Upon redirect the plaintiff testified as follows (Tr. p. 57):

Q. Just briefly name the different veterans' bureau hospitals, or offices, you have been in since you got out of the service.

A. The first one was Detroit; the next one Great Lakes, Illinois; examined in Indianapolis, Indiana; and the one in Philadelphia, Pennsylvania. I was in the University Hospital, Oklahoma, for stomach examination.

Q. How about Arizona?

A. I had several examinations in Arizona— Phoenix.

"I have been examined at Letterman's. Dr. Read examined me the last time I was examined. There were four doctors altogether examined me, looked at me through the fluoroscope.

"A diagnosis of pulmonary tuberculosis was made. That was after I went to Phoenix, Arizona."

Plaintiff, called in rebuttal, further testified (Tr. pp. 69 and 70):

"Dr. R. B. Hyatt, who examined me before I entered the service, was the same doctor that treated me after I got back. He lives at Herkimer. * * *"

Q. I am handing you Plaintiff's Exhibit "B" and call your attention to the report of the Adjutant General prior to your entering service, and ask if that bears your signature, at the bottom of the page?

A. Yes, sir.

Q. Now, in answer to this question: "Declaration of Soldier. Have you any reason to believe that at the present time you are suffering from any disability or impairment of health, whether or not incurred in the military service?" the answer is "no." Did you write that answer in?

A. No, sir; I never did.

Q. Was that there before you signed it, or not? When was it written in there? If you don't know, say so.

A. I really couldn't say for sure.

"I have no explanation to make to the jury about the signature that appears in answer to that question. I was then suffering from a physical disability. I was sick; I was discouraged; I thought if I could get out of the service and get home I would get better."

In support of plaintiff's contentions, the following testimony was introduced:

Mrs. A. J. Anderson, one of plaintiff's witnesses, testified as follows (Tr. p. 58):

"Mr. Anderson and I know Mr. Hill. We knew him and his family when they lived here. We met them about two years ago, the latter part of December. We were neighbors; they lived next door. I was in their home practically every day.

"I know Mr. Hill complained of his stomach all the time he lived there. Every time he ate a meal he had trouble afterwards. I know he wasn't working while he was there.

"I don't know what kind of trouble he seemed to have after eating; seemed like it burned his stomach. He always took some kind of medicine afterwards.

"During the period of time I saw him he was nervous; didn't look at all well; hasn't since I have met him.

"I have personal knowledge of his condition at home; I saw him there. He had some kind of spells after he ate. I know he had to go to bed several times. I saw him in bed in the daytime a short time, possibly three or four times."

And her husband, Mr. A. J. Anderson, testified (Tr. pp. 59, 60):

"I know Mr. Hill, the plaintiff here, and met him the same time as my wife, in December, 1929. They were next door neighbors.

"I was in and out of their home, sometimes every day, or every day or two. We were constantly in touch with them. If I wasn't there every day or so, the women visited back and forth.

"At this time I thought Mr. Hill was a sick man. He was complaining all the time I knew him; still is, that he was sick; and he looked sick. And different times I have seem him taking medicine. The last couple of weeks he has been continually taking medicine, and I surmised it was his stomach.

"Mr. Hill is very high strung; he is nervous. If he gets his mind set on any one thing, or tells you about something, one particular thing—pretty soon he gets so loud you can hear him a block away."

Q. Do you know what kind of nights he spends?

A. I have come home twelve, one or two o'clock, and see a light. I would drop in, and Mr. Hill was complaining he couldn't sleep. I tried to sympathize with him different ways; I felt sorry for him. * * *

"He has been at my place since this came on for trial. He also came to my place in August—or October—a year ago, for a visit. His condition has always been the same."

In Appellant's Brief, much is made of the fact that the record made by plaintiff does not include testimony from medical experts. Careful reading of the testimony will show that the major portion of plaintiff's time subsequent to discharge was spent in New York, Michigan, Pennsylvania, Indiana and Arizona. This plaintiff, ravaged by tuberculosis and ever in quest of health, could not, in the nature of things, produce the testimony of the physicians who had seen him through those years. It is apparent from a review of his industrial history that the plaintiff had not been able to make a livelihood throughout the years following release from service. From page 54, Transcript of Record, we learn that plaintiff, with his family, was living, at the time of the trial, on a homestead in Southern Oregon. The record made suggests why plaintiff was unable to supply medical evidence in support of his testimony.

However, the absence of medical testimony does not improve appellant's position for the reason that the plaintiff's own testimony constitutes substantial evidence sufficient to support this judgment.

In United States v. Tyrakowski (C. C. A.), 50 Fed. (2d) 766, 768, 771, the Court, in defining what constitutes substantial evidence, remarked:

"We do not wish to be understood as saying that the allegations of the complaint were proved by a preponderance of all the evidence, for that was a matter for the trial Court to decide; but we do say that appellee's testimony constituted substantial evidence of his total disability. The term 'substantial evidence' is not used in the sense of reliability, but rather in contradistinction to the term 'scintilla of evidence.' His evidence cannot be disregarded, although it is not such as to inspire complete confidence. * * * there is evidence tending to show that the disability was total and permanent, and we are compelled to hold that such evidence amounted to more than a scintilla and was substantial, regardless of what our views may be as to its weight and reliability.

"While realizing that the evidence is not as convincing as we might wish or as we might require if we were the trier of the facts instead of a reviewer of the trier's facts, yet we cannot say under this record that there is no substantial evidence to show that insured was so disabled prior to August 31, 1919, that he could not follow continuously any gainful occupation. That is the test. United States v. Phillips (C. C. A.), 44 F. (2d) 689; United States v. Eliasson (C. C. A.), 20 F. (2d) 821; United States v. Cox (C. C. A.) 24 F. (2d) 944; United States v. Sligh, (C. C. A.) 31 F. (2d) 735; United States v. Schweppe (C. C. A.), 38 F. (2d) 595."

The fact that several witnesses contradict a party's unsupported statement does not make his statement a mere scintilla of evidence so as to be insufficient to support a verdict in his favor. 23 C. J. 9, Sec. 1733.

Were appellant's contention in this regard correct, any veteran whose doctors, otherwise available, had died or were out of the country at the time of trial, would be barred from recovery, no matter how meritorious his case might be.

Furthermore, the Government's counsel might see fit to confess that the soldier plaintiff was and had been totally and permanently disabled for the past seven, eight or nine years, and thus bar such medical testimony as might be available to the soldier plaintiff.

We strenuously urge that the plaintiff himself offers substantial evidence that he came out of the service after a long period of sickness, and, at the time of his discharge, had the typical picture of one suffering from pulmonary tuberculosis. In addition he was then suffering from nervous disorders and stomach trouble. (Tr. p. 39.)

He continued in quest of continuous employment, and, at the same time, continued to seek good health. By reason of the condition which came upon him incident to his wartime service, he was unsuccessful in securing and achieving his objective in both regards.

He has continued sick and unable to work all these years. We find him at time of trial unable to do anything at all (Tr. pp. 44, 54, 56)—he is living on a homestead which he is unable to farm—in effect, he is a public charge.

His condition is accurately portrayed by Mr. and Mrs. Anderson and it would seem to be reasonable to conclude from this advantageous position of hindsight that, as the jury found, plaintiff, in April, 1919, was unable to work and was in a condition of total disability which was reasonably certain to continue throughout his lifetime. Time has proven this to be the fact.

As said by the Court in McGovern v. United States, 294 Fed. 108 (C. C. A.) 299 Fed. 302:

> "As permanency of any condition (here, total disability) involves the element of time, the event of its continuance during the passage of time is competent and cogent evidence."

In the case of Humble v. United States, 49 Fed. (2d) 600, there was, apparently, no statement of opinion as to the permanence of plaintiff's pulmonary tuberculosis. The only medical testimony referred to was contained in the diagnostic reports of the Veterans Bureau doctors as to the plaintiff's condition over a term of years. This testimony was amplified by that of lay observers who described the plaintiff's condition at various periods subsequent to the war. Referring to the time when plaintiff claimed he became disabled the Court said:

> "My conclusion, further, is that he was then permanently disabled within the meaning of the Act. It was then impossible to say that the disease would not continue active for the rest of his life. The disposition of the case could not await subsequent developments to determine whether it would. Besides, the possibility that it might thereafter cease to be active and become arrested did not affect the permanency of the disability, and that for two reasons. An arrested tuberculosis may become active again if the vitality is lowered—manual labor performed continuously and to the extent necessary

to the success of a substantially gainful occupation is calculated to lower the vitality—and plaintiff was adapted only to an occupation involving such labor. The other reason is that the Act seems to contemplate that a total disability may at the same time be permanent so as to cause the maturing of the policy notwithstanding it may subsequently turn out that it may not be permanent. * * *"

Another line of authorities dealing with personal injuries permits consideration of permanence of an injury or disability by a jury in the absence of expert testimony. In the case of B. & A. Electric Ry. Co. v. Cross, 142 Md. 500, 121 Atl. 374, there was no medical evidence. The trial was held two and a half years after the injury and testimony tended to show that there had been no recovery. The question of permanence was held for the jury on this alone. To like effect see Burns v. Polar Wave Ice & Fuel Co., 187 S. W. 145; Chapman v. Kansas City Ry. Co., 217 S. W. 623; Alabama Great Southern Ry. Co. v. Taylor, 71 So. 676.

Appellant would upset this judgment by reason of the fact that plaintiff introduced the Adjutant-General's office report and his own Honorable Discharge from the United States Army. It will be remembered that these documents were prepared by army officials, and that plaintiff, as did millions of others, signed when and where he was told. The circumstances under which plaintiff signed the Adjutant-General's report are eloquently pictured on page 70 of the Transcript of Record:

> "I have no explanation to make to the jury about the signature that appears in answer to that question. I was then suffering from a physical disability. I was sick; I was discouraged; I thought if I could get out of the service and get home I would get better."

The Courts have had this question to deal with before. Thus, in Nichols v. United States, 48 Fed. (2d) 293, 296, the Court remarked:

> "I see no escaping the conclusion that at the time of plaintiff's discharge he was afflicted with tuberculosis. * * * Nor is it affected by plaintiff's declaration at the time of his discharge. He may not have realized his condition and he may then have been feeling better in view of his prospect of getting home than he did whilst he was in the service."

Again, in Sprencel v. United States, 47 Fed. (2d) 501, 505, the Court said:

> "The circumstances of his having signed his discharge, and the other papers above mentioned in the manner indicated, were to be considered by the jury in determining the weight and effect of his testimony in this case along with all the other proof."

Also, in Clark v. United States, 48 Fed. (2d) 291, 293, the Court said:

> "Much is made of the fact that in his discharge it is stated that at that time his physical condition was good to which he gave consent by subscribing his name thereto. But the examination was more

or less superficial, and it is not unlikely that he did
not realize the serious condition in which he then
was."

See, also, to the same effect as foregoing decisions,
Hayden v. United States (C. C. A. 9th), 41 Fed. (2d)
614, 617.

In conclusion, plaintiff has run the gauntlet of Court
and jury. The jury who saw plaintiff and heard his
history found him to be totally and permanently disabled as of April 4, 1919. The trial Judge, after argument on a motion for new trial, decided that plaintiff
had introduced substantial evidence sufficient to support this verdict.

Keeping in mind the past expressions of this Circuit
Court of Appeals wherein the cases of Ford v. United
States, supra, and White v. United States, supra, are
cited with approval, we feel warranted in urging that
the judgment herein be affirmed.

Respectfully submitted,

ALLAN A. BYNON,
Attorney for Appellee.

No. 6807

United States
Circuit Court of Appeals
For the Ninth Circuit / 3

GIUSEPPE GRECO, alias JIMMY POLIZZI,

Appellant,

vs.

~~EDWARD L. HAFF, AS ACTING~~
~~JOHN D. NAGLE,~~ Commissioner of Immigration,
Port of San Francisco,

Appellee.

Transcript of Record

Upon Appeal from the United States District Court
for the Northern District of California,
Southern Division.

No. 6807

United States
Circuit Court of Appeals
For the Ninth Circuit

GIUSEPPE GRECO, alias JIMMY POLIZZI,

Appellant,

vs.

JOHN D. NAGLE, Commissioner of Immigration, Port of San Francisco,

Appellee.

Transcript of Record

Upon Appeal from the United States District Court for the Northern District of California, Southern Division.

INDEX

[Clerk's Note: When deemed likely to be of an important nature, errors or doubtful matters appearing in the original certified record are printed literally in italic; and, likewise, cancelled matter appearing in the original certified record is printed and cancelled herein accordingly. When possible, an omission from the text is indicated by printing in italic the two words between which the omission seems to occur.]

Page

Affidavit of E. Hanoff...................... 70

Assignment of Errors....................... 92

Certificate of Clerk to Transcript of Record.. 96

Citation on Appeal......................... 97

EXHIBITS:

    Exhibit "A" 9

    Exhibit "B" 11

    Exhibit "C" 19

    Exhibit "D" 67

Notice of Filing Respondent's Exhibits....... 71

    Respondent's Exhibit 1 73

    Respondent's Exhibit 2 75

    Respondent's Exhibit 3 77

    Respondent's Exhibit 4 78

    Respondent's Exhibit 5 79

    Respondent's Exhibit 6 87

Notice of Appeal........................... 90

Order Allowing Appeal...................... 94

Order to Show Cause........................ 68

Order Submitting Matter.................... 89

Order Denying Petition for Writ............. 89

Petition for Writ of Habeas Corpus.......... 1

Petition for Appeal........................ 91

Praecipe for Transcript of Record.......... 95

NAMES AND ADDRESSES OF ATTORNEYS.

JAMES F. BRENNAN, Esq., and NATHAN
MERENBACH, Esq., 701 Hearst Bldg., San
Francisco, California.

For Petitioner and Appellant.

GEORGE J. HATFIELD, United States Attorney,
San Francisco, Calif.

For Respondent and Appellee.

In the United States District Court for the Northern District of California, Southern Division.

No. 20,741-L.

In the Matter of the Application of
GIUSEPPE GRECO, alias JIMMIE POLIZZI,
For a Writ of Habeas Corpus.

PETITION FOR WRIT OF HABEAS CORPUS.

To the Honorable Judges of the United States District Court in and for the Northern District of California:

Your petitioner, Giuseppe Greco, alias Jimmy Polizzi, respectfully shows and represents to the Court the following facts:

That your petitioner is now unlawfully imprisoned and detained and confined and restrained of his liberty by one John D. Nagle, United States Immigration Commissioner at San Francisco, Northern District of California.

That your petitioner is not imprisoned, restrained or deprived of his liberty by or under any process, judgment or decree of any competent court or tribunal of civil jurisdiction.

That the true cause or pretense of the restraint and imprisonment of your petitioner as aforesaid, is a certain alleged "Warrant for Deportation of Alien," a copy of which said alleged warrant is annexed hereto, made a part hereof and marked "Exhibit A"; that the said warrant depends upon certain proofs submitted to the Department of Labor of the United States, and more particularly the Assistant Secretary of Labor who signed and issued said warrant.

The copies of the said proofs and testimony taken before [1*] the Immigration Inspectors and otherwise are attached hereto, made a part hereof, and marked Exhibits B and C, respectively.

That the said proofs do not state facts sufficient to constitute a crime against any law or laws of the United States, and do not constitute facts sufficient to invest said Department of Labor with jurisdiction to issue said warrant or to deport petitioner; that there is no evidence to show that this petitioner was guilty of any crime against the United States and there is no evidence to show that your petitioner was found, after entering, advocating or teaching anarchy or that he is a member of or affiliated with

---

*Page numbering appearing at the foot of page of original certified Transcript of Record.

an organization, association, society or group, that advises or advocates or believes in or teaches the overthrow of the Government of the United States by force or violence, or, of all or any forms of law; or that he is a member of and affiliated with an organization or association or society or group that writes or circulates or distributes or prints or publishes or displays or causes to be printed or written or published or displayed or circulated or has in its possession for the purpose of said circulation, publication, !distribution or issue, written or printed matter advising or advocating or teaching the overthrow of the Government of the United States or at all or any forms of law.

Your petitioner further shows that for the reasons hereinabove set forth, said detention and imprisonment by the said John D. Nagle, United States Immigration Commissioner, is illegal and without authority of justification of the law and is in violation of the Constitution of the United States of America and the amendments thereto, and contrary to the acts of Congress in such case made and provided, and that the said warrant of deportation was wrongfully and unlawfully issued against this petitioner. [2]

That your petitioner was arrested and taken into custody on the 11th day of September, 1930, at San Francisco, California, by officials of the United States Immigration Service of the Department of Labor without any warrant; that immediately after his said arrest your petitioner was questioned and a statement was taken from him; that your petitioner is ignorant of the English language and did not know or understand the nature or purpose of the questions asked him; that your petitioner was not informed at said time of the reason for his arrest or that he was entitled to be represented by counsel; that no copy of any evidence or papers upon which a warrant of arrest was issued was shown him; that no warrant of arrest was at said time issued for your petitioner's arrest; that a copy of the statement taken from said petitioner at said time and place is hereto attached and marked Exhibit "B"; that subsequent to the arrest of your petitioner and subsequent to the taking of the statement from your petitioner marked Exhibit "B" a warrant was issued for the arrest of your petitioner and was presented to your petitioner on or about the first day of October, 1930; that at no time prior to the hearing of your petitioner or at the hearing of your petitioner were the papers or evidence upon which said warrant was issued, submitted to your petitioner or his attorneys; that on or about the first day of October, 1930, and from time to time thereafter, your petitioner was given a hearing before Inspectors P. J. Farrelly and T. E. Borden of the United States Immigration Service at San Francisco, California; that a copy of all testimony adduced at said hearing is hereby attached and marked Exhibit "C"; that the evidence upon which the warrant of arrest was issued was not shown to your petitioner or to your petitioner's attorneys pursuant to Rule 22, subdivision 5b of the Rules of the [3] ·Immigration Service, by reason of which your petitioner was denied a fair and impartial hearing and due process of law within the meaning of the Constitution of the United States.

That on said hearing beginning November 1, 1930, the Inspectors in charge of said hearing arbitrarily marked in evidence certain statements taken from your petitioner by said Immigration officials on the 11th day of September, 1930, prior to the date upon which the warrant for arrest of petitioner was issued; that said statements were hearsay and were arbitrarily marked in evidence; that thereby your petitioner was denied a fair and impartial hearing and was denied due process of law within the meaning of the Constitution of the United States.

That during said hearing the Inspectors in charge exhibited to your petitioner a number of magazines and pamphlets, none of which magazines or documents your petitioner recognized; that the authorship of said magazines was not shown and it was not shown that said magazines were ever circulated or distributed by anybody; that there was no evidence to show from what source the Immigration Service came into possession of said magazines, or that your petitioner ever saw or knew about them; that by arbitrarily marking said magazines and pamphlets without in any way connecting the same with your petitioner, your petitioner was denied an impartial hearing and due process of law within the meaning of the Constitution of the United States.

That at the end of the hearing before Inspector P. J. Farrelly, said Inspector arbitrarily stated to your petitioner that an extra oral charge was made against your petitioner, as set forth on page 17 beginning line 12 of Exhibit "C", without directing his attention to the facts which constituted the reason for this additional charge. [4]

That said Immigration inspector arbitrarily incorporated into the record certain reports of Inspectors Brown, Neilson and Endicott, as set forth on page 17 beginning line 7 of Exhibit "C"; that said reports were hearsay; that none of said inspectors were produced or submitted to cross-examination; that the reports of said inspectors were not produced, nor was the reading of said reports waived, nor were said reports or the contents thereof incorporated in the record, a full copy of which record is attached hereto and marked Exhibit "C"; that by the arbitrary marking of said reports of said inspectors in evidence, your petitioner was denied a fair and impartial hearing and was denied due process of law within the meaning of the Constitution of the United States.

That certain pamphlets and magazines were exhibited to your petitioner, none of which your petitioner identified, nor were any of said magazines or pamphlets connected in any way with your petitioner; that said pamphlets and magazines were arbitrarily admitted in evidence over the objection of your petitioner; that in the admission of said magazines in evidence, as set forth on page 18 of Exhibit "C," your petitioner was denied a fair and impartial hearing and was denied due process of law within the meaning of the Constitution of the United States.

That said warrant for deportation of alien hereinabove referred to is at variance with the original warrant of arrest attached hereto and marked Exhibit "D," in that the original warrant of arrest said petitioner was charged with being a Communist, which charge does not appear in the warrant for deportation; that in issuing a warrant for deportation on a charge other than the one upon which the hearing was held, the Department of Labor denied your petitioner a fair and impartial hearing and he was denied due process of law within the meaning of the Constitution of the United States. [5]

That for the purpose of fully presenting the questions of law in this application, your petitioner begs leave to refer to all of the records of the proceedings held before the inspectors of the United States Immigration Service at San Francisco, California, in the above cause. Your petitioner has produced all of the records and proceedings that were furnished him and the same are hereto attached and marked exhibits "A," "B," "C" and "D." [6]

WHEREFORE, your petitioner prays that a writ of habeas corpus issue directing and commanding the said John D. Nagle, United States Commissioner of Immigration at San Francisco, California, and any and all persons under his direction and control, to produce and bring up said Giuseppe Greco, alias Jimmy Polizzi, before this court for hearing and determination by this court concerning his wrongful detention and restraint, and for such other and further relief as to this court may seem just in the premises; and that said John D. Nagle further produce the warrant of arrest and all evidence upon which said warrant of arrest was issued, if any, together with all records and files and return these proceedings and all orders, papers, files and testimony, of every nature, had and used before him, at such time and place as this honorable court may direct, and further why your petitioner should not be forthwith discharged from custody.

GIUSEPPE GRECO,
Petitioner.

JAS. F. BRENNAN &
NATHAN MERENBACH,
    Attorneys for Petitioner.

United States of America,
Northern District of California,
City and County of San Francisco.—ss.

Giuseppe Greco, alias Jimmy Polizzi, being first duly sworn, deposes and says that he is the petitioner named in the above entitled action; that the foregoing petition was read and explained to him and he knows the contents thereof, and that the same is true.

GIUSEPPE GRECO.

Subscribed and sworn to before me, this 9th day of October, 1931.

[Seal]   HELEN M. FLETCHER,

Notary Public in and for the City and County of San Francisco, State of California. [7]

EXHIBIT "A."

United States of America
Department of Labor
Washington

No. 12020-17739
No. 55711/802

To Commissioner of Immigration, Angel Island Station, San Francisco, Calif.

District Director of Immigration,

Or to any Officer or Employee of the United States Immigration Service:

WHEREAS, from the proofs submitted to P. F. Snyder, Assistant to the Secretary, after due hearing before Immigration Inspectors P. J. Farrelly and T. E. Borden held at San Francisco, California, the said P. F. Snyder has become satisfied that the alien

GIUSEPPE GRECO alias JIMMY POLIZZI

who landed at the port of New York ex SS "Barbarosa" on the 17th day of June, 1909, has been in the United States in violation Immigration Act of October 16, 1918, as amended by the Act of June 5, 1920, in that he is a member of an organization that believes in, advises, advocates and teaches the overthrow by force or violence of the government of the United States and that he is a member of an organization that circulates, distributes, publishes and displays printed matter advising, advocating and teaching the overthrow by force or violence of the government of the United States, and may be deported in accordance therewith,

I, W. N. SMELSER, Assistant to the Secretary of Labor, by virtue of power and authority vested in me by the laws of the United States, do hereby command you to return the said alien to Italy, the country whence he came, at the expense of the appropriation, "Salaries and Expenses, Bureau of Immigration, 1932," including the expenses of an attendant, [8] if necessary. Delivery of the alien and acceptance for deportation will serve to cancel the outstanding appearance bond.

For so doing, this shall be your sufficient warrant.

Witness my hand and seal this 31st day of July, 1931.

                    W. N. SMELSER,
                    Assistant to the Secretary of
                    Labor.   [9]

EXHIBIT "B."

U. S. Department of Labor
Immigration Service
District No. 30

12020/

Preliminary Statement taken from	City Office San Francisco, California September 11, 1930
GIUSEPPE GRECO alias JIMMY POLIZZI to determine his status.	Present: P. J. FARRELLY, Examining Inspector; C. J. SCANLON, Stenographer

Alien is sworn:

Q. What is your full and correct name?

A. Giuseppe Greco.

Q. Have you ever used any other name?

A. Yes, Jimmy Polizzi.

Q. When and where were you born?

A. In Licata, Sicily, Italy, on September 10, 1883.

Q. Were either of your parents ever residents in the United States?

A. No.

Q. What was your father's name?

A. "Polizzi."

Q. Do you know the first name of your father?

A. Yes, "Vincenze."

Q. Was your alleged father married to your mother?

A. No.

Q. What was your mother's name?

A. Angela Greco.

Q. Have you used the name "Greco" while residing in the United States?

A. Yes, all the time.

Q. What name did you use when you arrived in the United States?

A. Giuseppe Greco.

Q. When and where did you arrive in the United States?

A. On June 17, 1909, as a passenger on the SS "Barbarosa" at the port of New York.

Q. Have you left the United States since your arrival here in June, 1909?

A. Yes, I went to Alaska once.

Q. Have you ever applied to become a citizen of the United States?

A. Yes, once.

Q. When and where did you apply?

A. Here in San Francisco in 1919, I think.

Q. Under what name?

A. Giuseppe Greco.

Q. Was it before or after the war?

A. After the war.

Q. Where did you register for the Draft?

A. Here in San Francisco.

Q. What classification did you receive?

A. I was in the second Draft but the war was ended and so I was not called.

Q. Do you understand now that you are under oath and sworn to tell the truth?

A. Yes, I understand.

Q. Are you a member now of the Trade Union Unity League?

A. Yes.

Q. When did you join the organization?

A. In January this year.

Q. Are you a member of the Communist Party?

A. No.

Q. When you speak of the Trade Union Unity League, what do you mean?

A. It is an organization for better pay and better conditions.

Q. Did you ever read a pamphlet called the "Trade Union Unity League—its Program, Structure, Methods and History"?

A. No.

Q. Can you read English?

A. A little bit. [10]

Q. Can you read in the Italian language?

A. A little bit.

Q. Have you ever attended meetings at the Communist Headquarters, 145 Turk?

A. Yes.

Q. When?

A. A long time ago.

Q. When was it?

A. The last time I paid the dues.

Q. Are you in sympathy with the objects of the Trade Union Unity League?

A. I belong to them.

Q. Are you in sympathy with their objects and aims?

A. Yes I am.

Q. Do you attend the meetings of the Communist Party at 145 Turk Street?

A. No, I do not.

Q. Do you know that the Trade Union Unity League has as its program to struggle and fight against the capitalist—to war against the capitalist, and to force this country into a defense of the Soviet Union?

A. No.

Q. Do you know that the Trade Union Unity League organizes and educates the masses into fighting in defense of the Soviet Union?

A. No, I do not know that.

Q. Do you call the government, as we have it in the United States, as it is at the present time, a capitalistic government or is it a government of the workers?

A. I think it is a government of the people.

Q. Is it a government affiliated with the Soviet Union?

A. No, it is not.

Q. Is it not the policy of the Trade Union Unity League to organize the workers in order that each country shall change its organization and laws so that it becomes a member of the Soviet Union?

A. Yes, that is the policy.

Q. In other words, if you were a member of the Trade Union Unity League in San Francisco and another man who was a member of the Trade Union Unity League in Mexico you would both be working with the same ends and purposes in view—is that correct?

A. Yes, this is right.

Q. If your comrade in Mexico would want to make this country a party of the Soviet Union would you work toward that end also?

A. Yes.

Q. And if your comrades in the United States would want to change the institutions in this country so that it would become a member of the Soviet Union would you vote for such a change?

A. Yes.

Q. Then you, as a member of the Trade Union Unity League, were working to do your part to change this government to be a government affiliated with the Soviet Union as one of the Soviet Republics?

A. Yes, I want this to be a worker republic.

Q. How do you want to change the constitution of this country so that this country would become a member of the Soviet Union or a Soviet Republic?

A. By the votes of the people.

Q. Do you or do you not believe in the overthrow of the government of the United States by force of arms?

A. No.

Q. What is your reason for not believing in the overthrow of the government by force of arms?

A. No, I have none.

Q. Do you know that the Trade Union Unity League teaches the overthrow of the government of the United States by force of arms?

A. It never taught me.

Q. Can you explain how it is that when you were taken into custody you stated that you were not a member of the Trade Union Unity League?

A. It just happened.

Q. Why did you deny your membership in the Trade Union Unity League?

A. I had no reason at all. [11]

Q. Is membership in the Trade Union Unity League something to be ashamed of?

A. No, I just said "no".

Q. Do you believe in the principles of the Trade Union Unity League?

A. Yes.

Q. Did you take an oath when you joined the Trade Union Unity League?

A. No.

Q. Did you sign any pledge, paper or document of any kind?

A. No.

Q. Are you loyal to the principles of the Trade Union Unity League or are you loyal to the government of the United States?

A. Yes, I am loyal to the Trade Union Unity League and I am a good member.

Q. Have you ever applied to become an American citizen since 1919?

A. No.

Q. Can you read any English?

A. A little bit.

Q. Did you ever join the Communist party at any time?

A. No.

Q. Do you subscribe to the "Daily Worker"?

A. No.

Q. Did you ever distribute any leaflets issued by the Communist Party?

A. No.

Q. Did you ever have in your possession or in your home any leaflets issued by the Communist Party?

A. Yes, I have had them in my home.

Q. I show you a leaflet which was distributed by the Communist Party at the time the fleet of the United States was in port. This leaflet is headed "DEFEND THE SOVIET UNION! DEFEND SOVIET CHINA! FIGHT AGAINST IMPERIALISTIC WAR!" I ask if you ever had in your possession a leaflet similar to this one?

A. I do not know—a lot of times they gave them to me and I take them home and read them.

Q. You never distributed them did you?

A. No.

Q. Where did they generally give those leaflets to you?

A. On the streets sometimes.

Q. Did you ever make application to join the Communist Party?

A. No.

Q. Have you ever been arrested in the United States?

A. Yes, about a year ago.

Q. Where?

A. At Market and Stevenson Streets. I saw a bunch of people there and I was arrested.

Q. At that time was there a Communist meeting there?

A. Yes, a Communist meeting was going on there.

Q. Were you a speaker?

A. No.

Q. Were you carrying a banner?

A. No.

Q. Were you sentenced to any term of imprisonment?

A. No, I was taken out that night.

Q. Under what name were you arrested?

A. Guiseppe Greco.

Q. Are you sure you did not give the name of Jimmy Polizzi?

A. Yes.

Q. Who put up the bail money for you?

A. The Labor Defender.

Q. Is that the only time you were arrested?

A. Yes.

Q. Were you ever married?

A. No.

Q. Where are you employed at the present time?

A. By Mr. Barrons who operates a window cleaning organization on Turk Street near Taylor. It is 115 Turk Street.

Q.   You also have a shoe shining parlor—is that right?

A.   Yes.

DESCRIPTION OF ALIEN: Height, 5′ 8½″; weight, 180 lbs; brown eyes; dark brown hair. Marks: scar on forehead.

I hereby CERTIFY that the foregoing is a true and correct transcript of the notes taken in the above described case.

C. J. SCANLON, Stenographer.
Book 14,132. [12]

EXHIBIT "C".

U. S. Department of Labor
Immigration Service
District No. 30

In answering refer to
No. 12020/17739

Office of the Commissioner
Angel Island Station
Via Ferry Post Office
San Francisco, Calif.
October 30, 1930

Nathan Merenbach, Attorney at Law,
   703 Market Street, San Francisco, Cal.
      James F. Brennan, Attorney,
         Russ Building, San Francisco, Cal.

Sir:

This is to inform you that hearing in the case of your client Giuseppe Greco alias Jimmy Polizzi has been set for 10 AM on October 28, 1930, and will be held at this office, Room 65 Appraisers Building, Washington and Sansome Streets, San Francisco. Please be prepared to proceed with this matter at the time designated.

Respectfully

For the Commissioner

San Francisco District

W. E. WALSH

Inspector in Charge

City Office

JGG;NH   [13]

Form 607

U. S. Department of Labor

Immigration Service

File No. 12020/17739

REPORT OF HEARING

in the case of

GIUSEPPE GRECO, alias

JIMMY POLIZZI

Under Department warrant No. 55711/802.

Dated September 12, 1930.

Hearing conducted by Inspr. P. J. Farrelly.

At San Francisco, Calif.,   Date Oct. 1, 1930.

Alien taken into custody at San Francisco, Cali-
(place)

fornia,. October 1, 1930, at 1:00 P. M., by Inspector
(Date and Hour)

P. J. Farrelly, and released from custody under
(State if released on own recognizance or

bond in the sum of $1,000.00.
bail, or if detained, where.)

(Testimony of Guiseppe Greco.)

Testimony taken and transcribed by Clerk R. H. Rule.

Said alien, being able to speak and understand the English language satisfactorily, no interpreter.

At request of council however, Paul Di Martini, Jr., is allowed to be present and acts as Italian interpreter in order to facilitate the examination.

(Interpreter duly sworn)

(if other than regular Government employee, state as to being first duly sworn.)

Said alien was informed that the purpose of said hearing was to afford him an opportunity to show cause why he should not be deported to the country whence he came, said warrant of arrest being read and each and every allegation therein contained carefully explained to him. Said alien was offered an opportunity to inspect the warrant of arrest and the evidence upon which it was issued, which privilege was accepted. The alien being first duly sworn, the following evidence was presented:

Q. What is your correct name?

A. Guiseppe Greco. [14]

Q. Have you ever been known by another name?

A. Jimmy Polizzi.

Q. You are advised that under these proceedings you have the right to be represented by counsel. Do you desire to obtain the services of a lawyer?

A. Yes, I am represented by attorneys.

Q. Do you remember making a statement before me at this office under date of September 11th last?

A. Yes.

Q. Was that statement true to the best of your knowledge?

A. Certain things asked me I understood and certain things that were asked me I did not understand.

Q. Do you wish to have that statement read to you through the interpreter?

A. Not at this time.

By EXAMINING INSPECTOR.—The statement referred to is incorporated into and made a part of this record.

———

JOSEPH BARRON
called as a witness and duly sworn.

EXAMINING OFFICER TO WITNESS:

Q. What is your occupation?

A. Contractor.

ATTORNEY BRENNAN TO WITNESS:

Q. Do you know the alien here, Giuseppe Greco?

A. Yes.

Q. What has been his business?

A. I am now doing janitorial work.

Q. But you know the alien Giuseppe Greco?

A. Yes.

Q. How long have you known him?

A. About fifteen or twenty years.

Q. In what way have you known him?

(Testimony of Joseph Barron.)

A. In a business way and in a friendly way.

Q. Has he been employed by you during that time?

A. I don't think he has missed six months.

Q. How long has he been employed by you?

A. About fifteen years.

Q. And during that time he has not missed six months from his work?

A. I don't think he has missed six months.

Q. What sort of a man is he as far as you know, industrious and conscientious?

A. A very faithful worker.

Q. Has he any bad habits, such as drinking?

A. He never drinks, never smokes; has no bad habits at all.

Q. Have you ever had any difficulty or arguments of any kind with him?

A. Yes, I have heard him argue, but not anything concerning the Government.

Q. A kind of a free sort of a fellow?

A. He always helps the boys and is always ready to help the boys when he can and he has quite a few dollars outstanding among the boys now.

Q. What type of a man is he mentally?

A. Mentally he is a man, well I would say he is a man more like a boy—a man with a boy's brain. He listens to everyone and is easily influenced. He listens to some argument and he thinks and talks about it and it influences him and he thinks it over and it is something altogether different. He don't

(Testimony of Joseph Barron.)

have a mind of his own. He just listens from one to the other. He is easily influenced.

Q. He never created any disturbance?

A. No.

Q. In labor circles or otherwise?

A. No. We had a union strike in my business once [15] during the war time and they went around trying to pull things down, but he never came and bothered me like the rest of them did and he intended to work just the same.

Q. Do you believe he is a man worthy to become a citizen of the United States?

A. Yes.

Q. Are you a citizen of the United States?

A. Yes.

Q. What is your age?

A. Fifty.

Q. Have you any family?

A. I am married.

Q. How long have you been married?

A. Twenty-five years.

EXAMINING OFFICER TO WITNESS:

Q. Do you know to your own knowledge whether the alien is or is not a member of the Communist Party?

A. No, except that I would say this, that he belongs to the trade union, and he says the trade union was to make better wages.

Q. Were you present when I examined him at your office?

(Testimony of Joseph Barron.)

A. Yes.

Q. Did you hear me ask him the question if he belonged to the Trade Union Unity League?

A. No, although I understood you to say if he belonged to the Communist Party and he said no and you showed him the book.

Q. Did you tell me that he was weak minded and was always spreading propaganda and that you had warned him he was going to get in trouble if he did not cease talking like that?

A. I don't remember that.

Q. There was another officer present during the conversation and you told him you had warned him and said if he did not get away from the crowd around Turk St. that he was going to get in trouble. Where is your office?

A. 115 Turk St.

Q. Do you know where the Communist headquarters are located?

A. I understood it is next door. That is all I understand.

ATTORNEY MERENBACH TO WITNESS:

Q. Mr. Greco is still employed by you?

A. Yes.

Q. And you regard him as a very reliable employee?

A. He is a very good employee.

Q. And he is still employed by you?

A. Yes.

(Testimony of Joseph Barron.)

EXAMINING OFFICER TO WITNESS:

Q. Do you know if he has any other employment besides working for you?

A. I don't know.

Q. You know he goes and runs a bootblack stand when he quits work?

A. Yes.

Q. You have a distinct recollection of the day I was there?

A. Yes, I remember when you came in and I told you where he was working, and I said I would get him in like I did.

Q. Did you at his request communicate with any attorney in San Francisco after he had been taken into custody?

A. No. The only man I spoke to was the man that bailed him out.

Q. Do you know what the Trade Union Unity League stands for?

A. No. [16]

Q. If you knew that the Trade Union Unity League stands for the overthrow of the Government of the United States and if you had known that the alien was a member of it would that change your opinion about him?

A. It certainly would.

Q. Did he ever tell you he was a member of the Trade Union Unity League?

A. No, not to my recollection.

(Testimony of Joseph Barron.)

Q. Since he has been on bail has he ever talked to you about it?

A. No. He talked on the subject.

Q. Did he ever tell you that he became a member?

A. No.

Q. Did you ever ask him if he ever became a member?

A. No. Outside of my business I don't care what he does.

Q. If you knew that he was a member of the Trade Union Unity League, would you still have him in your employ?

A. If I knew what that meant no. If I knew it was against the government I would not have him in my employ. I never studied it enough to know what it is.

Q. After he was taken into custody you knew that he was charged with being a member of an organization that was opposed to the government of the United States?

A. No he told me that he did not belong to the Communist Party and thought the trade union was not part of the Communist party.

JOSEPH CYKLEN

called as a witness and duly sworn.

EXAMINING OFFICER TO WITNESS:

Q. What is your name?

A. Joseph Cyklen.

ATTORNEY BRENNAN TO WITNESS:

Q. Where do you live?

A. 1360 Webster Street. My business is at 1590 O'Farrell St.

Q. Are you married?

A. Yes.

Q. Have you any children?

A. I have five children.

Q. How old is the oldest?

A. Twenty-two years.

Q. Are you a citizen of the United States?

A. I came November 1, 1922.

Q. Do you know the alien Mr. Greco?

A. I knew him seven years.

Q. Did he ever live at your home?

A. He was in my home two years when I was living on O'Farrell Street.

Q. As a member of your family?

A. He had a room in my home and was like a member of the family, playing with the kids all the time, and my family is a musical family, singing all the time. This man rented a room and he took a great interest in music and singing, and so he became like a member of the family, always playing with the kids and singing, and he was taking singing lessons.

(Testimony of Joseph Cyklen.)

Q. What was he paying a lesson?

A. Three dollars a lesson.

Q. Is he quite an accomplished singer?

A. Oh no, he is just a lover of singing.

Q. Did you ever know of him to be in any trouble?

A. No.

Q. What portions of his evenings did he spend at your home?

A. He was there very often. He was in the house every evening cooking for himself and playing with the kids. [17]

Q. And since that time he has visited your home quite frequently?

A. Yes.

Q. Did you ever hear of him belonging to the Communist Party or any organization that was opposed to the Government of the United States?

A. No. If he did I would not have him in the house. I left Russia on account of my dislike for the Russian government. I went with my children to a small settlement just to get rid of that sort of thing.

ATTORNEY MERENBACH TO WITNESS:

Q. And lost considerable property?

A. Yes, I lost a house in Russia that I had had for twenty-two years.

ATTORNEY BRENNAN TO WITNESS:

Q. And you are one of the closest friends that Mr. Greco has in San Francisco.

(Testimony of Joseph Cyklen.)

A.   Yes sir.

Q.   When he got in trouble he immediately called upon you to furnish bail?

A.   Yes.

Q.   If you had believed that he belonged to any organization that was opposed to the government you would have nothing to do with him?

A.   No.

EXAMINING OFFICER TO WITNESS:

Q.   On what vessel did you arrive in San Francisco when you came from Russia?

A.   On the SS "Tenyo Maru."

Q.   Could you speak English when you arrived in the United States?

A.   A little.

Q.   When you knew Mr. Greco first could he speak well or poorly?

A.   Very poorly.

Q.   In your opinion how is his knowledge of English at the present time?   Can he understand questions propounded to him?

A.   Not so good.

Q.   Do you remember the day he was arrested?

A.   I can't remember the day.

Q.   Who told you he was arrested?

A.   His boss told me.

Q.   Did anybody go around in a machine to your place and tell you that he had been taken into custody?

(Testimony of Joseph Cyklen.)

A. After the boss left he came himself with two officers.

Q. Did you make the remark when you were told why he was arrested, did you say "I told him to stop talking about the Bolsheviks"?

A. I said maybe he was in trouble because he talked too much.

Q. Did you say "I told him to stop talking about the Bolsheviks"?

A. I said "Oh, the boy maybe talks something that does not belong to him."

Q. What did you mean by that remark?

A. He is something—he talks—he comes from the store and said he heard somebody talking like that.

Q. You have no sympathy have you with the Communist Party?

A. No.

Q. Did you know to your own knowledge that Greco was a member and was attending meetings?

A. No.

Q. Did you ever hear him talking in favor of the Communist Party?

A. No.

Q. Why did you say you advised him not to talk so much?

A. Because he talks so much and he listens to what they say and says maybe somebody was on Fillmore Street talking like that. [18]

(Testimony of Joseph Cyklen.)

Q. Who did he hear speaking on Fillmore or O'Farrell Street?

A. I don't know. I say sometimes he hears somebody talking on Fillmore or O'Farrell Street.

Q. About what?

A. Talking about working the people here in the United States, and he comes and says what——

Q. In your opinion is he a man that would be easily influenced?

A. I think so.

Q. Did he ever loan you any amount of money when you were going in business?

A. Yes.

Q. How much has he loaned you?

A. A few hundred dollars. He bought some stocks and I told him he had better get through and save his money.

Q. Is he interested in your business financially?

A. No.

Q. Do you owe him any money now?

A. I don't know. Maybe I owe him a few hundred dollars. He has no money in the business but sometimes he keeps a couple of hundreds——

ATTORNEY MERENBACH (interrupting). Is the bank book in his own name?

(Answer unintelligible.)

By ATTORNEY MERENBACH.—He has a bank book. Is it in his own name?

By WITNESS.—In his name.

(Testimony of Joseph Cyklen.)

EXAMINING OFFICER TO WITNESS:

Q. Do you owe him at the present time any sum of money, or has he any money loaned to you?

A. Yes.

ATTORNEY MERENBACH TO WITNESS:

Q. You said before that you believed him to be of low mentality and sometimes talked like a kid and would say something that wasn't right. Your interest in him was like a father or brother, was it not?

A. I knew he was a nice boy and didn't like to see him listen on the streets.

Q. And you knew Mr. Greco to be a hard working, thrifty and saving boy?

A. Yes.

ART OLANDAR

called as a witness and duly sworn.

EXAMINING OFFICER TO WITNESS:

Q. What is your name?

A. Art Olandar.

ATTORNEY BRENNAN TO WITNESS:

Q. Where do you live?

A. 1340 McAllister Street.

Q. What is your business?

A. I am retired.

Q. What was your business?

A. I had a store in Mariposa County.

(Testimony of Art Olandar.)

Q. Do you know Giuseppe Greco?

A. Yes, he worked in my store.

Q. How long ago?

A. A few months about five years ago.

Q. Are you a man of a family?

A. Yes, sir.

Q. Have you any children?

A. Yes, sir.

Q. Did he ever visit you in your home?

A. Yes.

Q. He always paid his rent?

A. He is a nice man and he paid. [19]

Q. He is a man that sings quite a bit?

A. Yes.

Q. A happy sort of a fellow?

A. He is foolish a little.

Q. Talks like a boy about eight or nine years old?

A. A boy you know, like a spoiled kid; talks like a man but like——

Q. But like a boy?

A. Yes.

EXAMINING OFFICER TO WITNESS:

Q. Are you a citizen of the United States?

A. Yes.

Q. Do you know if the alien here ever stated that he was a member of the Communist Party?

A. I never knew anything about that. I never talked to him about it in my house.

Q. Where were you born?

(Testimony of Art Olandar.)

A. In Russia-Poland, years ago.

Q. Have you any sympathy with the Communist Party?

A. I don't understand it.

Q. And if he spoke to you about the Communist Party then, you would not have known what he was talking about?

A. If he were talking against the government I think I would know.

ATTORNEY BRENNAN TO WITNESS:

Q. You believe he is a good man?

A. Yes.

Q. You don't think he would hurt the government in any way?

A. No.

Q. Do you know he was in the second Draft in the war and was ready to go to war for the American government?

A. That was before he came to my house.

———

PAULINE MARKEL

called as a witness and duly sworn.

EXAMINING OFFICER TO WITNESS:

Q. What is your name?

A. Pauline Markel.

Q. Where do you live?

A. On Post between Scott and Divisadero.

(Testimony of Pauline Markel.)

ATTORNEY BRENNAN TO WITNESS:

Q. And you are a housewife?

A. Yes, sir.

Q. A married woman?

A. Yes, sir.

Q. What does your husband do?

A. He is in the fruit business.

Q. Is he a citizen of the United States?

A. No.

Q. You are Greeks?

A. Yes.

Q. He tried to become a citizen but has not passed the examination yet?

A. He hasn't got his second papers yet.

Q. You have children have you?

A. Yes.

Q. How many?

A. Two boys and four girls.

Q. You know the alien here, Giuseppe Greco?

A. Yes. I have known him for three years.

Q. He has lived with you all the time?

A. Yes.

Q. Paid rent all the time?

A. Yes.

Q. Ever make any trouble?

A. No.

Q. Any bad habits?

A. No. [20]

Q. Has he ever visited with you in your home?

A. Yes.

(Testimony of Pauline Markel.)

Q. Did he play with the children?

A. Yes, he is nice to the children.

Q. Is he single?

A. Yes.

Q. You think he is a good man?

A. He never make any trouble.

Q. Is he home nights pretty much?

A. Every night he comes home.

Q. What time in the evening does he come home?

A. Six o'clock in the evening.

Q. Does he stay home after dinner?

A. Yes.

Q. And then visits in the home a great deal?

A. Yes.

EXAMINING OFFICER TO WITNESS:

Q. In your opinion can the alien speak English well?

A. He understands.

Q. Can he speak English as well as you can?

A. Yes.

Q. How long have you been in the United States?

A. Eighteen years.

Q. Did your husband apply to become a citizen of the United States?

A. Yes.

Q. Can you read English?

A. A little.

Q. Can your husband read English?

(Testimony of Pauline Markel.)

A.   Yes.

Q.   Who pays the subscription for the "Daily Worker"?

A.   My husband.

Q.   How do you know he pays the subscriptions for the "Daily Worker"

A.   I know.

Q.   And your husband applied one time to become a citizen of the United States?

A.   Yes.

Q.   Did you ever read the "Daily Worker?"

A.   Yes.

Q.   Who induced your husband to subscribe for that paper, if anyone?

A.   Some one came around.

Q.   Do you know that the "Daily Worker" is the official organ of the Communist Party?

A.   No.

Q.   Does your husband know that the "Daily Worker" is the official organ of the Communist Party?

A.   No. He never reads it.

Q.   He pays for it without reading it?

A.   Yes.

Q.   How long has he been receiving that paper?

A.   Several months.

ATTORNEY BRENNAN TO WITNESS:

Q.   You say he helped some people out?

A.   A woman came into the store and wanted him to help some people and says "you pay fifty

(Testimony of Pauline Markel.)

cents a month and get this paper." My husband said we had the Examiner and Chronicle and Daily News and the Greek papers in the store, and she say to him "for fifty cents you can get this" and he took it.

EXAMINING OFFICER TO ALIEN:

(Examination in English.)

Q. The official records show that you made a sworn statement before an officer of this Service at this office on September eleventh last. You are advised that this statement is now incorporated into and made a part of this record.

EXAMINING OFFICER TO ATTORNEY BRENNAN.—Do you desire to cross-examine the alien?

By ATTORNEY BRENNAN.—Yes. [21]

ATTORNEY BRENNAN TO ALIEN:

(In English.)

Q. You applied to become a citizen of the United States in 1919 or 1918?

A. I don't remember. I believe it was 1918 I believe. I think one or two——

Q. Now have you ever taken the examination to become a citizen?

A. No.

Q. Why?

A. I was not then—didn't know how to read or write English.

(Testimony of Giuseppe Greco.)

By ATTORNEY BRENNAN.—I want to note at this time the peculiar, unusual dialect that of course cannot be made a part of the record of the alien's testimony, and in order to have the evidence brought out clearly I think we had better take it through the interpreter.

ATTORNEY BRENNAN TO ALIEN:

(Through the Acting Italian Interpreter.)

Q. What was the reason that you did not become a citizen of the United States?

A. The reason was that I was afraid I could not pass the examination and also because I could not read or write in English, and about the same amount in Italian. I could not read or write that very well.

Q. You signed up for the war?

A. Yes.

Q. Were you willing to go to war for America?

A. Yes, I was ready to serve for the United States.

Q. What is your age now?

A. I am forty-seven years old now.

Q. You were at that time—that was about twelve years ago—you were about thirty-five then?

A. I signed up in the draft I think it was 1916 or 1917. I think I was about 33 or 34 years old.

Q. And you were in the second draft and were . not called?

A. The second class and was not called.

(Testimony of Giuseppe Greco.)

Q. Before you came to this country, did you serve in the Italian Army?

A. Yes.

Q. This Trade Union Unity League, did you join that organization?

A. No. It happened this way: I was at Fillmore and O'Farrell Street and a woman came up to me and said "do you want to join the Union for better pay and better conditions?" The lady wrote my name on a piece of paper and later she sent a letter to my office and sent me a read card, or paper.

ATTORNEY BRENNAN TO EXAMINING OFFICER.—Have you a book or card that you received from the landlady where Mr. Greco lives— have you that in your possession now?

By EXAMINING OFFICER.—Yes.

By ATTORNEY BRENNAN.—Will you please deliver it to us on behalf of the alien?

By EXAMINING OFFICER.—Yes.

By ATTORNEY BRENNAN.—It will be stipulated that the writing in the book is not the handwriting of the alien?

By EXAMINING OFFICER.—Yes.

ATTORNEY BRENNAN TO ALIEN:

Q. Is this the card that she sent you?

A. Yes.

Q. There is a name on there, Jimmie Polizzi. Is that your signature? Did you write that there?

A. No. [22]

(Testimony of Giuseppe Greco.)

Q. That is not your writing?

A. No.

Q. Did you tell anybody to write your name in that book?

A. No.

ATTORNEY BRENNAN TO EXAMINING OFFICER.—I will ask that this book be admitted in evidence and marked Exhibit No. 1 on behalf of the alien.

ATTORNEY BRENNAN TO ALIEN:

Q. Did you ever read this book?

A. No.

Q. At the time this lady put your name on this piece of paper or book, what kind of a lady was it?

A. A young woman about eighteen or nineteen.

Q. At the time she put your name on the piece of paper did you pay her any money at that time?

A. I gave her a dollar.

Q. Were you informed then what it would cost to belong to this trade union?

A. She said twenty-five cents a month.

Q. Did you make any oath or sign any paper of any kind at any time concerning this trade union?

A. No.

By ATTORNEY BRENNAN.—May I state for the record that it appears from the card, the membership card, that there is nothing in it that in any way indicates that there is any opposition to the

(Testimony of Giuseppe Greco.)

government or anything that indicates that he joined any organization that had for its purpose the overthrow of the American Government.

ATTORNEY BRENNAN TO ALIEN:

Q. Did you ever join the Communist Party?

A. No, I did not know anything about the Communist Party. I don't know what it is all about. I joined this organization because I thought it was a labor union.

Q. And did you ever read any pamphlets of any kind concerning this unity league—this Trade Union Unity League?

A. No.

Q. Can you read English?

A. Very little.

Q. Did you ever go up to the meeting at 145 Turk Street?

A. No. I went up there once for the purpose of paying my twenty-five cents dues, at which time I told them that I did not want to become a member —or did not want to belong to the union any longer because I was going into business for myself.

Q. How many months dues did you pay?

A. I don't remember whether it was four or five. I paid all at one time.

Q. And you told them at that time that you did not care to belong to it any longer?

A. Yes. I told them I no longer wanted to belong to it.

Q. Why?

(Testimony of Giuseppe Greco.)

A. Because I wanted to go into business for myself and I was going to open a business of my own.

Q. Did you open a business of your own?

A. Yes, I bought a bootblack stand.

Q. Where?

A. At Turk and Taylor Street.

Q. Do you own that bootblack stand now?

A. Yes. I work there at nights.

Q. That was the business you told them you
were going to buy when you told them you were
not going to belong to the union any longer?

A. Yes. [23]

Q. What did you understand this organization
that you joined—what kind of an organization did
you think this was that you joined, this Trade
Union Unity League?

A. I thought it was a union like all the rest of
them, for better conditions and better pay.

Q. Did you think at that time that it believed
in, advised, advocated or taught the overthrow of
the Government of the United States by force or
violence?

A. No, I never understood that.

Q. Did you believe that it was an organization
that circulated, published, printed or displayed
printed matter advising, advocating or teaching the
overthrow by force or violence of the Government
of the United States?

A. No.

Q. You just thought it was a union like any
other union?

(Testimony of Giuseppe Greco.)

A. I thought it was a union like all the rest of them.

Q. And you never went to but one meeting of this organization and you thought it was a union?

A. Yes.

Q. And that was the time you paid up your two bits a month and told them you didn't want to belong to it any longer because you were going into business for yourself?

A. Yes. I went there for the purpose of paying up my dues and to tell them that I no longer wanted to belong to the organization because I was going into business for myself; that then the organization of course would have no use for me.

Q. And you never paid any more dues?

A. No.

Q. Did you ever carry this red book in your pocket at any time?

A. Never.

Q. Now do you know what the Soviet Union is?

A. No.

Q. Did you ever hear the word English "Soviet Union" and understood what the term meant?

A. No, I never understood that or heard the expression.

Q. Do you know what communism means?

A. No.

By ATTORNEY BRENNAN.—I am referring to the question on page two. It is to be noted that it is in the form of a leading question and that the question is involved and compound.

(Testimony of Giuseppe Greco.)

ATTORNEY BRENNAN TO ALIEN:

Q. You were asked in this statement you are purported to have made to a Government officer, this question: "Is it not the policy of the Trade Union Unity League to organize the workers in order that each country shall change its organization and laws so that it becomes a member of the Soviet Union?" To that question you gave the following answer: "Yes, that is the policy." Now I want to ask you if you have any explanation to make of your answer; whether you understood the question and whether you understood the nature of the answer that you were giving to that question?

A. Perhaps I did answer that way because I may not have understood the sense of the question, and perhaps I did not understand the question as asked me and thought if I say yes maybe I am wrong and if I say no maybe I am wrong and so answered yes.

Q. You did not know nor did you believe at that time that this Trade Union Unity League had as its policy the purpose to organize the workers in order that each country should change its organization and laws so as to become a member of the Soviet Union?

A. No. [24]

(Alien continues). I didn't understand that term "Soviet."

Q. You did not believe at that time that this organization that you joined which you thought was

(Testimony of Giuseppe Greco.)

a trade union, intended to change the laws of this country did you?

A. No. I thought the purpose of the union was to better conditions for the laborers and make better pay, and the lady told me when I became a member of this union I would get better pay.

Q. You did not think the purpose of this organization was to change the organization or laws of the United States so that we should become a member of the Soviet Union?

A. I don't know what the meaning of the Soviet Union is.

Q. The next question you are purported to have answered in that statement is: "In other words, if you were a member of the Trade Union Unity League in San Francisco and another man who was a member of the Trade Union Unity League in Mexico you would both be working with the same ends and purposes in view?" Your answer was: "Yes, that is right." Now did you understand the question and did you intend to give the answer that is purported to be given there?

A. No, I didn't understand that question.

Q. Did you intend to tell the examiner at that time that if you were a member of the Trade Union Unity League in San Francisco and another man was a member of the Union Unity League in Mexico that you would both be working with the same ends and purposes in view?

(Testimony of Giuseppe Greco.)

A. No, that was not my intention. My understanding was that the union was a San Francisco union.

Q. You didn't think this union that you joined had anything to do with any union in Mexico?

A. No.

Q. In other words, you did not believe that anybody that belonged to any particular organization or union in Mexico was in any way connected with the union that you joined in San Francisco?

A. No, because Mexico is Mexico and the United States is the United States.

Q. The next question: "If your comrade in Mexico would want to make this country a part of the Soviet Union would you work toward that end also?" Your answer was "yes." I want to ask you if you understood that question and if you intended to make that answer?

A. I didn't understand that question for the reason that I don't understand English well.

Q. Do you know what the Soviet Union means?

A. No, I have not read anything about it.

Q. Now, I will give you the next question: "And if your comrades in the United States would want to change the institutions in this country so that it would become a member of the Soviet Union would you vote for such a change?" And your answer was "yes." Did you intend to make that answer to that question?

(Testimony of Giuseppe Greco.)

A. I didn't understand that because, because I remember well now when the question was asked me. He asked me if I wanted to change the government. My understanding of that was that if it was a change of Government, for instance, if Hoover was running for re-election and someone else running for election, as to whom I would give my vote.

Q. You wouldn't want to change the Government of the United States by force of arms or anything of that kind would you?

A. No, I believe if it is a change of Government it should be done by the votes, or from Republican to Democrat.

Q. Now you have given an answer along that same line to a question of Inspector Farrelly, and it is not a leading question: "How do you want to change the constitution of this country so that this country would become a member of the Soviet Union or a Soviet Republic?" Answer: "By votes of the people." [25] In other words for the Party, for instance, for the Republican Party or the other party?

A. Yes.

Q. You wouldn't want to change this Government by the votes of the people so that it would become a part of the Soviet Union or the Soviet Republic would you?

A. I never have been given to understand the purpose of the Soviet Government. I dont't know what you call it.

(Testimony of Giuseppe Greco.)

Q. Now at the time you were taken into custody Inspector Farrelly asked you if you belonged to the Communist Party didn't he?

A. Yes, he asked me if I belonged to the Communist Party and I said no.

Q. And you didn't think at that time that he was referring to the trade union that you thought you had joined?

A. No, I didn't understand that.

Q. You never subscribed to any paper of any kind did you, that was communistic or represented the Communist Party?

A. No, but many times going around the street men and women were distributing pamphlets and newspapers and so forth and I would take them and when I got home I would clean my pockets out.

Q. You never read any of these pamphlets did you?

A. No. I would put them in my pocket and then clean them out.

Q. In this statement you made to Inspector Farrelley you stated that you had been arrested once?

A. Yes.

Q. Tell us just how that happened.

A. I was in Leighton's cafeteria on Third Street. I don't know whether it was about seven thirty or eight o'clock, and I saw maybe a group of people outside, and, curious, I went out to see what was going on, and I went near the patrol wagon looking

(Testimony of Giuseppe Greco.)

around to see what I could see, and while I was there a police officer grabbed hold of me and threw me in.

Q. Were there some Filipinos put in the wagon too?

A. Yes.

Q. Anyone else?

A. No. There were women and men.

Q. Do you know how you got out of jail at that time?

A. About twelve o'clock an officer came and opened the door and let us out and I remember of him telling me to come back Tuesday. And afterwards I came to the Court and I was not called, and so that is all I know about it.

Q. You are perfectly satisfied with this country are you?

A. Yes.

Q. Are you against the capitalistic class here?

A. What do you mean by capitalistic class?

Q. Rich people?

A. I like to make money myself.

Q. You are not against the rich people are you?

A. No.

Q. You are perfectly satisfied to remain in this country are you?

A. Sure.

Q. And abide by the laws of this country?

A. With the American law.

Q. And you don't want to change the Government in any way, do you?

(Testimony of Giuseppe Greco.)

A. No, because this is a good government. It is the best government in the world.

Q. Do you intend now to study and endeavor to take an examination to become a citizen of the United States?

A. Sure. I want to do everything possible to become a citizen of the United States.

Q. Do you know whether that meeting that was had at the time that you were arrested, whether that was a Communist meeting or what kind of a meeting it was?

A. No, because I arrived there right at the end of the affair and the rest of them were arrested and the last one that was arrested was myself. And I don't know what it was about. [26]

Q. Did you ever got to school at all?

A. No I learned to write when I was in the Italian Army, because I had made application to become one of the caribanieri (police officer) and my Captain took a liking to me and so he checked up the military orders and said he would assist me and he sent me to school, and I showed improvements and got a recommendation to the police forces.

Q. You were raised in Palermo?

A. I was born in Licata but I was raised in Palermo.

Q. Do you know an attorney named Zwerin?

A. No.

(Testimony of Giuseppe Greco.)

Q. Did you ever authorize any other attorney to appear here except Mr. Merenbach and myself?

A. Never.

EXAMINING OFFICER TO ALIEN:

Q. When did you make application to become a citizen of the United States?

A. I don't remember now whether it was in 1918 or 1919. I believe it was 1918 but I am not sure.

Q. Had you filed your application when you registered for the second draft?

A. No, afterwards.

Q. Did you claim exemption as an alien when you registered for the second draft?

A. I told them that I was an Italian subject but that it was my intention to go to war for the United States.

Q. Did you claim exemption?

A. I want to say that at that time I didn't understand anything. I was more ignorant than I am right now.

Q. How old were you at the time of the second draft?

A. Perhaps thirty-three.

Q. Were you ever married?

A. No.

Q. What was your occupation at that time?

A. I was a laborer.

Q. Were you in the reserve of the Italian army at that time?

(Testimony of Giuseppe Greco.)

A. I had served three years military service in Italy and I came to America.

Q. Did you report to the Italian Consulate at any time during the war?

A. Never.

Q. Did you read the newspapers during the war?

A. I didn't have any interest in that. I worked all day and then would go home and go to bed.

Q. Did you know that Italy was engaged in the European War?

A. Yes.

Q. Did you know American regiments were over at the Italian front?

A. Yes, I heard people say and read that the American army was on the front fighting the Germans.

Q. Then why didn't you join the American army?

A. Because at that time they said they would call us.

Q. How much money have you got deposited in banks in Italy at the present time?

A. Two or three thousand dollars. I left the book with them and I don't know what the interest is.

A. Is that money deposited in a bank at Palermo?

A. It is deposited in the Bank of Italy and America at Palermo, with the point in view that

(Testimony of Giuseppe Greco.)

when the exchange got up even they would withdraw the money.

Q. How many positions do you hold at the present time in the United States?

A. Two.

Q. What time do you go to work in the morning?

A. About eight o'clock.

Q. What time do you get through?

A. I go home at five o'clock and if I am tired I eat at a restaurant and if I am not tired I go home and cook my own meals, for instance, after cleaning myself up about seven o'clock I go down to the barber shop, or my bootblack stand, and remain until nine or ten o'clock, as long as there is any business. [27]

Q. How long have you been operating that bootblack stand?

A. Four months.

Q. How many men do you employ there?

A. One.

Q. Is he an American?

A. I think he was born here but he has told me, or at least I think that he is of Mexican or Spanish extraction.

Q. What salary do you pay him?

A. Eighteen dollars a week and whatever tips he makes.

Q. What salary do you receive as a window cleaner?

(Testimony of Giuseppe Greco.)

A. Six dollars a day.

Q. At the time you were arrested who put up the bail for you?

A. I don't know. About twelve o'clock at night I got out.

Q. At the time you were asked on September 11th the question "Who put up the bail for you?" you answered "The labor defender." What did you mean by that answer?

A. One who defends the working men.

Q. Do you mean the public defender?

A. One who defends the working men.

Q. You are advised that the labor defender is known as the organ of the Trade Union Unity League, and the Public Defender is an official of the City and County of San Francisco. To whom did you refer when you spoke of the labor defender?

A. I didn't know then and I don't know now.

Q. I will show you a leaflet and ask you if you ever saw that leaflet before or a similar leaflet before?

A. I will say perhaps someone did give me that on the street and I put it in my pocket.

Q. Did you ever read it?

A. No.

Q. Do you believe in the overthrow of the Government of the United States by the votes of the people?

A. Why should they create a revolution? I don't know what they want to do.

(Testimony of Giuseppe Greco.)

Q. Do you believe in the principles of the Trade Union Unity League, the organization to which you belonged at one time?

A. I don't know what their program is. I have never read their program and don't know what the principle is. Neither have I any interest in it.

Q. You were shown a leaflet distributed by the Communist Party at the time the fleet of the United States was in port, and you were asked if you had a similar leaflet in your possession and you said "I don't know. Lots of time they give them to me and I take them home and read them." What did you mean by that answer?

Q. Perhaps I did say that, but if I did say that, my intention was to say that the papers, or what-it might have been, was given to me on the street and that I put them in my pocket and went home and laid them around the room and cleaned my pockets out, and that I did not read them and could not read them, because, knowing very little about the Italian and much less the English, I didn't understand them.

Q. Where is the headquarters of the Communist party in San Francisco?

A. I never have been there.

Q. Where do you work?

A. At 115 Turk Street, San Francisco.

Q. Do you mean to testify under oath that you have never been at the headquarters of the Communist party in San Francisco?

(Testimony of Giuseppe Greco.)

A. At this time I will swear that I was never at the Communist Headquarters.

Q. Were you ever at the headquarters of the Trade Union Unity League?

A. Once.

Q. Where have they got their office?

A. 145 Turk Street. [28]

Q. Are you sure about that?

A. Sure.

Q. Who did you see up at 145 Turk Street?

A. The girl there that I paid the 25¢ a month to for four or five months and to whom I told that I didn't want to belong to it any more.

Q. Did you ever attend any dances at 145 Turk Street?

A. No.

Q. When you were arrested around Stevenson Street, how many people were arrested with you?

A. A big bunch.

Q. I will show you the "Communist" for April, 1929, and ask you if you have ever read that magazine?

A. No.

Q. Have you ever seen the magazine for July, 1929?

A. No.   ·

Q. The magazine for March?

A. No. I have no interest in them.

By EXAMINING INSPECTOR.—The three magazines just mentioned are incorporated into

(Testimony of Giuseppe Greco.)
record and marked Exhibits "A," "B" and "C" respectively.

Q. I will show you the "Communist Manifesto" and ask you if you have ever read that document or saw it?

A. How could I read it when I can't read English?

By EXAMINING INSPECTOR.—Said pamphlet is incorporated into and made a part of this record and marked Exhibit "D."

Q. I will show you a pamphlet entitled "Gastonia, Citadel of the Class Struggle in the New South," and will ask if you have ever read that document?

A. I have seen this book, because they were selling them on the street and many times were giving them out gratis.

Q. Have you ever read that book?

A. No, because I didn't understand it.

By EXAMINING INSPECTOR.—Said pamphlet incorporated into and made a part of the record and marked Exhibit "E."

Q. I show you a book entitled "The Trade Union Unity League" and ask if you are familiar with the contents of that document?

A. No.

By EXAMINING INSPECTOR.—Said book incorporated into and made a part of the record and marked Exhibit "G."

(Testimony of Giuseppe Greco.)

Q. I show you the "Red International of Labour Unions" and ask if you have ever read that book?

A. No.

By EXAMINING INSPECTOR.—Said document incorporated into and made a part of the record and marked Exhibit "H."

Q. I show you a pamphlet entitled "Why Every Worker Should Join the Communist Party" and ask you if you have ever read or seen that pamphlet?

A. I have not read it, but I will say this, that many times on the street men and women were handing out the pamphlets and perhaps I may have taken one. I never read it.

By EXAMINING INSPECTOR.—Said pamphlet incorporated into and made a part of the rec-[29] ord and marked Exhibit "I."

Q. I show you a pamphlet entitled "Out of a Job" and ask if you are in sympathy with the contents of that document?

A. How could I be in sympathy with it when I don't know the contents?

By EXAMINING INSPECTOR.—Said document is incorporated into and made a part of this record and marked Exhibit "J." There are also incorporated into the record reports of Inspectors Brown, Neilson and Endicott, dated August, 1930, and marked Exhibits "K," "L" and "M," respectively.

(Testimony of Giuseppe Greco.)

Q. In addition to the charges contained in the warrant of arrest the following additional charges are now placed against you, to wit: That you are affiliated with the Communist Party of the United States of America, the Trade Union Unity League and the Red International of Labour Unions, which organizations believe in, advise, advocate and teach the overthrow by force or violence of the Government of the United States, and which organizations circulate, distribute, publish and display printed matter advising, advocating and teaching the overthrow by force or violence of the Government of the United States. Have you anything to say as to why you should not be deported on those charges?

By ATTORNEY BRENNAN.—In response to the question just asked, we submit that we have made our showing.

EXAMINING OFFICER TO ATTORNEY BRENNAN.—Do you wish to file a brief in this case?

ATTORNEY BRENNAN.—Yes.

EXAMINING OFFICER.—You will be allowed ten days from receipt of a transcript of the record to submit your brief in duplicate.

(Testimony of Giuseppe Greco.)

I hereby certify that the foregoing is a true and correct transcript of the record of hearing in this case.

R. H. RULE,

Stenographer. [30]

U. S. Department of Labor

Immigration Service

City Office,

San Francisco, Calif.

November 5, 1930.

12020/17739

Further hearing in the case of

GIUSEPPE GRECO alias

JIMMY POLIZZI

Present: T. M. BORDEN,

Examining Inspector

James F. Brennan, Attorney

L. F. Smith, Stenographer

Alien sworn:

INSPECTOR TO ATTORNEY:

Q. It appears that Paul DeMartini, Jr., was present at the former hearings in this case to act as Italian interpreter, in order to facilitate this examination. It is noted he is not present at this time, are you willing to proceed with the examination without an Italian interpreter being present?

A. Yes.

INSPECTOR TO ALIEN:

Q. What is your correct name?

A. Giuseppe Greco.

(Testimony of Giuseppe Greco.)

Q. Have you ever been known by any other name?

A. Jimmy Polizzi.

Q. Are you the same Giuseppe Greco alias Jimmy Polizzi who was served with Warrant of Arrest in this office, October 1, 1930?

A. Yes.

Q. There is introduced and made part of this record and marked Exhibit "N" a pamphlet entitled: "Programme of the Communist International" below which appears the following endorsement in ink: "Book bought in Communist Headquarters No. 734 Harrison Street, San Francisco, October 31, 1930, signed Arthur A. Jarrett, Clerk U. S. Immigration Service. [31]

BY ATTORNEY:

A. We want to make formal objection that this should not be admitted on the ground it is in no way connected with the alien. It has not been shown that he has ever seen the pamphlet and does not know anything about its contents.

BY INSPECTOR:

Q. There is also introduced and made a part of this record a list entitled "International Labor Defense in District No. 13, Financial Statement December 31, 1929 to March 31, 1930," containing eight pages marked 1-8, marked Exhibit "C."

BY ATTORNEY:

Q. I want to object to the introduction of this list upon the grounds that it has not been shown

(Testimony of Giuseppe Greco.)

that the alien ever intended to make any contribution to this organization or that he ever did make any contribution.

INSPECTOR TO ALIEN:

Q. On page No. 6 appears the name Jimmy Polizzi contribution of $25.00 does that name and amount contributed refer to you and the amount you contributed to the International Labor Defense, District No. 13?

A. Yes, I gave somebody $25.00.

ATTORNEY TO ALIEN:

Q. Do you remember who it was that you gave the $25.00 to?

A. No, it is pretty hard to remember. It was on the street I gave it.

Q. This labor place—you are a window washer and your boss has an office right next door to this labor place?

A. Between the labor place.

Q. One door is the labor place and next building is the office of your boss?

A. Yes. [32]

Q. Now after you finished your work did you ever go down to your boss' office at night?

A. Every night we go to the boss and he gives orders what to do in the morning.

Q. Who did you give this $25.00 to?

A. A girl came and asked if I wanted to help public defense. I no speak very good English, I hardly remember this $25.00.

(Testimony of Giuseppe Greco.)

Q. Did you ever get this $25.00 back?

A. Yes.

Q. When did you get this $25.00 back?

A. I saw the girl and asked when she was going to give me the $25.00 because I needed it. She told me she would bring it back.

Q. When did she bring it back?

A. She brought it back in September of this year.

Q. Was that after you were arrested down here?

A. No.

Q. But that was after you told the women that you would not belong and to get your money because you were going in business for yourself?

A. The same day I bought this business I told the girl I would not be able to do so and needed the money.

Q. Now in what way did you get this $25.00 back?

A. She brought it to me at night where I worked.

Q. Was that in cash or in check?

A. Check.

Q. It was a check was it, for how much?

A. $25.00.

Q. On what bank?

A. I cashed it in the Italian Bank, Market and Turk Streets.

Q. You mean the Bank of Italy at Market and Turk?

A. Yes.

(Testimony of Giuseppe Greco.)

Q. That is the bank that runs all night?

A. Yes.

Q. And did you sign your name on the back of the check?

A. Yes, why not, that is my money. [33]

Q. What name did you sign on the back of that check?

A. Jimmy Polizzi.

Q. Do you know whose name was signed to the check?

A. I do not know.

INSPECTOR TO ATTORNEY:

Q. Have you any evidence to offer in this case?

A. No further evidence.

Q. Will you file a brief?

A. I will file a brief within ten days after receipt of copy of this record.

Q. You are advised that this brief should be submitted in duplicate.

I certify that the foregoing is a true and correct transcript of the record of hearing in this case.

L. F. SMITH,

Stenographer. [34]

EXHIBIT "D"

Bureau of Immigration
 Form 8-A
   Warrant—Arrest of Alien
   United States of America
   Department of Labor
   Washington

No. 55711/802

To Commissioner of Immigration, Angel Island Station, San Francisco, Calif. or to any Immigration Inspector in the service of the United States.

WHEREAS, from evidence submitted to me, it appears that the alien

GIUSEPPE GRECO alias JIMMY POLIZZI

who landed at the port of New York, N. Y., ex SS. "Barbarosa," on the 17th day of June, 1909, has been found in the United States in violation of the immigration act of October 16, 1918, as amended by the act of June 5, 1920, for the following among other reasons:

That he is a member of the Communist party of the United States of America, an organization that believes in, advises, advocates, and teaches the overthrow by force or violence of the government of the United States and which circulates, distributes, publishes, and displays printed matter, advising, advocating, and teaching the overthrow by force or violence of the government of the United States,

I, W. N. Smelser, Assistant to the Secretary of Labor, by virtue of the power and authority vested in me by the laws of the United States, do hereby command you to take into custody the said alien and grant him a hearing to enable him to show cause why he should not be deported in conformity with law. The expenses of detention hereunder, if necessary, are authorized, payable from the appropriation "Expenses of Regulating Immigration, 1951." Pending further proceedings the alien may be released from custody under bond in the sum of $1,000.

For so doing, this shall be your sufficient warrant.

Witness my hand and seal this 12th day of September, 1930.

W. N. SMELSER,
Assistant to the Secretary of Labor.

PEJ

[Endorsed]: Filed Oct. 9, 1931. Walter B. Maling, Clerk. [35]

———

[Title of Court and Cause.]

ORDER TO SHOW CAUSE.

Upon reading and filing the petition of Giuseppe Greco, alias Jimmy Polizzi, for a writ of habeas corpus, and good cause appearing therefor,

IT IS HEREBY ORDERED that JOHN D. NAGLE, Immigration Commissioner, do appear before this court, Division ...... thereof, on the 19th day of October, 1931, at the courtroom thereof in the Postoffice Building, San Francisco, California, then and there to show cause why the writ of habeas corpus, as prayed for, should not be granted to the said Giuseppe Greco, alias Jimmy Polizzi, petitioner herein.

IT IS FURTHER ORDERED that petitioner be not deported during the pendency of this order to show cause or until the final determination thereof, and that no further action be taken on said warrant of deportation until the final determination of the petition herein.

AND IT IS FURTHER ORDERED that a copy of this order, together with a copy of the petition herein, be served upon said John D. Nagle at least three days prior to the said 19th day of October, 1931. [36]

ORDERED that petitioner be released from custody on bail in the sum of One Thousand ($1,000.00) Dollars, pending hearing, either in cash or surety bond.

Dated this 9th day of October, 1931.

HAROLD LOUDERBACK,

Judge.

[Endorsed]: Filed Oct. 19, 1931. Walter B. Maling, Clerk. [37]

State of California,
City and County of San Francisco.—ss.

E. Hanoff, being first duly sworn, deposes and says: That he is and was at all times hereinafter mentioned District Organizer of Trade Union Unity League, and as such is familiar with its principles and activities.

That Trade Union Unity League is interested in better economic conditions of labor, and is in no way affiliated with the Communist Party or any other party, its membership being open to all regardless of political affiliations. That as a matter of fact the overwhelming majority of its members are not members of Communist Party.

That at present its headquarters are located in a separate and distinct location from that of Communist Party. That at no time its headquarters were located at 734 Harrison St., San Francisco. That during the time mentioned in Greco case to which my attention was called, the office of Trade Union Unity League was maintained at 145 Turk Street, San Francisco, California, in the same building where Communist Party had its headquarters— such arrangement being for economy sake only. That at that time Trade Union Unity League had no book shop connected with the organization and the book shop which carried literature purchased by Immigration Inspectors: Brown, Neilson, and Endicott, or by any other person and introduced as evidence in said Greco case was operated by the Communist Party.

That as a further indication that the arrangement of having more than one different organization share in their overhead expenses is not unusual, affiant further states that even at present time the Trade Union Unity League shares its quarters with another organization, viz., Needle Trades Workers Industrial Union.

E. HANOFF.

Subscribed and sworn to before me this 17th day of November, 1931.

[Seal] MARY N. WICKERSHAM,

Notary Public in and for the City and County of San Francisco, State of California.

[Endorsed]: Filed Nov. 21, 1931. Walter B. Maling, Clerk. [38]

[Title of Court and Cause.]

NOTICE OF FILING RESPONDENT'S EXHIBITS.

To the Petitioner in the above entitled matter, and to James F. Brennan and Nathan Merenbach, his attorneys:

You and each of you will please take notice that on the hearing upon the order to show cause herein, respondent will file the annexed copies of proceedings and evidence before the Immigration authorities in the deportation proceedings relating to the petitioner herein, said annexed documents being additional to the portions of the Immigration proceedings filed herein as Petitioner's Exhibits:

Respondent's Exhibit 1—application for warrant for arrest.

Respondent's Exhibit 2—report of Inspector S. F. Brown (designated in the record of the Immigration hearing as "Exhibit K").

Respondent's Exhibit 3—report of Inspector Neilson (designated in the record of the Immigration hearing as "Exhibit L").

Respondent's Exhibit 4—report of Inspector Endicott (designated in the record of the Immigration hearing as "Exhibit M").

Respondent's Exhibit 5—summary and recommendation of the Examining Inspector T. E. Borden.

Respondent's Exhibit 6—warrant of deportation.

GEO. J. HATFIELD,
United States Attorney,
Attorney for Respondent. [39]

RESPONDENT'S EXHIBIT 1

Application for Warrant of Arrest Under Section
19 of the Act of February 5, 1917.

12020/17739

U. S. Department of Labor
Immigration Service

(Place) San Francisco, California,
September 11, 1930.

The undersigned respectfully recommends that
the Secretary of Labor issue his warrant for the
arrest of Giuseppe Greco alias Jimmy Polizzi,
male, aged 47, single, laborer, native and citizen
of Sicily, Italy, of the South Italian race, who last
entered the United States at New York ex SS
"Barbarosa" on June 17, 1909, as passenger. The
alien named in the attached certificate, upon the
following facts which the undersigned has carefully investigated, and which, to the best of his
knowledge and belief, are true:

(1) (Here state fully facts which show alien to
be unlawfully in the United States. Give sources
of information, and, where possible, secure from
informants and forward with this application duly
verified affidavits setting forth the facts within the
knowledge of the informants. Application for a
warrant based on conviction for a crime committed
in the United States should be accompanied by
a copy of the alien's commitment obtained from the
warden of the institution wherein he is confined, or

a certificate of conviction obtained from the clerk of the court wherein sentence was pronounced.)

Communist charge: [40]

The inclosed documents indicate that this alien is a member of the Trade Union Unity League of the United States of America, an organization that believes in, advises, advocates and teaches the overthrow by force or violence of the Government of the United States, and which circulates, distributes, publishes and displays printed matter advising, advocating and teaching the overthrow by force or violence of the Government of the United States. NOTE * * * THIS CONFIRMS TELEGRAPHIC APPLICATION OF THIS DATE.

This office is in possession of certain documents which will be introduced at time hearing is accorded this alien showing that the Trade Union Unity League of the United States, is an organization that believes in, advises, advocates and teaches the overthrow by force or violence of the Government of the United States, and which circulates, distributes, publishes and displays printed matter advising, advocating and teaching the overthrow by force or violence of the Government of the United States.

INCLOSURES. Transcript of alien's sworn statement dated at San Francisco, California, September 11, 1930.

(2) The present location and occupation of above-named are as follows:

At Large, San Francisco, California.

Pursuant to Rule 18 of the Immigration Regulations there is attached hereto and made a part hereof the certificate prescribed in subdivision B of said Rule, as to the landing or entry of said alien, duly signed by the immigration officer in charge at the port through which said alien entered the United States.

12020/17739   (Signature) ....

cjs

Incl. 7367   (Official title) ....

Commissioner. [41]

RESPONDENT'S EXHIBIT 2.

U. S. Department of Labor
Immigration Service
District No. 30

In answering refer to
No.

Office of the Commissioner
Angel Island Station
via Ferry Post Office
San Francisco, Calif
August 19, 1930

Commissioner of Immigration,
(Through Inspector in Charge—City Office)
San Francisco, California.

As instructed by this office, I called at No. 145 Turk Street, San Francisco, California, the headquarters of the Communist Party and the meeting place of the Trade Union Unity League, and purchased the following pamphlets, or magazines:

(1) The Red International of Labour Unions, December, 1929, issue.

(2) The Trade Union Unity League, its program, structure, methods and history.

(3) The Communist magazine for April and July, 1929.

I made a notation on the outside of the cover of the above-described pamphlets, showing the date and place where they were purchased, and initialed same.

S. F. BROWN,
Immigrant Inspector.

SFB/AAJ [42]

RESPONDENT'S EXHIBIT 3.

U. S. Department of Labor
Immigration Service
District No. 30

In answering refer to
No.

Office of the Commissioner
Angel Island Station
Via Ferry Post Office
San Francisco, Calif
August 19, 1930

Commissioner of Immigration
(Through Inspector in Charge, City Office)
San Francisco, California.

As instructed by this office, I called at No. 145 Turk Street, San Francisco, California, the headquarters of the Communist Party, and the meeting place of the Trade Union Unity League, and purchased the following pamphlet:

"Gastonia, Citadel of the Class Struggle in the New South   By Wm. F. Dunne"

I made a notation on the outside of the cover of the above-described pamphlet, showing the date and place where it was purchased, and initaled same.

J. A. NEILSON, JR.
Immigrant Inspector.

JAN/AAJ   [43]

RESPONDENT'S EXHIBIT 4.

U. S. Department of Labor
Immigration Service
District No. 30

In answering refer to
No.

Office of the Commissioner
Angel Island Station
via Ferry Post Office
San Francisco, Calif
August 19, 1930

Commissioner of Immigration,
Through Inspector in Charge, City Office,
San Francisco, California.

As per instructions by the San Francisco office, on August 9, 1930, I purchased in San Francisco a pamphlet called

"Communist Manifesto," by Karl Marx and Frederick Engels,

and on February 24, 1930, I purchased from the Communist Headquarters, 145 Turk St., San Francisco, California, a pamphlet called,

"Why Every Worker Should Join the Communist Party."

SAM ENDICOTT,
Immigrant Inspector.

SE   [44]

RESPONDENT'S EXHIBIT 5.

12020/17739

SUMMARY:

The alien, Guiseppe Greco, alias Jimmy Polizzi, 47 years of age, single, laborer, native of Sicily, subject of Italy, last entered the United States June 17, 1909, as a passenger on the SS "Barbarosa."

The record shows that this alien on January 11, 1930 joined The Trade Union Unity League at San Francisco, California, and that he paid dues to that organization for the months of January to May 1930, inclusive (See Membership Card marked Exhibit ONE for alien; page 10 of the record) Said membership card (Page No. 1) shows that the Trade Union Unity League is affiliated to the R. I. L. U. (Red International of Labour Unions) and that Wm. Z. Foster is General Secretary; Page No. 2 shows that this card shall be accepted as a free transfer into all organizations affiliated with the T. U. U. L. Page No. 3 shows that Jimmie Polizzi is a member of the T. U. U. L., and the months he paid dues; Page No. 4 shows some of the policies of the T. U. U. L., one of which is "Defend the Soviet Union."

There was introduced into the record a list of names (Marked Exhibit "O") showing this alien contributed $25.00 to the "International Labor Defense."

The alien admits membership in the Trade Union Unity League. This organization is affiliated with the Communist Party of America and the Red International of Labour Unions as shown by Exhibits "G" and "J" of this summary.

Exhibit "A" is identified as "The Communist" a magazine issued for the month of April, 1929; on Page 224 of said issue it is shown that said magazine is owned and published by The Communist Party of the United States of America. [45]

Exhibit "B" is identified as the magazine called "The Communist" for July, 1919. Quoting from Pages 356-57-58 of this magazine as follows:

"When Communists urge strikes and crippling of industry in time of war we are accused of trying to bring about the defeat of 'our own' government. To that charge we plead guilty. That is precisely our aim. A Government engaged in warfare is weaker than at other times, in spite of the fact that its savage repressions make it appear stronger to the superficial observer. At such a moment an organized drive to stop the production of war supplies, to cripple the transportation system may result in creating such difficulties that the imperialist forces may be defeated. But it is not sufficient in our drive against imperialist war merely to concentrate upon the war industries. We must be able to reach the masses in the armed forces of the nation with revolutionary agitation and propaganda calculated to cause defections and mutiny in the ranks. We do not indulge in the social-democratic twaddle about disarmament. We will not tell the soldiers in the army to throw away their guns and run home. We tell them to hold their guns in their hands and use them against their own capitalist oppressors.

When faced with an imperialist war as an accomplished fact we must be able to popularize definite revolutionary slogans among the armed forces. In case of a war between imperialist nations we raise the slogan of fraternization with the soldiers of the opposing army, refusal to obey commands of officers, mutinies, and other forms of disruptive work. In case of war against the Soviet Union [46] our main slogan will be different. We will then urge the soldiers in the imperialist armies to desert the army and with their guns and as much ammunition as they can get go over to the side of the Red Army against the imperialist forces. While the capitalists prepare for another imperialist war, we prepare to utilize the difficulties for capitalism arising out of such a war in order to initiate the next stage of the world revolution. We realize that such a conflict requires careful preparation under the leadership of a determined Bolshevik party. Turning an imperialist war between nations into a civil war against capitalism is not a simple matter, it is not a game for dilettantes to play. It requires the most highly developed revolutionary strategy and an ability to estimate the relative forces involved in the struggle as well as the precise moment for the launching of the insurrection. When a revolutionary situation is developing, as a result of

war or from any other cause, the Party of the proletariat must lend a direct attack against the capitalist state. The slogans put forth must be of such
a nature as to guide the movement in its development, which will take the form at first of mass
strikes and armed demonstrations. In that stage
there arises the question of arming of the working
class and disarming the capitalist class. Finally the
highest form of struggle is reached wherein it cul-
minates in the general strike and a merging of
large sections of the Military forces and the workers
for armed insurrection against the capitalist state
power." [47]

Exhibit "D" is identified as a book or pamphlet
entitled: "The Communist Manifesto" by Karl
Marx and Frederick Engles. Quoting from page
58 of the same pamphlet, as follows:

"In short, the Communists everywhere support
every revolutionary movement against the existing
social and political order of things—the Communists
disdain to conceal their views and aims. They
openly declare that their ends can be attained only
by the forcible overthrow of all existing conditions.
Let the ruling classes tremble at the prospects of
a Communist revolution. Proletarians have nothing
to lose but their chains. They have the world to
win. Proletarians of all countries unite."

Exhibit "E" is identified as a pamphlet entitled
"Gastonia—Citadel of the Class Struggle in the
New South—Wm. J. Dunne." This book contains a
recital of certain events that transpired between

the Textile Mills Owners and certain members of the National Textile Worker's Union at Gastonia, N. C.

Exhibit "G" is identified as a book or pamphlet called "The Trade Union Unity League, Its Program, Structure, Methods and History." Quoting from page 6 of said book or pamphlet as follows:

"The United States Government is the great instrument of the American ruling class to maintain this system of capitalistic exploitation. Its chief function is to hold the masses of workers in subjection to the capitalists. The capitalists own and control the Government. [48]

The two big parties are controlled by the employers, and even the Socialist Party, as we shall see further on, is their little brother. The Senate and the House are essentially representative of trustified capital. The Democratic pretenses of the Government are only sham to cover up its capitalistic character."

Quoting from page 12 of the said book or pamphlet as follows: "The Soviet Government is the advanced section of the world proletarian revolution which will finally wipe out the whole capitalistic system of exploitation."

Quoting from page 31 of said document as follows: "The Trade Union Unity League coordinates and binds all the revolutionary union forces into one united organization. It leads and directs the general struggle of the new union movement. It is the

American Section of the Red International of Labour Unions."

Exhibit "H" is identified as a magazine called "The Red International of Labour Unions" for December 1929. Quoting from page 70 of that issue: "Economic strikes in the present, third, period, invariably have a profound political character, bringing, as they do, the strikers into conflict with the whole machinery of the bourgeois state; employers' organizations, fascists, social democracy and the trade union bureaucracy in the service of the employers. Strike experience during the past few years has been so instructive in this regard that there can be little doubt on this hand. This in itself advances the question of raising each strike to a higher level and drawing fresh sections into the struggle, converting economic conflicts into mass political struggle." [49]

Exhibit "I" is identified as a pamphlet entitled "Why Every Worker Should Join the Communist Party." Quoting from page 6 of said pamphlet as follows: "The program of the Communist Party includes the organization of the working class in every phase of life. It leads the struggle of the workers, from the most simple everyday demand, clear up to the final struggle for the overthrow of capitalism and the establishment of the workers' government, the proletarian dictatorship."

Exhibit "J" is identified as a pamphlet entitled "Out of a Job" by Earl Browder. Quoting from page 20 of said document as follows: "—and capitalism can only be abolished by the working class, organizing its power in strong, fighting trade unions, under the leadership of the Communist Party, and overthrowing the state power of the capitalist class to replace it with a workers' government—the dictatorship of the proletariat,'' etc.

On pages 26, 29, 30 and 31, etc. is outlined how the Communist Party and the Trade Union Unity League is functioning together to this common purpose; and "together with Young Communist League intensify agitation amongst the new recruits to armed forces and around army, navy recruiting stations.''

All of the Exhibits introduced into the record were purchased by officers of this service at No. 145 Turk Street, then headquarters of The Communist Party of the United States of America.

In addition to the charges contained in the warrant of arrest there was introduced against the alien at the hearing additional charges; to wit: "That you are affiliated with the Communist Party of the United States of America—[50] the Trade Union Unity League and the Red International of Labour Unions, which organizations believe in, advise, advocate and teach the overthrow by force or violence of the Government of the United States, and which organizations circulate, distribute, publish and display printed matter advising, advocating and teaching the overthrow by force or violence of the Government of the United States.''

RECOMMENDATION:

The organizations mentioned believe in, advise and teach the overthrow by force or violence of the Government of the United States, and circulate, distribute, publish and display printed matter advising, advocating and teaching the overthrow by force or violence of the Government of the United States. Therefore the charges contained in the warrant of arrest, as well as the additional charges placed, have been sustained.

It is therefore recommended that the alien be deported.

T. E. BORDEN,
Immigrant Inspector.

I certify that the foregoing is a true and correct transcript of the record of hearing in this case.

L. F. SMITH,
Stenographer. [51]

RESPONDENT'S EXHIBIT 6.

Warrant—Deportation of Alien
United States of America
Department of Labor
Washington

No. 12020-17739
No. 55711/802

To Commissioner of Immigration, Angel Island Station, San Francisco, California,

District Director of Immigration, Galveston, Texas Or to any Officer or Employee of the United States Immigration Service.

WHEREAS, from proofs submitted to P. F. Snyder, Assistant to the Secretary, after due hearing before Immigrant Inspector P. J. Farrelly, and T. E. Borden, held at San Francisco, California, the said P. F. Snyder, has become satisfied that the alien Giuseppe Greco, alias Jimmy Polizzi, who landed at the port of New York, N. Y., ex SS "Barbarosa," on the 17th day of June, 1909, has been found in the United States in violation of the immigration act of October 16, 1918, as amended by the act of June 5, 1920, in that, he is a member of an organization that believes in, advises, advocates, and teaches the overthrow by force or violence of the government of the United States; and that he is a member of an organization that circulates, distributes, publishes, and displays printed matter advising, advocating, and teaching the overthrow by force or violence of the government of the United

States, and may be deported in accordance therewith:

I, W. N. Smelser, Assistant to the Secretary of Labor, by virtue of the power and authority vested in me by the laws of the United States, do hereby command you to return the said alien to Italy, the country whence he came, at the [52] expense of the appropriation "Salaries and Expenses, Bureau of Immigration, 1932," including the expense of an attendant, if necessary. Delivery of the alien and acceptance for deportation will serve to cancel the outstanding appearance bond.

For so doing, this shall be your sufficient warrant. Witness my hand and seal this 31st day of July, 1931.

MCV

Assistant to the Secretary of Labor.

[Endorsed]: Filed Oct. 19, 1931, 4:21 PM. Walter B. Maling, Clerk. [53]

At a stated term of the Southern Division of the United States District Court for the Northern District of California, held at the Court Room thereof, in the City and County of San Francisco, on Monday, the 19th day of October, in the year of our Lord One Thousand Nine Hundred and Thirty-one.

Present: The Honorable HAROLD LOUDERBACK, DISTRICT JUDGE, et al.

[Title of Cause.]

ORDER SUBMITTING MATTER.

This matter came on regularly for hearing, pursuant to an order to show cause heretofore signed and filed. Mr. Brennan was present on behalf of the Petitioner. F. J. Perry, Esq., Asst. U. S. Atty., was present for and on behalf of Respondent. Mr. Perry made a motion to incorporate in this case the exhibits heretofore filed in the case of the petition of Meikichi Nishimura, on Habeas Corpus, No. 20474, which said motion was submitted. After argument by attorneys for both sides, ordered that the parties herein be and are hereby granted 10 days for the petitioner and 5 for the United States within which time to file briefs upon the petition for writ of habeas corpus. [54]

————

AT A STATED TERM of the Southern Division of the United States District Court for the Northern District of California, held at the Court Room thereof, in the City and County of San Francisco, on Friday, the 22nd day of January, in the year of our Lord One Thousand Nine Hundred and Thirty-two.

Present: The Honorable HAROLD LOUDERBACK, DISTRICT JUDGE, et al.

[Title of Cause.]

The petition of Giuseppe Greco for a Writ of Habeas Corpus, having been heretofore heard and

submitted, and being now fully considered, IT IS
ORDERED that said petition for Writ of Habeas
Corpus be and the same is hereby denied. Ordered
that the petitioner, Giuseppe Greco, be and is here-
by remanded to custody of the Commissioner of
Immigration. [55]

[Title of Court and Cause.]
NOTICE OF APPEAL.

To the Clerk of the above entitled Court, to J. D.
    Nagle, commissioner of immigration and to
    Geo. J. Hatfield, U. S. Attorney, his attorney:

You, and each of you, will please take notice that
Giuseppe Greco, alias Jimmy Polizzi, the petitioner
in the above entitled matter hereby appeals to the
United States Circuit Court of Appeals for the
Ninth Circuit from the order and judgment
rendered, made and entered herein on the 21st day
of January, 1932, denying the petition for a writ
of habeas corpus herein.

Dated this 13th day of February, 1932.

                    JAMES F. BRENNAN and
                    NATHAN MERENBACH,
                            Attorneys for Appellant.

[Endorsed]: Filed Feb. 13, 1932. Walter B.
Maling, Clerk. [56]

[Title of Court and Cause.]

PETITION FOR APPEAL.

To the Honorable Harold Louderback, Judge of the District Court for the Northern District of California, Southern Division:

Giuseppe Greco, alias Jimmy Polizzi, the petitioner above named conceiving himself aggrieved by the order and judgment made and entered on the 21st day of January, 1932, in the above entitled proceeding, does hereby appeal from the said order and judgment to the United States Circuit Court of Appeals for the Ninth Judicial Circuit of the United States at San Francisco in the State of California, and files herewith his assignment of errors to be urged on appeal and prays that his appeal may be allowed and that a transcript of the record of all proceedings, and papers upon which said order and judgment was made duly authenticated may be sent to the United States Circuit Court of Appeals for the Ninth Judicial Circuit of the United States at San Francisco, in the State of California.

Dated this 13th day of February, 1932.

JAMES F. BRENNAN and
NATHAN MERENBACH,
Attorneys for Appellant.

GIUSEPPE GRECO,
JOE GRECO,
Petitioner.

[Endorsed]: Filed Feb. 13, 1932. Walter B. Maling, Clerk. [57]

[Title of Court and Cause.]

ASSIGNMENT OF ERRORS.

Comes now Giuseppe Greco, alias Jimmy Polizzi, the above named petitioner by his attorneys and says that in the record and proceedings, in the above entitled matter, there is manifest error and that the final judgment and order made and entered in said matter on the 21st day of January, 1932, is erroneous and against the just rights of the said petitioner Giuseppe Greco, alias Jimmy Polizzi, in this:

First. That the above entitled Court erred in denying the petition of the said Giuseppe Greco, alias Jimmy Polizzi, for a writ of habeas corpus;

Second. That the above entitled Court erred in refusing to discharge the petitioner from custody for the reason that the petitioner showed that there was no legal reason for the restraint and imprisonment of said petitioner;

Third. That the above entitled Court erred in holding that the proofs submitted upon which deportation warrant herein was issued were sufficient in law to vest the department of labor with jurisdiction to issue said warrant or to hold or deport said petitioner.

Fourth. That the Court erred in not holding that there [58] was no evidence before the immigration authorities to justify the conclusion that the petitioner herein was a deportable alien.

Fifth. That the Court erred in holding that the appellant was accorded a full and fair hearing before the immigration authorities.

Sixth. That the Court erred in admitting in evidence or considering the statement taken from said petitioner Giuseppe Greco, alias Jimmy Polizzi, on September 11, 1930.

Seventh. That the Court erred in admitting in evidence respondent's exhibits.

Eighth. That the Court erred in holding that Trade Union Unity League is an organization which "believes in, advises, advocates, and teaches the overthrow by force or violence of the government of the United States and which circulates, distributes, publishes and displays printed matter advising, advocating and teaching the overthrow by force or violence of the government of the United States."

The said Giuseppe Greco, alias Jimmy Polizzi, now prays that the order and judgment made and entered on the 21st day of January, 1932, herein above mentioned be reversed, annuled and held for naught and that he, the said petitioner, may have such further relief as may be meet in the premises.

Dated, February 13, 1932.

GIUSEPPE GRECO,
JOE GRECO,
Petitioner.

JAMES F. BRENNAN and
NATHAN MERENBACH,
His Attorneys.

[Endorsed]: Filed Feb. 13, 1932. Walter B. Maling, Clerk. [59]

[Title of Court and Cause.]

ORDER ALLOWING APPEAL.

It appearing to the above entitled court that Giuseppe Greco, alias Jimmy Polizzi, the petitioner herein, has this day filed and presented to the above court this petition praying for an order of this court allowing an appeal to the United States Circuit Court of Appeals for the Ninth Circuit from the judgment and order of this court denying a writ of habeas corpus herein and dismissing his petition for said writ, and good cause appearing therefor,

IT IS HEREBY ORDERED that an appeal be and the same is hereby allowed as prayed for herein; and

IT IS HEREBY FURTHER ORDERED that the Clerk of the above entitled court make and prepare a transcript of all the papers, proceedings and records in the above entitled matter and transmit the same to the United States Circuit Court of appeals for the Ninth Circuit within the time allowed by law; and

IT IS FURTHER ORDERED that the execution of the warrant of deportation of said Giuseppe Greco, alias Jimmy Polizzi, be and the same is hereby stayed pending this appeal that cost bond of

$250.00 be filed by petitioner, and that the said Giuseppe Greco, alias Jimmy Polizzi, be not removed [60] from the jurisdiction of this court pending this appeal.

AND IT IS FURTHER ORDERED that the proceedings herein be suspended until such time as said appeal is determined and that Giuseppe Greco, alias Jimmy Polizzi, be allowed his liberty pending this appeal on filing a good and sufficient bond in this cause in the sum of $1000.00 with the usual conditions of appeal bonds from this court.

Dated at San Francisco, California, this 13th day of February, 1932.

HAROLD LOUDERBACK,
U. S. District Judge.

[Endorsed]: Filed Feb. 13, 1932. Walter B. Maling, Clerk. [61]

[Title of Court and Cause.]

PRAECIPE FOR TRANSCRIPT OF RECORD.

To the Clerk of Said Court:

Sir: Please issue copies of the following papers to be used in preparing transcript on appeal:

1. Petition for Writ of Habeas Corpus together with exhibits attached thereto.

2. The affidavit of E. Hanoff contained in Appellant's Reply Brief to Respondent's Points and Authorities.

3. Order to Show Cause.

4. Notice of Filing of Respondent's Exhibits and Respondent's Exhibits.

5. Minute Order Submitting Cause. October 19, 1931.

6. Minute Order Denying Writ of Habeas Corpus.

7. Notice of Appeal.

8. Petition for Appeal.

9. Assignment of Errors.

10. Order Allowing Appeal.

11. Citation.

12. Praecipe for Record on Appeal.

JAMES F. BRENNAN and
NATHAN MERENBACH,
Attorneys for Appellant.

[Endorsed]: Filed Feb. 13, 1932. Walter B. Maling, Clerk. [62]

[Title of Court and Cause.]

CERTIFICATE OF CLERK TO TRANSCRIPT
OF RECORD ON APPEAL.

I, Walter B. Maling, Clerk of the United States District Court, for the Northern District of California, do hereby certify that the foregoing 62 pages, numbered from 1 to 62, inclusive, contain a full, true, and correct transcript of the records and proceedings in the matter of Giuseppe Greco, alias Jimmy Polizzi, on Habeas Corpus, No.

20741-L, as the same now remain on file and of record in my office.

I further certify that the cost of preparing and certifying the foregoing transcript of record on appeal is the sum of Seventeen Dollars and Fifty Cents ($17.50) and that the said amount has been paid to me by the attorneys for the appellant herein.

IN WITNESS WHEREOF, I have hereunto set my hand and affixed the seal of said District Court, this 11th day of March A. D. 1932.

[Seal]   WALTER B. MALING,
                                              Clerk.
                    By C. M. TAYLOR,
                              Deputy Clerk.   [63]

CITATION ON APPEAL.

United States of America.—ss.

The President of the United States of America.

To John D. Nagle, Commissioner of Immigration, Port of San Francisco, and George J. Hatfield, United States Attorney, GREETING:

YOU ARE HEREBY CITED AND ADMONISHED to be and appear at a United States Circuit Court of Appeals for the Ninth Circuit, to be holden at the City of San Francisco, in the State of California, within thirty days from the date hereof, pursuant to an order allowing an appeal,

of record in the Clerk's Office of the United States
District Court for the Northern District of California wherein Giuseppe Greco, alias Jimmy Polizzi, is appellant, and you are appellee, to show
cause, if any there be, why the decree or judgment
rendered against the said appellant, as in the said
order allowing appeal mentioned, should not be corrected, and why speedy justice should not be done
to the parties in that behalf.

WITNESS, the Honorable HAROLD LOUDER-
BACK, United States District Judge for the
Southern Division of the Northern District of Cali-
fornia, this 13th day of February, A. D. 1932.

[Seal]   HAROLD LOUDERBACK,
                    United States District Judge.

[Endorsed]: Filed March 2, 1932, 10:24 A. M.
Walter B. Maling, Clerk.   [64]

[Endorsed]: No. 6807. United States Circuit
Court of Appeals for the Ninth Circuit. Giuseppe
Greco, alias Jimmy Polizzi, Appellant, vs. John D.
Nagle, Commissioner of Immigration, Port of San
Francisco, Appellee. Transcript of Record. Upon
Appeal from the United States District Court for
the Northern District of California, Southern Di-
vision.

Filed Apr. 1, 1932.

.   PAUL P. O'BRIEN,
Clerk of the United States Circuit Court of Appeals
     for the Ninth Circuit.   '

No. 6807

IN THE

United States Circuit Court of Appeals

For the Ninth Circuit

GIUSEPPE GRECO, alias Jimmy Polizzi,

Appellant,

VS.

JOHN D. NAGLE, Commissioner of Immigration, Port of San Francisco,

Appellee.

BRIEF FOR APPELLANT.

JAMES F. BRENNAN,
Russ Building, San Francisco,

NATHAN MERENBACH,
Hearst Building, San Francisco,

GEORGE DE LEW,
Russ Building, San Francisco,

Attorneys for Appellant.

FILED

NOV 16 1932

PAUL P. O'BRIEN,
CLERK

PERNAU-WALSH PRINTING CO., SAN FRANCISCO

Subject Index

	Page
Statement of the case	1
Argument	6

I. Was there any evidence that appellant was a Communist? 8

   1. The appellant in the warrant for his arrest was charged with being a Communist (Exhibit D', Tr. 67) 8

II. Was there any evidence to justify the findings of the Commissioner of Immigration that appellant was a member of Trade Union Unity League? 9

   1. Time element 9

   2. Necessity of intelligent understanding of the program of the organization 10

III. Is Trade Union Unity League an organization the alien members of which are automatically subject to deportation? 11

   1. Is Trade Union Unity League an organization prohibited by law? 11

   2. Nature of the organization..................... 12

IV. Fair hearing 15

   1. Examination under circumstances amounting to duress makes the hearing unfair............... 16

   2. An interpreter should have been provided where the alien was a man of low intelligence and did not have sufficient knowledge of the English language to understand the technical, involved and confusing questions 20

   3. Arrest without a warrant is improper.......... 21

   4. No evidence upon which the warrant was issued was exhibited to appellant 22

   5. Request for a telegraphic warrant was unfair under the circumstances 22

   6. Discrepancy between the warrant of arrest and the warrant of deportation rendered the hearing unfair 24

Page

7. It was unfair to add additional charge against
   appellant, to-wit: 24

8. It was unfair to introduce numerous books and
   pamphlets, the ownership or possession of none of
   which had been charged to appellant............ 25

9. Error of law on the part of the District Court in
   considering the contents of books and pamphlets. 25

Conclusion 26

Table of Authorities Cited

Pages

Biloquomsky v. Tod, 263 U. S. 149.....................20, 21

Colyer v. Skeffington, 265 Fed. 17....................10, 16, 25

Eguci, Ex parte, 58 Fed. (2d) 417..................... 19

Firestein v. Conaty, 41 Fed. (2d) 53.................. 25

Hee, Charley, v. U. S., 18 Fed. (2d) 355.............. 20

Jouras v. Allen, 222 Fed. 758......................... 22

Radioeff, Ex parte, 278 Fed. 227......................15, 18

Ungar v. Seaman, 4 Fed. (2d) 80.......................15, 16

Whitfield v. Hanges, 222 Fed. 745.....................15, 19, 20

STATUTES, RULES AND PAMPHLETS CITED

Pages

Act of October 16, 1918, as amended by the Act of June 5,
   1920 ....8, 9, 15

Rule 22, Subdivision 5 (b)............................ 4

Trade Union Unity League 11, 12, 13

No. 6807

United States Circuit Court of Appeals
For the Ninth Circuit

GIUSEPPE GRECO, alias Jimmy Polizzi,
Appellant,

vs.

JOHN D. NAGLE, Commissioner of Immigration, Port of San Francisco,
Appellee.

BRIEF FOR APPELLANT.

STATEMENT OF THE CASE.

Mr. Giuseppe Greco has been a resident of this country for a period of over twenty-two years. He is industrious and kind-hearted, though not a very intelligent person, with a very limited knowledge of the English language. For fifteen years prior to his arrest, he was employed steadily by Mr. Barron, who operated a janitorial and window washing establishment. The limited number of men employed by Mr. Barron gave him an opportunity to know Mr. Greco intimately, and he is of the highest opinion as to Greco's character. In addition to his employment, Mr. Greco at the time of his arrest owned a shoe shine stand, employing another person during the day and devoting some time himself to the stand evenings at the conclusion of his own work. Thus he was not only industrious as a laborer, but was likewise an employer.

Some few months prior to his arrest, he happened to be in a crowd which listened to some street orator in the vicinity of O'Farrell and Fillmore streets. His presence there will be better understood if we are to take into consideration that the drug store and residence of Mr. Cykman, one of the witnesses and a good friend of Mr. Greco, was then located on the corner of Webster and O'Farrell streets and Mr. Greco used to visit Mr. Cykman and his family practically every evening and had to pass that particular vicinity.

At the conclusion of the address, an attractive young lady came up and asked Mr. Greco to join an organization—as he then understood, a labor union—and he gave her $1.00. At no time did he sign an application for membership or a pledge card of any sort. Subsequently a card was mailed to by him by Trade Union Unity League. It so happened that the headquarters of this particular organization were near Mr. Greco's place of employment, and he was approached by a young lady on one more occasion to make a loan of $25.00 for some defense fund. Being a very easy-going man with his funds (Tr. 23, Exhibit C), he gave her $25.00, with an express understanding that he was to get his money back. Shortly thereafter Mr. Greco bought a shoe shine stand and became an employer. He then notified the girl at the headquarters of Trade Union Unity League that he no longer desired to be a member of the organization. He then also asked for and received the $25.00 advanced by him for a defense fund.

At the time of his arrest, he was no longer a member of the organization, as evidenced not only by his testimony, but by the membership card seized by the immigration authorities, which card on its face shows that *no dues had been paid for several months* prior to Mr. Greco's arrest.

In connection with the membership card, it might be stated that the immigration officers found it not upon the person of appellant, but in his house, which was entered and searched without any warrant on September 11, 1930, and that same day Mr. Greco was arrested, with no definite charges placed against him. He was taken into custody, the oath was administered to him by the immigration officer, and he was forced, not only to make what amounts to a statement against himself, but the examining officer, who was the very person who arrested Greco, made every possible effort to confuse Mr. Greco by elaborate and tricky questions, instead of trying to ascertain the truth. In spite of the efforts of the examining officer to involve Mr. Greco and his limited knowledge of English, Mr. Greco stated that he understood Trade Union Unity League to be an organization for better wages (Tr. 13); that he was not a member of the Communist Party (Tr. 13); that he never understood that Trade Union Unity League educated the masses into fighting in defense of the Soviet Union (Tr. 14).

On the tricky question of whether the United States is a capitalistic government or a government of the workers, he answered it is the government of the people (Tr. 14). He also testified that he did not believe in violent measures, but believed in changes by the votes of the people (Tr. 15). He also stated that he worked as a window washer and owned a shoe shine stand (Tr. 18, 19), and that during the war he registered for the draft, but was not called because of his age (Tr. 12).

If it is kept in mind that petitioner was not given an opportunity to consult an attorney as to his rights, that he was not advised as to the exact nature of the charges against him, that he was examined by the same officer who arrested him,—the above answers stand out in still more favorable light for petitioner.

At the time of petitioner's arrest, no warrant for his arrest was ever issued, and none apparently was applied for until after Mr. Greco was made to testify. Only then apparently a telegraphic warrant was applied for and issued on the day following, to-wit, September 12, 1930. At no time prior to the actual hearing of the case was the warrant of arrest ever exhibited to petitioner or his attorneys, and at no time was either petitioner or his attorneys shown affidavits or other evidence upon which the warrant of arrest was issued (Rule 22, subdivision 5 (b)).

At the hearing held October 1, 1930, all the witnesses examined testified that Mr. Greco was industrious, kind, and of good character, and that he was not a Communist. Mr. Barron, his employer, testified that during a strike the petitioner was the only one who was loyal to him and refused to join the strikers (Tr. 24). The evidence of Mr. Cykman is likewise important because of his intimate acquaintanceship with Mr. Greco and because Mr. Cykman, who lost all his life savings in Russia due to the Bolshevik regime, as brought out in testimony, is very bitterly opposed to the Communist or Soviet form of government.

The petitioner himself testified that he believes this government to be the best in the world (Tr. 52), and that he has nothing against a capitalistic regime as such, as he himself believes in making money. *He testified that at the time of his arrest he did not belong to Trade Union Unity League, as he went into business for himself;* that even during the time he nominally belonged to the organization he did not believe it to be anything but a labor union (Tr. 47); that his joining the organization was purely accidental (Tr. 41); that he does not believe in the overthrow of the government by force or violence (Tr. 49); that he has a very limited knowledge of the English language, which, by the way, was the only reason why he did not become naturalized (Tr. 40); that he would like to become a citizen of the United States (Tr. 52); that he was willing to go to war for the United States (Tr. 40); that he never read any of the numerous pamphlets and books introduced by the examining officer in record (Tr. 58, 59, 60).

As against this testimony, the examining officer produced no direct testimony for the government, never connected the petitioner with the mass of literature introduced in evidence, and upon objection by one of the counsel for the petitioner (Mr. Merenbach) to such procedure, the examiner (Inspector Farrelly) admitted that these pamplets were not found in Mr. Greco's home, but that they must be introduced nevertheless. For some reason this objection was not recorded. In like manner, the examining officer introduced reports of Inspectors Brown, Neilson and Endicott, *dated August, 1930,* without disclosing the contents of such reports to said petitioner or his attorneys, without producing said inspectors for cross-examination, and without showing any connection between the appellant and the subject matter of the reports. The objection to the arbitrary admission in evidence of pamphlets not connected with appellant was again made by Attorney James F. Brennan, but to no avail (Tr. 63).

At the conclusion of the hearing held October 1, 1930, Inspector Farrelly made an additional oral charge against petitioner without directing his attention to the facts which constituted the reason for placing this additional charge (Tr. 61).

Finally, after a delay of about a year, the Department of Labor issued a warrant of deportation (Exhibit A), which on its face shows that the original charge against petitioner stated in the warrant of arrest (Exhibit D), that of being a Communist, was not sustained. Nevertheless, the Department of Labor issued a warrant of deportation on the charge for which the warrant of arrest was not issued.

ARGUMENT.

There are the following eight assignments of error: First. That the above entitled court erred in deny-

ing the petition of the said Giuseppe Greco, alias
Jimmy Polizzi, for a writ of habeas corpus.

Second. That the above entitled court erred in
refusing to discharge the petitioner from custody for
the reason that the petitioner showed that there was
no legal reason for the restraint and imprisonment of
said petitioner.

Third. That the above entitled court erred in holding that the proofs submitted upon which deportation
warrant herein was issued were sufficient in law to
vest the Department of Labor with jurisdiction to
issue said warrant or to hold or deport said petitioner.

Fourth. That the court erred in not holding that
there was no evidence before the immigration authorities to justify the conclusion that the petitioner herein
was a deportable alien.

Fifth. That the court erred in holding that the
appellant was accorded a full and fair hearing before
the immigration authorities.

Sixth. That the court erred in admitting in evidence or considering the statement taken from said
petitioner Giuseppe Greco, alias Jimmy Polizzi, on
September 11, 1930.

Seventh. That the court erred in admitting in evidence respondent's exhibits.

Eighth. That the court erred in holding that Trade
Union Unity League is an organization which ''believes in, advises, advocates, and teaches the overthrow by force or violence of the government of the
United States, and which circulates, distributes, pub-

lishes and displays printed matter advising, advocating and teaching the overthrow by force or violence of the government of the United States.''

The consideration of the above assignment of errors involves the following four questions:

I. Was there any evidence that appellant was a Communist?

II. Was there any evidence to justify the findings of the Commissioner of Immigration that appellant was a member of Trade Union Unity League?

III. Is Trade Union Unity League an organization the alien members of which are automatically subject to deportation under the Act of October 16, 1918, as amended by the Act of June 5, 1920, U. S. C. A., Sec. 137?

IV. Was appellant accorded a fair hearing?

I. WAS THERE ANY EVIDENCE THAT APPELLANT WAS A COMMUNIST?

1. The appellant in the warrant for his arrest was charged with being a Communist (Exhibit D, Tr. 67).

The best answer to the question listed as number I lies in the fact that the original charge against appellant was dropped and in its stead was substituted in the warrant of deportation a general charge that appellant ''is a member of an organization that believes in, advocates and teaches the overthrow by force and violence of the government of the United States,'' and that he ''is a member of an organization that circulates, distributes, publishes and displays printed matter advising, advocating and teaching the overthrow by force or violence of the government of the United States" (Tr. 10).

The general charge against appellant just cited will not stand unless the following two premises are correct:

(a) That the appellant at the time of his arrest was a member of Trade Union Unity League.

(b) That Trade Union Unity League is an illegal organization which comes under the provision of the Act of October 16, 1918, as amended by the Act of June 5, 1920, U. S. C. A., Sec. 137.

II. WAS THERE ANY EVIDENCE TO JUSTIFY THE FINDINGS OF THE COMMISSIONER OF IMMIGRATION THAT APPELLANT WAS A MEMBER OF TRADE UNION UNITY LEAGUE?

1. Time element.

Appellant at the time of his arrest was not a member of Trade Union Unity League. Petitioner was arrested on the 11th day of September, 1930, while actually engaged in his work of washing windows. The membership card, which at the request of appellant was introduced in evidence and marked Exhibit No. 1 (Tr. 42), on its face shows that no dues were paid since May, 1930. This corroborates the testimony of the appellant that he paid his dues and resigned from the organization at the time he purchased a bootblack stand, which was operated by him for a period of several months prior to his arrest (Tr. 43,

44, 55). It is clear, therefore, that at the time of his arrest Greco was no longer a member of Trade Union Unity League.

2. **Necessity of intelligent understanding of the program of the organization.**

It is definitely established by the decisions of the court that mere membership in a prohibited by law organization would not in itself automatically subject the member to deportation. The alien must fully understand the nature of the organization which he has joined. Joining under a mistaken idea as to the program or nature of the organization would not make one a member for the purpose of deportation proceedings. Even admission by the alien that he was a member of the Communist Party was held to be insufficient for the purpose of deportation, unless it could likewise be shown that he intelligently understood what the membership in the Communist Party implied (*Colyer v. Skeffington*, 265 Fed. 17, at pp. 23, 24).

In the instant case, the record is clear that appellant was an ignorant and practically illiterate Italian, from whom an attractive young lady had no difficulty in extracting one dollar. He would have just as readily given a dollar to any cause if approached by a charming saleslady. He signed no card and took no pledge of any kind. Whatever understanding he had as to the nature of the organization was that it was a labor union for better wages. His former record as the only employee who refused to take part in a strike, and his desire to better himself by purchasing a shoe shine business, and his present status as the owner of a window cleaning establishment (in fact, appellant has a contract with the United States Government to wash all the windows in the Post Office Building where this court is located), corroborate his testimony and that of the witnesses that at no time was he against the organized government. Had he understood Trade Union Unity League to be what the immigration authorities claim it to be, there is no doubt that he would not have joined it.

————

III. IS TRADE UNION UNITY LEAGUE AN ORGANIZATION THE ALIEN MEMBERS OF WHICH ARE AUTOMATICALLY SUBJECT TO DEPORTATION?

1. Is Trade Union Unity League an organization prohibited by law?

While maintaining that appellant, because of his ignorance, at no time understood Trade Union Unity League to be anything else but a labor union, and while repeating our stand that at the time of his arrest appellant was no longer connected with the organization, we wish to call the attention of the court to the fact that there is not a single decision by the Supreme Court of the United States which would definitely place Trade Union Unity League in the same category as the Communist Party, active membership in which would justify deportation of an alien.

The only connection between the two organizations was that for some period of time Trade Union Unity League occupied a small portion of the premises at 145 Turk Street, San Francisco, the remaining portion being occupied by the Communist Party. This arrangement was only due to a desire to economize in the rental of the hall, and is not at all unusual.

As it appears from the affidavit of E. Hanoff, an authority on the subject (Tr. 70, 71), Trade Union Unity League is in no way connected with the Communist Party, and that membership in the Trade Union Unity League is open to all, regardless of party affiliation. As a corroborative factor, the attention of the court is called to the fact that at the time said affidavit was made Trade Union Unity League was no longer at 145 Turk Street and shared its new quarters with Needle Trades Workers' Industrial Union.

Both from the affidavit of Hanoff, as well as from the reports of the immigration officers, it appears that the book shop which was operated at 145 Turk Street was operated exclusively by the Communist Party and that Trade Union Unity League had nothing to do with the sale or distribution of pamphlets introduced in evidence, none of which, by the way, were ever found in the possession of the appellant, or in any way directly connected with him.

Nature of the organization.

In order to understand better the nature of the organization, let us quote from the pamphlet introduced in evidence by the immigration authorities, entitled "Trade Union Unity League," p. 19:

"The TUUL unions discard the old local structure of craft unionism. They base themselves directly upon the shops, establishing shop committees and the shop delegate system. The building of shop committees, the carrying on of union work directly in the shop, draws the working masses into the life and struggle of the union. The new unions eliminate the autocracy of the craft unions and establish a real democracy among the workers. They wipe out the corrupting high salary practices of the old trade unions and pay their officials only the going wage of the industries. Instead of exorbitant dues and initiation fees, breeders of corruption and reaction, they have union rates within the reach of the lowest paid workers. They systematically carry on a work of education of their general membership as to the real meaning of capitalism and the struggle to abolish it."

It is a foregone conclusion that the United States Attorney in his reply brief will try to connect Trade Union Unity League with the Red Internationale of Labor Unions. While not admitting any direct affiliation between the two organizations, let us again quote from the program of the Red Internationale of Labor Unions as adopted at its fourth congress in 1928. The program is as follows:

"1· The maximum 7-hour day without a reduction in wages, and the 6-hour day for underground workers and for those engaged in dangerous and particularly strenuous occupations, as well as for workers under 18 years of age.

2. The rejection of overtime work; early closing before Sundays and holidays; an annual holiday of a fortnight and not less than a month for underground workers and for those engaged in dangerous trades and particularly strenuous occupations, with the payment of full wages.

3. The fight against wage reduction; the fight for raising real wages; the fight against bonus and piece-rate systems; an increased struggle against piece-rates on the conveyor. Where piece-rates are in force it is necessary to ask for guaranteed minimum wages; the restriction of the rates of output in the terms of the wage agreements; a struggle against the arbitrary regulation of the pace of conveyors; equal wages for equal work for men, women and youth.

4. The limitation of the speed of work by the introduction of rest pauses; the right to change the place of work; the struggle against the stop-watch system.

5. A worker may be discharged only by consent of the factory council, or the union local, with the payment of the discharge benefits, which should be particularly high in the case of mass dismissals; the shortening of the working hours in order to prevent dismissals, while paying the same wages as before. The struggle for enrolling the unemployed into the process of production: the payment of state benefits to the unemployed at the rate of the minimum wage without distinction of nationality and sex; the remuneration for so-called 'relief' work at the current rate of wages.

6. The introduction of legislative orders for the protection of the workers in the factories, as well as all kinds of social welfare measures.

7. The prohibition of the employment of pregnant women and nursing mothers in hard and unhealthy work.

8. The struggle against factory police, pecuniary fines, espionage, blacklist.''

This program might well have been that of the Republican or the Democratic party, as nothing shocking to our conscience is noted therein. In fact, shorter working hours have been advocated by the leaders of both of these major parties.

If Trade Union Unity League is declared an outlaw organization, it is but a step to declare the Socialist Party an outlaw organization, and but another step to declare all labor unions as being illegal. The safety of the government lies not in such extreme and oppressive measures, tending to kill all criticism of the present economic and political systems, but rather in the sound judgment of citizens.

IV. FAIR HEARING.

Should the court reach an unfortunate decision that:

1. Appellant was a member of Trade Union Unity League at the time of his arrest;

2. That he had full knowledge of the aims and purposes of Trade Union Unity League; and

3. That Trade Union Unity League is an illegal organization within the meaning of the Act of October 16, 1918, as amended by the Act of June 5, 1920;

The appellant still cannot be deported unless he had a fair hearing.

Ex parte Radivoeff, 278 Fed. 227;

Whitfield v. Hanges, 222 Fed. 745;

Ungar v. Seaman, 4 Fed. (2d) 80.

"But while the courts have no jurisdiction on
habeas corpus to substitute their judgment on
pure questions of fact for that of the Secretary
of Labor, it is equally well settled that if the proceedings in the Department of Labor are shown
to be unfair or otherwise lacking in the essential
elements of due process of law, or if the Secretary of Labor is proceeding on an erroneous view
of the law, then the courts must review."

Colyer v. Skeffington, 265 Fed. 17, at p. 23.

1. **Examination under circumstances amounting to duress
makes the hearing unfair.**

In the analogous case of *Ungar v. Seaman*, 4 F.
(2d) 80, Sanborn, Circuit Judge, also condemns such
tactics:

"The facts that these aliens were arrested and
immediately questioned by the arresting officer
while they were in custody, without notice by the
charges in the warrants of arrest or otherwise of
the simple charge against them, without counsel,
and without time or opportunity, before they
were interrogated upon the merits of their cases,
to prepare to meet the real charge against them,
violated the basic requirement of due process and
a fair hearing that the accused shall be notified
of the charge against him before he shall be required to answer or commit himself upon the
merits of his case, and that he shall be given time
and opportunity to obtain counsel and to prepare
to meet the charge against him. The introduction
in evidence against the accused of the reports and
affidavits of the officers who conducted these
secret examinations of the contents of these unfair and unjust examinations violated the indis-
pensable requirements of a fair trial, that the

witnesses against the accused shall confront them
and give the latter an opportunity to cross-
examine them, and that hearsay is neither competent nor fair evidence against the accused.
Backus v. Owe Sam Goon, 235 F. 847, 853, 149 C.
C. A. 159; Ex parte Radivoeff (D. C.), 278 F.
227, 228, 229, 230.''

* * * * * * ⹂

"It is not denied that the admission of aliens
when they are not under arrest, freely made to
officers or other persons, established by the oral
testimony of those officers or persons subject to
cross-examination by the accused, may be received in evidence against them at their hearings
before the immigration officers, and that such
hearings are not bound in all things by the strict
rules of evidence which prevail in the courts. But
the secret questioning of these aliens by the
arresting officers, immediately after their arrest,
without counsel or opportunity to procure it,
without plain notice of the specific violation of
an act of Congress they were required to meet,
and without opportunity or time to prepare to
meet it, the admission in evidence of the reports
of this secret questioning against them, without
the presence or testimony of the reporting officers
or any opportunity for the accused to cross-
examine them, the receipt by the Assistant Secretary of Labor after the hearing was closed of
hearsay evidence sought by him without the
knowledge of the alien or his counsel, and the
other proceedings to which reference has been
made, deprived these aliens of the essential elements of due process of law, and rendered their
hearings so unfair and unjust that they cannot be
sustained.''

In *Ex parte Radivoeff*, 278 Fed. 229, where petitioner was first examined without being told of his right to have counsel and to examine evidence upon which the warrant of arrest was based, the court held that such procedure constituted an unfair hearing:

"* * * That the proceedings were unfair and prejudicial, and denied due process of law to the alien, is clear. Not only general principles of law were violated, but also the department's rules. These latter, in so far as consistent with law, are themselves law, and, be it noted, law for government—for the department—as well as for aliens. In connection with the general law of the land, the rules constitute for aliens in deportation proceedings the due process of law guaranteed by the federal Constitution to all men. The object is obvious, viz., so that the 'vast power of the Secretary of Labor, judicial in its nature, capable of infinite abuse and tyranny, little restrained by the constitution, procedure, publicity, responsibilities, and traditions that hedge about a court, and little controlled, save by his honor and conscience' (Tam Chung (D. C.), 223 Fed. 802), shall 'be administered, not arbitrarily and secretly, but fairly and openly, under the restraints of the tradition and principles of free government applicable where the fundamental rights of men are involved.' Kwock Jan Fat v. White, 253 U. S. 464, 40 Sup. Ct. 566, 64 L. Ed. 1010. All to the end that trials result in justice, with what is of only lesser importance, an appearance of justice.

In addition to the unsupported warrant, the alien a witness against himself, quasi secret rather than open and public hearings, which it is not determined of themselves alone would be fatal to fairness, there is flagrant disregard of the department's rules and of the general law of evidence and procedure. The object of rule 22, to enable the alien to prepare for hearing and therein to have counsel, not partially, but throughout, was defeated, probably in conformity to the secret circular of the time, and set out in the Colyer Case (D. C.), 265 Fed. 46. * * *''

How much stronger is the present case, where petitioner was arrested without any warrant and was examined without any interpreter by the same officer who arrested him. In *Whitfield v. Henges,* 222 Fed. 745, the court says (p. 750):

"It will be noticed that the rule gives the inspector no authority secretly, in the presence of no one but himself and his police officers, whose presence and power unavoidably places the defenseless alien under fear and restraint, to examine or question him."

In *Ex parte Eguci,* 58 Fed. (2d) 417, the alien was held for six days incommunicado without any charges, the immigration officers not having sufficient information upon which to apply for a warrant. The alien was told that unless he told the truth it was impossible to say when his case would be reached, which apparently he did at the expiration of six days' confinement. In granting the writ, the court stated:

"The fairness required in deportation proceedings must mark the actions of the Immigration officers at all times. The detention of the alien and acts of the officers attending the same are a part of the proceeding equally with the formal

taking of evidence. Clearly petitioner was subjected to duress. He was coerced. Conceding that
he did not give correct information until he was
thus confined for a period of six days and that he
finally told a true story, the methods here employed are entirely unwarranted, constitute a
denial of due process of law and of that freedom
that must be accorded the humblest stranger
within our gates equally with the most distinguished citizen of the land" (p. 418).

In this case the alien was arrested and immediately
placed under oath and examined by the very man who
arrested him. He was not asked whether he was willing to make a statement. He was not informed that
there was any charge at all against him. He was still
laboring under such fright occasioned by his arrest
that the situation amounted in reality to duress. The
situation is amply stated by Judge Anderson in
Charley Hee v. U. S., 19 Fed. (2d) 335, when he says:

"To seize the person and search the memory of
the frightened victim is a far grosser invasion of
personal liberty and disregard of due process of
law than is the search for and the seizure of
papers even from a home or from an office as in
the Gould case." (*Whitfield v. Henges,* 222 Fed.
745.)

2. An interpreter should have been provided where the alien
was a man of low intelligence and did not have sufficient
knowledge of the English language to understand the
technical, involved and confusing questions.

In *Biloqumsky v. Tod,* 263 U. S. 149, we find the
following language:

"If the alien is unable to speak or understand
English, an interpreter should be employed where
practical."

3. Arrest without a warrant is improper.

It is a foregone conclusion that the appellee will cite *Biloqumsky v. Tod,* supra, as an authority for the proposition that the arrest without a warrant is immaterial and does not render the hearing unfair. However, a careful reading of the case convinces one that whatever was said by the court there, was not intended to apply to a case similar to the one now before the court. In the *Biloqumsky* case the alien was first arrested by the local police authorities, and at the time of his arrest he had in his possession for distribution a great deal of Communistic literature. While lawfully in custody he was interrogated by an immigration officer. The court said:

> "But mere interrogation under oath by a Government official of one *lawfully* in confinement is not a search and seizure."

In the instant case, when the first statement was taken from Greco he was not lawfully in custody, as there was no federal or local warrant of any sort for his arrest at that time. In *Biloqumsky v. Tod,* the court apparently recognizes that interrogation of one even in lawful custody may sometimes be improper. On page 157 the court says:

> "To render a hearing unfair, the defect or the practice complained of must have been such as might have led to the denial of justice, or there must have been absent one of the elements deemed essential to due process."

The court also says:

> "If the alien is unable to speak or understand English, an interpreter should be employed where practical."

How much that language could be applied to the instant case, where the petitioner, as stated already, was arrested without a warrant and examined by the same officer who arrested him, while he was in the state of fear, and without an opportunity being given to get an interpreter and without informing him of the charge against him.

4. **No evidence upon which the warrant was isssued was exhibited to appellant.**

5. **Request for a telegraphic warrant was unfair under the circumstances.**

In the instant case the petitioner was arrested without a warrant on September 11, 1930; that telegraphic warrant was received September 12; that in spite of a letter addressed September 13, 1930, to immigration inspector by Mr. Nathan Merenbach, one of the counsel for petitioner, asking for all data pertaining to the case, nothing was presented to him, and only on the date of the hearing upon the hearing to show cause and preliminary to the taking of testimany, the examining inspector, Mr. Farley, made a statement for the purpose of the record that the warrant and the evidence upon which it was based was shown to petitioner, there being no showing as to what that evidence consisted of, and as a matter of fact no evidence of any sort upon which the warrant was based was shown to either counsel or petitioner. In *Jouras v. Allen,* 222 Fed. 758, the court says:

> "Rule 22b of the Department of Labor requires that during the hearing the alien shall be allowed to inspect the warrant. The purposes of that portion of that rule are to inform the ac-

cused of the genuineness of the signature to the warrant and of the charges against him. But such a telegraphic warrant in a code of which the alien is ignorant accomplishes neither of these objects. The signature to it is not the genuine signature of the Secretary, or any officer, and the telegram gives the accused no information. Hence rule 22, subdivision 2, requires that 'Telegraphic application may be resorted to only in case of necessity.' There was neither necessity nor reason for a telegraphic application in this case. But the inspector having made a telegraphic application and procured the telegraphic warrant, at about 4 P. M. on Saturday, January 5, 1914, went to Jouras' restaurant, seized him, and caused him to be thrown into and kept in solitary confinement in a dark cell at police headquarters 'for investigation' during Saturday night, Sunday, Sunday night, and until Monday at 11 A. M. when he took him to his room, handcuffed him, and with a weapon at his command, gave him a hearing there without counsel or friend, which consisted of questioning him in an exceedingly threatening manner, and writing down what he succeeded in extracting from him. This course of action was arbitrary, contrary to the rule regarding telegraphic applications, a clear abuse of the discretion of the inspector, and a hearing thus conducted is unfair and contrary to the fundamental principles which inhere in due process of law. United States v. Ruiz, 203 Fed. 441, 443, 121 C. C. A. 551.''

6. **Discrepancy between the warrant of arrest and the warrant of deportation rendered the hearing unfair.**

In the instant case the warrant of arrest charged the appellant with being a Communist and his defense was based on this issue. Yet the warrant of deportation entirely omits this charge. In the instant case the discrepancy is of such a nature as amounting to a denial to petitioner of a fair hearing and due process of law. In the original warrant he was charged with being a Communist. To be on guard against such a charge is not the same as being warned against the extremely broad charge of belonging to an organization which believes in the overthrow of the government by force or violence, especially when by an ingenious process of reasoning many organizations which were formerly regarded by their members as entirely different from the Communist Party, are arbitrarily placed by the immigration inspectors in the same group with the Communist Party.

7. **It was unfair to add additional charge against appellant, to-wit:**

"that you are affiliated with the Communist party of the United States of America, the Trade Union Unity League and the Red International of Labour Unions, which organizations believe in, advise, advocate and teach the overthrow by force or violence of the Government of the United States, and which organizations circulate, distribute, publish and display printed matter advising, advocating and teaching the overthrow by force or violence of the Government of the United States."

It is elementary that when additional charges are placed against the alien during the hearing, the atten-tion of the alien should be directed to the facts which constitute the reason for such additional charges (*Colyer v. Skeffington,* supra.)

8. It was unfair to introduce numerous books and pamphlets, the ownership or possession of none of which had been charged to appellant.

A number of pamphlets were introduced which were purchased at 145 Turk Street, the headquarters of the Communist Party. There is no proof that Trade Union Unity League had anything to do with the distribution of the pamphlets or had any other connection with the Communist Party, except being located in the same building. None of the books or pamphlets belonged to or were in the possession of the appellant, and besides it appears that appellant had a limited knowledge of the English language and could not have read or understood said books or pamphlets, even if he had them.

9. Error of law on the part of the District Court in considering the contents of books and pamphlets.

In this connection we further charge that it was error of law on the part of the United States District Court to consider the books and pamphlets referred to, it being admitted by the United States Attorney, in respondent's brief, page 2, lines 29-32, that said books and pamphlets were kept at the time as a part of another case. In *Firestein v. Conaty,* 41 Fed. (2d) 53, the court stated:

"The appellee seems to contend that the court will take judicial notice of the character of the Communist party. No authority is cited in support of this contention. While the character of this organization has frequently been considered by the court, and in some very recent cases, Whitney v. California, 274 U. S. 357, 47 S. Ct. 641, 71 L. Ed. 1095; Anbolish v. Paul (C. C. A.), 283 Fed. 957; Skeffington v. Katzeff (C. C. A.), 277 F. 129; Ex parte Ingrams (D. C.), 17 F. (2d) 507, the decisions in these cases are based upon the evidence adduced before the court with reference to the character of this organization, the statements made in the opinion of the court with reference to that organization are based upon the testimony before court, and in no instance has the court attempted to take judicial notice of the character of this organization. * * *

"Reversed, with directions to try the issues de novo, as suggested in Chin Yow v. U. S. 208 U. S. 13; Whitfield v. Henges, 222 F. 745; Svarney v. U. S., 7 F. (2d) 799; Mourakis v. Noyle, 24 F. (2d) 799; In re Chan Foo Lin, 243 F. (2d) 80; Ng Fung Ho v. White, 259 U. S. 276."

CONCLUSION.

It is respectfully submitted that the appellant must be given his liberty if the court finds any one of the following premises to be correct:

1. That Trade Union Unity League is not an organization prohibited under the act in question.

2. That appellant was not at the time of his arrest a member of Trade Union Unity League.

3. That appellant did not understand Trade Union Unity League to be anything else but a labor union.

4. That appellant did not have a fair hearing.

In deportation cases the court is the final arbitrator. Even the President of the United States is powerless to act to remedy an admitted wrong. It is for that reason that we pray for careful and liberal consideration of the facts and law presented herein, so that a man who is an industrious and useful resident and an employer of other men may not, without justifiable cause, be torn apart from the country which he loves and which he has grown to think of as his own, and sent to a place which he had voluntarily forsaken more than twenty-four years ago.

Dated, San Francisco,
November 14, 1932.

Respectfully submitted,
JAMES F. BRENNAN,
NATHAN MERENBACH,
GEORGE DE LEW,
Attorneys for Appellant.

United States Circuit Court of Appeals

For the Ninth Circuit

GIUSEPPE GRECO, alias
JIMMY POLIZZI,

          Appellant,

  VS.

JOHN D. NAGLE, Commissioner of
Immigration, Port of San Francisco,

          Appellee.

BRIEF FOR APPELLEE.

GEO. J. HATFIELD,
United States Attorney.

LUCAS E. KILKENNY,
Asst. United States Attorney,
Attorneys for Appellee.

ARTHUR J. PHELAN,
*United States Immigration Service
on the Brief.*

FILED

DEC 16 1932

Parker Printing Company, 545 Sansome Street, San Francisco.

PAUL P. O'BRIEN,
CLERK

Subject Index

	Page
STATEMENT OF THE CASE	1
FACTS OF THE CASE	2
ARGUMENT	5
(1) The executive finding is sustained by the evidence	5
(2) There was no unfairness in the Immigration hearing	9

Table of Cases Cited

Pages

Bilokumsky v. Tod, 263 U. S. 149 at 155, 156, 157 .... 9, 10

Colyer v. Skeffington, 265 Fed. 17.................................... 6

Evanoff v. Bonham, (C. C. A. 9) 50 F. (2d) 756 ....8, 9, 11
Ex parte Guest, 287 Fed. 884 at 888........................... 13
Ex parte Hamiguchi, 161 Fed. 185 at 192.............. 12

Firestein v. Conaty, 41 F. (2d) 53.............................. 12

Ghiggeri v. Nagle, (C. C. A. 9) 19 F. (2d) 875...... 5

Japanese Immigrant Case, 189 U. S. 86 at 101, 102 ....12, 13

Kamiyama v. Carr, (C. C. A. 9) 44 F. (2d) 503.. 9
Kishimoto v. Carr, (C. C. A. 9) 32 F. (2d) 991..5, 9, 10
Kostenowczyk v. Nagle, (C. C. A. 9) 18 Fed. (2d) 834 12

Lee Choy v. United States, (C. C. A. 9) 49 F. (2d) 24 9
Li Bing Sun v. Nagle, (C. C. A. 9) 56 F. (2d) 1000 at 1002, 1003.. 9
Low Wah Suey v. Backus, 225 U. S. 460 at 470.....10, 11

Murdoch v. Clark, (C. C. A. 1) 53 F. (2d) 155..... 8, 11

Neils Christian Mikklesen Kjar v. Doak, et al., (C. C. A. 7) No. 4834..6, 8, 11
Ng Kai Ben v. Weedin, (C. C. A. 9) 44 F. (2d) 315 at 316 .... 5, 9

Plane v. Carr, (C. C. A. 9) 19 F. (2d) 470............. 10
Prentis v. Seu Leung, (C. C. A. 7) 203 F. 25 at 28 5

Pages

Siniscalchi v. Thomas, (C. C. A. 6) 195 Fed. 701 at 705 13

Skeffington v. Katzeff et al., (C. C. A. 1) 277 Fed. 129 at 132 .... 6, 8, 11

Sormunen v. Nagle, (C. C. A. 9) 59 F. (2d) 398 .... 9, 10, 11

Tisi v. Tod, 264 U. S. 131 7

U. S. ex rel Scimeca v. Husband, (C. C. A. 2) 6 F. (2d) 957 8

U. S. ex rel Lisafeld v. Smith, 2 F. (2d) 90 at 91 7

U. S. ex rel Rosen v. Williams, (C. C. A. 2) 200 Fed. 538 at 541 13

United States v. Tapolcsanyi, (C. C. A. 3) 40 F. (2d) 255 at 257 .... 7, 11

U. S. ex rel Yokinen v. Commissioner of Immigration, (C. C. A. 2) 57 F. (2d) 707 5

Vilarino v Garrity, (C. C. A. 9) 50 F. (2d) 582 .... 9, 10

Wolck v. Weedin, (C. C. A. 9) 58 F. (2d) 128 .... 9, 10

No. 6807

United States Circuit Court of Appeals

For the Ninth Circuit

GIUSEPPE GRECO, alias
JIMMY POLIZZI,

Appellant,

vs.

JOHN D. NAGLE, Commissioner of
Immigration, Port of San Francisco,

Appellee.

BRIEF FOR APPELLEE.

STATEMENT OF THE CASE.

This appeal is from an order of the United States
District Court for the Southern Division of the
Northern District of California denying appellant's
petition for a writ of habeas corpus (Tr. 89 and 90).

FACTS OF THE CASE.

The record flatly contradicts appellant's version of
the facts.

On September 11, 1930, appellant was questioned by an Immigrant Inspector (Tr. 11 to 19, inclusive). He then testified in part as follows:

"Q. *Are you a member now of the Trade Union Unity League?*
A. *Yes.*
Q. When did you join the organization?
A. In January this year.

*   *   *   *   *   *   *

Q. Have you ever attended meetings at the Communist Headquarters, 145 Turk?
A. Yes.
Q. When?
A. A long time ago.
Q. When was it?
A. The last time I paid my dues.
Q. *Are you in sympathy with the objects of the Trade Union Unity League?*
A. *I belong to them* (Tr. 13).
Q. *Are you in sympathy with their objects and aims?*
A. *Yes I am.*

*   *   *   *   *   *   *

Q. Is it not the policy of the Trade Union Unity League to organize the workers in order that each country shall change its organization and laws so that it becomes a member of the Soviet?
A. Yes that is the policy." (Tr. 14, 15.)

"Q. Can you explain how it is that when you were taken into custody you stated that you were not a member of the Trade Union Unity League?

A. It just happened.

Q. Why did you deny your membership in the Trade Union Unity League?

A. I had no reason at all.

Q. Is membership in the Trade Union Unity League something to be ashamed of?

A. No, I just said 'No.'

Q. *Do you believe in the principles of the Trade Union Unity League?*

A. *Yes.*

* * * * * * *

Q. Are you loyal to the principles of the Trade Union Unity League or are you loyal to the Government of the United States.

A. Yes, *I am loyal to the Trade Union Unity League and I am a good member"* (Tr. 16).

"Q. Did you ever have in your possession or in your home any leaflets issued by the Communist Party?

A. Yes, I have had them in my home.

Q. I show you a leaflet which was distributed by the Communist Party at the time the Fleet of the United States was in port. This leaflet is headed 'DEFEND THE SOVIET UNION! DEFEND SOVIET CHINA! FIGHT AGAINST IMPERIALISTIC WAR!' I ask you if you ever had in your possession a leaflet similar to this one?

A. I do not know—a lot of times they gave them to me and I take them home and read them." (Tr. 17.)

On September 12, 1930, the Secretary of Labor issued his warrant for appellant's arrest (Tr. 67 and 68).

On October 1, 1930, appellant was accorded a hearing, at which he was represented by counsel (Tr. 20-66, inclusive). The record of that hearing shows the following at the outset:

> "Said alien was informed that the purpose of said hearing was to afford him an opportunity to show cause why he should not be deported to the country whence he came, said warrant of arrest being read and each and every allegation therein contained carefully explained to him. Said alien was afforded an opportunity to inspect the warrant of arrest and the evidence upon which it was issued, which privilege was accepted." (Tr. 21)

On July 31, 1931, the Secretary of Labor ordered appellant deported under 8 U. S. C. A., Section 137, on the following grounds:

> "That he is a member of an organization that believes in, advises, advocates and teaches the overthrow by force or violence of the government of the United States.

> And that he is a member of an organization that circulates, distributes, publishes and displays printed matter advising, advocating and teaching the overthrow by force or violence of the government of the United States." (Tr. 9, 10)

ARGUMENT.

There is nothing new in this case. The points made by appellant have been many times passed upon by the courts adversely to his contentions.

(1) THE EXECUTIVE FINDING IS SUSTAINED BY THE EVIDENCE.

Regarding appellant's claim that he withdrew from the Trade Union Unity League (Tr. 43), his testimony of September 11, 1930 that he was *then* a member would justify a finding of the Secretary to that effect, despite appellant's later retraction.

> *Ng Kai Ben v. Weedin,* (C .C. A. 9) 44 F. (2d) 315, at 316;
>
> *Ghiggeri v. Nagle,* (C. C. A. 9), 19 F. (2d) 875;
>
> *Kishimoto v. Carr,* (C. C. A. 9) 32 F. (2d) 991;
>
> *Prentis v. Seu Leung,* (C. C. A. 7) 203 Fed. 25, at 28.

Furthermore, if appellant had been a member of the organization he is subject to deportation even though he might have ceased to be a member prior to his arrest.

> "Perhaps the sufficient answer is that had Congress intended membership at the time of arrest to be the criterion it would have said so."
>
> *United States ex rel. Yokinen v. Commissioner of Immigration,* (C. C. A. 2) 57 F. (2d) 707.

The statute provides for the deportation at any time after entry of any alien who is found to have been at the time of entry *"or to have become thereafter"* a member of any one of the classes of aliens enumerated (8 U. S. C. A., Sec. 137g).

Appellant contends that it has not been shown that he had knowledge of the nature of the Trade Union Unity League.

In

> *Neils Christian Mikklesen Kjar v. Doak et al.* (C. C. A. 7, No. 4834) decided October 18, 1932 and not yet reported,

the Court said:

> "Nor was it necessary to prove that appellant had knowledge of the contents of the programs of the several organizations or any one of them. It is sufficient if the evidence showed that he was a member of, or affiliated with, such an organization as contemplated by the Statute."

Appellant relies upon the decision of the District Court in

> *Colyer v. Skeffington,* 265 Fed. 17.

In reversing that decision the Circuit Court of Appeals stated that the declarations of purposes and program found in the manifesto and Constitution of the organization there involved

> "are binding upon a member of the latter for in the application for membership the applicant declares 'his adherence to the principles and tactics of the party * * * ' "

> *Skeffington v. Katzeff, et al.,* (C. C. A. 1) 277 F. 129, at 132.

Appellant in the case at bar in his testimony heretofore quoted declared his adherence to and sympathy with the objects and aims of the Trade Union Unity League of which he admitted he was a member.

See, also:

> United States ex rel. Lisafeld v. Smith, 2 F. (2d) 90, at 91;
> United States v. Tapolcsanyi, (C. C. A. 3) 40 Fed. (2d) 255, at 257.

The statute uses the word "knowingly" only when providing for the deportation of aliens who are found personally circulating or distributing literature, and *omits* the word "knowingly" in the subdivisions relative to aliens who are members of an organization that advocates the overthrow of the government by force or violence or of an organization that circulates literature containing such advocacy. Obviously the omission of the word "knowingly" when referring to the latter classes was intentional.

Moreover even in the cases in which proof of knowledge is made a condition of the right to deport it is settled that such knowledge may be inferred despite the alien's denial and even without direct evidence of such knowledge.

> Tisi v. Tod, 264 U. S. 131.

There is ample basis in the appellee's testimony quoted above for the inference that his knowledge of the character and aims of the Trade Union Unity League is greater than he now professes.

Appellant attempts to argue that the Trade Union
Unity League is not such an organization as is mentioned in the statute.

Of course the affidavit of E. Hanoff which was
never before the Immigration authorities and which
was not executed until after the institution of the
habeas corpus proceedings (Tr. 70 and 71) is no
proper part of the record and could not be considered
by the court.

> *United States ex rel. Scimeca v. Husband,* (C.
> C. A. 2) 6 F. (2d) 957.

At the immigration hearing a number of pamphlets
were introduced in evidence to show the nature and
program of the Trade Union Unity League (Tr. 58,
59, 60, 63). These exhibits have not been brought
before this court by appellant and hence it must be
presumed that the finding was supported by the evidence.

> *Evanoff v. Bonham,*(C. C. A. 9) 50 F. (2d) 756;
> *Skeffington v. Katzeff et al.,* 277 Fed. 129, at
> 132, supra.

If these exhibits were in the record we could point
out from them the aims of the Trade Union Unity
League and its connection with the Communist Party.
In their absence we will content ourselves with pointing out that the same documents have been held to
show that the Trade Union Unity League is such an
organization as is mentioned in the statute.

> *Murdoch v. Clark,* (C. C. A. 1) 53 F. (2d) 155;
> *Neils Christian Mikklesen Kjar v. Doak, et al.,*
> supra.

(2) THERE WAS NO UNFAIRNESS IN THE IMMIGRATION HEARING.

Appellant, although represented by counsel at the hearings, made no objection to the introduction in evidence of his preliminary statement (Tr. 21, 22, 39), nor (with the exception of two documents introduced at the final hearing) was any objection made to the introduction of any of the exhibits (Tr. 58, 59, 60, 63), nor to the procedure followed at the hearing.

Appellant therefore may not now complain regarding these matters.

> *Sormunen v. Nagle,* (C. C. A. 9) 59 F. (2d) 398;
> *Ng Kai Ben v. Weedin,* supra;
> *Li Bing Sun v. Nagle,* (C. C. A. 9) 56 F. (2d) 1000, at 1002, 1003;
> *Kamiyima v. Carr,* (C. C. A. 9) 44 F. (2d) 503.

Furthermore, there is no merit in the contentions that the statement was given under duress and that its reception in evidence constituted unfairness.

> *Bilokumsky v. Tod,* 263 U. S. 149, at 155, 156, 157;
> *Wolck v. Weedin,* (C. C. A. 9) 58 F. (2d) 128;
> *Kishimoto v. Carr,* supra;
> *Evanoff et al. v. Bonham,* supra;
> *Vilarino v. Garrity,* (C. C. A. 9) 50 F. (2d) 582;
> *Lee Choy v. United States,* (C. C. A. 9) 49 F. (2d) 24.

Appellant relies upon cases in which aliens were denied the right to have counsel at the hearing under the warrant of arrest. There is however, no right to representation by counsel at the preliminary examination before a warrant of·arrest is applied for or issued.

> *Low Wah Suey v. Backus,* 225 U. S. 460, at 470;
> *Bilokumsky v. Tod,* supra, at page 156;
> *Vilarino v. Garrity,* supra;
> *Kishimoto v. Carr,* supra;
> *Plane v. Carr,* (C. C. A. 9) 19 F. (2d) 470.

Irregularities prior to or in connection with the arrest are immaterial on habeas corpus.

> *Bilokumsky v. Tod,* supra;
> *Sormunen v. Nagle,* supra;
> *Wolck v. Weedin,* supra.

The notice of the placing of an additional charge against appellant (Tr. 61) is also immaterial since that charge has not been made a ground for the deportation order (Tr. 9 and 10).

A formal warrant of arrest was issued September 12, 1930 (Tr. 67, 68). It was read and explained to appellant and inspected by him at the hearing of October 1, 1930, at which his counsel were present (Tr. 20). He was also shown the evidence upon which it was issued (Tr. 20). All the evidence was formally introduced at that and a subsequent hearing. If counsel neglected to inspect the evidence as it was offered, the examining inspector was certainly not to blame.

The pamphlets (introduced without objection of counsel—Tr. 58, 59, 60) were purchased at the meet-

ing place of the Trade Union Unity League, in which
appellant admitted his membership (Tr. 75 to 78, inclusive). They were properly considered by the Immigration Authorities.

Neil Christian Mikklesen Kjar v. Doak, et al.,
supra;
Murdoch v. Clark, supra;
Sormunen v. Nagle, supra;
United States v. Tapolcsanyi, supra.

It is further contended that the court below erred
in considering these exhibits. In the first place the
record does not show that these exhibits were considered by the court below, and they are not in this
record on appeal. On the hearing in the court below appellee suggested that the exhibits which were
before the Immigration authorities be incorporated
in the proceedings before the court, these same exhibits being already on file in connection with another
habeas corpus case (Tr. 89). Appellant's counsel re-
sisted this suggestion, and so far as the record discloses it was not acted upon.

If appellant desired to have the executive finding
reviewed it was incumbent upon him to see that the
court had all the evidence which was before the executive officers.

Evanoff et al. v. Bonham, supra;
Skeffington v. Ketzeff, supra;
Low Wah Suey v. Backus, supra.

District Court Rule 50, Northern District of California.

Appellant not only failed to supply the court below
with the exhibits introduced at the Immigration hearing but opposed appellee's attempt to supply them.
The case of

Firestein v. Conaty, 41 F. (2d) 53,

cited by appellant has no application here. In that
case the Secretary of Labor had excluded the exhibits
from consideration on the ground that they had been
obtained by illegal seizure. That left no evidence before the Secretary as to the nature of the organization
of which Firestein was a member.

It is next contended that the hearing was unfair
because the warrant of arrest charged

"that he is a member of the Communist Party
of the United States of America, an organization
that believes in, advises, advocates and teaches
the overthrow, etc." (Tr. 67)

Whereas, the warrant of deportation simply
charges "that he is a member of an organization that
believes in, advises, advocates and teaches the overthrow, etc."

It is settled that in these deportation proceedings
if the alien has notice *"although not a formal one"* of
the purpose of the hearing it is sufficient.

The Japanese Immigrant Case, 189 U. S. 86,
at 101, 102;
Ex parte Hamiguchi, 161 Fed. 185, at 192;
Kostenowczyk v. Nagle, (C. C. A. 9) 18 F. (2d)
834;

United States ex rel. Rosen v. Williams, (C. C.
A. 2) 200 F. 538, at 541;
Siniscalchi v. Thomas, (C. C. A. 6) 195 F. 701,
at 705;
Ex parte Guest, 287 Fed. 884, at 888.

In the case at bar the fact of appellant's membership in the Trade Union Unity League "came from
his own mouth." No contention was made before the
Immigration authorities that he did not have adequate notice of the charges. The record shows that
he and his counsel had actual notice of the fact that
his admission of membership in the Trade Union
Unity League was relied upon as subjecting him to
deportation. This fully appears from the fact that
the proof of membership in the organization was
predicated solely on appellant's own statement of
September 11, 1930. At the hearing the defense of
appellant was devoted primarily to an attempt to
prove that he was not actually a member of the Trade
Union Unity League (Tr. 41, 42, 43, 44, 45, 46, 47,
48, 50).

If appellant felt that he had been prejudiced by
inadequate notice his recourse was to bring this fact
to the attention of the Secretary of Labor.

The decision in

The Japanese Immigrant Case, supra,

disposes of this contention of appellant as well as all
his other allegations of unfairness. We quote from
that decision:

"Besides, the record now before us shows that the appellant had notice, *although not a formal one,* of the investigation instituted for the purpose of ascertaining whether she was illegally in this country. The traverse to the return made by the Immigration Inspector shows upon its face that she was before that officer pending the investigation of her right to be in the United States, and made answers to questions propounded to her. It is true that she pleads a want of knowledge of our language; that she did not understand the nature and import of the questions propounded to her; that the investigation made was a 'pretended' one; and that she did not, at the time, know that the investigation had reference to her being deported from the country. *These considerations cannot justify the intervention of the courts. They could have been presented to the officer having primary control of such a case, as well as upon an appeal to the Secretary of the Treasury, who had power to order another investigation if that course was demanded by law or by the ends of justice.* It is not to be assumed that either would have refused a second or fuller investigation, if a proper application and showing for one had been made by or for the appellant. *Whether further investigation should have been ordered was for the officers, charged with the execution of the statutes, to determine. Their action in that regard is not subject to judicial review.* Suffice to say, it does not appear that appellant was denied an opportunity to be heard."

We submit that the order of the court below was correct and should be affirmed.

GEO. J. HATFIELD,
United States Attorney.

LUCAS E. KILKENNY,
Asst. United States Attorney,
Attorneys for Appellee.

ARTHUR J. PHELAN,
*United States Immigration Service
on the Brief.*

No. 6808

United States

Circuit Court of Appeals

For the Ninth Circuit. *1 6*

G. F. SLOAN, J. E. ADAMS, C. O. MIDDLETON,
J. A. ANDERSON, L. H. BARNHART, and
J. H. MILLER,

Petitioners,

vs.

COMMISSIONER OF INTERNAL REVENUE,

Respondent.

Transcript of Record.

**Upon Petition to Review an Order of the United States
Board of Tax Appeals.**

FILED

APR 1 1 1932

PAUL P. O'BRIEN,
CLERK

Filmer Bros. Co. Print, 330 Jackson St., S. F., Cal.

United States
Circuit Court of Appeals
For the Ninth Circuit.

G. F. SLOAN, J. E. ADAMS, C. O. MIDDLETON,
J. A. ANDERSON, L. H. BARNHART, and
J. H. MILLER,

Petitioners,

vs.

COMMISSIONER OF INTERNAL REVENUE,

Respondent.

Transcript of Record.

**Upon Petition to Review an Order of the United States
Board of Tax Appeals.**

Filmer Bros. Co. Print, 330 Jackson St., S. F., Cal.

INDEX TO THE PRINTED TRANSCRIPT OF RECORD.

[Clerk's Note: When deemed likely to be of an important nature, errors or doubtful matters appearing in the original certified record are printed literally in italic; and, likewise, cancelled matter appearing in the original certified record is printed and cancelled herein accordingly. When possible, an omission from the text is indicated by printing in italic the two words between which the omission seems to occur.]

	Page
Amended Answer (Docket No. 40,380)	31
Amended Answer (Docket No. 40,381)	60
Amended Answer (Docket No. 40,396)	78
Amended Answer (Docket No. 40,491)	97
Amended Answer (Docket No. 40,516)	115
Amended Answer (Docket No. 40,517)	134
Answer (Docket No. 40,380)	29
Answer (Docket No. 40,381)	58
Answer (Docket No. 40,396)	77
Answer (Docket No. 40,491)	95
Answer (Docket No. 40,516)	113
Answer (Docket No. 40,517)	132
Certificate of Clerk U. S. Board of Tax Appeals to Transcript of Record (Consolidated Cases)	164
Decision (Docket No. 40,380)	146
Decision (Docket No. 40,381)	147
Decision (Docket No. 40,396)	148
Decision (Docket No. 40,491)	149
Decision (Docket No. 40,516)	150
Decision (Docket No. 40,517)	151

Index.	Page
Docket Entries (No. 40,380)	1
Docket Entries (No. 40,381)	3
Docket Entries (No. 40,396)	6
Docket Entries (No. 40,491)	9
Docket Entries (No. 40,516)	11
Docket Entries (No. 40,517)	13

EXHIBITS:

Exhibit "A" Attached to Petition (Docket No. 40,381)—Notice of Deficiency 23

Exhibit "A" Attached to Petition (Docket No. 40,381)—Notice of Deficiency 41

Exhibit "A" Attached to Petition (Docket No. 40,396)—Notice of Deficiency ..., 70

Exhibit "A" Attached to Petition (Docket No. 40,491)—Notice of Deficiency 88

Exhibit "A" Attached to Petition (Docket No. 40,516)—Notice of Deficiency 107

Exhibit "A" Attached to Petition (Docket No. 40,517)—Notice of Deficiency 125

Exhibit "B" Attached to Petition (Docket No. 40,381)—Declaration of Trust ... 48

Exhibit "C" Attached to Petition (Docket No. 40,381)—Appointment of Trustees of Trust Known as Dominguez Harbor Tract No. 2, Dated November 25, 1914 51

Exhibit "D" Attached to Petition (Docket No. 40,381)—Appointment of Trustees of Trust Known as Dominguez Harbor Tract No. 2, Dated February 15, 1915 54

Index.   Page

Findings of Fact (Consolidated Cases) 138

Motion for Reconsideration (Consolidated
  Cases) 153

Opinion (Consolidated Cases) 143

Petition (Docket No. 40,380) 16

Petition (Docket No. 40,381) 34

Petition (Docket No. 40,396) 63

Petition (Docket No. 40,491) 81

Petition (Docket No. 40,516) 100

Petition (Docket No. 40,517) 118

Petition for a Review of the Decision of the
  United States Board of Tax Appeals (Consolidated Cases) 157

Praecipe for Transcript of Record (Consolidated Cases) 162

Stipulation to Amend Praecipe (Consolidated
  Cases) 163

DOCKET No. 40,380.

G. F. SLOAN,

Petitioner,

vs.

COMMISSIONER OF INTERNAL REVENUE,
Respondent.

APPEARANCES:

For Petitioner: FREDERICK O. GRAVES, Esq.
DANA LATHAM, Esq.
GEO. M. THOMPSON, Esq.
MELVIN D. WILSON, Esq.

For Respondent: J. M. LYONS, Esq.
E. L. UPDYKE, Esq.

DOCKET ENTRIES.

1928.

Aug. 21—Petition received and filed. Taxpayer
notified. (Fee paid.)

Aug. 22—Copy of petition served on General
Counsel.

Oct. 17—Motion for an extension of time to
1/21/29 to answer filed by General
Counsel—granted.

1929.

Jan. 21—Answer filed by General Counsel.

Jan. 23—Copy of answer served on taxpayer—circuit calendar.

---

*Page-number appearing at the top of page of original certified
Transcript of Record.

1931.

May   9—Hearing set June 1, 1931—Los Angeles,
         California.

May 15—Motion for leave to amend answer filed
         by General Counsel—amendment ten-
         dered. 5/20/31 granted.

May 15—Motion for order to produce records
         filed by General Counsel.

May 15—Motion to consolidate with dockets
         40,381, 40,391, 40,516, 40,517, and
         40,491 filed by General Counsel.
         5/19/31 copy served.

May 15—Application for subpoena *duces tecum*
         filed by General Counsel.

May 15—Subpoena *duces tecum* issued (G. F.
         Sloan). 5/16/31 subpoena served.

May 18—Order that petitioner produce at hearing
         certain written documents entered.

June 1—Hearing had before W. C. Lansdon on
         merits. Submitted. Subpoenas and
         proof of service of same for J. E.
         Adams, G. F. Sloan and C. O. Mid-
         dleton filed at hearing. Briefs due
         in 60 days.

June 20—Transcript of hearing of June 1, 1931,
         filed.

July 3—Brief filed by General Counsel.

July 24—Brief filed by taxpayer.

Sept. 21—Findings of fact and opinion rendered—
         Wm. C. Lansdon, Div. 8. Decision
         will be entered for the respondent.

Sept. 21—Decision entered—Logan Morris, Divi-
         sion 14.

1931.

Oct. 12—Motion for reconsideration of decision
filed by taxpayer. Denied 10/27/31.

1932.

Feb. 20—Notice of appearance of Frederick O.
Graves as counsel filed.

[2] 1932.

Feb. 20—Motion to fix amount of bond in the
amount of $4,000.00 filed by taxpayer.

Feb. 25—Order fixing the amount of bond at
$4,000.00 entered.

Mar. 5—Petition for review to U. S. Circuit
Court of Appeals (9) with assignments of error filed by taxpayer.

Mar. 5—Proof of service filed.

Mar. 5—Praecipe filed.

Mar. 5—Proof of service filed.

Mar. 22—Stipulation to amend praecipe filed.

---

[3]   DOCKET No. 40,381.

J. E. ADAMS,

Petitioner,

vs.

COMMISSIONER OF INTERNAL REVENUE,

Respondent.

APPEARANCES:

For Petitioner: FREDERICK O. GRAVES, Esq.
DANA LATHAM, Esq.
GEO. M. THOMPSON, Esq.
MELVIN D. WILSON, Esq.

For Respondent: J. M. LYONS, Esq.
E. L. UPDYKE, Esq.

DOCKET ENTRIES.

1928.

Aug. 21—Petition received and filed. Taxpayer notified. (Fee paid.)

Aug. 22—Copy of petition served on General Counsel.

Oct. 17—Motion for continuance to 1/21/29 to answer filed by General Counsel—granted.

1929.

Jan. 21—Answer filed by General Counsel.

Jan. 23—Copy of answer served on taxpayer—circuit calendar.

1931.

May 9—Hearing set June 1, 1931—Los Angeles, California.

May 15—Motion for order to produce records filed by General Counsel.

May 15—Motion for leave to amend answer filed by General Counsel—amendment tendered. 5/20/31 granted.

May 15—Motion to consolidate with dockets 40,380, 40,396, 40,516, 40,517 and 40,491 filed by General Counsel. 5/19/31 copy served.

May 15—Application for subpoena *duces tecum* filed by General Counsel.

May 15—Subpoena *duces tecum* (J. E. Adams) issued. 5/15/31 subpoena served.

May 18—Order that petitioner produce at hearing certain written documents entered.

1931.

June 1—Hearing had before Wm. C. Lansdon on merits. Submitted. Subpoenas and proof of service of same for J. E. Adams, G. F. Sloan and C. O. Middleton filed. Briefs due in 60 days. See docket 40,380.

June 20—Transcript of hearing of June 1, 1931, filed.

July 3—Brief filed by General Counsel.

July 24—Brief filed by taxpayer.

Sept. 21—Findings of fact and opinion rendered—Wm. C. Lansdon, Division 8. Decision will be entered for the respondent.

Sept. 21—Decision entered—Division 14, Logan Morris.

Oct. 12—Motion for reconsideration of decision filed by taxpayer. 10/27/31 denied.

[4] 1932.

Feb. 20—Motion to fix amount of bond in the amount of $4,000.00 filed by taxpayer.

Feb. 25—Order fixing the amount of bond at $4,000.00 entered.

Mar. 5—Petition for review to U. S. Circuit Court of Appeals (9) with assignments of error filed by taxpayer.

Mar. 5—Proof of service filed.

Mar. 5—Praecipe filed.

Mar. 5—Proof of service filed.

Mar. 22—Stipulation to amend praecipe filed.

[5] DOCKET No. 40,396.

C. O. MIDDLETON,

Petitioner,

vs.

COMMISSIONER OF INTERNAL REVENUE,

Respondent.

APPEARANCES:

For Petitioner: FREDERICK O. GRAVES, Esq.
DANA LATHAM, Esq.
GEO. M. THOMPSON, Esq.
MELVIN D. WILSON, Esq.

For Respondent: J. M. LYONS, Esq.
E. L. UPDYKE, Esq.

DOCKET ENTRIES.

1928.

Aug. 22—Petition received and filed. Taxpayer
notified. (Fee paid.)

Aug. 23—Copy of petition served on General
Counsel.

Oct. 17—Answer filed by General Counsel.

Oct. 30—Copy of answer served on taxpayer—
circuit calendar.

1931.

May   9—Hearing set June 1, 1931—Los Angeles,
California.

May 15—Motion for leave to amend answer filed
by General Counsel—amendment tendered. 5/20/31 granted.

1931.

May 15—Motion for order to produce records filed by General Counsel.

May 15—Motion to consolidate with dockets 40,380, 40,381, 40,516, 40,517 and 40,491 filed by General Counsel. 5/19/31 copy served.

May 14—Application for subpoena *duces tecum* filed by General Counsel.

May 15—Subpoena *duces tecum* (C. O. Middleton) issued. 5/16/31 subpoena served.

May 18—Order that petitioner produce at the hearing certain written documents entered.

June 1—Hearing had before Mr. Lansdon on merits. Submitted. Subpoenas and proof of service of same for J. E. Adams, G. F. Sloan and C. O. Middleton filed. 60 days for briefs. See docket 40,380.

June 20—Transcript of hearing of June 1, 1931, filed.

July 3—Brief filed by General Counsel.

July 24—Brief filed by taxpayer.

Sept. 21—Findings of fact and opinion rendered— Wm. C. Lansdon, Div. 8. Decision will be entered for the respondent.

Sept. 21—Decision entered—Logan Morris, Division 14.

Oct. 12—Motion for reconsideration of decision filed by taxpayer. 10/27/31 denied.

[6]   1932.

Feb. 20—Notice of appearance of Frederick O. Graves as counsel filed.

Feb. 20—Motion to fix amount of bond in the amount of $4,000.00 filed by taxpayer.

Feb. 25—Order fixing the amount of bond at $4,000.00 entered.

Mar. 5—Petition for review to U. S. Circuit Court of Appeals (9) with assignments of error filed by taxpayer.

Mar. 5—Proof of service filed.

Mar. 5—Praecipe filed.

Mar. 5—Proof of service filed.

Mar. 22—Stipulation to amend praecipe filed.

———

[7]   DOCKET No. 40,491.

J. A. ANDERSON,

Petitioner,

vs.

COMMISSIONER OF INTERNAL REVENUE,

Respondent.

APPEARANCES:

For Petitioner: FREDERICK O. GRAVES, Esq.
GEO. M. THOMPSON, Esq.
MELVIN D. WILSON, Esq.
DANA LATHAM, Esq.

For Respondent: J. M. LYONS, Esq.
E. L. UPDYKE, Esq.

DOCKET ENTRIES.

1928.

Aug. 29—Petition received and filed. Taxpayer notified. (Fee paid.)

Aug. 30—Copy of petition served on General Counsel.

Oct. 25—Motion for extension to Jan. 29, 1929, to file answer filed by General Counsel —granted.

1929.

Jan. 24—Answer filed by General Counsel.

Jan. 26—Copy served on taxpayer—circuit calendar.

1931.

May   9—Hearing set June 1, 1931—Los Angeles, California.

May 15—Motion for leave to amend answer filed by General Counsel—amendment tendered. 5/20/31 granted.

May 15—Motion for order to produce records filed by General Counsel.

May 15—Motion to consolidate with dockets 40,380, 40,381, 40,396, 40,516 and 40,517 filed by General Counsel. 5/19/31 copy served.

May 14—Application for subpoena *duces tecum* filed by General Counsel.

May 15—Subpoena *duces tecum* (J. A. Anderson) issued. 5/16/31 subpoena served.

1931.

May 18.—Order that petitioner produce at hearing certain written documents entered.

June 1—Hearing had before W. C. Lansdon on merits. Submitted. Subpoenas and proof of service of same for J. E. Adams, G. F. Sloan, and C. O. Middleton filed. Briefs due in 60 days. See #40,380.

June 20—Transcript of hearing of June 1, 1931, filed.

July 3—Brief filed by General Counsel.

July 24—Brief filed by taxpayer.

Sept. 21—Findings of fact and opinion rendered— Wm. C. Lansdon, Div. 8. Decision will be entered for the respondent.

Sept. 21—Decision entered—Logan Morris, Division 14.

Oct. 12.—Motion for reconsideration of decision filed by taxpayer. 10/27/31 denied.

[8] 1932.

Feb. 20—Notice of appearance of Frederick O. Graves as counsel filed.

Feb. 20—Motion to fix amount of bond in the amount of $4,000.00 filed by taxpayer.

Feb. 25—Order fixing the amount of bond at $4,000.00 entered.

Mar. 5—Petition for review to U. S. Circuit Court of Appeals (9) with assignments of error filed by taxpayer.

Mar. 5—Proof of service filed.

Mar. 5—Praecipe filed.

Mar. 5—Proof of service filed.

Mar. 22—Stipulation to amend praecipe filed.

———

[9]   DOCKET No. 40,516.

LEZZETTE H. BARNHART,

Petitioner,

vs.

COMMISSIONER OF INTERNAL REVENUE,

Respondent.

APPEARANCES:

For Petitioner: FREDERICK O. GRAVES, Esq.

MELVIN D WILSON, Esq.

DANA LATHAM, Esq.

GEO. M. THOMPSON, Esq.

For Respondent: J. M. LYONS, Esq.

E. L. UPDYKE, Esq.

———

DOCKET ENTRIES.

1928.

Sept. 1—Petition received and filed.   Taxpayer notified.   (Fee paid.)

Sept. 4—Copy of petition served on General Counsel.

Oct. 27—Motion for extension of time to 2/3/29 to answer filed by General Counsel—granted.

1929.

Jan. 24—Answer filed by General Counsel.

Jan. 26—Copy of answer served on taxpayer—circuit calendar.

1931.

May 9—Hearing set June 1, 1931—Los Angeles, California.

May 15—Motion for leave to amend answer filed by General Counsel—amendment tendered. 5/20/31 granted.

May 15—Motion for order to produce record filed by General Counsel.

May 15—Motion to consolidate with dockets 40,-380–81, 40,396, 40,491 and 40,517 filed by General Counsel.

May 14—Application for subpoena *duces tecum* filed by General Counsel.

May 15—Subpoena *duces tecum* (Lezzette Howard Barnhart) issued. 5/16/31 subpoena served.

May 18—Order that petitioner produce at hearing certain written documents entered.

June 1—Hearing had before Mr. Lansdon on merits. Submitted. Subpoenas served, proof of service of same for J. E. Adams, G. F. Sloan and C. O. Middleton filed. Briefs due in 60 days. See docket 40,380.

June 20—Transcript of hearing of June 1, 1931, filed.

July 3—Brief filed by General Counsel.

July 24—Brief filed by taxpayer.

Sept. 21—Findings of fact and opinion rendered—Wm. C. Lansdon, Div. 8. Decision will be entered for the respondent.

Sept. 21—Decision entered—Logan Morris, Division 14.

1931.

Oct. 12—Motion for reconsideration of decision filed by taxpayer. 10/27/31 denied.

[10] 1932.

Feb. 20—Notice of appearance of Frederick O. Graves as counsel filed.

Feb. 20—Motion to fix amount of bond in the amount of $4,000.00 filed by taxpayer.

Feb. 25—Order fixing the amount of bond at $4,000.00 entered.

Mar. 5—Petition for review to U. S. Circuit Court of Appeals (9) with assignments of error filed by taxpayer.

Mar. 5—Proof of service filed.

Mar. 5—Praecipe filed.

Mar. 5—Proof of service filed.

Mar. 22—Stipulation to amend praecipe filed.

---

[11]   DOCKET No. 40,517.

J. H. MILLER,

Petitioner,

vs.

COMMISSIONER OF INTERNAL REVENUE,
Respondent.

APPEARANCES:

For Petitioner: FREDERICK O. GRAVES, Esq.
DANA LATHAM, Esq.
GEO. M. THOMPSON, Esq.
MELVIN D. WILSON, Esq.

For Respondent: J. M. LYONS, Esq.
E. L. UPDYKE, Esq.

DOCKET ENTRIES.

1928.

Sept. 1—Petition received and filed. Taxpayer notified. (Fee paid.)

Sept. 4—Copy of petition served on General Counsel.

Oct. 27—Motion for extension of time to 2/3/29 to answer filed by General Counsel—granted.

1929.

Jan. 24—Answer filed by General Counsel.

Jan. 26—Copy of answer served on taxpayer—circuit calendar.

1931.

May 9—Hearing set June 1, 1931—Los Angeles, California.

May 15—Motion for leave to amend answer filed by General Counsel—amendment tendered. 5/20/31 granted.

May 15—Motion for order to produce record filed by General Counsel.

May 15—Motion to consolidate with docket 40,-380–81, 40,396, 40,491 and 40,516 filed by General Counsel. 5/19/31 copy served.

May 14—Application for subpoena *duces tecum* filed by General Counsel.

May 15—Subpoena *duces tecum* (J. H. Miller) issued. 5/16/31 subpoena served.

May 18—Order that petitioner produce at hearing certain written documents entered.

June 1—Hearing had before Mr. Lansdon on merits. Submitted. Subpoenas and proof of service of same for J. E. Adams, G. F. Sloan and C. O. Middleton filed. Briefs due in 60 days. See docket 40,380.

June 20—Transcript of hearing of June 1, 1931, filed.

July 3—Brief filed by General Counsel.

July 24—Brief filed by taxpayer.

Sept. 21—Findings of fact and opinion rendered—Wm. C. Lansdon, Div. 8. Decision will be entered for the respondent.

Sept. 21—Decision entered—Logan Morris, Division 14.

Oct. 12—Motion for reconsideration of decision filed by taxpayer. 10/27/31 denied.

[12] 1932.

Feb. 20—Notice of appearance of Frederick O. Graves as counsel filed.

Feb. 20—Motion to fix amount of bond in the amount of $4,000.00 filed by taxpayer.

Feb. 25—Order fixing the amount of bond at $4,000.00 entered.

Mar. 5—Petition for review to U. S. Circuit Court of Appeals (9) with assignments of error filed by taxpayer.

Mar. 5—Proof of service filed.

Mar. 5—Praecipe filed.

Mar. 5—Proof of service filed.

Mar. 22—Stipulation to amend praecipe filed.

[13]   Filed Aug. 21, 1928.

United States Board of Tax Appeals.

DOCKET No. 40,380.

G. F. SLOAN,

Petitioner,

vs.

COMMISSIONER OF INTERNAL REVENUE,

Respondent.

PETITION.

The above-named petitioner hereby petitions for a redetermination of the deficiency set forth by the Commissioner of Internal Revenue in his notice of deficiency bearing symbols IT:E:RR:280:60D–JEM, dated July 3, 1928, and as a basis of this proceeding alleges as follows:

(1)   Petitioner is an individual residing at 219 South Highland, Los Angeles, California.

(2)   The notice of deficiency, a copy of which is attached and marked Exhibit "A" was mailed to petitioner on July 3, 1928.

(3)   The taxes in controversy are income taxes for the years 1923, 1924, 1925 and 1926 as follows:

Year.	Tax.
1923	$1,045.58
1924	703.63
1925	279.83
1926	None
Total	$2,029.04

(4)   The determination of tax set forth in the said notice of deficiency is based upon the following errors:

(a) The Commissioner is erroneously and illegally holding the petitioner to be liable under the provisions of Section 280 of the Revenue Act of 1926 for a tax in the amount   [14] above stated as a transferee of the assets of "Dominguez Harbor Tract No. 2," a trust formed under the laws of the State of California, whereas the petitioner is not liable for any tax or other indebtedness of said "Dominguez Harbor Tract No. 2" under the said section of the law for the reason that:

(1)   Section 280 of the Revenue Act of 1926, as amended by the Revenue Act of 1928, is unconstitutional and void, being in violation of Section 2 of Article 1, Section 9 of Article 3, and Article 5 of the Constitution of the United States.

(2)   Section 280 of the Revenue Act of 1926, in so far as it purports to impose a tax on the former beneficiaries of a dissolved trust is unconstitutional in that the liability of the several beneficiaries is not definitely set forth.

(3)   Petitioner is not a transferee within the meaning of Section 280 of the Revenue Act of 1926.

(b)   The Commissioner of Internal Revenue is erroneously and illegally proposing to impose a tax upon "Dominguez Harbor Tract No. 2" as an association.

(c) The Commissioner of Internal Revenue is erroneously and illegally proposing to assess the petitioner, who is a beneficiary of a trust known as "Dominguez Harbor Tract No. 2," on account of income taxes for the calendar years of 1923 to 1925, inclusive, aggregating $2,029.04, which is claimed by the Commissioner to be the total tax liability of the said trust.

[15] (d) The Commissioner of Internal Revenue is erroneously and illegally proposing to assess the petitioner the total amount of income taxes for the calendar years 1923 to 1925, inclusive, purporting to be due from the "Dominguez Harbor Tract No. 2," disregarding the fact that even if this trust is held to be taxable as an association, the petitioner herein could not be held liable for a greater amount than that received in liquidation.

(e) The Commissioner of Internal Revenue is erroneously and illegally proposing to assess to the petitioner the total amount of income taxes purported to be due for the calendar year 1923 from the trust known as "Dominguez Harbor Tract No. 2" in the sum of $1,045.58, whereas the assessment of additional taxes for the calendar year 1923 to the beneficiary is barred by the statute of limitations.

(f) On information and belief petitioner alleges that in determining the net income for the calendar years 1923, 1924 and 1925 the Commissioner of Internal Revenue used an erroneous cost basis in determining the gross profit realized from sales of the trust property.

(g) Upon information and belief petitioner alleges that the net income of "Domingues Harbor Tract No. 2" as determined by the Commissioner of Internal Revenue for the calendar years 1923, 1924 and 1925 is erroneous.

(5) The facts upon which the petitioner relies as a basis of this proceeding are as follows:

[16] (a) Under date of September 1, 1913, P. H. O'Neil, J. E. Adams and J. H. Miller, as joint tenants, J. A. Anderson, Charles O. Middleton, G. F. Sloan and the Alisal Ranch Company caused to be created a certain trust known as "Dominguez Harbor Tract No. 2," naming Charles O. Middleton and J. E. Adams, Trustee, whereby certain property was transferred to the trustees for the purpose of securing certain indebtedness and for the purpose of doing other things set out fully in the Declaration of Trust, copy of which is attached as Exhibit "B" to petition filed by J. E. Adams.

(b) Under date of November 25, 1914 J. E. Adams and P. H. O'Neil were named as Trustees of trust known as "Dominguez Harbor Tract No. 2" created under date of September 1, 1913. (See copy of appointment attached as Exhibit "C" to petition filed by J. E. Adams.) Under date of February 15, 1915, J. E. Adams and G. F. Sloan were named as Trustees of trust known as "Dominguez Harbor Tract No. 2" created under date of

September 1, 1913. (See copy of appointment attached as Exhibit "D" to petition filed by J. E. Adams.)

(c)   The operations of "Dominguez Harbor Tract No. 2" and the rights and duties of the respective parties thereto are controlled by the Declaration of Trust hereinbefore referred to as Exhibit "B."

(d)   The Trust known as "Dominguez Harbor Tract No. 2" is not taxable as an association within the meaning of the Revenue Act of 1926. Therefore, there can be no liability to the petitioner herein under the provisions of [17]   Section 280, Revenue Act of 1926.

(e)   The Declaration of Trust does not provide for any periodical meetings of beneficiaries, for the election of officers of any kind, or the appointment of directors.

(f)   The "Dominguez Harbor Tract No. 2" is not an association within the meaning of the Revenue Acts of 1921, 1924 and 1926.

(g)   "Dominguez Harbor Tract No. 2" is a trust taxable to the beneficiaries as a joint venture.

(h)   The petitioner was a beneficiary under trust known as "Dominguez Harbor Tract No. 2," owning a 150/1000ths interest therein.

(i)   Petitioner filed income tax returns for the calendar years 1923, 1924 and 1925 and properly accounted therein his *pro rata* share of the income earned by trust designated "Dominguez Harbor Tract No. 2."

(j) On information and belief petitioner alleges that the Commissioner of Internal Revenue in determining net income of the trust known as "Dominguez Harbor Tract No. 2" used an erroneous cost in determining the amount of profit realized from sales of the trust property.

(k) Upon information and belief petitioner alleges that the net income of "Dominguez Harbor Tract No. 2" as determined by the Commissioner of Internal Revenue is erroneous.

(l) Section 280 of the Revenue Act of 1926 is unconstitutional and void, being in violation of Section 2 of [18] Article 1, Section 9 of Article 3 and Article 5 of the Constitution of the United States.

(6) Petitioner prays for relief from the deficiency asserted by the respondent on the following and each of the following particulars.

(a) Section 280 of the Revenue Act of 1926 is unconstitutional. Therefore, the petitioner is not liable as a transferee of the assets of the "Dominguez Harbor Tract No. 2." Therefore, there is no deficiency in tax.

(b) "Dominguez Harbor Tract No. 2" is not taxable as an association within the meaning of the Revenue Acts of 1921, 1924 and 1926, and therefore, there is no deficiency in tax.

WHEREFORE, petitioner prays that this board may hear and redetermine the deficiency herein alleged.

DANA LATHAM,
Counsel for Petitioner,
819 Title Insurance Building,
Los Angeles, California.

GEORGE M. THOMPSON,
Counsel for Petitioner,
505 Title Insurance Building,
Los Angeles, California.

State of California,
County of Los Angeles,—ss.

G. F. Sloan, being duly sworn, says that he is the petitioner above named; that he has read the foregoing petition or had the same read to him and is familiar with the statements therein contained; and that the facts therein stated are true except such facts as are recited to be upon information and belief and those facts he believes to be true.

G. F. SLOAN.

Subscribed and sworn to before me this 10th day of August, 1928.

[Seal]   MARSHALL D. HALL,
Notary Public in and for the County of Los Angeles, State of California.

My commission expires June 30, 1929.

[19]   EXHIBIT "A"

TREASURY DEPARTMENT,
WASHINGTON.

Office of
Commissioner of Internal Revenue.

July 3, 1928.

Mr. G. F. Sloan,
219 South Highland,
Los Angeles, California.

Sir:

In accordance with Section 274 of the Revenue Act of 1926 you are advised that the determination of your tax liability for the years 1923, 1924 and 1925, discloses a deficiency of $2,029.04, as shown in the attached statement, as transferree of the Dominguez Harbor Tract No. 2, Los Angeles, California, under Section 280 of said Act.

The section of the law above mentioned allows you an appeal to the United States Board of Tax Appeals within sixty days from the date of the mailing of this letter. However, if you acquiesce in this determination, you are requested to execute the inclosed Form A and forward it to the Commissioner of Internal Revenue, Washington, D. C., for the attention of IT:C:P–7.

Respectfully,

D. H. BLAIR,
Commissioner.

By C. B. ALLEN,
Deputy Commissioner.

Inclosures:
> Statement.
> Form A.
> Form 882.

[20] STATEMENT.

IT:E:RR:280:60D
> JEM.

> > In re: Mr. G. F. Sloan,
> > 219 South Highland,
> > Los Angeles, California.

Under authority of Section 280 of the Revenue Act of 1926 there is proposed for assessment against you the amount of $2,029.04, constituting your liability as transferee of the assets of the Dominguez Harbor Tract No. 2, c/o George M. Thompson, Title Insurance Building, Los Angeles, California, for unpaid income taxes in the above amount due from said corporation (plus any accrued penalty and interest) for the years 1923, 1924, and 1925, as shown in the following statement:

Year	Deficiency in Tax
1923	$ 1,045.58
1924	703.63
1925	279.83
1926	None

Total, $2,029.04

1923

Gross profit $9,062.25
Additions:
  Interest 2,752.14

                                        11,814.39
Deductions:
  Bookkeeping and miscella-
    neous expenses $1,074.82
  Discounts 296.02
  Taxes 78.90 1,449.74

Adjusted net income $10,364.65

Explanation.

The gross profit as shown above is computed as follows: (Installment sales basis.)
  155 lots sold at $565.00 each $87,575.00
  155 lots cost $340.00 each 52,700.00

                                          $34,875.00

Percentage of gross profit to sales .398 plus or
40%.

[21]   STATEMENT.

Mr. G. F. Sloan,
Los Angeles, California.

Collections received during the year $22,655.62—
40% of $22,635.62 equals $9,062.25.

Computation of Tax.

Net taxable income $10,364.65
Less:
  Credit 2,000.00

Balance taxable at 12½% $8,364.65

Tax at 12½% $1,045.58

Tax previously assessed .... None

_____

Deficiency $1,045.58

1924.

Gross profit $5,737.34

Additions:

Profit on repossession not
previously reported $1,741.98

Interest 1,568.66   3,310.54

_____

$9,047.88

Deductions:

Bookkeeping and miscella-
neous items $1,246.73

Discounts 117.67

Taxes 54.44   1,418.84

_____

Adjusted net income $7,629.04

Explanation.

The gross profit is computed as shown under
1923 income.

The total collections received during 1924
amounted to $14,343.35. 40% of $14,343.35 equals
$5,737.34.

Computation of Tax.

Net taxable income $7,629.04

[22] STATEMENT.

Mr. G. F. Sloan,
Los Angeles, California.

Brought forward $7,629.04

Less:

    Credit $2,000.00

Balance taxable at 13½% $5,629.04

Tax at 13½% 703.63

Tax previously assessed .... None

Deficiency .... $ 703.63

1925.

Gross profit $5,814.54

Additions:

    Interest .... $ 911.62

    Taxes 223.78 1,135.40

                           $ 6,949.94

Deductions:

    Bookkeeping and miscella-
neous items $2,748.33

    Discounts 49.10 2,797.43

Adjusted net income $4,152.51

Explanation.

Gross profit is determined in same manner as for prior years. Collections received during 1925, $14,536.34 at 40% equal $5,814.54.

Computation of Tax.

Net taxable income $4,152.51

Less:

    Credit 2,000.00

Balance taxable at 13% $2,152.51

Tax at 13% 279.83
Tax previously assessed .... None

Deficiency ....$ 279.83

[23] STATEMENT.

Mr. G. F. Sloan,
Los Angeles, California.

1926.

Gross profit ....$ 848.19
Additions:
  Interest 220.43

                                      $1,068.62
Deductions:
  Bookkeeping and miscella-
    neous expenses 2,298.12
  Discounts 5.57
  Taxes 298.37 2,602.06

Adjusted net loss $1,533.44

Explanation.

The adjustments are all of same character as for prior years.

Computation of Tax.

Since there is a net loss for this year, no tax is due. Hence case is closed no tax due.

Your protest in respect to the taxability of the so-called trust (taxpayer) has been duly considered. From evidence submitted it is held by this office that the taxpayer (Dominguez Harbor Tract No.

2) constitutes an association for income tax purposes for all the years involved.

Section 281 of the Revenue Act of 1926 provides that notice of a deficiency or other liability, if mailed to the taxpayer or other person subject to the liability at his last known address, shall be sufficient for the purposes of this title, even if such taxpayer or other person is deceased, or is under a legal disability, or, in the case of a corporation, has terminated its existence.

———

[24]   Filed Jan. 21, 1929.   United States Board of Tax Appeals.

United States Board of Tax Appeals.

DOCKET No. 40,380.

G. F. SLOAN,

Petitioner,

vs.

COMMISSIONER OF INTERNAL REVENUE,
Respondent.

ANSWER.

The Commissioner of Internal Revenue, by his attorney, C. M. Charest, General Counsel, Bureau of Internal Revenue, for answer to the petition of the above-named taxpayer, admits, denies and alleges as follows:

1.   Admits the allegations contained in Paragraph 1 of said petition.

2.   Admits that the notice of deficiency was mailed to taxpayer July 3, 1928, and that the copy with statement attached to said petition is a true and correct copy thereof.

3.   Admits the allegations contained in Paragraph 3 of said petition.

4.   Denies each and every allegation of error contained in Paragraph 4 of said petition.

5 (a) (b) (c).   Admits that a certain trust known as "Dominquez Harbor Tract No. 2" was created under date of September 1, 1913.   Alleges that the respondent is without knowledge or information as to the other matters and things alleged in subparagraphs (a), (b) and (c) of Paragraph 5 of said petition, hence denies the same.

(d) (e) (f) (g) (i) (j) (k) (l).   Denies each and every allegation contained in paragraphs (d), (e), (f), (g), (i), (j), (k), and (l), of Paragraph 5 of said petition.

[25]   (h) Admits the allegations contained in subparagraph (h) of Paragraph 5 of said petition.

Further answering respondent alleges that the notice of deficiency was mailed to petitioner within the time required by law.

WHEREFORE, it is prayed that the Commissioner's determination be in all things approved and that said petition be dismissed.

(Signed) C. M. CHAREST.

C. M. CHAREST,

General Counsel,

Bureau of Internal Revenue.

Of Counsel:
> J. E. MATHER,
> > Special Attorney,
> > > Bureau of Internal Revenue.

1/19/29.
EAT:LLD.

———

[26]   Filed May 20, 1931.

United States Board of Tax Appeals.

DOCKET No. 40,380.

G. F. SLOAN,

> Petitioner,

vs.

COMMISSIONER OF INTERNAL REVENUE,
> Respondent.

AMENDED ANSWER.

The Commissioner of Internal Revenue, by his attorney, C. M. Charest, General Counsel, Bureau of Internal Revenue, for amended answer to the petition filed in this proceeding admits, denies, and alleges as follows:

(1) Admits the allegation contained in Paragraph (1) of the petition.

(2) Admits the allegation contained in Paragraph (2) of the petition.

(3) Admits that the taxes in controversy are income taxes for the calendar years 1923, 1924, and 1925 in the respective amounts of $1,045.58, $703.63,

and $279.83. Denies that any taxes for the calendar year 1926 are in controversy.

(4) Denies that the Commissioner erred as alleged in Paragraph (4) of the petition.

(5) (a), (b), (c), (d), (e), (f), and (g). Denies the allegations contained in subdivisions (a) to (g), inclusive, of Paragraph (5) of the petition.

(5) (h). Admits that the petitioner owned a 150/1000ths interest in the "Dominguez Harbor Tract No. 2." Denies the remaining allegations contained in subdivision (h) of Paragraph (5) of the petition.

[27] (5) (i). Denies the allegations contained in subdivision (i) of Paragraph (5) of the petition.

(5) (j). Moves that subdivision (j) of Paragraph (5) of the petition be stricken therefrom, as the same is improperly pleaded, does not state a cause of action, and is too vague and indefinite to aid in framing an issue before this Board.

(5) (k) Moves that subdivision (k) of Paragraph (5) of the petition be stricken therefrom, as the same is improperly pleaded, does not state a cause of action, and is too vague and indefinite to aid in framing an issue before this Board.

(5) (1). Neither admits nor denies subdivision (1) of Paragraph (5) of the petition in that it sets forth a conclusion of law only.

(6) Denies generally and specifically each and every material allegation contained in the petition not hereinabove admitted, qualified, nor denied.

(7) The respondent alleges affirmatively:

1. The respondent determined that in the calen-

dar years 1923 to 1925, inclusive, "Dominguez Harbor Tract No. 2" was taxable as a corporation.

2. The respondent on his March, 1928, Special List #2, assessed deficiencies in income tax amounting to the respective sums of $1,045.58, $703.63, and $279.83 against the "Dominguez Harbor Tract No. 2" for the calendar years 1923, 1924, and 1925.

3. Collection of said assessments cannot be made because the properties of the said "Dominguez Harbor Tract No. 2" have been distributed to the holders of the certificates of interest therein.

[28] 4. The beneficial interest in the "Dominguez Harbor Tract No. 2" was divided into 1,000 shares, represented by certificates of interest.

5. That in the calendar years 1923 to 1928, inclusive, the petitioner herein was the owner of 150 shares out of a total of 1,000 shares outstanding in the said "Dominguez Harbor Tract No. 2."

6. That in the calendar years 1923 to 1928, inclusive, the "Dominguez Harbor Tract No. 2" distributed in liquidation to the petitioner, cash in a sum greatly in excess of the liability herein involved.

7. That as a result of said distributions, the "Dominguez Harbor Tract No. 2" became insolvent and is unable to pay the tax involved herein.

8. The petitioner is, therefore, liable for the unpaid income tax liability together with interest thereon as provided by law of the "Dominguez Harbor Tract No. 2" for the calendar years 1923, 1924, and 1925.

WHEREFORE, it is prayed that the respondent's determination be approved.

(Signed) C. M. CHAREST.

C. M. CHAREST,
General Counsel,
Bureau of Internal Revenue.

Of Counsel:
J. A. LYONS,
E. L. UPDIKE,
Special Attorneys,
Bureau of Internal Revenue.

ELU:MEP.
5-13-31.

----

[29]   Filed Aug. 21, 1928.

United States Board of Tax Appeals.

DOCKET No. 40,381.

J. E. ADAMS,

Petitioner,

vs.

COMMISSIONER OF INTERNAL REVENUE,

Respondent.

PETITION.

The above-named petitioner hereby petitions for a redetermination of the deficiency set forth by the Commissioner of Internal Revenue in his notice of deficiency bearing symbols IT:E:RR:280:60D–JEM, dated July 3, 1928, and as a basis of this proceeding alleges as follows:

(1)   Petitioner is an individual residing at 1901 West View Street, Los Angeles, California.

(2)   The notice of deficiency, a copy of which is attached and marked Exhibit "A" was mailed to petitioner on July 3, 1928.

(3)   The taxes in controversy are income taxes for the years 1923, 1924, 1925 and 1926 as follows:

Year.	Tax.
1923	$1,045.58
1924	703.63
1925	279.83
1926	None
Total	$2,029.04

(4)   The determination of tax set forth in the said notice of deficiency is based upon the following errors:

(a)   The Commissioner is erroneously and illegally holding the petitioner to be liable under the provisions of Section 280 of the Revenue Act of 1926 for a tax in the amount [30] above stated as a transferee of the assets of "Dominguez Harbor Tract No. 2," a trust formed under the laws of the State of California, whereas the petitioner is not liable for any tax or other indebtedness of said "Dominguez Harbor Tract No. 2" under the said section of the law for the reason that:

(1)   Section 280 of the Revenue Act of 1926, as amended by the Revenue Act of 1928, is unconstitutional and void, being in violation of

Section 2 of Article 1, Section 9 of Article 3, and Article 5 of the Constitution of the United States.

(2)   Section 280 of the Revenue Act of 1926, in so far as it purports to impose a tax on the former beneficiaries of a dissolved trust is unconstitutional in that the liability of the several beneficiaries is not definitely set forth.

(3)   Petitioner is not a transferee within the meaning of Section 280 of the Revenue Act of 1926.

(b)   The Commissioner of Internal Revenue is erroneously and illegally proposing to impose a tax upon "Dominguez Harbor Tract No. 2" as an association.

(c)   The Commissioner of Internal Revenue is erroneously and illegally proposing to assess the petitioner, who is a beneficiary of a trust known as "Dominguez Harbor Tract No. 2," on account of income taxes for the calendar years 1923 to 1925, inclusive, aggregating $2,-029.04, which is claimed by the Commissioner to be the total tax liability of the said trust.

[31]   (d)   The Commissioner of Internal Revenue is erroneously and illegally proposing to assess to the petitioner the total amount of income taxes for the calendar years 1923 to 1925, inclusive, purporting to be due from the "Dominguez Harbor Tract No. 2," disregarding the fact that even if this trust is held to be taxable as an association, the petitioner herein could not be held liable for a greater amount than that received in liquidation.

(e) The Commissioner of Internal Revenue is erroneously and illegally proposing to assess to the petitioner the total amount of income taxes purported to be due for the calendar year 1923 from the trust known as "Dominguez Harbor Tract No. 2" in the sum of $1,045.58, whereas the assessment of additional taxes for the calendar year 1923 to the beneficiary is barred by the statute of limitations.

(f) On information and belief petitioner alleges that in determining the net income for the calendar years 1923, 1924 and 1925 the Commissioner of Internal Revenue used an erroneous cost basis in determining the gross profit realized from sales of the trust property.

(g) Upon information and belief petitioner alleges that the net income of "Dominguez Harbor Tract No. 2" as determined by the Commissioner of Internal Revenue for the calendar years 1923, 1924 and 1925 is erroneous.

(5) The facts upon which the petitioner relies as a basis of this proceeding are as follows:

[32] (a) Under date of September 1, 1913, P. H. O'Neil, J. E. Adams and J. H. Miller, as joint tenants, J. A. Anderson, Charles O. Middleton, G. F. Sloan and the Alisal Ranch Company caused to be created a certain trust known as "Dominguez Harbor Tract No. 2," naming Charles O. Middleton and J. E. Adams, Trustees, whereby certain property was transferred to the Trustees for the purpose of securing certain indebtedness and for the purpose of doing

other things set out fully in the Declaration of Trust, copy of which is attached hereto and marked Exhibit "B."

(b)   Under date of November 25, 1914, J. E. Adams and P. H. O'Neil were named as Trustees of trust known as "Dominguez Harbor Tract No. 2" created under date of September 1, 1913. (See copy of appointment attached hereto marked Exhibit "C.") Under date of February 15, 1915, J. E. Adams and G. F. Sloan were named as Trustees of trust known as "Dominguez Harbor Tract No. 2" created under date of September 1, 1913. (See copy of appointment attached hereto and marked Exhibit "D.")

(c)   The operations of "Dominguez Harbor Tract No. 2" and the rights and duties of the respective parties thereto are controlled by the Declaration of Trust hereinbefore referred to as Exhibit "B."

(d)   The Trust known as "Dominguez Harbor Tract No. 2" is not taxable as an association within the meaning of the Revenue Act of 1926. Therefore, there can be no liability to the petitioner herein under the provisions of [33] Section 280, Revenue Act of 1926.

(e)   The Declaration of Trust does not provide for any periodical meetings of beneficiaries, for the election of officers of any kind, or the appointment of directors.

(f)   The "Dominguez Harbor Tract No. 2" is not an association within the meaning of the Revenue Acts of 1921, 1924 and 1926.

(g) "Dominguez Harbor Tract No. 2" is a trust taxable to the beneficiaries as a joint venture.

(h) The petitioner was a beneficiary under trust known as "Dominguez Harbor Tract No. 2," owning together with J. H. Miller, as joint tenants, with right of survivorship, a 400/1000ths interest therein.

(i) Petitioner filed income tax returns for the calendar years 1923, 1924 and 1925 and property accounted therein his *pro rata* share of the income earned by trust designated "Dominguez Harbor Tract No. 2."

(j) On information and belief petitioner alleges that the Commissioner of Internal Revenue in determining net income of the trust known as "Dominguez Harbor Tract No. 2" used an erroneous cost in determining the amount of profit realized from sales of the trust property.

(k) Upon information and belief petitioner alleges that the net income of "Dominguez Harbor Tract No. 2" as determined by the Commissioner of Internal Revenue is erroneous.

(l) Section 280 of the Revenue Act of 1926 is unconstitutional and void, being in violation of Section 2 of [34] Article 1, Section 9 of Article 3 and Article 5 of the Constitution of the United States.

(6) Petitioner prays for relief from the deficiency asserted by the respondent on the following and each of the following particulars:

(a)   Section 280 of the Revenue Act of 1926 is unconstitutional. Therefore, the petitioner is not liable as a transferee of the assets of the "Dominguez Harbor Tract No. 2." Therefore, there is no deficiency in tax.

(b)   "Dominguez Harbor Tract No. 2" is not taxable as an association within the meaning of the Revenue Acts of 1921, 1924 and 1926 and, therefore, there is no deficiency in tax.

WHEREFORE, petitioner prays that this Board may hear and redetermine the deficiency herein alleged.

> DANA LATHAM,
> Counsel for Petitioner,
> 819 Title Insurance Building,
> Los Angeles, California.

> GEORGE M. THOMPSON,
> Counsel for Petitioner,
> 505 Title Insurance Building,
> Los Angeles, California.

State of California,
County of Los Angeles,—ss.

J. E. Adams, being duly sworn, says that he is the petitioner above named; that he has read the foregoing petition or had the same read to him and is familiar with the statements therein contained; and that the facts therein stated are true except such facts as are recited to be upon information and belief and those facts he believes to be true.

> J. E. ADAMS.

Subscribed and sworn to before me this 10th day of August, 1928.

[Seal]   MARSHALL D. HALL,

Notary Public in and for the County of Los Angeles, State of California.

My commission expires June 30, 1929.

[35]   EXHIBIT "A."

TREASURY DEPARTMENT.
WASHINGTON.

Office of

Commissioner of Internal Revenue.

Address Reply to

Commissioner of Internal Revenue

and refer to

July 3, 1928.

Mr. J. E. Adams,

     1901 West View Street,

        Los Angeles, California.

Sir:

In accordance with Section 274 of the Revenue Act of 1926 you are advised that the determination of your tax liability for the years 1923, 1924 and 1925, discloses a deficiency of $2,029.04 as shown in the attached statement, as transferee of the Dominguez Harbor Tract No. 2, Los Angeles, California, under Section 280 of said Act.

The section of the law above mentioned allows you an appeal to the United States Board of Tax Appeals within sixty days from the date of the

mailing of this letter. However, if you acquiesce
in this determination, you are requested to execute
the inclosed Form A and forward it to the Commissioner of Internal Revenue, Washington, D. C.,
for the attention of IT:C:P-7.

Respectfully,

D. H. BLAIR,

Commissioner.

(Signed)   C. B. ALLEN,

Deputy Commissioner.

Inclosures:
> Statement.
> Form A.
> Form 882.

[36]   STATEMENT.

IT:E:RR:280:60D.
> JEM.

In re: Mr. J. E. Adams,
1901 West View Street,
Los Angeles, California.

Under the authority of Section 280 of the
Revenue Act of 1926, there is proposed for assessment against the amount of $2,029.04, constituting
your liability as transferee of the assets of the
Dominguez Harbor Tract No. 2, c/o George M.
Thompson, Title Insurance Building, Los Angeles,
California, for unpaid income taxes in the above
amount due from said corporation (plus any accrued penalty and interest) for the years 1923,
1924 and 1925, as shown in the following statement:

Year.	Deficiency in Tax.
1923	$1,045.58
1924	703.63
1925	279.83
1926	None

Total, $2,029.04

1923.

Gross profit	$ 9,062.25
Additions:	
Interest	2,752.14
	$11,814.39

Deductions:

Bookkeeping and miscella- neous expenses	$1,074.82	
Discounts	296.02	
Taxes	78.90	1,449.74

Adjusted net income	$10,364.65

Explanation.

The gross profit as shown is computed as follows: (Installment sales basis.)

155 lots sold at $565.00 each	$87,575.00
155 lots cost $340.00 each	52,700.00
Gross profit	$34,875.00

Percentage of gross profit to sales .398 plus or 40%.

[37] STATEMENT.

Mr. J. E. Adams,

Los Angeles, California.

Collections received during year $22,655.62—40%
of $22,655.62 equals $9,062.25.

Computation of Tax.

Net taxable income	$10,364.65
Less:	
Credit	2,000.00
Balance taxable at 12½%	$ 8,364.65
Tax at 12½%	$ 1,045.58
Tax previously assessed	None
Deficiency	$ 1,045.58

1924.

Gross profit		$ 5,737.34
Additions:		
Profit on repossession not previously reported	$1,741.98	
Interest	1,568.56	3,310.54
		$9,047.88
Deductions:		
Bookkeeping and miscellaneous items	$1,246.73	
Discounts	117.67	
Taxes	54.44	1,418.84
Adjusted net income		$ 7,629.04

Explanation.

The gross profit is computed as shown under 1923 income.

The total collections received during 1924 amounted to $14,343.35. 40% of $14,343.35 equals $5,737.34.

Computation of Tax.

Net taxable income $7,629.04

[38] STATEMENT.

Mr. J. E. Adams,
Los Angeles, California.

Brought forward	$7,629.04
Less:	
Credit	2,000.00
Balance taxable at 13½%	$5,629.04
Tax at 13½%	703.63
Tax previously assessed	None
Deficiency	$ 703.63

1925.

Gross profit		$5,814.54
Additions:		
Interest	$911.62	
Taxes	223.78	1,135.40
		$6,949.94

46   *G. F. Sloan et al. vs.*

Deductions:
  Bookkeeping and miscella-
    neous items $2,748.33
  Discounts 49.10
                                    ──────
                                    2,797.43
                                    ──────
Adjusted net income $4,152.51

Explanation.

Gross profit is determined in same manner as for prior years. Collections received during 1925, $14,536.34 at 40% equal $5,814.54.

Computation of Tax.

Net taxable income $4,152.51
Less:
  Credit $2,000.00
                                    ──────
Balance taxable at 13% $2,152.51
Tax at 13% 279.83
Tax previously assessed .... None
                                    ──────
Deficiency .... $ 279.83

[39] STATEMENT.

Mr. J. E. Adams,
Los Angeles, California.

1926.

Gross profit .... $ 848.19
Additions:
  Interest 220.43
                                    ──────
                                    $1,068.62

Deductions:

Bookkeeping and miscellaneous expenses ....,...	$2,298.12
Discounts	.5.57
Taxes	298.37

2,602.06

Adjusted net loss $1,533.44

Explanation.

The adjustments are all of same character as for prior years.

Computation of Tax.

Since there is a net loss for this year, no tax is due. Hence case is closed no tax due.

Your protest in respect to the taxability of the so-called trust (taxpayer) has been duly considered. From evidence submitted it is held by this office that the taxpayer (Dominguez Harbor Tract No. 2) constitutes an association for income tax purposes for all the years involved.

Section 281 of the Revenue Act of 1926 provides that notice of a deficiency or other liability, if mailed to the taxpayer or other person subject to the liability at his last known address, shall be sufficient for the purposes of this title, even if such taxpayer or other person is deceased, or is under a legal disability, or, in the case of a corporation, has terminated its existence.

[40]   EXHIBIT "B."

DECLARATION OF TRUST.

THIS INDENTURE made this first day of September, A. D. 1913, WITNESSETH: That CHARLES O. MIDDLETON and J. E. ADAMS of Los Angeles, California, herein designated the "trustees," have and hold the legal title in fee simple in joint tenancy with right of survivorship to the following described real estate, situated in the County of Los Angeles, State of California, to wit:

Property description omitted.

That the said real estate is held by said trustees in trust for the beneficiaries hereinafter named, their lawful assigns and legal representatives according to their respective interests, for the following uses and purposes with the following powers in said trustees, to wit:

To sell the whole or any part of said real estate and to that end to lay out and subdivide said lands or any part thereof; to pay commissions for the sale of said lands; to improve the same and to execute conveyances for said land or any part thereof; also to mortgage or lease said real estate or any part thereof; and to receive the rents and profits of said real estate and, as incidental to said powers, to prosecute and defend all actions at law or in equity relating to said property or any thereof; to collect moneys owing upon any sale or sales thereof and to satisfy judgments and claims relating thereto and to otherwise exercise full control and management of said property. When said property shall have been sold, to divide the proceeds of the sales thereof after deducting all necessary expenses, among the several beneficiaries or their lawful assigns or legal representatives according to their respective interests.

The said beneficiaries and their assigns and legal representatives shall not have or hold any title to said land or any part thereof and shall not be authorized to maintain any suit for partition thereof or to annul or terminate this trust, except as herein provided.

The beneficial interest in said property shall be divided into One Thousand shares among the following beneficiaries with the following number of respective shares to each:

P. H. O'Neil	One Hundred Shares
J. E. Adams & J. H. Miller, joint tenants with right of survivorship,	Three Hundred Shares
J. A. Anderson	One Hundred Shares
Charles O. Middleton	Two Hundred Fifty Shares
G. F. Sloan	One Hundred Fifty Shares
Alisal Ranch Company	One Hundred Shares

A separate certificate shall be issued to each beneficiary for his number of shares and upon surrender thereof, such certificate may be divided and separate certificates issued for such shares to those entitled thereto.

In case of the death, removal or inability to act of either of said trustees, the survivor shall fill such vacancy by proper conveyance.

Certificates of trust issued under this instrument may be transferred by assignment and delivery.

Three fourths of the beneficiaries in interest may by an instrument in writing, remove any trustee under this instrument and appoint another in his stead and may require such trust property to be conveyed to such surviving trustee and new trustee in joint tenancy by proper conveyance and in case of the death or inability of both said trustees, may fill such vacancies. Three fourths in interest in said beneficiaries may likewise terminate this trust *any* any time and partition said property by [41] their own act or by judicial proceeding for partition, but in any event this trust shall cease and determine upon the decease of all the natural persons in being named in this instrument.

The trustee shall be empowered at any time prior to the determination of this trust whenever in their judgment it may be expedient and proper, to declare dividends of money among the respective beneficiaries, derived from sales of real estate.

WITNESS our hands and seals.

(Signed)   CHARLES O. MIDDLETON.
(Seal)
(Signed)   J. E. ADAMS.   (Seal)

I, Marshall D. Hall, do hereby certify the foregoing to be a true and correct copy of the original dated and signed as above presented to me this

28th day of July, 1928, with the exception of omissions as stated.

[Seal]   MARSHALL D. HALL,

Notary Public in and for the County of Los Angeles, State of California.

My commission expires June 30, 1929.

[42] EXHIBIT "C."

THIS INDENTURE, made this twenty-fifth day of November, 1914, by and between J. E. Adams and Lillie E. Adams, his wife, and P. H. O'Neil, Trustee, both of Los Angeles, California, WITNESSETH,

WHEREAS J. E. Adams, and Charles O. Middleton executed their declaration of trust on Sept. 1st, 1913, declaring that they held the legal title as trustees in joint tenancy, with right of survivorship to the following described real estate, situated in the County of Los Angeles, State of California, to-wit:

(Property Description Omitted.)

WHEREAS, on the 19th day of October, 1914, said Charles O. Middleton by quitclaim deed conveyed to said P. H. O'Neil, Trustee, all his right, title and interest in and to said real estate, and terminated his trustee-ship therein;

NOW, THEREFORE, the said J. E. Adams and P. H. O'Neil, Trustee, hereby convey each to the other an equal interest in said real estate and in the whole thereof to hold in joint tenancy with right of survivorship each one with the other, and hereby declare that in and by this instrument they have

created said joint tenancy and further declare that
they hold said property in joint tenancy with right
of survivorship for the uses and purposes declared
in said instrument of Sept. 1st, 1913, and for the
benefit of the beneficiaries therein named and their
assigns and lawful representatives.

IT IS AGREED AND, UNDERSTOOD, that
the undersigned trustees respectively, are not to be
liable for any losses of said trust property or the
proceeds thereof, caused by any act or acts during
any period of time, while the undersigned, respectively, were not trustees for said property.

WITNESS our hands and seals the date first
above written.

P. H. O'NEIL, Trustee.   (Signed)

J. E. ADAMS.   (Signed)

LILLIE E. ADAMS.   (Signed)

By J. E. ADAMS,

Atty. in Fact.   (Signed)

State of California,
County of Los Angeles,—ss.

On this 27th day of November, in the year nineteen hundred and fourteen, A. D., before me, T. L.
Dudley, a Notary Public in and for said County
of Los Angeles, State of California, residing
therein, duly commissioned and sworn, personally
appeared P. H. O'Neil and J. E. Adams personally
known to me to be the person whose names are subscribed to the within instrument, and acknowledged
to me that they executed the same.

IN WITNESS WHEREOF, I have hereunto
set my hand and affixed my official seal in said

county the day and year in this certificate first above written.

[Seal]   T. L. DUDLEY, (Signed)

Notary Public in and for Los Angeles County, State of California.

[43]   State of California,
County of Los Angeles,—ss.

On this 27th day of November, A. D. 1914, before me, T. L. Dudley, a Notary Public in and for the said County and State, residing therein, duly commissioned and sworn, personally appeared J. E. Adams known to me to be the person whose name is subscribed to the within Instrument, as the Attorney-in-Fact of Lillie E. Adams and acknowledged to me that he subscribed the name of Lillie E. Adams thereto as principal and his own name as Attorney-in-Fact.

IN WITNESS WHEREOF, I have hereunto set my hand and affixed my official seal the day and year in this certificate first above written.

T. L. DUDLEY, (Signed)

Notary Public in and for said County and State.

I, Marshall D. Hall, a Notary Public in and for the County of Los Angeles, State of California, do hereby certify the foregoing to be a true and correct copy of the original dated and signed as above present to me this 3rd day of August, 1928, with the exception of omissions as stated.

[Seal]   MARSHALL D. HALL,

Notary Public in and for the County of Los Angeles, State of California.

My commission expires June 30, 1929.

[44]   EXHIBIT "D."

THIS INDENTURE, made this fifteenth day of
February, 1915, by and between J. E. ADAMS and
LILLIE E. ADAMS, his wife, and G. F. SLOAN
and MINNIE E. SLOAN, his wife, both of Los
Angeles, California, WITNESSETH,

WHEREAS J. E. ADAMS and Charles O. Middleton executed their declaration of trust on Sept.
1st, 1913, declaring that they held the legal title
as trustees in joint tenancy, with right of survivorship to the following described real estate, situated
in the County of Los Angeles, State of California,
to-wit:

(Property Description Omitted.)

WHEREAS, on the 19th day of October, 1914,
said Charles O. Middleton by quitclaim deed conveyed to P. H. O'Neil, Trustee, all his right, title
and interest in and to said real estate, and termined
his trustee-ship therein;

WHEREAS, on the 13th day of February, 1915,
said P. H. O'Neil by quitclaim deed conveyed to
G. F. Sloan all his right, title and interest in and
to said real estate, and terminated his trustee-ship
therein;

NOW, THEREFORE, the said J. E. Adams and
G. F. Sloan hereby convey each to the other an
equal interest in said real estate and in the whole
thereof to hold in joint tenancy with right of survivorship each one with the other, and hereby declare that in and by this instrument they have created said joint tenancy and further declare that

they hold said property in joint tenancy with right of survivorship for the uses and purposes declared in said instrument of Sept. 1st, 1913, and for the benefit of the beneficiaries therein named and their assigns and lawful representatives.

IT IS AGREED AND UNDERSTOOD, that the undersigned trustees respectively, are not to be liable for any losses of said trust property or the proceeds thereof, caused by any act or acts during any period of time, while the undersigned, respectively, were not trustees for said property.

WITNESS our hands and seals the date first above written.

J. E. ADAMS.	(Signed)
LILLIE E. ADAMS.	(Signed)
By J. E. ADAMS,	(Signed)
Atty. in Fact.	
G. F. SLOAN.	(Signed)
MINNIE E. SLOAN.	(Signed)
By G. F. SLOAN,	(Signed)
Atty. in Fact.	

State of California,
County of Los Angeles,—ss.

On this 17th day of February, in the year nineteen hundred and fifteen, A. D., before me, T. L. Dudley, a Notary Public in and for the said County of Los Angeles, State of California, residing therein, duly commissioned and [45] sworn, personally appeared J. E. Adams and G. F. Sloan, personally known to me to be the persons whose names are subscribed to the within instrument, and acknowledged to me that they executed the same.

IN WITNESS WHEREOF, I have hereunto set my hand and affixed my official seal in said county the day and year in this certificate first above written.

[Seal]   T. L. DUDLEY, (Signed)
Notary Public in and for Los Angeles County,
     State of California.

My commission expires Sept. 18, 1916.

State of California,
County of Los Angeles,—ss.

On this 17th day of February, in the year nineteen hundred and fifteen, A. D., before me, T. L. Dudley, a Notary Public in and for the said County of Los Angeles, State of California, residing therein, duly commissioned and sworn, personally appeared J. E. Adams personally known to me to be the person described in and whose name is subscribed to the within instrument, as the attorney in fact of Lillie E. Adams and acknowledged to me that he subscribed the name of Lillie E. Adams thereto as principal and his own name as attorney in fact.

IN WITNESS WHEREOF, I have hereunto set my hand and affixed my official seal in said county the day and year in this certificate first above written.

[Seal]   T. L. DUDLEY (Signed)
Notary Public in and for Los Angeles County,
     State of California.

My commission expires Sept. 18, 1916.

State of California,
County of Los Angeles,—ss.

On this 17th day of February, in the year nineteen hundred and fifteen, A. D., before me, T. L. Dudley, a Notary Public in and for the said County of Los Angeles, State of California, residing therein, duly commissioned and sworn, personally appeared G. F. Sloan personally known to me to be the person described in and whose name is subscribed to the within instrument, as the attorney in fact of Minnie E. Sloan and acknowledged to me that he subscribed the name of Minnie E. Sloan thereto as principal and his own name as attorney in fact.

IN WITNESS WHEREOF, I have hereunto set my hand and affixed my official seal in said county the day and year in this certificate first above written.

[Seal]   T. L. DUDLEY (Signed)
Notary Public in and for *the* Los Angeles County,
    State of California.

My commission expires Sept. 18, 1916.

I, Marshall D. Hall, a Notary Public in and for the County of Los Angeles, State of California, do hereby certify the foregoing to be a true and correct copy of the original dated and signed as above presented to me this 3d day of August, 1928, with the exception of omissions as stated.

[Seal]   MARSHALL D. HALL,
Notary Public in and for the County of Los Angeles,
    State of California.

My commission expires June 30, 1929.

[46]   Filed Jan. 21, 1929.   United States Board
of Tax Appeals.

United States Board of Tax Appeals.

DOCKET No. 40,381.

J. E. ADAMS,

                                    Petitioner.

                vs.

COMMISSIONER OF INTERNAL REVENUE,

                                    Respondent.

ANSWER.

The Commissioner of Internal Revenue by his
attorney, C. M. Charest, General Counsel, Bureau
of Internal Revenue, for answer to the petition of
the above-named taxpayer, admits, denies and
alleges as follows:

1. Admits the allegations contained in Paragraph 1 of said petition.

2. Admits that the notice of deficiency was
mailed to taxpayer July 3, 1928, and that the copy
with statement attached to said petition is a true
and correct copy thereof.

3. Admits the allegations contained in Paragraph 3 of said petition.

4. Denies each and every allegation of error
contained in Paragraph 4 of said petition.

5 (a) (b) (c).   Admits that a certain trust known
as "Dominquez Harbor Tract No. 2" was created
under date of September 1, 1913. Alleges that the
respondent is without knowledge or information as

to the other matters and things alleged in subparagraphs (a), (b) and (c) of Paragraph 5 of said petition, hence denies the same.

(d) (e) (f) (g) (i) (j) (k) (l). Denies each and every allegation contained in subparagraphs (d), (e), (f), (g), (i), (j), (k), and (l), of Paragraph 5 of said petition.

[47] (h). Admits the allegations contained in subparagraph (h) of Paragraph 5 of said petition.

Further answering respondent alleges that the notice of deficiency was mailed to petitioner within the time required by law.

WHEREFORE, it is prayed that the Commissioner's determination be in all things approved and that said petition be dismissed.

(Signed) C. M. CHAREST.

C. M. CHAREST,
General Counsel,
Bureau of Internal Revenue.

Of Counsel:
J. E. MATHER,
Special Attorney,
Bureau of Internal Revenue.

1/19/29.
EAT:LLD.

[48]   Filed May 20, 1931.

United States Board of Tax Appeals.

DOCKET No. 40,381.

J. E. ADAMS,

Petitioner,

vs.

COMMISSIONER OF INTERNAL REVENUE,

Respondent.

AMENDED ANSWER.

The Commissioner of Internal Revenue, by his attorney, C. M. Charest, General Counsel, Bureau of Internal Revenue, for amended answer to the petition filed in this proceeding admits, denies, and alleges as follows:

(1)   Admits the allegation contained in Paragraph (1) of the petition.

(2)   Admits the allegation contained in Paragraph (2) of the petition.

(3)   Admits that the taxes in controversy are income taxes for the calendar years 1923, 1924, and 1925 in the respective amounts of $1,045.58, $703.63, and $279.83. Denies that any taxes for the calendar year 1926 are in controversy.

(4)   Denies that commissioner erred as alleged in Paragraph (4) of the petition.

(5) (a), (b), (c), (d), (e), (f), and (g). Denies the allegations contained in subdivisions (a) to (g), inclusive of Paragraph (5) of the petition.

(5) (h). Admits that the petitioner, together with J. H. Miller as joint tenants, owned a 400/1000ths interest in the "Dominguez Harbor Tract No. 2." Denies the remaining allegations contained in subdivision (h) of Paragraph (5) of the petition.

[49] (5) (i). Denies the allegations contained in subdivision (i) of Paragraph (5) of the petition.

(5) (j). Moves that subdivision (j) of Paragraph (5) of the petition be stricken therefrom, as the same is improperly pleaded, does not state a cause of action, and is too vague and indefinite to aid in framing an issue before this Board.

(5) (k). Moves that subdivision (k) of Paragraph (5) of the petition be stricken therefrom, as the same is improperly pleaded, does not state a cause of action, and it too vague and indefinite to aid in framing an issue before this Board.

(5) (l). Neither admits nor denies subdivision (l) of Paragraph (5) of the petition in that it sets forth a controversy of law only.

(6) Denies generally and specifically each and every material allegation contained in the petition not hereinabove admitted, qualified, nor denied.

(7) The respondent alleges affirmatively:

1. The respondent determined that in the calendar years 1923 to 1925, inclusive, "Dominguez Harbor Tract No. 2" was taxable as a corporation.

2. The respondent on his March, 1928, Special List #2, assessed deficiencies in income tax amounting to the respective sums of $1,045.58, $703.63, and $279.83 against the "Dominguez Harbor Tract No. 2" for the calendar years 1923, 1924, and 1925.

3. Collection of said assessments cannot be made because the properties of the said "Dominguez Harbor Tract No. 2" have been distributed to the holders of the certificates of interest therein.

[50] 4. The beneficial interest in the "Dominguez Harbor Tract No. 2" was divided into 1,000 shares, represented by certificates of interest.

5. That in the calendar years 1923 to 1928, inclusive, the petitioner herein, together with J. H. Miller as joint tenants, was the owner of 400 shares out of a total of 1,000 shares outstanding in the said "Dominguez Harbor Tract No. 2."

6. That in the calendar years 1923 to 1928, inclusive, cash amounting to a sum greatly in excess of the liability herein involved was distributed in liquidation to the petitioner by the "Dominguez Harbor Tract No. 2."

7. That as a result of said distribution, the "Dominguez Harbor Tract No. 2" became insolvent and is unable to pay the tax involved herein.

8. The petitioner is, therefore, liable for the unpaid income tax liability together with interest thereon as provided by law of the "Dominguez Harbor Tract No. 2" for the calendar years 1923, 1924, and 1925.

WHEREFORE, it is prayed that the respondent's determination be approved.

(Signed) C. M. CHAREST.

C. M. CHAREST,
General Counsel,
Bureau of Internal Revenue.

Of Counsel:
    J. A. LYONS,
    E. L. UPDIKE,
        Special Attorneys,
           Bureau of Internal Revenue.
ELU:MEP.
5-11-31.

———

[51] Filed Aug. 22, 1928.

United States Board of Tax Appeals.

DOCKET No. 40,396.

C. O. MIDDLETON,
                        Petitioner,
        vs.

COMMISSIONER OF INTERNAL REVENUE,
                        Respondent.

PETITION.

The above-named petitioner hereby petitions for a redetermination of the deficiency set forth by the Commissioner of Internal Revenue in his notice of deficiency bearing symbols IT:E:RR:280:60D–JEM. dated July 3, 1928, and as a basis of this proceeding alleges as follows:

(1) Petitioner is an individual residing at the Roosevelt Building, Los Angeles, California.

(2) The notice of deficiency, a copy of which is attached and marked Exhibit "A" was mailed to petitioner on July 3, 1928.

(3)   The taxes in controversy are income taxes
for the years 1923, 1924, 1925 and 1926 as follows:

Year.	Tax.
1923	$1,045.58
1924	703.63
1925	279.83
1926	None

Total, $2,029.04

(4)   The determination of tax set forth in the
said notice of deficiency is based upon the following errors:

(a)   The commissioner is erroneously and
illegally holding the petitioner to be liable
under the provisions of Section 280 of the
Revenue Act of 1926 for a tax in the amount
[52]   above stated as a transferee of the assets
of "Dominguez Harbor Tract No. 2," a trust
formed under the laws of the State of California, whereas the petitioner is not liable for
any tax or other indebtedness of said "Dominguez Harbor Tract No. 2" under the said
section of the law for the reason that:

(1)   Section 280 of the Revenue Act of 1926,
as amended by the Revenue Act of 1928, is unconstitutional and void, being in violation of
Section 2 of Article 1, Section 9 of Article 3,
and Article 5 of the Constitution of the United
States.

(2)   Section 280 of the Revenue Act of 1926,
in so far as it purports to impose a tax on the

former beneficiaries of a dissolved trust is unconstitutional in that the liability of the several beneficiaries is not definitely set forth.

(3) Petitioner is not a transferee within the meaning of section 280 of the Revenue Act of 1926.

(b) The Commissioner of Internal Revenue is erroneously and illegally proposing to impose a tax upon "Dominguez Harbor Tract No. 2" as an association.

(c) The Commissioner of Internal Revenue is erroneously and illegally proposing to assess the petitioner, who is a beneficiary of a trust known as "Dominguez Harbor Tract No. 2," on account of income taxes for the calendar years 1923 to 1925, inclusive, aggregating $2,-029.04, which is claimed by the Commissioner to be the total tax liability of the said trust.

[53] The Commissioner of Internal Revenue is erroneously and illegally proposing to assess to the petitioner the total amount of income taxes for the calendar years 1923 to 1925, inclusive, purporting to be due from the "Dominguez Harbor Tract No. 2," disregarding the fact that even if this trust is held to be taxable as an association, the petitioner herein could not be held liable for a greater amount than that received in liquidation.

(e) The Commissioner of Internal Revenue is erroneously and illegally proposing to assess to the petitioner the total amount of income taxes purported to be due for the calendar year

1923 from the trust known as "Dominguez Harbor Tract No. 2" in the sum of $1,045.58, whereas the assessment of additional taxes for the calendar year 1923 to the beneficiary is barred by the statute of limitations.

(f) On information and belief petitioner alleges that in determining the net income for the calendar years 1923, 1924 and 1925 the Commissioner of Internal Revenue used an erroneous cost basis in determining the gross profit realized from sales of the trust property.

(g) Upon information and belief petitioner alleges that the net income of "Dominguez Harbor Tract No. 2" as determined by the Commissioner of Internal Revenue for the calendar years 1923, 1924 and 1925 is erroneous.

(5) The facts upon which the petitioner relies as a basis of this proceeding are as follows:

(a) Under date of September 1, 1913, P. H. O'Neil, [54] J. E. Adams and J. H. Miller, as joint tenants, J. A. Anderson, Charles O. Middleton, G. F. Sloan and the Alisal Ranch Company caused to be created a certain trust known as "Dominguez Harbor Tract No. 2," naming Charles O. Middleton and J. E. Adams Trustees whereby certain property was transferred to the Trustees for the purpose of securing certain indebtedness and for the purpose of doing other things set out fully in the Declaration of Trust, copy of which is attached as Exhibit "B" to petition filed by J. E. Adams.

(b) Under date of November 25, 1914, J.

E. Adams and P. H. O'Neil were named as Trustees of trust known as "Dominguez Harbor Tract No. 2" created under date of September 1, 1913. (See copy of appointment marked Exhibit "C" attached to petition filed by J. E. Adams.) Under date of February 15, 1915, J. E. Adams and G. F. Sloan were named as Trustees of trust known as "Dominguez Harbor Tract No. 2" created under date of September 1, 1913. (See copy of appointment marked Exhibit "D" attached to petition filed by J. E. Adams.)

(c) The operations of "Dominguez Harbor Tract No. 2" and the rights and duties of the respective parties thereto are controlled by the Declaration of Trust hereinbefore referred to as Exhibit "B" and attached to petition filed by J. E. Adams.

(d) The Trust known as "Dominguez Harbor Tract No. 2" is not taxable as an association within the meaning of the Revenue Act of 1926. Therefore, there can be no [55] liability to the petitioner herein under the provisions of Section 280, Revenue Act of 1926.

(e) The Declaration of Trust does not provide for any periodical meetings of beneficiaries, for the election of officers of any kind, or the appointment of directors.

(f) The "Dominguez Harbor Tract No. 2" is not an association within the meaning of the Revenue Acts of 1921, 1924 and 1926.

(g) "Dominguez Harbor Tract No. 2" is

a trust taxable to the beneficiaries as a joint venture.

(h)   The petitioner was a beneficiary under trust known as "Dominguez Harbor Tract No. 2," owning a 250/1000ths interest therein.

(i)   Petitioner filed income tax returns for the calendar years 1923, 1924 and 1925 and subsequently accounted for his *pro rata* share of the income earned by trust designated as "Dominguez Harbor Tract No. 2."

(j)   On information and belief petitioner alleges that the Commissioner of Internal Revenue in determining net income of the trust known as "Dominguez Harbor Tract No. 2" used an erroneous cost in determining the amount of profit realized from sales of the trust property.

(k)   Upon information and belief petitioner alleges that the net income of "Dominguez Harbor Tract No. 2" as determined by the Commissioner of Internal Revenue is erroneous.

(l)   Section 280 of the Revenue Act of 1926 is unconstitutional and void, being in violation of Section 2 of   [56]   Article 1, Section 9 of Article 3 and Article 5 of the Constitution of the United States.

(6)   Petitioner prays for relief from the deficiency asserted by the respondent on the following and each of the following particulars:

(a)   Section 280 of the Revenue Act of 1926 is unconstitutional. Therefore, the petitioner is not liable as a transferee of the assets of the "Dominguez Harbor Tract No. 2." Therefore, there is no deficiency in tax.

(b) "Dominguez Harbor Tract No. 2" is not taxable as an association within the meaning of the Revenue Acts of 1921, 1924 and 1926 and, therefore, there is no deficiency in tax.

WHEREFORE, petitioner prays that this Board may hear and redetermine the deficiency herein alleged.

DANA LATHAM,
Counsel for Petitioner,
819 Title Insurance Building,
Los Angeles, California.

GEORGE M. THOMPSON,
Counsel for Petitioner,
505 Title Insurance Building,
Los Angeles, California.

State of California,
County of Los Angeles,—ss.

C. O. Middleton, being duly sworn, says that he is the petitioner above named; that he has read the foregoing petition or had the same read to him and is familiar with the statements therein contained; and that the facts therein stated are true except such facts as are recited to be upon information and belief and those facts he believes to be true.

C. O. MIDDLETON.

Subscribed and sworn to before me this 17th day of August, 1928.

[Seal]   LILLIAN WRIGHT,

Notary Public in and for the County of Los Angeles, State of California.

My commission expires July 17, 1932.

[57]   EXHIBIT "A."

TREASURY DEPARTMENT,
WASHINGTON.

Office of
Commissioner of Internal Revenue.

July 3, 1928.

Mr. C. O. Middleton,
    Roosevelt Building,
        Los Angeles, California.

Sir:

In accordance with Section 274 of the Revenue Act of 1926, you are advised that the determination of your tax liability for the years 1923, 1924, and 1925, discloses a deficiency of $2,029.04, as shown in the attached statement, as transferee of the Dominguez Harbor Tract No. 2, Los Angeles, California, under Section 280 of said Act.

The section of the law above mentioned allows you an appeal to the United States Board of Tax Appeals within sixty days from the date of the mailing of this letter. However, if you acquiesce in this determination, you are requested to execute the enclosed Form A and forward it to the Commissioner of Internal Revenue, Washington, D. C., for the attention of IT:C:P-7.

Respectfully,

D. H. BLAIR,

Commissioner.

By C. B. ALLEN,

Deputy Commissioner.

Inclosures:

Statement.

Form A.

Form 882.

[58]   STATEMENT.

IT:E:RR:280:60D.

JEM.

In re: Mr. C. O. Middleton,

Roosevelt Building,

Los Angeles, California.

Under authority of Section 280 of the Revenue Act of 1926 there is proposed for assessment against you the amount of $2,029.04, constituting your liability as transferee of the assets of the Dominguez Harbor Tract No. 2, c/o George M. Thompson, Title Insurance Building, Los Angeles, California, for unpaid income taxes in the above amount due from said corporation (plus any accrued penalty and interest) for the years 1923, 1924, and 1925, as shown in the following statement:

Year.	Deficiency in Tax
1923	$1,045.58
1924	703.63
1925	279.83
1926	None

Total, $2,029.04

1923.

Gross profit	$ 9,062.25
Additions:	
Interest	2,752.14

$11,814.39

Deductions:

Bookkeeping and miscella- neous expenses	$1,074.82	
Discounts	296.02	
Taxes	78.90	1,449.74

Adjusted net income $10,364.65

Explanation.

The gross profit as shown above is computed as follows:

(Installment sales basis.)

155 lots sold at $565.00 each	$87,575.00
155 lots cost $340.00 each	52,700.00

Gross profit $34,875.00

Percentage of gross profit to sales .398 plus or 40%.

[59] STATEMENT.

Mr. C. O. Middleton,
Los Angeles, California.

Collections received during the year $22,655.62—
40% of $22,655.62 equals $9,062.25.

Computation of Tax.

Net taxable income	$10,364.65
Less:	
Credit	2,000.00
Balance taxable at 12½%	$ 8,364.65
Tax at 12½%	1,045.58
Tax previously assessed	None
Deficiency	$ 1,045.58

1924.

Gross profit		$ 5,737.34
Additions:		
Profit on repossession not previously reported	$1,741.98	
Interest	1,568.56	3,310.54
		$9,047.88
Deductions:		
Bookkeeping and miscellaneous item	1.246.73	
Discounts	117.67	
Taxes	54.44	1,418.84
Adjusted net income		$ 7,629.04

Explanation.

The gross profit is computed as shown under 1923
income.

The total collections received during 1924 amounted to $14,343.35. 40% of $14,343.35 equals $5,737.34.

Computation of Tax.

Net taxable income 7,629.04

[60] STATEMENT.

Mr. C. O. Middleton,
Los Angeles, California.

Brought forward	$7,629.04
Less:	
Credit	2,000.00
Balance taxable at 13½%	$5,629.04
Tax at 13½%	703.63
Tax previously assessed	None
Deficiency	$ 703.63

1925.

Gross profit		$5,814.54
Additions:		
Interest	$911.62	
Taxes	223.78	1,135.40
		$6,949.94
Deductions:		
Bookkeeping and miscellaneous items	$2,748.33	
Discounts	49.10	2,797.43
Adjusted net income		$4,152.51

Explanation.

Gross profit is determined in same manner as for prior years. Collections received during 1925, $14,536.34 at 40% equal $5,814.54.

Computation of Tax.

Net taxable income	$4,152.51
Less:	
Credit	2,000.00
Balance taxable at 13%	$2,152.51
Tax at 13%	279.83
Tax previously assessed	None
Deficiency	$ 279.83

[61] STATEMENT.

Mr. C. O. Middleton,
Los Angeles, California.

1926.

Gross profit		$ 848.19
Additions:		
Interest		220.43
		$1,068.62
Deductions:		
Bookkeeping and miscellaneous expenses	$2,298.12	
Discounts	5.57	
Taxes	298.37	2,602.06
Adjusted net loss		$1,533.44

Explanation.

The adjustments are all of same character as for prior years.

Computation of Tax.

Since there is a net loss for this year, no tax is due. Hence case is closed no tax due.

Your protest in respect to the taxability of the so-called trust (taxpayer) has been duly considered. From evidence submitted it is held by this office that the taxpayer (Dominguez Harbor Tract No. 2) constitutes an association for income tax purposes for all the years involved.

Section 281 of the Revenue Act of 1926 provides that notice of a deficiency or other liability, if mailed to the taxpayer or other person subject to the liability at his last known address, shall be sufficient for the purposes of this title, even if such taxpayer or other person is deceased, or is under a legal disability, or, in the case of a corporation, has terminated its existence.

---

[62]   Filed Oct. 17, 1928.

United States Board of Tax Appeals.

DOCKET No. 40,396.

C. O. MIDDLETON,

Petitioner,

vs.

COMMISSIONER OF INTERNAL REVENUE,

Respondent.

ANSWER.

The Commissioner of Internal Revenue, by his attorney, C. M. Charest, General Counsel, Bureau of Internal Revenue, for answer to the petition filed by above-named taxpayer, admits and denies as follows:

(1) Admits the averments in Paragraph (1) of the petition.

(2) Admits the averments in Paragraph (2) of the petition.

(3) Admits that the taxes in controversy are income taxes for 1923, 1924 and 1925; denies that any tax is in controversy for 1926.

(4) Denies the averments contained in Paragraph (4) of the petition.

(5) Admits the averments in Paragraph (5)(a), (5)(b), and (5)(c); denies the averments in Paragraph (5)(d), (5)(e), (5)(f) and (5)(g); admits the averments in Paragraph (5)(h), lacks sufficient information to form an opinion as to the averments contained in Paragraph (5)(i) and therefore denies the said averments and will demand proof thereof upon the trial of this case; denies the averments in Paragraph (5)(j), (5)(k) and (5)(l) of the petition.

WHEREFORE, it is prayed that the taxpayer's petition be denied.

(Signed) C. M. CHAREST,
General Counsel,
Bureau of Internal Revenue.

Of Counsel:
HAROLD ALLEN,
Special Attorney,
Bureau of Internal Revenue.

---

[63]   Filed May 20, 1931.

United States Board of Tax Appeals.

DOCKET No. 40,396.

C. O. MIDDLETON,

Petitioner,

vs.

COMMISSIONER OF INTERNAL REVENUE,

Respondent.

AMENDED ANSWER.

The Commissioner of Internal Revenue, by his attorney, C. M. Charest, General Counsel, Bureau of Internal Revenue, for amended answer to the petition filed in this proceeding admits, denies, and alleges as follows:

(1) Admits the allegation contained in Paragraph (1) of the petition.

(2) Admits the allegation contained in Paragraph (2) of the petition.

(3) Admits that the taxes in controversy are income taxes for the calendar years 1923, 1924, and 1925, in the respective amounts of $1,045.58, $703.63, and $279.83. Denies that any taxes for the calendar year 1926 are in controversy.

(4) Denies that the Commissioner erred as alleged in Paragraph (4) of the petition.

(5), (a), (b), (c), (d), (e), (f), and (g). Denies the allegations contained in subdivisions (a) to (g), inclusive, of Paragraph (5) of the petition.

(5) (h). Admits that the petitioner owned a 250/1000ths interest in the "Dominguez Harbor Tract No. 2." Denies the remaining allegations contained in subdivision (h) of Paragraph (5) of the petition.

[64] (5) (i). Denies the allegations contained in subdivision (i) of Paragraph (5) of the petition.

(5) (j). Moves that subdivision (j) of Paragraph (5) of the petition be stricken therefrom, as the same is improperly pleaded, does not state a cause of action, and is too vague and indefinite to aid in framing an issue before this Board.

(5) (k). Moves that subdivision (k) of Paragraph (5) of the petition be stricken therefrom, as the same is improperly pleaded, does not state a cause of action, and is too vague and indefinite to aid in framing an issue before this Board.

(5) (l). Neither admits nor denies subdivision (l) of Paragraph (5) of the petition in that it sets forth a conclusion of law only.

(6) Denies generally and specifically each and every material allegation contained in the petition not hereinbefore admitted, qualified, nor denied.

(7) The respondent alleges affirmatively:

1. The respondent determined that in the calendar years 1923 to 1925, inclusive, "Dominguez Harbor Tract No. 2" was taxable as a corporation.

2. The respondent on his March, 1928, Special List #2, assessed deficiencies in income tax amounting to the respective sums of $1,045.58, $703.63, and $279.83 against the "Dominguez Harbor Tract #2" for the calendar years 1923, 1924, and 1925.

3. Collection of said assessments cannot be made because the properties of the said "Dominguez Harbor Tract No. 2" have been distributed to the holders of the certificates of interest therein.

[65] 4. The beneficial interest in the "Dominguez Harbor Tract No. 2" was divided into 1,000 shares, represented by certificates of interest.

5. That in the calendar years 1923 to 1928, inclusive, the petitioner herein was the owner of 250 shares out of a total of 1,000 shares outstanding in the said "Dominguez Harbor Tract No .2."

6. That in the calendar years 1923 to 1928, inclusive, the "Dominguez Harbor Tract No. 2" distributed in liquidation to the petitioner, cash in a sum greatly in excess of the liability herein involved.

7. That as a result of said distributions, the "Dominguez Harbor Tract No. 2" became insolvent and is unable to pay the tax involved herein.

8. The petitioner is, therefore, liable for the unpaid income tax liability, together with interest thereon as provided by law, of the "Dominguez Harbor Tract No. 2" for the calendar years 1923, 1924, and 1925.

WHEREFORE, it is prayed that the respondent's determination be approved.

(Signed) C. M. CHAREST.

C. M. CHAREST,

General Counsel,

Bureau of Internal Revenue.

Of Counsel:

    J. A. LYONS,

    E. L. UPDIKE,

        Special Attorneys,

           Bureau of Internal Revenue.

ELU:MEP.

5–14–31.

---

[66]   Filed Aug. 29, 1928.

United States Board of Tax Appeals.

DOCKET No. 40,491.

J. A. ANDERSON,

Petitioner,

        vs.

COMMISSIONER OF INTERNAL REVENUE,

Respondent.

PETITION.

The above-named petitioner hereby petitions for a redetermination of the deficiency set forth by the Commissioner of Internal Revenue in his notice of deficiency bearing symbols IT:E:RR:280:60D—JEM, dated July 3, 1928, and as a basis of this proceeding alleges as follows:

(1)   Petitioner is an individual residing at 112 North Rampart Boulevard, Los Angeles, California.

(2)   The notice of deficiency, a copy of which is attached and marked Exhibit "A" was mailed to petitioner on July 3, 1928.

(3)   The taxes in controversy are income taxes for the years 1923, 1924 and 1925 as follows:

1923	$1,045.58
1924	703.63
1925	279.83
Total	$2,029.04

(4)   The determination of tax set forth in the said notice of deficiency is based upon the following errors:

(a)   The Commissioner of Internal Revenue is erroneously and illegally holding the petitioner to be liable under the provisions of Section 280 of the Revenue Act of 1926 for a tax in the amount above stated as a transferee [67] of the assets of "Dominguez Harbor Tract No. 2," a trust formed under the laws of the State of California, whereas the petitioner is not liable for any tax or other indebtedness of said Dominguez Harbor Tract No. 2 under the said section of the law for the reason that

(1)   Section 280 of the Revenue Act of 1926, as amended by the Revenue Act of 1928, is unconstitutional and void, being in violation of Section 2 of Article 1, Section 9 of Article 3,

and Article 5 of the Constitution of the United States.

(2) Section 280 of the Revenue Act of 1926, in so far as it purports to impose a tax on the former beneficiaries of a dissolved trust is unconstitutional in that the liability of the several beneficiaries is not definitely set forth.

(3) Petitioner is not a transferee within the the meaning of Section 280 of the Revenue Act of 1926.

(b) The Commissioner of Internal Revenue is erroneousl*u* and illegally proposing to impose a tax upon Dominguez Harbor Tract No. 2 as an association.

(c) The Commissioner of Internal Revenue is erroneously and illegally proposing to assess the petitioner, who is a beneficiary of a trust known as Dominguez Harbor Tract No. 2, on account of income taxes for the calendar years 1923, 1924 and 1925, aggregating $2,029.04, which is claimed by the commissioner to be the total tax liability of the said trust.

(d) The Commissioner of Internal Revenue is erroneously and illegally proposing to assess to the petitioner the total [68] amount of income taxes for the calendar years 1923, 1924 and 1925, purporting to be due from the Dominguez Harbor Tract No. 2, disregarding the fact that even if this trust is held to be taxable as an association, the petitioner herein could not be held liable for a greater amount than that received in liquidation.

(e) The Commissioner of Internal Revenue is erroneously and illegally proposing to assess to the petitioner the total amount of income taxes purported to be due for the calendar year 1923 from the trust known as Dominguez Harbor Tract No. 2 in the sum of $1,045.58, whereas the assessment of additional taxes for the calendar year 1923 to the beneficiary is barred by the statute of limitations.

(f) On information and belief, petitioner alleges that in determining the net income for the calendar years 1923, 1924 and 1925 the Commissioner of Internal Revenue used an erroneous cost basis in determining the gross profit realized from sales of the trust property.

(g) Upon information and belief, petitioner alleges that the net income of Dominguez Harbor Trust No. 2 as determined by the Commissioner of Internal Revenue for the calendar years 1924, 1925 and 1925 is erroneous.

(5) The facts upon which the petitioner relies as a basis of this proceeding are as follows:

(a) Under date of September 1, 1913, P. H. O'Neil, J. E. Adams and J. H. Miller, as joint tenants, J. A. Anderson, Charles O. Middleton, G. F. Sloan and the Alisal Ranch Company caused to be created a certain trust known as Dominguez Harbor Tract No. 2, naming Charles O. Middleton and [69] *and* J. E. Adams, Trustees, whereby certain property was transferred to the Trustees for the purpose of securing certain indebtedness and for the purpose of doing other things set out fully in the Declaration of Trust, copy of which is attached as Exhibit "B" to petition filed by J. E. Adams.

(b) Under date of November 25, 1914, J. E. Adams and P. H. O'Neil were named as Trustees of trust known as Dominguez Harbor Tract No. 2, created under date of September 1, 1913. (See copy of appointment marked Exhibit "C" attached to petition filed by J. E. Adams.) Under date of February 15, 1915, J. E. Adams and G. F. Sloan were named as Trustees of trust known as Dominguez Harbor Tract No. 2 created under date of September 1, 1913. (See copy of appointment marked Exhibit "D" attached to petition filed by J. E. Adams.)

(c) The operations of Dominguez Harbor Tract No. 2 and the rights and duties of the respective parties thereto are controlled by the Declaration of Trust hereinbefore referred to as Exhibit "B" and attached to petition filed by J. E. Adams.

(d) The trust known as Dominguez Harbor Tract No. 2 is not taxable as an association within the meaning of the Revenue Act of 1926. Therefore, there can be no liability to the petitioner herein under the provisions of section 280, Revenue Act of 1926.

(e) The Declaration of Trust does not provide for any periodical meetings of beneficiaries, for the election of officers of any kind, or the appointment of directors.

(f) The Dominguez Harbor Tract No. 2 is not an [70] association within the meaning of the Revenue Acts of 1921, 1924 and 1926.

(g) Dominguez Harbor Tract No. 2 is a Trust taxable to the beneficiaries as a joint venture.

(h) The petitioner was a beneficiary under trust known as Dominguez Harbor Tract No. 2, owning a 100/1000ths interest therein.

(i) Petitioner filed income tax returns for the calendar years 1923, 1924 and 1925 and accounted for his *pro rata* share of the income earned by trust designated Dominguez Harbor Tract No. 2.

(j) On information and belief petitioner alleges that the Commissioner of Internal Revenue in determining net income of the trust known as Dominguez Harbor Tract No. 2, used an erroneous cost in determining the amount of profit realized from sale of the trust property.

(k) Upon information and belief petitioner alleges that the net income of Dominguez Harbor Tract No. 2 as determined by the Commissioner of Internal Revenue is erroneous.

(l) Section 280 of the Revenue Act of 1926 is unconstitutional and void, being in violation of Section 2 of Article 1, Section 9 of Article 3 and Article 5 of the Constitution of the United States.

(6) Petitioner prays for relief from the deficiency asserted by the respondent on the following and each of the following particulars:

(a) Section 280 of the Revenue Act of 1926 is unconstitutional. Therefore, the petitioner is not liable as a transferee of the assets of the Dominguez Harbor Tract No. 2. Therefore, there is no deficiency in tax.

[71] (b) Dominguez Harbor Tract No. 2 is not taxable as an association within the meaning of the Revenue Acts of 1921, 1924 and 1926, and, therefore, there is no deficiency in tax.

WHEREFORE, petitioner prays that this Board may hear and redetermine the deficiency herein alleged.

DANA LATHAM,
Counsel for Petitioner,
819 Title Insurance Building,
Los Angeles, California.

GEORGE M. THOMPSON,
Counsel for Petitioner,
505 Title Insurance Building,
Los Angeles, California.

State of California,
County of Los Angeles—ss.

J. A. Anderson, being duly sworn, says that he is the petitioner above named; that he has read the foregoing petition or had the same read to him and is familiar with the statements therein contained; and that the facts therein stated are true except such facts as are recited to be upon information and belief and those facts he believes to be true.

                         J. A. ANDERSON.

Subscribed and sworn to before me this 25 day of August, 1928.

[Seal]   TRENT G. ANDERSON,
Notary Public in and for the County of Los Angeles, State of California.

[72]   EXHIBIT "A."

TREASURY DEPARTMENT,
WASHINGTON.

Mailed
Jul. 3, 1928.

Office of
Commissioner of Internal Revenue.

IT:E:RR:280:60D.

   JEM

Mr. J. A. Anderson,
    112 North Rampart Boulevard,
       Los Angeles, California.

Sir:

In accordance with Section 274 of the Revenue Act of 1926 you are advised that the determination of your tax liability for the years 1923, 1924, and 1925, discloses a deficiency of $2,029.04, as shown in the attached statement, as transferee of the Dominguez Harbor Tract No. 2, Los Angeles, California, under Section 280 of said Act.

The section of the law above mentioned allows you an appeal to the United States Board of Tax

Appeals within sixty days from the date of the mailing of this letter. However, if you acquiesce in this determination, you are requested to execute the inclosed Form A and forward it to the Commissioner of Internal Revenue, Washington, D. C., for the attention of IT:C:P–7.

Respectfully,

D. H. BLAIR,

Commissioner.

By ————————————,

Deputy Commissioner.

Inclosures:

    Statement.

    Form A.

    Form 882.

[73] STATEMENT.

IT:E:RR:280:60D.

    JEM.

In re: Mr. J. A. Anderson,

112 North Rampart Boulevard,

Los Angeles, California.

Under authority of Section 280 of the Revenue Act of 1926 there is proposed for assessment against you the amount of $2,029.04, constituting your liability as transferee of the assets of the Dominguez Harbor Tract No. 2, c/o George M. Thompson, Title Insurance Building, Los Angeles, California, for unpaid income taxes in the above amount due from said corporation (plus any accrued penalty and interest) for the years 1923, 1924, and 1925, as shown in the following statement:

Year	Deficiency in Tax.
1923	$1,045.58
1924	703.63
1925	279.83
1926	None

Total $2,029.04

1923.

Gross profit .... $ 9,062.25

Additions:

  Interest 2,752.14

$11,814.39

Deductions:

  Bookkeeping and miscella-

    neous expenses $1,074.82

  Discounts 296.02

  Taxes 78.90   1,449.74

Adjusted net income $10,364.65

Explanation.

The gross profit as shown above is computed as follows:

(Installment sales basis.)

155 lots sold at $565.00 each $87,575.00

155 lots cost $340.00 each 52,700.00

Gross profit $34,875.00

Percentage of gross profit to sales .398 plus or 40%.

[74] STATEMENT.

Mr. J. A. Anderson,

Los Angeles, California.

Collections received during year $22,655.62 –40% of $22,655.62 equals $9,062.25.

Computation of Tax.

Net taxable income	$10,364.65
Less:	
Credit	2,000.00
Balance taxable at 12½%	$ 8,364.65
Tax at 12½%	1,045.58
Tax Previously assessed	None
Deficiency	$ 1,045.58

1924.

Gross profit		$ 5,737.34
Additions:		
Profit on repossession not previously reported	$1,741.98	
Interest	1,568.56	3,310.54
		$ 9,047.88
Deductions:		
Bookkeeping and miscellaneous item	$1,246.73	
Discounts	117.67	
Taxes	54.44	1,418.84
Adjusted net income		$7,629.04

Explanation.

The gross profit is computed as shown under 1923 income.

The total collections received during 1924 amounted to $14,343.35. 40% of $14,343.35 equals $5,737.34.

Computation of Tax.

Net taxable income $7,629.04

[75] STATEMENT.

Mr. J. A. Anderson,
Los Angeles, California.

Brought forward .... $ 7,629.04
Less:
  Credit 2,000.00
<hr>
Balance taxable at 13½% .... $ 5,629.04
Tax at 13½% 703.63
Tax previously assessed .... None
<hr>
Deficiency .... $ 703.63

1925.

Gross profit .... $ 5,814.54
Additions:
  Interest $911.62
  Taxes 223.78   1,135.40
<hr>
          $ 6,949.94

Deductions:

Bookkeeping and miscella-
neous items $2,748.33
Discounts ....$ 49.10

2,797.43

Adjusted net income ....$ 4,152.51
Explanation.

Gross profit is determined in same manner as for prior years. Collections received during 1925, $14,-536.34 at 40% equal $5,814.54.

Computation of Tax.

Net taxable income ....$ 4,152.51
Less:
Credit 2,000.00

Balance taxable at 13% ....$ 2,152.51
Tax at 13% 279.83
Tax previously assessed .... None

Deficiency ....$ 279.83

[76]   STATEMENT.

Mr. J. A. Anderson,
Los Angeles, California.

1926.

Gross profit ....$ 848.19
Additions:
Interest 220.43

$ 1,068.62

Deductions:

Bookkeeping and miscella-
neous expenses $2,298.12
Discounts 5.57
Taxes 298.37
                        _____
                              2,602.06
                        _____

Adjusted net loss ....$ 1,533.44

Explanation.

The adjustments are all of same character as for prior years.

Computation of Tax.

Since there is a net loss for this year, no tax is due. Hence case is closed no tax due.

Your protest in respect to the taxability of the so-called trust (taxpayer) has been duly considered. From evidence submitted it is held by this office that the taxpayer (Dominguez Harbor Tract No. 2) constitutes an association for income tax purposes for all the years involved.

Section 281 of the Revenue Act of 1926 provides that notice of a deficiency or other liability, if mailed to the taxpayer or other person subject to the liability at his last known address, shall be sufficient for the purposes of this title, even if such taxpayer or other person is deceased, or is under a legal disability, or, in the case of a corporation, has terminated its existence.

_____

[77] Filed Jan. 24, 1929. United States Board of Tax Appeals.

United States Board of Tax Appeals.

DOCKET No. 40,491.

J. A. ANDERSON,

Petitioner,

vs.

COMMISSIONER OF INTERNAL REVENUE,
Respondent.

ANSWER.

The Commissioner of Internal Revenue by his attorney, G. M. Charest, General Counsel, Bureau of Internal Revenue, for answer to the petition of the above-named taxpayer, admits, denies and alleges as follows:

1. Admits the allegations contained in Paragraph 1 of said petition.

2. Admits that the notice of deficiency was mailed to petitioner July 3, 1926, and that the copy with statement attached to said petition is a true and correct copy thereof.

3. Admits the allegations contained in Paragraph 3 of said petition.

4. Denies each and every allegation of error contained in Paragraph 4 of said petition.

5. (a) (b) (c). Admits that a certain trust known as "Dominquez Harbor Tract No. 2" was created under date of September 1, 1913. Alleges that the respondent is without knowledge or information sufficient to form a belief as to the other matters and things alleged in subparagraphs (a),

(b) and (c) of Paragraph 5 of said petition, hence denies the same.

(d) (e) (f) (g) (i) (j) (k) (l). Denies each and every allegation contained in subparagraphs (d), (e), (f), (g), (i), (j), (k), and (l), of Paragraph 5 of said petition.

[78] (h). Admits the allegations contained in subparagraph (h) of Paragraph 5 of said petition.

Further answering respondent alleges that the notice of deficiency was mailed to petitioner within the time required by law.

WHEREFORE, it is prayed that the Commissioner's determination be in all things approved and that said petition be dismissed.

(Signed) C. M. CHAREST.

C. M. CHAREST,

General Counsel,

Bureau of Internal Revenue.

Of Counsel:

J. E. MATHER,

Special Attorney,

Bureau of Internal Revenue.

1/21/29.

EAT:LLD.

[79] Filed May 20, 1931.

United States Board of Tax Appeals.

DOCKET No. 40,491.

J. A. ANDERSON,

Petitioner,

vs.

COMMISSIONER OF INTERNAL REVENUE,

Respondent.

AMENDED ANSWER.

The Commissioner of Internal Revenue, by his attorney C. M. Charest, General Counsel, Bureau of Internal Revenue, for amended answer to the petition filed in this proceeding admits, denies, and alleges as follows:

(1) Admits the allegation contained in Paragraph (1) of the petition.

(2) Admits the allegation contained in Paragraph (2) of the petition.

(3) Admits that the taxes in controversy are income taxes for the calendar years 1923, 1924, and 1925 in the respective amounts of $1,045.58, $703.63, and $279.83. Denies that any taxes for the calendar year 1926 are in controversy.

(4) Denies that the Commissioner erred as alleged in Paragraph (4) of the petition.

(5) (a), (b), (c), (d), (e), (f), and (g). Denies the allegations contained in subdivisions (a) to (g), inclusive, of Paragraph (5) of the petition.

(5) (h). Admits that the petitioner owned a

100/1000ths interest in the "Dominguez Harbor
Tract No. 2." Denies the remaining allegations
contained in subdivision (h) of Paragraph (5) of
the petition.

[80]   (5) (i). Denies the allegations contained
in subdivision (i) of Paragraph (5) of the petition.

(5) (j). Moves that subdivision (j) of Paragraph (5) of the petition be stricken therefrom, as
the same is improperly pleaded, does not state a
cause of action, and is too vague and indefinite
to aid in framing an issue before this Board.

(5) (k). Moves that subdivision (k) of Paragraph (5) of the petition be stricken therefrom, as
the same is improperly pleaded, does not state a
cause of action, and is too vague and indefinite to
aid in framing an issue before this Board.

(5) (1). Neither admits nor denies subdivision
(1) of Paragraph (5) of the petition in that it sets
forth a conclusion of law only.

(6)   Denies generally and specifically each and
every material allegation contained in the petition
not hereinabove admitted, qualified nor denied.

(7)   The respondent alleges affirmatively:

1.   The respondent determined that in the calendar years 1923 to 1925, inclusive, "Dominguez
Harbor Tract No. 2" was taxable as a corporation.

2.   The respondent on his March, 1928, Special
List #2, assessed deficiencies in income tax amounting to the respective sums of $1,045.58, $703.63, and
$279.83 against the "Dominguez Harbor Tract No.
2" for the calendar years 1923, 1924, and 1925.

3.   Collection of said assessments cannot be made

because the properties of the said "Dominguez Harbor Tract No. 2" have been distributed to the holders of the certificates of interest therein.

[81] 4. The beneficial interest in the "Dominguez Harbor Tract No. 2" was divided into 1,000 shares, represented by certificates of interest.

5. That in the calendar years 1923 to 1928, inclusive, the petitioner herein was the owner of 100 shares out of a total of 1,000 shares outstanding in the said "Dominguez Harbor Tract No. 2."

6. That in the calendar years 1923 to 1928, inclusive, the "Dominguez Harbor Tract No. 2" distributed in liquidation to the petitioner, cash in a sum greatly in excess of the liability herein involved.

7. That as a result of said distributions, the "Dominguez Harbor Tract No. 2" became insolvent and is unable to pay the tax involved herein.

8. The petitioner is, therefore, liable for the unpaid income tax liability together with interest thereon as provided by law of the "Dominguez Harbor Tract No. 2" for the calendar years 1923, 1924, and 1925.

WHEREFORE, it is prayed that the respondent's determination be approved.

(Signed) C. M. CHAREST.

C. M. CHAREST,

General Counsel,

Bureau of Internal Revenue.

Of Counsel:
    J. A. LYONS,
    E. L. UPDIKE,
        Special Attorneys,
            Bureau of Internal Revenue.
ELU: MEP.
5–14–31.

---

[82]   Filed Sept. 1, 1928.

United States Board of Tax Appeals.

DOCKET No. 40,516.

LEZZETTE HOWARD BARNHART,

                                    Petitioner,

            vs.

COMMISSIONER OF INTERNAL REVENUE,

                                    Respondent.

PETITION.

The above-named petitioner hereby petitions for a redetermination of the deficiency set forth by the Commissioner of Internal Revenue in her notice of deficiency bearing symbols IT:E:RR:280:60D–JEM., dated July 3, 1928, and as a basis of this proceeding alleges as follows:

(1)   Petitioner is an individual residing at 742 Lake Shore, Oakland, California.

(2)   The notice of deficiency, a copy of which is attached and marked Exhibit "A" was mailed to petitioner on July 3, 1928.

(3)   The taxes in controversy are income taxes for the year 1923, 1924 and 1925 as follows:

1923	$1,045.58
1924	703.63
1925	279.83
Total	$2,029.04

(4)   The determination of tax set forth in the said notice of deficiency is based upon the following errors:

(a)   The Commissioner of Internal Revenue is erroneously and illegally holding the petitioner to be liable under the provisions of section 280 of the Revenue Act of 1926 for a tax in the amount above stated as a transferee [83] of the assets of Dominguez Harbor Tract No. 2, a trust formed under the laws of the State of California, whereas the petitioner is not liable for any tax or other indebtedness of said Dominguez Harbor Tract No. 2 under the said Section of the law for the reason that

(1)   Section 280 of the Revenue Act of 1926, as amended by the Revenue Act of 1928, is unconstitutional and void, being in violation of Section 2 of Article 1, Section 9 of Article 3, and Article 5 of the Constitution of the United States.

(2)   Section 280 of the Revenue Act of 1926, in so far as it purports to impose a tax on the former beneficiaries of a dissolved trust is unconstitutional in that the liability of the several beneficiaries is not definitely set forth.

(3)   Petitioner is not a transferee within the meaning of Section 280 of the Revenue Act of 1926.

(b)   The Commissioner of Internal Revenue is erroneously and illegally proposing to impose a tax upon Dominguez Harbor Tract No. 2 as an association.

(c)   The Commissioner of Internal Revenue is erroneously and illegally proposing to assess the Petitioner, who is a beneficiary of a trust known as Dominguez Harbor Tract No. 2, on account of income taxes for the calendar years 1923, 1924 and 1925, aggregating $2,029.04, which is claimed by the Commissioner to be the total tax liability of the said trust.

(d)   The Commissioner of Internal Revenue is erroneously and illegally proposing to assess to the petitioner the total   [84]   amount of income taxes for the calendar years 1923, 1924 1925, purporting to be due from the Dominguez Harbor Tract No. 2, disregarding the fact that even if this trust is held to be taxable as an association, the petitioner herein could not be held liable for a greater amount than that received in liquidation.

(e)   The Commissioner of Internal Revenue is erroneously and illegally proposing to assess to the petitioner the total amount of income taxes purported to be due for the calendar year 1923 from the trust known as Dominguez Harbor Tract No. 2 in the sum of $1,045.58, whereas the assessment of additional taxes for the calendar year 1923 to the beneficiary is barred by the statute of limitations.

(f)   On information and belief, petitioner alleges that in determining the net income for the calendar years 1923, 1924 and 1925 the Commissioner of Internal Revenue used an erroneous cost basis in determining the gross profit realized from sales of the trust property.

(g)   Upon information and belief, petitioner alleges that the net income of Dominguez Harbor Tract No. 2 as determined by the Commissioner of Internal Revenue for the calendar years 1924, 1925 and 1926 is erroneous.

(5)   The facts upon which the petitioner relies as a basis of this proceeding are as follows:

(a)   Under date of September 1, 1913, P. H. O'Neil, J. E. Adams and J. H. Miller, as joint tenants, J. A. Anderson, Charles O. Middleton, G. F. Sloan and the Alisal Ranch Company caused to the created a certain trust known as Dominguez Harbor Tract No. 2, naming Charles O. Middleton and [85] and J. E. Adams, Trustees, whereby certain property was transferred to the Trustees for the purpose of securing certain indebtedness and for the purpose of doing other things set out fully in the Declaration of Trust, copy of which is attached as Exhibit "B" to petition filed by J. E. Adams,

(b)   Under date of November 25, 1914, J. E. Adams and P. H. O'Neil were named as Trustees of trust known as Dominguez Harbor Tract No. 2, created under date of September 1, 1913. (See copy of appointment marked Exhibit "C"

104   *G. F. Sloan et al. vs.*

attached to petition filed by J. E. Adams,)
Under date of February 15, 1915, J. E. Adams
and G. F. Sloan were named as Trustees of
trust known as Dominguez Harbor Tract No. 2
created under date of September 1, 1913. (See
copy of appointment marked Exhibit "D" attached to petition filed by J. E. Adams.)

(c)   The operations of Dominguez Harbor
Tract No. 2 and the rights and duties of the
respective parties thereto are controlled by the
Declaration of Trust hereinbefore referred to
as Exhibit "B" and attached to petition filed
by J. E. Adams.

(d)   The trust known as Dominguez Harbor
Tract No. 2 is not taxable as an association
within the meaning of the Revenue Act of 1926.
Therefore, there can be no liability to the petitioner herein under the provisions of Section
280, Revenue Act of 1926.

(e)   The Declaration of Trust does not provide for any periodical meetings of beneficiaries,
for the election of officers of any kind, or the
appointment of directors.

(f)   The Dominguez Harbor Tract No. 2 is
not an [86] association within the meaning
of the Revenue Acts of 1921, 1924 and 1926.

(g)   Dominguez Harbor Tract No. 2 is a
Trust taxable to the beneficiaries as a joint
venture.

(h)   The petitioner was a beneficiary under
Trust known as Dominguez Harbor Tract No. 2,
owning a 100/1000ths interest therein.

(i) Petitioner filed income tax returns for the calendar years 1923, 1924 and 1925 and accounted for her *pro rata* share of the income earned by trust designated Dominguez Harbor Tract No. 2.

(j) On information and belief petitioner alleges that the Commissioner of Internal Revenue in determining net income of the trust known as Dominguez Harbor Tract No. 2, used an erroneous cost in determining the amount of profit realized from sale of the trust property.

(k) Upon information and belief petitioner alleges that the net income of Dominguez Harbor Tract No. 2 as determined by the Commissioner of Internal Revenue is erroneous.

(1) Section 280 of the Revenue Act of 1926 is unconstitutional and void, being in violation of Section 2 of Article 1, Section 9 of Article 3 and Article 5 of the Constitution of the United States.

(6) Petitioner prays for relief from the deficiency asserted by the respondent on the following and each of the following particulars:

(a) Section 280 of the Revenue Act of 1926 is unconstitutional. Therefore, the petitioner is not liable as a transferee of the assets of the Dominguez Harbor Tract No. 2. Therefore, there is no deficiency in tax.

[87] (b) Dominguez Harbor Tract No. 2 is not taxable as an association within the meaning of the Revenue Acts of 1921, 1924 and 1926, and, therefore, there is no deficiency in tax.

WHEREFORE, petitioner prays that this Board may hear and redetermine the deficiency herein alleged.

DANA LATHAM,
Counsel for Petitioner,
819 Title Insurance Building,
Los Angeles, California.

GEORGE M. THOMPSON,
Counsel for Petitioner,
505 Title Insurance Building,
Los Angeles, California.

State of California,
County of Los Angeles,—ss.

John T. Riley, being duly sworn, on oath deposes and says:

That he is attorney for Lezzette Howard Barnhart and has authority to verify this petition in behalf of said Lezzette Howard Barnhart; that he has read said petition and the facts stated therein are true, except those which are stated to be on information and belief; and as to those facts, he believes them to be true.

JOHN T. RILEY.

Subscribed and sworn to before me this 27th day of August, 1928.

[Seal]   MARSHALL HALL,
Notary Public in and for the County of Los Angeles,
State of California.

My commission expires June 30, 1929.

[88] EXHIBIT "A."

TREASURY DEPARTMENT,
WASHINGTON.

Mailed

Office of   Jul. 3, 1928.

Commissioner of Internal Revenue.

IT:E:RR:280:60D.

JEM.

Lezzette Howard Barnhart,
742 Lake Shore Avenue,
Oakland, California.

Madam:

In accordance with Section 274 of the Revenue of 1926 you are advised that the determination of your tax liability for the years 1923, 1924, and 1925, discloses a deficiency of $2,029.04, as shown in the attached statement, as transferee of the Dominguez Harbor Tract No. 2, Los Angeles, California, under Section 280 of said Act.

The section of the law above mentioned allows you an appeal to the United States Board of Tax Appeals within sixty days from the date of the mailing of this letter. However, if you acquiesce in this determination, you are requested to execute the inclosed Form A and forward it to the Commissioner of Internal Revenue, Washington, D. C., for the attention of IT:C:P–7.

Respectfully,

D. H. BLAIR,
Commissioner,
By C. B. ALLEN,
Deputy Commissioner.

Inclosures:
   Statement.
   Form A.
   Form 882.

[89]   STATEMENT.

IT:E:RR:280:60D.
   JEM.

   In re: Lezzette Howard Barnhart,
         742 Lake Shore Avenue,
         Oakland, California.

Under authority of Section 280 of the Revenue
Act of 1926, there is proposed for assessment against
you the amount of $2,029.04, constituting your lia-
bility as transferee of the assets of the Dominguez
Harbor Tract No. 2, c/o George M. Thompson,
Title Insurance Building, Los Angeles, California,
for unpaid income taxes in the above amount due
from said corporation (plus any accrued penalty
and interest) for the years 1923, 1924, and 1925,
as shown in the following statement:

Year	Deficiency in Tax.
1923	$1,045.58
1924	703.63
1925	279.83
1926	None
Total,	$2,029.04

1923.

Gross profit $9,062.25

Additions:

Interest 2,752.14

                                    _____

                                    $11,814.39

Deductions:

Bookkeeping and miscellan-

eous expenses $1,074.82

Discounts 296.02

Taxes 78.90   1,449.74

                        _____   _____

Adjusted net income $10,364.65

Explanation.

The gross profit as shown above is computed as follows:

(Installment sales basis.)

155 Lots sold at $565.00 each $87,575.00

155 lots cost $340.00 each 52,700.00

                                        _____

Gross profit $34,875.00

Percentage of gross profit to sales .398 plus or 40%.

[90]   STATEMENT.

Lezette Howard Barnhart,

742 Lake Shore Avenue,

Oakland, California.

Collections received during year $22,655.62—40% of $22,655.62 equals $9,062.25.

Net taxable income $10,364.65

Computation of Tax.

Less:

Credit 2,000.00

Balance taxable at 12½% .... $ 8,364.65
Tax at 12½% 1,045.58
Tax previously assessed .... None

Deficiency ....$ 1,045.58

1924.

Gross profit ....$ 5,737.34
Additions:
Profit on repossession not
  previously reported $1,741.98
Interest 1,568.56   3,310.50

                                 $9,047.88
Deductions:
Bookkeeping and miscella-
  neous items $1,246.73
Discounts 117.67
Taxes 54.44   1,418.84

Adjusted net income ....$ 7,629.04

Explanation.

The gross profit is computed as shown under 1923 income.

The total collections received during 1924 amounted to $14,343.35. 40% of $14,343.35 equals $5,737.34.

Computation of Tax.

Net taxable income $7,629.04

[91] STATEMENT.

Lezzette Howard Barnhart,
742 Lake Shore Avenue,
Oakland, California.

Brought forward $7,629.04
Less:
  Credit 2,000.00

Balance taxable at 13½% $5,629.04
Tax at 13½% 703.63
Tax previously assessed .... None

Deficiency .... $ 703.63

1925.

Gross profit $5,814.54
Additions:
  Interest $911.62
  Taxes 223.78   1,135.40

                                      $6,949.94
Deductions:
  Bookkeeeping and miscella-
    neous items $2,748.33
  Discounts 49.10

                                       2,797.43

Adjusted net income $4,152.51

Explanation.

Gross profit is determined in same manner as for prior years. Collections received during 1925 $14,536.34 at 40% equal $5,814.54.

G. F. Sloan et al. vs.

Computation of Tax.

Net taxable income $4,152.51
Less:
   Credit 2,000.00
   ───────────
Balance taxable at 13% $2,152.51
Tax at 13% 279.83
Tax previously assessed .... None
   ───────────
Deficiency .... $ 279.83

[92] STATEMENT.

Lezzette Howard Barnhart,
742 Lake Shore Avenue,
Oakland, California.

1926.

Gross profit .... $ 848.19
Additions:
   Interest 220.43
   ───────────
                                       $1,068.62

Deductions:
   Bookkeeping and miscella-
      neous expenses $2,298.12
   Discounts 5.57
   Taxes 298.37
   ───────────
                                       2,602.06
                                       ───────────
Adjusted net loss $1,533.44

Explanation.

The adjustments are all of same character as for prior years.

Computation of Tax.

Since there is a net loss for this year, no tax is due, Hence case is closed no tax due.

Your protest in respect to the taxability of the so-called trust (taxpayer) has been duly considered. From evidence submitted it is held by this office that the taxpayer (Dominquez Harbor Tract No. 2) constitutes an association for income tax purposes for all the years involved.

Section 281 of the Revenue Act of 1926 provides that notice of a deficiency or other liability, if mailed to the taxpayer or other person subject to the liability of his last known address, shall be sufficient for the purpose of this title, even if such taxpayer or other person is deceased, or is under a legal disability, or, in the case of a corporation, has terminated its existence.

––––––

[93]   Filed Jan. 24, 1929.   United States Board of Tax Appeals.

United States Board of Tax Appeals.

DOCKET No. 40,516.

LEZZETTE HOWARD BARNHART,

Petitioner,

vs.

COMMISSIONER OF INTERNAL REVENUE,

Respondent.

ANSWER.

The Commissioner of Internal Revenue by his attorney, C. M. Charest, General Counsel, Bureau of Internal Revenue, for answer to the petition of the above-named taxpayer, admits, denies and alleges as follows:

1. Admits the allegations contained in Paragraph 1 of said petition.

2. Admits that the notice of deficiency was mailed to petitioner July 3, 1928, and that the copy with statement attached to said petition is a true and correct copy thereof.

3. Admits the allegations contained in Paragraph 3 of said petition.

4. Denies each and every allegation of error contained in Paragraph 4 of said petition.

5 (a) (b) (c). Admits that a certain trust known as "Dominquez Harbor Tract No. 2" was created under date of September 1, 1913. Alleges that the respondent is without knowledge or information sufficient to form a belief as to the other matters and things alleged in subparagraph (a), (b) and (c) of Paragraph 5 of said petition, hence denies the same.

(d) (e) (f) (g) (i) (j) (k) (l). Denies each and every allegation contained in subparagraphs (d), (e), (f), (g), (i), (j), (k), and (l), of Paragraph 5 of said petition.

[94] (h) Admits the allegations contained in subparagraph (h) of Paragraph 5 of said petition.

Further answering respondent alleges that the

notice of deficiency was mailed to petitioner within the time required by law.

WHEREFORE, it is prayed that the Commissioner's determination be in all things approved and that said petition be dismissed.

> (Signed) C. M. CHAREST.
>
> C. M. CHAREST,
>
> General Counsel,
>
> Bureau of Internal Revenue.

Of Counsel:

> J. E. MATHER,
>
> Special Attorney,
>
> Bureau of Internal Revenue.

1/21/29.

EAT:LLD.

———

[95]   Filed May 20, 1931.

United States Board of Tax Appeals.

DOCKET No. 40,516.

LEZZETTE HOWARD BARNHART,

> Petitioner,

vs.

COMMISSIONER OF INTERNAL REVENUE,

> Respondent.

AMENDED ANSWER.

The Commissioner of Internal Revenue, by his attorney, C. M. Charest, General Counsel, Bureau of Internal Revenue, for amended answer to the petition filed in this proceeding admits, denies, and alleges as follows:

(1) Admits the allegation contained in Paragraph (1) of the petition.

(2) Admits the allegation contained in Paragraph (2) of the petition.

(3) Admits that the taxes in controversy are income taxes for the calendar years 1923, 1924, and 1925, in the respective amounts of $1,045.58, $703.63, and $279.83. Denies that any taxes for the calendar year 1926 are in controversy.

(4) Denies that the Commissioner erred as alleged in Paragraph (4) of the petition.

(5) (a), (b), (c), (d), (e), (f) , and (g). Denies the allegations contained in subdivisions (a) to (g) inclusive, of Paragraph (5) of the petition.

(5) (h). Admits that the petitioner owned a 100/1000ths interest in the "Dominguez Harbor Tract No. 2." Denies the remaining allegations contained in subdivision (h) of Paragraph (5) of the petition.

[96] (5) (i). Denies the allegations contained in subdivision (i) of Paragraph (5) of the petition.

(5) (j). Moves that subdivision (j) of Paragraph (5) of the petition be stricken therefrom, as the same is improperly pleaded, does not state a cause of action, and is. too vague and indefinite to aid in framing an issue before this Board.

(5) (k). Moves that subdivision (k) of Paragraph (5) of the petition be stricken therefrom, as the same is improperly pleaded, does not state a cause of action, and is too vague and indefinite to aid in framing an issue before this Board.

(5) (l). Neither admits nor denies subdivision

(1) of Paragraph (5) of the petition in that it sets forth a conclusion of law only.

(6)   Denies generally and specifically each and every material allegation contained in the petition not hereinabove admitted, qualified, nor denied.

(7)   The respondent alleges affirmatively:

1.   The respondent determined that in the calendar years 1923 to 1925, inclusive, "Dominguez Harbor Tract No. 2" was taxable as a corporation.

2.   The respondent on his March, 1928 Special List #2, assessed deficiencies in income tax amounting to the respective sums of $1,045.58, $703.63, and $279.83 against the "Dominguez Harbor Tract No. 2" for the calendar years 1923, 1924, and 1925.

3.   Collection of said assessments cannot be made because the properties of the said "Dominguez Harbor Tract No. 2" have been distributed to the holders of the certificates of interest therein.

[97]   4.   The beneficial interest in the "Dominguez Harbor Tract No. 2" was divided into 1,000 shares, represented by certificates of interest.

5.   That in the calendar years 1923 to 1928, in-inclusive, the petitioner herein was the owner of 100 shares out of a total of 1,000 shares outstanding in the said "Dominguez Harbor Tract No. 2."

6.   That in the calendar years 1923 to 1928, inclusive, the "Dominguez Harbor Tract No. 2" distributed in liquidation to the petitioner, cash in a sum greatly in excess of the liability herein involved.

7.   That as a result of said distributions, the "Dominguez Harbor Tract No. 2" became insolvent and is unable to pay the tax involved herein.

8.   The petitioner is, therefore, liable for the unpaid income tax liability together with interest thereon as provided by law of the "Dominguez Harbor Tract No. 2" for the calendar years 1923, 1924, and 1925.

WHEREFORE, it is prayed that the respondent's determination be approved.

(Signed) C. M. CHAREST.

C. M. CHAREST,

General Counsel,

Bureau of Internal Revenue.

Of Counsel:

    J. A. LYONS,

    E. L. UPDIKE,

       Special Attorneys,

         Bureau of Internal Revenue.

ELU:MEP.

5–13–31.

---

[98]   Filed Sept. 1, 1928.

United States Board of Tax Appeals.

DOCKET No. 40,517.

J. H. MILLER,

Petitioner,

vs.

COMMISSIONER OF INTERNAL REVENUE,

Respondent,

PETITION.

The above-named petitioner hereby petitions for

a redetermination of the deficiency set forth by the Commissioner of Internal Revenue in his notice of deficiency bearing symbols IT:E:RR:280:60D–JEM, dated July 3, 1928, and as a basis of this proceeding alleges as follows:

(1) Petitioner is an individual residing at 1901 West View Street, Los Angeles, California.

(2) The notice of deficiency, a copy of which is attached and marked Exhibit "A" was mailed to petitioner on July 3, 1928.

(3) The taxes in controversy are income taxes for the years 1923, 1924, 1925 and 1926 as follows:

1923	$1,045.58
1924	703.63
1925	279.83
1926	–0–
Total	$2,029.04

(4) The determination of tax set forth in the said notice of deficiency is based upon the following errors:

(a) The Commissioner is erroneously and illegally holding the petitioner to be liable under the provisions of Section 280 of the Revenue Act of 1926 for a tax in the amount [99] above stated as a transferee of the assets of Dominguez Harbor Tract No. 2, a trust formed under the laws of the State of California, whereas the petitioner is not liable for any tax or other indebtedness of said Dominguez Harbor Tract No. 2 under the said Section of the law for the reason that

(1) Section 280 of the Revenue Act of 1926, as amended by the Revenue Act of 1928, is unconstitutional and void, being in violation of Section 2 of Article 1, Section 9 of Article 3, and Article 5 of the Constitution of the United States.

(2) Section 280 of the Revenue Act of 1926, in so far as it purports to impose a tax on the former beneficiaries of a dissolved trust is unconstitutional in that the liability of the several beneficiaries is not definitely set forth.

(3) Petitioner is not a transferee within the meaning of Section 280 of the Revenue Act of 1926.

(b) The Commissioner of Internal Revenue is erroneously and illegally proposing to impose a tax upon "Dominguez Harbor Tract No. 2" as an association.

(c) The Commissioner of Internal Revenue is erroneously and illegally proposing to assess the petitioner, who is a beneficiary of a trust known as Dominguez Harbor Tract No. 2, on account of income taxes for the calendar years 1923, to 1925, inclusive, aggregating $2,029.04, which is claimed by the Commissioner to be the total tax liability of the said trust.

[100] (d) The Commissioner of Internal Revenue is erroneously and illegally proposing to assess to the petitioner the total amount of income taxes for the calendar years 1923 to 1925, inclusive, purporting to be due from the Dominguez Harbor Tract No. 2, disregarding

the fact that even if this trust is held to be taxable as an association, the petitioner herein could not be held liable for a greater amount than that received in liquidation.

(e) The Commissioner of Internal Revenue is erroneously and illegally proposing to assess to the petitioner the total amount of income taxes purported to be due for the calendar year 1923 from the trust known as Dominguez Harbor Tract No. 2 in the sum of $1,045.58, whereas the assessment of additional taxes for the calendar year 1923 to the beneficiary is barred by the Statute of Limitations.

(f) On information and belief petitioner alleges that in determining the net income for the calendar years 1923, 1924 and 1925 the Commissioner of Internal Revenue used an erroneous cost basis in determining the gross profit realized from sales of the trust property.

(g) Upon information and belief, petitioner alleges that the net income of Dominguez Harbor Tract No. 2 as determined by the Commissioner of Internal Revenue for the calendar years 1923, 1924 and 1925 is erroneous.

(5) The facts upon which the petitioner relies as a basis of this proceeding are as follows:

[101] (a) Under date of September 1, 1913, P. H. O'Neil, J. E. Adams and J. H. Miller, as joint tenants, J. A. Anderson, Charles O. Middleton, G. F. Sloan and the Alisal Ranch Company caused to be created a certain trust known as "Dominguez Harbor Tract No. 2,"

naming Charles O. Middleton and J. E. Adams Trustees, whereby certain property was transferred to the Trustees for the purpose of securing certain indebtedness and for the purpose of doing other things set out fully in the Declaration of Trust, copy of which is attached as Exhibit "B" to petition filed by J. E. Adams.

(b) Under date of November 25, 1914, J. E. Adams and P. H. O'Neil were named as Trustees of trust known as Dominguez Harbor Tract No. 2 created under date of September 1, 1913. (See copy of appointment marked Exhibit "C" attached to petition filed by J. E. Adams.) Under date of February 15, 1915, J. E. Adams and G. F. Sloan were named as Trustees of trust known as Dominguez Harbor Tract No. 2, created under date of September 1, 1913. (See copy of appointment marked Exhibit "D" attached to petition filed by J. E. Adams.)

(c) The operations of Dominguez Harbor Tract No. 2 and the rights and duties of the respective parties thereto are controlled by the Declaration of Trust hereinbefore referred to as Exhibit "B." and attached to petition filed by J. E. Adams.

(d) The trust known as Dominguez Harbor Tract No. 2 is not taxable as an association within the meaning of the Revenue Act of 1926. Therefore, there can be no [102] liability to the petitioner herein under the provisions of Section 280, Revenue Act of 1926.

(e) The Declaration of Trust does not provide for any periodical meetings of beneficiaries, for the election of officers of any kind, or the appointment of directors.

(f) The Dominguez Harbor Tract is not an association within the meaning of the Revenue Acts of 1921, 1924 and 1926.

(g) Dominguez Harbor Tract No. 2 is a trust taxable to the beneficiaries as a joint venture.

(h) The petitioner was a beneficiary under trust known as "Dominguez Harbor Tract No. 2," owning together with J. H. Miller, as joint tenants, with right of survivorship, a 400/1000ths interest therein.

(i) Petitioner filed income tax returns for the calendar years 1923, 1924 and 1925 and properly accounted therein his *pro rata* share of the income earned by trust designated Dominguez Harbor Tract No. 2.

(j) On information and belief petitioner alleges that the Commissioner of Internal Revenue in determining net income of the trust known as Dominguez Harbor Tract No. 2 used an erroneous cost in determining the amount of profit realized from sales of the trust property.

(k) Upon information and belief petitioner alleges that the net income of Dominguez Harbor Tract No. 2 as determined by the Commissioner of Internal Revenue is erroneous.

(l) Section 280 of the Revenue Act of 1926

is unconstitutional and void, being in violation of Section 2 of [103] Article 1, Section 9 of Article 3 and Article 5 of the Constitution of the United States.

(6) Petitioner prays for relief from the deficiency asserted by the respondent on the following and each of the following particulars:

(a) Section 280 of the Revenue Act of 1926 is unconstitutional. Therefore, the petitioner is not liable as a transferee of the assets of the Dominguez Harbor Tract No. 2. Therefore, there is no deficiency in tax.

(b) Dominguez Harbor Tract No. 2 is not taxable as an association within the meaning of the Revenue Acts of 1921, 1924 and 1926 and, therefore, there is no deficiency in tax.

WHEREFORE, petitioner prays that this Board may hear and redetermine the deficiency herein alleged.

DANA LATHAM,
Counsel for Petitioner,
819 Title Insurance Building,
Los Angeles, California.

GEORGE M. THOMPSON,
Counsel for Petitioner,
505 Title Insurance Building,
Los Angeles, California.

State of California,
County of Los Angeles,—ss.

John T. Riley, being duly sworn, on oath deposes and says:

That he is attorney for J. H. Miller and has authority to verify this petition in behalf of said J. H. Miller; that he has read said petition and the facts stated therein are true, except those which are stated to be on information and belief; and as to those facts, he believes them to be true.

JOHN T. RILEY.

Subscribed and sworn to before me this 27th day of August, 1928.

[Seal]   MARSHALL D. HALL,
Notary Public in and for the County of Los Angeles, State of California.

My commission expires June 30, 1929.

[104] EXHIBIT "A."

TREASURY DEPARTMENT,
WASHINGTON.

Office of
Commissioner of Internal Revenue
Address reply to
Commissioner of Internal Revenue
and refer to

July 3, 1928.

Mr. J. H. Miller,
1901 West View Street,
Los Angeles, California.

Sir:

In accordance with Section 274 of the Revenue Act of 1926 you are advised that the determination of your tax liability for the years 1923, 1924 and 1925, discloses a deficiency of $2,029.04, as shown in the attached statement, as transferee of the Dominguez Harbor Tract No. 2, Los Angeles, California, under Section 280 of said Act.

The section of the law above mentioned allows you an appeal to the United States Board of Tax Appeals within sixty days from the date of the mailing of this letter. However, if you acquiesce in this determination, you are requested to execute the inclosed Form A and forward it to the Commissioner of Internal Revenue, Washington, D. C., for the attention of IT:C:P-7.

Respectfully,

D. H. BLAIR,

Commissioner.

By C. B. ALLEN (Signed),

Deputy Commissioner.

Inclosures:
    Statement.
    Form A.
    Form 882.

[105]   STATEMENT.

IT:E:RR:280:60D.
    JEM.

In re: Mr. J. H. Miller,
            1901 West View Street,
            Los Angeles, California.

Under authority of Section 280 of the Revenue Act of 1926 there is proposed for assessment against you the amount of $2,029.04, constituting your liability as transferee of the assets of the Dominguez Harbor Tract No. 2, c/o George M. Thompson, Title Insurance Building, Los Angeles, California, for unpaid income taxes in the above amount due from said corporation (plus any accrued penalty and interest) for the years 1923, 1924, and 1925, as shown in the following statement:

Year.	Deficiency in Tax.
1923	$1,045.58
1924	703.63
1925	279.83
1926	None
Total,	**$2,029.04**

1923.

Gross profit	$9,062.25
Additions:	
Interest	2,752.14
	$11,814.39

Deductions:

Bookkeeping and miscellaneous expenses	$1,074.82	
Discounts	296.02	
Taxes	78.90	1,449.74

Adjusted net income $10,364.65

Explanation.

The gross profit as shown above is computed as follows:

(Installment sales basis.)

155 lots sold at $565.00 each	$87,575.00
155 lots cost $340.00 each	52,700.00
Gross profit	$34,875.00

Percentage of gross profit to sales, .398 plus 40%.

[106]   STATEMENT.

Mr. J. H. Miller,

Los Angeles, California.

Collections receiver during year $22,655.62—40%
of $22,655.62 equals $9,062.25.

Computation of Tax.

Net taxable income $10,364.65
Less:
    Credit 2,000.00
                                       _____

Balance taxable at 12½% .... $ 8,364.65
Tax at 12½% 1,045.58
Tax previously assessed ....   None
                                       _____

Deficiency ....$ 1,045.58

1924.

Gross profit ....$ 5,737.34
Additions:
    Profit on repossession not
        previously reported......$1,741.98
    Interest 1,568.56   3,310.54
                              _____   _____

                                         $ 9,047.88

Deductions:
    Bookkeeping and miscella-
        neous items $1,246.73
    Discounts 117.67
    Taxes 54.44   1,418.84
                              _____   _____

Adjusted net income ....$ 7,629.04

Explanation.

The gross profit is computed as shown under 1923 income.

The total collections received during 1924 amounted to $14,343.35   40% of $14,343.35 equals $5,737.34.

Computation of tax.

Net taxable income ....$ 7,629.04

[107] STATEMENT.

Mr. J. H. Miller,
Los Angeles, California.

Brought forward $7,629.04
Less:
  Credit 2,000.00
  _____
Balance taxable at 13½%...............$5,629.04
Tax at 13½% 703.63
Tax previously assessed .... None
  _____
Deficiency 703.63

1925.

Gross profit $5,814.54
Additions:
  Interest $911.62
  Taxes 223.78   1,135.40
  _____   _____
                                     $6,949.94

Deductions:

Bookkeeping and miscella-
neous items $2,748.33
Discounts 49.10   2,797.43

Adjusted net income $4,152.51

Explanation.

Gross profit is determined in same manner as for prior years.

Collections received during 1925 $14,536.34 at 40% equals $5,814.54.

Computation of Tax.

Net taxable income $4,152.51
Less:
Credit 2,000.00

Balance taxable at 13% $2,152.51
Tax at 13% 279.83
Tax previously assessed .... None

Deficiency ....$ 279.83

[108] STATEMENT.

Mr. J. H. Miller,
Los Angeles, California.

1926.

Gross profit ....$ 848.19
Additions:
Interest 220.43

$1,068.62

Deductions:

Bookkeeping and miscella-
neous expenses $2,298.12
Discounts 5.57
Taxes 298.37   2,602.06

Adjusted net loss $1,533.44

Explanation.

The adjustments are all of same character as for prior years.

Computation of Tax.

Since there is a net loss for this year, no tax is due. Hence case is closed no tax due.

Your protest in respect to the taxability of the so-called trust (taxpayer) has been duly considered. From evidence submitted it is held by this office that the taxpayer (Dominguez Harbor Tract No. 2) constitutes an association for income tax purposes for all the years involved.

Section 281 of the Revenue Act of 1926 provides that notice of a deficiency or other liability, if mailed to the taxpayer or other person subject to the liability at his last known address, shall be sufficient for the purposes of this title, even if such taxpayer or other person is deceased, or is under a legal disability, or, in the case of a corporation, has termined its existence.

---

[109] Filed Jan. 24, 1929. United States Board of Tax Appeals.

United States Board of Tax Appeals.

DOCKET No. 40,517.

J. H. MILLER,

                              Petitioner,

vs.

COMMISSIONER OF INTERNAL REVENUE,

                              Respondent.

ANSWER.

The Commissioner of Internal Revenue by his attorney, C. M. Charest, General Counsel, Bureau of Internal Revenue, for answer to the petition of the above-named taxpayer, admits, denies and alleges as follows:

1. Admits the allegations contained in Paragraph 1 of said petition.

2. Admits that the notice of deficiency was mailed to petitioner July 3, 1928, and that the copy with statement attached to said petition is a true and correct copy thereof.

3. Admits the allegations contained in Paragraph 3 of said petition.

4. Denies each and every allegation of error contained in Paragraph 4 of said petition.

5 (a) (b) (c). Admits that a certain trust known as "Dominguez Harbor Tract No. 2" was created under date of September 1, 1913. Alleges that the respondent is without knowledge or information sufficient to form a belief as to other matters and things alleged in subparagraphs (a),

(b) and (c) of Paragraph 5 of said petition, hence denies the same.

(d) (e) (f) (g) (i) (j) (k) (l). Denies each and every allegation contained in subparagraph (d), (e), (f), (g), (i), (j), (k), and (l), of Paragraph 5 of said petition.

[110] (h) Admits the allegations contained in subparagraph (h) of paragraph 5 of said petition.

Further answering respondent alleges that the notice of deficiency was mailed to petitioner within the time required by law.

WHEREFORE, it is prayed that the Commissioner's determination be in all things approved and that said petition be dismissed.

(Signed) C. M. CHAREST.

C. M. CHAREST,
General Counsel,
Bureau of Internal Revenue.

Of Counsel:

J. E. MATHER,
Special Attorney,
Bureau of Internal Revenue.

1/21/29.

EAT:LLD

[111] Filed May 20, 1931.

United States Board of Tax Appeals.

DOCKET No. 40,517.

J. H. MILLER,

Petitioner,

vs.

COMMISSIONER OF INTERNAL REVENUE,
Respondent.

AMENDED ANSWER.

The Commissioner of Internal Revenue, by his attorney, C. M. Charest, General Counsel, Bureau of Internal Revenue, for amended answer to the petition filed in this proceeding admits, denies, and alleges as follows:

(1) Admits the allegation contained in Paragraph (1) of the petition.

(2) Admits the allegation contained in Paragraph (2) of the petition.

(3) Admits that the taxes in controversy are income taxes for the calendar years 1923, 1924, and 1925 in the respective amounts of $1,045.58, $703.63, and $279.83. Denies that any taxes for the calendar year 1926 are in controversy.

(4) Denies that the Commissioner erred as alleged in Paragraph (4) of the petition.

(5) (a), (b), (c), (d), (e), (f), and (g). Denies the allegations contained in Subdivisions (a) to (g), inclusive, of Paragraph (5) of the petition.

(5) (h). Admits that the petitioner, together

with J. E. Adams as joint tenants, owned a 400/1000ths interest in the "Dominguez Harbor Tract No. 2." Denies the remaining allegations contained in Subdivision (h) of Paragraph (5) of the petition.

[112] (5) (i). Denies the allegations contained in Subdivision (i) of Paragraph (5) of the petition.

(5) (j). Moves that Subdivision (j) of Paragraph (5) of the petition be stricken therefrom, as the same is improperly pleaded, does not state a cause of action, and is too vague and indefinite to aid in framing an issue before this Board.

(5) (k). Moves that Subdivision (k) of Paragraph (5) of the petition be stricken therefrom, as the same is improperly pleaded, does not state a cause of action, and is too vague and indefinite to aid in framing an issue before this Board.

(5) (l). Neither admits nor denies Subdivision (l) of Paragraph (5) of the petition in that it sets forth a conclusion of law only.

(6) Denies generally and specifically each and every material allegation contained in the petition not hereinabove admitted, qualified, nor denied.

(7) The respondent alleges affirmatively:

1. The respondent determined that in the calendar years 1923 to 1925, inclusive, "Dominguez Harbor Tract No. 2" was taxable as a corporation.

2. The respondent on his March, 1928, Special List #2, assessed deficiencies in income tax amounting to the respective sums of $1,045.58, $703.63, and $279.83 against the "Dominguez Harbor Tract No. 2" for the calendar years 1923, 1924, and 1925.

3. Collection of said assessments cannot be made because the properties of the said "Dominguez Harbor Tract No. 2" have been distributed to the holders of the certificates of interest therein.

[113] 4. The beneficial interest in the "Dominguez Harbor Tract No. 2" was divided into 1,000 shares, represented by certificates of interest.

5. That in the calendar years 1923 to 1928, inclusive, the petitioner herein, together with J. E. Adams as joint tenants, was the owner of 400 shares out of a total of 1,000 shares outstanding in the said "Dominguez Harbor Tract No. 2."

6. That in the calendar years 1923 to 1928, inclusive, the "Dominguez Harbor Tract No. 2" distributed in liquidation to the petitioner, cash in a sum greatly in excess of the liability herein involved.

7. That as a result of said distributions, the "Dominguez Harbor Tract No. 2" became insolvent and is unable to pay the tax involved herein.

8. The petitioner is, therefore, liable for the unpaid income tax liability together with interest thereon as provided by law of the "Dominguez Harbor Tract No. 2" for the calendar years 1923, 1924, and 1925.

WHEREFORE, it is prayed that the respondent's determination be approved.

(Signed) C. M. CHAREST.

C. M. CHAREST,
General Counsel,
Bureau of Internal Revenue.

Of Counsel:
  J. A. LYONS,
  E. L. UPDIKE,
     Special Attorneys,
        Bureau of Internal Revenue.
ELU :MEP.
5–13–31.

———

[114]   24 B. T. A. ——.

United States Board of Tax Appeals.

DOCKET Nos. 40380, 40381, 40396, 40491, 40516 and 40517.

Promulgated September 21, 1931.

*G. F. SLOAN et al.,

                              Petitioners,

          vs.

COMMISSIONER OF INTERNAL REVENUE,
                              Respondent.

In the taxable years the petitioner conducted a business for profits and for such years was an association taxable as a corporation.   Hecht vs. Malley, 265 U. S. 144.

———

*Sloan, G. F.
Adams, J. E.
Middleton, C. O.
Anderson, J. A.
Barnhart, Lazzette H.
Miller, J. H.

FINDINGS OF FACT.

MELVIN D. WILSON, Esq., for the Petitioners.

J. A. LYON, Esq., and E. L. UPDIKE, Esq., for the Respondent.

In his notices to the petitioners herein the respondent has asserted liabilities under Section 280 of the Revenue Act of 1926 for the years 1923, 1924 and 1925, in the identical amounts of $1,045.58, $703.63 and $279.83, respecting alleged unpaid income taxes of Dominguez Harbor Tract No. 2, which was a trust instituted to subdivide and sell a certain tract of real estate. The only question at issue is whether such trust was an association taxable as a corporation in the years under review. The several proceedings have been consolidated for hearing and report. The parties have stipulated that if the trust is an association taxable as a corporation the several petitioners are liable as set forth in the letters of the respondent.

A true copy:

[Seal]   Teste: B. D. GAMBLE,
                    Clerk U. S. Board of Tax Appeals.

[115] The several petitioners are individuals residing in or near the city of Los Angeles, California.

Prior to 1907, certain real estate operators had subdivided a parcel of land containing 108 acres situated between Long Beach and Wilmington, California, and known as the Dominguez Tract, and had sold a few lots. In the panic of 1907, the subdividers failed and the property reverted to the mortgage holders, the Henry Matson Estate. A representative of such estate later asked petitioner C. O. Middleton to take over the property for the purpose of liquidation.

In 1912, Middleton made a nominal payment and in 1913, after inviting several others to join him in the matter, he took title to the property in the name of Charles O. Middleton and J. E. Adams as joint tenants and as Trustees for all the parties interested in the acquisition and disposition thereof, and on September 1, 1913, Middleton and Adams executed the following Declaration of Trust:

[116] THIS INDENTURE made this first day of September, A. D. 1913, WITNESSETH: That CHARLES O. MIDDLETON and J. E. ADAMS of Los Angeles, California, being designated the "Trustees," have and hold the legal title in fee simple in joint tenancy with right of survivorship to the following described real estate, situated in the County of Los Angeles, State of California, to wit:

All that property conveyed to Charles O. Middleton and J. E. Adams, as joint tenants, with right of survivorship, by Frank R. Bell, in Deed of Grant, dated March 1, 1913, and recorded in Book 5742 at Page 94 of Deeds, Records of Los Angeles County, being certain lots in the Dominguez Harbor Tract, as per map of said tract, recorded in Book 12, Pages 14 & 15 of Maps, Records of Los Angeles County, and all of Dominguez Harbor Tract, Sheet #2, as per map recorded in Book 22,

140   *G. F. Sloan et al. vs.*

Page 176 of Maps Records of Los Angeles
County.

Subject to an existing incumbrance in the
amount of $139,345.00.

That the said real estate is held by said trustees
in trust for the beneficiaries hereinafter named,
their lawful assigns and legal representatives according to their respective interests, for the following uses and purposes with the following powers
in said trustees, to wit:

To sell the whole or any part of said real estate
and to that end to lay out and subdivide said lands
or any part thereof; to pay commissions for the
sale of said lands; to improve the same and to execute conveyances for said land or any part thereof;
also to mortgage or lease said real estate or any
part thereof; and to receive the rents and profits of
said real estate and, as incidental to said powers, to
prosecute and defend all actions at law or in equity
relating to said property or any thereof; to collect
moneys owing upon any sale or sales thereof and to
satisfy judgments and claims relating thereto and
to otherwise exercise full control and management
of said property. When said property shall have
been sold, to divide the proceeds of the sales thereof
after deducting all necessary expenses, among the
several beneficiaries or their lawful assigns or legal
representatives according to their respective
interests.

The said beneficiaries and their assigns and legal
representatives shall not have or hold any title to

said land or any part thereof and shall not be authorized to maintain any suit for partition thereof or to annul or terminate this trust, except as herein provided.

The beneficial interest in said property shall be divided into One Thousand shares among the following named beneficiaries with the following number of respective shares to each:

[117] P. H. O'Neil,	One Hundred Shares
J. E. Adams & J. H. Miller, joint tenants with right of survivorship,	Three Hundred Shares
J. A. Anderson,	One Hundred Shares
Charles O. Middleton,	Two Hundred Fifty Shares
G. F. Sloan,	One Hundred Fifty
Alisal Ranch Company,	One Hundred Shares Shares

A separate certificate shall be issued to each beneficiary for his number of shares and upon surrender thereof, such certificate may be divided and separate certificates issued for such shares to those entitled thereto.

In case of death, removal or inability to act of either of said trustees, the survivor shall fill such vacancy by proper conveyance.

Certificates of trust issued under this instrument may be transformed by assignment and delivery.

Three fourths of the beneficiaries in interest may by an instrument in writing, remove any trus-

142   *G. F. Sloan et al. vs.*

tee under this instrument and appoint another in
his stead and may require such trust property to
be conveyed to such surviving Trustee and new
Trustee in joint tenancy by proper conveyances and
in case of the death or inability of both said Trustees,
may fill such vacancies. Three fourths in interest
of said beneficiaries may likewise terminate this
trust at any time and partition said property by
their own act or by judicial proceedings for partition, but in any event this trust shall cease and
determine upon the decease of all the natural persons in being named in this instrument.

The Trustee shall be empowered at any time
prior to the determination of this trust whenever
in their judgment it may be expedient and proper,
to declare dividends of money among the respective beneficiaries, derived from sales of real estate.

WITNESS our hands and seals.

                CHARLES O. MIDDLETON. (Seal)
                J. E. ADAMS. (Seal)

[118] Certificates of beneficial interest were issued in conformity with the trust instrument.
Two of such certificates were assigned to other parties and such assignments were recognized by the
Trustees.

On November 25, 1914, Middleton resigned as
Trustee and Adams appointed P. H. O'Neil as
his successor. On February 15, 1915, O'Neil resigned and Adams appointed G. F. Sloan as his
successor.

On February 29, 1924, March 9, 1925, and March
15, 1926, respectively, the Trustees filed fiduciary

returns for the years 1923, 1924 and 1925. On March 15, 1929, the Trustees executed and caused to be filed with the Collector of Internal Revenue at Los Angeles and with the Revenue Agent in Charge at the same city, an election to be taxed for the years 1923, 1924 and 1925 as a trust under the provisions of section 704 (b) of the Revenue Act of 1928.

The Trustees never acquired any land in addition to the lots taken over in 1913 and through agents sold all such lots prior to 1923. Throughout the taxable years they sold no lots and their activities were limited to collecting installment payments on sales contracts previously made, paying expenses, executing deeds for lots covered by paid-up contracts, and distributing proceeds of collections to the beneficiaries. None of the receipts from sales was reinvested or retained as working capital.

[119] The beneficiaries never held a meeting, removed or appointed a Trustee, terminated the trust or petitioned the law.

OPINION.

LANSDON.—The petitioner contends that the sole function of the trust herein was to liquidate a certain parcel of real property which came into the possession of one of the beneficiaries in a manner and at a cost not clearly disclosed by the record. In support of this theory it relies on Blair vs. Wilson Syndicate Trust, 39 Fed. (2d) 43; Lucas vs. Extension Oil Company, 47 Fed. 65; Lansdowne Realty Trust, C. C. A. First Circuit,

¶9397, C. C. H.; C. H. Atherton et al, Trustees, C. C. A. Ninth Circuit, ¶9452, C. C. H.; Max Wolf et al, Trustees of Nord Hop Ranch, 10 B. T. A. 835; Gonzolus Creek Oil Co., 12 B. T. A. 310; Myers Long & Co., 14 B. T. A. 460; Terminal Properties Company, 19 B. T. A. 584; The Royal Syndicate, 20 B. T. A. 255; Dauphin Deposit Trust Company, Trustee of Estate of James M. McCormick, 21 B. T. A. 1214.

A careful study of these cases indicates that the real test applied in each was not that there was a liquidation of real estate, but that there was no continuing business operation carried on for profit. This is the rule laid down in Hecht vs. Malley, 265 U. S. 144, in which it is clearly set forth that a trust transacting business for profit is liable to excise tax as a corporation. Upon this principle the courts and this Board have uniformly held that a [120] trust operating a business for profit is an association taxable as a corporation. Little Four Oil and Gas Co. vs. Lewellyn, 29 Fed. (2d) 1082; White vs. Hornblower, 27 Fed. (2d) 777; E. A. Landreth, 11 B. T. A. 1; Alexander Trust Co., 12 B. T. A. 1226; Durfee Mineral Company, 7 B. T. A. 231; Pritchett et al, 17 B. T. A. 1064; Rochester Theater Trust, 16 B. T. A. 1275; Woodrow Lee Trust, 14 B. T. A. 1420.

In the light of the opinions and decisions cited above, it remains only for us to determine whether this petitioner was engaged in business for profit. The petitioner contends that its operation had no other purpose than the liquidation of the real estate involved. Liquidation means realization or conversion of property for the benefit of its owners. If such a liquidation is effected through a trust the owners of the property are the beneficiaries of the trust and certificates of beneficial interest issued to them represent their former ownership of assets that have become the *corpus* of the trust. Up to the date of the declaration of trust, only two, if any, of the beneficiaries herein were owners of any interest in the parcel of land. The others came into the trust by invitation or solicitation and presumably paid for their certificates of beneficial interest with cash which was used to purchase the land from its [121] original owners or from the receivers in charge of the liquidation of their affairs. Everything in the record indicates that the beneficiaries herein entered into a voluntary association for the purpose of acquiring, subdividing, improving and selling Dominguez Harbor Tract No. 2, with the expectation of realizing a profit therefrom. Through a period of ten years or more they engaged in the activities necessary to accomplish their purposes. This state of facts discloses a situation far different from the institution of a trust merely to conserve or liquidate property already owned by the beneficiaries.

Decision will be entered for the respondent.

[122]   United States Board of Tax Appeals,
Washington.

DOCKET No. 40,380.

G. F. SLOAN,

Petitioner,

vs.

COMMISSIONER OF INTERNAL REVENUE,
Respondent.

DECISION.

Pursuant to the determination of the Board, as set forth in its report promulgated September 21, 1931,—

IT IS ORDERED AND DECIDED: That the liability of the petitioner at law or in equity as a transferee in respect of the tax of Dominguez Harbor Tract No. 2 for the years 1923, 1924 and 1925 is $1,045.58, $703.63 and $279.83, respectively, together with interest thereon as provided by law.

(Signed) LOGAN MORRIS,
Member.

Entered Sep. 21, 1931.

A true copy.
[Seal]   Teste: B. D. GAMBLE,
Clerk U. S. Board of Tax Appeals.

[123]   United States Board of Tax Appeals,
Washington.

DOCKET No. 40,381.

J. E. ADAMS,

Petitioner,

vs.

COMMISSIONER OF INTERNAL REVENUE,
Respondent.

DECISION.

Pursuant to the determination of the Board, as set forth in its report promulgated September 21, 1931,—

IT IS ORDERED AND DECIDED: That the liability of the petitioner at law or in equity as a transferee in respect of the tax of Dominguez Harbor Tract No. 2 for the years 1923, 1924 and 1925 is $1,045.58, $703.63 and $279.83, respectively, together with interest thereon as provided by law.

(Signed) LOGAN MORRIS,
Member.

Entered Sep. 21, 1931.

A true copy.
[Seal]   Teste: B. G. GAMBLE,
Clerk U. S. Board of Tax Appeals.

[124]   United States Board of Tax Appeals,
Washington.

DOCKET No. 40,396.

C. O. MIDDLETON,

Petitioner,

vs.

COMMISSIONER OF INTERNAL REVENUE,
Respondent.

DECISION.

Pursuant to the determination of the Board, as set forth in its report promulgated September 21, 1931,—

IT IS ORDERED AND DECIDED: That the liability of the petitioner at law or in equity as a transferee in respect of the tax of Dominguez Harbor Tract No. 2 for the years 1923, 1924 and 1925 is $1,045.58, $703.63 and $279.83, respectively, together with interest thereon as provided by law.

(Signed) LOGAN MORRIS,
Member.

Entered Sep. 21, 1931.

A true copy.
[Seal]   Teste: B. G. GAMBLE,
Clerk U. S. Board of Tax Appeals.

[125]   United States Board of Tax Appeals,
Washington.

DOCKET No. 40,491.

J. A. ANDERSON,

Petitioner,

vs.

COMMISSIONER OF INTERNAL REVENUE,

Respondent.

DECISION.

Pursuant to the determination of the Board, as set forth in its report promulgated September 21, 1931,—

IT IS ORDERED AND DECIDED: That the liability of the petitioner at law or in equity as a transferee in respect of the tax of Dominguez Harbor Tract No. 2 for the years 1923, 1924 and 1925 is $1,045.58, $703.63 and $279.83, respectively, together with interest thereon as provided by law.

(Signed) LOGAN MORRIS,

Member.

Entered Sep. 21, 1931.

A true copy:

[Seal]   Teste: B. D. GAMBLE,

Clerk U. S. Board of Tax Appeals.

[126]   United States Board of Tax Appeals,
Washington.

DOCKET No. 40,516.

LAZZETTE H. BARNHART,

Petitioner,

vs.

COMMISSIONER OF INTERNAL REVENUE,

Respondent.

DECISION.

Pursuant to the determination of the Board, as set forth in its report promulgated September 21, 1931,—

IT IS ORDERED AND DECIDED: That the liability of the petitioner at law or in equity as a transferee in respect of the tax of Dominguez Harbor Tract No. 2 for the years 1923, 1924 and 1925 is $1,045.58, $703.63 and $279.83, respectively, together with interest thereon as provided by law.

(Signed) LOGAN MORRIS,

Member.

Entered Sep. 21, 1931.

A true copy:

[Seal]   Teste: B. D. GAMBLE,

Clerk U. S. Board of Tax Appeals.

[127]   United States Board of Tax Appeals,
Washington.

DOCKET No. 40,517.

J. H. MILLER,

Petitioner,

vs.

COMMISSIONER OF INTERNAL REVENUE,
Respondent.

DECISION.

Pursuant to the determination of the Board, as set forth in its report promulgated September 21, 1931,—

IT IS ORDERED AND DECIDED: That the liability of the petitioner at law or in equity as a transferee in respect of the tax of Dominguez Harbor Tract No. 2 for the years 1923, 1924 and 1925 is $1,045.58, $703.63 and $279.83, respectively, together with interest thereon as provided by law.

(Signed) LOGAN MORRIS,
Member.

Entered Sep. 21, 1931.

A true copy:
[Seal]   Teste: B. D. GAMBLE,
Clerk U. S. Board of Tax Appeals.

[128]   Filed Oct. 12, 1931.

United States Board of Tax Appeals.

24 B. T. A.

September 21, 1931.

DOCKET No. 40,380.

G. F. SLOAN,

Petitioner,

vs.

COMMISSIONER OF INTERNAL REVENUE,
Respondent.

DOCKET No. 40,381.

J. E. ADAMS,

Petitioner,

vs.

COMMISSIONER OF INTERNAL REVENUE,
Respondent.

DOCKET No. 40,396.

C. O. MIDDLETON,

Petitioner,

vs.

COMMISSIONER OF INTERNAL REVENUE,
Respondent.

DOCKET No. 40,491.

J. A. ANDERSON,

Petitioner,

vs.

COMMISSIONER OF INTERNAL REVENUE,
Respondent.

DOCKET No. 40,516.

LEZZETTE H. BARNHART,

Petitioner,

vs.

COMMISSIONER OF INTERNAL REVENUE,

Respondent.

DOCKET No. 40,517.

J. H. MILLER,

Petitioner,

vs.

COMMISSIONER OF INTERNAL REVENUE,

Respondent.

[129] MOTION FOR RECONSIDERATION.

To the Honorable Chairman and Members of the United States Board of Tax Appeals:

Petitioners, G. F. Sloan, J. E. Adams, C. O. Middleton, J. A. Anderson, Lezzette H. Barnhart, and J. H. Miller, respectfully move for a reconsideration of the decision in this case, promulgated September 21, 1931.

While the taxes involved in these cases are small amounts, still, the question of whether a "real estate subdivision trust" is an association is an extremely important question which, in our opinion, merits the undivided attention of the full Board. See Section 704 of the Revenue Act of 1928 and its Legislative History.

The grounds for the motion for reconsideration are as follows:

(1) The decision does not indicate that it was reviewed by the Board. We respectfully suggest that the principle involved warrants a thorough consideration by the entire Board.

(2) The decision does not answer petitioners' contention that the case for 1923 is governed by section 704 (a) of the Revenue Act of 1928. We respectfully suggest that the point deserves consideration.

(3) The decision does not answer petitioners' contention that the case for 1924 and 1925 is governed by section 704 (b) of the Revenue Act of 1928. We believe this point deserves consideration.

(4) The decision does not give any weight to the transactions of the trust during the taxable years. No property was bought or sold in the taxable years. The trust did nothing but collect accounts receivable and pay taxes and made distributions during the years involved in this appeal. To hold that these actions constitute the doing of business is contrary to all the Board and Court decisions.

(5) The decision assumes that, looking at the entire life of the trust, it was conducting a permanent business. In fact, it was a venture limited to a specific property, and as such a joint venture, and not an association. 33 C. J. 841; Peterson vs. Nichols, 156 Pac. 406; Sander vs. Newman, 171 N. W. 822; Central Trust Co. vs. Crul, 211 S. W.

421; Camp vs. U. S., 15 Court of Claims 469; Berg vs. Mead, 100 N. Y. S. 792, 115 App. Div. 288; Discus vs. Sherer, 115 N. E. 161.

[130] (6) The decision does not give due weight to the fact that the beneficiaries, of whom there were six only, neither had nor exercised any voice in the management of the affairs of the trust. Since this trust merely collected money, in the taxable years, and the beneficiaries had no control over the trust, it is a strict trust under Art. 1314 of Regulations 74.

Petitioner respectfully requests the Board to consider, in connection with this case, the following decisions, in addition to those mentioned in the brief:

> Robert H. Gardiner et al., Trustees, vs. U. S., C. C. A. 1st, 5/28/31.
> White vs. Hornblower, 27 F. (2d) 777.
> F. E. M. Glone et al., 22 B. T. A. 358.
> Morriss Realty Company Trusts 1 and 2, 23 B. T. A. 1076.
> I. T. 2583, Internal Revenue Bulletin X–30–5151, August, 1931.
> Jackson-Wermich Trust, 24 B. T. A., September 24, 1931.

We respectfully submit:

(1) That since the beneficiaries neither had nor exercised any control, and the trust did nothing but collect accounts receivable, and the venture was limited to a single property:

> The trust is a strict trust for 1923 under section 704 (a) of the Revenue Act of 1928.

The trust is a strict trust under section 704 (b) of the 1928 Act, for all years.

The trust is a strict trust or joint venture within the meaning of art. 1314 of Regulations 74, and the Board and court cases.

Accordingly, we respectfully submit that a reconsideration should be had and the decision revised; that a reconsideration of the law and facts will result in a reversal of the decision herein, and that a miscarriage of justice will occur if this decision is not reversed.

Respectfully submitted,

(Signed) MELVIN D. WILSON,

819 Title Insurance Bldg.,

Los Angeles, California.

Counsel for Petitioners,

MILLER, CHEVALIER, PEELER & WILSON,

Of Counsel.

DENIED—OCT. 27, 1931.

(S) W. C. LANSDON,

Member, U. S. Board of Tax Appeals.

---

[131] Filed Mar. 5, 1932. United States Board of Tax Appeals.

In the United States Circuit Court of Appeals for the Ninth Circuit.

DOCKET Nos. 40,380, 40,381, 40,396, 40,491, 40,516, and 40,517.

G. F. SLOAN, J. E. ADAMS, C. O. MIDDLE-TON, J. A. ANDERSON, L. H. BARN-HART, and J. H. MILLER,

Petitioners,

vs.

DAVID BURNET, Commissioner of Internal Revenue,

Respondent.

PETITION FOR A REVIEW OF THE DECI-SION OF THE UNITED STATES BOARD OF TAX APPEALS.

To the Honorable, the Judges of the United States Circuit Court of Appeals for the Ninth Circuit:

G. F. Sloan, J. E. Adams, C. O. Middleton, J. A. Anderson, L. H. Barnhart, and J. H. Miller, in support of this, their joint petition, filed in pursuance of section 1001 of the Revenue Act of 1926 (44 Stat. 109) for the review of the decision of the United States Board of Tax Appeals which was rendered on the 21st day of September, 1931, approving deficiencies in income taxes in the case of each petitioner as transferee of Dominguez Harbor Tract No. 2, in the amounts of $1,045.58 for

1923, $703.63 for 1924, and $279.83 for 1925, show
to this honorable Court as follows:

I.

STATEMENT OF THE NATURE OF THE CONTROVERSY.

On July 3, 1928, the Commissioner of Internal
Revenue mailed deficiency letters to each of the
petitioners herein, stating that the Dominguez
Harbor Tract No. 2 was taxable as a corporation
and claiming that each petitioner was individu-
ally liable at law or in [132] equity as transferee for alleged unpaid taxes of said Dominguez
Harbor Tract No. 2 for the years 1923, 1924 and
1925 in the amounts of $1,045.58, $703.63, and
$279.83, respectively.

Each petitioner within the proper time, filed a
petition with the United States Board of Tax Appeals in pursuance of section 280 of the Revenue
Act of 1926. It was the principal contention of
the petitioners that Dominguez Harbor Tract No.
2 was not an association taxable as a corporation,
but that it was a trust or a joint venture and that
its income was taxable to its beneficiaries.

The appeals were consolidated for hearing and
decision, and on September 21, 1931, the Board of
Tax Appeals promulgated its findings of facts and
opinion, holding that Dominguez Harbor Tract
No. 2 was an association taxable as a corporation.
Final orders were entered in each case on September 21, 1931, sustaining the deficiency as de-

termined by the Commissioner of Internal Revenue.

II.

DESIGNATION OF COURT OF REVIEW.

The petitioners, all of whom are residents of the city of Los Angeles, California, except L. H: Barnhart who is a resident of Piedmont, California, desire a review of the said findings of fact, opinion and orders of the Board of Tax Appeals in accordance with the provisions of section 1001 of the Revenue Act of 1926 (44 Stat. 109) by the United States Circuit Court of Appeals for the Ninth Circuit, within which circuit is located the office of the Collector of Internal Revenue to whom tax returns were filed on behalf of Dominguez Harbor Tract No. 2 for the years 1923, 1924 and 1925, and to whom tax returns were filed by the petitioners.

[133] III.

ASSIGNMENTS OF ERRORS.

The petitioners, as a basis for review, make the following assignments of error:

1. The Board erred in holding that Dominguez Harbor Tract No. 2, was an association taxable as a corporation for the years 1923, 1924 and 1925.

2. The Board erred in failing to hold that Dominguez Harbor Tract No. 2 was taxable as a trust rather than as a corporation, for the years 1923, 1924 and 1925 in accordance with the provisions of section 704 (b) of the Revenue Act of 1928.

3. The Board erred in failing to hold that Dominguez Harbor Tract No. 2 was taxable as a trust rather than as a corporation for the year 1923, in accordance with section 704 (a) of the Revenue Act of 1928.

4. The Board erred in holding that Dominguez Harbor Tract No. 2 was conducting a continuing business operation.

5. The Board erred in holding that Dominguez Harbor Tract No. 2 was carrying on business during the years 1923, 1924, and 1925.

6. The Board erred in affirming the determination of the respondent.

WHEREFORE, your petitioners pray that this Honorable Court may review said findings, decision, opinion and orders and reverse and set aside the same, and for such further relief as the Court may deem proper in the premises.

MELVIN D. WILSON.

MELVIN D. WILSON,

819 Title Insurance Building,

Los Angeles, California.

(S.)   FREDERICK O. GRAVES.

FREDERICK O. GRAVES,

922 Southern Building,

Washington, D. C.,

Attorneys for Petitioners.

Messrs. MILLER & CHEVALIER,

922 Southern Building,

Washington, D. C.,

Of Counsel.

[134]   State of California,
County of Los Angeles,—ss.

Melvin D. Wilson, being duly sworn, deposes and says:

That I am an attorney at law, authorized to practice before the United States Board of Tax Appeals, and the United States Circuit Court of Appeals for the Ninth Circuit, and have my office at 819 Title Insurance Building, Los Angeles, California.

That I was the attorney of record for the petitioners named in the foregoing petition, before the United States Board of Tax Appeals.

That I am familiar with the facts stated in the foregoing petition and allege them to be true.

MELVIN D. WILSON.

Subscribed and sworn to before me this 26 day of February, 1932.

[Seal]   MILDRED K. ROGERS,
Notary Public in and for the County of Los Angeles, State of California.

---

[135]   Filed   Mar.   5,   1932.   United   States Board of Tax Appeals.

United States Board of Tax Appeals.

DOCKET Nos. 40,380, 40,381, 40,396, 40,491, 40,516
and 40,517.

G. F. SLOAN, J. E. ADAMS, C. O. MIDDLETON,
J. A. ANDERSON, L. H. BARNHART,
and J. H. MILLER,

Petitioners,

vs.

DAVID BURNET, Commissioner of Internal
Revenue,

Respondent.

PRAECIPE FOR TRANSCRIPT OF RECORD.

To the Clerk of the United States Board of Tax
Appeals:

You will please prepare and transmit to the
Clerk of the United States Circuit Court of Appeals for the Ninth Circuit certified copies of the
following documents which are necessary in connection with the joint petition for review which has
been filed this day.

1. The docket entries of proceedings before the
   United States Board of Tax Appeals in the
   above-entitled cases.
2. Pleadings before the Board.
3. Findings of fact, opinion and decision of the
   Board.
4. Petition for review.
5. This designation.

[136] The foregoing to be prepared, certified, and transmitted as required by law and the rules of the United States Circuit Court of Appeals for the Ninth Circuit.

> FREDERICK O. GRAVES.
> FREDERICK O. GRAVES,
>> Attorney for Petitioners.

March 5, 1932.

---

[137] Filed Mar. 22, 1932. United States Board of Tax Appeals.

United States Board of Tax Appeals.

DOCKET Nos. 40,380, 40,381, 40,396, 40,491, 40,516 and 40,517.

G. F. SLOAN, J. E. ADAMS, C. O. MIDDLE-TON, J. A. ANDERSON, L. H. BARN-HART, and J. H. MILLER,

> Petitioner,

vs.

DAVID BURNET, Commissioner of Internal Revenue,

> Respondent.

STIPULATION TO AMEND PRAECIPE.

It is hereby agreed by and between counsel for the respective parties that the praecipe for the record which was filed on behalf of the petitioners on March 5, 1932, may be amended to include the

motion for reconsideration, which was filed on behalf of the petitioners on October 12, 1931.

(Signed) F. O. GRAVES.

F. O. GRAVES,

922 Southern Building,

Washington, D. C.,

Attorney for Petitioners.

C. M. CHAREST.

J. A L.

C. M. CHAREST,

General Counsel,

Bureau of Internal Revenue,

Attorney for Respondent.

March 22, 1932.

---

[138] DOCKET Nos. 40,380–81, 40,396, 40,491,
40,516 and 40,517.

G. F. SLOAN, J. E. ADAMS, C. O. MIDDLE-
TON, J. A. ANDERSON, L. H. BARN-
HART, and J. H. MILLER,

Petitioners,

vs.

COMMISSIONER OF INTERNAL REVENUE,

Respondent.

CERTIFICATE OF CLERK U. S. BOARD OF
TAX APPEALS TO TRANSCRIPT OF
RECORD.

I, B. D. Gamble, Clerk of the U. S. Board of Tax
Appeals, do hereby certify that the foregoing pages 1

to 137, inclusive, contain and are a true copy of the transcript of record, papers and proceedings on file and of record in my office as called for by the Praecipe in the appeal (or appeals) as above numbered and entitled.

IN TESTIMONY WHEREOF, I hereunto set my hand and affix the seal of the United States Board of Tax Appeals, at Washington, in the District of Columbia, this 25th day of March, A. D. 1932.

[Seal]   B. D. GAMBLE,

Clerk.

[Endorsed]: No. 6808. United States Circuit Court of Appeals for the Ninth Circuit. G. F. Sloan, J. E. Adams, C. O. Middleton, J. A. Anderson, L. H. Barnhart, and J. H. Miller, Petitioners, vs. Commissioner of Internal Revenue, Respondent. Transcript. of Record. Upon Petition to Review an Order of the United States Board of Tax Appeals.

Filed April 1, 1932.

PAUL P. O'BRIEN,

Clerk of the United States Circuit Court of Appeals for the Ninth Circuit.

No. 6808.

United States
Circuit Court of Appeals,
FOR THE NINTH CIRCUIT.

G. F. Sloan, J. E. Adams, C. O. Middleton, J. A. Anderson, L. H. Barnhart
and J. H. Miller,

Appellants,

vs.

Commissioner of Internal Revenue,

Appellee.

BRIEF ON BEHALF OF APPELLANTS.

MELVIN D. WILSON,
Title Ins. Bldg., 433 S. Spring St., Los Angeles,

Counsel for Appellants.

FILED

OCT 12 1932

PAUL P. O'BRIEN,

Parker, Stone & Baird Co., Law Printers, Los Angeles.

TOPICAL INDEX.

PAGE

Statement of the Case.. 3

Question Involved... 4

Statutes Involved... 4

Statement of Facts... 5

Errors Relied Upon... 9

Argument 10

I.
In the Taxable Years Involved, the Trustees of
Dominguez Harbor Tract No. 2 Were Merely
Holding Contracts Receivable and Collecting the
Income Therefrom and Distributing. the Same to
the Beneficiaries and the Adventure Is a Strict
Trust 10

II.
Dominguez Harbor Tract No. 2 Is a Strict Trust
Under the Provisions of Section 704(a) of the
Revenue Act of 1928 for the Taxable Year 1923...... 16

III.
Dominguez Harbor Tract No. 2 Is, for the Years 1923,
1924 and 1925, Governed by the Provisions of Section 704(b) of the Revenue Act of 1929..................... 19

IV.
This Trust Can Be Distinguished on the Facts From
Trusts 5833 and 123-B N. S., Heretofore Considered
by This Court.. 21

Summary 24

TABLE OF CASES AND AUTHORITIES CITED.

PAGE

Blair v. Wilson Syndicate Trust, 39 Fed. (2d) 43....11, 19

Commercial Trust Co. case, 18 B. T. A. 1248.............. 18

33 Corpus Juris, 907.. 20

Gardiner v. U. S., 49 Fed. (2d) 992, 996...................... 11
G. C. M. 6677, C. B. VIII-2, p. 172...................... 20

E. A. Landreth Co., 15 B. T. A. 655.............................. 16
Lansdowne Realty Trust v. Commissioner, 50 Fed.
    (2d) 56.. 11
Llewellyn v. Pittsburgh B. & L. E. R. Co., 222 Fed.
    177 13

Merchants Trust Co. v. Welch............................ 21

Revenue Act of 1921, Article 1504 of Regulations 62.... 10
Revenue Acts of 1921, 1924 and 1926, Secs. 2(2)...... 4
Revenue Act of 1928, Sec. 704(a)....................14, 15, 16
Rollin S. Sturgeon, *et al.,* 25 B. T. A. 368.................14, 15

Security First National Bank v. Welch, 54 F. (2) 323.. 21

Terminal Properties Co., 19 B. T. A. 584...................... 11
Tiffany, Real Property, p. 370........................... 20
Tiffany, Real Property, p. 372........................... 20

U. S. v. Emery, Bird, Thayer Realty Co., 237 U. S. 28.. 12
U. S. v. Hotchkiss Redwood Co., 25 Fed. (2d) 958...... 12

Van Cleave Trust, 18 B. T. A. 486............................ 17

White v. Hornblower, 27 Fed. (2d) 777...................... 12
Wilson Syndicate Trust, 14 B. T. A. 508...................... 18

Yukon Alaska Trust v. Commissioner, 26 B. T. A.
    635 18

Zonne v. Minneapolis Syndicate, 220 U. S. 187............ 12

No. 6808.

IN THE

United States

Circuit Court of Appeals,

FOR THE NINTH CIRCUIT.

G. F. Sloan, J. E. Adams, C. O. Middleton, J. A. Anderson, L. H. Barnhart and J. H. Miller,

Appellants,

vs.

Commissioner of Internal Revenue,

Appellee.

BRIEF ON BEHALF OF APPELLANTS.

STATEMENT OF THE CASE.

This is a petition for the review of a decision of the United States Board of Tax Appeals in favor of the appellee, dated September 21, 1931, wherein the Board of Tax Appeals found that each of the appellants owed additional taxes as follows:

1923—	$1,045.58
1924—	703.63
1925—	279.83

The Board's decision was entered September 21, 1931.

The appellants were the beneficiaries and are the transferees of the Dominguez Harbor Tract No. 2.

The Commissioner of Internal Revenue held that the Dominguez Harbor Tract No. 2 was an association taxable as a corporation and the Board of Tax Appeals upheld the Commissioner's determination.

QUESTION INVOLVED.

The only question involved is whether or not, during the years 1923, 1924 and 1925, the Dominguez Harbor Tract No. 2 was an association taxable as a corporation.

STATUTES INVOLVED.

Sections 2(2) of the Revenue Acts of 1921, 1924 and 1926 provide as follows:

"The term 'corporation' includes associations, joint-stock companies, and insurance companies."

Section 704 of the Revenue Act of 1928 provides:

"(a) If a taxpayer filed a return as a trust for any taxable year prior to the taxable year 1925 such taxpayer shall be taxable as a trust for such year and not as a corporation, if such taxpayer was considered to be taxable as a trust and not as a corporation either (1) under the regulations in force at the time the return was made or at the time of the termination of its existence, or (2) under any ruling of the Commissioner or any duly authorized officer of the Bureau of Internal Revenue applicable to any of such years, and interpretative of any provision of the Revenue Act of 1918, 1921, or 1924, which had not been reversed or revoked prior to the time the return was made, or under any such ruling made after the return was filed which had not been reversed or revoked prior to the time of the termination of the taxpayer's existence.

"(b) For the purpose of the Revenue Act of 1926 and prior Revenue Acts, a trust shall, at the option of the trustee exercised within one year after the enactment of this Act, be considered as a trust the income of which is taxable (whether distributed or not) to the beneficiaries, and not as an association, if such trust (1) had a single trustee, and (2) was created and operated for the sole purpose of liquidating real property as a single venture (with such powers of administration as are incidental thereto, including the acquisition, improvement, conservation, division, and sale of such property), distributing the proceeds therefrom in due course to or for the benefit of the beneficiaries, and discharging indebtedness secured by the trust property, and (3) has not made a return for the taxable year as an association."

STATEMENT OF FACTS.

The several appellants are individuals residing in or near the city of Los Angeles, California.

Prior to 1907 certain real estate operators had subdivided a parcel of land containing 108 acres situated between Long Beach and Wilmington, California, and known as Dominguez Tract, and had sold a few lots. In the panic of 1907, the subdividers failed and the property reverted to the mortgage holders, the Henry Matson Estate. A representative of such estate later asked petitioner C. O. Middleton to take over the property for the purpose of liquidating it. In 1912, Middleton made a nominal payment and in 1913, after inviting several others to join him in the matter, he took title to the property in the name of Charles O. Middleton and J. E. Adams as joint tenants and as trustees of all the parties interested in the acquisition and disposition thereof, and on September 1, 1913, Middleton and Adams executed the following Declaration of Trust:

"This Indenture made this first day of September, A. D. 1913, Witnesseth: That Charles O. Middleton and J. E. Adams of Los Angeles, California, herein designated the 'Trustees,' have and hold the legal title in fee simple in joint tenancy with right of survivorship to the following described real estate, situated in the County of Los Angeles, State of California, to wit:

"All that property conveyed to Charles O. Middleton and J. E. Adams, as joint tenants, with right of survivorship, by Frank R. Bell, in Deed of Grant, dated March 1, 1913, and recorded in Book 5742 at Page 94 of Deeds, Records of Los Angeles County, being certain lots in the Dominguez Harbor Tract, as per map of said tract, recorded in Book 12, Pages 14 & 15 of Maps, Records of Los Angeles County, and all of Dominguez Harbor Tract, Sheet #2, as per map recorded in Book 22, Page 176 of Maps, Records of Los Angeles County.

"Subject to an existing incumbrance in the amount of $139,345.00.

"That the said real estate is held by said trustees in trust for the beneficiaries hereinafter named, their lawful assigns and legal representatives according to their respective interests, for the following uses and purposes with the following powers in said trustees, to wit:

"To sell the whole or any part of said real estate and to that end to lay out and subdivide said lands or any part thereof; to pay commissions for the sale of said lands; to improve the same and to execute conveyances for said land or any part thereof; also to mortgage or lease said real estate or any part thereof; and to receive the rents and profits of said real estate and, as incidental to said powers, to prosecute and defend all actions at law or in equity relating to said property or any thereof; to collect moneys owing upon any sale or sales thereof and to satisfy judgments and claims relating thereto and to otherwise exercise full control and management of said property. When said property shall have been sold, to divide the proceeds of the sales thereof after deducting all necessary expenses, among the several beneficiaries or their lawful assigns or legal representatives according to their respective interests.

"The said beneficiaries and their assigns and legal representatives shall not have or hold any title to said land or any part thereof and shall not be authorized to maintain any suit for partition thereof or to annul or terminate this trust, except as herein provided.

"The beneficial interest in said property shall be divided into One Thousand shares among the following named beneficiaries with the following number of respective shares to each:

"P. H. O'Neil,	One Hundred Shares
J. E. Adams & J. H. Miller, joint tenants with right of survivorship,	Three Hundred Shares
J. A. Anderson,	One Hundred Shares
Charles O. Middleton,	Two Hundred Fifty Shares
G. F. Sloan,	One Hundred Fifty Shares
Alisal Ranch Company,	One Hundred Shares

"A separate certificate shall be issued to each beneficiary for his number of shares and upon surrender thereof, such certificate may be divided and separate certificates issued for such shares to those entitled thereto.

"In case of the death, removal or inability to act of either of said trustees, the survivor shall fill such vacancy by proper conveyance.

"Certificates of trust issued under this instrument may be transferred by assignment and delivery.

"Three fourths of the beneficiaries in interest may by an instrument in writing, remove any trustee under this instrument and appoint another in his stead and may require such trust property to be conveyed to such surviving Trustee and new Trustee in joint tenancy by proper conveyances and in case of the death or inability of both said Trustees, may fill such vacancies. Three fourths in interest of said beneficiaries may likewise terminate this trust at any time and partition said property by their own act or by judicial proceedings for partition, but in any event this trust shall cease and determine upon the decease of all the natural persons in being named in this instrument.

"The Trustee shall be empowered at any time prior to the determination of this trust whenever in their judgment it may be expedient and proper, to declare dividends of money among the respective beneficiaries, derived from sales of real estate.

"Witness our hands and seals.

CHARLES O. MIDDLETON.   (Seal)

J. E. ADAMS.   (Seal)"

Certificates of beneficial interest were issued in conformity with the trust instrument. Two of such certificates were assigned to other parties and such assignments were recognized by the trustees.

On November 25, 1914, Middleton resigned as trustee and Adams appointed P. H. O'Neil as his successor. On February 15, 1915, O'Neil resigned and Adams appointed G. F. Sloan as his successor.

On February 29, 1924, March 9, 1925, and March 15, 1926, respectively, the trustees filed fiduciary returns for the years 1923, 1924 and 1925. On March 15, 1929, the trustees executed and caused to be filed with the Collector of Internal Revenue at Los Angeles and with the Revenue Agent in Charge at the same city, an election to be taxed for the years 1923, 1924 and 1925 as a trust under the provisions of section 704(b) of the Revenue Act of 1928.

The trustees never acquired any land in addition to the lots taken over in 1913 and through agents sold all such lots prior to 1923. Throughout the taxable years they sold no lots and their activities were limited to collecting installment payments on sales contracts previously made, paying expenses, executing deeds for lots covered by paid-up contracts, and distributing proceeds of collections to the beneficiaries. None of the receipts from sales were reinvested or retained as working capital.

The beneficiaries never held a meeting, removed or appointed a trustee, terminated the trust or partitioned the land.

The parties have stipulated that if the trust is an association taxable as a corporation, several appellants are liable for the taxes of the trust by reason of being transferees of its assets.

ERRORS RELIED UPON.

The appellants submit that the Board of Tax Appeals erred in the following respects:

(1) The Board erred in holding that Dominguez Harbor Tract No. 2 was an association taxable as a corporation for the years 1923, 1924 and 1925.

(2) The Board erred in failing to hold that Dominguez Harbor Tract No. 2 was taxable as a trust rather than as a corporation for the year 1923, in accordance with section 704(a) of the Revenue Act of 1928.

(3) The Board erred in failing to hold that Dominguez Harbor Tract No. 2 was taxable as a trust rather than as a corporation for the years 1923, 1924 and 1925, in accordance with the provisions of section 704(b) of the Revenue Act of 1928.

(4) The Board erred in holding that Dominguez Harbor Tract No. 2 was, during the taxable years involved, conducting a continuing business operation.

(5) The Board erred in holding that Dominguez Harbor Tract No. 2 was carrying on business during the years 1923, 1924 and 1925.

ARGUMENT.

I.

In the Taxable Years Involved, the Trustees of Dominguez Harbor Tract No. 2 Were Merely Holding Contracts Receivable and Collecting the Income Therefrom and Distributing the Same to the Beneficiaries and the Adventure Is a Strict Trust.

Whatever may have been the taxable status of this trust in the years in which the trustees held, subdivided and sold the property, it surely was a strict trust passively holding contracts receivable during the taxable years involved.

Prior to 1923, all of the real property had been sold and during the taxable years 1923, 1924 and 1925, the trustees merely collected the money due on the contracts of sale, paid the taxes, and distributed the balance to the beneficiaries. Such conduct does not amount to doing business either under the rulings of the Commissioner of Internal Revenue, the Board of Tax Appeals, or the courts.

Article 1504 of Regulations 62, promulgated under the provisions of the Revenue Act of 1921, distinguished associations from trusts in the following manner:

"Association distinguished from trust. Where trustees hold real estate subject to a lease and collect the rents, doing no business other than distributing the income less taxes and similar expenses to the holders of their receipt certificates, who have no control except the right of filling a vacancy among the trustees and of consenting to a modification of the terms of the trust, no association exists and the *cestui que trust* are liable to tax as beneficiaries of a trust the income of which is to be distributed periodically, whether or not at regular intervals. But in such a trust if the trustees pursuant to the terms thereof have the right to hold the income for future distribution, the net income is taxed to the trustees instead of

to the beneficiaries. See section 219 of the statute
and articles 341-348. If, however, the *cestui que
trust* have a voice in the conduct of the business of
the trust, whether through the right periodically to
elect trustees or otherwise, the trust is an association
within the meaning of the statute."

From the foregoing statement of facts, it is apparent
that the trustees of Dominguez Harbor Tract No. 2 were
fully as inactive as the trustees were in the case mentioned
in article 1504, above. Furthermore, the beneficiaries of
the Dominguez Harbor Tract No. 2 had no control over
the trustees, or the affairs of the trust. Article 1504 recognized that the right of filling a vacancy among the
trustees and consenting to the modification of the terms
of the trust, did not amount to control by the beneficiaries
over the trustees.

The Circuit Court of Appeals for the Fifth Circuit, in
the case of *Blair v. Wilson Syndicate Trust,* 39 Fed. (2d)
43, held that the power to remove the trustee did not give
the beneficiaries control over the fundamental policies of
the trust. Dominguez Harbor Tract No. 2, therefore,
meets all the requirements of Article 1504. The trust was
passively holding contracts receivable and its beneficiaries
could not control the trustees or the affairs of the trust.
It may be pointed out that the beneficiaries never exercised any of the powers given to them. Specifically, they
never removed the trustees, appointed a new trustee, held
a meeting, or modified the terms of the trust indenture.
The powers exercised determine the status of the trust
rather than the powers conferred.

> *Gardiner v. U. S.,* 49 Fed. (2d) 992, 996;
> *Terminal Properties Co.,* 19 B. T. A. 584;
> *Lansdowne Realty Trust v. Commissioner,* 50 Fed.
> (2d) 56.

The Board of Tax Appeals and the courts have frequently held that activities such as were engaged in by the Dominguez Harbor Tract No. 2, do not constitute the doing of business. In *U. S. v. Hotchkiss Redwood Co.*, 25 Fed. (2d) 958, this Honorable Court held that a company organized solely to own and hold timber land and resell same at a profit was not doing business.

In the case of *Zonne v. Minneapolis Syndicate*, 220 U. S. 187, the Supreme Court held that a corporation organized for the purpose of owning and renting an office building, but which had wholly parted with the control and management of the property, and by the terms of a reorganization had disqualified itself from any activity in respect to it, its sole authority being to hold title subject to a lease for 130 years, and to receive and distribute the rentals which might accrue under the terms of the lease, or the proceeds of any sale of the land, if it should be sold, was not doing business within the meaning of the 1909 Excise Tax Act imposing an excise upon the doing or carrying on of business in a quasi-corporate capacity.

Similarly, in the case of *U. S. v. Emery, Bird, Thayer Realty Co.*, 237 U. S. 28, the Supreme Court held that a real estate corporation whose powers were limited very nearly to the necessary incidents of holding a specific tract of land, and whose characteristic charter function and the only one that it was carrying on was the collection and distribution of the rent received from a single lessee, was not engaged in business within the meaning of the Federal Corporation Tax Law of 1909.

In the case of *White v. Hornblower*, 27 Fed. (2d) 777, the United States Circuit Court of Appeals for the First

Circuit, held that a trust organized to liquidate an embarrassed corporation was not an association. In that case the trustees merely owned securities in a corporation and the power of the trustees to manage the company's affairs was limited to their power to liquidate the corporation.

Hon. Wm. C. Lansdon, the member of the United States Board of Tax Appeals when considering the case at bar, apparently failed to take into consideration the fact that during the taxable years involved the trust was merely holding contracts and liquidating them by receiving the payments due on the contracts and distributing the proceeds. Whatever may have been done in preceding years, the activities of the trust were certainly limited to the liquidation of contracts in the taxable years involved.

In *Llewellyn v. Pittsburgh B. & L. E. R. Co.,* 222 Fed. 177, the United States Circuit Court of Appeals for the Third Circuit, defined the doing of business under the 1909 Federal Corporation Excise Tax Law, as follows:

> "The three expressions, 'engaged in business,' 'carrying on business,' and 'doing business,' either separately or connectedly *convey the idea of progression, continuity or sustained activity.* 'Engaged in business' means occupied in business; employed in business. 'Carry on business' does not mean the performance of a single disconnected business act. It means conducting, prosecuting, or continuing business by performing progressively all the acts normally incident thereto, and likewise the expression 'doing business,' when employed as a description of an occupation, conveys the idea of business being done, not from time to time, but all the time."

Surely no one could say that merely in holding contracts and receiving and distributing the proceeds therefrom that Dominguez Harbor Tract No. 2 was continuously, progressively conducting, transacting and carrying on a permanent business.

The United States Board of Tax Appeals has, in many other cases, held that organizations much more active than was Dominguez Harbor Tract No. 2 during the taxable years involved, were not engaged in business and were, therefore, not taxable as associations. In fact, the appellants doubt that the decision of Hon. Wm. C. Lansdon, the sole member of the United States Board of Tax Appeals to consider this case, either originally or upon the motion for reconsideration, is in line with the other decisions of the full Board. For example, see the decision of *Rollin S. Sturgeon, et al.,* 25 B. T. A. 368. That case involves very closely analogous facts. It was promulgated in January, 1932, subsequent to the decision in the case at bar. In that case Sturgeon, a motion picture director, and Hubbard, an author of scenarios, decided to produce one motion picture based on a story written by Hubbard. They organized a trust and became the trustees. They contributed a substantial part of the capital needed by the trust to produce the picture, and raised the balance of the necessary capital by selling certificates of beneficial interest to several other persons. The trustees owned approximately two-thirds of the beneficial interests of the trust. The trust produced a picture which was sold, in 1923, for $75,000, payable in installments. The sum of $10,000 was reserved to protect possible censorship requirements. No other picture was contemplated or produced. Subsequent to the sale the trustees did nothing but collect and distribute the moneys due on the contract of sale. The Board of Tax Appeals found that the trust was governed by section 704(a) of the Revenue Act of

1928 for 1923. As to the years 1924 and 1925, the Board used the following language:

> "This Board has held that the significant tests to be applied in determining whether an alleged trust is a trust, or an association taxable as a corporation, are whether (1) the beneficiaries of the alleged trust have voluntarily associated themselves together in the general form and mode of procedure of a corporation, and (2) are organized to, and in fact are, engaged in the active conduct of a business for profit, or (3) whether the trustees are merely holding the property and collecting the income therefrom and distributing to those beneficially interested. *Extension Oil Co.*, 16 B. T. A. 1028, affd., 47 Fed. (2d) 65; *Jackson-Wermich Trust*, 24 B. T. A. 150; *E. B. Galbreath, et al.*, 24 B. T. A. 1107.

> "During the years 1924 and 1925 the trustees did nothing more than collect installments of reserved purchase money and distribute them to the beneficiaries. The retention of $10,000 from the purchase price was necessitated by the possible prohibitions of censorship authorities. The trust was continued in 1924 and 1925 solely to meet that contingency. The nominal actions of the trustees during those years do not signify that the petitioner was engaged in the active conduct of a business for profit, but rather that the funds of the trust were merely received and held for distribution. *Gardiner v. United States*, 49 Fed. (2d) 992; *Lansdowne Realty Trust v. Commissioner*, 50 Fed. (2d) 56; *Zenith Real Estate Trust v. Commissioner*, 54 Fed. (2d) 29.

> "Under these facts, therefore, the petitioner is taxable as a trust during all the years under consideration."

While the Commissioner of Internal Revenue has announced his non-acquiescence in the Sturgeon case, he has taken no appeal and the time therefor has run.

This decision indicates that the activities engaged in by an organization in the years prior to the taxable years involved, are not to be taken into consideration, but only the activities engaged in during the taxable years.

II.

Dominguez Harbor Tract No. 2 Is a Strict Trust Under the Provisions of Section 704(a) of the Revenue Act of 1928 for the Taxable Year 1923.

The trustees of Dominguez Harbor Tract No. 2 filed a fiduciary return for the year 1923 on February 29, 1924. At the time that the 1923 fiduciary return was filed, the Dominguez Harbor Tract No. 2 was considered to be taxable as a trust and not as a corporation, under Reg. 62, Sec. 1504, set out above.

The Board of Tax Appeals, in the case of *Rollin S. Sturgeon, et al.,* 25 B. T. A. 368, in construing the applicability of section 704(a) of the Revenue Act of 1928 for the trust there involved, said:

> "In *Commercial Trust Co.,* 18 B. T. A. 1248, we pointed out that in all cases in which the shareholders did not control the actions of the trustees, irrespective of whether or not the taxpayer was engaged in business under corporate form, the rulings of the Bureau of Internal Revenue, in effect up to July 1, 1924, consistently held that the taxpayer was taxable as a trust. See also *E. A. Landreth Co.,* 15 B. T. A. 655; *Van Cleave Trust,* 18 B. T. A. 486."

In the case of *E. A. Landreth Co.,* 15 B. T. A. 655, the Board of Tax Appeals reviewed all of the rulings of the Commissioner, the Bureau of Internal Revenue, and of the Solicitor of Internal Revenue and the Treasury decisions, and analyzed them as follows:

"It is sufficient to say that beginning in the year
1919 and up to and including the period July-December, 1922, the Bureau of Internal Revenue was consistently ruling that irrespective of whether the taxpayer was engaged in business under the corporate
forms, it was taxable as a trust in all cases where
the shareholders could not control the actions of the
trustees."

In that case the beneficiaries, by a majority vote, could
remove the trustee for misconduct or breach of trust, and
a majority of the beneficiaries could appoint a new trustee
in the case of vacancies. Nevertheless, the Board held
that the beneficiaries could not control the trust and that
it was therefore governed by the provisions of section
704(a) of the Revenue Act of 1928.

In the case at bar there was less evidence of control
than in the Landreth case, as a majority of the beneficiaries could remove the trustee in the Landreth case,
while it would take three-fourths (¾) of the beneficiaries
to remove the trustees in the case at bar.

In the case of *Van Cleave Trust,* 18 B. T. A. 486, the
Board considered the application of section 704(a) of the
Revenue Act of 1928 to the taxable status of the trust for
the taxable year 1923. The Board said:

"Our decision in Wilkens & Lange, 15 B. T. A.
1183, followed that in Landreth, *supra,* but inasmuch
as our pronouncement went only so far as the period
ended with December, 1922, and, further, there being
involved in the instant case the tax return for 1923,
filed, as stipulated for the purposes of this proceeding only, on or before March 15, 1924, therefore we
have examined Cumulative Bulletins suceeding the
year 1922 and have found no ruling, and none has
been cited, reversing or revoking earlier rulings on
this point, but rather, those so found have reiterated

or been confirmatory of them. Therefore, we extend our pronouncement in the Landreth case, as set forth above, to include the period to July 1, 1924, and we find for the petitioner on this point and hold that for the year 1923 it was entitled to be taxed as a trust."

In the *Commercial Trust Co.* case, 18 B. T. A. 1248, the trust was created in 1920 and property of the value of $100,000 was transferred to a sole trustee. Two-thirds (⅔) of the holders of beneficial interests could terminate the trust. The trust was actively engaged in carrying on a business during the years 1922, 1923 and 1924, and filed fiduciary returns for those years. The trustee with the written consent of two-thirds (⅔) of the holders of beneficial interests, had power to amend the trust. The trust was to continue for twenty-one years after the death of the last surviving original beneficiary. The Board held that the trust should be taxed as a pure trust under the provisions of section 704(a) of the Revenue Act of 1928.

In *Yukon Alaska Trust v. Commissioner,* 26 B. T. A. 635, the Board of Tax Appeals held that the beneficiaries did not control the trust and that therefore it came under the provisions of section 704(a) of the Revenue Act of 1928, even though the holders of three-fourths of the beneficial interests had the power to terminate the trust and could appoint trustees if the remaining trustees did not do so.

In *Wilson Syndicate Trust,* 14 B. T. A. 508, the holders of five-sevenths (5/7) of the beneficial interests had power to remove the trustee with or without cause. The Board of Tax Appeals held that this power did not give them any voice in, or control over the fundamental policies of the organization. This principle was offered in *Blair v. Wilson Syndicate Trust,* 39 Fed. (2d) 43.

Since the only test recognized by the Commissioner of Internal Revenue, prior to July 1, 1924, was whether or not the beneficiaries had positive control over the trustees and the affairs of the trust, and inasmuch as the beneficiaries of the Dominguez Harbor Tract No. 2 did not have control over the trustees and the affairs of the trust, this trust is governed by the provisions of section 704(a) of the Revenue Act of 1928, as to the year 1923.

III.

Dominguez Harbor Tract No. 2 Is, for the Years 1923, 1924 and 1925, Governed by the Provisions of Section 704(b) of the Revenue Act of 1929.

In order for section 704(b) to be applicable, the following prerequisites are necessary:

(1) Created to liquidate real property as a single venture.

(2) Has not filed a corporation return for the taxable year.

(3) Filed an election under 704(b) before June 28, 1929.

(4) Had a single trustee.

Section 704(b) was enacted at the instance of real estate subdividers. Consequently, there can be no question but that a real estate subdivision is created to liquidate real property, as a single venture. That was certainly true of Dominguez Harbor Tract No. 2.

The Statement of Facts shows that Dominguez Harbor Tract No. 2 filed fiduciary and not corporation returns for the years involved.

On February 15, 1929, the trust filed an election to be taxed under section 704(b).

The first three prerequisites have, therefore, undoubtedly been complied with.

The only remaining question is whether or not the trust had a single trustee.

As long as the joint tenancy exists, there is but a single owner of the property. The essential elements of joint tenancy are that the ownership of property is in a single entity; that there is unity of interest, unity of title, unity of time, unity of possession. *33 C. J.* 907.

> "In the case of a joint tenancy, all the tenants have together, in the theory of the law, *but one estate in the land,* and to this are to be traced the various characteristics of the tenancy. Furthermore, all the tenants, whether only two, or more than two, *constitute* for some purposes *but one tenant.* * * *"
> *Tiffany, Real Property,* p. 370.

> "* * * the leading characteristic of a joint tenancy is the fact that, on the death of one joint tenant, the other joint tenant or tenants who may survive him, * * * have the whole estate. Thus, if there be three joint tenants, on the death of one the two survivors have the whole, and, on the death of one of these survivors, the last survivor has the whole * * *. This doctrine is based on the fact, before referred to, that all the tenants together, * * * were *regarded as constituting but one tenant,* and that this fictitious personality was considered as existent as long as any one of the tenants was alive."
> *Tiffany, Real Property,* p. 372.

See also:
G. C. M. 6677, C. B. VIII-2, p. 172.

Since the trust had but a single trustee, and meets all the other requirements, section 704(b) applies, and requires that it be taxed as a trust for 1923, 1924 and 1925.

IV.

This Trust Can Be Distinguished on the Facts From Trusts 5833 and 123-B N. S., Heretofore Considered by This Court.

The appellants submit that the activities, during the taxable years involved, really govern its status for tax purposes. Looking at the taxable years involved in this case then, we find joint tenancy trustee holding contracts receivable, collecting installments due under the contracts, and distributing the proceeds to seven beneficiaries who neither had nor exercised any control over the fundamental affairs of the trust. During the taxable years involved the trustees did not own land, did not sell any land, did not subdivide, or otherwise improve any real property. They had no employees, no agents; they did not retain any of the capital of the trust. The trust had no office, place of business, seal, stationery, officers, or official name.

During the taxable years, therefore, this trust differed greatly from Trusts 5833 and 123-B N. S., heretofore considered by this Honorable Court in the cases of Trust 5833, *Security First National Bank v. Welch,* 54 F. (2) 323, and *Merchants Trust Co. v. Welch,* June 13, 1932. This court is so familiar with the activities of those trusts that it would be a waste of time to analyze their activities in this brief.

Assuming, without conceding, that the entire history of the trust should be considered in determining its taxable status for 1923, 1924 and 1925, the facts are so different in this case and the real estate trust cases heretofore decided by this court as to render the decisions therein inapplicable.

In Trusts 5833 and 123-B N. S., a bank, with a full staff of accountants, attorneys and trust officers, was appointed as executive agent or officer to carry out the multitudinous affairs of the trust. The trusts in those cases used the existing personnel of the trust company in place of organizing a corporation and assembling a large staff of office workers. They were, in effect, great business organizations actually conducting business, through the staffs of the trust companies, on a large scale. The cost and sales prices of lots in the two cases mentioned were many times greater than in the case at bar. A large group of persons, 30 to 40, invested in the certificates of beneficial interests in the other two cases, while only six beneficiaries originally participated in Dominguez Harbor Tract No. 2.

Trusts 5833 and 123-B N. S. used the form and mode of corporations to a considerable extent, while such form was entirely lacking in Dominguez Harbor Tract No. 2. In Trust 5833 there was a board of five syndicate managers who conducted the affairs of the trust in a manner similar to the board of directors of a corporation. In Trust 123-B N. S. the beneficiaries delegated their authority to a single agent, which fact this Honorable Court decided did not distinguish it from the board of managers of Trust 5833.

As to Dominguez Harbor Tract No. 2, two individuals were appointed trustees in joint tenancy with right of survivorship, and *were given authority to exercise full control and management of said property.* There was no board of syndicate managers, nor any beneficiary who had power or authority delegated to him by the other beneficiaries to give instructions to the trustees.

In Trusts 5833 and 123-B N. S., real property was held during the taxable years and portions thereof were sold in those years. Numerous transfers of beneficial interests were made; huge sums of money were collected and disbursed; and various activities carried on, including the continuous attempt to sell the property throughout the taxable year.

In Dominguez Harbor Tract No. 2, during the taxable years involved, the trustees were merely holding the contracts receivable for the purpose of liquidating them. They were merely receiving moneys paid in under the contracts and disbursing the proceeds to the beneficiaries. While Trusts 5833 and 123-B N. S. were engaging, in the taxable year involved, in the operation of a business, holding, subdividing and selling real estate, Dominguez Harbor Tract No. 2 was merely holding contracts for the purpose of collecting payments thereon and distributing them to the beneficiaries.

While Trusts 5833 and 123-B had quasi-corporate forms, were engaged in the taxable years in doing business, and the beneficiaries had control of the affairs of the trusts in the Dominguez Harbor Tract No. 2, there were no corporate forms, the trustees were not engaging in business in the taxable years, and the beneficiaries had no control.

The cases, therefore, were entirely different and distinguishable.

SUMMARY.

Appellants respectfully request this Honorable Court to find:

(1) That Dominguez Harbor Tract No. 2 was a passive trust not engaged in business, but merely. holding contracts for the collection and distribution of the proceeds.

(2) That the trust was not, during the taxable years, engaged in business; that it used no corporate forms and that its beneficiaries had no control over the fundamental policies of the trust.

(3) That since the beneficiaries did not control the affairs of the trust, it was taxable as a strict trust for 1923 under the provisions of section 704(a) of the Revenue Act of 1928.

(4) That the trust was taxable as such during the years involved, and not as an association, under the provisions of section 704(b) of the Revenue Act of 1928.

(5) The trust was, during the taxable years involved, passively holding contracts for liquidation and, therefore, distinguishable from the decisions of this court respecting Trusts 5833 and 123.

Dated: October 10, 1932.

MELVIN D. WILSON,
Counsel for Appellants.

INDEX

Page

Previous opinion _____ 1
Jurisdiction _____ 1
Question presented _____ 2
Statutes and regulations involved _____ 2
Statement of facts _____ 2
Summary of argument _____ 7
Argument:
    I. The respondent concedes error with respect to the taxable
       year 1923 _____ 9
    II. The Board of Tax Appeals properly held petitioners to
        be an association taxable as a corporation during the
        years 1924 and 1925 _____ 12
Conclusion _____ 20
Appendix _____ 21

CITATIONS

Cases:
    Bank of Commerce v. *Tennessee,* 161 U. S. 134 _____ 19
    Blair v. *Wilson Syndicate Trust,* 39 F. (2d) 43 _____ 15, 17
    Brewster v. *Gage,* 280 U. S. 327 _____ 13
    Burk-Waggoner Oil Assn. v. *Hopkins,* 269 U. S. 110 _____ 15
    Cornell v. *Coyne,* 192 U. S. 418 _____ 19
    Crocker v. *Malley,* 249 U. S. 223 _____ 10
    Edwards v. *Chile Copper Co.,* 270 U. S. 452 _____ 16
    Flint v. *Stone Tracy Co.,* 220 U. S. 107 _____ 16
    Harmar Coal Co. v. *Heiner,* 34 F. (2d) 725 _____ 15, 17
    Hecht v. *Malley,* 265 U. S. 144 _____ 7, 8, 10, 11, 12, 13, 15
    Heiner v. *Colonial Trust Co.,* 275 U. S. 232 _____ 13
    Hemphill v. *Orloff,* 277 U. S. 537 _____ 15
    Landreth Co., E. A., 15 B. T. A. 655 _____ 11
    Little Four Oil & Gas Co. v. *Lewellyn,* 35 F. (2d) 149 _____ 15
    McCaughn v. *Hershey Chocolate Co.,* 283 U. S. 488 _____ 13
    Merchants' Trust Co. v. *Welch,* 59 F. (2d) 630 _____ 9, 16
    National Lead Co. v. *United States,* 252 U. S. 140 _____ 13
    Riverdale Co.-op. Creamery Ass'n. v. *Commissioner,* 48 F. (2d)
      711 _____ 19
    Trust No. 5833, Security-First Nat. Bank v. *Welch,* 54 F. (2d)
      323 _____ 9, 16, 17
    Van Cleave Trust, 18 B. T. A. 486 _____ 11
    Willis v. *Commissioner,* 58 F. (2d) 121 _____ 9, 18, 19
    Woodrow Lee Trust, 17 B. T. A. 109 _____ 11

Statutes: **Page**

Revenue Act of 1921, c. 136, 42 Stat. 227—

    Sec. 2 _____ 21

    Sec. 1303 _____ 9

Revenue Act of 1924, c. 234, 43 Stat. 253—

    Sec. 2 _____ 21

    Sec. 1001 _____ 9

Revenue Act of 1926, c. 27, 44 Stat. 9—

    Sec. 2 _____ 21

    Sec. 1101 _____ 9

Revenue Act of 1928, c. 852, 45 Stat. 791, Sec. 704 ___ 7, 8, 10, 21

Miscellaneous:

    Corporation Tax Act of 1909 _____ 16

    G. C. M. 6417, III–1 C. B. 152 _____ 10

    H. R. 1882, 70th Cong., 1st Sess., p. 24 _____ 11

    S. R. 960, 70th Cong., 1st Sess., p. 40 _____ 11

    T. D. 3595, VIII–1 C. B. 489 _____ 10

    T. D. 3748, IV–2 C. B. 7 _____ 12

    Treasury Regulations 62—

        Art. 1502 _____ 9, 22

        Art. 1504 _____ 10, 11, 23

    Treasury Regulations 65—

        Art. 1502 _____ 13, 23

        Art. 1504 _____ 8, 12, 13, 23

    Treasury Regulations 69—

        Art. 1502 _____ 13, 24

        Art. 1504 _____ 13, 24

    Treasury Regulations 74—

        Art. 1312 _____ 13

        Art. 1314 _____ 13

In the United States Circuit Court of Appeals for the Ninth Circuit

No. 6808

G. F. SLOAN, J. E. ADAMS, C. O. MIDDLETON, J. A. Anderson, L. H. Barnhart, and J. H. Miller, petitioners

v.

COMMISSIONER OF INTERNAL REVENUE, RESPONDENT

ON PETITION FOR REVIEW OF DECISION OF THE UNITED STATES BOARD OF TAX APPEALS

BRIEF FOR RESPONDENT

PREVIOUS OPINION

The only previous opinion is that of the United States Board of Tax Appeals (R. 137), which is reported in 24 B. T. A. 61.

JURISDICTION

The petition for review in the above case involves deficiencies in income taxes asserted against the petitioners as transferees of the Dominguez Harbor Tract No. 2 for the years 1923, 1924, and 1925 in the amounts of $1,045.58, $703.63, and $279.83, respectively, and is taken from decisions (orders of redetermination) of the United States Board of Tax Appeals entered against the separate petitioners on September 21, 1931. (R. 146-151.) The several proceedings were consolidated for hearing and determination before the Board of Tax Appeals (R. 138), and the case is brought before this Court by a single petition for review filed March 5, 1932 (R. 157-161), pursuant to the provisions of the Revenue Act of 1926, c. 27, 44 Stat. 9, 109, 110, Sections 1001, 1002, and 1003.

QUESTION PRESENTED

Whether the so-called Dominguez Harbor Tract No. 2 was an association taxable as a corporation for the calendar years 1923, 1924, and 1925, as determined by the respondent and held by the Board of Tax Appeals, or a strict trust, as contended by petitioners. (Error is confessed on behalf of the respondent with reference to the year 1923.)

STATUTES AND REGULATIONS INVOLVED

The statutes and regulations involved will be found in the Appendix annexed to this brief, pp. 21-25.

STATEMENT OF FACTS

The findings of fact made by the Board of Tax Appeals are not disputed and may be abridged for present purposes as follows (R. 138-143):

The several petitioners are individuals residing in or near the city of Los Angeles, California.

Prior to 1907 certain real-estate operators had subdivided a parcel of land containing 108 acres situated between Long Beach and Wilmington, California, and known as the Dominguez Tract, and had sold a few lots. In the panic of 1907 the subdividers failed and the property reverted to the mortgage holders, the Henry Matson Estate. A representative of such estate later asked petitioner, C. O. Middleton, to take over the property for the purpose of liquidation.

In 1912 Middleton made a nominal payment, and in 1913, after inviting several others to join him in the matter, he took title to the property in the name of Charles O. Middleton and J. E. Adams as joint tenants and as Trustees for all the parties interested in the acquisition and disposition thereof, and on September 1, 1913, Middleton and Adams executed the following Declaration of Trust:

THIS INDENTURE made this first day of September, A. D. 1913, WITNESSETH: That CHARLES O. MIDDLETON and J. E. ADAMS, of Los Angeles, California, being designated the "Trustees," have and hold the legal title in fee simple in joint tenancy with right of survivorship to the following-described real estate situated in the County of Los Angeles, State of California, to wit:

(Description.)

"Subject to an existing incumbrance in the amount of $139,345.00."

That the said real estate is held by said trustees in trust for the beneficaries hereinafter named, their lawful assigns and legal representatives according to their respective interests, for the following uses and purposes with the following powers in said trustees, to wit:

To sell the whole or any part of said real estate and to that end to lay out and subdivide said lands or any part thereof; to pay commissions for the sale of said lands; to improve the same and to execute conveyances for said land or any part thereof; also to mortgage or lease said real estate or any part thereof; and to receive the rents and profits of said real estate and, as incidental to said powers, to prosecute and defend all actions at law or in equity relating to said property or any thereof; to collect moneys owing upon any sale or sales thereof and to satisfy judgments and claims relating thereto and to otherwise exercise full control and management of said property. When said property shall have been sold, to divide the proceeds of the sales thereof after deducting all necessary expenses, among the several beneficiaries or their lawful assigns or legal representatives according to their respective interests.

The said beneficiaries and their assigns and legal representatives shall not have or hold any title to said land or any part thereof and shall not be authorized to maintain any suit for partition thereof or to annul or terminate this trust, except as herein provided.

The beneficial interest in said property shall be divided into One Thousand shares

among the following named beneficiaries
with the following number of respective
shares to each:

    P. H. O'Neil, One Hundred Shares.

    J. E. Adams & J. H. Miller, joint tenants
    with right of survivorship, Three
    Hundred Shares.

    J. A. Anderson, One Hundred Shares.

    Charles O. Middleton, Two Hundred
    Fifty Shares.

    G. F. Sloan, One Hundred Fifty
    Shares.

    Alisal Ranch Company, One Hundred
    Shares.

A separate certificate shall be issued to
each benficiary for his number of shares and
upon surrender thereof such certificate may
be divided and separate certificates issued
for such shares to those entitled thereto.

In case of death, removal, or inability to
act of either of said trustees, the survivor
shall fill such vacancy by proper conveyance.

Certificates of trust issued under this instrument may be transformed [transferred]
by assignment and delivery.

Three-fourths of the beneficiaries in interest may by an instrument in writing, remove any trustee under this instrument and
appoint another in his stead and may require such trust property to be conveyed to
such surviving Trustee and new Trustee in
joint tenancy by proper conveyances and in
case of the death or inability of both said
Trustees, may fill such vacancies. Three-
fourths in interest of said beneficiaries may

likewise terminate this trust at any time and partition said property by their own act or by judicial proceedings for partition, but in any event this trust shall cease and determine upon the decease of all the natural persons in being named in this instrument.

The Trustee shall be empowered at any time prior to the determination of this trust whenever in their judgment it may be expedient and proper to declare dividends of money among the respective beneficiaries derived from sales of real estate.

WITNESS our hands and seals.

CHARLES O. MIDDLETON. [SEAL.]

J. E. ADAMS. [SEAL.]

Certificates of beneficial interest were issued in conformity with the trust instrument. Two of such certificates were assigned to other parties and such assignments were recognized by the Trustees.

On November 25, 1914, Middleton resigned as Trustee and Adams appointed P. H. O'Neil as his successor. On February 15, 1915, O'Neil resigned and Adams appointed G. F. Sloan as his successor.

On February 29, 1924, March 9, 1925, and March 15, 1926, respectively, the Trustees filed fiduciary returns for the years 1923, 1924, and 1925. On March 15, 1929, the Trustees executed and caused to be filed with the Collector of Internal Revenue at Los Angeles and with the Revenue Agent in Charge at the same city, an election to be taxed for the years 1923, 1924, and 1925 as a trust under the provisions of Section 704 (b) of the Revenue Act of 1928.

The Trustees never acquired any land in addition to the lots taken over in 1913 and through agents sold all such lots prior to 1923. Throughout the taxable years they sold no lots and their activities were limited to collecting installment payments on sales contracts previously made, paying expenses, executing deeds for lots covered by paid-up contracts, and distributing proceeds of collections to the beneficiaries. None of the receipts from sales was reinvested or retained as working capital.

The beneficiaries never held a meeting, removed or appointed a Trustee, terminated the trust, or petitioned the law [partitioned the land].

Upon the basis of these facts the Board of Tax Appeals held the organization to be an association taxable as a corporation, and confirmed the deficiencies asserted by the respondent. (R. 143–145.)

SUMMARY OF ARGUMENT

The decision of the Supreme Court in *Hecht* v. *Malley,* 265 U. S. 144, marked the adoption of a standard for determining the taxable status of trusts not theretofore recognized. The treasury regulations and administrative rulings, in conformity with the principles thus announced, rejected the criterion of beneficiary control in favor of that of organization of trustees in quasi-corporate form for the conduct of a business enterprise. In order to relieve taxpayers from the hardships entailed by a retrospective application of the principles of *Hecht* v. *Malley,* the Congress enacted Section 704 (a) of the Revenue Act of 1928, which retroactively enables a given taxpayer who has filed a trust return for a year prior to 1926 to secure the benefit of the prevailing treasury practice at the time the return was filed or the trust dissolved. For administrative purposes August 11, 1924, has been recognized as the effective date of *Hecht* v. *Malley.* The respondent concedes error with respect to the deficiencies asserted for 1923.

Treasury regulations having the force and effect of law govern in determining the status of taxpayers either as pure trusts or as associations taxable as corporations where return was made subsequent to August 11, 1924. In the present case the organization was markedly quasi corporate in form, with concentration of management, transferable certificates of interest, and discretion in the trustees to determine the amount of distributions. The trustees were "associated together in much the same manner as directors in a corporation." (Treasury Regulations 65, Art. 1504.) Furthermore, the organization was for the purpose of carrying on a business enterprise for profit, and was in fact so engaged for a period of more than ten years. It was not a mere trust for conservation or liquidation of property already owned by the beneficiaries. The facts clearly bring the case within

the principles announced and applied by this Court
in *Trust No. 5833, Security-First Nat. Bank* v.
Welch, 54 F. (2d) 323, certiorari denied, 286 U. S.
544; *Merchants' Trust Co.* v. *Welch,* 59 F. (2d) 630;
and *Willis* v. *Commissioner,* 58 F. (2d) 121.

ARGUMENT

I

The respondent concedes error with respect to the taxable year 1923

The single question presented to this Court for
review is whether the so-called Dominguez Harbor
Tract No. 2 was an association taxable as a corporation for the years 1923, 1924, and 1925, as determined by the Commissioner and held by the
Board of Tax Appeals, or a strict trust, as contended by the petitioners. It will be necessary to
treat the taxable year 1923 separately.

The term "corporation" is defined by Section 2
of the Revenue Acts of 1921, 1924, and 1926, *infra,*
to include associations. The term "association"
is not defined in any of the revenue laws. It has
been defined in the regulations promulgated by the
Commissioner from time to time, pursuant to
statutory authority.[1] Article 1502 of Treasury
Regulations 62, *infra,* promulgated under the Revenue Act of 1921, defines "association" to include
"common-law trusts * * * which act or do

---

[1] Such authority is expressly given by Section 1303, Revenue Act of 1921; Section 1001, Revenue Act of 1924; Section
1101, Revenue Act of 1926.

business in an organized capacity." Article 1504 of the cited regulation, *infra,* distinguishes "association" from "trust." While it is not as clearly drawn as might be desired, it purports to make the presence or absence of control by the beneficiaries the standard for determining whether an organization is a trust or an association within the meaning of the statute.

The entire administrative viewpoint was changed by the decision of the Supreme Court in *Hecht* v. *Malley,* 265 U. S. 144. Theretofore the Treasury Department, in reliance upon the earlier decision in *Crocker* v. *Malley,* 249 U. S. 223, had ruled that control by the beneficiaries was essential in order that a trust should be classified as an association. In *Hecht* v. *Malley, supra,* the Supreme Court departed from the earlier criterion of beneficiary control, holding that a trust is to be treated as an association irrespective of such control where organized in corporate form for the conduct of a business enterprise. The decision in *Hecht* v. *Malley,* was adopted and published as T. D. 3595, III–1 C. B. 489, on August 11, 1924, and the Treasury Department has adopted that date [2] as marking the change from the prior practice based upon the existence of beneficiary control to the new rule made necessary by the more recent decision of the Supreme Court.

Section 704 (a) of the Revenue Act of 1928, *infra,* was designed to afford retroactive relief to

---

[2] G. C. M. 6417, VIII–1 C. B. 152.

taxpayers from the consequences of a retrospective application of the principles of *Hecht* v. *Malley, supra,* which would have subjected them to tax as associations, although they would have been taxable as trusts under the administrative rulings in effect at the time the return was filed or the trust was dissolved. This clearly appears by reference to the legislative history of the statute.[3] The language of the act is broad and relief is extended in respect of any taxpayer who filed a return as a trust for a taxable year prior to 1925 who would have been considered (by the Treasury Department) taxable as a trust under regulations in force and under any applicable ruling of the Bureau effective when the return was filed.

The return for 1923 was filed on February 29, 1924. (R. 142–143.) Whatever question may exist as to the proper interpretation of Article 1504 of Treasury Regulations 62, we concede that under applicable Treasury rulings in effect when the return was filed the petitioners were taxable as a trust and not as an association.[4] On behalf of the respondent error is therefore confessed in so far as the Board of Tax Appeals held the petitioners taxable as an association for the year 1923.

[3] S. R. 960, 70th Cong., 1st Sess., pp. 40–45; H. R. 1882, 70th Cong., 1st Sess., p. 24.

[4] Many of the cognate rulings are set forth and discussed in the opinion of the Board of Tax Appeals in *Woodrow Lee Trust,* 17 B. T. A. 109. See also *E. A. Landreth Co.,* 15 B. T. A. 655, and *Van Cleave Trust,* 18 B. T. A. 486, cited by petitioners. (Br. 16–18.)

II

**The Board of Tax Appeals properly held petitioners to
be an association taxable as a corporation during the
years 1924 and 1925**

A very different situation is presented with respect to the taxable years 1924 and 1925. The return for the year 1924 was filed on March 9, 1925.
By that time the views of the Treasury Department
had crystallized along the line of the principles announced in *Hecht* v. *Malley, supra.* Article 1504
of Treasury Regulations 65, *infra,* promulgated under the Revenue Act of 1924, provided that—

> Operating trusts, whether or not of the Mas-
> sachusetts type, in which the trustees are not
> restricted to the mere collection of funds and
> their payment to the beneficiaries, but are
> associated together in much the same man-
> ner as directors in a corporation for the pur-
> pose of carrying on some business enterprise,
> are to be deemed associations within the
> meaning of the Act, regardless of the control
> exercised by the beneficiaries.

On August 31, 1925, the article above quoted was
amended and amplified by T. D. 3748,[5] providing—

> Even in the absence of any control by the
> beneficiaries, where the trustees are not re-
> stricted to the mere collection of funds and
> their payment to the beneficiaries, but are
> associated together with similar or greater
> powers than the directors in a corporation

---

[5] IV-2 C. B. 7.

for the purpose of carrying on some business enterprise, the trust is an association within the meaning of the statute.

The matter above quoted was incorporated as a part of Article 1504, Treasury Regulations 69, *infra,* under the Revenue Act of 1926.

The Treasury regulations have been carried over in substantially unchanged form since 1924.[6] During this period the Congress has thrice reenacted without change the provisions of the revenue act upon which the Treasury regulations were based. The regulations are therefore to be accorded the force and effect of law. *National Lead Co.* v. *United States,* 252 U. S. 140, 146; *Heiner* v. *Colonial Trust Co.,* 275 U. S. 232, 235; *Brewster* v. *Gage,* 280 U. S. 327, 337; *McCaughn* v. *Hershey Chocolate Co.,* 283 U. S. 488, 492–493.

With respect to the tax years 1924 and 1925 we are to determine, then, whether the trustees were "associated together in much the same manner as directors in a corporation for the purpose of carrying on some business enterprise."[7]

---

[6] Compare Treasury Regulations 65, Articles 1502 and 1504; Treasury Regulations 69, Articles 1502 and 1504; Treasury Regulations 74, Articles 1312 and 1314, promulgated under the Revenue Act of 1928.

[7] The Supreme Court, in *Hecht* v. *Malley, supra,* adopted the following definition of " association " (p. 157):

" * * * a term ' used throughout the United States to signify a body of persons united without a charter, but upon the methods and forms used by incorporated bodies for the prosecution of some common enterprise.' "

14

The trustees were vested with legal title to the Dominguez Harbor lands for purposes of subdivision and ultimate sale. (R. 139.) They were empowered to pay commissions, improve the land, and execute conveyances. They were also empowered to mortgage or lease the land, to receive rentals, profits, and payments of purchase price, to prosecute and defend all legal proceedings and "to otherwise exercise full control and management of said property." After sale they were authorized to pay expenses and make distribution to the *cestuis que trustent* upon the basis of their beneficial interest. (R. 140.) The beneficial interest was divided into 1,000 shares and separate transferable certificates were issued to the six beneficiaries, with the privilege of reissuing certificates in smaller denominations. In case of death, removal, or inability to act the surviving trustee could fill the vacancy so occurring. (R. 141.) The trustees had discretionary power in the declaration of dividends. (R. 142.)

The entire organization and management of the business was in all respects confided to the trustees. The sole powers reserved to the beneficiaries were those of removal and replacement of a trustee by action of three-fourths of their number in interest and the termination of the trust by similar action. It is clear that the trustees in the instant case were "associated together in much the same manner as directors in a corporation." The

organization was markedly quasi-corporate in
form, with concentration of management, trans-
ferable certificates and discretion in the trustees
to determine the amount of distributions. See
Hecht v. *Malley, supra,* pp. 157, 161; *Little Four
Oil & Gas Co.* v. *Lewellyn,* 35 F. (2d) 149, 151
(C. C. A. 3d), certiorari denied, 280 U. S. 613.
Cf. *Hemphill* v. *Orloff,* 277 U. S. 537, 550; *Burk-
Waggoner Oil Assn.* v. *Hopkins,* 269 U. S. 110,
114.

There remains for discussion the question
whether the trustees were associated together "for
the purpose of carrying on some business enterprise." We believe it to be clearly established that
in order to meet this test it is not necessary that
any great volume of business be conducted. In
Blair v. *Wilson Syndicate Trust,* 39 F. (2d) 43
(C. C. A. 5th), the court said (p. 45):

> * * * it may be considered settled, within
> the meaning of the taxing laws, that, if a
> corporation is doing that for which it was or-
> ganized, for the purpose of earning profit,
> very slight activity is sufficient to constitute
> the doing of business. * * *

Similarly, in *Harmar Coal Co.* v. *Heiner,* 34 F. (2d)
725 (C. C. A. 3d), certiorari denied, 280 U. S. 610,
the court said (p. 728):

> * * * a corporation, organized for a defi-
> nite though limited business purpose involv-
> ing profits, that pursues activities to carry

out that purpose, no matter how few or small they may be, is carrying on or doing business within the meaning of the statute. * * * These decisions conform to the rule announced by the Supreme Court in *Edwards* v. *Chile Copper Co.,* 270 U. S. 452, 455, and are believed to be in accord with the principles applied in the earlier cases arising under the Corporation Tax Act of 1909, of which *Flint* v. *Stone Tracy Co.,* 220 U. S. 107, is the prototype.

The trust in this case was organized for the purpose of subdividing real estate and selling lots for profit. It actually engaged in the subdivision, improvement, and sale of real estate in lots, doing everything necessary to that end which might have been done by a corporation organized for similar purposes. It is scarcely open to question that the trustees were associated for the purpose of carrying on a business enterprise.

Petitioners endeavor to distinguish the earlier decisions of this Court in *Trust No. 5833, Security-First Nat. Bank* v. *Welch,* 54 F. (2d) 323, certiorari denied, 286 U. S. 544; and *Merchants' Trust Co.* v. *Welch,* 59 F. (2d) 630. (Br. 21, *et seq.*)[8] The

---

[8] In this connection petitioners state that the trustees " had no employees, no agents; they did not retain any of the capital of the trust. The trust had no office, place of business, seal, stationery, officers, or official name." These statements are wholly gratuitous so far as the present record shows and have no proper place in the consideration of the case.

petitioners place emphasis, in this part of their argument, upon the size of the organization and volume of the business transacted. Such a standard we believe to be palpably unsound. (See discussion, *supra,* citing and quoting *Blair* v. *Wilson Syndicate Trust* and *Harmar Coal Co.* v. *Heiner.*)

· We believe our position in this case to be entirely consistent with the views of this Court in several decisions dealing with the same general question. In *Trust No. 5833, Security-First Nat. Bank* v. *Welch, supra,* this Court determined that a syndicate formed by a declaration of trust for the purpose of purchasing, subdividing, improving, and selling a large tract of land was engaged in doing business for profit and was properly an association taxable as a corporation under the Revenue Act of 1928. While it is true the venture was organized and conducted upon a larger and more elaborate scale than Dominguez Harbor Tract No. 2, there appears to be little difference in principle. Significantly, this Court in the *Security-First Nat. Bank case* quoted with approval from the opinion of the Board in the present case, which was characterized as concerning "a California subdivision real-estate syndicate similar to that involved" in the *Security-First Nat. Bank case. Merchants' Trust Co.* v. *Welch, supra,* presenting a similar fact situation, was decided upon the authority of *Security-First Nat. Bank* v. *Welch, supra.*

Willis v. *Commissioner*, 58 F. (2d) 121, is one of the most recent expressions of this Court in a similar case. There the trust property consisted of real estate received by devisees under a will who pooled their interests to form a trust in the absence of a suitable market to absorb the property at once. This Court stated the question as follows (p. 122):

> * * * did the trustees manage and operate the property in their charge as a business, with the purpose to accumulate a profit by the use of it, or was their sole purpose, intended and pursued, to dispose of it as rapidly as possible, market conditions considered, and divide the proceeds among the beneficiaries?

After an analysis of the conduct of the enterprise and the powers of the trustees the court concluded that the acts went beyond transactions carried on for the single purpose of effecting a liquidation of assets and that the organization was an association taxable as such. It is difficult to conceive of any other conclusion where an enterprise functions over a long period of years and contemplates improvements on real property, the execution of leases, mortgages, and all the usual steps toward realization of profit through the subdivision, development, and sale of land.

It is also suggested by the petitioners (Br. 16) that only the activities engaged in during the actual taxable years are significant. This proposi-

tion is believed clearly unsound. The fundamental
test in this respect is the purpose for which the
individuals are associated, and it is unthinkable
that when an organization is created for the purpose of conducting a business for profit along corporate lines and in fact enters upon the conduct
of such business, its status as a trust or an association may change, chameleonlike, from year to year,
responsive to the periodic variation in sales or
receipts. No sales of land were made during 1925,
the second of the taxable years involved in the
Willis case, supra (p. 122).

No extended reply seems necessary to so much
of the petitioners' argument (Br. 19–20) as is devoted to an effort to show that the two trustees were
in fact one trustee for the purpose of bringing the
case within the purview of Section 704 (b) of the
Revenue Act of 1928. Trust property is frequently held by trustees in joint tenancy, and if
the petitioners are correct twenty trustees could be
counted as one quite as readily as two could be so
treated. The law is subject to no such reproach.
The taxpayer who seeks classification in a privi-
leged group must bring himself within the fair in-
tendment of the statute. *Bank of Commerce* v.
Tennessee, 161 U. S. 134, 146; *Cornell* v. *Coyne,* 192
U. S. 418; *Riverdale Co-op. Creamery Ass'n.* v.
Commissioner, 48 F. (2d) 711 (C. C. A. 9th).

CONCLUSION

For the foregoing reasons it is respectfully submitted that the decision of the United States Board of Tax Appeals should be affirmed in so far as relates to the deficiencies asserted for the taxable years 1924 and 1925.

G. A. YOUNGQUIST,
Assistant Attorney General.
SEWALL KEY,
WM. CUTLER THOMPSON,
Special Assistants to the Attorney General.

NOVEMBER, 1932.

APPENDIX

Revenue Act of 1921, c. 136, 42 Stat. 227:

SEC. 2. That when used in this Act—

* * * * *

(2) The term "corporation" includes associations, joint-stock companies, and insurance companies;

(This provision is repeated in identical terms in like numbered sections of the Revenue Acts of 1924, c. 234, 43 Stat. 253, and 1926, c. 27, 44 Stat. 9.)

Revenue Act of 1928, c. 852, 45 Stat. 791:

SEC. 704. TAXABILITY OF TRUSTS AS CORPORATIONS—RETROACTIVE.

(a) If a taxpayer filed a return as a trust for any taxable year prior to the taxable year 1925, such taxpayer shall be taxable as a trust for such year and not as a corporation, if such taxpayer was considered to be taxable as a trust and not as a corporation either (1) under the regulations in force at the time the return was made or at the time of the termination of its existence, or (2) under any ruling of the Commissioner or any duly authorized officer of the Bureau of Internal Revenue applicable to any of such years and interpretative of any provision of the Revenue Acts of 1918, 1921, or 1924, which had not been reversed or revoked prior to the time the return was made, or any such ruling made after the return was filed which had not been reversed or revoked prior to the time of the termination of the taxpayer's existence.

(b) For the purpose of the Revenue Act of 1926 and prior Revenue Acts, a trust shall, at the option of the trustee exercised within one year after the enactment of this Act, be considered as a trust the income of which is taxable (whether distributed or not) to the beneficiaries, and not as an association, if such trust (1) had a single trustee, and (2) was created and operated for the sole purpose of liquidating real property as a single venture (with such powers of administration as are incidental thereto, including the acquisition, improvement, conservation, division, and sale of such property), distributing the proceeds therefrom in due course to or for the benefit of the beneficiaries, and discharging indebtedness secured by the trust property, and (3) has not made a return for the taxable year as an association.

Treasury Regulations 62:

ART. 1502. *Association.*—Associations and joint-stock companies include associations, common-law trusts, and organizations by whatever name known, which act or do business in an organized capacity, whether created under and pursuant to State laws, agreements, declarations of trust, or otherwise, the net income of which, if any, is distributed or distributable among the members or shareholders on the basis of the capital stock which each holds or, where there is no capital stock, on the basis of the proportionate share or capital which each has or has invested in the business or property of the organization. A corporation which has ceased to exist in contemplation of law but continues its business in corporate form is an association or corporation within the meaning of section 2, but if it continues its business in the form of a trust, it becomes subject to the provisions of section 219.

ART. 1504. *Association distinguished from trust.*—Where trustees hold real estate subject to a lease and collect the rents, doing no business other than distributing the income less taxes and similar expenses to the holders of their receipt certificates, who have no control except the right of filling a vacancy among the trustees and of consenting to a modification of the terms of the trust, no association exists and the cestuis que trust are liable to tax as beneficiaries of a trust the income of which is to be distributed periodically, whether or not at regular intervals. But in such a trust if the trustees pursuant to the terms thereof have the right to hold the income for future distribution, the net income is taxed to the trustees instead of to the beneficiaries. See section 219 of the statute and articles 341–348. If, however, the cestuis que trust have a voice in the conduct of the business of the trust, whether through the right periodically to elect trustees or otherwise, the trust is an association within the meaning of the statute.

Treasury Regulations 65:
Article 1502 repeats the language of Article 1502, Treasury Regulations 62.

ART. 1504. *Association distinguished from trust.*—Holding trusts, in which the trustees are merely holding property for the collection of the income and its distribution among the beneficiaries, and are not engaged, either by themselves or in connection with the beneficiaries, in the carrying on of any business, are not associations within the meaning of the law. The trust and the beneficiaries thereof will be subject to tax as provided in articles 341–347. Operating trusts, whether or not of the Massachusetts type, in which the trustees are not restricted to the mere

collection of funds and their payments to
the beneficiaries, but are associated together
in much the same manner as directors in a
corporation for the purpose of carrying on
some business enterprise, are to be deemed
associations within the meaning of the Act,
regardless of the control exercised by the
beneficiaries.

Treasury Regulations 69:

ART. 1502. *Association.*—Associations and
joint-stock companies include associations,
common law trusts, and organizations by
whatever name known, which act or do business in an organized capacity, whether
created under and pursuant to State laws,
agreements, declarations of trust, or otherwise, the net income of which, if any, is distributed or distributable among the shareholders on the basis of the capital stock
which each holds, or, where there is no
capital stock, on the basis of the proportionate share or capital which each has or has
invested in the business or property of the
organization. A corporation which has
ceased to exist in contemplation of law but
continues its business in quasi-corporate
form is an association or corporation within
the meaning of section 2.

ART. 1504. *Association distinguished from
trust.*—Where trustees merely hold property
for the collection of the income and its distribution among the beneficiaries of the
trust, and are not engaged, either by themselves or in connection with the beneficiaries,
in the carrying on of any business, and the
beneficiaries have no control over the trust,
although their consent may be required for
the filling of a vacancy among the trustees
or for a modification of the terms of the
trust, no association exists, and the trust and

the beneficiaries thereof will be subject to
tax as provided by section 219 and by articles
341–347. If, however, the beneficiaries have
positive control over the trust, whether
through the right periodically to elect trustees or otherwise, an association exists
within the meaning of section 2. Even in
the absence of any control by the beneficiaries, where the trustees are not restricted to
the mere collection of funds and their payment to the beneficiaries but are associated
together with similar or greater powers than
the directors in a corporation for the purpose of carrying on some business enterprise, the trust is an association within the
meaning of the statute.

6811

In the United States Circuit Court of Appeals

FOR THE NINTH CIRCUIT

UNITED STATES OF AMERICA,
> Appellant,

vs.

CARROL TILLMAN McCREARY,
> Appellee.

Transcript of Record

Upon Appeal from the United States District Court for the District of Oregon

Names and Addresses of Attorneys of Record:

GEORGE NEUNER,
United States Attorney for the District of Oregon.

CHAS. W. ERSKINE,
Assistant United States Attorney
Federal Building, Portland, Ore.
> For Appellant.

C. G. SCHNEIDER,
ALLAN A. BYNON,
Portland, Oregon
> For Appellee.

FILED

APR 4 - 1932

In the United States Circuit Court of Appeals

FOR THE NINTH CIRCUIT

UNITED STATES OF AMERICA,

Appellant,

vs.

CARROL TILLMAN McCREARY,

Appellee.

Transcript of Record

Upon Appeal from the United States District Court
for the District of Oregon

Names and Addresses of Attorneys of Record:

GEORGE NEUNER,

United States Attorney for the District of Oregon.

CHAS. W. ERSKINE,

Assistant United States Attorney

Federal Building, Portland, Ore.
For Appellant.

C. G. SCHNEIDER,

ALLAN A. BYNON,

Portland, Oregon
For Appellee.

INDEX

Page

Answer 11

Assignments of Error 22

Bill of Exceptions 24

Citation on Appeal.. 5

Complaint 7

Judgment 16

Notice of Appeal 20

Order Allowing Appeal................................. 20

Petition for Order of Appeal....................... 18

Praecipe for Transcript of Record........... 157

Reply 14

Stipulation as to What Transcript of Record Shall
    Contain 156

Verdict 15

DISTRICT COURT OF THE UNITED STATES OF AMERICA, DISTRICT OF OREGON

To CARROL TILLMAN McCREARY, the above-named plaintiff, and C. G. SCHNEIDER and ALLAN A. BYNON, his attorneys, Greetings:

WHEREAS, the United States of America has lately appealed to the United States Circuit Court of Appeals for the Ninth Circuit from a judgment rendered in the District Court of the United States for the District of Oregon, in your favor, and has given the security required by law;

YOU ARE THEREFORE HEREBY CITED AND ADMONISHED to be and appear before said United States Circuit Court of Appeals for the Ninth Circuit, at San Francisco, California, within thirty days from the date hereof, to show cause, if any there be, why the said judgment should not be corrected, and speedy justice should not be done to the parties in that behalf.

Given under my hand, at Portland, in said District, this 28th day of December, in the year of our Lord, one thousand nine hundred and thirty-one.

JAMES ALGER FEE, Judge.

UNITED STATES OF AMERICA, ⎱
⎰ ss.
District of Oregon.

Due and legal service of the within CITATION
ON APPEAL is hereby admitted and accepted in the
State and District of Oregon, this 28th day of December, 1931, by receiving a copy thereof, duly
certified to be a true and correct copy of the original,
by Chas. W. Erskine, Assistant United States Attorney.

ALLAN A. BYNON, L. C.
Of Attorneys for Plaintiff.

Endorsed:
U. S. DISTRICT COURT
District of Oregon
Filed Dec. 28, 1931
G. H. Marsh, Clerk
By F. L. Buck, Chief Deputy

IN THE DISTRICT COURT OF THE UNITED
STATES FOR THE DISTRICT OF OREGON
July Term, 1930

BE IT REMEMBERED, That on the 17th day of
September, 1930, there was duly filed in the District
Court of the United States for the District of Ore-
gon, a

COMPLAINT
in words and figures as follows, to-wit:

IN THE DISTRICT COURT OF THE UNITED
STATES FOR THE DISTRICT OF OREGON

L11137

COMPLAINT

CARROL TILLMAN McCREARY,
                    Plaintiff,

vs.

UNITED STATES OF AMERICA,
                    Defendant.

Comes now the plaintiff and for cause of action against the defendant complains and alleges:

I.

Plaintiff is now a bona fide resident and inhabitant of the County of Multnomah, State of Oregon, and is a citizen of the United States of America.

II.

Heretofore, and upon the 20th day of February, 1918, plaintiff joined the Marine Corps of the United States of America, and thereafter served with said Marine Corps during the late World War and was transferred to inactive duty on the 19th day of August, 1919, and thereafter was honorably discharged from said service on or about the 19th day of September, 1922.

III.

During said service with said Marine Corps, plaintiff applied for and received a policy of War Risk Insurance from the United States of America in the sum of Ten Thousand Dollars ($10,000.00), by the

terms and conditions of which the defendant agreed
to pay the plaintiff, in case of permanent and total
disability, the sum of Fifty-seven and 50/100 Dollars
($57.50) per month during the continuation of said
condition of permanent total disability, all on the
condition that the plaintiff pay to the defendant premiums on said policy of insurance as provided by
law, and said premiums were duly paid by said plaintiff on said policy of insurance to and including the
date upon which plaintiff was transferred to inactive
service, as is hereinbefore set forth, and upon the
date of said transfer to inactive service, said policy
was in full force and effect and so continued for a
period of thirty-one days thereafter.

IV.

On or about June 1, 1918, plaintiff contracted the
mumps; thereafter, and on or about July 18, 1918,
plaintiff was shell shocked and became afflicted with
acute enteritis, dysentery and amoebiasis; thereafter,
and on or about August 24, 1918, plaintiff was
stricken with influenza, and thereafter developed
heart trouble, the exact nature of which was and is
unknown to plaintiff; thereafter, and on or about
November 9, 1918, plaintiff became afflicted again
with acute enteritis, dysentery and amoebiasis;
shortly thereafter plaintiff developed and suffered
from hyperchlorhydria and ulcers of the duodenum;
and shortly thereafter plaintiff developed and suf-

fered psychoneurosis, neurasthenia and severe headaches. Said disabilities persisted and grew worse
and by reason thereof plaintiff was, at the time of
his said transfer to inactive service, permanently and
totally disabled in that he was at that time, and has
been at all times subsequent thereto, is now, and will
ever be, unable to follow continuously any substantially gainful occupation. Said disabilities and said
conditions so existing at the date of plaintiff's said
transfer to inactive service were founded on conditions reasonably certain to prevail throughout his
lifetime.

V.

Prior to the filing of this action, plaintiff made
due proof to the defendant of his condition of permanent and total disability, but the defendant has
disagreed with the plaintiff as to his claim and has
disallowed his claim and now disagrees with the
plaintiff and a disagreement exists between said
plaintiff and said defendant by reason thereof.

WHEREFORE, plaintiff prays for judgment
against the defendant that he be adjudged to have
been permanently and totally disabled upon the date
of his transfer to inactive service, and for judgment
at the rate of Fifty-seven and 50/100 Dollars ($57.50)
per month from the said date of his transfer to inactive service, to-wit, August 19, 1919, to the date of

judgment, and for plaintiff's costs and disbursements
incurred herein.

C. L. SCHNEIDER
EMMONS, LUSK & BYNON
Attorneys for Plaintiff.

STATE OF OREGON, } ss.
County of Multnomah,

I, CARROL TILLMAN McCREARY, being first
duly sworn, depose and say that I am the plaintiff
in the above entitled action; and that the foregoing
Complaint is true, as I verily believe.

(Sgd.) CARROL TILLMAN McCREARY.

Subscribed and sworn to before me this 17th day
of Sept. 1930.

(Sgd.) ALLAN A. BYNON.
Notary Public for the State of Oregon.
My commission expires July 8, 1931.
(Notarial Seal)

STATE OF OREGON, } ss.
County of Multnomah.

Due, timely and legal service by copy admitted
at Portland, Oregon, this 17th day of Sept. 1930.

GEORGE NEUNER.
U. S. District Attorney.

Endorsed:

U. S. DISTRICT COURT

11

District of Oregon
Filed Sept. 17, 1930
G. H. Marsh, Clerk
By F. L. Buck, Chf. Deputy.

And Afterwards, to-wit, on the 12th day of February, 1931 there was duly Filed in said Court, an

ANSWER

in words and figures as follows, to-wit:

COMES NOW the United States of America, by George Neuner, United States Attorney for the District of Oregon, and Chas. W. Erskine, Assistant United States Attorney, and for its Answer to the Bill of Complaint of plaintiff herein admits, denies and alleges as follows:

I.

Alleges that the defendant herein has no information or knowledge sufficient to enable it to form a belief as to the truth or falsity of any of the allegations contained in Paragraph I of plaintiff's complaint, and, therefore, denies the same and puts the plaintiff on proof thereof.

II.

Admits the allegations of Paragraph II of plaintiff's complaint.

III.

Admits the allegations of Paragraph III of plaintiff's complaint.

IV.

Denies the allegations of Paragraph IV of plaintiff's complaint.

V.

Denies the allegations of Paragraph V of plaintiff's complaint, except it is admitted that a disagreement exists between plaintiff and defendant.

For a further and separate answer, defendant alleges:

That the plaintiff, effective July 1, 1927, was granted a reinstatement contract of insurance in the sum of $5,000 and that this reinstatement contract was on said date converted into a five-year convertible term insurance policy K-703573, on which premiums were paid during the month of October, 1930.

WHEREFORE, defendant having fully answered plaintiff's complaint, demands:

FIRST: That plaintiff take nothing thereby and that the defendant go hence without day and recover of and from the plaintiff its costs and disbursements herein.

SECOND: That if the plaintiff be found entitled to recover on the contract sued upon, that before judgment to him is entered he be required to surrender the reinstated and converted contract of insurance.

GEORGE NEUNER,
United States Attorney.
CHAS. W. ERSKINE,
Assistant United States Attorney.

STATE OF OREGON, ⎫
⎬ ss.
County of Multnomah, ⎭

I, Chas. W. Erskine, being first duly sworn, depose and say:

That I am a duly appointed, qualified and acting Assistant United States Attorney for the District of Oregon; that I am possessed of information concerning the above-named plaintiff, from which I have prepared the foregoing ANSWER; that I have prepared and read the foregoing Answer and that the allegations therein contained are true, as I verily believe.

CHAS. W. ERSKINE,
Assistant United States Attorney.

Subscribed and sworn to before me this 11th day of February, 1931.

FRANK L. BUCK,
Notary Public for Oregon.

My Commission Expires October 16, 1932.
(Seal)
Endorsed:
U. S. DISTRICT COURT
District of Oregon

Filed Feb. 12, 1931

G. H. Marsh, Clerk

By F. L. Buck, Chf. Deputy

And Afterwards, to-wit, on the 30th day of September, 1931 there was duly Filed in said Court, a

REPLY

in words and figures as follows, to-wit:

Come now the plaintiff and for his reply to the defendant's further and separate answer herein:

I.

DENIES each and every allegation therein contained, and the whole thereof.

WHEREFORE, having fully replied, plaintiff reiterates the prayer of his Complaint and demands judgment as therein prayed for.

> (Sgd.) C. G. SCHNEIDER,
> (Sgd.) ALLAN A. BYNON,
> Attorneys for Plaintiff.

STATE OF OREGON,   ⎫
                   ⎬ ss.
County of Multnomah, ⎭

I, CARROL TILLMAN McCREARY, being first duly sworn, depose and say that I am the plaintiff in the above entitled action; and that the within Reply is true, as I verily believe.

> (Sgd.) CARROL TILLMAN McCREARY.

Subscribed and sworn to before me this 26th day of September, 1931.

(Sgd.) ALLAN A. BYNON,
Notary Public for the State of Oregon.

My commission expires July 2, 1935.

(Notarial Seal)

Endorsed:

U. S. DISTRICT COURT

District of Oregon

Filed Sept. 30, 1931

G. H. Marsh, Clerk

And Afterwards, to-wit, on the 1st day of October, 1931, there was duly Filed in said Court, a

VERDICT

in words and figures as follows, to-wit:

We, the jury, duly impaneled and sworn to try the above entitled cause, do find in favor of the plaintiff and against the defendant, and find that the above named plaintiff was, on the 19 day of Sept., 1919, and ever since has been, totally and permanently disabled.

Dated at Portland, Oregon, this 1 day Oct., 1931.

HANS P. LARSEN,
Foreman.

Endorsed:

U. S. DISTRICT COURT

District of Oregon

Filed Oct. 1, 1931

G. H. Marsh, Clerk

And Afterwards, to-wit, on Thursday, the 1st day of October, 1931, the same being the 65th Judicial day of the Regular July Term of said Court; present the Honorable John H. McNary, United States District Judge, presiding, the following proceedings were had in said cause, to-wit:

JUDGMENT

This cause coming on for trial upon the 30th day of September, 1931, before the Honorable John H. McNary, Judge of the above entitled Court, plaintiff appearing in person and by his counsel, C. G. Schneider and Allan A. Bynon, the defendant, United States of America, appearing by its counsel, Charles W. Erskine and Metta G. Walker, a jury having been duly impaneled and sworn to try said cause, the opening statements of counsel having been made, witnesses having been sworn and heard, the closing arguments of respective counsel having been made, the jury, having been instructed by the Court, did, upon the 1st day of October, 1931, return its verdict that the plaintiff above named was, on the 19th day of September, 1919, and ever since has been, permanently and totally disabled;

NOW, THEREFORE, the Court, being advised in its premises, and according to said verdict, does enter its judgment; and

IT IS ORDERED AND ADJUDGED that Carrol Tillman McCreary became totally and permanently disabled upon the 19th day of September, 1919, and ever since said date has been and now is permanently and totally disabled, and judgment is entered herein in favor of the plaintiff, and against the defendant, United States of America, and that there is now due said Carrol Tillman McCreary upon said policy of War Risk Insurance carried by him which is referred to in the Complaint herein, the accrued payments of Fifty-seven and 50/100 Dollars ($57.50) per month from the 19th day of September, 1919, until this date; and

IT IS FURTHER ORDERED AND ADJUDGED that a certain reinstated and converted policy, known as a Five-Year Convertible Term Insurance Policy, numbered K-703573, issued on July 1, 1927, on the life of plaintiff, in the amount of Five Thousand Dollars ($5,000.00), which said policy was duly and regularly surrendered and tendered into Court contemporaneously with the return of the verdict made, entered and filed herein, be and the same is hereby declared to be surrendered, cancelled, set aside and held for naught; and

IT IS FURTHER ORDERED AND ADJUDGED that there be and hereby is allowed to said plaintiff's attorneys, C. G. Schneider and Allan A. Bynon, as a reasonable attorneys' fee herein, ten per centum of the amount recovered by the plaintiff herein, that is to say, ten per centum of each payment the plaintiff shall hereunder and hereafter collect from such insurance, to be paid to said C. G. Schneider and Allan A. Bynon by the Veterans' Bureau of the United States out of the payments to be made under this judgment at the rate of one-tenth of each of such payments;

AND IT IS SO ORDERED.

Dated this 1st day of October, 1931.

(Sgd.)   JOHN H. McNARY,

Judge.

Endorsed:

U. S. DISTRICT COURT

District of Oregon

Filed Oct. 1, 1931

G. H. Marsh, Clerk

And Afterwards, to-wit, on the 28th day of December, 1931 there was duly Filed in said Court, a

PETITION FOR ORDER OF APPEAL

in words and figures as follows, to-wit:

The above-named defendant, United States of America, conceiving itself aggrieved by the judgment flied and entered on the 1st day of October, 1931, in the above-entitled action, does hereby appeal from said judgment, and the whole thereof, to the United States Circuit Court of Appeals for the Ninth Judicial Circuit, for the reasons and upon the grounds specified in the Assignments of Error filed herewith, and prays that this, its appeal, be allowed; that a citation issue as provided by law, and that a transcript of the record and proceedings of said cause, duly authenticated, may be sent to the United States Circuit Court of Appeals for the Ninth Judicial Circuit, sitting at San Francisco, California.

Dated at Portland, Oregon, this 28th day of December, 1931.

> GEORGE NEUNER,
> United States Attorney for the
> District of Oregon
> CHAS. W. ERSKINE,
> Assistant United States Attorney.

Endorsed:
U. S. DISTRICT COURT
District of Oregon
Filed Dec. 28, 1931
G. H. Marsh, Clerk
By F. L. Buck, Chief Deputy

And Afterwards, to-wit, on Monday, the 28th day of December, 1931, the same being the 43rd Judicial day of the Regular November Term of said Court; present the Honorable James Alger Fee, United States District Judge, presiding, the following proceedings were had in said cause, to-wit:

ORDER ALLOWING APPEAL

Upon petition of the United States of America, defendant in the above-entitled cause,

IT IS ORDERED that the appeal of said defendant from the judgment herein to the United States Circuit Court of Appeals for the Ninth Circuit be, and the same is hereby, allowed.

Dated at Portland, Oregon, this 28th day of December, 1931.

JAMES ALGER FEE,
Judge.

Endorsed:

U. S. DISTRICT COURT
District of Oregon
Filed Dec. 28, 1931
G. H. Marsh, Clerk
By F. L. Buck, Chf. Deputy

And Afterwards, to-wit, on the 28th day of December, 1931, there was duly Filed in said Court, a

NOTICE OF APPEAL

in words and figures as follows, to-wit:

To the above-named plaintiff, CARROL TILLMAN McCREARY, and his attorneys, C. G. SCHNEIDER and ALLAN A. BYNON:

You, and each of you, will take notice that the defendant, United States of America, appeals to the

United States Circuit Court of Appeals for the Ninth Circuit from that certain judgment and decree made and entered in the above-entitled cause and court and signed by the Honorable John H. McNary, one of the judges of said District, on the 1st day of October, 1931, which judgment and decree was and is to the effect that the plaintiff, Carrol Tillman Mc-Creary, became totally and permanently disabled upon the 19th day of September, 1919, and ever since said date has been and now is permanently and totally disabled and that judgment be entered in favor of the plaintiff, Carrol Tillman McCreary, and against the defendant, United States of America, and that there is now due said Carrol Tillman McCreary upon the policy of war risk insurance carried by him the accrued payments of Fifty-seven and 50/100 ($57.50) Dollars per month from the 19th day of September, 1919, and which judgment and decree

was and is to the further effect that a certian reinstated and converted policy, known as a Five-Year Convertible Term Insurance Policy, numbered K-703573, issued on July 1, 1927, on the life of the plaintiff, in the amount of Five Thousand Dollars ($5,000.00), which said policy was duly and regularly surrendered and tendered into court contemporaneously with the return of the verdict made, entered and filed herein be declared to be surrendered, cancelled, set aside and held for naught, and the defendant appeals from the whole of said judgment and decree.

Dated this 28th day of December, 1931.

> GEORGE NEUNER,
> United States Attorney for the
> District of Oregon
> CHAS. W. ERSKINE,
> Assistant United States Attorney

Endorsed:

U. S. DISTRICT COURT

District of Oregon

Filed Dec. 28, 1931

G. H. Marsh, Clerk

By F. L. Buck, Chief Deputy

And Afterwards, to-wit, on the 28th day of December, 1931 there was duly Filed in said Court,

ASSIGNMENTS OF ERROR

in words and figures as follows, to-wit:

The United States of America, being the defendant in the above-entitled cause, and appearing by George Neuner, United States Attorney for the District of Oregon, and Chas. W. Erskine, Assistant United States Attorney, and having filed a notice of appeal, as required by law, that the defendant appeals to the United States Circuit Court of Appeals for the Ninth Circuit from the final order and judgment made and entered in said cause against said defendant herein, now makes and files in support of said appeal the following assignments of error, upon which it will rely for a reversal of said final order and judgment upon the said appeal, and which said error is to the great detriment, injury and prejudice of this defendant, and said defendant says that in the records and proceedings upon the hearings and determination thereof in the District Court of the United States for the District of Oregon, there is manifest error, in this, to-wit:

I.

That the court erred in overruling the motion of the defendant for a directed verdict, for the reason that the evidence adduced at the trial of the above-entitled cause was insufficient to justify a verdict for the plaintiff.

II.

That the court erred in overruling the motion of the defendant for a directed verdict, for the reason that the evidence adduced at the trial of the above-entitled cause establishes the fact that plaintiff was not permanently and totally disabled on or before the 19th day of September, 1919.

WHEREFORE, on account of the errors above assigned, defendant prays that the judgment of this Court be reversed and that this case be remanded to said District Court and that such directions be given that the above errors may be corrected and the law and justice be done in the matter.

Dated at Portland, Oregon, this 28th day of December, 1931.

GEORGE NEUNER,
United States Attorney for the
District of Oregon
CHAS. W. ERSKINE,
Assistant United States Attorney

Endorsed:

U. S. DISTRICT COURT
District of Oregon
Filed Dec. 28, 1931
G. H. Marsh, Clerk
By F. L. Buck, Chf. Deputy

And Afterwards, to-wit, on the 16th day of March, 1932 there was duly Filed in said Court, a

BILL OF EXCEPTIONS

in words and figures as follows, to-wit:

BE IT REMEMBERED; That on the 30th day of September, 1931, at 10 o'clock A.M., the above-entitled cause came on for trial before John H. McNary, District Judge, Allan A. Bynon and C. G. Schneider, Attorneys at Law, of Portland, Oregon, appearing as attorneys for plaintiff, and Chas. W. Erskine, Assistant United States Attorney, and Metta D. Walker, of the United States Veterans' Bureau, appearing as attorneys for the defendant;

WHEREUPON, the following proceedings were had:

F. G. LEARY, called and sworn as a witness on behalf of plaintiff, testified as follows:

(Direct Examination by Mr. Bynon.)

I am in the fuel business and the wrecking business. I live in Portland. I know Mr. McCreary, the plaintiff, and should say the first time I knew him was in 1929. In 1929 I had a joint contract with the O.K. & Rose City Wrecking Co., tearing down a building, the old Weinhardt Brewery between 12th and 13th on Couch Street, and McCreary was brought upon the job by Mr. White who is the foreman of the O.K. & Rose City Wrecking Co. He furnished one-half the help and I furnished the other half. I gave him employment at that time.

Part of the time he was working under Mr. White and most of the time under me. He worked under my supervision, I would say, between five and eight weeks. I can not give you the exact length of time.

From my observation of Mr. McCreary during that period of time I would say he did the best he could — the work he was given to do. He was an ex-soldier and I noticed him and observed his work. He wasn't able to do the heaviest work we had. Part of the work was using paving breakers, and under the condition of his health during this time I thought he was having a trying time. He was doing the best he could and we favored him every chance we had, and I can say that honestly, aside from the sentiment connected with the case, knowing him as I did, he was not actually able to do as much work as the other men on the job, although he received the same pay.

He did not do as much work as the other men. I noticed that his strength was not as much as it would have to be to do the work required of him. I didn't notice anything special of a nervous condition.

As I remember it, he was off two or three different times, until finally he left the job entirely. I never knew why he left; he wasn't discharged; he just didn't come back.

"Q. What was his condition when he quit? As you observed it?

A. He was very weak and unable to do a day's work."

(Cross Examination by Mr. Erskine.)

"Q. I believe the last answer should be stricken, Your Honor. I do not believe this man, as a layman, can answer that sort of question in the manner in which he answered it.

THE COURT: I think probably that is correct. He

did or he did not do a day's work?

A. I have hired men for twenty years and I have
always had to discharge a certain number of
men for the efficiency of the work in order to
come out on the contracts I have been engaged
in. I would say, aside from knowing his condition, I would not have kept him on the job
at all.

THE COURT: The motion will be allowed."

I am in the fuel and wrecking business. It
was in the summer of 1929 that Mr. McCreary worked
for me, and he continued working for something like
a period of six weeks. It was during July and August, and we were wrecking a part of the old Weinhardt Brewery, over on 12th and Couch Streets.
Mr. McCreary's work, during that entire period, was
there.

The building was a steel frame with concrete
and brick along with it. The work was more or
less heavy. On a job of that kind, the men who are
employed have to do different things. There are no
two days alike. We do some lumber wrecking along
with the brick and concrete wrecking. Windows
have to be taken out, doors taken out and rubbish
burned up — everything like that. Mr. McCreary
was doing all those sorts of jobs; he was doing all
sorts of jobs that naturally you would ask any labor-

er to do on the job.

He got fifty cents an hour for an eight-hour day.
I don't remember that there was any over-time. I
didn't actually look up that information; I don't remember. That was the same wages paid to the other
laborers, except the truck drivers; they received over
that — $4.50; the laborers received fifty cents an
hour.

I can't remember exactly just when he was off
during the time he was working there, but probably
some couple of times he didn't show up at work;
he was away two or three times. That sort of condition very seldom applied to any of the other laborers,
but did happen once in a great while.

(Redirect Examination by Mr. Bynon.)

Of my own knowledge I can not say why he
wasn't working during the times he was absent. I
can't tell whether I inquired of him or not. I knew
in my own mind why he wasn't there, but I don't
know that I can tell you. I don't know it. I do,
but I don't legally know it.

A. H. BURNS, called and sworn as a witness on
behalf of plaintiff, testified as follows:

I live at Troutdale, Oregon, and have lived there
since the fall of 1905. I am a farmer.

I know Carrol McCreary and have known him

since the spring of 1906. I knew him well up to the time he went to war. He worked for me.

I recall the time when he went to war. I saw him within a week after he came back from the service. That was in the early fall of 1919; it was the last days of August or the first of September of 1919.

He came down to visit with us and stayed about a week or ten days — a few days more or less. He said, "I have to have a job." I had work for him to do there, but I couldn't put him to work because his condition showed he was more ready for the hospital than he was to work. He was very nervous. He could only eat certain things and otherwise it disagreed with him. My wife had to work to figure out what he could eat. He was a school mate to both of us, and that was his reason for coming to visit us. We had to be very careful what he ate and how he ate it. He didn't do any work for me, but went to help my brother about a quarter of a mile from our residence, and helped him thresh. On one particular instance when I was present he started pitching in, and I am positive he had not pitched in over fifteen minutes when my brother went up on the stack and put him in the shade and told him to stay there and he wasn't to do any more threshing. Carrol McCreary was trembling like a leaf. He did not work any more for my brother, nor did he work any more for me.

From then on I saw him on an average of about once a month.

"Q. Before we leave that first part of his time, when he got back from the service — was there anything else that would describe what his condition was? Did you see anything whatever that would indicate his condition?

A. Yes, sir. One night we were in Gresham. I never realized what shell-shock was before. There was a celebration, a fete for the queen, and a fire-cracker went off behind him and I was standing beside McCreary. It was pitiful to see his condition after that.

Q. What did he say?

A. He seemed to jump right up off the side walk. He said, "My God, Art, let's get out of here."

He was very weak, and his face was pinched and drawn and very pale, compared with how it was before he went to war.

I saw him in his attempts to find employment after that. He would work two or three days here and there and would have to quit on account of his condition. He spoke to me about going to work, too, for the Robert Strebin Dairy. That was the first dairy he went to. I saw him there when he was there. He acted all of the time very tired and very weak, very tired, and continued nervous. Up to the last two years I saw him every month so; for the last two years I haven't seen him as often as in the past. It seemed like he was failing more all the time; in other words, getting weaker.

He had not done any more work for me. So far as I noticed there has been no change in his nervous condition, nor in his condition of strength and vigor.

Cross Examination by Mr. Erskine.)

Mrs. Burns and I went to school with Mr. Mc-Creary, and when he came back from the service he made a visit at my home. We had a farm out there. This was in September, 1919.

I could have given him employment at that time, but I didn't think his condition warranted it.

"Q. Still you took him up and hired him out to your brother?

A. No sir.

Q. How did he happen to come up there?

A. He was a friend of his and he said, 'Jack, I will come up and help you.'

Q. You didn't say anything to your brother about Mr. McCreary wasn't able to do that work?

A. No."

This work for my brother was shortly after or during the time McCreary was visiting at my home.

It is a fact that Mr. McCreary went into the army from Eastern Oregon. I saw him shortly before the time of his enlistment.

This bundle pitching I spoke of was from the stack, and there were two men on each stack. I was not one of the men on the stack, but was working around the threshing machine, carrying the grain. I was carrying the sacks and dumping it in the granary. The granary was probably seventy-five to one hundred feet from the threshing outfit, and I would take it over there and dump it. The threshing lasted there about three hours.

Since that time I have seen Mr. McCreary on the average of about once a month up until the last two years; somewhere near it; that would not be accurate; some months I would not see him at all. But it averaged that throughout the years.

The experience at Gresham when the fire-cracker went off occurred probably a week after he worked for my brother, I can't say. It might not have been that long and it may have been a few days before or after. When this fire-cracker went off, it scared me for an instant before I was over it; I started — sort of jumped, too.

I can't say how soon after this incident it was

that Mr. McCreary went to work for the Strebin Dairy, probably a week or ten days after that; sometime the latter part of September, or October — I can't say.

This Strebin Dairy is about two miles and a half from my residence. This dairyman and I were friends; we did not have any business dealings. The place was right on the road to Troutdale. I did not stop there whenever I went to Troutdale; once in a while I did.

I had occasion to see McCreary occasionally going from my place to Troutdale and passing this dairy where he was working. He had charge of the dairy herd. By that I mean feeding and milking, and he took care of the milk. I just can't say whether that was quite a good-sized dairy; they were milking around eighteen or twenty cows. He had the supervision of the milking and the dairy, the feeding, and things of that sort. He had experience along that line.

I can't say how long he worked there. I saw him probably a year or a year and half when going from my ranch into Troutdale, and think he probably worked there somewhere near that time. I don't know what kind of wages he was getting.

I don't know when he left this dairy and went over to the Fernwood Dairy. I knew when he was at the Fernwood Dairy. I can't tell whether it was shortly after quitting work for the Strebin Dairy.

"Q. And you saw him on an average of about once a month?

A. It might have been I didn't see him. I can't say definitely when he made the change. It was between the time — I don't know how long it was.

Q. What would you say was the next job after leaving the Strebin Dairy?

A. I can't answer that.

Q. You can't answer that? Do you know how long he worked for the Fernwood people?

A. No sir."

I lived about a mile and a quarter from him when he lived on the ranch. I can't say how long he lived there — about a year or a year and a half. He and his wife lived there.

It was not a little dairy ranch, it was a little cleared place.

I don't remember when he worked for the Davidson Packing Company. I did not see him during that period of time any more than to say "Hello!" in passing.

I can't say just when he came back to the farm

again after he worked for the Davidson Company, but I know he wasn't able to run the farm when he did come back.

The farm he came back to was on Hickory Heights; it was the same one as he owned, and is the same one he was on for that year's period. I can't say what year it was he came back there.

I don't remember when he went up to Bend, and therefore don't know how long he was up there.

When he was working for Strebin there he was very tired and very weak.

(Redirect Examination by Mr. Bynon.)

I had work I could have given McCreary to do if he had been in condition to do it when he came back from the service, and subsequent to that.

He has been about the same in his appearance since the war until now.

(Recross Examination by Mr. Erskine.)

"Q. Now, I understood you, when you were first being examined by Mr. Bynon, to say that during the last few years he had been getting worse. Is that the fact?

A. Yes. He don't look — he is getting worse all of the time.

Q. He is getting worse all the time?

A. Yes, sir.

Q. Then he is in a worse condition now than he was after the war?

A. No, I would say he seemed to recuperate a short time afterwards."

(Redirect Examination by Mr. Bynon.)

I visited him when he was sick at home. I have seen Carrol McCreary home sick, when he could have been working, at least three or four times while he was working at Strebin's Dairy. I saw him in that condition myself.

DR. H. H. HUGHES, called and sworn as a witness on behalf of plaintiff, testified as follows:

(Direct Examination by Mr. Bynon.)

I live at Gresham, and my business is physician and surgeon. (Qualifications admitted.) I have been practicing my profession twenty years.

I have known Carrol T. McCreary since 1913, and recall having seen him on frequent occasions from 1913 until he went to war. I was not the family doctor and never took care of the McCrearys at that time. I examined him for life insurance about 1914.

I knew what his condition was at that time. I saw him off and on out around and I saw him two or three days before he went into the service. He came and talked to me.

After he got back from the service I saw Mc-Creary in the early part of October, 1919. He consulted me at my office about his condition.

At that time I found he had lost a good deal of weight, and he looked somewhat anemic and stooped, and his voice had changed a good deal, and he did not have the strength that he used to have. He complained of having suffered diarrhea and pain in the abdomen. Those were about the things he complained about. He also had a tenderness in the abdomen and he had a diarrhea at that time. He complained of not being able to digest his food, of having a good deal of gas and a sour stomach.

I took the usual history taken in such cases and interrogated him about what he had been through. I diagnosed his trouble as dysentery, and he had an inflamed or sore bowel at that time. We called that a colitis.

I didn't determine the cause of the dysentery because I have no way, out in the country, of determining the cause of dysentery. That is done in hospitals and laboratories. But I found he had such.

It was the fore part of October, 1919, I examined him. McCreary hadn't been home from the service very long at that time; probably a month or two.

On the occasion of my first examination of him after he left the service, he seemed very nervous and

restless as he was sitting in the chair; he was restless and nervous and he had a cough at that time,
and was raising some material.

"Q. Did you ever find out what had caused this
nervous condition, Doctor?

A.   Oh, I talked to him about the war. He had been
to see me before he went to war, and we talked
over the war. He had been in France and he
told me he had been up on the firing line and
I told him I had been in the Medical Corps in
France and so forth and I didn't hear anything
of the fighting around there, but he, when there
was any fighting going on, — he described a
good deal of what he went through and the guns
and so forth and I took it for granted that was
the cause of his nervousness."

I can't say just how frequently I have seen this
man since that first visit right after service, but a
good many times. I think that nervousness is about
the same as it was then; yes, it has persisted.

"Q. Doctor, what was the next time you saw this
man professionally?

A.   I remember of seeing him again in — he was at
my office off and on. I remember one particular time he came to the office in 1921 and he
complained of more pain at that time than usual
in his right side and I diagnosed it as appendi-

citis. I referred him to Portland surgeons. He came back and said that the doctor told him that he should have the appendix removed."

That was done at the Good Samaritan Hospital by Dr. J. M. Short.

After that, I did see him professionally. At one time he came into the office; I don't remember the exact date, but I remember telling him that he should come to the Veterans' Bureau and he should see them and I helped him, too, to get in there, and I think at one time I reported his condition to the Red Cross, and I believe later they came out and saw him.

I can't tell you the date I was called to aid Mc-Creary, but it was several years ago. A man 'phoned me one evening that McCreary was very sick; he was having a hard time to breathe. I was called to his house. I told him what to do before I arrived. I told him to put his feet in hot water, and so forth, because he was short of breath, and when I arrived he was sitting in a chair with a blanket around him and his feet in hot water. He was bothered with his heart.

I examined Mr. McCreary just a few days ago. He was in the office. This man has a dysentery which has weakened him, and he is very nervous and he has had a weak heart; he has lost weight and he is not what I would say is a strong man; this is because of the weakening condition due to the dysentery. From what he said, the dysentery has persisted since I first saw him in 1919. I have been there when he had dysentery. I didn't see the stools passed, but that is the report.

Dystentery is caused by different things, different bacteria and parasites. There is no cure. They are better for a while and then they are worse.

It leaves a man in a weakened condition. It explains the loss of weight and his nervousiness and his weak heart.

Based upon my examination and knowledge of this man and his history I have taken, I think this man is totally and permanently unable to follow continuously a substantially gainful occupation. I would say he was totally and permanently disabled, as defined, at the time he came back from the service, August, 1919, and I would say that the condition he is in is reasonably certain to continue throughout his lifetime.

(Cross Examination by Mr. Erskine.)

I have known Mr. McCreary since 1913, and in 1914 I examined him for life insurance. I do not remember treating him for what is known as walking typhoid just after that time. I don't remember having anything to do with sending him up to Eastern Oregon for his health.

I saw him a short time after he came home and he came to my office in October, 1919. We discussed, as comrades, our army experiences, and I noticed the same nervous condition that the boy has today. He told me something about the guns and shell-fire, and so forth, which I said, in my opinion, could account for the nervousness then disclosed.

At that time he said he was having a dysentery or diarrhea. That was his history.

"Q. And ever since that time, October, 1919, of your own knowledge of the diarrhea or dysentery he had, has he been in the hospital?

A. Well, I didn't see him have a bowel movement. No.

Q. You didn't put him in a hospital or anything like that? So that you could make a determination?

A. Yes, I did. I advised him to go to the Veterans' Bureau Hospital where they would make that examination.

Q. But you made no such observation personally?

A. We don't do that in the country; that is done in the laboratories.

Q. I am not criticising you, Doctor, but it wasn't done?

A. No. I didn't do it."

At the time of that first visit, in addition to this nervousness and dysentery, there was a slight coughing. I did not at that time give him a tentative diagnosis of tuberculosis. He had some rales in the chest; rales may be from tuberculosis or may be from bronchial trouble, but he had some rales in the chest.

"Q. And at that time, these rales you found there — you were of the opinion, weren't you, Doctor, that it was tuberculosis?

A. No. I never make a diagnosis that quick. We have the X-ray and all those things to aid us.

Q. But you had such suspicions, didn't you?

A. Yes. Whenever a man hears rales in a chest — a Doctor naturally thinks there is an infection.

Q. But from subsequent examinations and histories, as you have been told and took from this young man, you have proven your original suspicion, if you had such, was erroneous?

A. Yes, I don't think he has T.B.

Q. The last time I believe you say you saw him was when he came to your office for examination in 1921, when you say you diagnosed appendicitis?

A. The last time? I believe that is the only time I remember. I may have seen him in between.

Q. From October, 1919 until 1921, you don't now recall whether you had seen him professionally or not?

A. I don't remember any outstanding thing or change or symptoms that would impress that upon my mind. No, I don't.

Q. You may have or you may not? A. Yes."

At the time I made this diagnosis, and to confirm it, I sent him to an expert — a specialist in Portland, and it was so done and the operation was performed. I don't remember about informing him that he could go to work when he had sufficiently recovered from the operation itself. I don't remember how soon after that he was able to work or how soon I saw him after that.

I don't remember just how long after that it was that I was called to his home, but I imagine it was three or four years after that; along about 1924 or 1925 some time.

"Q. And that is the first time you distinctly recall having treated this boy since the appendicitis trouble, is it?

A. That stands out in my memory the best. Very often when he came to town he came up and visited and talked over the places he had been in the war. He said, 'I have been back to the

Veterans' Hospital and I have been out two months trying to hold down a job. One was in Washington.' He said he had been working on a pump job up there.

Q. That was recently, wasn't it?

A. I don't remember the dates.

Q. This time, in 1924 or 1925, as nearly as you can fix it, was the only time since 1919 that you ever professionally treated Carrol McCreary in his own home, wasn't it?

A. As I remember it, yes. I have always referred him to the Portland Veterans' Hospital."

I think he was just as thin and had lost just as much weight when I first saw him in October, 1919, as I see him today. I really don't see much change.

This nervous condition was exhibited continually — not exactly jerking but just getting up and going to the window and coming back and sitting and lighting a cigarette and smoking a puff or two and throwing it down.

As a physician, I would not consider just that indication of nervousness — sitting down a while and getting up and smoking a cigarette a short time — a sufficient disability to keep a man from working; I would consider that a result.

I have never had any experience in dysentery in

the laboratory but I see them in my country practice. I see them with the dysentery and then, later, they are sent or find their way to the hospital where the dysentery is determined from the stool, under the microscope. Dysentery can not be differentiated. They have all much the same symptoms. They are an irritation to the bowel, a cramping and going to the stool and so forth and you can not determine which kind of bacteria or parasite it is.

I never made such determination in this case. He told me he had dysentery — diarrhea — and from the symptoms he gave me I would say that he had dysentery.

"Q. Now, in what way was the heart weak? What was his pulse and blood pressure the other day when you examined him?

A. I didn't take his blood pressure.

Q. You didn't take his blood pressure? A. No."

I took his pulse, and it was ninety. We don't say that a pulse is normal. We say that the average pulse is say, seventy-two — so that we would say his pulse was rapid. For a man of his size and age it should not be ninety.

I did not take his blood pressure, but I did listen to his heart by the stethoscope, and the rapidness of the heart was the only thing I found wrong with the heart. I didn't find any heart lesion. A rapid heart or pulse is tackicardia; that would be my diagnosis. Of course, I have to think back of the condition that he had in 1924 or 1925 — that night I saw him. With a little exertion a man of his strength or size and trying to carry a new born calf and being so short of breath he could not — scarcely breathe — why you would just naturally say that that man has a weak heart. That one time is the only time I saw him under that condition.

In 1919 and 1921, when I saw him, there was nothing that impressed me about his heart except that it was rapid. I remember it was rapid way back there; I made an examination at that time.

"Q. I didn't understand from your diagnosis of October, 1919, that you found anything wrong with his heart.

A. He was weakened all over; when a man is weakened from diarrhea, that is he has to go a good many times in twenty-four hours, it weakens his heart the same as it weakens him in other ways. It weakens the muscles.

Q. And that weakens the heart? That weakness of the heart caused by diarrhea makes a rapid heart; is that what it does?

A. A weak heart is usually a rapid heart.
Q. It is?   A. It is with him.

Q. A rapid heart in itself, is not totally disabling, is it, to such a degree as you find in this man?

A. It depends upon each individual case.

Q. And in this man, a rapid heart alone, —

A. It is his general condition, yes.

Q. Well, a rapid heart alone, would it be so severe as to prevent him doing some kind of work?

A. Well, I don't know what some kind of work would be. He could sit at a desk and write. He could do some such work, but I don't believe he is in any condition to do manual labor.

Q. Say that he knows all about the dairy business and how to feed the cows and how and when they should be fed and milked and so forth, and knows how to direct the work to be done; is his heart condition such that he could direct the work of the dairy?

A. It has probably been, at times.

Q. Is it now?

A. No. I don't think he is in condition now to do dairy work. Dairy work is very hard.

Q. I am giving an illustration of directing the affairs of a dairy. Not a man doing the feeding, but a man who has charge of and directing men when to do the work of feeding and milking.

A. Yes, he could do that.

Q. He could do that today?

A. Yes, I think he could.   Yes, sir.

Q. Now, Dr. Hughes, you said also that this condition — this dysentery condition — was one that would tend to make him nervous. Is that what you mean?

A. The weakness from it would make him nervous, yes.

Q. Now, which do you think was the primary cause of the nervousness you found — the dysentery or the experience he related to you there in your office, when he first came back there?

A. Well, I don't know. I think that it is the combination. Either one has been enough to put the average man out."

(Redirect Examination by Mr. Bynon.)

"Q. Now, Dr. Hughes, Counsel very cleverly asked you if this heart condition was such as to prevent him from carrying on the job of Director of a Dairy. I don't know what the Director of a Dairy is — with all these conditions disabling him, would you consider him totally and permanently disabled? Or do you take just the one condition — just the heart? Which is it you take?

MR. ERSKINE: The final question I asked the doctor was: 'Do you find his condition now such as he could do the foreman's work?'

THE COURT: Let counsel ascertain what the foundation of that question was. I understood that his opinion is based upon his heart condition. Is that opinion based upon his heart condition alone or upon his entire condition?

A. Yes, his entire condition, Your Honor.

Q. All right, Doctor. Do you consider, taking into consideration all his disability, that he is able to go out and act as Director of a Dairy?

A. He is not the type of man. He has not the vigor of the type of man — of the man who usually runs men. No. I suppose he could stand there and tell them what to do, but he is not the type of man I would pick out to do that type of work.

Q. The heart itself might not disable him to that extent?

A. How is that?

Q. What I am getting at is — consider this man's total and permanent disability — you are considering all of the disabilities he is now possessed of and has been since he came from the service?

A. Yes sir.

Q. All right. You say that you think that what brought about the nervousness may be a combination of shell-shock and dysentery?

A. Either one was enough to cause his nervousness.

Q. They might both of them have contributed to it?

A. Yes sir.

Q. Doctor, is it not true that in addition to these army experiences which bring on nervousness, as you testified, that the infection which goes with this dysentery also produces nervousness?

A. Any septic poisoning—

Q. That is my point.

A. Yes, sure it may.

THE COURT: You talked about his pulse. Is seventy-two a normal pulse for a man of his age or does it vary with the age?

A. It may vary. We don't say that the pulse is normal, but it is average and a man of sixty-four may have just as good a heart as a younger man and it may be eighty, —

THE COURT: The pulse of the elder man is usually greater than that of a young man."

I had heard that he had an ulcer, but I have not

examined him for that.

DR. EDWIN P. FAGAN, called and sworn as a witness on behalf of plaintiff, testified as follows:

(Direct Examination by Mr. Bynon.)

I am a physician and surgeon, regularly licensed to practice my profession in Oregon, and am associated with the Portland Clinic of Doctors. (Qualifications admitted.)

"Q. Dr. Fagan you and — or Dr. Joyce examined Mr. McCrary? A. Yes.

Q. When did you first examine him?

A. September 8, 1930.

Q. The reason I mentioned Dr. Joyce — is he able to be here as a witness? A. No he is away."

I think the date we first examined this plaintiff, McCreary, was September 8, 1930. He came in as a patient, for diagnosis and treatment, complaining of stomach trouble. I don't assume he came in for the purpose of having us testify.

We took a history of his case and he was given a thorough physical examination and such laboratory work as was deemed necessary.

From our examination we diagnosed his condition as ulcer and renal glycosuria — duodenal ulcer. Duodenal ulcer is an ulcer of the peloric portion of the stomach — of the duodenum.

There are several different causes of it. It may come about by burns or infectious disease, debilitating diseases, and it causes cramps or may cause obstructions in that region, depending upon the location in the stomach.

This duodenal ulcer would be where the duodenum is — that portion of the end of the stomach between the stomach and the small bowel. It is located in the right upper portion of the abdomen.

I said McCreary has an ulcer there. He gave the subjective sensations of ulcer. The symptoms were a dull, gnawing, burning sensation located in the right upper side of the abdomen. He had a typical history that comes on three or four hours after they eat and goes away after they eat food or take soda bicarbonate. The usual thing is pain and discomfort.

We determined that he had a duodenal ulcer from the symptoms and fluoroscopy of the stomach. By fluoroscopy of the stomach I mean you put an X-ray back of them and it shows up on a screen. They drink a barium meal and the barium meal fills the alimentary canal; he stands before the X-ray machine with the fluoroscope. I have read in the dark room what the condition of the stomach is and what the condition of the duodenum is; it fills out the outline and contour of the stomach.

"Q. Dr. Fagan, did this man complain of a history and diagnosis — any part of it dysentery and diarrhea?

A. I questioned him and he told me about having dysentery some time in France which continued some time after he came back and it was diagnosed as dysentery at the Veterans' Hospital at Portland.

MR. ERSKINE: What is that?

A. He gave a history of having dysentery and diarrhea with cramps while in France, and after he came back to this country it was diagnosed as dysentery in this country. I think he told me that.

MR. ERSKINE: He told you that?

A. Yes sir. He said that. He gave that history.

MR. ERSKINE: You think he told you that?

A. No, I know he told me that.

Q. Based upon that history, doctor, it is your opinion that he has this — or had the infection you spoke of?

A. I presume that he had. I have his word only for it.

Q. Do you know what the infection was that caused this condition — the diarrhea or dysentery?

A. Nothing aside from what I heard. We made a test there and found nothing in his stool.

Q. Can you tell from your diagnosis, Doctor, what, if anything, they claimed he had been suffering prior to this time?

A. Nothing, only some form of dysentery — from his history."

Geardia is a fusiform-like organism found in the small intestinal tract of man and animals, equipped with a sucking disc on one end and eight pairs of wings. Some claim it to be pathogenic with man and others claim that it is not. This organism has a sucking disc on one end and eight pairs of wings on the side — like this (illustrating on board). These flagella are located on either side; eight pairs on either side, with a sucking disc on either end. This sucking disc attaches itself to the wall of the intestine.

This dysentery is parasitic, so to speak. If it produces the disease it is a parasite. It does not produce the disease; that is, it lives on the host; it is a parasite; it lives there. When it produces disease it is a parasite. Anything that lives at the expense of some other animal is a parasite.

Supposing that McCreary has this geardia in his intestines, it is more than one; there are indefinite numbers of them. Nobody can say as to how many of them there are in a normal case, but the average run of people have them in the intestinal tract all of the time; it is like any other of these things — some are present.

According to some doctors, when people have them in such numbers they cause diarrhea and cramps and those are the main symptoms. They are usually picked up through water, or they may be transmitted through food.

"Q. Now, is there any relation between the time that Mr. McCreary has this trouble — this diarrhea which was the first thing that he complained of, and the geardia?

A. If he had that it might have been possible that was the cause of it, yes.

Q. Is there any relation between that and the duodenal ulcer?

A. I can not say as to that."

According to the authorities, there is no cure for this geardia. Some men claim that they get desired results, but the majority of them claim that they do not. There is no permanent way to get rid of it.

This man was very nervous when I examined him. The history he gave might account for some of his nervousness; any person with that much trouble in their stomach — it would account for some of their nervousness. I should think dysentery would produce nervousiness; it would. The fact that a person has to go — it keeps him sort of walking, until he is actually nervous. There is a toxicity — a condition caused by diarrhea which causes nervousness. In other words, they get dehydrated because of the loss of so much fluid.

Aside from his history he gave of having these different things that may have been the cause of the nervousiness, the present condition of the stomach may be an added factor in bringing about that condition of nervousness. The duodenal ulcer can make a person nervous.

I examined this man four or five days ago and could see no change in his condition.

Based upon my examination and the history that I took, and with my knowledge of these conditions, I would say that this man in his present condition is totally and permanently disabled from following continuously any substantially gainful occupation; that is, he is permanently and totally disabled.

Assuming that these conditions have prevailed and persisted at least since he was released from active service in August, 1919, I would say he was totally and permanently disabled from that time on; this is a permanent and total disability and has been ever since that time.

(Cross Examination by Mr. Erskine.)

The first time I examined this man was September 8, 1930. I don't know whether it was at the request of Mr. Bynon I examined him, but it was at Dr. Joyce' — he was sent in as Dr. Joyce' patient. I don't know who requested Dr. Joyce to examine him.

During the course of this examination I did not know that the plaintiff contemplated this suit; I made a complete and thorough examination.

As a result of that examination I found he had a duodenal ulcer and renal glycosauria. That is an infection of the kidneys.

"Q. And, at that time, September 8, 1930, or whenever it was,—between about that time and the time your examination was completed—I suppose it covered several days—as a result of your diagnosis you knew on that day, whenever it was, that he was permanently and totally disabled?

A. Yes.

Q. And that the man was disabled by a duodenal ulcer?

A. Yes, and Renal Glycosuria.

Q. There were only two things wrong with the man —the duodenal ulcer and this kidney infection?

A. That was the diagnosis of his condition at that time.

Q. You say that was the extent of your diagnosis at that time? At that time, based upon that diagnosis, you say that he was permanently and totally disabled?

A. Yes, sir.

Q. Now, this duodenal ulcer you found, was the man disabled by it?

A. That was the thing he complained of at that time, for which he was examined.

Q. Was that the main disability upon which you base your judgment that he was permanently and totally disabled?

A. That, yes—and the fact that he was nervous."

I would not state that the duodenal ulcer was a permanent condition, because no one can say as to that. The ulcer he has had for a long period of time and—yes—it would be permanent, probably. Some duodenal ulcers yield to treatment.

I would treat duodenal ulcer as most doctors do; they treat it medically—with medical treatments— and if they find that it does not respond to that treatment, then they resort to surgical treatment. This ulcerous condition is not necessarily eliminated by surgical treatment. We resort to surgical treatment because they don't have any chance to get well after medical treatment fails, and this is the only thing left to resort to.

Dr. Joyce and I had performed many duodenal ulcer operations. It doesn't eliminate the ulcer in all cases.

No one can say as to whether the fact that a person has duodenal ulcer means that he is permanently and totally disabled. Some people clear up and some do not. It means a permanent condition so far as you can ascertain; you can't say that it will clear up.

I have been practicing medicine since 1929, and was admitted in this state in 1929.

When a person is afflicted with a duodenal ulcer it is not necessarily a permanent condition; some respond and some do not. It is permanent so far as you can tell; you can't tell whether it will clear up. Nobody can tell whether it is a permanent condition.

Duodenal ulcers can be cured by medical science; they have been. I can't say as to the percentage that are. Some duodenal ulcers are cured by surgery.

"Q. Do you want to say, Doctor, that the present diagnosis, duodenal ulcer, can't be cured by medicine?

A.   I would not say that it can't be or can be cured.
Some are and some are not.

Q.   Some can be cured by medicine though?

A.   Yes, sir.

Q.   All right.   Do you want to say that some can be
cured by surgery?   A.   Yes sir.

Q.   All right. Taking that as a basis, that some duodenal ulcers can be cured, either by medicine or
by surgery, how can you tell, when you diagnose a case of duodenal ulcer, whether it is a
permanent one or can be cured?

A.   If you give them a chance with medical treatment and that does not cure them, then you can
resort to surgery.

Q.   That doesn't answer my question.

THE COURT: How do you determine that this
plaintiff's condition is not curable, if some instances can be cured?

A.   I don't know as to that.   Some people clear up
with the use of one kind of treatment and some
won't, and some with another.

Q.   If you don't know, then you can say so.   When
you first diagnosed this patient as having duodenal ulcer, did you diagnose it as a permanent
one?

A. So far as the facts are concerned, he had medical treatment for a period of years and it has not cleared up and he has his ulcer still.

Q. You couldn't say in this case, diagnosing this man as having duodenal ulcer, at that time, that it was a permanent condition?

A. This man had had medical treatment only. Unless he resorted to surgery nobody could tell as to that. As I said, he had had medical treatment only.

Q. Did you resort to surgery in this case?

A. It was what he was advised.

Q. And until after he resorted to surgery you would not say it could not be cured?

A. I said that the fact that he had treatment for a number of years but he did not improve —

Q. Answer this question: If he had resorted to surgery as you recommended in this case, could it have been cured?

A. I didn't advise him on that. Dr. Joyce advised him as to what he should do.

Q. Doctor, I was asking you in connection with the permanence of the condition of the duodenal ulcer, at the time it was diagnosed by you, of this patient, and as I remember your testimony, you said the condition of it when you first diagnosed it was that it might be cured by medicine or by surgery. That is correct is it not?

A. Yes.

Q. And you recommended surgery to the plaintiff in this case, didn't you?   A. Yes.

Q. So that at the time you made the diagnosis of this plaintiff's condition, of the duodenal ulcer, you could not then say at that time that it was a permanent condition, could you?

A. Well, it had been permanent. That is all I could say of its chances being one way or another. There was no reason to assure him that his condition could be cured by surgery except that this was the only chance he had.

Q. But it can be cured by surgery?

A. Some cases can be, yes.

Q. But you did not know whether his condition could be cured by surgery or not?

A. I couldn't assure him it would be, no.

Q. Therefore, you could not say at the time you diagnosed his case that it was a permanent condition, could you?

A. I will ask you to answer me that question.

THE COURT: Answer yes or no, if you can do so.

Then you may explain.

A. I don't know as it can be answered yes or no. You could qualify either one statement or the other. You could not assure him one could cure him.

Q. If there is a possibility of its being cured by surgery, and you diagnosed him and found this ulcer then you cannot say that it is a permanent condition, if it is possible to be cured?

A. No, you could not say that at that time. You could not assure him that it could be cured by surgery because there are a certain number of cases that do not respond to surgery and at the time of the diagnosis he had symptoms that might not be overcome by the operation if it was successful.

Q. Is that the only explanation that you wish to make?

A. Yes.

Q. Now then, doctor, since you cannot tell at the time you diagnosed him whether his condition was permanent or not, and since he has not responded to your suggestion for a surgical operation how can you now say that this condition is a permanent one?

A. You can say that on the strength that it has not

responded to medicine.

Q. We are forgetting the medicine and going to the surgery. How can you say, if he has not had this surgical operation which you recommended, that his condition is a permanent one?

A. All you can say as to that is that there are a certain number that do not respond to treatment.

Q. Then you can't say?

A. No, only based on other cases of a similar nature as to what they did.

Q. Then I say again, you can't tell, can you?

A. Well, if a person had symptoms it is permanent until some change takes place.

Q. Now the duodenal ulcer, as I understand your explanation, is not in the stomach at all, is it?

A. Well, the stomach is a different portion and the duodenum is between the stomach and the small intestine.

Q. Will you step down here to the blackboard, doctor, and show us where the duodenum is?

(Doctor left the witness chair and drew a picture of the stomach and duodenum on the blackboard.)

A. This is the stomach here, and this is the length, about ten or twelve inches, and this is a continuation of the intestine tract from the stomach proper.

Q. Where is the duodenum?

A. Here. (Pointing to the small picture.)

Q. And where is the pylorus? A. It is here.

Q. Is that the main sack of the stomach?

A. It is the opening of the stomach into the duodenum. The pulorus is the way they speak of it.

Q. Where is the cardiac end? A. Right here.

Q. Where on that was the duodenal ulcer that you found?

A. On the cap here.

Q. Now an ulcer on that portion is much less difficult to eliminate by surgery than down on the bigger portion is it not?

A. What is that?

(Question repeated by Court Reporter.)

A. Well, yes, from a surgical point of view. We make an opening between this and the stomach.

Q. Is that done quite often —

A. (Interrupting) You mean for ulcers?

Q. Yes.

A. It is done in those cases where medical treatment does not answer.

Q. And that is what you would have done in this case if he had followed your advice?

A. If his condition had warranted.

Q. And that would have eliminated that trouble up there in the duodenum?

A. It might have, but not necessarily.

Q. It might have?

A. Yes, but not necessarily."

I have a report of the examination made at that time. (Hands counsel paper.)

Albumen zero in the laboratory report of the urine means no albumen present. Sugar plus means there was sugar present. No diacetic acid in the urine means there was none present, which was normal. 4-9 WBC to field is pus in the urine. S.G.1020 means specific gravity; that was normal. Acid reaction depends on the alkaline or acid in his urine at that time, and does not mean anything.

There was no amoebae in the stools; that was what they were tested for. I made the examination and tried to find out what was wrong with this boy. From an examination of the stools, I found nothing wrong — nothing pathological or showing evidence of any disease.

I found no geardia parasite; it is found in from six to twenty per cent. That parasite in itself does not necessarily mean anything. Certain organisms are pathological and some are not. Some cause disease in the intestinal tract all the time unless there are enough defensive factors to overcome the organisms. To my knowledge that has no connection with the duodenal ulcer at all.

He was nervous when he was examined; I think more so than the average person going through a clinic. I found no pathological reason for this nervousness aside from his ulcer in the stomach, which was found later; that might have a tendency to make him nervous.

"Q. But that condition of nervousness which you found was not such that it would prevent him from working?

A. I don't know what kind of work he was doing.

Q. Any kind of work — there are some kinds of work that his nervous condition would not prevent him from doing?

A. Well, that is a matter of degree. His nervousness displayed there — he may be more or less nervous at different times.

Q. But the nervousness displayed to you during the course of this examination would not prevent him from doing some kinds of work?

A. I don't think I am qualified to say whether it would.

Q. Well, you attempted to qualify, doctor, when Mr. Bynon asked you if he was unable to work?

A. He is unable to work so far as his stomach is concerned.

Q. His stomach was the only thing you based your answer upon?

A. That and his history. You can't take just what you find wrong with the man. You must also take into account what was found wrong with the man just previous to the time he became ill.

Q. Then you based your answer on the question of whether or not this boy was able to work now, as much upon the history that the boy gave you as upon the diagnosis?

A. You can't disregard the history.

Q. I will ask you to answer the question.

A. Yes, what is it?

Q. I will have it repeated to you. (The reporter read the question.)

A. No.

Q. Then you take your diagnosis mostly into account?

A. No, you have to take them both into account.

Q. Which predominated in your mind when you gave the answer he was totally and permanently disabled, the diagnosis or the history the boy gave you?

A. The diagnosis, of course."

(Redirect Examination by Mr. Bynon.)

"Q. Doctor, just one or two more questions, please, if you don't mind. You said in answer to Mr. Erskine's question about this operation, that he might respond or might not to a surgical operation. You said if conditions were such he might not respond to a surgical operation. What condition did you refer to?

A. Well, his general condition. You can't come out and state that a man, having the trouble he is having, and his pain, would be overcome. Chances are that he would, but he still might continue to have pain.

Q. I am referring to the trouble he was suffering from at that time.

A. Well, from the findings that he was nervous and that he complained of pain in his stomach, and in the region of his abdomen, as far as the pains there, the chances are he would be benefitted by this operation."

From the history I took I found he had been given medication for several years, and that he had been suffering from this disorder for a number of years, and that he had suffered with this nervousness for some time.

He gave me the history of these different attacks he had in France, and also the fact that he had been overseas and was engaged in several major engagements, as he gave it, might account for some of this nervousness. His internal trouble would induce this nervousness, and being under shell fire, which he told me about, would induce nervousness.

"Q. The question of finding the ova in the stool, doctor, is it not true that upon one examination of the stool, that you might not have found it, while you might have upon the next examination of the stool. A. Yes.

Q. In other words, doctor, if you caught him at a time when it was active you would have found it?

A. Yes."

MR. BYNON, addressing the Court: "Your Honor, I have just learned that Doctor Tucker of Forest Grove is sick in bed and will not be able to be present, and for that reason I would like to have Doctor Fagan give us the definition of a few medical terms that I would have asked Doctor Tucker. May I?

THE COURT: Yes, I think that will be all right.

MR. BYNON: Thank you."

Enteritis is the inflammation of the intestines and especially of its mucous coat. Diarrhea is a condition where the evacuations are very frequent, and more or less watery. Dysentery is a name applied to the same group of symptoms caused by different organisms. There are a number of different diseases that cause dysentery; bacillary and amoebic. These are two different types. Types caused by diphtheria. Different diseases may cause this. Amoeba is the type that causes dysentery. Amoeba is the specific organism that causes it. It is a one-cell animal. It causes ulcers in the large bowel, with a tendency to form abscesses in the liver. Both these animals are so small you can't see them with the naked eye, and they exist in very large numbers.

"Q. What is hyperacidity?

A.   It's an excessive amount of acid.

Q.   Well, suppose a man had an excessive amount of acid — if that condition existed and he had a duodenal ulcer how would that affect him?

A.   Well, they are usually found together.

Q.   Suppose a man has a duodenal ulcer and a

hyperchloydria, would you find that condition in the stomach?

A. That is why they give alkaline to neutralize it."

Psychoneurosis is a term given to a number of disorders caused by the mental state of the patient. It is rather a broad term. It covers the whole family of nerves.

Neuresthenia is a functional nervous disorder. A patient is often unable to do some of his work and unable to carry on some of his tasks, and it is brought about by acute upsets and strain. I did not say neuresthenia could be brought about by shell-shock or a disturbance, or both; but, according to different theories, neuresthenia is a nervous state of any kind and may be brought about by prolonged fears or infection over a long period of time, or by any kind of shell-shock.

(Recross Examination by Mr. Erskine.)

The amoebae is not a bug, it is an animal. The geardia is also an animal. It is a different kind of animal, but they are both of the same specie. They both live in the bowel, but cause altogether different kinds of diseases. In fact, the latter one, some authorities think, does not cause disease at all, whereas some think it does. There are no schools who say the amoebae does not cause disease; it has been proven to be a definite disease in itself.

"Q. You didn't find this condition at the time of your and Dr. Joyce's examination, did you?

Q. Now then, this hyper-acidity is that not just an over-acid condition in the stomach?   A.   Yes.

Q. Sometimes we eat a fried steak and we afterwards have to take some soda.

A. (Interrupting.)   It's not so much the acid as a rule but we take a little soda to relieve the condition.   When we eat we have more acids but you would not say that that was the cause of the trouble.   It may be some other thing.

Q. We usually relieve that by taking a little soda?

A. Yes."

When a person has hyperacidity, doctors usually give alkaline to reduce it.   Some may give soda. Duodenal ulcer and the acid condition in the stomach usually exist at the same time, but one is not dependent on the other.

"Psychoneurosis" is a broad term used to include all disorders caused by the mental state of the patient. One suffering from psychoneurosis is apt to enlarge his imagination.   I did not find such a condition when I examined this boy.

ROBERT S. STRUBIN, called and sworn as a witness on behalf of plaintiff, testified as follows:

(Direct Examination by Mr. Bynon.)

My name is Robert S. Strubin, and I live at Troutdale, Oregon. I am the same Mr. Strubin who gave the first employment to Carrol McCreary.

I have known Carrol McCreary ever since we were small boys and went to school together. We went through the grade school together and we played together practically every day.

I saw him some time after he came back from the service. I could not state just how soon. I remember going up to see him when he was at Mr. Burn's place. He was back then only a short time; I could not state the exact time; I imagine a few weeks.

I don't know what part of the year it was when I started him in there. My sister kept the books and there isn't any record now.

I don't think he was working at Mr. Burns' when I went up there for him, except to help a day in threshing. My place was between two and three miles northwest of the Burns place.

I was doing practically all dairying at that time.

That was the first time I had seen him after he returned from the service. I noticed a big change in him. He didn't seem to be the same man that went away. He stooped more and his eyes were hollow, and he had the general appearance of being nervous. I doubted very much if he could stand the work, but I needed someone there to help me very much and I insisted on him coming down anyway.

I don't know whether we talked over his condition at that time or not, but I think I remember Mr. McCreary told me he didn't think he could stand the work but that he would come down and try it, and I took him to my place.

"Q. What did you notice as he proceeded with his duties? Just tell the jury; they want to know.

A. Mr. McCreary — well I had to have a man to do the heavy work. I employed two men, and I had to have one man do the heavy work. I milked forty-eight cows at the time, and I used the milking machines and McCreary was to over-see the milking machines, and he was to attend to the mixing of the feed for the cattle because much money can be lost and wasted in a herd of that size, and your profits can be thrown away if you don't watch out. The other man got in the grain and the other feed and he cleaned the stables and put in the cows. Carroll had time off each day, which he had to take, and in fact many times he was so nervous we could not get him off on time for his evening chores. When we would call him he would come up with a jump and throw his hands into the air and he would come to the barn with his eyes glaring — they would be so glary — and he would go about his work and would carry on principally on his nerves."

I had to have a man to assist him. He could never have carried on a week alone.

I can't say how long he worked for me — I would be guessing. I know it was a considerable time. Whether it was a year or more or less I can't say. It must have been somewhere around a year from the time he started until he stopped.

"Q. Was that continuous employment or not?

A. He went away one time when he had to give up the work entirely."

He had to give up the work; he could not stand it; he was broken up completely.

Aside from that time there were many times when he could not carry on. Sometimes I had to assist him and sometimes my sister had to assist him. Sometimes he had to fill the silo. Many times my sister had to help.

"Q. What was the matter with him when he had to lay off?

A. He just did not have the strength, and he was nervous and he could not stand it — the work he was doing. He couldn't carry on."

Many times he had to lay off part of some days when he did not go away entirely.

The reason I continued this course with him was that his experience was worth so much to me in the work I had. You see I used the milking machines on my herd of cows, and Mr. McCreary had had some experience with the use of milking machines. He worked at the Sundahl place before he went to war, and it was almost impossible to get a man with milking-machine experience.

The first time there was a big interruption in his work, I tried to replace him and I couldn't do it. My herd went to pieces. As far as he was concerned, I hunted him up. I don't remember where I found him; I don't remember whether it was here in Portland or not. I hunted him up and offered him a great increase in wages, either fifteen or twenty dollars, if he would come back to me.

I don't remember exactly how much he was receiving all told, but after the raise I think McCreary was getting somewhere around one hundred and ten dollars a month; I don't remember. I can't state how long he received that salary.

I don't believe he was working when I induced him to come back.

"Q. What was his condition when you talked to him and urged him to come back?

A. Well, you see Mr. McCreary did not like to refuse to come back. I had been good to him
there. My folks had always known him and
my mother was good to him, and he saw I was
in a pinch and he knew I was losing money,
and he said he would come back but he doubted
that he could stand it — he doubted that he
could stand the work again. He showed a little
improvement from a few days' rest but he still
showed that nervous appearance that he always
had.

Q. How long did he carry on?

A. This time?

Q. — this time until he had to lay off again in the
afternoon.

A. I could not say. I am only guessing at these
periods because it has been many years ago.
Whether it was a month or two months I could
not say."

He did not regain his health. He finally had to
give the work up. He couldn't stand it. His condition then was about as poor as a man could be in.

Any little thing would startle Carrol — any little
noise. After any little noise you would see him going up into the air. I guess you would only see him
coming down. Around the barn or at the house —
when my mother would call him — sometimes it was

almost dangerous to call him. Many times we did not call him. Sometimes we would let him sleep until the milking was practically done. He was such a nervous wreck we did not like to disturb him.

"Q. Do you remember anything that happened. Anything that remains in your mind?

A. Yes, I remember once or — well I remember one or two things that I never will forget. One time we were walking back of the cows and his shoulder brushed the cow's tail and the cow pails were hanging back there, and I looked around there and I just saw him coming down. He must have been up a considerable distance.

Q. Where had he been — you said he was coming down?

A. Well, he jumped up in the air. He had been walking along there and I just saw him coming down, and then another time one of the boys fired a shotgun back of the stable at some crows and Carrol let out a yell as loud as he could and he came over the cows with his bucket and he didn't get over that for several days. These two instances and when we would call him or arouse him out of his sleep, I perhaps will never forget, and I don't think anybody else would ever forget — the look he carried at these times."

I have seen this man quite a number of times since I gave him employment. I have never employed him since that time.

If Carroll could have stood the work we would have been glad to have had him back. I stated that to him when he left — that if he could ever do the work we would be glad to have him back.

On these occasions that I have seen him since he quit there, I can't see where he was ever any better.

He has been employed a few places since the war, but I could not say where.

I believe I saw Carroll on the little farm he had up there one time when I went by. He was making an attempt to farm the place, but he could not stand the work there. I think he told me that day that the work was too much for him.

(Cross Examination by Mr. Erskine.)

Mr. McCreary and I have been friends since our boyhood days, and we grew up together in that part of the country.

It wasn't because of my early acquaintance with him, or my friendship, that I first employed him after the war. It was because of his knowledge and experience in the handling of milking machines. I went to Mr. Burns' place and sought him out for that purpose.

At that time we were milking somewhere near forty-eight cows. The other man employed by me did not come at the exact time that Mr. McCreary did.

Up to the time I employed Mr. McCreary I was attending to the dairy herds myself. My sisters were helping me. I could not get any help except an old broken down man I had there. I couldn't trust them to any exacting work.

Later I got hold of Mr. McCreary, who had some knowledge of milking machines, and I had to get another man, too. I devoted myself to farm work, and I did considerable hunting that winter and took considerable rest.

It was right after threshing time in the fall of 1919 when he went to work for me; just about threshing time. It may have been two years he worked for me; I have no way of telling at all. I don't like to say it was not less than a year; I don't like to guess on those things.

The first wages I paid him were somewhere around $75. No, I don't think it could have been $90. I think Carroll drew $75 as near as I can tell. That included his board and room as well.

"Q. And after he worked for you a while he was gone, how long was he gone?

A. Well — about that $75 or $90 question, I can't answer that. It has been years ago. I have no records.

Q. It may have been either seventy-five or ninety dollars?   A. Yes.

Q. That was the starting wages?   A. Yes.

Q. And then he worked for you again — how long a period was it until you went after him again?

A. Well, now that would be guessing again. When I get to guessing I would be making one guess for you and one guess for Mr. Bynon.

THE COURT: Just give it the best you can.

A. Well, I don't have the least idea. He had been there quite a long while when he had to give it up.

Q. Was that the first time or the second time?

A. The first time.

Q. And then how much of an interval was there between the two times that he worked for you?

A. I don't remember but not very long, I believe.

Q. And during that interval you were losing money, your herd had become disorganized and so you went to get Mr. McCreary to come back and re-organize your herd and help you out so that you would not be losing so much money? Is that right?   A.   Yes.

Q.   He had such an adaptability to operate your herd that instead of your being on the debit side of your ledger you were on the credit side of your ledger when he was there; is that right?

A.   Yes, that is right, except the boy sacrificed himself for me — he sacrificed his health for my benefit, and I did not feel so good about that at the time.

Q.   But he did operate your business while he was there to such an extent that you were making money as against losing money when he was not there?

A.   Yes, that is true.   He was capable of handling milking machines.

THE COURT: What year was that?

A.   I can't tell you that exactly.

Q.   Do you know about what year it was?

A.   Well, it was right after the war.

Q.   1919 or 1920 was it?

A.   Yes, I think it was.

MR. ERSKINE: Q.   And your purpose of employing him was because of his ability to run your herd and not because you had sympathy for the boy?

A. No, I didn't have sympathy for him. He was employed for his experience. I didn't know when he came there that he couldn't handle this other work as well—this heavy part, but that he could not do. I had to hire another man or do it myself, and I hired another man."

Well, I don't know as I made very much money in addition to hiring another man to get in the grain and clean the stables, with Mr. McCreary there, but I didn't lose any.

When he came back the second time, in order to induce him to help me reorganize my herd I raised his salary ten, fifteen or twenty dollars.

"Q. If it was seventy-five dollars that he had been receiving, and you increased his wages ten or fifteen or twenty dollars, then he was receiving ninety or ninety-five dollars, and if it was ninety dollars when he left it was one hundred and ten dollars when he came back?

A. Well, I think it was one hundred and ten dollars that I offered him when he came back so it must have been ninety. I gave him a ten or fifteen dollar raise when he came back, I remember that."

FRED T. WILSON, called and sworn as a witness on behalf of plaintiff, testified as follows:

(Direct Examination by Mr. Schneider.)

My name is Fred T. Wilson; address, 504 E. 27th St., No., this city. I have lived here in the city of Portland about twenty-three years.

During the past ten or fifteen years I have been engaged in the business of selling cream and milk.

I have employed the plaintiff in this case, Carroll T. McCreary, since the fall of 1919. I employed him soon after the war. I think I employed him for a matter of several months.

"Q. You may state what his condition was with reference to his being able to do the class of work that you employed him to do? Was he able to perform it in a good and workmanlike manner?

What was his physical condition?"

A. I think the first time he was in my employ, when he first came to work, that he was able to do his work, but I could not say how long he worked there, but he worked for some time, and then he gradually became weaker and weaker and in fact got so he could not do his work.

Q. What was he doing?

A. I think he was checking. He was either checking or working; working inside my plant."

I had a milk plant at that time, and I had some

45 people working for me. The work he was doing could be classified as fairly heavy work.

I don't remember so much about his condition with reference to being nervous. He was unable later to do his work, because he was sick. He was weak, but he made a supreme effort to do it, but I requested him to—I called him in and I asked him to quit until he could get in shape so that he could do his work, and he quit.

He came back again and stayed a very short time. His physical condition then was not very good.

I don't remember his physical condition when he finally left my employment the last time, only that I do remember he had to quit on account of his health.

"Q. What did you say to him when you asked him to quit?

A.　The first time?

Q.　Yes, the first time.

A.　Well, the second time I think he came in and re-signed, and the first time—I think I asked him to lay off until he could get in shape so that he could handle his work. He was all run down and weak. So far as we were concerned we wanted to keep him."

I did not know him previous to his war experience. The name of my firm at that time was the Fernwood Dairy.

(Cross Examination by Mr. Erskine.)

This firm was located at the corner of Union and Ash Streets, this city. The nature of the dairy business was manufacturing, wholesale, and retail. It had nothing to do with herds or milking.

I am unable to state whether it was some time in 1920 that he went to work for me. I think I did know that he had had some previous experience working on a dairy farm before I hired him.

I am unable to state what the nature of his work for my firm was. I had forty-five people working for me, and I think he was either in the checking room, checking out routes of the wagons and checking in the returns, or doing general extra work.

Sometimes he would help load the wagons. A case of milk would weigh fifty-five pounds. These wagons were built up three or four cases.

I don't know what wages he received there at that time; I think probably $120 or $135 a month. It might be as much as $150. It was whatever the going wages were; I think we were paying $120, $135, or possibly $150. I am unable to state the length of time he was employed there. Just a few months elapsed between the two times he worked for me.

The second time he worked for me it was at the Fernwood. Later I sold to the Damascus.

LEON CODDEY, called and sworn as a witness on behalf of plaintiff, testified as follows:

I make my home out at Gresham. I have a mail box in Gresham and Troutdale both. I am a patrolman in the city of Portland.

I know Carrol T. McCreary. The first time that I ever saw Carrol T. McCreary that I remember was about 1913 or along there. Up to the time he went to war, I knew him whenever I saw him out with the boys and things like that.

"Q. How soon after he came back from the service did you see him?

A. I came back the 15th of June, and I was walking on the streets here in Portland and I saw him on the street, and he had on his army overcoat and I saw him standing on the street, and he was feeling weak like, and his eyes were glassy and wasted away, and his face was thin, drawn in, and I said, 'Carrol, what is the matter with you?' and he said, 'Well, I don't know' and I said 'Are you trying to do anything for yourself,' and he said 'I don't know what is the matter,' and I told him to see a doctor and he said he was coming to town and that was the last time I seen him that time."

I don't remember just how soon after that I saw him. I have seen him frequently since the war.

I have been at his house when he was sick. I was the one that called the doctor—at the time I went over there; his wife came over there three days before this little boy was born and she said "Mr. Coddey, can't you come over?" So I went to his house. When I got over there he was sitting on a chair and he was having a hard time to breathe and I said, "What's the matter" and he said "I can't get any air" and so I gave him a drink of water and I rubbed him as fast as I could to keep his circulation up until the doctor got there. Before the doctor got there I didn't know what he would do. He was all bent over, and the nurse gave him a shot in the arm. My opinion is that he would have fainted in the next five minutes if she hadn't given him the shot in the arm. I took him to the Veterans' Hospital.

"Q. During the different periods of time that you have been in his home, have you ever worked with him?

A. Why, I went and got Carrol a job once. I got him the easiest job with the city of Portland. I got a job for him watching rocks on the road at Bull Run, and he was home a few days and then he had to come down and his father was up there two or three days, and then he came back, and then they found another easy job for him, but Carrol played out on that job, too, and he had to give that up. I believe you asked me if I had seen him working. I went home another evening and he was down in the field, and he had been attempting to clear some ground and he had his father's sled up there, eight or ten feet long, and he was down on his hands by this sled, and he was waving and hollering to me to come over there and I left my job and I went over there, and so I got my arm around his shoulder and I got him to the house the best I could. He was walking, and I put him to bed and I took his team and put it in the barn and I took the harnesses off the horses. That was another episode that happened at that time."

(Cross Examination by Mr. Erskine.)

I lived close to where he lived when he lived out on that little place. I did not live there in 1923; I lived up there in 1925. I was not living up there when he lived on that place the first time; he lived there and I lived on the old place and then I moved over there.

"Q. And during the second time that you lived out there on the place, that would be in 1926, or 1925?

A. Well, I moved up on the place in 1925. I was

working for the city of Portland; and I was living about two miles south of there."

When I got him the job with the City of Portland on the road, we were living approximately within six hundred feet of each other. That was in 1925; that was up on Victory Heights. I worked up on Dodge Heights.

I could not swear that he came home nights. He started home but some nights I didn't know where he went. I would see a light there but I don't know whether he came home or not. I did not go up there.

I didn't live there. I went back and forth. He would ride with me as much as he could. He had a Ford car at that time and I used to take him with me and bring him back as much as I could. Sometimes I was attending to other work on the pipe work that I had to attend to.

"Q. And he could not go with you these times?

A. No, he would get somebody else to bring him along.

Q. But you finished that job in 1925, didn't you?

A. Well, he didn't. He played out before the job was finished. I stayed there and worked with two other follows."

The crew on which he was working was not continued all winter. I don't think he went back the

next winter when it started up again on that construction work. If he could do the work I would
have him with me today.

"Q. You don't know when he went back to work for
the city in April, 1926?

A. There was some work up there. I don't just
remember—in April, 1926—whether Jake worked there at that time or not. If I don't know
the date or the time I would rather not answer
it.

Q. Well, it was in 1925, when you got him that
first position and you don't recall whether he
went back the next spring or not?

A. I don't recall."

JOHN EVERLE, called and sworn as a witness
on behalf of plaintiff, testified as follows:

(Direct Examination by Mr. Bynon.)

My name is John Everle. I live five miles southeast of Troutdale.

"Q. Do you know the plaintiff here, Carroll Mc-
Creary?

A. Yes, I know Jake. That isn't his name but we
call him that.

Q. How long have you known him?

A. Ever since 1904 (or 1914)."

I knew him pretty well—since before he went to war. I saw him shortly after he came back. I don't know just when.

I noticed he looked a whole lot different when he came back than when he went away. He didn't look like the same man at all. He was all humped up. His eyes were all swollen out, and he looked all worn out.

He worked for me a little off and on on occasions. It was just day work, but he could not hold out. He would try to help me but he would give out. I tried to get him to help me clear a little land and drive a horse and he gave out. I wanted him to drive the stump machine. Every time I employed him after he came back from the war he gave out.

I employed him before the war. He was a great man before the war. If he could have done the work, I would have had work for him after the war.

Yes, I saw some manifestation of nervousness. I had some blasting to do and every time I set off a blast he would duck and try to get away from it, and he was very nervous-like.

I have never seen him work for anybody else that I can recall.

He has not been any different since he got back; he is about the same.

(Cross Examination by Mr. Erskine.)

The first work Jack did for me when he came back, as near as I can recall, was along about 1926 or 1927—somewhere in there. He tried to help me a little, haying. That was the first work he did for me after he got back from the war.

The next work he tried to help me with was with the stumping machine, in the fall of 1928. His work was to drive the horse; it was his work to bring the horse there and throw the machine out of gear and in gear. He was assisting in stump pulling. I was using blasting power at that time, and some of the stumps I could not pull were blasted.

He continued to work with me for two or three days, and then he gave out.

We were not blasting during all that time. We were pulling stumps. Sometimes I did when I could not pull and then I had to blast. During this time and during some time each day we did some blasting. Some days we used more blasting power than others. It depended on how we got hung up.

In 1926, when he helped me haul hay, he gave out. I reemployed him in 1928 because it was a light job, and I thought he might be able to help out. He wanted to earn a few dollars.

T. E. GABODE, called and sworn as a witness on behalf of plaintiff, testified as follows:

(Direct Examination by Mr. Schneider.)

I know Mr. McCreary. I became acquainted with him in May, 1923. I hired him to work for me at that time as a general roustabout—a pickup man. He was so employed for about ten months, or until March, 1924.

He was under my direct supervision all that time. He worked steadily, with the exception of a few days, but it was almost steady during all that time.

He was able to do the work that was assigned him well enough to keep him on the job. We had his brother there on the job working and we tried to keep him working, but many times when we had heavy work to do we always had to send somebody with him.

I did not consider him good, first class, from a physical standpoint.

Regarding his nervous condition, you could notice there was a nervous strain. You could see he was bothered with something. We knew he was not exactly right physically but we tried to help him along.

I don't remember anything in particular that attracted my attention to his nervous condition. It was a sort of all the time that he did not appear to be able—well, he could do light jobs all right, but when it came to heavy jobs he just petered out and we had to give him help.

He would not lay off for more than a couple of days at a time.

When he quit he came in and said he could not handle the work and he felt that we were just keeping him on and he felt the best thing to do was to quit. I would say we were just helping him along.

(Cross Examination by Mr. Erskine.)

We usually paid these men four dollars a day, and I would say that was what he got at that time, although I don't remember exactly. I have not made a search of my payroll records to see what I was paying him at that time, but I know we usually paid these men that amount of money. I did not look it up.

He was first employed in May, 1923, and he worked until March, 1924. During that time I would say he would average $100 a month—at four dollars a day, with the exception of a few days off. Including the days he was off he would average pretty close to $100 a month.

I couldn't tell you what he earned in the month of June, 1923. I didn't look it up; I don't know; I suppose $104 would be about the right amount.

I don't know how much he earned in March, 1924,

the last month he was there, unless I would base it on the average. I wouldn't say it was as much as $117.00; would say it was somewhere between $96 and $100.

He was a pick-up man. The duties of a pick-up man were driving the truck around and picking up various things at the different docks and depots. Of course, that was just part of his work. He attended to the janitor work and moving supplies around. He was not supposed to fire the ovens. It was mostly roustabout work. He may have done some of that, but as I remember it, he did not.

His time off there was just a few days occasionally, due to his condition, as I remember it. He would be sick and to that I attributed it at that time —to his nervous condition. I don't know whether he went to the Veterans' Hospital or not at the time. I remember he was having some examination but whether it was time off for that I don't remember.

MR. J. H. COOPER, called and sworn as a witness on behalf of plaintiff, testified as follows:

(Direct Examination by Mr. Bynon.)

My name is J. H. Cooper, and my residence is Portland, Oregon.

I have known the plaintiff ever since he was a boy. The first time I ever gave him any employment was at Potlatch, Washington, with the Phoenix Logging Company.

I saw him after he came back from the service; I had seen him once down at his place. He was trying to clear his land and he was pretty sick and weak and he couldn't do much. That was the first time I had seen him after he came back.

He came up to Potlatch, Washington, to the logging company, in the fall of 1926. I guess he came up there to work. He was there eight or ten days before he was able to do anything. I was foreman there and I gave him a job of what I thought he could do.

He made it fairly well until Christmas time and then he had to lay off. He couldn't stand it. We shut down about the 20th of December. I suppose he worked a little better than a month there—a little better than a month and a half.

He worked first on the slack line, but he couldn't stand that. It was too heavy for him. Then I put him to trucking wood. The first was a five dollar a day job and the second was a four dollar a day job. He worked at that the rest of the time he was there.

There was work for him there if he could have continued; he could have worked as long as he wanted to.

He did not continue to work because he was not able to stand it any longer. After Christmas he got sick and he laid off for about a week.

He would topple over, he got so weak he could not get around. There was something the matter with his stomach and his heart. He was taking stimulants for his heart. I didn't know he was as bad as he really was. He was always nervous and he seemed as though he couldn't get any rest. That was not before the war; it was while he was up there. Before the war he was a big, husky lad.

(Cross Examination by Mr. Erskine.)

The first time I saw him after the war was out there on his place. That was in 1924 some time. He had been back some time then. He had just bought his little place and he was trying to do some clearing on it. I didn't see much of him then untli 1929, until up at Potlatch; I had only seen him once or twice between that time.

Then I got him a job in that logging camp at five dollars a day.

"Q. What did this logging job consist of?

A. Well, we had seven-eighths line there, about two hundred and fifty or three hundred feet long—

Q. (interrupting) What were these lines?

A. Steel lines, and they were to be pulled around

by hand and fastened to the top of a tree, and
there was a block to hang onto the tree and—

Q. (interrupting) And was he supposed to go up
into the tree?

A. No, he was supposed to shuffle these steel ropes
around there—"

That was a pretty heavy job; it took no particular
experience. There was one head man there who
inspected what was to be done. Three men worked
there together.

From that job I got him a job bucking wood. He
was not splitting wood; he was sawing it into three
and one-half to four feet lengths. One man was sawing it. After the wood was sawed, there was a man
there to split it.

He continued that work until about December
20, and then the mill closed down until after New
Years, and we started up again after the first of the
year.

He came back to work after the first of the year
and was up there until the last of February.

He went to work there about the first of November and worked there until the 20th of December,
and then went to work again the first of January,
when the camp started up, and he worked until the
last of February.

(Redirect Examination by Mr. Bynon.)

He did not work steadily from the first of the year until the last of February. He had four or five days off once because he had to rest up. His heart was bothering him and he was all doubled up. He couldn't eat anything.

M. H. DAHL, called and sworn as a witness on behalf of plaintiff, testified as follows:

(Direct Examination by Mr. Schneider.)

My name is M. H. Dahl; residence, Troutdale, Oregon. I have lived there on the same farm for thirteen years last past.

I had occasion to employ the plaintiff, Carroll T. McCreary, about eight or ten times since the war. Some of the jobs were fairly long jobs. By long jobs I mean a week or two, but not steady. None of these occasions were for more than two weeks.

Some of his work was light work and some was heavy work, like haying.

He was very willing to work and made a great effort, but in a short time—that is, in a few days— you could see the effect on his person. He was very badly worn out after he worked hard for a time. After that, as a rule he went back to his father's or up home where he lived, close to his father. That was near my place.

Regarding his nervous condition — if anyone stepped up close by him—I had two boys and they were a little bit unruly at times, and if they touched him quick it would send him up in the air.

I did not know Carroll before the war. My observation of him has been since the war.

(Cross Examination by Mr. Erskine.)

The first time Mr. McCreary was employed by me was in the spring of 1922. The first time he worked for me he was running a hand cultivator, about this size or width (indicating), and it had shovels on it and shears to cut the small weeds. He motivated the power; you would have to get the shovels down into the ground to cut the weeds out. That was in the spring of 1922.

He continued on that job until it was finished, and he trimmed rhubarb for me for a week for a while, breaking it off the plant and trimming it up.

He did not stay with me until whatever I had to do was completed. Mr. McCreary was not very well. That was partly why I did not have much more work for him to do. The rest of it was pretty heavy work. The most of my work was pretty heavy.

I employed him at various times for various short jobs I had there. He did not always stay until the jobs I had for him were completed. I would say he did half the time. The other half of the time there was work for him to do if he could have done it.

MRS. HELEN LYONS, called and sworn as a witness on behalf of plaintiff, testified as follows:

(Direct Examination by Mr. Bynon.)

My name is Mrs. Helen Lyons; I live at Forest Grove, Oregon.

I work for Dr. Tucker in his office, as technician, and have been working for him three and one-half or nearly four years. Dr. Tucker is now confined to his home.

I know Mr. McCreary, the plaintiff in this case. I met him in Dr. Tucker's office a little over two years ago.

Mr. McCreary certainly has been consulting with Dr. Tucker personally since the time I first met him over two years ago. Since that time I should say, to the best that I can recall, he has been there twenty or twenty-five times. I know of my own knowledge that the doctor was treating him for heart trouble and stomach trouble or dysentery.

"Q. Mrs. Lyons, can you describe briefly the trouble or the condition you observed this young man to be in when he came to the doctor's office on these several occasions which you have testified about?

A. Yes, I can because he impressed me the very first time I saw him as he came into the office there and then I was called into the office to be with him as he was extremely weak. In fact, it was with some difficulty we were able to take care of him for a little while because he had to rest up and be cared for. He was suffering then with his heart."

In a way he would respond to treatment. He would become a little stronger, and then perhaps the very next day or the day after that, perhaps, he would be back there and tell us of another severe attack he had had, and of the night spells with his heart.

I was with the doctor during the time he was treating this man.

(Cross Examination by Mr. Erskine.)

The main trouble Dr. Tucker was treating this man for was his heart. It was hard to treat him with this other trouble he had also. This stomach or dysentery trouble that came on. It made it a little bad. He had to be careful in treating his heart. His heart and this dysentery trouble seemed to be the main trouble; his heart was the main trouble.

I know that he was treating for his heart and for the dysentery trouble, and that is all that I know. That is all that I can truthfully say. I am not trying to tell more than I know. I am just telling you what I know. I know he was in a very weakened condition, and my business there at that time was in doing as any office assistant would do that was with the doctor.

I am a technician in Dr. Tucker's office. I do laboratory work, but principally my work is psychotherapy. My business is to give these treatments.

I have taken this man's pulse and his blood pressure, too. I am not prepared now to give you any information or data on that. His blood pressure was very low. It naturally would be. Anybody would know that with his condition and with his heart as bad as it was—. I have no records here with me; I could give it if I had the records here.

Blood pressure varies. His would be very low and that he would improve and would feel better and he would come in and we would take his blood pressure and we would be encouraged because it was up. I remember one time it was down as low as 91, and then he would get better and it would come up again. His blood pressure was not bothering the doctor. It was the cause of the low blood pressure. The low blood pressure was a symptom and therefore he did not lay much stress on it. You asked me if I had take his blood pressure, and I say yes, I have.

I am prepared to say low pressure is sometimes

very hard to bring up and if your blood pressure is very low why you are in as much danger, and I think in more danger, in one way, than it is to have high blood pressure.

His low blood pressure was due to his low vitality; due to his sickness or trouble.

"Q. You usually find high blood pressure in a nervous person, don't you?

A. Well, you can find low pressure in a nervous person also."

CARROLL T. McCREARY, called and sworn as a witness in his own behalf, testified as follows:

(Direct Examination by Mr. Bynon.)

My full name is Carroll T. McCreary. I live at Forest Grove, Oregon, at the present time. I am a resident and inhabitant of Multnomah County, Oregon, and have been ever since I filed my complaint.

Prior to entering the service I worked in Eastern Oregon, something like two years and three or four months before I came here. I left there December 20, 1917, a few days before Christmas. I made my home before that with my parents here in Oregon, at Troutdale. My folks are farmers in the eastern end of this county.

I went into the Marines.

I made my living as a laborer before I entered the service. I had an eighth grade education.

After I joined the United States Marine Corps I was sent to Virginia, and from there I went to Hoboken and embarked for Brest, France.

Before entering the service I had not suffered any disability nor been sick at any time. I suppose I had the croup, and other childhood diseases, but after I grew up to manhood I had no disabilities that I know of. During the first months I was in the army I enjoyed the life of a normal man physically and mentally.

My first sickness was when I got the mumps when I was on the boat going over, and I was left at the hospital barracks at Brest, France. The mumps were bad with me; they went down on me. I got out of the hospital one day and went to the convalescent camp in Brest, and the mumps went down that night, and I went back to the hospital after that the next morning. That time I was kept there something in the neighborhood of three weeks.

After I was discharged from the hospital I went back to the convalescent camp and from there they sent me to the army replacement camp at St. Agnes. From there I went to the Marine Replacement Camp. It was only a short distance from there; I don't remember exactly the town. From there I was sent to join the 45th Marines on the Marne on the 5th of July, I think it was.

"Q. I will hand you Plaintiff's Exhibit 'A' for identification and will ask you to tell us what that is, if you know?

A. That is my discharge from the service."

(Plaintiff's Exhibit "A" offered in evidence without objection.)

PLAINTIFF'S EXHIBIT "A"
UNITED STATES MARINE CORPS
To all whom it may concern:

Know ye, that CARROL TILLMAN McCREARY, a Private (Provisional) of the MARINE CORPS RESERVE, Class 4, who was enrolled the Twentieth day of February, 1918, at Mare Island, Calif., to serve FOUR years, IS HEREBY HONORABLY DISCHARGED from the United States Marine Corps and from the service of the United States BY REASON OF "Expiration of Enrollment."

Said Carrol T. McCreary was born May 19th, 1895, at Florence, Ind., and when enrolled was 74 inches high, with Blue eyes, Light Brown hair, Ruddy complexion, occupation Farmer; citizenship, US.

GIVEN under my hand and delivered at Washington, D. C., this 19th day of February, 1922.

Johne A. Lyume,

Major General Commandant.

CHARACTER Excellent.

MILITARY RECORD

Foreign service: France from 6-7-18 to 8-2-19.
Battles, engagements, affairs, or skirmishes:

Aisne-Marne from 7-18-18 to 7-19-18. St. Mihiel from 9-12-18 to 8-16-18. Meuse-Argonne from 10-1-18 to 10-9-18 and from 11-1-18 to 11-9-18.

G.—Bishop, Jr.
Lt. Col. U. S. M. C.,
Commanding Marines."

"MR. BYNON: I suppose I may refer to this without reading it to the Jury at this time. There will be no objection to that, will there?

MR. ERSKINE: No."

My first recollection of the first time I was in fear is we were in a certain amount of shell fire all the time from the time we joined the Marines at the Marne. We went in there on the 12th of July, 1918, and I joined the company there, or somewhere near that time. I can't say for sure.

We left there and we went to Soissons Sector, and we went on that drive on the 18th, I think it was. I was with the Second Division of the Fifth Company at that time.

About that time—the 15th or 18th of July—was

the first time I got sick or bothered with this dysentery and diarrhea.

"Q. Immediately prior to that had anything happened to you in regard to fire—shell fire or action, or—

A. Oh, we were under shell fire there. We went into a dug-in in a hill and we dug into what was called 'Dead Man's Hill.' I think there was something over two hundred of us fellows dug in there and there wasn't a hundred of us left, and we were there only four hours.

Q. What happened to you at that time and place in this Dead Man's Hill?

A. Shells exploded within ten or fifteen feet of me and the man next to me died. He was dead before I was able to get up.

Q. What happened to you?

A. It shot the wind out of me and I was thrown down on the ground like a feather."

Shortly after that time this dysentery broke out on me, and I was so sick from that I didn't notice any great change. The dysentery was—the bowels run off. It was the diarrhea; that is what I think it was. It was from the water or something we got to eat. At that time we were eating with the French troops. We had to eat their rations. I think it was canned horse meat and we had hard tack. And we had rotten coffee.

"Q. As a result of this dysentery, what was done with you?

A. Well, I was able to stay with the company a few days when we moved back of the lines. I had been on guard but they relieved me. A sergeant thought I was drinking but I told him I had nothing to drink and then they put me on sick bed and I was there for two or three days. They had no convalescent's camp to send me to or a hospital, and then from there I joined the company and went into the town of Nancy.

Q. Were you in the hospital there for some time— or were you in the hospital at any time until you went into the hospital at St. Mihiel?

A. I was in the hospital in Selincourt."

I don't know whether I was in the hospital there for flue, or this trouble, or what it was. I was in the hospital there two weeks or a little better. I think they called it influenza. Following that I was weak and run down.

After I got out of the hospital at Selincourt I went back and joined the company. I came back only two days before we went on the St. Mihiel offensive. They detailed me to guard duty there. That was along in the fall. I know it rained like blazes when we went there. It was maybe in September some time.

The reason I was detailed to guard duty there at that time, I guess, was they figured I wasn't fit for anything else. I was bothered with dysentery and diarrhea and I couldn't carry my pack. I couldn't keep up with the outfit.

After the St. Mihiel offensive I went into the kitchen. I figured I could maybe get better stuff to eat; better stuff for my condition than I could get on the outside, and I couldn't stand the trip. I couldn't carry my pack. I did not get better; I was able to get by and that was all.

"Q. Did you go to any sick bed until you went into the Champoigne offense?

A. I went sometimes four and five times a day. Sometimes I would be excused from duty and sometimes I would not be. I think they gave me aspirin tablets.

Q. Did you get any relief with that medicine from your sickness?

A. I can't say that I did.

Q. What actions did you take part in?

A. After St. Mihiel it was the Champoigne.

Q. Were you on shell fire there?

A. I was."

My condition was very poor during that time. I volunteered to go into the lines and they wouldn't take me. The captain laughed at me. He said he was having trouble enough with well men without taking sick men along into the lines.

From October 1, 1918, to October 9, 1918, is what I refer to as the Champoigne offensive, or the Mont Blanc offensive. We were in reserve there behind this line until just a few days before we went into the Argonne Sector, over on the Verdun.

"Q. How long were you on the Argonne Drive?

A. I left the outfit two days before the Armistice was signed."

I left two days before the Armistice was signed because I was not physically able to carry on.

From there I went to the hospital. I was there when the Armistice was signed. We moved 17 kilometers back to Hospital No. 1, and I got back there, and I was left there, and from there I went back from the hospital to Contrexeville, France, Base 36. I don't remember the exact number of days I was in the hospital at Contrexeville. I left there some time after the first of January, 1919.

In the hospital there I believe they treated me for intra-colitis, or inflammation of the bowels, or dysentery.

When I went into the service I was slightly under-weight; I weighed only about 165 pounds. When I left California I weighed sometimes over 200 pounds. I recall being weighed for over-seas service when I left Virginia. I weighed about 208 pounds at Ponet-cal, Virginia. I was six feet, two inches tall.

During this period of time while I was sick, commencing some time in July, 1918, and continuing until January, 1919, I was weighed while in the hospital at Contrexeville, France, and I weighed 130 pounds at that time.

I was very weak at that time and presume I was pretty much run down.

Then I was sent back to my organization in Germany. My company was there in a little town called Waterbuton. I came home with my outfit.

While I was with my company in Germany I did regular duty for a short time. I went back to the outfit and went into the kitchen and was in the kitchen for about two months. I don't know exactly, but I acted as a helper for the mules; three of us. We took care of four head of mules. I stayed with that until May, 1919, and then I was transferred back to straight duty. I was not on duty for a great part of the time.

When I came home I was discharged from Pon-tical, Virginia. From there I came home.

"Q. What was your condition when you got home?

A. On the trip home on the water I picked up, but the trip across the continent weakened me.

Q. Did you have any more spells of dysentery?

A. Yes; I had spells after that.

Q. When did you first notice the neurasthenia of which you complain?—in these pleadings.

A. I don't know what caused it. I don't know whether it was from being shook up caused by the motion of the wheels or whether it was from being sick so long. I can't say what it was.

Q. I asked you when you first noticed the neurasthenia? Of its bothering you? When did you first notice that you were nervous, or that you had been nervous, when you had not been previously?

A. I can't say as to that. I know I had it when I started home.

Q. When did you start home from France?

A. Well, you see I was practically in or within the sound of guns from the time I joined the outfit until the Armistice was signed. We would move back a short time but all our training quarters were within hearing of the guns.

Q. The point I want to make here is—when did you

first realize that you had this nervous disorder?

A. I can't say as to that.

Q. Was it prior to leaving France?

A. Oh, yes, yes.

Q. When did you first discover that you were having trouble with your heart?

A. Well, it bothered me some at the time we got out but not a great deal. I think it has got worse in the last two years.

Q. It bothered you some when you first got out?

A. Yes.

Q. You talk about an acute enteritis—?

A. Yes.

Q. —do you know that that was what you had when you got back into civil life?

A. No, I thought it was the grub I was eating.

Q. When did you first discover that your stomach was bothering you?

A. Well, my stomach was bad when I was in the service.

Q. Did you have any of these disabilities before you entered the service?

A. Not to my knowledge.

Q. Well, you should know.

A. Well, I think I could eat nails before I went in.

Q. After you were mustered out, you came back here to your people in the east end of this county, is that right?

A. Yes."

The first work I did was I helped one of the neighbors out there. That was Mr. Burns. I helped him possibly four or five hours. I did not work with the rest of the crew until the work was done; I played out; it was one of my days.

I heard Mr. Burns testify here yesterday. I was around with Mr. Burns for possibly a week or ten days. I believe I helped him with the chores while I was there.

I think Bob Strubin came and asked me to assist him in 1919. He asked me to come and help him and I said I didn't know whether I could or not but that I would try, and I went down and made a try, and for a while I got along fairly good, and then this

trouble bothered me and I had two or three light attacks, and then after two or three light attacks I had a bad attack, and I went to the doctor; to Dr. Hughes, at Gresham. That was about the first part of October, 1919.

At that time I was bothered with dysentery, and

I was very weak, and I had bad night sweats, and I didn't know what was wrong with me. I also was bothered with severe headaches at that time—something awful. It would catch me through the temple and the back of the head.

I was nervous at that time, and I understood Bob used to have quite a time with me there. They had one old gasoline engine that they used to grind ensilage with for feed, and also grind other grain for the cows, and Bob used to play with that and get it to backfire to see me jump, and I would hit the deck on all fours. It would catch me when I didn't know it was going to do it. If I had known it I could have controlled myself but if I didn't I would go right up in the air and come down.

"Q. Why would you go up in the air?

A.   I guess it was a matter of habit. That is one thing that a fellow learns to do when he is in the army —that's to duck when a shell goes off."

The first three or four weeks I had to take very little time off. The doctor told me to lay around for four or five days the first time I took sick and then go back to work, and at different times I had to take time off. I think there was five or six days that I did nothing until toward the last.

"Q. Did he have anybody there to assist you?

A. Well, he had one man there first and then a boy to help me. He helped to clean out the barn and get the feed in. Later on he done away with the milking machines and he got a man there to help me.

Q. This work you did there and the work done by this man and this boy later, could you have done it all if you had been well?

A. Well, one man should take care of 30 or 40 cows.

Q. Could you have done that if you had been as well as you had been before you went into the service?

A. I had done it before."

I have made an attempt to get the payroll records or the amounts that have been paid me by the Fernwood Dairy and these other people, but have not been successful.

The first time I was at Mr. Strubin's I got $75 a month and board. He did not dock me for the time I was laid off, sick.

I worked there until about the first of April, 1920, and then I gave it up and was away five or six weeks; I don't remember which. Then he saw me again about asking me to resume my employment, and he said he would have a man help me all the time, and that I would have to do the feeding, and that he would give me an increase over what he had been paying. He had been paying me $75 and he said he would give me $110 or $115; I don't remember it now.

I don't think anything was said about my condition at that time. I told him I would try. I didn't say I would keep it up; I said I would try.

The second time I worked there, I think, until about the 15th of August that same year. The last four or five days I was there I did not do but very little. I was not feeling just right and I wasn't able to get around. I wanted to do my end of the work and the rest of the work the other lad did. There were two of us taking care of the dairy herd at that time.

I helped with the milking and the other boy did the heavy work. Some days I could carry on my share of the work pretty well and other days I couldn't very well.

The first time I quit Mr. Strubin was because I could not carry on, and the second time was because I was on the sick list, and I believe it was partly because I was just married. I was married a few days after I left there.

After I left Bob Strubin I worked for Mr. Wilcox of the Fernwood Dairy. I can't recall how much time elapsed between the time I worked for Mr. Strubin and the time I worked for Mr. Wilcox, but think somewhere between three and four weeks; something like that.

I was with Mr. Wilcox of the Fernwood Dairy a little over a year. I was off eight weeks in the summer of 1921, with an operation. I had this operation because this trouble was still bothering me and I could not get any relief for it. The operation did not relieve it.

Besides the eight weeks, I lost a few days now and then. I think four days was the longest I was off. I lost a few days now and then because I was not able to carry on. It was the same trouble.

After the operation I went back and went to work for Mr. Wilcox. Mr. Wilcox came to me himself and asked me to quit. He said I wouldn't last a year if I kept on with that work. He told me to quit. I was sick at that time.

After that I did practically nothing all that winter, or until the spring of 1922.

I lived out on 97th Street, in Portland. I forget the exact number of the house. I think it was 64 something on 97th Street. During that time I was not well by any means.

Next I bought a little place out near Gresham—

the place that has been referred to here several times. I attempted to farm that place, with very poor success.

I did some of the work on the place, and my father did some, and I hired some of the work done. I hired some plowing done by John Strubin. My wife did some work there; she helped me, of course.

"Q. Were you sick while you were out there?

A. I was.

Q. How long were you in the hospital at that time?

A. At the time of the

Q. At the time of the operation?

A. August, 1922.

Q. And what hospital was that?

A. The old veterans' hospital.

Q. The old hospital '77' across the river?

A. Yes.

Q. What occasioned your going to the hospital?

A. Well, Dr. Rockey sent me there. He sent me there for observation and treatment.

Q. What was your treatment at that time?

A. I was still bothered with abdominal trouble and this diarrhea.

Q. And what about your nervous condition?

A. Yes, sure.

Q. You still had that?

A. Yes, sure.

Q. And what about your headaches?

A. Several headaches of the same kind.

Q. What else? Was it just the same condition that you have told us about before?

A. Yes."

The next job I had was with the Davidson Bakery Company. I went to work there in May of 1923, I believe. I got along pretty well but when it came to the heavy work I had to have help, but the light work I could get along with pretty well.

I had a brother working there at that same time, and he is still there.

I worked at that place somewhere around eight or ten months.

There were interruptions in that employment. I was off part of the time because I was sick.

During that period of time I was under Dr. Edson's care—at least a good part of the time; Dr. Edson of the Veterans' Hospital. I don't just remember what other doctors.

I left the bakery and went into the hospital—No. 77. Dr. C. C. Campbell, of the Veterans' Hospital, treated me while I was there. I went through the routine examination while I was there, and I think I was under Dr. Campbell's care practically all the time I was there.

After I was discharged from the Veterans' Hospital I think I felt better. I was feeling pretty good when I left and from then until the fall.

The only work I did after that amounted to anything was for the City of Portland; that was the job of watching the rocks coming down the hill.

My stomach gave me an awful lot of trouble during all that time. I can't tell you exactly how long I continued that work. I worked on that job watching this road until it was completed, and then I worked one day running a wheelbarrow, and then I went to the Veterans' Hospital for an examination and treatment, and was there possibly two weeks or better. Then I got discharged.

At the hospital I went through the routine examination before the Board. I was not treated at that particular time. I think Dr. Marcellas and Dr. Schauffler examined me at that time.

I worked for a few days with Mr. Dahl in the summer of 1922, and a few days off and on since then. I had a job over near Siletz, Camp No. 12. I think I was there two or three weeks. I think that was 1927.

Prior to that time I was on my farm. At that place I had the heart attack that Leon testified to yesterday. After that I was in the hospital again— in Veterans' Hospital No. 77. I don't recall all the doctors who examined me. I was under Dr. Schauffler at that time, I believe.

I quit work at the logging camp because I played out; I could not fill the bill. I think I worked somewhere around two or three weeks before I played out. I am not sure.

In March, 1928, I went up to Bend, and got employment there. I worked there somewhere in the neighborhood of six or eight weeks. I had been off two weeks while I was there, on the sick list, and the last three or four days, and then I quit the last time and came home. I was not able to carry on. I was not so well. I was not in bed.

When I came home sick, my wife was staying out at her folks' home, and I stayed out there for a while, and then we stayed with my folks for a while—at Troutdale.

After July, 1928, I think I was called in for an examination then.

In the summer of 1929, I worked for the Rose

City & McKay (or O'Kay) Logging Company. I got along fairly good for a while, and then I went to pieces. I was there for possibly two months. I was off some. I quit because I played out two or three days right in succession.

In November, 1929, I did some work with the Phoenix Logging Company. That was the work Mr. Cooper testified about. His story of what happened up there is correct. My condition when I quit that job was very poor.

After that I came home and went through a routine examination at the Veterans' Hospital. I did not get any cure for my troubles then.

I moved out to Forest Grove, I think, the 7th of October, 1930.

I heard Mrs. Lyons tell about my consulting Dr. Tucker. I was under his care for something like six weeks last year. I had a pain in my left side and he said it was a heart condition, but I forget just what he called it. I don't believe he treated me for my stomach condition. I was in to see him a couple of years ago when I was bothered with the dysentery trouble.

The last year I have done no work at all, and my dysentery has bothered me very little. I had to lay off because of it, that was all. If I get out and exert myself my bowels run off more frequently than if

I lay around. If I don't do much exercise, why they're better.

"Q. Now, I have attempted to cover the field of your work in your service. Have I overlooked anything that you can recall? Is there anything that you have not told us here with reference to your getting employment or your attempt to get it?

A. I don't believe so.

Q. Will you tell us now what other doctors, other than those you have mentioned, treated you at the Veterans' Bureau?

A. In the Veterans' Bureau?

Q. Yes.

A. Dr. Touesey."

I was under him for examination. At that time he was a Veterans' Hospital doctor. I don't remember what he told me my trouble was. I asked him for training, and he said he would not recommend it. He said I would not be able to carry on if I had it.

In the spring of 1924 or 1925, sometime during that year, when I was in the Veterans' Hospital, treating for inflammation of the gall bladder, as they termed it, I asked Dr. Marcellas what my trouble was, and he said I had amoebic dysentery, and that that was what my trouble was and had been all along.

This amoebic dysentery that I was being treated

for was the same as I had when I was first treated for a disorder in France, and I have been suffering from the same thing ever since.

(Cross Examination by Mr. Erskine.)

The first illness after I joined the military service was this attack of mumps. I think I was in the hospital about five days then, and on sick list on the boat, and about that number of days on rest, and when they went down I think it was something like three weeks after that. I don't think there has been any serious or permanent injury from the mumps.

My first shell fire was on the Marne. I think we were two days on that drive. I joined the outfit on the 12th of July. We went in there the 18th and 19th.

"Q. And then from there you went to some other sector?

A. To Soissons.

Q. Well, you went to the Marne Sector first?

A. Yes. Yes, I think we called it the Soissons.

Q. It was off in the Marne District, was it?

A. Yes.

Q. And then when you left the Marne District you went to Nancy?

A. Yes.

Q. And while you were there were you under shell fire?

A. No, not at Nancy; and then we went to Ponya and we laid in a quiet sector there for a week or two.

Q. All the time after—from the time you were two days on the Marne, you were never in direct shell fire were you?

A. Well, we were not in the line but we were under shell fire to a certain extent. We could hear the shells all the time.

Q. You could hear them but as far as immediate activity with your outfit, except for the two days that you were up on the Marne, you were not under active shell fire?

A. Not continuous, no.

Q. Well, not at all, were you?

A. Well, now in Nancy they bombed that with shell practically every night that we were there and we were there three or four nights, and from there we went up on the Ponzon (?) Reserve, and we were under shell fire there continuously.

Q. You could just hear them, couldn't you?

A .No, there was always a few shells around now and then.

Q. The next offense that you were actually on was the two days that you were on the Marne, that you were actually on was—

A. What do you mean?

Q. Well, you know what offensive means?

A. Yes.

Q. That was the only time that you were on the offensive, were these two days?

A. No.

Q. When were you on any other? The Argonne?

A. The Argonne. When I was on the Argonne, I was under shell fire, sure.

Q. I understood you to say you were in the kitchen, that you could hear the reports of the guns, and things like that, but that you were not up in line?

A. No, I was not in the front line, no.

Q. You were never in the front line after the two days on the Marne, were you?

A. No."

I believe it was in August some time when I had the influenza. That was the first sickness I had after I had the mumps for which I had to go to the hospital. That was in August. I was on sick leave then a good many times before I went to the hospital in August for the flu. I was in the hospital at the time I had the influenza.

"Q. And then later on, the 12th day of November, the day after the Armistice, you went to Field Hospital 32, didn't you?

A. It was somewhere in that neighborhood. I don't know exactly.

Q. And when was the next time you were in the hospital after the influenza? Was that the next time?

A. Yes.

Q. And at that time you were there for intro-colitis?

A. Yes.

Q. And you stayed there until the 21st day of November, didn't you, About ten days or two weeks.

A. I left there in January.

Q. Base Hospital 32?

A. Yes, we were at Contrexeville, France."

Then I went to Germany with my outfit in the Army of Occupation and went back to my regular duty. My regular duty at that time was work in the kitchen. This work in the kitchen was not the heaviest work they had to do. It was the easiest. They were drilling nine hours a day, so I imagine the kitchen was easier than that.

After I quit the kitchen, I and two or three others took care of three or four mules. I couldn't say whether there was anything wrong with the other two or three boys.

Then I came home and came out to Troutdale and worked part of one day for Mr. Burns. That was shortly after I came home.

"Q. Well, going back just a little bit—Counsel asked you concerning your experience before you enlisted and you said you had been in Eastern Oregon about two years prior to that time— prior to the time you enlisted?

A. Two years or a little better."

I had not gone to high school before I went to Eastern Oregon. I didn't go to high school at all. I did not go over there because of the condition of my health. A man would not go to work on a ranch for his health, I presume. My health was all right at that time.

Then in September, 1919, I went to work for Mr. Strubin, and worked for him until April, at $75 per month. Then I was off until some time in May and he came after me; it was April or the first of May. Then I worked until August 15, 1920. The second time I worked for him I got an increase up to $110 or $115 a month.

Mr. Strubin had sold his milking machines before I went there. I came back to help him milk those cows. I don't think there were 48 cows. I think there were 42 cows milking while I was there.

We would milk the cows twice a day. We would start at 4 o'clock in the morning, and I and the other man who worked there would be through by seven or seven-thirty for breakfast.

In the afternoon we started around 4 o'clock.

While I was out there I was bothered with this weakness and diarrhea.

"Q. At that time you had no trouble with your stomach?

A. Well, I could not eat. I did not know what was the matter with me. When I was out there in 1919 and 1920 I went through a complete examination and when I got through I never knew what was the matter with me or what was not.

Q. It was not until 1925, that you had anything wrong with your stomach?

A. Yes; I knew I had something wrong but what I had or what was wrong I didn't know.

Q. The stomach did not bother you while you were over in France, did it?

A. It sure did.

Q. Now then, in October, 1919, after six weeks, is when you went to see Dr. Hughes, and you had been off two or three days at that time—after you had been working six weeks?

A. Yes.

Q. And the next time that you had off was while you were working for Mr. Strubin, during the ten or eleven months, five or six days one time, and that was when you had your examination?

A. I was off once for six weeks.

Q. Between the two periods you were off six weeks?

A. Yes.

Q. While you were working there?

A. I was off several times, four or five days."

I quit in August, 1920, to get married.

After about three or four weeks I went to work for Mr. Wilcox at the Fernwood Dairy in town.

I continued to work for him for about a year— with the time I was off a little better than a year. I was off eight weeks at one time for an appendix operation.

I was on different salaries there. I think I started at $33 and I was raised to $35, and then I was cut down to $30. That was weekly. I washed bottles and I checked.

Assuming I went to work there in September, 1920, I worked there until—I believe it was in October, 1921.

"Q. Then the rest of the year you have not accounted for your work? Did you work the rest of the year?

A. Yes, I worked. Let me see—I worked at the saw mill for ten days or two weeks."

The saw mill work was at Prescott, Oregon. I went up there in 1922—January or February.

Before I went onto my own place I worked for Mr. Bowman on his place east of Gresham. I did dairying work there. I think I continued that work something like three weeks.

Then I bought my own little place, and my wife and I went onto that little place to live for about a year; about 11 months, from May, 1922, until about the 1st of April, 1923.

I worked a few days at the neighbors when I went out there first and during the summer of 1922 I done very little work, but my main business was running the ranch during that year, outside of a few days that I may have worked for some neighbors.

During that summer I made my first trip to Hospital No. 77. I went over there for observation and treatment. I was there something like two or three weeks.

I believe it was May, 1923, I went to work for the Davidson Bakery Company, and I continued the work for eight or ten months.

(Following amounts of wages received were put in the record upon stipulation.)

Commencing with

May 21, 1923, 8 days, earned	$ 32.00
June, 1923, lost 2 days, earned	104.00
July, 1923, lost 2 days, earned	102.00
August, 1923, lost 3 days, earned	108.00
September, 1923, lost 5 days, earned	100.00
October, 1923, lost 4 days, earned	104.00
November, 1923, lost 4 days, earned	104.00
December, 1923, lost 5 days (worked 1 day extra)	104.00
January, 1924, lost 16 days	68.00
February, 1924, lost 9 days	86.00
March, 1924, lost 5 days	117.00
Did not work after the 31st day of March, earned a total of	$1029.00

I went to the United States Veterans' Hospital for observation and treatment, either in January or February, I am not sure. It was during that time that Dr. Campbell examined me. That would account for part of the loss of time while I was working for the Davidson Bakery Company.

I don't necessarily remember what my wages were while I was firing or docketing for about six weeks during that year. It was the average wage they were paying at that time; usually about $4.25.

Then in the spring of 1925 my wife and I went back to our place for about two years, but I do not remember the dates. We lived there about two years and during that time I worked for the City of Portland and did a few other small jobs. But my main occupation was living there on my place during that two-year period.

I went to Brooks-Scanlon in March, 1928; I was out there at Camp No. 4, falling logs and barking. My companion in falling was a man by the name of Armstrong.

I was paid by the foot. I think the best scale I made was somewhere in the neighborhood of nineteen thousand or something; it was something less than twenty thousand.

"Q. You mean for one month?

A. Oh, I don't know for the month. This was for one day.

Q. It would hardly go twenty thousand any day, would it?

A. I said that was for one day but we had some from another day on that. I am giving you the —I think—I think it was about five or five and quarter or something like that—I am not sure.

Q. I don't think it went that high. I find the highest here is eleven thousand in one day."

After that I worked for something like two months. I don't remember what I was paid for those two months.

Dr. Tousey examined me at one time; I think he is dead now. I think Dr. Schauffler is deceased also.

I don't remember that I went to see Dr. Joyce at the request of Mr. Bynon. After I finished Dr. Joyce's clinic a recommendation was made to me for an operation for this ulcer in my duodenum. I never had that operation because I am afraid of it. I think it would be quite a gamble. I have seen many of them who have had that operation performed and they were no better afterward. I believe I have seen a few the other way.

(Redirect Examination by Mr. Bynon.)

Not all these doctors whom I have mentioned are dead. I think the two he mentioned are dead. I think Dr. Marcellas is in Palo Alto, California.

When I quit Strubin the second time I was not very husky. I was not able to carry on with my work; I lost out three or four days before I quit there. Since I have been separated from the service some days I would feel good and some I would not.

(Defendant's Exhibit 2 offered in evidence without objection.)

Defendant's Exhibit 2

1. Full Name: Carrol T. McCreary.

2. Address: Gresham, Oregon.

9. Date and place of last discharge: Aug. 19, 1919, Quantico, Va.

10. Cause of discharge: Transfer to inactive status M. C. R.

11. Nature and extent of disability claimed: Pain in right side and nervousness.

12. Date disability began: June 1st, 1918.

13. Cause of disability: Mumps, gassed and exposure.

14. When and where received: June 1st, 1918, on USS "HENDERSON."

15. Did you receive treatment at an Army or Navy hospital? Yes.

    (a) If so, state name and location of the hospital: From June 1, 1918 on USS "Henderson" in Sick Bay on way to France, then taken to hospital at Brest, France, and was there until June 27, 1918; gassed in July, 1918; sent to Field Hosp. No. 16 in Toule Sector Aug. 1918 for two weeks; from Nov. 9, 1918 to Jan. 8, 1919, in Evac. Hospitals and then Base No. 32 at Contrecinville, France.

16. Occupations and wages before entering service: Stock farming $75.00 (monthly), (dates) 1915-1918-Feb. 20, 1918; farming at home.

17. Last two employers before entering service: Hilton & Burgess, Fossil, Oregon, 2½ yrs. (time employed).

18. Occupation since discharge, dates of each, and wages received. If less than before, why? Dairy work, Sept. 6, 1919, to April 1, 1920, $75.00; dairy work, May 1, 1920, $110.00.

19. Present employer: Robert Strevin, Portland, Ore.

20. Name and address of attending physician: None.

21. Are you confined to bed? No. Do you require constant nursing or attendance? No.

23. Are you willing to accept medical or surgical treatment if furnished? Yes.

I make the foregoing statements as part of my claim with full knowledge of the penalty provided for making a false statement as to a material fact in a claim for compensation or insurance.

(Signed) Carrol T. McCreary.

Subscribed and sworn to before me this 22nd day of May, 1922, by Carrol T. McCreary, claimant, to whom the statements herein were fully made known and explained.

(Signed) Meta M. Dekkar,
Notary Public for Oregon.

"Q. The Government has offered Defendant's Exhibit 2 in evidence, being the application you made (showing witness paper) is that your signature on the bottom of that, on the last page? It is, is it not?

A. Yes."

I don't know who made it out for me. I believe it was made out in the Veterans' Bureau Building.

Plaintiff rests.

Deposition of DR. CHARLES GEORGE RATTNER, taken on behalf of defendant on oral interrogatories submitted by Mr. Clark on behalf of defendant; no appearance for plaintiff:

My full name is Charles George Rattner, and my present address is 3760 88th Street, Jackson Heights, Long Island, New York.

I am a physician—a graduate of Oregon University Medical School, in 1916. I have taken European courses in surgery as post graduate courses. I have practiced my profession for fifteen years and have specialized in general surgery.

The document you have handed me is a report of physical examination which I made on Carrol T. McCreary at the United States Veterans' Hospital in the City of Portland, Oregon, on August 31, 1922.

I do not recall, independently of this report of the medical examination, my findings made at the time of that examination.

The document above referred to bears my signature, and correctly reports my examination of the findings at that time.

Refreshing my memory from the report of examination, I made no findings at all at that time. I mean by that that at that time there was no disability and the man was entirely well.

"Q. Doctor, how do you proceed with this examination. State in detail just what you do from the time a man comes into the office for an examination; state how you went about making your findings.

A. FIRST: There was an examination on his admission at the hospital. He came in for observation for intestinal condition. His only complaint was gas in the stomach. He was quite anguished and nervous at the time when he came in, but during the stay in the hospital the nervousness entirely disappeared, and the laboratory findings for gastro-intestinal observations were negative. Therefore, he was discharged as a patient without any disability."

This man was under my immediate observation. I conducted a full and complete examination of him, using a stethoscope, and in the laboratory work, the X-ray.

The diagnosis, as made by me of the results of my findings, as given, was negative; no diagnosis as far as his intestinal condition was concerned.

As far as the gastro-intestinal canal was concerned, the prognosis in this case was good.

I am familiar with the general duties of various civilian occupations, such as farmers, loggers, bricklayers, factory laborers.

"Q. Doctor, basing your knowledge upon the findings made by you in your report of the examination made by you on Carrol T. McCreary, on or about August 31st, 1922, and on your knowledge of the general duties of various civilian occupations named by you, state whether it was your opinion that Carrol T. McCreary was suffering from any impairment of mind or body at the time of the examination, which rendered it impossible for him to follow continuously any substantially gainful occupation?

A.   No sir."

In my opinion he could follow the occupation of farming. At the time I examined this man, he was in such physical condition that he could engage in farming in competition with the average farmer; absolutely yes.

Deposition of DR. C. C. CAMPBELL, taken on behalf of defendant on oral interrogatories submitted by Ernest D. Fooks, appearing for defendant; no appearance for plaintiff:

My name is Clayton C. Campbell, and my address 808 Professional Building, Long Beach, California.

I am a physician; a graduate of the Indiana University School of Medicine in 1904. I have practiced my profession since 1904 continuously.

"Q. Have you taken any post-graduate courses?

A.   Assistant to the Chair of Medicine, Indiana University; Chief of Medicine, Base Hospital, Fort Benjamin Harrison, Indianapolis, Indiana, and Surgeon of the 44th Engineers, Chief General Inspecting Officer 44th Division Somure, France, and after being discharged from the Army I went into the United States Public

Health Service Hospital No. 52, Baltimore, Maryland, as chief of medicine; Clinical Director, Boise Idaho Veterans' Bureau Hospital; Chief Consultant United States Veterans' Hospital, Portland, Oregon No. 77."

I have specialized in diagnosis, diseases of the heart, and the gastro-intestinal tract. I have specialized about 18 years in diseases of the heart, and about 10 years in gastro-intestinal tract.

I was with the Public Health Service from September 1st, 1920, until 1925. The Public Health was taken over by the Veterans' Bureau and I went over with them.

During the time I was a member of the staff of the United States Public Health Service and the United States Veterans' Bureau I had occasion to make a physical examination or examinations of Carrol T. McCreary at United States Veterans' Hospital No. 77, Portland, Oregon.

I do not have any independent recollection of Carrol T. McCreary.

I made notes of my examinations at the time of examination of Carrol T. McCreary. I have those notes with me.

Refreshing my memory from the notes and records I kept of the examinations of Carrol T. Mc-

Creary, I will state that he entered the hospital at Portland, Oregon — United States Veterans' Hospital — on February 4, 1924, and remained until February 9, 1924, undergoing a complete G.I. examination which took all of this time.

Referring to my notes — a fractional gastric analysis was made on the 5th and the highest acidity reported was 96; blood count on the 5th was negative; stool examination was asked for but patient did not comply so that his stool examination could be made; X-ray Gastro-Intestinal series was begun on the 6th and not completed until the 9th. That was negative. A spinal X-ray examination on the 5th was made and it was negative except Spina Bifida Occulate was found and patient given credit for same. The barium examination was negative and Wasserman was negative and the urine was negative.

Gastro-Intestinal series is a modern method of ascertaining the condition of the stomach and the gastro-intestinal tract by giving barium per mouth and watching with the fluoroscope the barium pass down into the stomach and out into the bowels. Every so often prints are made of the barium and the barium is traced through the entire gastro-intestinal tract and we know the normal reaction, how long it takes for the barium normally to pass down through, and when we have an abnormal slowing or rapidity that indicates certain things.

Spina Bifida means there is an abnormal outgrowth of bone that interferes with the movement of the vertebrae, impedes the movement of the vertebrae. This is considered a serious impairment by the medical profession if it progresses far enough. It depends greatly on how many vertebrae are affected.

I would not be able to answer regarding my finding in the case of Carrol T. McCreary if I were not allowed to refresh my memory by looking at my examination report.

The document you hand me is United States Veterans' Bureau Medical Division Physical Examination 2545, made by me and signed by me on June 27, 1924. I can identify the signature on this record as my own. The examination to which I have just referred was made by me.

Referring to this examination, I find that I stated the claimant was able to resume pre-war occupation with a handicap. The claimant was not bed-ridden. He was able to travel. Hospitalization was not advised at this time. The patient would accept hospitalization if it was necessary. An attendant was not necessary, training was feasible, showing that the previous findings of Spina Bifida condition had not developed to cause a great handicap at that time.

The handicap for pre-war occupations was on account of the Spina-Bifida and would interfere to some extent with the duties of hard, manual work.

Referring to my examination of Carrol T. McCreary, dated June 27, 1924, which I have just previously identified as my report, I will state that the diagnosis made at the time of this examination was hyperchlorhydria, mild; spina bifide occulata, neurasthenia, neurasthenic type, varicose veins, slight.

My prognosis was guarded; the reason for that was that any one of these four diagnoses could improve or get materially worse.

Referring to my notes and report of the examination made of Carrol T. McCreary on January 20, 1925, will state that Mr. McCreary came in complaining of gall-bladder trouble and a gall-bladder examination was made and found negative on this date. There was no diagnosis; diagnosis was negative; no prognosis was made.

By referring to my notes and records of the examination of Carrol T. McCreary on March 24, 1924, I find the patient was complaining of pain in the region of his gall bladder and another gall-bladder drainage was done, which was negative. No disease was found.

Referring to my notes and records of examination of Carrol T. McCreary on May 4, 1925, will state that his complaint at that time was precordial pain, giddiness, palpitation and cough, giving a history of having had tonsilitis. The pulse rate recumbent 80, blood pressure, Systolic 128, Diastolic 76; Pulse Pressure 52; Respiration 15; Pulse rate standing 100; Pulse after 50 hops 120; Systolic 134, Diastolic 70; Pulse Pressure 64; respiration 21. Two minutes after exercising pulse 80, full and regular. Relative cardiac dullness 8 c.m.'s left, and 3 c.m.'s right. P.M.I. was in the 5th interspace. No apparent increase over normal cardiac dullness. No thrill. No palpitation. No dyspnoea. No dizziness. No murmurs that are abnormal. Diagnosis 1096. No cardiac disease.

No cardiac disease was the diagnosis made at that time. There was no prognosis made on that examination.

Hyperchlorhydria means there is just a little bit too much acid in the stomach; not in his case a great amount but we gave him credit for a slight increase. That is a similar condition to the medical term known as hyperacidity. This is a mild type, as the examination at no time ran over 96, which is not very high.

Spina Bifida might be either a progressive or a fixed condition, but the proportion it has progressed is only to be determined by repeated X-rays.

The usual symptoms of that disease or condition are pain in the back, inability to move the vertebrae in stooping over or moving from side to side, etc., discomfort when lying on the back. In fact, it may be of such a character that there is hardly no time but when one is conscious of their back. This was discovered in the course of our examination; it was not complained of by the patient.

I am familiar with the general duties of various civilian occupations. In my examinations of Carrol T. McCreary I did not find any impairment of mind or body that would altogether preclude him from following a gainful, substantial occupation. He could follow a gainful occupation with a handicap.

Reverting to my findings of the various examinations made of Mr. McCreary, there was no indication of enteritis. We tried to cover this at the time. It was my intention, in examining these cases at this time, to give them credit for everything that they might have in the way of disease, so in outlining this work sheet I covered everything as near as it was possible. I requested that this patient give us his stool and you will notice in my first notes that the patient never gave us a stool so we were unable to report as to whether or not he had enteritis.

To my knowledge there was no indication of dysentery. There was no indication of amoebiasis, but we could not rule this out definitely because the patient did not cooperate with us to the extent of giving us a stool for the examination.

From the carbon copy of my heart examination, there was no indication at the time of any of my examinations of Mr. McCreary having any heart trouble.

There was no indication of ulcers of the stomach, as proven by our gastro-intestinal examination and X-rays at that time.

I diagnosed Mr. McCreary as a neurasthenic type. In referring to my notes I see he is a nervous, excitable fellow, and yet with the physical findings as given under the heart examination of May 4, 1925, one can readily see that it did not disturb the circulatory system so very much or he would have a pulse rate of more than 80 per minute and after 50 hops it would have been up around 140 or 150, whereas it was just 112, practically normal. I think on account of his nervous manifestations during his examination we gave him credit for a neurasthenia— of a neurasthenic type.

The copy of my report of the examination of Carrol T. McCreary, date June 27, 1924, contains the following findings:

General appearance male, white, well developed. Height 6 ft., 3 in., Weight present: 170 lbs. — normal 175 lbs. Eyes, ears, nose apparently normal. Tongue coated; Teeth good repair. Throat apparently normal; tonsils small. Lungs apparently normal; no rales. Heart apparently normal; no murmur. Blood pressure S. 110, D. 60; P.P. 50; Pulse 80 full reg. Abdomen apparently normal; unable to find any abnormal condition. Intestines, liver, spleen, kidneys, apparently normal. Skin apparently normal — scar appendectomy 8 cm long — well healed, non-adherent. Mucous membranes, bones, joints apparently normal, except spine as mentioned in 2545 Jan. 30, 1924. Glandular system, genito-urinary system apparently normal. Nervous system see 2545 dated Jan. 30, 1924. No hernia; no hemorrhoids. Urinalysis: Amber acid mucus 3 plus, albumin negative, crystals calcium oxalate, sp. gr. 1.029, negative sugar, W.B.C. one plus. Varicose veins slight both lower legs.

Fractional Gastric Analysis:

Free	Total	Blood Trace	Bile	Mucus	Starch	Diplo. cocci	Leuco- cytes
18	28	"	Neg	Neg	Pos	Pos	Two plus
42	50	"	Pos	"	"	"	
50	62	"	Neg	"			
76	78	"	"				
76	84	"	"	"			
84	96	"	"				

"Q. Doctor, I will give you the definition of permanent and total disability as defined by the

War Risk Insurance Act. It is deemed to be any impairment of mind or body which would prevent the sufferer therefrom from following continuously any substantial gainful occupation and that it is reasonable to believe that such a condition would remain throughout the life of the person suffering from said condition. Bearing in mind, Doctor, that definition, I will ask you if there is anything in your findings made in the examinations of Carrol T. McCreary which would indicate that he is permanently and totally disabled?

A. No sir; I do not think he was."

"MR. ERSKINE: The only other testimony the Government had is its affirmative allegation in the answer where it alleges the reinstatement of the old war risk insurance policy which had expired, that it was reinstated and converted to a five-year term policy, K-703573, during the month of October, 1930. Now if counsel will stipulate that —

MR. BYNON: I think I covered that yesterday when I made my statement, but I will put Mr. Mc-Creary on to show what this understanding is. We will admit that was done."

CARROL T. McCREARY, called in rebuttal in his own behalf, testified as follows:

I recall the instance of my having reinstated that policy. I was at the Veterans' Hospital 77 when that occurred. I happened to take that action as they wrote to me a number of times and I was asked by their contact man to reinstate.

I had never seen my original policy and was not aware of the provisions in that policy. I did not know what my rights were under the policy. I was not aware at that time that if my policy had matured when I came out I was entitled to benefits from it. I never knew of those provisions until I consulted my attorneys.

The first time I was in the hospital in 1922, when Dr. Rattner was there, I went through a routine examination in the Bureau, and I was sent to Dr. Ratner. He was a stomach specialist and he sent me to the Veterans' Hospital for observation and treatment.

"Q. Dr. Rattner sent you there? Which doctor sent you?

A. It was the father I believe.

Q. And was it following your entrance to the hospital that you met this doctor?

A. Yes."

"MR. ERSKINE: Comes now the defendant and moves the Court to direct a verdict in favor of the defendant and against the plaintiff for the reason that the plaintiff has failed to prove the allegations charged in his complaint in that he has failed to prove that he was totally and permanently disabled and unable to continuously follow a substantially gainful occupation on the 18th day of August, 1919, the date named in his complaint.

THE COURT: Motion denied and exception allowed."

Thereupon counsel for plaintiff and defendant argued the case to the jury, and at the conclusion of such arguments, the court instructed the jury as to the law. No exceptions to the court's instructions were noted.

IT IS HEREBY CERTIFIED that the foregoing proceedings were had upon the trial of this cause, and that the Bill of Exceptions contains all the evidence produced at said trial.

IT IS FURTHER CERTIFIED that the foregoing exceptions asked and taken by the defendant were allowed by the Court, and that this bill of exceptions was duly presented within the time fixed by law and the order of this court, and is by me duly allowed and signed this 16 day of March, 1932.

JOHN H. McNARY,

One of the Judges of the District Court of the United

States for the District of Oregon.

Endorsed:

U. S. DISTRICT COURT

District of Oregon

Filed March 16, 1932

G. H. Marsh, Clerk

By F. L. Buck, Chief Deputy.

And Afterwards, to-wit, on the 16th day of March, 1932, there was duly Filed in said Court, a

STIPULATION

in words and figures as follows, to-wit:

IT IS HEREBY STIPULATED by and between the respective parties to the above-entitled action that the record and transcript to be prepared by the Clerk of the Court and transmitted to the United States Circuit Court of Appeals for the Ninth Circuit shall consist of the following:

Citation on Appeal

Complaint

Answer

Reply

Verdict

Judgment

Petition for Order of Appeal

Order Allowing Appeal

Notice of Appeal

Assignments of Error

Bill of Exceptions

Stipulation as to what Transcript of Record
shall contain

Praecipe for Transcript of Record,
omitting titles, verifications, and acceptance of service on all said documents, except Citation on Appeal and Complaint.

> ALLAN A. BYNON,
> > Of Attorneys for Plaintiff.
> CHAS. W. ERSKINE,
> > Assistant United States Attorney.

Endorsed:

U. S. DISTRICT COURT

District of Oregon

Filed March 16, 1932

G. H. Marsh, Clerk

By H. S. Kenyon, Deputy

And Afterwards to-wit, on the 16th day of March, 1932, there was duly Filed in said Court, a

PRAECIPE

in words and figures as follows, to-wit:
To the Clerk of the above-entitled Court:

You are hereby directed to please prepare and certify the record of the above cause for transmission to the United States Circuit Court of Appeals for the Ninth Circuit, including therein a certified copy of all papers filed and proceedings had in the above-entitled cause, which are necessary to a determination thereof in said Appellate Court, and especially including therein the following documents:

Citation on Appeal

Complaint

Answer

Reply

Verdict

Judgment

Petition for Order of Appeal

Order Allowing Appeal

Notice of Appeal

Assignments of Error

Bill of Exceptions

Stipulation as to what Transcript of Record shall contain

Praecipe for Transcript of Record,

omitting titles, verifications, and acceptance of service on all said documents, except Citation on Appeal and Complaint.

Dated this 16th day of March, 1932.

CHAS. W. ERSKINE,

Assistant United States Attorney.

Endorsed:

U. S. DISTRICT COURT

District of Oregon

Filed March 16, 1932

G. H. Marsh, Clerk

By H. S. Kenyon, Deputy

INDEX

	Page
Statement of the Case	1
Assignment of Errors	2
Pertinent Statutes and Regulations	4
Argument:	
(1) Maturity of Insurance by Disability	23
(2) Attempted Combination of Disabilities	25
(3) Opinion Testimony	29

CASES CITED

Eggen v. *U. S.*, decided April 30, 1932, not reported	23
Long v. *U. S.*, decided June 13, 1932, not reported	23
Nalbantian v. *U. S.*, 54 Fed. (2d) 63	31
Nicolay v. *U. S.*, 51 Fed. (2d) 170	30
Roberts v. *U. S.*, 57 Fed. (2d) 514	23
United States v. *Barker*, 36 Fed. (2d) 556	5
United States v. *Crume*, 54 Fed. (2d) 556	5, 23
United States v. *Cole*, 45 Fed. (2d) 339	23, 24
United States v. *Harrison*, 49 Fed. (2d) 227	31
United States v. *Le Duc*, 48 Fed. (2d) 789	31
United States v. *Martin*, 54 Fed. (2d) 554	23
United States v. *Rice*, 47 Fed. (2d) 749	31
United States v. *Seattle Title Trust Co.*, 53 Fed. (2d) 435	23, 24
United States v. *Thomas*, 53 Fed. (2d) 192	23
United States v. *Wilson*, 50 Fed. (2d) 1062	23

OTHER CITATIONS

Sec. 13, War Risk Insurance Act, 49 Stat. 555	4
Treasury Decision No. 20	4

In the United States Circuit Court of Appeals for the Ninth Circuit

THE UNITED STATES OF AMERICA, APPELLANT

v.

CARROLL TILLMAN MCCREARY, APPELLEE

APPEAL FROM THE UNITED STATES DISTRICT COURT FOR THE DISTRICT OF OREGON

BRIEF FOR APPELLANT

STATEMENT OF THE CASE

Carroll Tillman McCreary, appellee, hereinafter called plaintiff, brought suit to recover on a contract of War Risk Insurance.

The complaint (R–7) alleged the existence of a $10,000 contract, payment of premiums thereon to include the 19th day of August 1919, maturity of insurance by permanent total disability on August 19, 1919, and a disagreement in the claim between plaintiff and defendant.

The answer (R–11) admitted the contract, payment of premiums as alleged and the existence of a disagreement; denied that plaintiff was totally permanently disabled and denied liability under the contract.

The cause came on for trial the 30th day of September, 1931. After all the evidence had been introduced by both sides, the defendant moved for a directed verdict for the reason that plaintiff had failed to prove that he was permanently and totally disabled and unable to follow continuously any substantially gainful occupation, as alleged. The motion was denied and an exception noted. The case was submitted to the jury and a verdict returned that the plaintiff was permanently and totally disabled on the 19th day of September, 1919. (R–15.)

Upon the verdict of the jury judgment was entered for the plaintiff on the first day of October, 1931. (R–16.)

Thereafter and in due time the appellant presented its petition for appeal and Assignments of Error and this appeal was duly allowed. (R–20.)

ASSIGNMENT OF ERRORS

The United States of America, being the defendant in the above entitled cause, and appearing by George Neuner, United States Attorney for the District of Oregon, and Chas. W. Erskine, Assistant United States Attorney, and having filed a notice of appeal, as required by law, that the defendant appeals to the United States Circuit Court of Appeals for the Ninth Circuit from the

final order and judgment made and entered
in said cause against said defendant herein,
now makes and files in support of said appeal the following assignments of error, upon which it will rely for a reversal of said
final order and judgment upon the said appeal, and which said error is to the great
detriment, injury and prejudice of this defendant, and said defendant says that in the
records and proceedings upon the hearings
and determination thereof in the District
Court of the United States for the District
of Oregon, there is manifest error, in this,
to-wit:

I

That the court erred in overruling the
motion of the defendant for a directed verdict, for the reason that the evidence adduced at the trial of the above entitled cause
was insufficient to justify a verdict for the
plaintiff.

II

That the court erred in overruling the motion of the defendant for a directed verdict,
for·the reason that the evidence adduced at
the trial of the above entitled cause establishes the fact that plaintiff was not permanently and totally disabled on or before
the 19th day of September, 1919.

WHEREFORE, on account of the errors
above assigned, defendant prays that the
judgment of this Court be reversed and that
this case be remanded to said District Court

and that such directions be given that the above errors may be corrected and the law and justice be done in the matter.

Dated at Portland, Oregon, this 28th day of December, 1921.

GEORGE NEUNER,
United States Attorney for the
District of Oregon.

CHAS. W. ERSKINE,
Asst. U. S. Attorney.

(Endorsed:) U. S. District Court, District of Oregon. Filed Dec. 28, 1931. G. H. Marsh, Clerk. By E. L. Buck, Chf. Deputy.

PERTINENT STATUTES AND REGULATIONS

The contract sued upon was issued pursuant to the provisions of the War Risk Insurance Act and insured against death or total permanent disability. (40 Stat. 409.) Section 13 of the War Risk Insurance Act (40 Stat. 555) provided that the Director, Bureau of War Risk Insurance—

> * * * shall administer, execute, and enforce the provisions of this Act, and, for that purpose have full power and authority to make rules and regulations not inconsistent with the provisions of this Act necessary or appropriate to carry out its purposes. * * *

Pursuant to this authority there was promulgated on March 9, 1918, Treasury Decision No. 20 reading:

> Any impairment of mind or body which renders it impossible for the disabled person

5

to follow continuously any substantially gainful occupation shall be deemed, in Articles III and IV, to be total disability.

Total disability shall be deemed to be permanent whenever it is found upon conditions which render it reasonably certain that it will continue throughout the life of the person suffering from it. Whenever it shall be established that any person to whom any installments of insurance has been paid as provided in Article IV on the ground that the insured has become totally and permanently disabled has recovered the ability to continuously follow any substantially gainful occupation, the payment of installments of insurance shall be discontinued forthwith and no further installments thereof shall be paid so long as such recovered ability shall continue.

ARGUMENT

For plaintiff to recover in this suit it was necessary for the evidence to show that during the life of the insurance contract he was suffering from an impairment of mind or body which rendered it impossible for him to pursue continuously any substantially gainful occupation and that such impairment was reasonably certain to continue throughout his life. (Treas. Dec. 20; *U. S.* v. *Barker,* 36 Fed. (2d) 556; *U. S.* v. *Crume,* 54 Fed. (2d) 556.)

F. G. LEARY testified (R–25) that he first knew plaintiff in 1929, at which time plaintiff worked for him five or eight weeks. Plaintiff was not able to do the heavy work, or as much work as the other men on the job, although he was paid the same wages. He did all sorts of jobs as a laborer and was paid 50¢ an hour for an eight-hour day. He was away two or three times and finally left the job entirely. He was not discharged but just did not come back.

A. H. Burns testified (R–28): Plaintiff visited him in August or September, 1919. He was nervous and had to be careful of what he ate. On one occasion he was trembling like a leaf and unable to do anything more after 15 minutes work. On another occasion during a celebration when a firecracker exploded behind him plaintiff seemed to jump right off the sidewalk. Plaintiff was weak and his face drawn and pinched and pale in comparison with his pre-war appearance. He went to work for the Robert Strubin Dairy and "acted all of the time very tired and continued nervous."

On cross-examination (R–31) the witness testified he did not think plaintiff's condition warranted employment in September, 1919. When he attended the celebration with plaintiff and the firecracker exploded "it scared me for an instant before I was over with it; I started—sort of jumped too." In September or October, 1919, plaintiff worked for the Strubin Dairy where he had charge of the herd and supervision of the feeding and milking. He worked for about a year and a half.

After an interval of other employment plaintiff returned to a farm he owned. He was not able to run it. Plaintiff was tired and weak while working for the Strubin Dairy.

On redirect examination (R–36) the witness testified that he had visited plaintiff when he was sick at home and had seen him at home sick three or four times when he could have been working at the Strubin Dairy.

Dr. H. H. HUGHES testified (R–36) he saw plaintiff early in October, 1919. Plaintiff had lost a good deal of weight, looked somewhat anemic and stooped, his voice had changed a good deal and he did not have the strength he used to have. He complained of diarrhea and pain in the abdomen, inability to digest food, gas, and a sour stomach. The witness diagnosed plaintiff's trouble as dysentery and colitis. (R–37.) Plaintiff seemed very nervous and restless. He had a cough and was raising some material. The witness assumed that the nervousness was a result of service. He has seen plaintiff since and the nervousness has persisted. He saw plaintiff at his office in 1921 when he complained of more than usual pain in his right side, which the witness diagnosed as appendicitis. He saw plaintiff professionally at his office another time but could not remember the date. Several years ago he was called to plaintiff's house and found him bothered with his heart. (R–39.) He had examined plaintiff a few days before the trial

131542—32——2

and found dysentery, nervousness, and a weak heart. From what plaintiff told him the dysentery has persisted since 1919.

The witness testified that dysentery is caused by different bacteria and parasites; that there is no cure; that it leaves one in a weakened condition and explains loss of weight, nervousness, and a weak heart; that based on his examination and knowledge of plaintiff and the history taken plaintiff was permanently totally disabled in August, 1919, and that the condition was reasonably certain to continue throughout his lifetime.

On cross-examination Dr. Hughes testified (R–40): Plaintiff came to his office in October, 1919. He noticed the same nervous condition plaintiff has to-day. Plaintiff told him he was having dysentery or diarrhea and the witness advised him to go to a Veterans' Bureau Hospital for examination. He did not make the diagnosis of dysentery himself. He found râles but made no diagnosis. He did not recall that he had seen plaintiff professionally from August, 1919, until 1921, when he made a diagnosis of appendicitis. (R–43.) He did not recall having treated plaintiff again until he was called to his home some time in 1924 or 1925, although he had seen plaintiff very often.

The nervous condition which he had observed was "exhibited continually—not exactly jerking but just getting up and going to the window and coming back and sitting and lighting a cigarette

and smoking a puff or two and throwing it down."
(R–44.)

The witness never made a determination of dysentery. Plaintiff " told me he had dysentery—diarrhea—and from the symptoms he gave me I would say that he had dysentery." Plaintiff's pulse was rapid. He did not take the blood pressure but listened to the heart with a stethoscope. The heart was rapid but he found no lesion or anything else wrong with the heart. From his observation of plaintiff during a heart attack in 1924 or 1925 when plaintiff was short of breath and could hardly breathe he would say that plaintiff had a weak heart. He had seen him in that condition only one time. (R–46.)

The witness testified that diarrhea weakens the heart muscles; that a weak heart is a rapid heart; that plaintiff could do some such work as sitting at a desk and writing but in his opinion could not do manual labor, although the plaintiff's heart condition has probably been so that he could direct the work of a dairy; that dairy work is hard and in his present condition plaintiff could not do it; that he could direct the work at the dairy; that he thought plaintiff's nervousness came from the combination of his war experiences and the dysentery.

Dr. EDWIN P. FAGAN testified (R–51) he first examined the plaintiff September 8, 1930. Plaintiff was complaining of stomach trouble and was given a thorough physical examination. Plaintiff's condition was diagnosed as duodenal ulcer and renal glycosuria. Plaintiff gave a history of dysentery. The record shows (R–53–54):

> Q. Based upon that history, Doctor, it is your opinon that he has this—or had the infection you spoke of?
>
> A. I presume that he had. I have his word only for it.
>
> Q. Do you know what the infection was that caused this condition—the diarrhea or dysentery?
>
> A. Nothing aside from what I heard. We made a test there and found nothing in his stool.
>
> Q. Can you tell from your diagnosis, Doctor, what, if anything, they claimed he had been suffering prior to this time?
>
> A. Nothing, only some form of dysentery—from his history.

In further reference to dysentery the record show (R–55):

> Q. Is there any relation between that and the duodenal ulcer?
>
> A. I can not say as to that.

The witness testified that there is no cure for dysentery; that plaintiff was nervous when he examined him; that dysentery or duodenal ulcer would cause nervousness; that he had examined plaintiff four or five days ago and could see no change in his condition; that upon his examination and the history taken plaintiff is now permanently totally disabled; that "assuming that these conditions have prevailed and persisted at least since he was released from active service in August, 1919, I would say that he was totally and permanently disabled from that time on; this is a permanent and total disability and has been ever since that time."

On cross-examination the witness testified: The only conditions found on examination of September 8, 1930, were the duodenal ulcer and the kidney condition (renal glycosuria); that the main disability on which his opinion of permanent total disability was based was the duodenal ulcer and the fact that plaintiff was nervous. (R–58.) He testified that no one can say that duodenal ulcer is a permanent condition; that "from an examination of the stools I found nothing wrong—nothing pathological or showing evidence of any disease." (R–66.) He testified that plaintiff was nervous when he was examined, "I think more so than the average person going through a clinic. I found no pathological reason for this nervousness aside from his ulcer in the stomach, which was found later; that might have a tendency to make him nervous."

ROBERT S. STRUBIN testified (R–73) he saw plaintiff shortly after service and noticed a big change in him. He was more stooped, his eyes were hollow, and he had the general appearance of being nervous. He employed plaintiff for a considerable time, "a year more or less." There were many times when plaintiff required help. Plaintiff was to oversee the milking and attend to the milling of the feed. Other men got in the grain and feed.

Plaintiff cleaned stables and put in the cows. He had time off every day which he had to take. Plaintiff left him and he tried to replace him and could not do so. "I hunted him up and offered him a great increase in wages, either fifteen or twenty dollars, if he would come back to me." (R–77.) After the raise he thought he paid plaintiff about $110 per month and room and board. When plaintiff returned to him he was still nervous. He did not regain his health. He could not stand the work and finally had to give it up. Any little noise would startle him.

On cross-examination (R–80) Mr. Strubin testified he and plaintiff were boyhood friends. He had sought out and employed plaintiff because of his experience and knowledge and not because of friendship. The witness had about 48 cows which he had handled with the help of his sisters and an old man. After he employed plaintiff and another man he devoted himself to farming and hunting and took considerable rest. He paid plaintiff about $75 per month, room, and board. In the interval between the two periods of plaintiff's employment the witness lost money. After plaintiff's reemployment he was paid about $110 per month.

Fred T. Wilson testified (R–84) he employed plaintiff soon after the war for several months; that when plaintiff first came to work he was able to do his work and then he gradually became weaker and got so he could not do his work (R–85); that he did not "remember so much about his condition with reference to his being nervous" (R–86) ; that plaintiff's work "was either in the checking room, checking out routes of the wagons and checking in the returns, or doing general extra work." Concerning plaintiff's wages the witness testified (R–87) : "I don't know what wages he received there at that time; I think probably $120 or $135 a month. It might be as much as $150. It was whatever the going wages were; I think we were paying $120, $135, or possibly $150. I am unable to state the length of time he was employed there. Just a few months elapsed between the two times he worked for me."

LEON CODDEY testified (R–88) he first saw plaintiff in Portland just after service; that plaintiff was "standing on the street, and he was feeling weak like, and his eyes were glassy and wasted away, and his face was thin"; that he had been at plaintiff's house when he was sick. The witness described plaintiff's condition during a heart attack, as of a date not given. (R–89), (Elsewhere fixed as 1924–1925), (Tr. 43.) He testified that plaintiff "had played out" on two jobs. He described an occasion when plaintiff was working in the field and required the assistance of the witness to get to the house. (R–90.) He did not give the date of this incident nor indicate the nature of plaintiff's condition requiring assistance, but on cross-examination testified: (R–90) "I lived close to where he lived. I did not live there in 1923; I lived up there in 1925."

JOHN EVERLE testified (R–92) that plaintiff looked a whole lot different when he came back than when he went away. "He was all humped up. His eyes were all swollen out, and he looked all worn out." He testified that plaintiff worked for him a little off and on; that every time he employed him after the war he gave out. That he saw some manifestations of nervousness. "I had some blasting to do and every time I set off a blast he would duck and try to get away from it, and he was very nervous-like."

On cross-examination, the witness testified (R–94) that the first work plaintiff did for him was about 1926 or 1927.

T. E. GABODE testified (R–94) that he became acquainted with plaintiff in 1923 and hired him as general roustabout or pick-up man, driving a truck and picking up various things (R–97); that plaintiff worked steadily, with the exception of a few days, for 10 months; that he was "able to do the work that was assigned to him well enough to keep him on the job" (R–95). The witness did not consider plaintiff "good, first class, from a physical standpoint." "You could notice there was a nervous strain. You could see he was bothered with something." (R–95.) The witness did not remember "anything in particular that attracted my attention to his nervous condition." He tried to help plaintiff along. He could do the light jobs but on the heavy jobs he just petered out. (R–95 and 96.)

Plaintiff's employment by the witness extended from May, 1923, to March, 1924. He averaged $100 per month at $4.00 a day. "Including the days he was off he would average pretty close to $100 per month." (R–96.)

J. H. COOPER testified (R–97) that he had known plaintiff as a boy; that after plaintiff's service he had seen him trying to clear his land; that plaintiff was pretty sick and weak and could not do much; that plaintiff worked for him in the fall of 1926 about a month and a half, first on a $5.00 a day job and then on a $4.00 a day job (R–98); that plaintiff could have worked as long as he wanted to and quit because he could not stand it. "After Christmas he got sick and laid off about a week." (R–99.) There was something the matter with his stomach and heart. He was taking stimulants for his heart. "He was always nervous and he seemed as though he could not get any rest." (R–99.)

On cross-examination (R–99) the witness testified that after the war he first saw plaintiff sometime in 1924. (R–99.) That the job he had given plaintiff was pretty heavy. That the mill closed down about December 20, (1926) and reopened about the first of the year (R–100); that plaintiff started work about November 1 and resumed work after the lay-off about the first of the year; that he worked to the last of February; that plaintiff did not work steadily but was off four or five days once.

M. H. DAHL testified (R–101) that he had employed plaintiff at odd jobs eight or ten times after the war; that none of these jobs were for more than two weeks (R–101); that some of the work was light and some of it heavy; that plaintiff was "badly worn out after he worked hard for a time" (R–101); that he first employed plaintiff in 1922; that plantiff was not very well—that was partly why he did not have more work for him to do; that "most of my work was pretty heavy" (R–102).

Mrs. HELEN LYONS testified (R–103) that she had worked as a technician for Dr. Tucker; that she first met plaintiff in Dr. Tucker's office "a little over two years ago"; that plaintiff had consulted Dr. Tucker twenty or twenty-five times; that she knew the doctor was treating him for heart trouble and stomach trouble or dysentery; that plaintiff impressed her the first time she saw him as extremely weak; that he would respond to treatment and become stronger, then the next day or so come back and tell of severe attacks or spells with his heart; that the main trouble was with his heart (R–104). That his blood pressure was low (R–105); that she did not have the records but remembered at one time his blood pressure was as low as 91. The witness further testified that plaintiff's low blood pressure was due to low vitality, sickness, or trouble.

CARROLL TILLMAN McCREARY testified (R–106): He was a laborer before service and had an eighth-grade education. He had mumps on the boat going to France and spent about three weeks in a hospital in Brest, France. He went to a replacement camp and then joined the 4th Marines on the Marne. (R–108.) Shells exploded within 10 feet or 15 feet of him, "It shot the wind out of me and I was thrown down on the ground like a feather." Shortly afterward he had dysentery. (R–110.) He was sick two or three days and then rejoined his company. Thereafter he was in a hospital in Selincourt for about two weeks for what he thought was the flu. (R–111.) He returned to his outfit and was "bothered with dysentery and diarrhoea." He could not carry his pack or keep up with the outfit. After the St. Mihiel offensive he went in the kitchen. (R–112.)

> I figured I could maybe get better stuff to eat; better stuff for my condition than I could get on the outside, and I could not stand the trip. I could not carry my pack. I did not get better; I was able to get by and that was all.

Two days before the armistice he went to a hospital where he thought they treated him for "intra-colitis, inflammation of the bowels or dysentery." (R–113.) He weighed about 165 pounds when he entered service, about 208 pounds before he went overseas, about 130 pounds in the hospital. In January, 1919, he rejoined his organization in Germany. He was in the kitchen about two months, a helper with mules until May, 1919, and then was transferred back to "straight duty." (R–114.)

He was not on duty a great part of the time. He
picked up on his trip back home on the water but
the trip across the continent weakened him. He
had spells of dysentery after that. (R–115.)

Asked on direct examination:

> Q. When did you first notice the neuras-
> thenia of which you complain?—in these
> pleadings.

he answered:

> A. I don't know whether it was from be-
> ing shook up caused by the motion of the
> wheels or whether it was from being sick
> so long.

He did not know when he first noticed that he was
nervous. His heart bothered him some when he
first got out, "but not a great deal. I think it has
gotten worse in the last two years." His stomach
was bad in service. (R–116.)

He worked for Bob Strubin and for a while got
along very well and then had two or three light
attacks and then had a bad attack, (presumably of
dysentery) and went to see Dr. Hughes. (R–117.)
He was bothered with dysentery, weakness, night
sweats, and severe headaches. He was "nervous at
that time" and understood that his employer used
to have "quite a time with him"; that his employer
would "play" with an old engine and "get it to
backfire to see me jump"; it would catch him unex-
pectedly—if he had known about it he could have
controlled himself. The doctor told him "to lay
around for four or five days the first time I took

sick and then go back to work, and at different times I had to take time off." (R–118.)

He worked for Mr. Strubin the first time until about April 1, 1920, for $75 per month and board with no deduction from pay for the time he was sick. (R–119.) He returned to employment with Strubin and remained until about August 15, 1920, at $110 or $115 per month.

> The first time I quit Mr. Strubin was because I could not carry on, and the second time was because I was on the sick list, and I believe it was partly because I was just married. I was married a few days after I left there. (R–120.)

After a lapse of three or four weeks he worked for Mr. Wilcox of the Fernwood Dairy for a little over a year. He was off from work 8 weeks in the summer of 1921 for an operation. Besides the 8 weeks he lost a few days now and then. He thought 4 days was the longest. (R–121.) After the operation Mr. Wilcox asked him to quit, "I was sick at that time." After that he did practically nothing until the spring of 1922 when he attempted to farm with poor success. In 1922 he was still bothered with abdominal trouble and was nervous and had headaches. In 1924 he was in a Veterans' Hospital under the care of Dr. C. C. Campbell. (R–124.)

During a period of work for the City of Portland plaintiff's stomach gave him an "awful lot of trouble." (R–124.)

Prior to 1927 he had a heart attack. In March, 1928, he was on the sick list. (R–128.) When he quit work for the Phoenix Logging Co. in 1929 his conditon was "very poor." (R–126.)

For six weeks in the year preceding the trial he was under the care of Dr. Tucker. He testified (R–127):

> I had a pain in my left side and he said it was a heart condition, but I forget just what he called it. I don't believe he treated me for my stomach condition. I was in to see him a couple of years ago when I was bothered with the dysentery trouble.

In the Spring of 1924 or 1925, "sometime during that year," Dr. Marcellus told him he had amoebic dysentery. "This amoebic dysentery that I was being treated for was the same as I had when I was first treated for a disorder in France, and I have been suffering from the same thing ever since."

On cross-examination, plaintiff testified: After the two days on the Marne he was never in the front line. He worked for Mr. Strubin from September, 1919, to April, 1920, at $75 per month and from sometime in April or the first of May until August 15, 1920, at $110 or $115 per month. (R–132.) He worked for the Fernwood Dairy at weekly wages of $33, $35, and $30 from September, 1920, to October, 1921, during which time he was off eight weeks for an appendicitis operation. (R–134–35.) He worked at a sawmill for 10 days or two weeks and a dairy for about three weeks. He bought a place of his own and lived there for about a year working for neighbors and himself. (R–135.) He worked for the Davidson Bakery and received the following wages for the periods indicated.

May 21, 1923, 8 days, earned_____	$32. 00
June, 1923, lost 2 days, earned_____	104. 00
July, 1923, lost 2 days, earned_____	102. 00
August, 1923, lost 3 days, earned_____	108. 00
September, 1923, lost 5 days, earned_____	100. 00
October, 1923, lost 4 days, earned_____	104. 00
November, 1923, lost 4 days, earned_____	104. 00
December, 1923, lost 5 days (worked 1 day extra)_____	104. 00
January, 1924, lost 16 days_____	68. 00
February, 1924, lost 9 days_____	86. 00
March, 1924, lost 5 days_____	117. 00

Did not work after the 31st day of March, earned a total of__ 1, 029. 00

He went to a Veterans' Hospital in January or February, 1924, for observation and treatment, accounting for part of the time lost from the bakery. In the Spring of 1925 he returned to his own place and stayed there for about two years, during which time he worked for the City of Portland and did a few other jobs. His main occupation was on his own place. (R–137.) In 1928 he worked for a logging company for about 2 months.

The above résumé contains the substance of the testimony offered for plaintiff.

Dr. Charles George Rattner, a physician, testified by deposition. (R–141.)

The witness identified the report of a physical examination made by him August 31, 1922. Plaintiff entered U. S. Veterans' Hospital, Portland, Oregon, for observation for an intestinal condition.

Plaintiff's only complaint was gas on the stomach. He was quite nervous when admitted but the nervousness disappeared during his stay in the hospital. The laboratory findings were negative for gastro-intestinal trouble. He was discharged as having no disability. Plaintiff was under his immediate observation. The witness made a complete examination using stethoscope and X ray.

In the opinion of the witness plaintiff was not on August 31, 1922, suffering from any impairment of mind or body which rendered it impossible for him to follow continuously any substantially gainful occupation. (R–143.)

Dr. Clayton C. Campbell, a physician, testified from examination records. (R–144.)

Plaintiff was in U. S. Veterans' Hospital, Portland, Oregon, from February 4, 1924 to February 9, 1924. A series of gastro-intestinal X rays were negative. A spinal X ray was negative except for Bifida Occulate, an outgrowth of bone interfering with the movement of the vertebrae, considered a serious impairment if far enough progressed. On March 24, 1924, plaintiff complained of pain in the region of his gall bladder. A gall-bladder drainage was negative; no disease was found.

From the record of an examination made June 27, 1924, plaintiff was able to resume his pre-war occupation with a handicap from the Spina Bifida which would interfere to some extent with hard manual labor. The diagnoses were hyperchlorhydria, mild; spina bifide occulata, neurasthenia, neu-rasthenic type, varicose veins, slight. The progno-sis was guarded as any of these conditions could im-prove or get worse.

Examination report of January 20, 1925, dis-closed complaints of gall-bladder trouble but no disease was found or diagnosis made.

Examination report of May 4, 1925, disclosed no abnormalities.

In the various examinations there was no indica-tion of enteritis, dysentery or amoebiasis. No ex-amination of the stools was made. There was no indication of heart trouble or of stomach trouble; plaintiff was nervous and excitable but the circula-tory system was not disturbed.

In the opinion of the witness plaintiff was not permanently totally disabled.

The above résumé contains the substance of all testimony in the case.

(1) Maturity of insurance by disability

War Risk Term Insurance is not matured by a total disability which is not permanent (*Rob-erts* v. *U. S.,* 57 Feb. (2d) 514; *United States* v. *Crume,* 54 Fed. (2d) 556; and *Long* v. *United States,* recently decided by the Fourth Circuit Court of Appeals), nor by a permanent disability which is not total (*United States* v. *Algie Thomas,* 53 Fed. (2d) 192; *United States* v. *John Bela Mar-tin,* 54 Fed. (2d) 554; and *United States* v. *Wilson,*

50 Fed. (2d) 1062), even though such permanent disability becomes a total permanent disability later (*United States* v. *Cole,* 45 Fed. (2d) 339; *United States* v. *Seattle Title Trust Co.,* 53 Fed. (2d) 435; *Eggen* v. *United States,* decided April 30, 1932, unreported).

In the case of Eggen vs. United States the court said in sustaining a directed verdict for defendant.

> If, upon a trial, all of the evidence, taking that view of it most favorable to the plaintiff, fails to disclose that the conditions which actually existed at the time the policy lapsed for the nonpayment of premiums made it then reasonably certain that the disability of the insured would continue throughout his life, a finding that he was permanently disabled, regardless of events subsequent to lapse, can not be sustained.

The evidence in this case does not disclose in the life of the insurance contract the existence of any disability then reasonably certain to be totally disabling throughout life. The plaintiff was examined by a physician in October, 1919. The physician testified that he diagnosed plaintiff's condition as dysentery and colitis. (R–37.) On cross-examination (R–40), the physician testified that he did not make the diagnosis of dysentery himself. Dr. Rattner who examined plaintiff in August, 1922 (R–143), and Dr. Campbell who examined him in 1924 and 1925 (R–150), witnesses for the defendant, found no indication of dysentery. Dr. Fagan

(R–54) plaintiff's other medical witness found no evidence of dysentery in 1930 and 1931.

Apparently plaintiff's condition in 1919 did not impress the physician as one that was total and likely to so continue, for plaintiff testified that the doctor told him to lay around four or five days the first time he took sick and then go back to work. (R–118.)

(2) Attempted combination of disabilities

In the case of *United States* v. *Crume,* 54 Fed. (2d) 556, the court said, in reversing judgment for plaintiff:

> This evidence must not merely show that he was at the time of his discharge totally disabled, but that he has continued and will continue to be so, not as the result of successive maladies making their onset from time to time, but as the result of the same malady, which then totally disabling, has continued and will continue permanently to be so.

Two physicians testified for the plaintiff. From their reported findings Dr. Hughes and Dr. Fagan might have been testifying about two different persons. Dr. H. H. Hughes testified (R–36) that he saw the plaintiff professionally five times between the date of alleged permanent and total disability and the date of trial—first, early in October, 1919, when he found the symptoms and took a history of dysentery (R–37); second, in 1921 when plaintiff had appendicitis (R–38); third, in 1924 or 1925 when plaintiff had some heart condition (R–39 & 43); fourth, a few days before the trial, concerning which the physician testified:

> From what he said, the dysentery has persisted since I first saw him in 1919. I have been there when he had dysentery. I didn't see the stools passed, but that is the report. (R–39–40.)

fifth, as of some date uncertain, concerning which the physician offers no testimony as to his findings. (R–39.)

Dr. Fagan examined plaintiff twice—September 8, 1930 (R–51) and four or five days before the trial. (R–56.) He testified that on September 8, 1930, plaintiff had a duodenal ulcer and renal glycosuria, the latter being an infection of the kidney (R–51), and that he could see no change in his condition a few days before the trial. He found no dysentery, testifying (R–66):

> From an examination of the stools, I found nothing wrong—nothing pathological or showing evidence of any disease.

Neither of the conditions found by Dr. Fagan are shown to have existed during the life of the contract or prior to 1930, and the conditions to which Dr. Hughes testified are not shown to have existed upon the occasions of Dr. Fagan's examinations. The only condition to which both physicians testified was nervousness. Dr. Hughes testified (R-37) in reference to his first examination of plaintiff:

> He seemed very nervous and restless as he was sitting in the chair, * * *.

and (R-44).

> This nervous condition was exhibited continually—not exactly jerking but just getting up and going to the window and coming back and sitting and lighting a cigarette and smoking a puff or two and throwing it down.

Dr. Fagan testified (R-67):

> He was nervous when he was examined; I think more so than the average person going through a clinic. I found no pathological reason for this nervousness aside from his ulcer in the stomach, which was found later; that might have a tendency to make him nervous.

That plaintiff was nervous is established by the testimony of Dr. Rattner (R-143) and Dr. Campbell (R-151), but that such nervousness could have constituted a permanent total disability is without support in the evidence. Dr. Rattner testified (R-143) that the nervousness disappeared during plaintiff's stay in the hospital. Dr. Campbell testified (R-151) that plaintiff was nervous and excitable but that his nervousness did not disturb the circulation or greatly accelerate the pulse rate.

There was lay testimony that plaintiff was nervous in 1919 and thereafter but it was apparently not a major disability or his employer, Robert S. Strubin, would not have played with a back-firing engine to make plaintiff jump as the latter testified that he did. (R–118.)

Medical testimony that plaintiff suffered from dysentery is given only by Dr. Hughes, who also testified (R–44):

> I have never had any experience in dysentery in the laboratory but I see them in my country practice. I see them with the dysentery and then, later, they are sent or find their way to the hospital where the dysentery is determined from the stool, under the microscope. * * * I never made such determination in this case. He told me he had dysentery—diarrhœa—and from the symptoms he gave me I would say that he had dysentery.

The appendicitis is not shown to have been other than an acute condition corrected by operation in the Summer of 1921 (R–121) or 1922 (R–43 & 122).

Concerning the heart condition which Dr. Hughes testified he found in 1924 or 1925, he said (R–46): "That is the only time I saw him under that condition," and

> In 1919 and 1921, when I saw him, there was nothing that impressed me about his heart except that it was rapid. I remember it was rapid way back there; I made an examination at that time.

(3) Opinion testimony

Dr. Hughes expressed an opinion based on examination and knowledge of the plaintiff and "his history I have taken" that plaintiff was permanently and totally disabled from August, 1919. (R–40.) His opinion must have been based entirely on "his history I have taken," as he did not testify to any continuity of findings or symptoms from which it could reasonably be concluded that total permanent disability existed, nor did he identify the particular impairment which in his opinion precluded the continuous pursuit of substantially gainful employment.

Dr. Fagan testified to an opinion, based on examination and history, that plaintiff was permanently and totally disabled at the time of the trial and that "Assuming that these conditions have prevailed and persisted" since August, 1919, that he was then permanently and totally disabled. Inasmuch as the only conditions shown to have existed since August, 1919, were a nervousness and a slightly rapid pulse with no evidence of duodenal ulcer and renal glycosuria until September, 1930, the opinion of Dr. Fagan based on an assumption as to the plaintiff's condition prior to his examination appears valueless in determining the condition of the plaintiff as of August, 1919.

In the case of *Nicolay* v. *United States,* 51 Fed.
(2d) 170, this court referred to the—

> further settled principle that 'when the tes-
> timony of a witness is positively contradicted
> by the physical facts, neither the court nor
> the jury can be permitted to credit it.'
> *American Car & Foundry Co.* v. *Kindermann*
> (C. C. A. 8) 216 F. 499, 502; *Missouri, K. &*
> *T. Ry. Co.* v. *Collier* (C. C. A. 8) 157 F.
> 347, cert. denied, 209 U. S. 545, 28 S. Ct.
> 571, 52 L. Ed. 920. Cases from many juris-
> dictions are gathered in a note in 8 A. L. R.
> 798, supporting the proposition that uncon-
> tradicted evidence which is contrary to phys-
> ical facts should be disregarded. Judg-
> ments can not and should not stand if they
> are entered upon testimony that can not be
> true. *Woolworth Co.* v. *Davis* (C. C. A. 10)
> 41 F. (2d) 342, 347.

The facts show that plaintiff worked at substantially gainful occupations for a period of years,
under circumstances wholly inconsistent with any
condition of total permanent disability. He worked
from September, 1919, until April, 1920, at $75 per
month, room and board and worked so successfully
that his employer after a few weeks reengaged
him at a substantial increase in pay. He worked
from April or May until August, 1920, at $110 or
$115 per month. (R–152.) He was married and
then worked for a Dairy from September, 1920, to
October, 1921, at weekly wages of $30 to $35. He
worked at odd jobs for a time then worked from

May, 1923, to March, 1924, in a bakery earning $1,029.00. These several periods of employment, selected from others of lesser duration, definitely establish plaintiff's ability to work and conclusively refute the allegation of permanent total disability. (*U. S.* v. *Rice,* 47 Fed. (2d) 749; *Nalbantian* v. *U. S.,* 54 Fed. (2d) 63; *U. S.* v. *Harrison,* 49 Fed. (2d) 227.)

The insurance is not matured by a present permanent total disability even though such disability be considered to have had its origin in service. Total permanent disability must occur during the life of the contract. *U. S.* v *McPhee,* 31 Fed. (2d) 243; *White* v. *U. S.,* 53 Fed. (2d) 565; *U. S.* v. *McLaughlin,* 53 Fed. (2d) 450. In the latter case the court said in reversing judgment for plaintiff:

> The evidence fails to show any total and permanent disability on or prior to May 31, 1919, the date of lapse of the policy.   *   *   * The most that can be said of the evidence is that the cause of subsequent disability arose during the service, and, it may be fairly presumed, progressed in intensity until total and permanent disability resulted in March, 1920, about ten months after the lapse of the policy.

In the case of *United States* v. *Le Duc,* 48 Fed. (2d) 789, the court said in reversing judgment for plaintiff:

> After all, the right of recovery in these War Risk Insurance cases is dependent on con-

tract, and it is not within the province of the jury to award from the public funds, gratuities to relatives of deceased ex-soldier; neither can we, under the guise of liberal construction, close our eyes to the undisputed facts disclosed by the record in this case.

It is respectfully submitted that the judgment herein should be reversed.

GEORGE NEUNER,
United States Attorney.
CHAS. W. ERSKINE,
Assistant U. S. Attorney.

W. C. PICKETT,
Attorney, Veterans' Administration.

TABLE OF CASES CITED

PAGE

Bangor v. Aroostook R. R. v. Jones, 36 F. (2d) 886   8

23 C. J. 9, Sec. 1733   7

Ford v. United States, 44 Fed. (2d) 754......... 8-9

Gray, Administratrix, v. Davis, Director General of
R. R., 294 F. 57   8

Gunning v. Cooley, 74 U. S. (L. Ed.) 720........   4

Heisson v. Dickinson, 35 F. (2d) 270............   8

Hickman v. Jones, 19 U. S. (L. Ed.) 551, 553....   3

Louisville N. & R. Co. v. Woodson, 33 U. S. (L.
Ed.) 1032, 1035   4

Marathon Lumber Co. v. Dennis, 296 F. 471......   6

McNalley v. United States, 52 Fed. (2d) 440, 443.   8

Mt. Adams & E. P. Inclined Ry. Co. v. Lowery, 74
F. 463, 20 C. C. A. 596.....................   5

Norfolk & W. Ry. Co. v. Hauser, 211 Fed. 567, 572   2

Quinn v. United States, 58 Fed. (2d) 19..........   3

Rochford v. Pennsylvania Co., 174 F. 81, 98 C. C.
A. 105   5

Smith-Booth-Usher Co. v. Detroit Copper Mining
Co., 220 F. 600, 136 C. C. A. 58..............   5

Southwestern Brewery & Ice Co. v. Schmidt, 57 U.
S. (L. Ed.) 170   3

Sudbury v. Penn Worsted Co., 263 Fed. 76, 77....   3

Third National Bank & Trust Co. v. United States,
53 Fed. (2d) 599, 603   2

Travelers' Ins. Co. v. Randolph, 78 F. 754, 24 C. C.
A. 305   5

TABLE OF CASES CITED—Continued

PAGE

United States Fidelity & Guaranty Co. v. Blum, 270 F. 946 5

United States v. Burke, 50 Fed. (2d) 653, 655, 656 4

United States v. Cox, 24 F. (2d) 944.......... 7

United States v. Eliasson, 20 F. (2d) 821....... 7

United States v. Lesher, 59 Fed. (2d) 53..... 9-42

United States v. Phillips, 44 F. (2d) 689....... 7

United States v. Scarborough, 57 Fed. (2d) 137.. 8

United States v. Schweppe, 38 F. (2d) 595...... 7

United States v. Sligh, 31 F. (2d) 735.......... 7

United States v. Stewart, 58 Fed. (2d) 520...... 7

United States v. Tyrakowski, 50 Fed. (2d) 766, 768, 771 6

United States v. Woltman, 57 Fed. (2d) 418.... 8

White v. United States, 270 U. S. 175, 180, 46 S. Ct. 274, 275, 70 L. Ed. 530.................. 8

In the United States Circuit Court of Appeals

For the Ninth Circuit

UNITED STATES OF AMERICA,
  Appellant,

vs.

CARROL TILLMAN McCREARY,
  Appellee.

APPELLEE'S BRIEF

Upon Appeal from the United States District Court
for the District of Oregon

Names and Addresses of Attorneys of Record:

GEORGE NEUNER,
  United States Attorney for the District of
  Oregon,

CHARLES W. ERSKINE,
  Assistant United States Attorney,
  Federal Building, Portland, Oregon,
    For Appellant.

C. G. SCHNEIDER,
ALLAN A. BYNON,
  Portland, Oregon,
    For Appellee.

ARGUMENT

The sole question involved in this appeal is whether the lower Court erred in overruling defendant's Motion for a Directed Verdict. It is the contention of the defendant that its motion should have been allowed by reason of the fact that plaintiff had failed to prove that he was permanently and totally disabled and unable to follow continuously any substantially gainful occupation on and after the 19th day of September, 1919, within the meaning of his War Risk Insurance policy.

Before examining the sufficiency of the evidence to support the verdict in this case, we wish to call to the Court's attention certain established principles that control the Federal Appellate Courts in passing upon the question as to whether the trial Court erred in refusing to direct a verdict, especially in cases involving War Risk Insurance policies.

In Norfolk & W. Ry. Co. v. Hauser, (C. C. A.) 211 Fed. 567, 572, the Court remarked:

> "* * * the responsibility for determining whether the issue shall be submitted to the jury is largely devolved upon the trial Judge. Where he declines to take the case from the jury and refuses a peremptory instruction, the Appellate Court will seldom interfere. The jury is the proper tribunal to determine a question of fact, and if the trial Judge upon the testimony commits the case to the jury, the Appellate Court will seldom interfere."

Again in Third National Bank & Trust Co. v. United States, (C. C. A.) 53 Fed. (2d) 599, 603, a case involving an action on a War Risk Insurance policy, the Court said:

> "* * * it ought not to be necessary to say that

it is not the province of this Court to determine
the weight of the evidence as between conflicting
theories."

Also, in Sudbury v. Penn Worsted Co., (C. C. A.)
263 Fed. 76, 77, the Court said:

"* * * if there be evidence to support the issue
tendered by a party, it is the right of the jury to
pass on it, whether it be strong or weak."

Again, the Supreme Court of the United States in
Southwestern Brewery & Ice Co. v. Schmidt, 57 U. S.
(L. Ed.) 170, said:

"Whether there is credible evidence to sustain
the verdict is a question for the jury, and not for the
Appellate Court."

Also, in Hickman v. Jones, 19 U. S. (L. Ed.) 551,
553, the Supreme Court said:

"In this case the evidence was received without
objection, and was before the jury. It tended to
maintain on the part of the plaintiff the issue, which
they were to try. Whether weak or strong, it was
their right to pass upon it. It was not proper for
the Court to wrest this part of the case, more than
any other, from the exercise of their judgment."

In Quinn v. United States, 58 Fed. (2d) 19, the
Court, in a War Risk Insurance case, says:

"Testimony was offered on both sides on the
question of the appellee's injuries and disabilities,
and whether they were total and permanent during
the life of the policy. The jury was carefully instructed by the Court as to the essential elements
in the plaintiff's case and the burden of proof resting upon him to establish these several elements.

It was the peculiar province of the jury to pass upon the conflicting evidence and render a decision on the facts, in harmony with the law, as given to them by the Court. The jury reached a verdict in plaintiff's favor, and, giving due effect to the findings of the jury, we are not prepared to say that their judgment was erroneous.

"The judgment should therefore be affirmed."

In Louisville N. & R. Co. v. Woodson, 33 U. S. (L. Ed.) 1032, 1035, the Court said:

"The truth of the facts and circumstances offered in evidence in support of the allegations on the record must be determined by the jury."

Also, in Gunning v. Cooley, 74 U. S. (L. Ed.) 720, the Court remarked:

"Issues that depend on the credibility of witnesses, and the effect or weight of evidence are to be decided by the jury. And in determining a motion of either party for a peremptory instruction, the Court assumes that the evidence for the opposing party proves all that it reasonably may be found sufficient to establish, and that from such facts there should be drawn in favor of the latter all the inferences that fairly are deducible from them."

In this Circuit, the rules governing the question as to when a given case should be left to the decision of a jury, are laid down in United States v. Burke, (C. C. A., 9th Circuit) 50 Fed. (2d) 653, 655, 656, where Judge Sawtelle says:

"The question is whether the evidence tending to establish total and permanent disability while

the policy was in effect was sufficient to take the
case to the jury. We do not weigh the evidence,
but inquire merely whether there was sufficient evidence to sustain the verdict and judgment. * * *

"Courts often experience great difficulty in determining whether a given case should be left to
the decision of the jury or whether a verdict should
be directed by the Court. Fortunately, however,
the rule in this Circuit has been definitely settled
and almost universally observed. Judge Gilbert,
for many years and until recently the distinguished
senior Judge of this Court, whose gift for expression was unsurpassed, has stated the rule as follows:

" 'Under the settled doctrine as applied by all
the Federal Appellate Courts, when the refusal to
direct a verdict is brought under review on writ of
error, the question thus presented is whether or
not there was any evidence to sustain the verdict,
and whether or not the evidence to support a directed verdict as requested, was so conclusive that
the trial Court in the exercise of a sound judicial
discretion should not sustain a verdict for the opposing party.

" 'And on a motion for a directed verdict the
Court may not weigh the evidence, and if there is
substantial evidence both for the plaintiff and the
defendant, it is for the jury to determine what
facts are established even if their verdict be against
the decided preponderance of the evidence. Trav-
elers' Ins. Co. v. Randolph, 78 F. 754, 24 C. C. A.
305; Mt. Adams & E. P. Inclined Ry. Co. v.
Lowery, 74 F. 463, 20 C. C. A. 596; Rochford v.
Pennsylvania Co., 174 F. 81, 98 C. C. A. 105;
United States Fidelity & Guaranty Co. v. Blum
(C. C. A.) 270 F. 946; Smith-Booth-Usher Co. v.
Detroit Copper Mining Co., 220 F. 600, 136 C. C.
A. 58. In the case last cited this Court said:

" ' "The right to a jury trial is guaranteed by
the Constitution, and it is not to be denied, except
in a clear case." ' * * *

"Again, 'such an instruction would be proper
only where, admitting the truth of the evidence for
the plaintiff below, as a matter of law, said plaintiff
could not have a verdict.' Marathon Lumber Co.
v. Dennis, 296 F. 471 (C. C. A. 5)."

In the Federal Courts there must be some substantial evidence to support an issue as distinguished
from a mere scintilla. However, the Court in United
States v. Tyrakowski, (C. C. A.) 50 Fed. (2d) 766,
768, 771, in defining what constituted substantial evidence, remarked:

"We do not wish to be understood as saying
that the allegations of the complaint were proved
by a preponderance of all the evidence, for that was
a matter for the trial Court to decide; but we do
say that appellee's testimony constituted substantial evidence of his total disability. The term 'substantial evidence' is not used in the sense of reliability, but rather in contradistinction to the term
'scintilla of evidence.' His evidence can not be disregarded, although it is not such as to inspire complete confidence. * * * there is evidence tending
to show that the disability was total and permanent,
and we are compelled to hold that such evidence
amounted to more than a scintilla and was substantial, regardless of what our views may be as to
its weight and reliability.

"While realizing that the evidence is not as convincing as we might wish or as we might require if
we were the trier of the facts instead of a reviewer
of the trier's facts, yet we cannot say under this
record that there is no substantial evidence to show

that insured was so disabled prior to August 31, 1919, that he could not follow continuously any gainful occupation. That is the test. United States v. Phillips, (C. C. A.) 44 F. (2d) 689; United States v. Eliasson, (C. C. A.) 20 F. (2d) 821; United States v. Cox, (C. C. A.) 24 F. (2d) 944; United States v. Sligh, (C. C. A.) 31 F. (2d) 735; United States v. Schweppe, (C. C. A.) 38 F. (2d) 595."

The fact that several witnesses contradict a party's unsupported statement does not make his statement a mere scintilla of evidence so as to be insufficient to support a verdict in his favor. 23 C. J. 9, Sec. 1733.

The Court of Appeals of the District Court in the recent case of United States v. Stewart, 58 Fed. (2d) 520, has expressed the law applicable hereto as follows:

"The evidence is very lengthy, and we have only referred to it briefly. We think, however, taken as a whole, there was quite enough to take it to the jury, and we have already said in several cases that the mere fact that a former soldier holding a War Risk policy of insurance may have worked for considerable periods of time during which he claimed to be permanently disabled is not conclusive, and that the real question is not whether he worked but whether he was able to work without material injury to his health, and so in this case the issue is not foreclosed because it appears that plaintiff did some work. That fact was material and proper for consideration by the jury, but should not defeat his right to recover if the jury should find that, in spite of temporary work, even for substantial periods of time, the disability which the statute covers in fact existed, and that question was, as we have already stated, under all the circumstances for the jury to decide.

"In this view, we are unable to say that the evidence taken as a whole, when viewed in the light most favorable to the plaintiff, does not justify the conclusion of the jury that he was totally and permanently disabled, and therefore we feel it our duty to affirm the judgment below."

In Ford v. United States, (C. C. A.) 44 Fed. (2d) 754, the Court said:

"It is well settled that, on such a question as is here presented, the plaintiff is entitled to the most favorable construction that a jury might be warranted in putting on the evidence. Heisson v. Dickinson, (C. C. A.) 35 F. (2d) 270, and cases cited; Bangor & Arrostook R. R. v. Jones, (C. C. A.) 36 F. (2d) 886; Gray, Administratrix v. Davis, Director General of R. R., (C. C. A.) 294 F. 57.

"And the act itself is to be liberally construed in favor of such claimants. In White v. United States, 270 U. S. 175, 180, 46 S. Ct. 274, 275, 70 L. Ed. 530, Mr. Justice Holmes said of such contracts: 'The insurance was a contract, to be sure, for which a premium was paid, but it was not one entered into by the United States for gain. All soldiers were given a right to it and the relation of the Government to them if not paternal was at least avuncular. It was a relation of benevolence established by the Government at considerable cost to itself for the soldier's good.'"

See to same effect, McNalley v. United States, (C. C. A.) 52 Fed. (2d) 440, 443; also, United States v. Woltman, 57 Fed. (2d) 418.

In the recent case of United States v. Scarborough, (C. C. A., 9th Circuit) 57 Fed. (2d) 137, Judge Sawtelle states the law as follows:

"The sole question to be determined is the sufficiency of the evidence to support the judgment; in other words, whether there is substantial evidence to establish plaintiff's claim that the deceased veteran was totally and permanently disabled prior to the date upon which the policy lapsed.

"The applicable rules of law in cases of this character are so familiar and have been so often announced by this and other Courts in recent cases that it would seem futile to refer to or repeat them here. It is fundamental that this Court, in determining the question here presented, must view the evidence in the light most favorable to the appellee, and must affirm the findings and conclusions of the trial Court if they are supported by any substantial evidence."

The last expression on this subject by the Circuit Court of Appeals for this Circuit appears in the case of United States v. Lesher, 59 Fed. (2d) 53, wherein Judge Neterer states the law as follows:

"Under the Seventh Amendment to the Constitution, a jury trial is guaranteed in a civil action; and that it is error to direct a verdict for defendant if there is any substantial evidence is stare decisis. * * *

"The Court does not weigh the evidence, but considers whether there is any or sufficient evidence to sustain a verdict. See Ford v. United States, (C. C. A.) 44 F. (2d) 754. And in war risk cases the most favorable construction should be given the evidence that is produced. Ford v. United States, supra. The trial Judge must, in the exercise of sound discretion, determine whether upon the evidence produced a verdict can be sustained, not weigh the evidence. If there is evidence, it must be submitted; if not, it is pronouncedly his duty to direct a verdict."

Keeping in mind the rules as laid down in the foregoing decisions, let us examine the evidence in this case
in order to ascertain whether there is substantial evidence that on or before the 19th day of September,
1919, plaintiff had an impairment of mind or body
which rendered it impossible for him to follow continuously any substantially gainful occupation and that
such impairment was then founded on conditions which
rendered it reasonably certain that it would continue
throughout his life.

Plaintiff, Carrol T. McCreary, gave the following
substantial evidence:

He tells us (Tr. p. 107) that he had never suffered
from any disability or been ill at any time prior to entering the army.

We find him with the second division of the Marines
(Tr. p. 109) going into the Soissons Sector and that
was the time that he became ill or, as he expresses it
(Tr. p. 110) "the first time I got sick or bothered with
the dysentery and diarrhea."

Immediately prior to that time he was under shell
fire and we quote the testimony at this point verbatim
(Tr. pp. 110, 111, 112, 113): "Q. Immediately prior
to that had anything happened to you in regard to fire
—shell fire or action, or— A. Oh, we were under shell
fire there. We went into a dug-in in a hill and we dug
into what was called 'Dead Man's Hill.' I think there
was something over two hundred of us fellows dug in

there and there wasn't a hundred of us left, and we were there only four hours. Shells exploded within ten or fifteen feet of me and the man next to me died. He was dead before I was able to get up. It shot the wind out of me and I was thrown down on the ground like a feather. Shortly after that time this dysentery broke out on me, and I was so sick from that I didn't notice any great change. The dysentery was—the bowels run off. It was the diarrhea; that is what I think it was. It was from the water or something we got to eat. At that time we were eating with the French troops. We had to eat their rations. I think it was canned horse meat and we had hard tack. And we had rotten coffee. Well, I was able to stay with the company a few days when we moved back of the lines. I had been on guard but they relieved me. A sergeant thought I was drinking but I told him I had nothing to drink and then they put me on a sick bed and I was there for two or three days. They had no convalescent's camp to send me to or a hospital, and then from there I joined the company and went into the town of Nancy. Q. Were you in the hospital there for some time—or were you in the hospital at any time until you went to the hospital at St. Mihiel? A. I was in the hospital in Selincourt. I don't know whether I was in the hospital there for flu, or this trouble, or what it was. I was in the hospital there two weeks or a little better. I think they called it influenza. Following that I was weak and run down. After I got out of the hospital at Selincourt I went back and joined the company. I came back only two

days before we went on the St. Mihiel offensive. They
detailed me to guard duty there. That was along in
the fall. I know it rained like blazes when we went
there. It was maybe in September some time. The
reason I was detailed to guard duty there at that time,
I guess, was they figured I wasn't fit for anything else.
I was bothered with dysentery and diarrhea and I
couldn't carry my pack. I couldn't keep up with the
outfit. After the St. Mihiel offensive I went into the
kitchen. I figured I could maybe get better stuff to
eat; better stuff for my condition than I could get on
the outside, and I couldn't stand the trip. I couldn't
carry my pack. I did not get better; I was able to get
by and that was all. Q. Did you go to any sick bed
until you went into the Champoigne offense? A. I went
sometimes four or five times a day. Sometimes I would
be excused from duty and sometimes I would not be.
I think they gave me aspirin tablets. Q. Did you get
any relief with that medicine from your sickness. A.
I can't say that I did. Q. What actions did you take
part in? A. After St. Mihiel it was the Champoigne.
Q. Were you on shell fire there? A. I was. My condition was very poor during that time. I volunteered
to go into the lines and they wouldn't take me. The
captain laughed at me. He said he was having trouble
enough with well men without taking sick men along
into the lines. Q. How long were you on the Argonne
Drive? A. I left the outfit two days before the Armistice
was signed. From there I went to the hospital. I was
there when the Armistice was signed. We moved 17

kilometers back to Hospital No. 1, and I got back there, and I was left there, and from there I went back from the hospital to Contrexeville, France, Base 36. I don't remember the exact number of days I was in the hospital at Contrexeville. I left there some time after the first of January, 1919. In the hospital there I believe they treated me for intra-colitis, or inflammation of the bowels, or dysentery."

Again (Tr. p. 115) he was asked this question and gave the following reply: "Q. Did you have any more spells of dysentery? A. Yes, I had spells after that."

Referring to Appellee's heart condition (Tr. pp. 116, 117, 118, 119) we again quote verbatim as follows: "Q. When did you first discover that you were having trouble with your heart? A. Well, it bothered me some at the time we got out but not a great deal. I think it has got worse in the last two years. Q. It bothered you some when you first got out? A. Yes. Q. You talk about an acute enteritis—? A. Yes. Q.—do you know that that was what you had when you got back into civil life? A. No, I thought it was the grub I was eating. Q. When did you first discover that your stomach was bothering you? A. Well, my stomach was bad when I was in the service. Q. Did you have any of these disabilities before you entered the service? A. Not to my knowledge. Q. Well, you should know. A. Well, I think I could eat nails before I went in. * * * The first work I did was I helped one of the neighbors out there. That was Mr. Burns. I helped him possibly four or five hours. I did not work with the rest of the crew until the work was done; I played out; it was one of my days. I heard Mr. Burns testify here yesterday. I was around with Mr. Burns for possibly a week or ten days. I believe I helped him with the chores while I was there. I think Bob Strubin came and asked me to assist him in 1919. He asked me to come and help him and I said I didn't know whether I could or not but that I would try, and I went down and made a try, and for a while I got along fairly good, and then this trouble bothered me and I had two or three light attacks, and then after two or three light attacks I had a bad attack, and I went to the doctor; to Dr. Hughes, at Gresham. That was about the first part of October, 1919. At that time I was bothered with dysentery, and I was very weak, and I had bad night sweats, and I didn't know what was wrong with me. I also was bothered with severe headaches at that time—something awful. It would catch me through the temple and the back of the head. I was nervous at that time, and I understood Bob used to have quite a time with me there. They had one old gasoline engine that they used to grind ensilage with for feed, and also grind other grain for the cows, and Bob used to play with that and get it to backfire to make me jump, and I would hit the deck on all fours. It would catch me when I didn't know it was going to do it. If I had known it I could have controlled myself but if I didn't I would go right up in the air and come down. Q. Why would you go up in the air? A. I guess it was a matter of habit. That is one thing that a fellow learns to do when he is in the army—that's to duck when a shell goes off. The first three or four weeks I had to take very little time off. The doctor told me to lay around for four or five days the first time I took sick and then go back to work, and at different times I had to take time off. I think there was five or six days that I did nothing until toward the last. Q. Did he have anybody there to assist you? A. Well, he had one man there first and then a boy to help me. He helped to clean out the barn and get the feed in. Later on he done away with the milking machines and he got a man there to help me. Q. This work you did there and the work done by this man and this boy later, could you have done it all if you had been well? A. Well, one man should take care of 30 or 40 cows. Q. Could you have done that if you had been as well as you had been before you went into the service? A. I had done it before."

McCreary realized his condition but showed his good intention by trying to work for Mr. Strebin a second time as seen in his testimony (Tr. pp. 119-120): "I worked there until about the first of April, 1920, and then I gave it up and was away five or six weeks; I don't remember which. Then he saw me again, about asking me to resume my employment, and he said he would have a man help me *all the time,* and that I would have to do the feeding, and that he would give me an increase over what he had been paying. He had been paying me $75 and he said he would give me $110 or $115; I don't remember it now."

Questioned as to his reason for leaving Mr. Wilcox's employ, we quote McCreary's testimony (Tr. p. 121) as follows: "I was with Mr. Wilcox of the Fernwood Dairy a little over a year. I was off eight weeks in the summer of 1921, with an operation. I had this operation because this trouble was still bothering me and I could not get any relief for it. The operation did not relieve it. Besides the eight weeks, I lost a few days now and then. I think four days was the longest I was off. I lost a few days now and then because I was not able to carry on. It was the same trouble. After the operation I went back and went to work for Mr. Wilcox. Mr. Wilcox came to me himself and asked me to quit. He said I wouldn't last a year if I kept on with that work. He told me to quit. I was sick at that time."

Some time after leaving Mr. Wilcox's employ, McCreary bought a small farm out near Gresham and we quote from his testimony (Tr. pp. 122, 123, 124) to show his condition at that time: "I did some of the work on the place, and my father did some, and I hired some of the work done. I hired some plowing done by John Strebin. My wife did some work there; she helped me, of course. Q. Were you sick while you were out there? A. I was. Q. How long were you in the hospital at that time? A. at the time of the Q. At the time of the operation? A. August, 1922. Q. And what hospital was that? A. The old veterans' hospital. Q. The old hospital '77' across the river? A. Yes. Q. What occasioned your going to the hospital? A. Well, Dr.

Rockey sent me there. He sent me there for observation and treatment. Q. What was your treatment at that time? A. I was still bothered with abdominal trouble and this diarrhea. Q. And what about your nervous condition? A. Yes, sure. Q. And what about your headaches? A. Several headaches of the same kind. Q. What else? Was it just the same condition that you have told us about before? A. Yes. The next job I had was with the Davidson Bakery Company. I went to work there in May of 1923, I believe. I got along pretty well but when it came to the heavy work I had to have help, but the light work I could get along with pretty well. I had a brother working there at that same time, and he is still there. I worked at that place somewhere around eight or ten months. There were interruptions in that employment. I was off part of the time because I was sick. I left the bakery and went into the hospital— No. 77. Dr. C. C. Campbell, of the Veterans' Hospital, treated me while I was there. I went through the routine examination while I was there, and I think I was under Dr. Campbell's care practically all the time I was there. After I was discharged from the Veterans' Hospital I think I felt better. I was feeling pretty good when I left and from then until the fall. The only work I did after that amounted to anything was for the City of Portland; that was the job of watching the rocks coming down the hill. My stomach gave me an awful lot of trouble during all that time. I can't tell you exactly how long I continued that work. I worked on that job watching this road until it was completed, and then I worked one day running a wheelbarrow and then I went to the Veterans' Hospital for an examination and treatment, and was there possibly two weeks or better. Then I got discharged."

In 1927 we find McCreary working in a logging camp for a short time and his testimony (Tr. p. 125) explains quite clearly his reason for being compelled to quit that employment: "I quit work at the logging camp because I played out; I could not fill the bill. I think I worked somewhere around two or three weeks before I played out. I am not sure."

The following testimony is substantial evidence that plaintiff's disabilities have persisted from date of discharge from the army to date of judgment (Tr. pp. 127, 128) : "This amoebic dysentery that I was being treated for was the same as I had when I was first treated for a disorder in France, and I have been suffering from the same thing ever since."

Dr. Marcellas (Tr. pp. 127-128) diagnosed McCreary's condition as amoebic dysentery. Concerning this plaintiff testified: "In the spring of 1924 or 1925, sometime during that year, when I was in the Veterans' Hospital, treating for inflammation of the gall bladder, as they termed it, I asked Dr. Marcellas what my trouble was, and he said I had amoebic dysentery, and that that was what my trouble was and had been all along."

Under cross-examination (Tr. p. 133) we call the Court's attention to the following testimony. "While

I was out there (Strebin's Dairy, 1919-1920) I was bothered with this weakness and diarrhea. Q. At that time had you no trouble with your stomach? A. Well, I could not eat. I did not know what was the matter with me. When I was out there in 1919 and 1920 I went through a complete examination and when I got through I never knew what was the matter with me. Q. It was not until 1925, that you had anything wrong with your stomach? A. Yes. I know I had something wrong but what I had or what was wrong I didn't know. Q. The stomach did not bother you while you were over in France, did it? A. It sure did."

In support of plaintiff's contentions, the following lay testimony was introduced:

Mr. A. H. Burns testified (Tr. p. 29) that he had known the plaintiff from boyhood, in fact that he and Mrs. Burns had attended school with the plaintiff, and that as soon as plaintiff was discharged from the service he came to visit at the farm home of Mr. and Mrs. Burns in September, 1919, and it is safe to assume that this was immediately after he was discharged from the service. He said (Tr. pp. 29, 30), "I knew him well up till the time he went to war. He worked for me. I recall the time when he went to war. I saw him within a week after he came back from service. That was in the early fall of 1919; it was the last days of August or the first of September of 1919.

"He came down to visit with us and stayed about a week or ten days—a few days more or less. He said,

'I have to have a job.' I had work for him to do there, but I could not put him to work because his condition showed he was more ready for the hospital than he was to work. He was very nervous. He could only eat certain things and otherwise it disagreed with him. My wife had to work to figure out what he could eat. He was a school mate to both of us, and that was his reason for coming to visit us. We had to be very careful what he ate and how he ate it. He did not do any work for me but went to help my brother about a quarter of a mile from our residence and help him thresh. On one particular instance when I was present he started pitching in, and I am positive he had not pitched in over fifteen minutes when my brother went up on the stack and put him in the shade and told him to stay there and he wasn't to do any more threshing. Carrol McCreary was trembling like a leaf. He didn't work any more for my brother, nor did he work any more for me. From then on I saw him on an average of about once a month."

Again (Tr. p. 30) : "One night he was in Gresham. I never realized what shell-shock was before. There was a celebration, a fete for the queen, and a firecracker went off behind him and I was standing beside McCreary. It was pitiful to see his condition after that. He seemed to jump right up off the side-walk. He said, 'My God, Art, let's get out of here.' He was very weak, and his face was pinched and drawn and very pale, compared with how it was before he went to war."

Mr. Burns was in quite close touch with McCreary for sometime after that as evidenced by his testimony when he tried to work for Mr. Strebin (Tr. pp. 30, 31): "I followed him in his attempts to find employment after that. He would work two or three days here and there and would have to quit on account of his condition; he spoke to me about going to work, too, for the Robert Strebin Dairy. That was the first dairy he went to. I saw him there when he was there. He acted all the time tired and very weak, and continued nervous."

Again, under cross-examination, Mr. Burns testified as follows (Tr. p. 31): "We had a farm out there. This was in September, 1919. I could have given him employment at that time, but I didn't think his condition warranted it."

Again, under cross-examination (Tr. p. 35) Mr. Burns testified as follows: "When he was working for Strebin there he was very tired and very weak."

On redirect examination (Tr. p. 35) Mr. Burns testified as follows: "I had work I could have given McCreary to do if he had been in a condition to do it when he came back from the service and subsequent to that. He has been about the same in his appearance since the war until now.

"I visited him when he was sick at home. I have seen Carrol McCreary home sick, when he could have been working, at least three or four times while he was working at Strebin's Dairy. I saw him in that condition myself."

Counsel for Appellant lay some stress upon the testimony of Mr. Strebin. Let us examine Mr. Strebin's testimony in some detail. Referring to the time that he was first employed by Mr. Strebin, also immediately after McCreary was discharged from the service, we quote from Mr. Strebin's testimony (Tr. pp. 74, 75, 76, 77, 78, 79, 80): "That was the first time I had seen him after he returned from the service. I noticed a big change in him. He didn't seem to be the same man that went away. He stooped more and his eyes were hollow, and he had the general appearance of being nervous. I doubted very much if he could stand the work, but I needed someone there to help me very much and I insisted on him coming down anyway. I don't know whether we talked over his condition at that time or not, but I think I remember Mr. McCreary told me he didn't think he could stand the work but that he would come down and try it, and I took him to my place. * * * Mr. McCreary—well I had to have a man to do the heavy work. I employed two men, and I had to have one man do the heavy work. I milked forty-eight cows at the time, and I used the milking machines and McCreary was to over-see the milking machines, and he was to attend to the mixing of the feed for the cattle because much money can be lost and wasted in a herd of that size, and your profits can be thrown away if you don't watch out. The other man got in the grain and the other feed and he cleaned the stables and put in the cows. Carrol had time off each day, which he had to take, and in fact many times he was so nervous we could not get him off on time for his evening chores. When we would call him he would come up with a jump and throw his hands into the air and he would come to the barn with his eyes glaring—they would be so glary—and he would go about his work and would carry on principally on his nerves. I had to have a man to assist him. He could never have carried a week alone.

" * * * He went away one time when he had to give up the work entirely. He had to give up the work; he could not stand it; he was broken up completely. Aside from that time there were many times when he could not carry on. Sometimes I had to assist him and sometimes my sister had to assist him. Sometimes he had to fill the silo. Many times my sister had to help. * * * He just did not have the strength and he was nervous and he could not stand it—the work he was doing. He couldn't carry on. Many times he had to lay off part of some days when he did not go away entirely. The reason I continued this course with him was that his experience was worth so much to me in the work I had. You see I used the milking machines on my herd of cows, and Mr. McCreary had had some experience with the use of milking machines. He worked at the Sundahl place before he went to war, and it was almost impossible to get a man with milking machine experience. The first time there was a big interruption in his work, I tried to replace him and I couldn't do it. My herd went to pieces. As far as he was concerned, I hunted him up. I don't remember where I found him; I don't remember whether it was here in Portland or not. I hunted him up and offered him a great increase in wages, either fifteen or twenty dollars, if he would come back to me. * * * Well, you see Mr. McCreary did not like to refuse to come back. I had been good to him there. My folks had always known him and my mother was good to him, and he saw I was in a pinch and he knew I was losing money, and he said he would come back but he doubted that he could stand it—he doubted that he could stand the work again. He showed a little improvement from a few days' rest but he still showed that nervous appearance that he always had. Q. How long did he carry on? A. This time? Q.—this time until he had to lay off again in the afternoon. A. I could not say. I am only guessing at these periods because it has been many years ago. Whether it was a month or two months I could not say.

"He did not regain his health. He finally had to give the work up. He couldn't stand it. His condition then was about as poor as a man could be in. Any little thing would startle Carrol—any little noise. After any little noise you would see him going up into the air. I guess you would only see him coming down. Around the barn or at the house—when my mother would call him—sometimes it was almost dangerous to call him. Many times we did not call him. Sometimes we would let him sleep until the milking was practically done. He was such a nervous wreck we did not like to disturb him. Q. Do you remember any thing that happened. Anything that remains in your mind? A. Yes, I remember once or—well I remember one or two things that I never will forget. One time we were walking back of the cows and his shoulder brushed the cow's tail and the cow pails were hanging back there, and I looked around there and I just saw him coming down. He must have been up a considerable distance. Q. Where had he been—you said he was coming down? A. Well, he jumped up into the air. He had been walking along there and I just saw him coming down, and then another time one of the boys fired a shotgun back of the stable at some crows and Carrol let out a yell as loud as he could and he came over the cows with his bucket and he didn't get over that for several days. These two instances and when we would call him or arouse him out of his sleep, I perhaps will never forget, and I don't think anybody else would ever forget—the look he carried at these times. I have seen this man quite a number of times since I gave him employment. I have never employed him since that time. If Carrol could have stood the work we would have been glad to have had him back. I stated that to him when he left— that if he could ever do the work we would be glad to have him back. On these occasions that I have seen him since he quit there, I can't see where he was ever any better."

Under cross-examination (Tr. p. 83) Mr. Strebin testified as follows: "Yes, that is right, except the boy sacrificed himself for me—he sacrificed his health for my benefit, and I did not feel so good about that at the time."

Mr. Fred T. Wilson of the Fernwood Dairy also employed McCreary for a short time (Tr. pp. 85, 86) and his testimony also throws some light upon Mc-Creary's condition shortly after his return from the service: "I think the first time he was in my employ, when he first came to work, that he was able to do his work, but I could not say how long he worked there, but he worked for some time, and then he gradually became weaker and weaker and in fact got so he could not do his work. Q. What was he doing? A. I think he was checking. He was either checking or working; working inside my plant. * * * I don't remember so much about his condition with reference to being nervous. He was unable later to do his work, because he was sick. He was weak, but he made a supreme effort to do it, but I requested him to—I called him in and I asked him to quit until he could get in shape so that he could do his work, and he quit. He came back again and stayed a very short time. His physical condition then was not very good. * * * Well, the second time I think he came in and resigned, and the first time—I think I asked him to lay off until he could get in shape so that he could handle his work. He was all run down and weak. So far as we were concerned we wanted to keep him."

Mr. Leon Coddey (Tr. pp. 88, 89, 90) had known McCreary prior to the war and met him on the streets of Portland some months after he (Coddey) had returned from the service and we quote from his testimony as follows: "I came back the 15th of June, and I was walking on the streets here in Portland and I saw him on the street, and he had on his army overcoat and I saw him standing on the street, and he was feeling weak like, and his eyes were glassy and wasted away, and his face was thin, drawn in, and I said, 'Carrol, what is the matter with you?' and he said, 'Well, I don't know' and I said, 'Are you trying to do anything for yourself?' and he said, 'I don't know what is the matter,' and I told him to see a doctor and he said he was coming to town and that was the last time I seen him that time. * * * Why, I went and got Carrol a job once. I got him the easiest job with the City of Portland. I got a job for him watching rocks on the road at Bull Run, and he was home a few days and then he had to come down and his father was up there two or three days, and then he came back, and then they found another easy job for him, but Carrol played out on that job, too, and he had to give that up. I believe you asked me if I had seen him working. I went home another evening and he was down in the field, and he had been attempting to clear some ground and he had his father's sled up there, eight or ten feet long, and he was down on his hands by this sled, and he was waving and hollering to me to come over there and I left my job and I went over there, and so I got my arm around his shoulder and I got him to the house the best I could. He was walking, and I put him to bed and I took his team and put it in the barn and I took the harnesses off the horses. That was another episode that happened at that time."

Mr. Coddey's testimony (Tr. pp. 91, 92) also throws some light on McCreary's condition in 1925. Cross-examination by Mr. Erskine: "But you finished that job in 1925, didn't you? A. Well, he didn't. He played out before the job was finished. I stayed there and worked with two other fellows. The crew on which he was working was not continued all winter. I don't think he went back the next winter when it started up again on that construction work. If he could do the work I would have him with me today."

Mr. John Everle, a farmer living near Troutdale, employed McCreary for a short time, but he, too, was unable to retain him in his employ because of his physical condition and inability to do ordinary work. And we quote from Mr. Everle's testimony (Tr. p. 93): "I noticed he looked a whole lot different when he came back than when he went away. He didn't look like the same man at all. He was all humped up. His eyes were all swollen, and he looked all worn out. He worked for me a little off and on, on occasions. It was just day work, but he could not hold out. He would try to help me but he would give out. I tried to get him to help me clear a little land and drive a horse and he gave out. I wanted him to drive the stump machine. Every time I employed him after he came back from the war he gave out. I employed him before the war.

He was a great man before the war. If he could have done the work, I would have had work for him after the war. Yes, I saw some manifestation of nervousness. I had some blasting to do and every time I set off a blast he would duck and try to get away from it, and he was very nervous-like. I have never seen him work for anybody else that I can recall. He has not been any different since he got back; he is about the same."

Mr. T. E. Gabode employed McCreary for a short time and like all other employers, was compelled to let him go. And we cite his experience with McCreary (Tr. pp. 95, 96) as follows: "He was able to do the work that was assigned him well enough to keep him on the job. We had his brother there on the job working and we tried to keep him working, but many times when we had heavy work to do we always had to send somebody with him. I did not consider him good, first class, from a physical standpoint. Regarding his nervous condition, you could notice there was a nervous strain. You could see he was bothered with something. We knew he was not exactly right physically but we tried to help him along. I don't remember anything in particular that attracted my attention to his nervous condition. It was a sort of all the time that he did not appear to be able—well, he could do light jobs all right, but when it came to heavy jobs he just petered out and we had to give him help. He would not lay off for more than a couple of days at a time. When he quit he came in and said he could not handle the work and he felt that we were just keeping him on and he felt the best thing to do was to quit. I would say we were just helping him along."

Mr. J. H. Cooper (Tr. p. 98) saw McCreary trying to do some work on his own place and his own words described McCreary's condition as follows: "I saw him after he came back from service; I had seen him once down at his place. He was trying to clear his land and he was pretty sick and weak and he couldn't do much. That was the first time I had seen him after he came back."

Again we refer to Mr. Cooper's testimony (Tr. p. 99): "He did not continue to work because he was not able to stand it any longer. After Christmas he got sick and he laid off for about a week. He would topple over. He got so weak he could not get around. There was something the matter with his stomach and his heart. I didn't know he was as bad as he really was. He was always nervous and he seemed as though he couldn't get any rest. That was not before the war; it was while he was up there. Before the war he was a big, husky lad."

Mr. Dahl, a farmer living near Troutdale, had work for McCreary, but he, like McCreary's other employers, was compelled to dispense with services. (Tr. pp. 101, 102, 103): "He was very willing to work and made a great effort, but in a short time—that is, in a few days—you could see the effect on his person. He was very badly worn out after he worked hard for a time. After that, as a rule, he went back to his father's or up home where he lived, close to his father. That was near my place. Regarding his nervous condition—if anyone stepped up close by him—I had two boys and they were a little bit unruly at times, and if they touched him quick it would send him up in the air. * * * I employed him at various times for various short jobs I had there. He did not always stay until the jobs I had for him were completed. I would say he did half the time. The other half of the time there was work for him to do if he could have done it."

Substantial evidence which supports this verdict came from the medical experts as follows:

Dr. H. H. Hughes, a physician maintaining an office and with a practice in Gresham, in the vicinity of which McCreary had lived prior and subsequent to the war, testified that he had known McCreary (Tr. p. 36) since 1913; and that he saw him two or three days before he went into the service. He also testified that he saw him after his return from the service in the early part of October, 1919, when he came to consult him professionally about his condition. Let us examine Dr. Hughes' statement more in detail. He testified (Tr. pp. 37, 38) in part as follows: "At that time I found he had lost a good deal of weight, and he was somewhat anemic and stooped, and his voice had changed a good deal, and he did not have the strength that he used to have. He complained of having suffered diarrhea and pain in the abdomen. These were about the things he complained about. He also had a tenderness in the abdomen and he had a diarrhea at that time. He complained of not being able to digest his food, of having a good deal of gas and a sour stomach.

"I took the usual history taken in such cases and interrogated him about what he had been through. I diagnosed his trouble as dysentery, and he had an inflamed or sore bowel at that time. We called that a colitis. I didn't determine the cause of the dysentery because I have no way, out in the country, of determining the cause of dysentery. That is done in hospitals and laboratories. But I found he had such. It was the fore part of October, 1919, I examined him. McCreary had not been home from service very long at that time; probably a month or two. On the occasion of my first examination of him after he left the service, he seemed very nervous and restless as he was sitting in the chair; he was restless and nervous and he had a cough at that time and was raising some material. * * * He described a good deal of what he went through, and the guns and so forth, and I took it for granted that was the cause of his nervousness.

"I can't say just how frequently I have seen the man since that first visit right after service, but a good many times. I think that nervousness is about the same as it was then; yes, it has persisted."

Again, quoting from Dr. Hughes (Tr. pp. 39, 40) we find the Doctor very emphatic as to Appellee's condition at the present time and gave it as his opinion that the condition of dysentery had continued ever since Appellee was discharged from the service.

"I examined Mr. McCreary just a few days ago. He was in the office. This man has a dysentery which has weakened him, and he is very nervous and he has had a weak heart; he has lost weight and he is not what I would say is a strong man; this is because of his weakened condition due to the dysentery. From what he said, the dysentery has persisted since I first saw him in 1919. I have been there when he had dysentery. * * * Dysentery is caused by different things, different bacteria and parasites. There is no cure. They are better for a while and then they are worse. It leaves a man in a weakened condition. It explains his loss of weight, his nervousness, and his weak heart."

We now come to what is unquestionably the most emphatic and most important part of Dr. Hughes' testimony. Quoting from Tr. p. 40 we want to call particular attention to this portion of the Doctor's testimony: "Based upon my examination and the knowledge of this man and his history I have taken, I think this man is totally and permanently unable to follow continuously a substantially gainful occupation. I would say he was totally and permanently disabled, as defined, at the time he came back from the service, August, 1919, and I would say that the condition he is in is reasonably certain to continue throughout his lifetime."

Under cross-examination (Tr. pp. 43, 44) Dr. Hughes testified as follows: "Very often when he came to town he came up and visited and talked over the places he had been in the war. He said, 'I have been back to the Veterans' Hospital and I have been out two months trying to hold down a job. One was in Washington.' He said he had been working on a pump job up there. * * * I have always referred him to the Portland Veterans' Hospital. I think he was just as thin and has lost just as much weight when I first saw him in October, 1919, as I see him today. I really don't see much change."

Again, quoting from Tr. p. 46: "Mr. Erskine: I did not understand from the diagnosis of October, 1919, that you found anything wrong with his heart. Dr. Hughes: He was weakened all over; when a man is weakened from diarrhea, that is, he has to go a good many times in twenty-four hours, it weakens his heart the same as it weakens him other ways. It weakens the muscles." (Tr. p. 47.)

Dr. Hughes, under cross-examination, was asked whether the dysentery condition was one that would tend to make McCreary nervous to which he replied (Tr. p. 48): "The weakness from it would make him nervous, yes. Q. Now, which do you think was the primary cause of the nervousness you found—the dysentery or the experience he related to you there in your office, when he first came back there? A. Well, I don't know. I think that it is the combination. Either one has been enough to put the average man out."

Under redirect examination the following testimony was given: "Q. Doctor, is it not true that in addition to these army experiences which bring on nervousness, as you testified, that the infection which goes with this dysentery also produces nervousness? A. Any septic poisoning— Q. That is my point. A. Yes, sure it may."

Dr. Edwin P. Fagan testified that as an associate of the Portland Clinic of Doctors he, with Dr. Joyce, first examined McCreary in September, 1930. He again examined him a short time before the trial and we quote from his testimony (Tr. p. 56) as follows: "I examined this man four or five days ago and could see no change in his condition. Based upon my examination and the history that I took and with my knowledge of these conditions, I would say that this man in his present condition is totally and permanently disabled from following continuously any substantially gainful occupation; that is, he is permanently and totally disabled. Assuming that these conditions have prevailed and persisted at least since he was released from active service in August, 1919, I would say he was totally and permanently disabled from that time on; this is a permanent and total disability and has been ever since that time."

Again (Tr. p. 68) we quote from Dr. Fagan's testimony: "A. He is unable to work so far as his stomach is concerned. Q. His stomach was the only thing you based your answer upon? A. That and his history. You can't take just what you find wrong with the man. You must also take into account what was found wrong with the man just previous to the time he became ill. Q. Then you based your answer on the question of whether or not this boy was able to work now, as much upon the history that the boy gave you as upon the diagnosis? A. You can't disregard the history."

Dr. Fagan was questioned in some detail (Tr. pp. 69, 70) with reference to the question of whether or not McCreary would be benefited by an operation, also with reference to his nervousness. We quote as follows: "Well, from the findings that he was nervous and that he complained of pain in his stomach, and in the region of his abdomen, as far as the pains there, the chances are he would be benefited by this operation. From the history I took I found he had been given medication for several years, and that he had been suffering from this disorder for a number of years, and that he had suffered with this nervousness for some time. He gave me the history of these different attacks he had in France, and also the fact that he had been overseas and was engaged in several major engagements, as he gave it, might account for some of this nervousness. His internal trouble would induce this nervousness, and being under shell fire, which he told me about, would induce nervousness."

Referring again to McCreary's condition from a medical standpoint it is interesting to examine the testimony of Mrs. Helen Lyons, technician in the office of Dr. Tucker at Forest Grove. Speaking of Mr. McCreary's condition while under treatment with Dr. Tucker (Tr. pp. 103, 104) she testified as follows: "Mr. McCreary certainly has been consulting with Dr. Tucker personally since the time I first met him over two years ago. Since that time I should say, to the best that I can recall, he has been there twenty or twenty-five times. I know of my own knowledge that the doctor was treating him for heart trouble and stomach trouble and dysentery. Q. Mrs. Lyons, can you describe briefly the trouble or the condition you observed this young man to be in when he came to the doctor's office on these several occasions which you have testified about? A. Yes, I can because he impressed me the very first time I saw him as he came into the office there and then I was called into the office there to be with him as he was extremely weak. In fact, it was with some difficulty we were able to take care of him for a little while because he had to rest up and be cared for. He was suffering then with his heart. In a way he would respond to treatment. He would become a little stronger, and then perhaps the very next day or the day after that, perhaps, he would be back there and tell us of another severe attack he had had, and of the night spells with his heart. * * * I know that he was treating for his heart and for the dysentery trouble, and that is all that I know. That is all that I can truthfully say."

The foregoing resume of pertinent evidence establishes that there was substantial evidence to support plaintiff's Complaint and to show that he was, as the jury found, totally and permanently disabled at the date of his discharge from service.

In Appellant's argument (Brief, pp. 23, 24) claim is made that "the evidence in this case does not disclose in the life of the insurance contract the evidence of any disability then reasonably certain to be totally disabling throughout life." This issue was decided by the jury when they heard the substantial evidence hereinbefore quoted.

It is clear from this evidence that during service, plaintiff developed and suffered from certain disabilities which have persisted ever since. Included in these disabilities are stomach, heart, bowel and nerve disorders. As illustrative, may we repeat plaintiff's testimony on one point (Tr. pp. 127, 128): "This amoebic dysentery that I was being treated for was the same as I had when I was first treated for a disorder in France and I have been suffering from the same thing ever since."

Appellant claims (Brief, p. 24) for the evidence as follows: "On cross-examination the physician (Dr. Hughes) testified that he did not make the diagnosis of dysentery." The record does not support this claim and the fact is that Dr. Hughes testified (Tr. pp. 37-39, 40, 45) that his diagnosis in this case was dysentery. What apparently confused counsel is the difference between the diagnosis and the cause of the disability. Dr. Hughes pointed out that this field of endeavor, to-wit, determination of cause, is done in hospital and in laboratory and that he went no further than to make the diagnosis of dysentery.

It is interesting at this point to recall another part of Dr. Hughes' testimony brought out on this same cross-examination (Tr. p. 48):

Q. Now, Dr. Hughes, you said also that this condition—this dysentery condition—was one that would tend to make him nervous. Is that what you mean?

A. The weakness from it would make him nervous, yes.

Q. Now, which do you think was the primary cause of the nervousness you found—the dysentery or the experience he related to you there in your office, when he first came back there?

A. Well, I don't know. I think that it is the combination. Either one has been enough to put the average man out.

Appellant's argument includes this statement (Brief, p. 25): "Dr. Fagan, plaintiff's other medical witness, found no evidence of dysentery in 1930 and 1931."

Dr. Fagan testified as follows (Tr. pp. 53, 54, 55, 56):

A. I questioned him and he told me about having dysentery some time in France which continued some time after he came back and it was diagnosed as dysentery at the Veterans' Hospital at Portland.

Mr. Erskine: What is that?

A. He gave a history of having dysentery and diarrhea with cramps while in France, and after he came back to this country it was diagnosed as dysentery in this country. I think he told me that.

Mr. Erskine: He told you that?

A. Yes, sir. He said that. He gave that history.

Mr. Erskine: You think he told you that?

A. No, I know he told me that.

* * * * *

A. * * * This man was very nervous when I examined him. The history he gave might account for some of his nervousness; any person with that much trouble in their stomach—it would account for some of their nervousness. I should think dysentery would produce nervousness; it would. The fact that a person has to go—it keeps him sort of walking, until he is actually nervous. There is a toxicity—a condition caused by diarrhea which causes nervousness. In other words, they get dehydrated because of the loss of so much fluid.

In answer to appellant's argument headed "Attempted combination of disabilities" (Brief, p. 25), we have this to say: There was medical testimony from Drs. Hughes and Fagan and from Dr. Tucker, by his office technician, Mrs. Lyons, and from Dr. Marcellas, Veterans Bureau doctor, by the plaintiff's statement of what this doctor told him, all of which shows a continuous complaint of similar disabilities from plaintiff. While Dr. Fagan found other things wrong with the plaintiff, it should be kept in mind that throughout the entire period with which we are concerned in this record, the plaintiff has complained of, suffered from and been treated for disorders of the bowels, stomach, heart and nerves. It will be remembered that Dr. Campbell, defendant's medical expert (Tr. p. 151) "diagnosed Mr. McCreary as a neurasthenic type" and "gave him credit for a neurasthenia—of a neurasthenic type."

We cannot agree with Appellant that, in order for plaintiff to prevail, it must be established that one or more isolated disabilities must be paramount in importance and dominant in character. We submit that plaintiff should be taken as he was on his return from service, and that a combination of disabilities, if permanent in nature and sufficient in combined severity to prevent him from following continuously any substantially gainful occupation, would be enough to sustain this recovery. An examination of this record leaves the reader satisfied that the disabilities with which plaintiff left the service have persisted continuously thereafter.

Concerning the appendicitis referred to in Appellant's Brief, on page 28, we respectfully call attention to plaintiff's testimony (Tr. p. 121):

> "I was off eight weeks in the summer of 1921 with an operation. I had this operation because this trouble was still bothering me and I could not get any relief for it. The operation did not relieve it."

Appellant in its argument entitled "Opinion testimony" (Brief, p. 29) says: "Dr. Hughes' opinion that 'plaintiff was permanently and totally disabled from August, 1919, * * * must have been based entirely on' the history he took, for, says Appellant's Brief, 'he did not testify to any continuity of findings or symptoms from which it could reasonably be concluded that total permanent disability existed, nor did he identify the particular impairment which in his opinion precluded the continuous pursuit of substantially gainful employment'."

This rather remarkable declaration convinces us that the writer of this Brief entirely overlooked Dr. Hughes' testimony as follows (Tr. pp. 38, 39, 40):

"I can't say just how frequently I have seen this man since that first visit right after service, but a good many times. I think that nervousness is about the same as it was then; yes, *it has persisted.*
* * *

"I examined Mr. McCreary just a few days ago. He was in the office. This man has a dysentery which has weakened him, and he is very nervous, and he has had a weak heart; he has lost weight and he is not what I would say is a strong man; this is because of the weakening condition due to the dysentery. From what he said, the *dysentery has persisted since I first saw him in 1919.* I have been there when he had dysentery. I didn't see the stools passed, but that is the report.
"Dysentery is caused by different things, different bacteria and parasites. There is no cure. They are better for a while and then they are worse.
"It leaves a man in a weakened condition. It explains the loss of weight and his nervousness and his weak heart."

Dr. Fagan's opinion is likewise attacked by reason of the hypothetical question put to him. As was said in the case of Lesher v. United States, supra:

"The trial Judge can say whether there is substantial evidence to support the hypothetical question and therefore the conclusion of the expert."

We submit there was ample lay and medical testimony to support the hypothetical question put to Dr. Fagan, and, by reason of the fact that plaintiff went to Dr. Fagan as a patient, it was proper for Dr. Fagan to place reliance upon the medical history which he took, all of which combines to support the expert opinion given by the doctor.

Appellant contends that plaintiff worked at substantially gainful occupations for a period of years under circumstances wholly inconsistent with any condition of total permanent disability (Brief, p. 30). We repeat that throughout this record it appears that plaintiff has been continuously sick and disabled since discharge from service, that he has never been well and has never been free from the disabilities which have repeatedly prevented him from carrying on without interruption. Each and every period of employment which is referred to in this record was terminated by reason of plaintiff's disabilities and the work he did was undoubtedly such as to aggravate his condition. This is evidenced by plaintiff's own testimony (Tr. p. 126):

"The last year I have done no work at all and my dysentery has bothered me very little. I had to lay off because of it, that was all. If I get out and exert myself, my bowels run off more frequently than if I lay around. If I don't do much exercise, why they're better."

In conclusion, the record is replete with substantial evidence sufficient to support this verdict. The trial Court, at the conclusion of this evidence, denied defendant's motion. The jury found for the plaintiff, and we submit their verdict should not be disturbed and the judgment entered should be affirmed.

Respectfully submitted,

C. G. SCHNEIDER,
ALLAN A. BYNON,
Attorneys for Appellee.

In the United States
Circuit Court of Appeals

FOR THE NINTH CIRCUIT

UNITED STATES OF AMERICA,
Appellant,

vs.

CARROL TILLMAN McCREARY,
Appellee.

68I

Petition for Rehearing on Behalf of the Appellee,
Carrol Tillman McCreary

Names and Addresses of Attorneys of Record:

GEORGE NEUNER,
United States Attorney for the District of Oregon,

CHAS. W. ERSKINE,
Assistant United States Attorney for the District of
Oregon,
Federal Bldg., Portland, Oregon,
For Appellant.

CLIFFORD G. SCHNEIDER,
Corbett Bldg.,

ALLAN A. BYNON,
American National Bank Bldg., Portland, Oregon,
For Appellee.

THE IVY PRESS, PORTLAND

TABLE OF AUTHORITIES CITED

Page

Bangor & Arrostook R. R. v. Jones (C. C. A.)
36 F. (2d) 886 21

Ford v. United States, 44 Fed. (2d) 754 21

Gray, Administratrix, v. Davis, Director General
of R. R. (C. C. A.), 294 F. 57.............. 21

Heisson v. Dickinson (C. C. A.), 35 F. (2d) 270. 21

United States v. Burke, 50 Fed. (2d) 653....... 15

United States v. Griswold, No. 6804............ 20

White v. United States, 270 U. S. 175, 180,
46 S. Ct. 274, 275, 70 L. Ed. 530.......... 21

In the United States Circuit Court of Appeals

FOR THE NINTH CIRCUIT

UNITED STATES OF AMERICA,
                              Appellant,

     vs.

CARROL TILLMAN McCREARY,
                              Appellee.

Petition for Rehearing on Behalf of the Appellee,
Carrol Tillman McCreary

To the Honorable Curtis D. Wilbur, Presiding Judge,
and the Associate Judges of the above entitled
Court:

COMES NOW Carrol Tillman McCreary, appellee
in the above entitled cause, and hereby most respectfully
petitions your Honors for a rehearing of said cause for
the reasons and upon the following grounds, to-wit:

I.

The opinion of this Court rendered on the 14th day
of November, 1932, is not based on facts disclosed by
the record, in that there is substantial evidence to sup-

port the verdict of the jury finding the appellee totally and permanently disabled on the 19th day of September, 1919.

II.

The opinion of this Court is contrary to the statutes and the law, as heretofore interpreted and applied by the Courts of this Circuit and Courts of other Circuits in similar cases.

It is difficult to urge our objections to the Court's opinion in this Petition because of the manner in which the opinion is written. Excerpts from the testimony are so woven together that we feel required to point out additional portions of the testimony, which are not included in the printed opinion and which, we feel, are necessary fully to estimate the worth of plaintiff's case.

Disabilities Incurred in France

Plaintiff suffered severely from his experiences in France. In addition to the testimony covering this phase of the case incorporated in the Court's opinion, the following excerpts from plaintiff's testimony help to make up the whole picture:

"My first sickness was when I got the mumps when I was on the boat going over, (June, 1918) and I was left at the hospital barracks at Brest, France. The mumps were bad with me; they went down on me. I got out of the hospital one day and went to the convalescent camp in Brest, and the mumps went down that night, and I went back to the hospital after that the next morning. That time I was kept there something in the neighborhood of three weeks. * * (Tr. p. 107).

"About * * * —the 15th or 18th of July— was the first time I got sick or bothered with this dysentery and diarrhea.

"Q. Immediately prior to that had anything happened to you in regard to fire—shell fire or action, or—

"A. Oh, we were under shell fire there. * * *

"Q. What happened to you?

"A. It shot the wind out of me and I was thrown down on the ground like a feather.

"Shortly after that time this dysentery broke out on me, and I was so sick from that I didn't notice any great change. * * * It was from the water or something we got to eat. * * * (Tr. pp. 109, 110.)

"The reason I was detailed to guard duty there at that time, I guess, was they figured I wasn't fit for anything else. I was bothered with dysentery and diarrhea and I couldn't carry my pack. I couldn't keep up with the outfit. * * * (Tr. p. 112.)

"My condition was very poor during that time. I volunteered to go into the lines and they wouldn't take me. The captain laughed at me. He said he was having trouble enough with well men without taking sick men along into the lines. * * * (Tr. p. 113.)

Plaintiff's Honorable Discharge (Tr. p. 109) shows that plaintiff was on the battlefronts from July 18, 1918, to November 9, 1918, and under cross-examination plaintiff testified (Tr. pp. 128, 129, 130):

"* * * My first shell fire was on the Marne. * * * Then * * * we laid in a quiet sector there for a week or two. * * *

"Q. All the time after * * * the Marne, you were never in direct shell fire, were you?

"A. Well, we were not in the line but we were under shell fire to a certain extent. We could hear the shells all the time. * * *

"* * * In Nancy they bombed that with shell practically every night that we were there * * * and from there we went up on the Ponzon(?) Reserve, and we were under shell fire there continuously. * * * There was always a few shells around. * * * When I was on the Argonne, I was under shell fire, sure.

"I recall being weighed for overseas service when I left Virginia. I weighed about 208 pounds at Ponetcal, Virginia. I was six feet, two inches tall.

"During this period of time while I was sick, commencing some time in July, 1918, and continuing until January, 1919, I was weighed while in the hospital at Contrexeville, France, and I weighed *130 pounds* at that time.

"I was very weak at that time and presume I was pretty much run down. * * * (Tr. p. 114.)

"Q. I asked you when you first noticed the neurasthenia? Of its bothering you? When did you first notice that you were nervous, or that you had been nervous, when you had not been previously?

"A. I can't say as to that. I know I had it when I started home. * * *

"Q. The point I want to make here is—when did you first realize that you had this nervous disorder?

"A. I can't say as to that.

"Q. Was it prior to leaving France?

"A. Oh, yes, yes. * * *

"Q. When did you first discover that your stomach was bothering you?

"Well, my stomach was bad when I was in the service.

"Q. Did you have any of these disabilities before you entered the service?

"A. Not to my knowledge. * * *" (Tr. pp. 115, 116.)

Plaintiff's Work Record

The Court says, "* * * Appellee was practically continuously employed from September, 1919, to March, 1924, * * *." We believe the following substantial evidence will certainly show plaintiff did not work continuously and was not able to do what he did do without serious injury to his health and aggravation of his condition.

Plaintiff testified (Tr. p. 117):

"The first work I did was I helped one of the neighbors out there. That was Mr. Burns. I helped him possibly four or five hours. I did not work with the rest of the crew until the work was done; I played out; it was one of my days. * * *"

Plaintiff's witness, A. H. Burns, who had known plaintiff intimately from boyhood and saw him immediately after his return from the service either late in August or early in September, 1919, testified (Tr. p. 29):

"* * * I had work for him to do there, but I couldn't put him to work because his condition showed that he was more ready for the hospital than he was to work. He was very nervous. He could only eat certain things and otherwise it disagreed with him. My wife had to figure out what he could eat. * * * We had to be very careful what he ate and how he ate it. * * *"

"A. * * * One night we were in Gresham. I never realized what shell-shock was before. There was a celebration * * * and a fire-cracker went off behind and I was standing beside McCreary. It was pitiful to see his condition after that. * * *

"He was very weak, and his face was pinched and drawn and very pale, compared with how it was before he went to war. * * * He would work two or three days here and there and would have to quit on account of his condition. * * * He acted all of the time very tired and very weak, very tired, and continued nervous. * * * It seemed like he was failing more all the time; in other words, getting weaker. * * *

"I could have given him employment at that time, but I didn't think his condition warranted it."

He also tells us (Tr. p. 35) that when plaintiff was working for Bob Strubin that he was very tired and very weak and further testified that plaintiff "has been about the same in his appearance since the war until now" and that he had (Tr. p. 36) seen plaintiff "home sick, when he could have been working, at least three or four times while he was working at Strubin's Dairy."

In September, 1919, plaintiff went to work for Robert S. Strubin and remained there until April, 1920, and in May resumed that work until August 15, 1920 (Tr. p. 132). Concerning this period plaintiff testified (Tr. pp. 117, 118, 120):

"At that time I was bothered with dysentery, and I was very weak, and I had bad night sweats, * * * severe headaches at that time—something awful. * * *

"I was nervous at that time, and I understood Bob used to have quite a time with me there. * * *

"The first time I quit Mr. Strubin was because I could not carry on, and the second time was because I was on the sick list, and I believe it was partly because I was just married. * * *"

Mr. Strubin, who also had known plaintiff since boyhood (Tr. p. 74) testified as follows (Tr. pp. 75-77):

"* * * He didn't seem to be the same man that went away. He stooped more and his eyes were hollow, and he had the general appearance of being nervous. I doubted very much if he could stand the work, but I needed someone there to help me very much and I insisted on him coming down anyway. * * * Mr. McCreary told me didn't think he could stand the work but that he would come down and try it. * * *

"* * * McCreary was to oversee the milking machines, and he was to attend to the mixing of the feed for the cattle. * * * Carrol had time off each day, which he *had to take,* and in fact many times he was so nervous we could not get him off on time for his evening chores. When we would call him he would come up with a jump and throw his hands into the air and he would come to the barn with his eyes glaring—* * * and he would go about his work and would carry on principally on his nerves. * * *

"I had to have a man to assist him. *He could never have carried on a week alone.*

" * * * *He had to give up the work; he could not stand it; he was broken up completely.*

"* * * He just did not have the strength, and he was nervous and he could not stand it—the work he was doing. He couldn't carry on.

"Many times he had to lay off part of some days when he did not go away entirely. * * *"

Concerning the second period of employment, Mr. Strubin testified (Tr. pp. 78, 79):

"* * * He said he would come back but he doubted that he could stand it—he doubted that he could stand the work again. He showed a little improvement from a few days' rest but he still showed that nervous appearance that he always had. * * *

"He did not regain his health. He finally had to give the work up. He couldn't stand it. His condition then was *about as poor as a man could be in.*

"Any little thing would startle Carrol—any little noise. After any little noise you would see him going up into the air. * * * Sometimes it was almost dangerous to call him. Many times we did not call him. Sometimes we would let him sleep until the milking was practically done. He was such a nervous wreck we did not like to disturb him. * * *

"* * * These two instances, and when we would call him or arouse him out of his sleep, I perhaps will never forget, and I don't think anybody else would ever forget—the look he carried at these times. * * * "

Some three or four weeks following the employment with Mr. Strubin, plaintiff went to work for the Fernwood Dairy and remained there a little over a year, during which time he was off eight weeks, in the summer of

1921, with an operation (Tr. p. 121). Plaintiff testified (Tr. pp. 121):

"* * * I had this operation because this trouble was still bothering me and I could not get any relief for it. The operation did not relieve it.

"Besides the eight weeks, I lost a few days now and then. I think four days was the longest I was off. I lost a few days now and then because I was not able to carry on. It was the same trouble.

"After the operation I went back. * * * Mr. Wilcox came to me himself and asked me to quit. He said I wouldn't last a year if I kept on with that work. He told me to quit. I was sick at that time."

Fred T. Wilcox (misspelled "Wilson" in the Transcript), testified concerning this period (Tr. pp. 85-87):

"I think the first time he was in my employ, when he first came to work, that he was able to do his work, but I could not say how long he worked there, but he worked for some time, and then he gradually became weaker and weaker and in fact got so he could not do his work. * * *

"He was either checking or working; working inside my plant. * * *

"I don't remember so much about his condition with reference to being nervous. He was unable later to do his work, because he was sick. He was weak, but he made a supreme effort to do it, but I requested him to—I called him in and I asked him to quit until he could get in shape so that he could do his work, and he quit.

"He came back again and stayed a very short time. His physical condition then was not very good.

"* * * I *do* remember he *had to quit* on account of his health. * * *"

Plaintiff then testified (Tr. p. 121):

"After that I did practically nothing all that winter or until the spring of 1922. * * *

"Next I bought a little place out near Gresham. * * *

"I did some of the work on the place, and my father did some, and I hired some of the work done. I hired some plowing done by John Strubin. My wife did some work there; she helped me, of course."

In August, 1922, plaintiff again went to the hospital "still bothered with abdominal trouble and this diarrhea" (Tr. p. 122), his nervous condition and his headaches (Tr. p. 123).

His next job was with the Davidson Bakery Company (Tr. p. 123) from May, 1923, to March, 1924 (Tr. p. 136). As appears by the figures incorporated in the Court's opinion, the plaintiff lost from 2 to 16 days a month while so employed. His explanation for this loss of time appears on Page 123, Transcript:

"There were interruptions in that employment. I was off part of the time because I was sick.

"During that period of time I was under Dr. Edson's care—at least a good part of the time; Dr. Edson of the Veterans' Hospital. I don't just remember what other doctors.

"I left the bakery and went into the hospital— No. 77. Dr. C. C. Campbell, of the Veterans' Hospital, treated me while I was there. * * *"

T. E. Gabode, who employed him at this time, testified (Tr. pp. 95, 96, 97):

"* * * I did not consider him good, first class, from a physical standpoint.

"Regarding his nervous condition, you could notice there was a nervous strain. You could see he was bothered with something. We knew he was not exactly right physically but we tried to help him along.

"When he quit he came in and said he could not handle the work. * * * I would say we were just helping him along. * * *

"His time off there was just few days occasionally, due to his condition, as I remember it. He would be sick and to that I attributed it at that time—to his nervous condition. * * *"

Interspersed during this time were odd jobs running from a few days to eight weeks at a time and which were terminated because he "played out," "couldn't fill the bill," "was not able to carry on" (Tr. p. 125), his "condition was very poor" (Tr. p. 126).

"The last year," plaintiff testified (Tr. pp. 126, 127), "I have done no work at all, and my dysentery has bothered me very little. I had to lay off because of it, that was all. If I get out and exert myself my bowels run off more frequently than if I lay around. If I don't do much exercise, why they're better. * * *"

The testimony given by Messrs. F. G. Leary (Tr. p. 25), Leon Coddey (Tr. p. 88), John Everle (Tr. p. 92), J. H. Cooper (Tr. p. 97) and M. H. Dahl (Tr. p. 101) all supports plaintiff's statement that his work was spasmodic and always interrupted by his service connected disabilities.

The following excerpts from the testimony which outline plaintiff's different periods of hospitalization since service, lend color to his claim that his work has been interrupted by his disabilities:

(1) "I was off eight weeks in the summer of 1921, with an operation. I had this operation because this trouble was still bothering me and I could not get any relief for it. The operation did not relieve it." (Tr. p. 121).

(2) "Q. What occasioned your going to the hospital? (August, 1922).

"A. Well, Dr. Rocky sent me there. * * * I was still bothered wth abdominal trouble and this diarrhea.

"Q. And what about your nervous condition?

"A. Yes, sure.

"Q. You still had that?

"A. Yes, sure." (Tr. pp. 122, 123).

(3) "I went to the United States Veterans' Hospital for observation and treatment, either in January or February, (1924) I am not sure." (Tr. p. 136).

(4) "I left the bakery and went into the hospital—No. 77." (March 31, 1924.) (Tr. p. 124).

(5) Dr. Campbell finds record of examination of plaintiff dated June 27, 1924. (Tr. p. 148).

(6) "The only work I did after that amounted to anything was for the City of Portland; * * * I worked on that job watching this road until it was completed * * * and then I went to the Veterans' Hospital (January 20, 1925, see Tr. p. 148) for an examination and treatment and was there possibly two weeks or better." (Tr. p. 124).

(7) "Prior to that time (1927) I was on my farm. At that place I had the heart attack that Leon testified to yesterday. After that I was in the hospital again—in Veterans' Hospital No. 77." (Tr. p. 125).

(8) "After July, 1928, I think, I was called in for an examination then." (Tr. p. 125).

(9) "In November, 1929, I did some work for the Phoenix Logging Company. * * * After that I came home and went through a routine examination at the Veterans' Hospital. I did not get any cure for my troubles then." (Tr. p. 126).

Medical Testimony

Critical analysis of the opinion shows the Court gave considerable attention to the evidence offered by defendant through its witness, Dr. Campbell. Three observations seem pertinent here:

First, the opinion says, "Dr. Campbell, *although available,* was not produced by plaintiff but for the defense." The facts are that Dr. Campbell was not available to plaintiff. He had left Oregon some years before this case was brought and his whereabouts were unknown to plaintiff. The defendant chose to present his testimony by way of deposition and plaintiff, by reason of his circumstances, was unable to secure representation when the deposition was taken at Long Beach, California, and no cross-examination of Dr. Campbell was attempted.

Second, Dr. Campbell said, "I do not have any independent recollection of Carrol T. McCreary." (Tr. p. 145).

Third, plaintiff should not be bound by the defendant's witnesses, and we remind the Court that the jury chose not to believe Dr. Campbell but saw fit to follow the testimony given on behalf of plaintiff.

As we understand the law, this Court's decision in *United States vs. Burke,* 50 Fed. (2d) 653, is applicable:

"And on motion for a directed verdict, the Court may not weigh the evidence, and if there is substantial evidence *both for the plaintiff and the defendant,* it is for the jury to determine what facts are established, even if their verdict be against the decided preponderance of the evidence. * * *"

Dr. H. H. Hughes, plaintiff's family physician, who had known plaintiff since 1913, examined him first in the early part of October, 1919 (Tr. pp. 36, 37). Concerning his condition then Dr. Hughes testified that at that time he found plaintiff had lost a good deal of weight, and he looked anemic and stooped, and his voice had changed a good deal, and he did not have the strength that he used to have; that he complained of having suffered diarrhea and pain in the abdomen (Tr. p. 37). The doctor continued (Tr. p. 37, 38, 39, 40, 44):

"* * * He also had a tenderness in the abdomen and he had a diarrhea *at that time.* He complained of not being able to digest his food, of having a good deal of gas and a sour stomach.

"*I took the usual history taken* in such cases and interrogated him about what he had been through. I diagnosed his trouble as dysentery, and he had an inflamed or sore bowel at that time. We called that colitis.

"I didn't determine the *cause* of the dysentery because I have no way, out in the country, of determining the cause of dysentery. This is done in hospitals and laboratories. *But I found he had such.* * * *

"On the occasion of my first examination of him after he left the service, he seemed very nervous and restless as he was sitting in the chair; he was restless and nervous * * *.

"Q. Did you ever find out what had caused this nervous condition, Doctor?

"A. Oh, I talked to him about the war. * * * He had been in France and he told me he had been up on the firing line * * * he described a good deal of what he went through and the guns and so forth and I took it for granted that was the cause of his nervousness. * * *

"I remember one particular time he came to the office in 1921 and he complained of more pain at that time *than usual* * * * and I diagnosed it as appendicitis.

"* * * This man has a dysentery which has weakened him, and he is very nervous and he has had a weak heart; he has lost weight and he is not what I would say is a strong man; this is because of the weakening condition due to the dysentery. From what he said, the dysentery had persisted since I first saw him in 1919. I have been there when he had dysentery. * * *

"* * * There is no cure. They are better for a while and then they are worse.

"It leaves a man in a weakened condition. It explains the loss of weight and his nervousness and his weak heart.

"Based upon my examination and knowledge of this man and his history I have taken, I think this man is totally and permanently unable to follow continuously a substantially gainful occupation. I would say he was totally and permanently disabled, as defined, at the time he came back from the service, August, 1919, and I would say that the condition he is in is reasonably certain to continue throughout his lifetime. * * *

"This nervous condtion *was exhibited continually*—not exactly jerking but just getting up and going to the window and coming back and sitting and lighting a cigarette and smoking a puff or two and throwing it down.

"As a physician, I would not consider just that indication of nervousness—sitting down a while and getting up and smoking a cigarette a short time—a sufficient disability to keep a man from working; I would consider that *a result.* * * *

"* * * From the symptoms he gave me I would say that he had dysentery. * * *"

Dr. Hughes testified that "several years ago" he had been called to plaintiff's home and on that time "he was bothered with his heart" (Tr. p. 39). As to this condition the Doctor further testified (Tr. pp. 46, 47):

"In 1919 and 1921, when I saw him, there was nothing that impressed me about his heart except that it was rapid. * * * I made an examination at that time. * * *

"He was weakened all over; when a man is weakened from diarrhea, that is he has to go a good many times in twenty-four hours, it weakens his heart the same as it weakens him in other ways. It weakens the muscles.

"Q. A rapid heart in itself, is not totally disabling, is it, to such a degree as you find in this man?

"A. It depends upon each individual case.

"Q. And in this man, a rapid heart alone—

"A. It is his general condition, yes.

"Q. Well, a rapid heart alone, would it be so severe as to prevent him doing some kind of work?

"A. Well, I don't know what some kind of work would be. He could sit at a desk and write. He could do some such work, but I don't believe he is in any condition to do manual labor. (Plaintiff testified (Tr. p. 107): "I made my living as a laborer before I entered the service. I had an eighth grade education.")

The Doctor continued (Tr. pp. 47, 48, 50):

"I don't think he is in condition now to do dairy work. Dairy work is very hard. * * *

"Q. Now, which do you think was the primary cause of the nervousness you found—the dysentery or the experience he related to you there in your office, when he first came back there?"

"A. Well, I don't know. I think that it is the combination. Either one has been enough to put the average man out. * * *

"Q. Doctor, is it not true that in addition to these army experiences which bring on nervousness, as you testified, that the infection which goes with this dysentery also produces nervousness?

"A. Any septic poisoning—

"Q. That is my point.

"A. Yes, sure it may." * *

The last expression of this Court covering a similar situation appears in the case of *United States v. Hallie L. Griswold,* No. 6804, decided November 7, 1932, in which the Court said:

"* * * There was substantial evidence to go to the jury upon the proposition that although plaintiff actually worked for long periods of time, he was not then able to do so nor to do so continuously."

In this last mentioned case, this Court relied, in part, upon the fact that the medical testimony showed that Griswold's disability, like this plaintiff's, moved in a "vicious circle." As we see it, the testimony adduced in the McCreary case plainly shows that when plaintiff worked he stimulated and aggravated his service connected disability, known as dysentery, for, said the plaintiff (Tr. p. 126), "If I get out and exert myself my bowels run off more frequently than if I lay around. If I don't do much exercise, why they're better."

Dr. Hughes confirmed this in his testimony.

Plaintiff made a valiant effort to earn a living from the date of discharge from the service until a year or two before trial. The record shows that he sought out and attempted to do many different kinds of work in the hope that he could secure and keep continuously some employment which would be substantially gainful. In each instance his work was interrupted and at last terminated because of his service connected disabilities.

It would seem that these repeated attempts to overcome his handicaps, followed, as we have said, by plaintiff's failure in each instance, would tend to establish that he has been, in fact, totally and permanently disabled within the meaning of his War Risk Insurance policy, and that plaintiff was, therefore, entitled to have his case passed upon by the jury.

Because we think it is good law and helpful here to the Courts and litigants alike, we beg leave to repeat an excerpt from *Ford v. United States,* 44 Fed. (2d) 754:

> "It is well settled that, on such a question as is here presented, the plaintiff is entitled to the most favorable construction that a jury might be warranted in putting on the evidence. *Heisson v. Dickinson* (C.C.A.), 35 F. (2d) 270, and cases cited; *Bangor & Arrostook R. R. v. Jones* (C.C.A.), 36 F. (2d) 886; *Gray, Administratrix, v. Davis, Director General of R. R.* (C.C.A.), 294 F. 57.
>
> "And the act itself is to be liberally construed in favor of such claimants. In *White v. United States,* 270 U. S. 175, 180, 46 S. Ct. 274, 275, 70 L. Ed. 530, Mr. Justice Holmes said of such contracts: 'The insurance was a contract, to be sure, for which a premium was paid, but it was not one entered into by the United States for gain. All soldiers were given a right to it and the relation of the Govern-

ment to them if not paternal was at least avuncular. It was a relation of benevolence established by the Government at considerable cost to itself for the soldier's good.' "

We firmly and honestly believe that upon an examination of the entire record this Honorable Court will conclude that we are entitled to a rehearing of this cause.

Respectfully submitted,

CLIFFORD G. SCHNEIDER,
ALLAN A. BYNON,
Attorneys for Appellee.

United States of America,
District of Oregon—ss.

I hereby certify that I am one of the attorneys for the appellee and petitioner in the above entitled cause, and that, in my judgment, the foregoing Petition for Rehearing is well founded in point of law as well as in fact, and that said petition is not interposed for delay.

ALLAN A. BYNON,
Of Attorneys for Appellee,
Petitioner herein.